THE HUMAN MIND

THE LONGER I LIVE THE MORE DO HUMAN beings appear to be fascinating and full of interest. . . .

Foolish and clever, mean and almost saintly, diversely unhappy — they are all dear to my heart; it seems to me that I do not properly understand them and my soul is filled with an inextinguishable interest in them. Many of them whom I knew are dead, I am afraid that except me there is no one who will tell their story as I would like to do and dare not; it will seem as though such men had never existed on earth at all. . . .

The people I am most fond of are those who are not quite achieved; who are not very wise, a little mad, "possessed." "The people of a sound mind" have little interest for me. The achieved man, the one perfect like an umbrella, does not appeal to me. I am called and doomed, you see, to describe — and what could I say of an umbrella but that it is of no worth on a sunny day?

A man slightly possessed is not only more agreeable to me; he is altogether more plausible, more in harmony with the general tune of life, a phenomenon unfathomed yet, and fantastic, which makes it at the same time so confoundedly interesting.

MAXIM GORKI: *Two Stories*

The Dial, September 1927, pp. 197–8

THE

HUMAN

MIND

KARL A. MENNINGER

THIRD EDITION
CORRECTED, ENLARGED, & REWRITTEN

ALFRED A KNOPF : *NEW YORK*

1971

THIS IS A BORZOI BOOK,
PUBLISHED BY ALFRED A. KNOPF, INC.

PUBLISHED FEBRUARY 1930
SECOND EDITION, RESET, PUBLISHED OCTOBER 1937

THIRD EDITION, REVISED, PUBLISHED MAY 1945
REPRINTED SIXTEEN TIMES
EIGHTEENTH PRINTING, JANUARY 1971

DEDICATED TO

MY FATHER AND MOTHER

AN INVINCIBLE LAIUS

AND A DISCERNING JOCASTA

PREFACE

Seven more years have elapsed. The war predicted in the preface to the second edition came to pass on precisely the problem there predicated; the conflict between theories of hereditary superiority and theories of environmental determination. Psychiatry, since the discoveries of Sigmund Freud, has been dominated by the environmental philosophy and hence finds itself wholly in accord with the spirit of the Allied Nations in World War II. On account of that war millions of people have been killed and millions more evicted, orphaned, widowed, wounded, transported, incarcerated. For everyone mercifully spared these greater tragedies, the difficulties of life adjustment have become greater. A better understanding of the nature of the human mind was never more necessary and psychiatry has rapidly advanced from a minor and relatively unpopular specialty of medicine to one of the great fields of scientific and popular interest.

Both the psychiatric casualties from battle and the rejections by the Selective Service for psychiatric reasons have far exceeded expectations. It is difficult for the average man to realize the immensity of the problem. There are available in the United States less than 4,000 psychiatrists. The Army and Navy alone could use all of these and more. Meanwhile, civilian hospitals, mental hygiene clinics, institutions for the delinquent and criminal, universities, colleges and public schools, general hospitals and private psychiatric practices, entirely aside from military needs, could use at the present time 10,000 psychiatrists (the estimate of the Director of the National Committee for Mental Hygiene, October 1944). The time required to train a physician in psychiatry following his graduation from medical school is at least four years. If all the medical students graduating from all the medical schools for the next three years were to elect psychiatry as their major interest, we would have only enough psychiatrists to meet the present needs by 1951. However, probably not one-twentieth of these students will make this choice, and to this we must add the further bad news that there do not exist in the whole world training facilities and teachers for even this minimum of prospective psychiatrists.

Obviously other ways to meet this need must be sought, beyond that of training more psychiatrists. For one thing an orientation in psychiatry must be provided for physicians in general practice and in the other specialties. They must be given an opportunity to acquire techniques for recognizing and dealing with the psychological elements in the illnesses of the patients whom they are now treating only by the time-honored but inadequate traditional methods of physics and chemistry. The teaching of medicine must be reorganized along these lines so as to include for the student a proper consideration of the human mind as well as of the human body. Psychiatrists must use new methods of diagnosis and of treatment which will enable them to carry heavier patient loads and do so more efficaciously. This will certainly include the greater utilization of trained aides — psychologists, social workers, occupational and recreational therapists, nurses and group leaders. To these ends research as well as training must be stimulated and fostered.

Just what the function of this book will be in this program of rapidly extended psychiatric education, which has become the fervid preoccupation of many of us, I do not know. I have tried, however, to make it an accurate and fairly complete summary of the essential facts, terms, methods and concepts of modern psychiatry to serve as a general introductory survey. Over and beyond this also I have tried to preserve in the book something which for me many texts lack: I mean the *spirit* of psychiatry. I feel that it is more important to inspire a student with an interest in the subject, a vision of its scope and significance and the desire to learn more about it, than to supply him with all of the pertinent facts. I have felt that if psychiatry could be presented to medical students in this way more of them would see the great opportunities it offers before it is too late for them to elect it as a field of life work toward which they could plan their training programs.

In this I have been encouraged by colleagues who have written me regarding their experiences with the use of this book in their teaching and also by medical students with whom I have had personal conferences. In the past year, under the auspices of the Menninger Foundation, I have visited about a dozen representative university medical schools, and I have talked at length with students, deans and faculty members. Everywhere I met the same situation — earnestness, eagerness, alertness, idealism and a relative open-mindedness in the younger students regarding the opportunities of psychiatry and the importance of the psychological factor in medicine. Generally, however, this attitude tended to be obliterated as the student progressed through the years of medical training; false impressions of psychiatry as an eccentric, unessential, impractical, discouraging specialty had replaced the original enthusiasm. The handicapped efforts of good psychiatrists on the faculty came too late in the curriculum or were counteracted by too much misunderstanding and depreciation by other members of the faculty. Often the students were discouraged by the impressions gained from advanced, extreme, hopeless-looking cases shown them to illustrate classical syndromes. These impressions and the textbook descriptions tend to eclipse the principles of psychological medicine so that the bizarre features and the gloomy prognoses are more outstanding in the minds of the students than are the social significance of the problems and the hopeful possibilities of early treatment and of prevention. The integration of psychiatry with general medicine is as yet so incomplete that it is not surprising to find it almost entirely lacking in the concepts of many of these students who are the hope of the immediate future of medical practice.

On the basis of these experiences I wrote to many of my psychiatric friends and co-workers and asked them for their advice and help in making this third revision of *The Human Mind*. I had so many helpful replies that it would be a practical impossibility to make an acknowledgment here to each one of them. But I would like to say again that it is no false modesty that leads me to insist that the credit for the content of this book belongs not to me alone or even to those of us who work here together at our Clinic, but to many psychiatric pioneers, practitioners, research men, psychologists, psychiatric social workers and, last but not least, physicians in other fields who have recognized and furthered the integration of psychiatry with general medicine.

In preparing the present revision the exigencies of the War made it necessary to restrict the changes to fundamentals. The paging has not been changed; the content of many pages, on the other hand, has been radically changed in accordance with developments within the field during the past seven years. Among these I would particularly emphasize: 1) the increased cooperation of psychiatrists with psychologists in diagnosis and with social workers in treatment; 2) the interrelations of psychiatry with general medicine; 3) advances and innovations in treatment methods; and 4) new books. Concerning the latter I should add that requests for a list of the basic or fundamental books requisite to a thorough psychiatric training come to me often, and we have had the need for such a list in our own Clinic for the purposes of resident physician training. For these reasons much time and pains were spent on this section and the assistance of numerous psychiatric colleagues solicited.

I am indebted for assistance in making this revision to Dr. Robert P. Knight, Chief of the Psychotherapy Service of the Menninger Clinic, to Dr. David Rapaport, Chairman of the Research Committee of the Menninger Foundation, Dr. Ruth I. Barnard and Dr. Joseph Dimont of the resident staff of the Menninger Psychiatric Hospital, Miss Lucille Cairns, of the Department of Psychiatric Social Work, Miss Clara Louise Meckel, our librarian, Mrs. Alice Dangerfield, my secretary, Mrs. Ida Malcolm, my research assistant, and to Jean Lyle Menninger, my wife and best critic. Mr. Samson Horn of New York was of valuable assistance in proof reading. Dr. Smith Ely Jelliffe called my attention to certain earlier errors in the history of psychoanalysis.

Finally, at this late date I want to make an overdue acknowledgment of indebtedness to Professor Charles E. Rogers, now of Iowa State College and formerly professor of journalism at Kansas State College. It was he whose discernment and encouragement were responsible for the original appearance of this book in 1930. He called the manuscript to the attention of Mr. Carl Van Doren, then one of the editors of the Literary Guild, which resulted in a rather wide initial distribution. The publishers tell me that well over 200,000 copies have now been sold and I am happy to know that it is still in considerable demand, latterly in medical schools. For whatever part the book may have or may have had in the dissemination of knowledge about or interest in psychiatry, Professor Rogers deserves this share of credit.

Karl Menninger, M.D.

Topeka, November 1, 1944

PREFACE

Seven years have passed since the first edition of this book was published, years of change in which the world has been shaken with economic crises, political realignments, and the rumblings of war. The human mind is not static either, nor is our knowledge of it, and this account of it had to be revised. In this revision I have had in mind, first, the new things that have been learned in the field of psychiatry and the related fields of psychology and sociology since the first edition; second, the changing attitude of the medical profession in the direction of greater appreciation of the validity of psychological data.

The question of the relative importance of heredity and environment in personality formation is an old question and an important one. For if what we are or may become is largely predetermined before our birth, by the heritage of our parents from their parents' parents, there is little use in any efforts we may make to improve our lot. If this be true we should know it and abide by the logical consequences; but so far as our most recent knowledge goes, it is *not* true. Yet the next war will undoubtedly crystallize about emotional attitudes essentially related to and reflected in this problem of heredity and environment. Because of this importance, and this timeliness, and the current misinformation about it, I have discussed it at some length throughout the book and have given more consideration to determining social factors.

Suicide is a logical step for one who believes in the inevitability of a hereditary fate to which he has been cursed; but since valid evidence of this is lacking, the question arises as to why anyone should *want* to think it? This wish to die, the wish to destroy oneself and blame science or society or one's ancestors for it, is so complex a phenomenon that we can only deal with it briefly here — but it serves to introduce a new point of view in the scientific study of the human being.

The passage of years and the extension of experience has made me *more* optimistic, not less, about the possibilities of helping those who want help. One of the suggestions most frequently made in the many letters that came to me after the book's first appearance was that I tell more about treatment methods and results. It is not easy to do this to the satisfaction

xi

of everyone because treatment is necessarily technical, and the evaluation of results cannot at the same time encourage everyone and yet tell the whole truth. But I was finally impelled to enlarge the section on treatment through the insistent requests of many of my medical colleagues, whose greatest difficulty in carrying out psychiatric principles with their patients is often the unfamiliarity of these patients with the methods or the purposes of such treatment. For the intelligent patients of intelligent doctors, I have, therefore, rewritten the section on treatment and made it more specific.

Not only as a treatment method, but as a scientific psychology, psychoanalysis has made rapid strides in the seven years. I have therefore rewritten this section and included a more systematic and comprehensive account of it.

And because I do not believe in hereditary damnation but do believe in education and in the fruitful possibilities of improving educational methods by applying some of the principles of psychiatry, I have expanded the section dealing with this theme. This is the only real mental hygiene I know of.

In response to the awakening interest in psychiatry on the part of clergymen and to repeated requests, I have inserted a brief section on its religious applications.

To assist the doctors, medical students, and young psychiatrists who have made use of the book as a text, I have greatly increased the references to sources and more technical discussions, and have expanded and reclassified the bibliography.

* * * * * * * *

Many readers have said to me: " I was afraid I would find myself in your book," or " I almost imagined I had some of those abnormal conditions myself." To such persons I usually reply quite gravely: " I hope so." For if one has a mind at all, his mental processes are subject to some of the faults and failings that characterize the human mind. If someone does not find himself at all in this book, it is either that he is not human or that some pages have been left out (or torn out). That curious emotional defence which impels some people to believe themselves exempt from all failure, from all weakness, from the taboo of " abnormality," is perhaps the greatest enemy of healthy mindedness.

One need waste no pity on those whom some consider unfortunate enough to be receiving psychiatric treatment, within the walls of a hospital or in the consultation offices of psychiatrists, psychoanalysts, and neurologists, for they are often much wiser and much more courageous than that larger group of persons who need help no less sorely, but who lack the intelligence that tells them what to do, the wisdom that leads them to do it, or the courage to ignore the ridicule of their ill-informed friends to obtain it!

I was much impressed that so many people wrote me that they had received benefit from reading *The Human Mind,* that they had been relieved of various symptoms as the result of the little knowledge thus gained of themselves. Medical colleagues even wrote me that they often prescribed it. I had not written it with any thought of its having therapeutic value and it surprised (and pleased) me to hear these things. Our theory that a better knowledge of oneself enables one to make a better social adjustment in life was thus happily verified. The whole matter of *bibliotherapy,* of the relief of suffering by the psychological processes induced by reading, is a field in which we have little scientific knowledge. But our intuition and our experience tell us that books may indeed "minister to a soul diseased" and come to the aid of the doctor or even precede him.

I have had in mind, therefore, in revising the first edition of this book, that it must serve the purposes of doctors, patients, medical students, nurses, teachers, psychologists, clergymen, and intelligent lay readers interested in science or in human beings. These are the people who read it before, and who I hope will feel that the revisions accurately represent the changes in fact, theory, or emphasis which the passage of time and the further experience of seven years have made necessary.

K. A. M.

Topeka, April 15, 1937

ACKNOWLEDGMENTS

I am indebted for assistance in the preparation of this second edition to numerous persons: All of my colleagues in the Menninger Clinic, especially Dr. Norman Reider, Dr. Byron Stewart, and my brother, William. In addition, Jeanetta Lyle, editorial secretary of the Clinic, assisted by Peggy Linn, librarian, and Alice Dangerfield, typist, did much of the necessary detail work. Dean John Warren Day and Rabbi Hyman Iola helped me with the section on religious applications. Messrs. Preston and Jacobs of Alfred A. Knopf, Inc., and W. A. Dwiggins, in reducing the complicated manuscript corrections to readable and well-ordered print have accomplished a difficult task with skill, thoroughness, and patience, for which I am grateful.

K. A. M.

PREFACE

TO THE FIRST EDITION

I have tried to put down in a systematic fashion the conception I have of the human personality. I have tried to keep it objective and specific, and to write it so it could be understood. I think it represents approximately the views of the younger group in American psychiatry. But I don't claim this. I take all the responsibility, because no other psychiatrist saw a page of it until it came from the press. It is full of my own ideas, my own views, my own prejudices, my own mistakes. But it's what I teach my students and it's what I tell my patients.

The adjuration to be "normal" seems shockingly repellent to me; I see neither hope nor comfort in sinking to that low level. I think it is ignorance that makes people think of abnormality only with horror and allows them to remain undismayed at the proximity of "normal" to average and mediocre. For surely anyone who achieves anything is, *a priori,* abnormal; this includes, not only the geniuses, but the presidents, the leaders, and the great entertainers. I presume most of the people in *Who's Who in America* would resent being called normal.

And while I haven't had much opportunity to examine personally those celebrities, I have had under close observation a considerable number of persons almost as interesting, just as abnormal, and a great deal more accessible to study. And, having spent my academic and professional life trying to discover the meaning of these people's troublesome abnormalities and the best ways to set them right, and at the same time observing the occurrence of the same formulas in my friends and neighbours and books and newspapers, I wanted to write down my ideas about this curious human mind. Not the mind as a machine operating perfectly and invariably in a quiet little laboratory, but the mind as a collection of enormously complex possibilities for variation, most of the variations being called abnormal by people with some other kind of variation. Unless these variations get one into difficulties or into distinction, they are apt to be unnoticed. Yet it is they that determine the personality. It is they that differentiate the human being from the robot.

The case histories cited in this book from my own experience are all true in essence, although carefully disguised to conceal the identity of the originals. My patients who read the book may not recognize themselves; but even if they do, it will cause them no distress. It is only the " normal " people who might worry about the revealing of the abnormal symptoms of other people. Those who have suffered the more painful kinds of abnormality have more wisdom. They know that no one is immune from the variations; some, only, are immune from the consciousness of them.

One can't stop living to write a book, and I've had to put together this manuscript under difficulties. I have rolled off pages of it in the cabooses of freight trains and in the lounge of the Twentieth Century. Parts of it were conceived in railroad depots and in the wards of the hospital. There are passages that still retain the flavour of the coal-oil lamp on the farmer's kitchen table.

Then there have been so many interruptions. No one but doctors and mothers know what it means to have interruptions. Mrs. Jones has a headache, Mr. Smith has obsessions, Helen Thompson perplexes the dean, and George Hall has just been arrested. Telephone calls demand to know if mother may have some oranges, if daughter rested well last night, and if chiropractic is a cure for epilepsy. Interruptions by the assault of sticky little hands and the most imperative news about the neighbour's dog. All sorts of interruptions.

But finally, with much help, I got it together. Please remember it's a book about the mind. Once men were concerned about their souls. In time the priests yielded to the medicine-men and science turned people's attention from their souls to their bodies. Long afterwards, and only of late, some of them gave thought to their minds. But only a small minority. To most people dietetics is still more important than psychometrics, and appendicitis more interesting than neurasthenia.

I am indebted to so many people that I don't know where to begin to enumerate them all. Scores of my colleagues put case material at my disposal. My patients and personal friends gave anonymous but invaluable help. Several of my college students lent me time and service—especially my painstaking artist, David Hale. My friends Nelson Antrim Crawford and Harry J. Colburn made invaluable editorial criticisms. I owe much to my incomparable secretary, Bess Cowdrey. And, finally, there is my long-time friend Logan Clendening, author of *The Human Body*. He has advised me from time to time, which he can do with perspicacity because he knows nothing about The Human Mind.

Ernest Southard of Harvard was the inspiration of this book. He told me to write it, just before he died, ten years ago, when I was one of his many disciples. Smith Ely Jelliffe is written into this book, and William Alanson White and Lawson Lowrey and Herman Adler and Adolf Meyer and William Healy and Frankwood Williams, Charles Frederick Menninger, my own father, and all those friends who have been at once my teachers and my companions. I hope I have done them credit.

K. A. M.

Topeka, July 22, 1929

CONTENTS

CHAPTER I PRINCIPLES   1

INTRODUCTORY SECTION, *dealing with modern conceptions of mind and health*

CHAPTER II PERSONALITIES   19

SYNTHETIC SECTION, *dealing with the external appearances of the assembled machine in action*

CHAPTER III SYMPTOMS   159

ANALYTIC SECTION, *dealing with the parts of the machine, dismantled*

CHAPTER IV MOTIVES   265

DYNAMIC SECTION, *dealing with the sources and distribution of the power that drives the machine*

CHAPTER V TREATMENTS   363

PRAGMATIC SECTION, *dealing with the technique of making repairs*

CHAPTER VI APPLICATIONS   417

PHILOSOPHIC SECTION, *dealing with extensions of psychiatric theory*

BIBLIOGRAPHY   489

INDEX   *follows page* 517

CHAPTER I

PRINCIPLES

INTRODUCTORY SECTION, DEALING WITH MODERN
CONCEPTIONS OF MIND AND HEALTH

*Let us define mental health as the adjustment of human beings
to the world and to each other with a maximum of effectiveness
and happiness. Not just efficiency, or just contentment — or the
grace of obeying the rules of the game cheerfully. It is all of
these together. It is the ability to maintain an even temper, an
alert intelligence, socially considerate behaviour, and a happy
disposition. This, I think, is a healthy mind.*

—K. A. M.

CHAPTER I

PRINCIPLES

When a trout rising to a fly gets hooked on a line and finds himself unable to swim about freely, he begins a fight which results in struggles and splashes and sometimes an escape. Often, of course, the situation is too tough for him.

In the same way the human being struggles with his environment and with the hooks that catch him. Sometimes he masters his difficulties; sometimes they are too much for him. His struggles are all that the world sees and it usually misunderstands them. It is hard for a free fish to understand what is happening to a hooked one.

Sooner or later, however, most of us get hooked. How much of a fight we have on our hands then depends on the hook, and, of course, on us. If the struggle gets too violent, if it throws us out of the water, if we run afoul of other strugglers, we become "cases" in need of help and understanding. Statistics say that one out of every twenty of us is, or has been, or will be, in a hospital for mental illness; and the other nineteen of us don't feel any too comfortable all of the time, even if we have no fears of such an extremity. The minor symptoms of the struggle are legion; mental ill health is certainly as common as physical ill health and probably much more so. Cicero said: "The diseases of the mind are more numerous and more destructive than those of the body." He was right. But they are not always recognized as such.

When a man is promoted to a new job and it worries him so much that he has to quit it; when a woman gets married, finds herself unfitted for married life, and becomes depressed; when a student goes to college with high hopes, but fails in half his subjects; when a soldier goes to war and develops shell-shock at the sound of the first gun; when a lad of promise spurns opportunities of achievement in favour of cheque-forging or automobile-stealing — then these people are mentally unhealthy; they are unable to adjust themselves to their environment. They are

3

inept and they are unhappy; some of them will end their lives in tragedy.

Consider some more specific examples of hooked fish. Remember that you might not have thought of them so. " Eccentric," you might have said, " queer," perhaps even " just mean." But these are the sorts of struggle that indicate to the psychiatrist a fish hooked and in peril.

The man who is always sick

Henry Clay is a clerk. He has always been a clerk. He will always be a clerk. When he isn't clerking, which he does mechanically, accurately, satisfactorily, he is contemplating his imminent death. He regards himself as suffering from tuberculosis, diabetes, rheumatism, heart-trouble, and goitre. He confidently expects that one or all of these will get the upper hand any minute and put him in his grave. He has never been able to get married because he spends all his savings on doctors' bills and new remedies.

The scoffer

Weston Williams was the brilliant and handsome son of a wealthy father. Everything was done to afford opportunity for developing his intellectual talent. He was sent to the best schools and provided with the best of companions.

At twenty-seven he was a hard-boiled, scoffing, idle cynic. To exemplify his contempt for sentiment he married a girl thirty minutes after he met her; he did not even know her name. He divorced her and married a derelict, whom he picked up from the street, and upon whom he spent thousands of dollars, only to have her elope with another man after she became a presentable human being. He contemptuously rejected an opportunity to take the lead in a large business owned by his family and now lives anonymously on a small allowance sent to him by his family on condition that he stay away from home.

The nagging wife

Mrs. Watson is regarded by the women of her community as a brilliant, talented, charming woman. She presides over her committees, her clubs, and her parties with enviable grace and poise. Everyone assumes and believes that she is a beautiful wife and mother.

At home she nags the children, quarrels with her husband, mismanages her household, and points to her outside success as an indication that the fault is anyone's but hers.

The incendiary

Helen Wilson had married well. Her husband made money and she made friends who were prominent in the social circles of her city.

It was not until several mysterious fires had occurred that it dawned upon her husband that his wife had deliberately set them. When he accused her of it, she calmly and demurely denied it; even when indisputable proof was brought, she remained obdurate in her denials. For a time the fires ceased, but one night her husband awoke to see their garage in flames and to find his wife's place in bed empty.

The merchant turned criminal

Howard Gilchrist is the false name for a well-known prisoner in the Kansas state penitentiary. Four years ago he was the owner of a Ford agency, which was making him about forty thousand dollars a year. He played pool in the evenings for amusement and met at the poolroom some gentlemen of fortune who induced him to lend them a car and later join them in half a dozen escapades of bank-robbing and car-stealing which netted him about five hundred dollars and ten years in the state prison.

The man-haters

Mary's parents had done everything they could to break up a crush between her and her pal Nell, but in spite of tears and lectures and threats and scoldings Mary and Nell were steadfast. No other girls interested them; all men disgusted them. They were happy with each other even when they were quarrelling most bitterly.

The impulsive thief

Helen Marsden was about to be married. Her friends congratulated and envied her and said that she had made a very good match.

Helen spent the few weeks prior to her marriage visiting her husband's relatives. These people began to miss little trinkets and articles of wearing-apparel. When it became almost certain that the prospective member of the family, whom they were fêting, was the guilty party, it was decided to let an outsider present the matter to her in an effort to clear up the embarrassment. In spite of excellent proof, however, she flatly denied the accusations and made a great stir about the "insulting suspicions." Her room was entered during her absence, however, and most of the loot recovered.

When she was faced with this, she confessed frankly that she was the victim of an impulse to steal which she could not control. Her fiancé took her immediately to a psychiatrist and arranged for treatment which was recommended. Realizing that she had come near to losing her husband-to-be and her bright future, the girl entered earnestly into the plan for her reformation. Three weeks after treatment had begun, however, the doctor discovered that half a dozen books, ten dollars' worth of stamps, a valuable paper-weight, and numerous other articles and small change had disappeared from the reception-room of his office, in spite of the vigilance of the office assistants.

The scholar

Evelyn Hawkins made Phi Beta Kappa. Three months before she was to be graduated, she left school. This is what she told her roommate:

" I went to school nearly four years. I was supposed to be one of the most popular girls in school. I made good grades, as you know; I was at the head of committees; I was president of my sorority. But during all that time I had just exactly three dates with men. One of them I myself invited to one of our own parties, and one of them was got for me by a mutual friend. What is there about me that makes me so uninteresting to men? I went and asked some of my friends. They told me I was too intellectual; they told me I didn't flirt enough or put myself out. They told me I was a prude and didn't do enough necking.

" So I did my best to change all these things, but without the slightest results that I could see. If I'm not capable of interesting men, I'm not capable of being a wife; and if I can't be a wife and mother, I don't care to live at all. What's all this intellectual development worth? I'm not going to spend my life teaching other folks' kids; I want my own."

The accusing physician

Dr. Jones was the leading physician in his community. His indefatigable industry, his natural skill, and his utter self-confidence gave him immediate prestige. His conceit rose to the highest degree and his peculiarities began to be increasingly offensive. He criticized the older physicians as being ignoramuses, asses, and quacks.

One of them sued him for these compliments and a long-drawn-out contest ensued. In order to help his own case he studied law and was even admitted to the bar. In the meantime, however, he came into acrimonious conflict with his own lawyers, refused to pay them, and brought suit against one of them. He began to believe that the courts were prejudiced against him and published bitter attacks upon them in certain radical journals, which in turn involved him in contempt charges. Before things came to a climax, there were forty-one suits in progress and he had accused hundreds of people of mischief and malice.

THE EVOLUTION OF THE DEVIL

What is the matter with these people?

Ever since the dawn of history society has been trying to decide. They have been called one thing and another; they have been pushed from pillar to post. All sorts of explanations have held popular sway.

Two thousand years ago it was *devils*. Persons and things were " possessed of devils." Jesus and others in the Bible cast out these devils. Some of the native Australians and Africans still interpret misbehaviour as demoniac possession.

But this Devil has undergone evolution. In the Middle Ages some of these people would have been called *witches* and others *bewitched*. The witches had sold themselves to Satan. And this amiable theory of misbehaviour and unhappiness still persists, not only in certain parts of Africa, but among certain groups in civilized countries.[1]

A little later the Devil became *original sin*. Sincere, devout people still exist who regard the misbehaviour of mankind as nothing but the evidence of sinfulness. Their solution is religious salvation. Instead of burning and exiling these strange actors as the devil-believers did, or hanging them and drowning them as the witch-believers did, they would have them prayed with, exhorted, cajoled, threatened, frightened, and told to repent and believe in God.

Then there is a less religious but more practical-minded point of view which regards all misbehaviour as representing *orneriness*, or *pure cussedness*. Because this is simple, because it is less pretentious, it has a great following, especially among policemen, army sergeants, and the superintendents of girls' reformatories. Unfortunately it, too, is much of a pessimistic theory based on a sentimental rather than on an intellectual attitude toward the problem, so that its application is as fruitless as the application of the theories of witchcraft and devil-possession.

A little more recent in origin were the moralists. They linked up all behaviour, good and bad, with a mystical metaphysical essence called responsibility. According to this solemn theory, it isn't God or lack of God, or sin or the Devil or witches or anything celestial or mundane that makes men saints or sinners. It is a single, solemn imponderable called *responsibility*. Millions of dollars are spent annually to determine who has it or who hasn't it. If one is found to have it, he is locked up; if he is found not to have it, he is also locked up. Thus is demonstrated

---

[1] See Theda Kenyon: *Witches Still Live* (New York: Ives Washburn, Inc., 1929) , and " Witches Win in York," by Dudley Nichols, in the *Nation* January 23, 1929.

the pragmatic beauty of the doctrine, which is neither fish nor fowl, but which is still the shibboleth and the fallacy of the lawyers just as the doctrine of original sin was the fallacy of the clergy.

And next came the fallacy of the psychologists. When they discovered tests a few years ago which in a general way measured the amount of intelligence a person has, and began applying this test to people far and wide, they found out that many people had less of it than had been supposed. Accordingly they began to suspect that a person who got into trouble did so because he hadn't enough brains to keep out of trouble. *Feeble-mindedness* became the explanation of all the woes of mankind, from bed-wetting to bootlegging. The psychologists no longer cling, officially, to this fallacy. They know, as does everyone else, that there is far more to the human mind than intelligence.

Then came the eugenists, for whom the Devil took the form of bad *heredity*. The fact that the children of feeble-minded parents sometimes become college professors and the fact that superior parents are often afflicted with inferior progeny has discouraged most of them.

The philosophers all this while were explaining it all as *human nature* (to which they assign numerous titles). Nations may rise and fall, social forms and economic systems may change ever so much, but something called human nature — so they insisted — remains unchanged. But what is this human nature? The same old Devil we have been discovering in the fallacious thinking of every group. As John Dewey says,

" ' Give a dog a bad name and hang him.' Human nature has been the dog of professional moralists, and consequences accord with the proverb. Man's nature has been regarded with suspicion, with fear, with sour looks, sometimes with enthusiasm for its possibilities but only when these were placed in contrast with its actualities. . . . It has been supposed that morality would be quite superfluous were it not for the inherent weakness, bordering on depravity, of human nature. Some writers with a more genial conception have attributed the current blackening to theologians who have thought to honor the divine by disparaging the human. Theologians have doubtless taken a gloomier view of man than have pagans and secularists. But this explanation doesn't take us far. For after all these theologians are themselves human, and they would have been without

influence if the human audience had not somehow responded to them." [2]

We have good reasons for believing that there is no such thing as human nature, certainly not in the sense of a human nature independent of social-psychological-biological laws.[3] And these are not something we can get moralistic about. This is a long-time philosophical fallacy.[4]

And finally there came the great fallacy of the psychiatrists, who found yet another cloak for His Satanic Majesty. His new name was *insanity*. People who misbehaved seriously must be crazy, sometimes with craziness type A, sometimes craziness type X; sometimes benign, sometimes malignant. But always human misbehaviour was explained on the assumption that something from the outside world got into the inside of a hapless soul and made him do and feel as he shouldn't do and feel.

And this in general is the trouble with all these theories. They all assume that something mysterious and malignant floating in the ether or transmitted in the germ plasm gets into the individual and makes him go wrong. And then he gets called names. Calling people witches or devils or psychopathic personalities doesn't help. To do so doesn't indicate any real understanding of why they are what they are, why they do what they do, or what can be done to help matters. If any names are to be called, they ought to be names which imply something as to treatment.

SCIENCE VERSUS COMMON SENSE

I can hear somebody say: " Well, why not just treat them by the rules of common sense? Why not drop all theories — or leave them to scientists — and just use plain common sense in handling these problems? "

Well, what passes for " common sense " is usually tried without yielding the help it would seem to promise. Here are a few examples that I know of, fictitious names — except in one celebrated case — being used instead of the real ones. Observe how " common sense " worked out with these cases.

[2] John Dewey: *Human Nature and Conduct* (New York: Henry Holt & Co., 1922), p. 1.

[3] See J. F. Brown: *Psychology and the Social Order* (New York: McGraw-Hill Book Co., 1936), Chapter XIV.

[4] One could go further and point out that the Devil theory is invoked officially or unofficially by nearly everyone. Karl Marx's devil was the capitalist, Hitler's devil is the Jew, the American bourgeois devil is the communist, the Christian Scientists' devil is the doctor.

Annabel Martin was always the life of the party. Everyone thought she was the loveliest, happiest, sweetest child they had ever known. She bubbled over with good spirits.

In her senior year in college she had a slight disappointment over a school honour. Her parents assured her that it was of no consequence and urged her to ignore it. But despite this " common sense " treatment by her parents, she became very sad, lost interest in everything, cried a great deal, and finally had to be taken to a psychiatric hospital for another kind of treatment.

George Dickens was a thoughtful, intelligent child who took things quite seriously and delighted his parents because of his good judgment and common sense. During the latter part of his high-school career he worried about family finances. He wanted very much to go to college, but he felt that it would be an unbearable drain on his father. His parents thought that he was a little depressed and attempted to cheer him up by back-slappings and exhortations to " snap out of it." They insisted that everything would be all right and told him to forget it. One evening, when the rest of the family had gone to a show, he killed himself with a revolver.

Edward Hickman was a brilliant student in school; he won second place in an oratorical contest and was editor of his high-school paper. A few years later he had forged many cheques (an offence which was treated by " common sense "), committed many hold-ups, and, having killed at least one man, perpetrated the murder of Marian Parker.

" Common sense " did not avert these tragedies. Nor did " common sense " do anything for such everyday problems as the following, each of which represents the end result of a struggle in which common sense, or what was thought to be common sense, was used in vain.

Whenever little Harry wanted something that wasn't immediately forthcoming, he whined and pouted. This might or might not succeed. Harry learned — but no matter; it's his method, and has been for thirty-five years. For Harry is now forty years old.

Mary Martin was so shy that she would hide behind her mother's skirts when the postman came. She never learned to meet people on their own level. A husband found her and keeps her, but she still hides, now behind him and behind their daughter.

Miss Ritchey is a college graduate who is proficient in interior decoration and design. Her talents make her much in demand, but certain mannerisms and nervous habits are so unpleasant for her friends and associates that she leads a lonely life. She has a persistent hacking cough and a habit of sniffing. She twitches and jerks her hands and is constantly fingering something or someone. She has little idea of the reasons for her unpopularity and even less idea what to do about it. Plenty of common sense, but —

Mr. Johnston would long ago have been promoted to the vice-presidency of his firm, many believe, had he not been so constantly gloomy and self-deprecatory. He is always sighing and apologizing for himself and prophesying failure. His work is excellent, but he can't see it. Indeed, he is ashamed of it. He makes all about him uncomfortable and distrustful. His common sense doesn't work.

Mr. Allen is a successful banker. His knowledge of investments and finance has made his bank very prosperous and has inspired the confidence of thousands. In his home, however, he is so autocratic, so dictatorial, so critical of the efforts of his wife and children to please him, that his family life is in a constant turmoil of anger, resentment, quarrelling, and unhappiness. Common sense?

Gertrude, a girl of nineteen, came from a celebrated family, members of which had done everything from entering the foreign mission field to becoming leaders of the most frivolous social set. Seclusiveness was certainly Gertrude's outstanding symptom. It was ascribed by her to a slight facial blemish, which she thought to be much more conspicuous than it really was. She was given to excessive day-dreaming, always sinking into reverie at the slightest opportunity. This she said she had always done because she had been left alone so much — never had had any playmates, any tasks, or any purposes. Her childhood had been full of actively imaginative play, but in contact with social reality she was self-conscious, diffident, seclusive, and constantly fearful as to her popularity. " Why is it? " she asked. " I wish someone would tell me why it is that I have no social life, no dates, and practically no girl friends. It must be my fault; the others chum together all right. But no one wants to do what I want to do when I want to do it. If I suggest a thing, it's a kind of a hoodoo — everyone's suddenly busy or can't go or won't go unless they can get reserved seats, and there are no more reserved seats, and so forth."
What's common sense here?

Common sense cannot solve these problems. This is no reflection upon common sense; it is what we have to rely upon in many of the decisions of life, and until science has provided us with something better in any given field, common sense is all we have — and some do not even have that. As soon as science has discovered enough definite facts to make new constructions possible, however, common-sense rules of thumb must be superseded by more useful methods based upon these scientific findings. The common-sense way to travel would be by foot or horseback; once it would have been thought to be a violation of common sense even to imagine any other way to get about. Now we should regard anyone who walks from one city to another as violating common sense, rather than utilizing it.

In the same way all the older theories of the treatment of human beings in distress based upon common-sense concepts are now giving way to theories and practices based upon increasing scientific knowledge of human behaviour. We no longer treat appendicitis or rheumatism by instructing the victim to wear a metallic belt or to dose himself with purgatives. And not only are physical ills now better understood and better treated, but the same is true of mental ills. It is much more recently, however, that science has been applied to the afflictions of the human mind, because it is only recently that we have come to apply scientific method to the study of human behaviour.

This statement will come as a surprise to many readers. Is not psychology the science of the mind? — and surely psychology is an old science. Does not all this study of human thought and emotions and actions belong in the old well-known science of psychology?

In the broad sense of the word, of course it does. But the trouble is that the word " psychology " is used in so many senses. There are psychologies and psychologies.[5] In the sense in which it has generally been used, however, the academic sense, psychology is (or has been) the scientific study of the human mind shut up in a laboratory.

Now, no human mind is ever shut up in a laboratory; at least no mind lives so. Human beings live in constant contact and interaction with other human beings, and the vast majority of mental processes concern these interactions. Consequently the information that we get from observing and describing and testing an individual in a laboratory, while very valuable as groundwork, is of little practical advantage in understanding the human

---

[5] See, for example, *Psychologies of 1925*, and also *Psychologies of 1930*; excellent summaries of various schools by competent representatives, published by Clark University (Worcester).

being. Your family physician had an elaborate course in anatomy, seventy-five per cent of which he has forgotten. The anatomy of a cadaver is of relatively little practical importance in the treatment of Grandmother's diabetes or in deciding upon a climate for Uncle John. Anatomy is not medical science, and psychology is not mental science; it is merely one of the foundation-stones on which mental science is built.

Psychology teaches us, for example, that we are made aware of the world by means of certain nerves and certain brain areas; that impressions are stored up and can be recalled under certain circumstances; that the organization of these memories constitutes, in a sense, what we call intelligence and that this can be measured by a relatively simple series of questions and answers. Psychology teaches us, further, that in addition to intelligence we have emotions and that this intelligence is affected by these emotions, and vice versa, and that both of them affect the motor acts of an individual — in other words, his behaviour. Psychology has measured the rapidity with which certain phases of this process take place. It has classified the varieties of response. It has even studied the various abnormalities in these responses. These, which are of great importance to psychiatry, are presented in Chapter III of this book.

But all this is from a practical standpoint far removed from the actual everyday behaviour of human beings. Psychologists know this, and for the most part they don't care any more than an anatomist cares what the doctors decide to do about preventing the grippe. Some of them, on the other hand, have felt the practical urge and have traced the relationship of certain nerves and certain habits to certain human activities, particularly the processes of learning and the processes of industry. This is the origin of what is called educational psychology and industrial psychology. The latter is the basis of the extraordinary work of efficiency engineers such as Frank and Lillian Gilbreth, Harrington Emerson, and others. Some, deploring the fact that psychology was so little interested in the scientific study of behaviour, went to the extreme of formulating a doctrine that there is nothing to mind and to life *but* behaviour. Such a revolt from academic psychology, which, to be sure, had become both dull and sterile, was accompanied by other reactions such as that of the psychometrists, who, following the lead of workers in the physical sciences, applied themselves to measuring some of the psychological functions. This, of course, could not touch the problem of *feeling*, which has only recently become the focus of psychological research. A few psychologists ventured into the field of clinical work — that is, the treatment of people with obvious psychological inhibitions and distortions — but in this the psychologists are handicapped, traditionally because the treatment of the sick has always been a function of physicians and scientifically because it is impossible to separate mind from body, and most psychologists have not had technical instruction concerning the body in relation to disease.

Nevertheless, it was this tendency toward the closer union of medicine and psychology that gave rise to the modern conception of a rational scientific treatment of the " hooked fish," the conception I shall endeavour to elaborate in this book.

PSYCHIATRY

Cloistered within the forbidding walls of mysterious castles on the outskirts of a few villages scattered over the country there have dwelt for the past century a strange and esoteric order known as psychiatrists. They were the keepers of the " insane " — physicians, scientists, medical men, to be sure, but medical men with so extraordinary and incredible an interest that they were apologized for by the rest of the profession as being almost as questionable as the patients they cared for. Yet with the passage of years and with the assistance of the psychologists and sociologists, the chemists and anatomists, who from time to time worked with them, these men accumulated an experience with the behaviour of queer people which gave them an understanding of why people do things, which opened up entirely new vistas in the science of the human mind.

Watching smooth-running automobiles purring along the highways or studying these cars minutely as they pose in the sales-room might supply a considerable body of knowledge about automobiles; it would certainly never give the understanding of why automobiles work and why they don't work, such as does the study made by a humble mechanic in the greasy back rooms of a garage repair shop. And this is precisely why psychiatrists who have studied the " wrecks " that came to them became enabled to say something definite, positive, and useful about the queer behaviour of queer people. And then about the queer behaviour of normal people. They discovered that there were general laws governing behaviour, laws as definite as those gov·

erning breathing or digestion. They discovered the ways in which a knowledge of these laws might be used to rehabilitate some of the wrecks and to prevent many other wrecks. And after they had been doing this with increasingly gratifying results, known only to themselves, the World War came along and they had a chance to prove their theories.

It was psychiatry that introduced first the idea of treating sick minds and then the idea of preventing mental ill health. In fact it is from the idea of preventing mental ill health that a more useful conception of the nature of the mind took its origin.

Preventing mental ill health has, in fact, become a movement [6] with a definite objective for an increasingly large group of informed people — laymen and scientists. It assumes at the outset that mental health and ill health actually exist and can be understood. It assumes that the distress of a personality struggling with an environment is simply struggle and not a matter of devils and witches, sin and " orneriness," or yet a matter of feeble intellect or feeble will.

It further assumes that mental health is attainable, and our failure to attain it and retain it is to some extent dependent upon our ignorance of general principles. For while health has always been one of the chief concerns of mankind, health has meant by implication the health of the body. Few people give any attention to the climate of their emotions or to brushing their mental teeth or to giving their minds a bath or their memories a cathartic.

---

[6] Mental hygiene as a movement has had several parents; in its present form it was initiated through the efforts of Clifford Beers whose book, *A Mind That Found Itself* (1908) eventuated in a National Committee for Mental Hygiene (1909) . This organization, now under the direction of Dr. George S. Stevenson, issues many publications and has initiated and assisted in many surveys and other projects aiming at the promotion of the mental health of the community. In 1843 a book was published in New York by Dr. William Sweetser, of the University of Vermont, entitled *Mental Hygiene*. Eleven years earlier a Dr. Amariah Brigham, later the first Superintendent of the Utica State Hospital, published a book entitled *Remarks on the Influence of Mental Cultivation and Mental Excitement upon Health*. In 1859 Dr. George Cook, superintendent of a private psychiatric hospital, published two articles on mental hygiene. In 1860 Dr. William M. Connell wrote *How to Enjoy Life, or Physical and Mental Hygiene,* and in 1863 Dr. Isaac Ray, one of the founders of American psychiatry, published a book entitled *Mental Hygiene*. In 1880 a National Association for the Protection of the Insane and the Prevention of Insanity was organized, whose policies were essentially the same as those of its successor, the National Committee for Mental Hygiene. This organization died about 1886. For a longer review see Albert Deutsch on " Mental Hygiene " in *One Hundred Years of American Psychiatry* (New York: Columbia University Press, 1944) .

And until recently they have had little help from either the scientists or public officials. Much money is spent by the federal government and by every state government and many municipal governments for the ensuring of healthy bodies in the citizenry; only a few states spend as much as a dime for the promotion of mental health, and the federal government spends nothing. The teeth, the tonsils, the eyes, and the ears of thousands of school-children are meticulously examined each year by physicians and their assistants, and much clatter and fuss are made over elaborate statistical reports of the damage found, repaired, or averted. Meanwhile, how much thought is given to the examining of the *minds* [7] of these same children? Are teeth and tonsils more important than minds?

Railroads and industries have medical services commonly; only a few of these, until recently, took account of the mental health of their employees. One large railroad sends a fully equipped ophthalmological office and staff over its entire system; every employee must pass certain rigid eye-tests. This same railroad makes no effort to examine the minds behind those eyes.

PROSPECTUS

The following chapters of this book endeavor to present the psychiatrist's conception of the human mind, with illustrations of the material from which he has derived this conception. It is only his; it does not preclude the truth of psychologists' laboratory views or philosophers' metaphysical views.

This book is devoted to an exposition of the theme that such cases as have been cited are samples of human distress comparable to the splashing of the fish described in the opening paragraph, that these splashings represent jams in the mental machinery, and that both the machinery and the jams are common to all and can be better understood with a better knowledge of the machinery and its jamming propensities. From such a study, our thesis holds, some jams may be relieved and the wheels restarted.

What factors, internal and external, bring about these jams? What are the tendencies in the personality which result in disaster in certain situations? And what do the disasters look like, and what are the signals of distress? What underlies these signals

[7] " Minds " is not equivalent to " intellects."

(the symptoms) and how can their language be understood? How can the failures be averted, and the victims rehabilitated? And, finally, how do the philosophy and techniques of psychiatry as here presented relate to theories of education, industry, law, and medicine?

The answers to these questions form the content of the succeeding chapters.

CHAPTER II

PERSONALITIES

SYNTHETIC SECTION, DEALING WITH THE EXTERNAL APPEAR-
ANCES OF THE ASSEMBLED MACHINE IN ACTION AND
PARTICULARLY IN DISASTER

*"All our lives long, every day and every hour, we are engaged
in the process of accommodating our changed and unchanged selves
to changed and unchanged surroundings; living, in fact, is
nothing else than this process of accommodation; when we fail
in it a little we are stupid, when we fail flagrantly we are mad,
when we suspend it temporarily we sleep, when we give up the
attempt altogether we die. In quiet, uneventful lives the changes
internal and external are so small that there is little or no strain
in the process of fusion and accommodation; in other lives there
is great strain, but there is also great fusing and accommodating
power; in others great strain with little accommodating power.
A life will be successful or not, according as the power of accommodation is equal to or unequal to the strain of fusing and
adjusting internal and external changes."*

— SAMUEL BUTLER in *The Way of All Flesh*

CHAPTER II

PERSONALITIES

The function of the mind has never been better phrased than in the words of Samuel Butler in *The Way of All Flesh,* quoted on page 19. This process of accommodation to the various forces and laws of the universe is accomplished by a great complexity of devices. Rivers adjust themselves to the terrain they traverse, rocks are beholden to the laws of gravity, and trees respond to the stimuli of the sun and the need for water. Grass, trodden upon, rises up again; birds of passage fly south to avoid cold weather. All these are " accommodations " — adjustments to environment. Living beings adjust themselves to their needs, they adapt their needs to their environments, and they derive from the environment satisfaction for their needs.

Now, the higher in the scale of life we go, the more complex are the needs, the more complex the mechanism for gratifying them. But the mental process in all beings — men and dogs, trees and earthworms — is essentially the same. Everyone knows, for example, that if a dog is hungry, he calls upon his memories of where food is to be had and betakes himself thither, and this is precisely what trees and earthworms and bank presidents do. The food selected will vary — the method of securing it will vary — the method of digestion will vary. But it is all to the same end.

If the essential *similarity* in the " minds " of all creatures is the gratifying of the instincts of each (the laws of nature) by some sort of an adaptation to what the world has to offer him at any particular time, what is the essential *difference*? The essential difference is merely one of complexity. The dog can remember more things than the earthworm, the child can remember more things than the dog, and the bank president remembers more things than the child. There are certain ways in which these memories are stored and certain ways in which they are recalled and used; this makes up the process of thinking, which is correspondingly more complicated in human beings. We shall discuss this more fully later on.

THE HUMAN MIND

Because we have a large memory storehouse, we are able to recognize and appreciate and crave vast numbers of opportunities for gratifying our instincts which are entirely denied to trees, dogs, and earthworms. But mind is more than merely memory and thinking. These gratifications utilize in the end the same simple physical equipment which dogs, and to some extent earthworms, have in common with us. (Here of course the plant kingdom is different.) Walking and fighting and feeling and breathing, listening to a concert, making love, or running for the legislature, all require physical as well as psychological machinery. They are the products of stimuli acting — through the mind — on muscles and glands.

In fact, the interaction of psychological and physical factors is such that except for theoretical purposes they are almost inseparable. There used to be hot disputes among psychologists as to whether a man ran because he was afraid or was afraid because he ran. Now we know that both are true, that running is a part of the mind's action in the affair just as much as the blanching of the skin or the palpitating of the heart, the standing of the hair on end, or the illusion of having seen a ghost.

For this reason it is impossible to discuss profitably different types of minds without reference to all the various factors that go to make up different types of human beings. Psychologists used to think that the mind was simply the performance of the brain, just as bile is the product of the liver, and breathing is the function of the lungs. We know now that it takes much more than a pair of lungs to effect breathing (it takes a nose and a windpipe and some chest muscles and a diaphragm and a regulating centre). In the same way we know now that the brain is only one of the organs of the mind — that is, only part of the machinery which helps in the adjustment of an individual. The mind depends to a certain extent upon the memory storehouse of the brain, but it also depends upon the sensory nerve endings in the skin, and the motor nerve endings in the muscles; it depends upon the muscles themselves and to some extent upon all the physical structures of the body.

This leads straight to the conclusion that in writing about

" the human mind " we have to abandon the project of writing about it in the sense of its being the brain's little bag of tricks. We must write about the mind as an adjustment process. And there we meet the difficulty that writing about processes is thin soup; what people are interested in is human beings and how these processes apply to them. How can we indicate that our focus of interest is in the human being as a bundle of instincts, habits, memories, organs, muscles, and sensations, all going through a process, a process of constantly changing itself in an effort to make itself more comfortable, constantly changing its environment for the same purpose, and constantly being changed by its environment, sometimes for better, sometimes for worse?

The word " personality " serves our purpose. Of course it has been used to describe almost everything from the attributes of the soul to those of a new talcum powder. As I shall use it, it means the individual as a whole, his height and weight and loves and hates and blood-pressure and reflexes; his smiles and hopes and bowed legs and enlarged tonsils. It means all that anyone is and all that he is trying to become. This is the modern psychiatric meaning of the term " personality."

What, more specifically, are the components of personality?

HEREDITY

Personality must be considered to possess an inherited nucleus, a nucleus of physical and psychological potentialities. Just how much or how little this hereditary part is, no one really knows; all we are sure of is that it is less than we used to think. It is probably confined to physical structure, including brain patterns. Functional propensities are usually acquired rather than inherited. This includes such things as nervousness, indigestion, alcoholism, a sense of humour, temper tantrums, and behaviour patterns in general. It is hard for the public and the eugenists to believe this, trained as they are to think in terms of " unit characters " as applied to structure. For we all know that tall parents are apt to have tall sons, that red hair runs in families, that children may be seen to have the same profile or the same skin texture or the same shape of hand as one of their parents. The wonderful results of breeding in domesticated animals are eloquent proof of the importance of heredity so far as *structure* is concerned.

But structure is not behaviour, and determines behaviour only within very wide limits. And while we know that many children imitate their parents in small things as well as in larger, and in attitudes as well as in general types of emotional reactions, we do not have any evidence that they inherit these similarities, and there is much evidence that we do *not* inherit them. We are apt to jump to the conclusion that, because these structural details are often the same in parent and child and are known to be inherited, behaviouristic tendencies which are similar in parent and child are likewise inherited. Furthermore, as I have said, some few scientists still believe that they are.

There are plenty of historical examples that ought to discourage such a theory. The monster Caligula, for example, was the son of Germanicus, who was a magnificent character; Germanicus was also the father of Agrippina, a despicable female, and the grandfather of Nero, whose reputation needs no citation. The cruel Domitian was the son of the wise, kindly Vespasian; and Commodus, who was a gross criminal, was the son of the noble Marcus Aurelius Antoninus. The father of Augustine was a rascal; Francis Bacon's mother was called insane, and both of the parents of John Kepler (the forerunner of Newton) were very queer.[1] Even Jesus, according to Matthew, came of a line on whose escutcheon there were some inconsistent blots.

> Considering your heredity, O my Savior,
> And that your ancestor Roboam was a bad man,
> And begat Abia, a bad son;
> And that the said Abia, a bad father,
> Begat Asa, a good son;
> And that Asa, a good father,
> Begat Josophat, a good son;
> And that Josophat begat Joram,
> Of whom nothing is known;
> Who in turn begat Ozias, of whom nothing is known;
> And on down, until your father Joseph was born,
> Of whom nothing is known,
> Except that it took an angel from heaven
> To keep him from divorcing your mother Mary —
> Seeing all this, and that my father was a drunkard,
> And I a leader in the church, a man of substance,
> I must conclude from your case and my own

[1] Arthur C. Jacobson: *Genius* (New York: Greenberg, 1927), p. 145.

That neither piety nor impiety
Is hereditary —
Which makes me fear for my son! [2]

In spite of what I have just said, a great many people believe
and will go on believing that not only personality traits but personality defects and personality diseases are inherited. This is
not confined to laymen; I have listened many times to dissertations by scientists of considerable standing who proceeded upon
the assumption that mental disease was hereditary. " Insanity in
the family " is pronounced as if it were an ominous warning or
condemnation. One of the most distinguished authors on stomach diseases frequently introduces into his otherwise erudite and
sensible medical addresses a digression concerning the probable
influence on stomach disease of this dreadful, lurking menace
— " insanity somewhere in the family tree." In several states,
including my own, patients in state hospitals who show some evidence of recovery from temporary illness, with a prospect of
returning to private life, are rendered sterile by an operation on
the dubious theory that this will decrease the incidence of mental disease in the community. In some instances sterilization is
undoubtedly desirable, but its wholesale application tends to
nourish the false comfort that something important is being
done by the state in the direction of preventive medicine.[3]

The truth is that at the present time we have no convincing
scientific evidence that " insanity " or any generally prevalent
form of mental disease likely to result in insanity is definitely
transmitted by heredity. There are a few exceptions to be noted
— one or two degenerative conditions of the nerve tissue which
seem to run in families but which are very rare. Epilepsy is
often described as hereditary but the trend of scientific opinion
is against this (see Myerson, *cit. infra.,* pp. 57–72) . Even feeble-
mindedness, which we once felt to be quite definitely and regularly hereditary in certain forms, is in the vast majority of cases,
not transmitted.

This problem was thoroughly investigated and reported upon
by Abraham Myerson [4] in a book which, while technical, is in-

[2] Edgar Lee Masters: " Ezekias Painter " in *The New Spoon River* (New York:
Boni & Liveright, 1924) .

[3] For a good summary of the present status of sterilization, see Jerome M.
Schneck: " The Problem of Sterilization in the Mentally Unfit," *Medical Record,*
April 1944.

[4] Abraham Myerson: *The Inheritance of Mental Diseases* (Baltimore: Williams & Wilkins Co., 1925) .

telligible to any educated layman and should be consulted by anyone, patient or physician, who suffers from the dread of the heredity bugaboo. A highly authoritative technical study of this subject was made by a committee of the American Neurological Association with particular reference to the sterilization program,[5] which weighs all the arguments and cites many books. The conclusions are essentially those implied above.

As a matter of fact, it is no longer considered scientific to speak of heredity and environment as sharply separated categories. The terms are useful as descriptive concepts, but they cannot be accurately defined except " operationally," and in this sense they describe characteristics of phenomena which are essentially continuous. We can *define* environmental forces, as Brown says,[6]

". . . as those over which we have potential control, and hereditary forces as those over which we have as yet no possibility of control. From this definition many things which we might control but do not are still to be considered as environmental. One thing is certain: If we may judge the future by past successes, the frontier's control will be pushed farther back as science grows. Hence, from this viewpoint no single trait is for all time determined by any specific hereditary force. The slogan, ' There is no heredity without environment, no environment without heredity,' may be taken to mean that no trait exists over which we are without some power to control, but for no trait are we able to bring about complete manipulatory control."

Many readers will be asking themselves: " If mental disease is not inherited, how is to be accounted for that Mr. Jones had melancholia and two of his sons had the same affliction; that Mrs. Brown had some nervous affliction, all of her children were nervous and three of her grandchildren too; that Mrs. Smith's aunt has precisely the same form of eccentricity that she has? " Such family histories are known to all of us, and the easiest assumption to make is that something is conveyed through the germ plasm. Such a theory conveniently relegates the responsibility for such afflictions to the ancestors. There may be a germ of truth in it; some brain structure defects *may* prove to be trans-

5 *A Report of the Committee of the American Neurological Association* . . . *composed of Abraham Myerson, M.D., James B. Ayer, M.D., Tracy J. Putnam, M.D., Clyde E. Keeler, Sc.D., and Leo Alexander, M.D.* (New York: The Macmillan Co., 1936) .

6 J. F. Brown: *Psychology and the Social Order* (New York; McGraw-Hill Book Co., 1936) , pp. 263, 264.

missible. But we cannot ignore the incalculable potency of the factors of unconscious imitation and suggestion.

It would be a mistake, however, to err in the opposite direction and assume that *nothing* is inherited. In addition to the structural patterns already referred to, there are probably peculiar neural arrangements which facilitate certain types of reaction. The point is that at the present time we know so little about this, so much less than is popularly assumed, that it were better to concentrate on what we do know about environmental factors than blindly and superstitiously to ascribe things to heredity.

THE PERSONALITY

Whatever nucleus is inherited is soon acted upon by a great variety of powerful influences. There are the teaching, training, and example of the parents, and the reactions to brothers and sisters; there are climate and weather, the architecture of the home, the food, fashions; there is the influence of the school, church, newspapers, playmates, society in general.[7] Economic laws and social laws are brought to bear and modify behaviour patterns. Then come the accidents of life, physical and mental, the illnesses, the wounds, the griefs, the disappointments, the shocks of all kinds that come to all people. All of these mould the personality. All of these things go to make up a personality.

When we proceed to study a personality scientifically, we go about it in a systematic way, securing first a history of the progenitors with their general mould, accomplishments, propensities, and so on; likewise of the other members of the family. We secure the history of the individual — of his birth, his infancy and childhood, his school life, vocational life, social life, sexual life, and health. Then we proceed to the examinations, which may be thought of as falling into four kinds, or made upon four levels (White). First there is the body *physics* to consider, its structure, its organs, its neurones, its glands; secondly the body *chemistry*, the blood, urine, cerebrospinal fluid, metabolism, and so forth; thirdly there is the *psychology* of the individual, his temperament, his memory, his intelligence, his obsessions, and many such considerations, to be taken up later

[7] For a masterful analysis of the way in which personality is determined by the social organization, see J. F. Brown: *Psychology and the Social Order* (New York: McGraw-Hill Book Co., 1936).

on in this book, perhaps best summarized in the phrase " behaviour patterns "; finally there must be an investigation of the *social* capacities of the individual — how does he get along with his fellows? [8]

And after we have studied these component parts of the personality, we attempt to evaluate them as a whole. (That the whole is more than the sum of all its parts is the basis of psychiatric practice, as well as of the most modern trend in psychology, Gestalt psychology.) Having obtained these data, we must ask ourselves how, in this complex world, does one use the physics and chemistry and psychology that go to make him a human being. What are the usual results of this person's efforts to adjust himself to situations? Is he in the habit of succeeding, or in

[8] To have dealt in a thorough or systematic way with the components of the personality at this point, or even to have entered into a discussion of the theories of personality which have dominated scientific thought during the development of scientific knowledge would have made the text unendurably long. It is interesting to consider, however, that the earliest conceptions of personality (Empedocles, 450 B.C., and Hippocrates, 400 B.C.) were essentially *psychological;* Galen (about A.D. 170) elaborated the *chemical* theory of personality, ascribing it to various internal secretions, a theory which even yet has a few representatives who think of personality largely in terms of the structural and functional results of glandular secretions, forgetting that the glands themselves have a structure and function which are surely determined by something. This confusion of mechanisms with basic purposes is typical of much thinking in regard to human behaviour. Along with this, Kant's (1798) emphasis on the psychological aspect of personality instead of the physiological was continued by the psychologists; the first extensive psychological study of character was made by Bain in 1861. For a long period this continued in the form of experimental psychology and later as psychometry, and was most fruitfully developed by the psychoanalytic additions of material from the unconscious.

Finally, the *physical* study of character and its representatives, probably began with Albrecht Dürer, who in a book published after his death by a friend (1528) developed the idea that " One finds in the human species various (physical) types which may be used for different figures according to the complexion of the individual. . . . By means of outward proportions, one can indicate the natures of men. . . ." Galton in England proposed the first anthropological approach to the study of personality and character (1877), which was closely related to the criminal theories of Lombroso (1866) and the only slightly less absurd doctrine of phrenology which followed it, to be replaced by a sober, thoughtfully conceived, but, in my opinion, almost equally undemonstrated version of physical types introduced by Kretschmer (1921). The characteristic of modern psychiatry is its emphasis upon the inseparability of the psychological, physical, chemical, and social constituents of the personality, and it is this concept that is assumed as definitive in the text of this book.

It is evidence of the interest in the study of the personality and extent of published works on the subject that at least one entire book has been published for the purpose of listing the books and articles which have appeared in this field (A. A. Roback: *A Bibliography of Character and Personality* [Cambridge, Mass.: Sci-Art Publishers, 1927], a comprehensive, accurate guide from which the above summary is taken in part).

the habit of failing, and if so, how? What happens, we inquire, when that which this person *is* attempts adjustments to situations which this person *meets?*

THE SITUATION

The situation is that part of the external environment to which the personality has to adjust itself. It is the particular phase of life presented at a particular moment. It is a composite of requirements, a game with a set of rules, the game we must play in order to live.

The rules of life are made up of physical laws, chemical laws, economic laws, social customs, legal enactments, and many local regulations. This is a far cry from the simplicity of savage life, and it is getting harder to live each day. The laws grow more and more complicated. It is no wonder there are so many failures. Some players apparently have no difficulty with any of the rules; some have difficulty with all of them. Still others fail only in certain particulars — socially, or financially, or physically, or in mental elasticity.

This complexity is made still more difficult by the fact that the " situation " as a whole is always changing. Sometimes it changes greatly within a short space of time. These sudden changes are called " *new* situations " — although no situation is ever entirely new. They always put unusual stress and strain upon the adaptive powers of the personality, and hence it is frequently new situations that evoke breaks in the smoothness of the process of adaptation. Marriage is such a new situation, the death of one's mother is another, election to office, dismissal from a position, going to college — these are others quite familiar.

THE ADJUSTMENT EFFORT

Now, what happens when a *personality* meets a *situation?* An attempt at mutual adjustment, with success, failure, or compromise as the outcome.

So long as a person is successful — that is, manages his adaptations to a succession of situations without damage to either himself or the environment — he probably won't attract any attention. We shall never know much about the real factors of those situations or about the essential elements in that personality. All that we shall know as outside observers is that Mrs.

Smith is a happy wife, or that Mr. Jones is a money-making banker, or that Miss Edwards won the tournament, or that Mr. Blake was given a promotion.

Most of the adjustments will probably be far less conspicuous even than these. They will probably be just the ordinary going-along of everyday existence. If his office is too hot, Mr. Brown will open the window; if an order comes in, he will fill it; if his stenographer resigns, he will advertise for another one; if the manager criticizes something he has done, he will change his procedure in that direction. When he is hungry, he goes out for lunch; when evening comes, he stops at the store for steak, as his wife has requested, and takes it home for her to cook; when he has eaten his dinner and read the paper and listened to the radio and become sleepy, he goes to bed. His personality adjusts itself smoothly to his environment; he fulfils the necessities of the situations which arise and that's all there is to it. Consequently we don't know very much about him.

But let some extraordinary situation arise — and such situations are always arising — then what happens to Mr. Brown? Let his house burn down, for example, or let his daughter become ill, or his wife die; let him be thrown out of employment, or let him get a typhoid infection, or let him be asked by the president to undertake a very difficult and responsible task, or let him suddenly receive an unexpected inheritance. What happens then?

He may still make a success of it. This may require considerable effort. He may have to change the situation somewhat and he may have to change himself somewhat. And he may do both. By one means and another he may manage the adjustment successfully.

He may, on the other hand, after more or less of a struggle, find the requirements imposed by the situation too great for his adjustment capacity. " Failure " is a broad term to describe this result.

There are two kinds of failure. Finding himself incapable of fulfilling the requirements of the situation, the personality essaying the adjustment may resort to flight, or he may resort to an attack on the situation. He may retreat from the situation or he may attempt its destruction. Ordinarily both flights and attacks are disastrous, the former resulting in damage to the personality, the latter in damage to the situation.

Consider, for example, a certain personality, let us say a man,

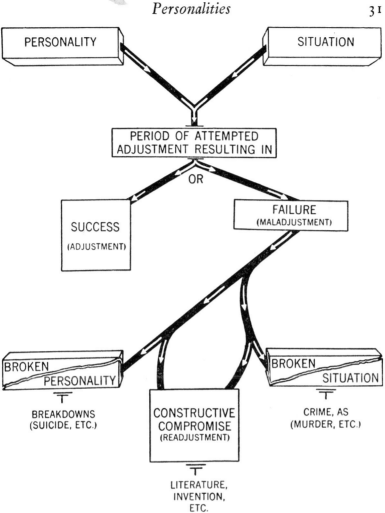

DIAGRAM OF ADJUSTMENT AND MALADJUSTMENT

FIG. 1

faced with a certain situation, let us say marriage. He may make a successful go of it. On the other hand, he may not; he may fail. Unhappy with his wife, he may resort to drinking. Or he may resort to an attack on his wife such that *she* is driven to drink. He may make life so difficult for her that she seeks a divorce. He may even kill her.

But this is not always so. The necessity for retreat may be utilized in a constructive attack on the situation such that the failure is turned into success. This is what we have called, in Figure 1 (see page 31) , a constructive compromise. It is really a secondary adjustment.

To illustrate the way in which a constructive compromise might be made out of the failure, the man just described may be driven by his marital unhappiness to find satisfaction and self-expression in painting or scientific research or organizing a labour-union or a Sunday-school class. He may do all this without experiencing unhappiness, but he *would* experience unhappiness if it were not for the successful outcome he makes of his secondary adjustment project.

The attacks

Attacks which the failing personality makes on the situation in an effort to achieve internal peace are apt to result in damage to or destruction of the situation.

These may be such behaviour as fighting, arrogant independence, the smashing of convention, antagonistic attitudes, contentiousness, defiance of authority, and, in children particularly, disobedience and temper tantrums. Still more serious are such destructive attacks on the situation as refusal to work and refusal to abide by economic and statutory laws. In other words, indolence and crime may be conceived of as an attack on the situation resulting in damage to it, brought about by the inability of certain personalities to adjust themselves to situations too difficult for them.

Some personalities can do criminal things, can break the situation to bits, can inflict immeasurable damage upon society, with apparent impunity. They may even achieve immortality by so doing. Napoleon and Alexander might be cited as examples, though such enormous failures are so exceptional as to be generally accounted successes. Adolf Hitler, the arch criminal of the century, is still the idol of millions.

Failing personalities who injure the environment have always been easier to understand than those whose failure results in injury to themselves. At least, they have *appeared to be* easier to understand. We all think we know why people steal and why they forge cheques. Actually the problems involved are just as complicated as are those of the woman who develops hysteria or the man who kills himself. But because, as members of society, we are personally injured by the stealing and the cheque-forging. we have an emotional reaction to it which makes us judge the offender in a very different way from the invalid. Both of them are slackers in a sense; both of them are evading or declining an adjustment to life of which they are incapable or of which they believe themselves to be incapable. One retreats, one attacks. We have been discussing the attackers; now we shall consider the retreaters.

The flights

Instead of damaging the situation to which it cannot adjust itself, the personality may withdraw into various kinds of re treat, by all of which and in all of which the personality itself suffers. These flights are of various sorts and are accomplished in various ways. They may take the form of undesirable character traits such as seclusiveness, timidity, fears, suspicions, and other emotional symptoms which act as protective devices. Or they may appear as such dodges as inefficiency, " passing the buck," refusal to accept responsibility, and depending upon luck, tricks, routine, or rules of thumb instead of intelligent solutions.

More obvious, because more extreme, are the flights into disease, " nervousness," alcohol and drug addiction, and suicide. Failure may have physical or chemical or psychological mani festations. If a man has a very hard task to perform and the task does him up, he may be said to have failed to make an adjust ment to it and retreated into a state of illness. A football-player who gets benched early in the season because of a broken shoul der has unintentionally accomplished failure; the result of his encounter with the football situation was a damage to his per sonality on the *physical* side. If the same player instead of hav ing broken his shoulder had become depressed in spirits because the coach had not seemed to appreciate his ability, his depression (which might even lead to his quitting the game) was a damage to his personality on the *psychological* side. It is conceivable that our football-player might have fumbled the ball in a very im portant game and in an effort to drown his chagrin and regret might have got drunk. This is a damage to the personality, a retreat of a *chemical* sort; which, however, also has psychological and physical aspects.

Constructive compromises

Sweet are the uses of adversity, and many are the successes of failure. Failing personalities are often forced to achieve success of another sort. They accomplish this by disavowing the per sonality-destroying escapes already discussed in favour of creative or constructive efforts to change the environment to their liking, or, perhaps we should say, in a direction which they find not only pleasing but possible for them to utilize and even exploit. It is safe to say, for example, that many authors who write about life are doing so in response to the stimulus which their own failure to negotiate life has afforded them. In other words, having been faced with situations in which they felt themselves inadequate, they retreat into the role of a writer about life and make a success of that, whereas they had made a failure of the former. The failure may never become apparent. Many men who have achieved fame and riches for their discoveries, inventions, organizations, reforms, would surely have been colossal failures at accomplishing much simpler things, and as a matter of fact may have succeeded as they did only after having failed at the more simple projects.

The out and out failures, however, have the great advantage of showing us these mechanisms. Automobiles by the thousands roll along highways Sunday afternoons and remain unnoticed and unknown as individual cases. No one notices anything about their insides. It is only when a car fails to make the grade or fails to stay in the road that we have a chance to see who is in the car, how good the tires are, and what kind of carburettor it has. Only then do we discover the engine trouble, the leaking radiators, the poorly adjusted brakes, and the broken axles. Only in a comparable way do we learn how human machines are built and how they go to pieces and how they can be reconstructed.

BROKEN PERSONALITIES

Broken *situations* involve problems referable to the field of sociology — crime, delinquency, dependency, etc. Broken *personalities,* on the other hand, are the concern of psychiatry and, generally, of all physicians. From long experience, from the observation of many wrecks, we have become familiar with certain tendencies, certain weaknesses, which seem to predispose to failure. With personalities that succeed, psychiatrists have less experience, but from a study of the failures we can understand the successes.

Experience has shown that the personalities which are likely to fail may be grouped into various major categories, and for purposes of studying them this is a helpful device. Classifications must never be taken too seriously — they ruin much thinking — but the fear to use them has prevented much more thinking.

The following classification does not correspond exactly to those in any of the systems described in the historical account of personality concepts in the footnote on page 28. The types do correspond in general to clinical concepts, but the names in italics are popular designations suggested by myself, and the whole classification is practical and descriptive rather than strictly systematic.

These, then, are personality types prone to have unusual difficulties on being put to adaptational strain:

1. The somatic type — *physical illness personalities;*
2. The hypophrenic type — *stupid personalities;*
3. The isolation type — *lonely personalities;*
4. The schizoid type — *queer personalities;*
5. The cycloid type — *moody personalities;*
6. The neurotic type — *frustrated personalities;*
7. The antisocial type — *perverse personalities.*

Each of these types will now be presented with illustrations taken from many sources — my practice, my friends, my enemies, my newspapers, my imagination. Some examples will be given of each personality type before any troubles have been met with; some will be cited which will be seen to have suffered only a little; still others will be given which will appear as total wrecks.

After we have surveyed these seven personality types prone to failure, and the kinds of wrecks they make, we shall take the wrecks apart, in the section on symptoms, and learn what parts the cars are made of, and then in the succeeding section (on motives) what makes them run.

1. THE SOMATIC TYPE

(PHYSICAL ILLNESS PERSONALITIES)

For a quarter of a century psychiatrists have been proclaiming the *holistic* theory, which simply means that physical, chemical, and psychological aspects of personality must all be considered for a useful scientific evaluation of the " total personality." The practical inference of this for the physician is that all physical diseases have psychological elements which must be considered in both diagnosis and treatment.

This point of view made small headway in general medicine, despite the voice of a few prophets crying in the wilderness (Groddeck, Jelliffe, White, Draper, Cannon, Alvarez, Ritter, Meyer, Coghill, Heyer, von Bergmann, Crookshank). Suddenly, however, under the label of " psychosomatic medicine " the conception caught on and spread rapidly. Physicians in general practice were quick to concede that from a third to a half of the patients they saw from day to day suffered more conspicuously from emotional pathology than from physical pathology. The publication of research studies showing that gastric ulcer, colitis, asthma, some skin diseases, and numerous other conditions could be cured by the means of psychological treatment only awakened the medical profession to the realization that the standard conceptions of pathology were in many instances all wrong, that psychological factors might be even more important in many physical conditions than bacteria. Doctors everywhere began to talk and think about " psyche and soma."

The fact remains that some people go to see their doctor because their eyes are inflamed or their joints ache, and others go to see their doctor because they are sleepless or depressed. This practical differentiation between the predominantly or conspicuously psychological symptom and the predominantly physical symptom will probably remain. Some people seem to get sick one way and some another. This book is *primarily* devoted to those who get sick in the *one* way (with manifest psychological disturbances). Of the seven personalities listed above, the latter six refer to personalities subject to different forms of this type of illness. We cannot omit some discussion, however, of those prone to that other form of illness.

I take pardonable (I hope) pride in the fact that I anticipated the present great interest in " psychomatic medicine." The first edition of this book (1930) listed an " organic disease personality type." The name " psychosomatic medicine " is an unfortunate one since it still implies a duality of mind and body which is contrary to the conception that the field intends to promote, but it is a better term than mine. The conception, not the word, is the important thing and it will certainly be expanded within the decade, since many research studies are in progress and pub. lished reports are appearing constantly. What they all add up to is that psychological factors enter into both the etiology and the therapy of illnesses characterized chiefly by physical symptoms,[9] and that a knowledge of these is therefore necessary to the general practitioner, the internist, and the surgeon, however much they may wish not to become contaminated with psychiatry.

Since 1930 our thinking has become a little more clear on the subject and it is necessary to subdivide this group into three parts. In the first place, it is obvious that accidents, diseases, or defects which primarily affect the physical structure of the body impair the adaptive capacity of the individual. A man who has lost an arm or his eyes has a handicap in his adjustment to reality that definitely differentiates his behaviour and his reactions from those of the normal individual. Assuming that these accidents were incurred under circumstances which preclude any responsibility on the part of the victim, we can say that something happened to him that caused him to change his way of living, his attitudes, his techniques, perhaps even his whole life program. This is the type of personality which one might call a (physically) crippled personality with the full recognition of the fact that psychological over-compensations may occur which make his accomplishments superior to those of many of his fellow men, but, on the other hand, may cause him to fall by the wayside as a definitely wrecked car.

It has been shown,[9a] however, that many accidents are *not* accidental, but are brought about by a more or less unconscious wish on the part of the patient. "Accident-prone" individuals have been shown statistically to be the victims of ninety per cent of all accidents. In a similar way it is quite certain that many physical illnesses are based on a definite, although unconscious, wish to fall ill (see references cited above). The unconscious wish to be sick may be expressed in mental symptoms, but it is very frequently expressed in physical symptoms and actual physical diseases. Such a wish is, of course, "abnormal," but that does not mean that it is illogical or reprehensible. It is the only thing that some personalities can do because of previous experiences and pre-existing drives, conflicts, fears, and frustrations.

[9] For books on the subject see the new section of the Bibliography. See also the special journal *Psychosomatic Medicine,* first issued in 1939, and for a sample application of the new concept to one field, that of obstetrics and gynecology, see the *Bulletin of the Menninger Clinic* for January 1943.

[9a] Flanders Dunbar: *Psychosomatic Diagnosis* (New York: Paul B. Hoeber, 1943); Karin Stephen: *Psychoanalysis and Medicine; A Study of the Wish to Fall Ill* (New York: Macmillan Co., 1933); Karl A. Menninger: *Man against Himself* (New York, Harcourt, Brace & Co., 1938).

Such individuals certainly differ in a practical way from those whose unconscious trends lead them in the direction of a depression or a neurosis. For this reason a definite personality type would seem to be indicated, which might be called the *sickness-prone type*. For just as accident-prone persons find slippery steps and speeding cars to co-operate with their inner wishes, so the sickness-prone type finds noxious agents in the external world with which to co-operate. We used to consider that the tuberculosis bacillus was the cause of tuberculosis, but it is now well known that persons who fall ill of it do so very often under circumstances which indicate that they were unconsciously anxious to do so. I recall a physician, for example, who was an excellent student in medical school, graduating with honours; he had always suffered, however, from an enormous fear of social contacts and dreaded the day when he would have finished his internship and have to go into practice. All of this was settled very definitely when one month after he had opened up his office and was waiting in terror for his first patients, he developed tuberculosis and had to repair to a sanitarium. After a time he improved definitely, but when the possibility of his returning to his office was mentioned, he immediately became worse.

The same sort of thing is now known to be true of a great many physical illnesses. The whole subject is one of great obscurity, into which many scientific researches are now being made, some of which have already been published in medical literature. For the purposes of this book we can summarize it by saying that there seem to be rather definite asthma personalities, peptic ulcer personalities, chronic constipation personalities, arthritis (rheumatism) personalities, repeated-surgical-operations personalities, high-blood-pressure personalities, and heart disease personalities. Almost certainly there are others, but those named have been fairly well delineated.

We have now discussed (1) the accident or disease crippled personalities (which really do not constitute a personality type of any distinctive kind until after the accident or physical illness) and (2) the illness-prone personalities, which are quite distinctive. Space limitation unfortunately precludes illustrating these here.

A third type of psychosomatic problem remains to be considered. There are certain physical diseases the first lesions and often the first symptoms of which are physical, but which soon manifest themselves conspicuously in disorders of perception, thinking, feeling, and behaviour. It has long been assumed that the psychological symptoms in such diseases were directly dependent upon the physical disorder. From the point of view of psychosomatic (or biodynamic [10]) medicine, this time-honoured interpretation must be rejected as naïvely inadequate and replaced with a conception of a basic injury of the personality reflected in physical and psychological reactions. In this instance the difference in point of view may not seem significant, but in the case of brain syphilis, to take another example, it is a very important distinction. There has never been an adequate explanation of the fact that of the many persons who acquire syphilis, so few acquire brain syphilis, and of those who acquire brain syphilis not all manifest the disease known as general paresis. Psychiatry thought it had made great progress when the paretic picture was definitely shown to be regularly associated with syphilitic involvement of the brain, but we know now that the theoretical problem remains unsolved, as do many others connected with this field. For the practical purposes of this book it must be sufficient merely to indicate what kind of cases belong here and to illustrate some of the more important varieties.

a. *Endocrine gland disorder*

Except for irritability and stubbornness through childhood, Joe Harrison had shown no unusual trait. He completed two years in high school and then took up a trade, which he carried on very successfully. Following an operation for appendicitis at thirty, he increased in weight from 140 to 200 pounds within a few months. During the next four years his weight went on up to 270 pounds. During this time he suffered from repeated severe headaches and had occasional sleepy spells, lasting from twelve to forty-eight hours, from which he could not be roused. Soon after this he became involved in a number of delinquencies, such as writing bad checks, which led to a psychiatric examination.

Physical examination, psychological examination, and chemical tests of metabolic functioning all confirmed the diagnosis of endocrine (chiefly pituitary) gland disturbance.[11]

b. *Brain tumour*

Many persons think much queerness and misbehaviour is explainable on the basis of a " growth on the brain." Although such growths are common, such *manifestations* of them are rare. The usual symptoms of brain tumours are paralyses, convulsions,

[10] Iago Galdston: " Biodynamic Medicine versus Psychosomatic Medicine," *Bulletin of the Menninger Clinic,* July 1944. See also J. F. Brown and K. A. Menninger: *Psychodynamics of Abnormal Behavior* (New York: McGraw-Hill, 1940) .
[11] See W. C. Menninger, *J.A.M.A.,* September 29, 1928.

visual disturbances, and severe headaches. Misbehaviour may occur, however, and here is an interesting illustrative case reported by Dr. Frederick Moersch of the Mayo Clinic: [12]

A minister, aged fifty-two years, was brought to the clinic on November 14, 1923. In the fall of 1922 the patient had been despondent, owing, his wife considered, to his various duties. About January 1923 he began to complain of severe headaches, which occurred from two to three times a week. About the middle of April it was noted that his sermons were incoherent, and that he stumbled through them, but always in an unconcerned manner. He preached his last sermon, which was an utter failure, but with which he was immensely pleased, in August. He was asked to resign, and went on a campaigning tour to raise funds. He was gone twenty days and returned dirty and dishevelled and gave a rambling account of his trip, of having lost himself, and of getting into various difficulties. His letters while he was away were incoherent. His memory now failed markedly; his attention, interest, and ability to concentrate were also impaired. He was unable to remember details; speech was slow and dragging, so that he became unable to carry on a conversation; he would break off suddenly and did not seem to realize what he was saying. He developed peculiar mannerisms, such as kicking with his right foot, or tapping on objects with his right forefinger. He read signs over and over again. During the month prior to his examination at the clinic he would sit about uninterested; he was careless about his habits and dress, soiled his clothes, and on one occasion urinated into his slipper, pouring the urine out of the window, much to his own amusement, but to the chagrin of his wife. The general lack of interest was one of the most outstanding features of his case.

The neurologic examination proved to be practically negative for any focal evidence of tumour. The eyes showed some blurring of the optic nerves, and X-ray of the skull showed destruction of the sella.

The patient gradually became worse and a right frontal exploration was made on December 4, but the tumour was not located. Two weeks later the left side was explored and a huge glioma (a rapidly growing

---

[12] *American Journal of Psychiatry*, Vol. IV, pp. 705 et seq. (April 1925). See also Harry N. Roback: "Behavior Disorder Associated with Brain Tumor," *Bulletin of the Menninger Clinic,* Vol. I, pp. 91–6 (January 1937), and further references there given. (Neurosurgery is that special technical development of surgery which enables us to relieve by surgical operations many formerly incurable neurological conditions, including certain types of brain tumour. It is one of the most brilliant developments of modern medicine, and one in which American workers are pre-eminent.)

tumour) about five centimetres in diameter, extending into the upper posterior portion of the frontal lobe, was exposed.

c. *Encephalitis* (inflammation of the brain) [13]

Harold is a boy of fifteen years whose behaviour is so unpredictably and dangerously impulsive that his family cannot keep him at home. He must always live in an institution.

He presents a strange, almost uncannily freakish appearance. He is short and squat in stature and has a short, squarish head that is oversized for his body. He walks with an awkward, shambling gait, a little like a monkey. As you watch him, he sidles toward another child in a gingerly, apparently affectionate manner. Suddenly he grasps the child's finger and bends it backward mercilessly; then he slinks impishly away, laughing and chuckling. In a moment he raises his bitten nails to his mouth and stares at the cloudless sky as though abruptly transported, and mutters some incoherent remark about a " terrible storm coming that will break all the limbs of the trees." A few minutes later with tears streaming from his eyes he presents an appearance of genuine remorse. He puts his arms around the same child's neck and suddenly chokes the child painfully with a tremendous hug. When a teacher pries him away he tries to bite her hand. He murmurs to the teacher: " I hurt you, didn't I? Can you whip? Whip me." Perhaps awhile later he may be seen to shuffle stealthily toward the same teacher and whisper to her in a childlike manner: " I like you." Then quick as a flash he may poke his finger into her eye and cry again: " Can you whip? Whip me."

He did not thrive well in his childhood, for he was beset with many illnesses. His physical and mental development was markedly retarded. He failed to adjust himself to school and at home became uncontrollably provocative and destructive. Very much distraught, the parents resorted to beatings to discipline him, but they were of no avail.

His mental age is about eight years (I.Q. 60). Emotionally he is very unstable; often he unaccountably bursts into tears. The most striking aspects of his behaviour are his uncontrolled impulsive cruelties and his perverted craving to suffer pain himself. Like the rest of us, he wants love and affection, but he seeks it in a strange way. He torments and

[13] Since the first edition of this book was published, a large amount of literature has accumulated in regard to the personality deformities wrought by encephalitis. The reader is especially recommended on the theoretical side to *Postencephalitic Respiratory Disorders* by Dr. Smith Ely Jelliffe (New York: Nervous and Mental Disease Publishing Co., 1927) and on the practical side to *The Treatment of Behavior Disorders Following Encephalitis* by Dr. Earl D. Bond and Dr. Kenneth E. Appel (New York: The Commonwealth Fund Division of Publications, 1931).

hurts others so they may do the same to him. He appears to derive an erotic pleasure from the pain which he provokes from others in lieu of love. To such injuries he adds those which he inflicts upon himself.

This is a strange boy indeed. His disordered behaviour is the consequence of an inflammatory illness of the brain, encephalitis, which complicated a contagious disease in infancy. Harold can be helped, but not cured.

d. *General paresis*

The encephalitis just described is a close relative of the well-known "flu." There is another kind of encephalitis, due to syphilis of the brain. Many people who have syphilis don't know they have it. Those who do know it rarely suspect the possibility of its affecting the nervous system. Brain syphilis follows the original infection usually by many years. It is difficult for the public to realize that syphilis far more frequently betrays itself by queer conduct than by startling skin eruptions. Brain syphilis may exist for years without being suspected by anyone, least of all by the victim. Yet it could be discovered and successfully treated if the proper examinations were made. This is the reason we advocate the routine examination of railroad engineers, several of whom are known to have suddenly "gone insane" from a brain syphilis long present, but unsuspected.

"Major Isaac Thompson, M.D., was a character. He had been regarded as eccentric for many years prior to his death at 63. In fact, it seems that there had been more or less definite symptoms and signs about his fortieth year. The doctor himself had a ready explanation for his Argyll-Robertson pupils [an eye symptom of brain syphilis]; he explained that he had had a peculiarly heavy smallpox at about the age of 27. . . .

"The doctor had a good secondary education. He had gone through the Civil War as a hospital steward, went into business after the war, married, and then went to the medical school, graduating at the age of 34. He continued in practice for a dozen years, and then gave it up. For years he had been especially interested in certain literary lines and he had published any number of pamphlets, all of a somewhat striking description, often with a political color and intended to stir up reform measures.

"It is possible that a fall on the ice in his 61st year actually started the fatal process, since after that time the patient had difficulty in walking and a few months later developed periods of excitement with peremptory insistence on obedience to his wishes. Whereas formerly the doctor had finished up one literary piece of work after another, he now began to do very scattering work. He appeared in public to denounce certain financial schemes with great force and unusual eloquence. His eloquence was greatly complimented, and these compliments induced the doctor to a remarkable crusade against a certain corporation; there was so much truth mixed with the fiction of his eloquence that he obtained a considerable following in his campaign. He wanted to start a bureau of information for the instruction of the public on these matters, and he planned to put up a building adjoining his own home for the accommodation of the various clerks and writers in this bureau. . . .

" One morning the doctor was very excitable and noisy over the telephone, ordering typewriters and giving directions to mechanics. He repaired to Boston in connection with certain resources that he supposed (and gave others reason to believe) had been supplied by the Government and by a large newspaper. One evening he returned very late. It appeared that he had had a fracas at a hotel and had knocked down one or two colored porters, acting as though drunk. Upon being put to bed, the doctor talked incessantly of religious matters, proposing to undertake a Sunday School class. His interlocutor did not exhibit a particular interest in this scheme, whereupon Dr. Thompson threatened him with violence. Police and doctors were called in and a constant stream of conversation lasted for hours. The patient was finally brought to the hospital upon representation by physicians, to whom he told that his luck had turned, that he was about to be made senator from the district, and that he and Roosevelt were going to break up the trusts and that, as a matter of fact, he was a relative of Mr. Roosevelt."

Dr. Thompson was found upon examination at the hospital to be suffering from general paresis (brain syphilis) of many years' standing.[14]

Two other examples of the same condition:

Anna is a rather pretty young married woman. She came of a healthy family. Until the present trouble began she had always been considered of excellent health. Two years previously a little girl had been born to her whose head was abnormally large and who had never learned to walk, but even this had not made the doctors suspicious. (The child is, in fact, a congenital syphilitic and has been improving under treatment.)

[14] E. E. Southard and H. C. Solomon: *Neurosyphilis* (Boston: W. M. Leonard, 1917) , pp. 289–92.

One day Anna's husband came home and found her sitting in the cellar, unwilling to tell him why she sat there. She continued to do many queer things. She hid behind the bed, saying that someone was after her — someone that looked just like the Devil. She would go to bed right after breakfast, neglecting her baby and housework. She thought people followed her and once chased a boy down a block with a butcher-knife and once bought some carbolic acid with which to kill herself.

At this time several doctors were called, none of whom made a blood examination or a correct diagnosis. She became progressively worse. She dyed her clothes bright colours, daubed splotches of paint all over the kitchen, ordered ten dollars' worth of toys from the ten-cent store, ordered a bouquet from the florist to surprise her husband, who certainly needed his money for something else. She called up a great many of her girl friends and told them she was going to start a millinery shop, in which she wanted them to work. She said she had hired the first floor of a large office-building and was going to have the biggest shop in town. She announced that she and her husband owned five hundred cottages and that her husband's income had been increased to fifty thousand dollars a year.

Her husband said that he had noticed that she had had increasing difficulty in speaking. He also noticed that she made very serious mistakes in calculating the simplest figures sometimes and could not be relied upon to do any of the family purchasing. She became very gay and made bad breaks under very embarrassing circumstances without the least shame. She insisted that she never felt better in her life, laughed and joked and seemed to have not the least concern in what was obviously the greatest anxiety to everyone else.

Physically she seemed perfect. A neurological examination, however, showed that her pupils did not react normally to light and that, while her arm reflexes were exaggerated, knee-jerks were absent. An examination of the blood and spinal fluid gave typical findings of general paresis.

Carl Larson was the industrious son of poor, hard-working, immigrant parents. After graduating from high school with the highest honours in his class, he left home in order to find a job, save up his money, and continue his studies in college. He worked for the few years following graduation from high school as a truck-driver, as a section hand on a railroad, and finally as an actor in a stock company.

Here he fell in love with and married a young actress, from whom he contracted syphilis. The young couple quarrelled frequently and soon obtained a divorce. Carl went back home, enrolled in the university and promptly " forgot " his unhappy marriage and the fact that he had had only a few months of anti-luetic treatment.

He worked his way through college and law school and graduated once more with the highest honours in his class. Being popular, industrious, and clever, he made rapid progress in his profession. At the death of a judge of the Superior Court the State Bar Association unanimously recommended the young man to the Governor for appointment to the vacancy, and at the age of thirty-two he took over his new duties, the youngest man ever to have held such a high judicial position in the state.

For a year he fulfilled his duties with wisdom and scholarliness. Then one day he approached a lawyer for whose client he had rendered a favourable decision and suggested that the client might like to remunerate him for having rendered such a decision. The lawyer, a good friend of the young judge, was somewhat taken aback by this irregular request and asked the reason for it. The judge explained that he was in need of money. The lawyer accepted this explanation and arranged a personal loan for his friend.

A few months later Judge Larson visited at night the home of the plaintiff in a law case being tried by him and proposed that if he decided the case in his favour the plaintiff was to remunerate the jurist. The plaintiff reported the incident to his attorney, who immediately called the matter to the attention of the Bar Association and the Governor, and the young jurist was immediately disbarred and disrobed.

Public opinion was so strong against him that he left town and went to a near-by city, where he obtained a job as a taxi-driver. Several of his fares complained that he was taking them to their destinations by circuitous routes. Actually he was losing his memory and could not remember how to get around the town, but he laughingly remarked to his customers that the longer the trip, the more money he made. Complaints from customers soon led to his dismissal. A friend of the young man urged him to go to a doctor for an examination. The doctor referred the case to a hospital, where unmistakable signs of paresis were observed. He was given treatment and six months later was again employed in a law office, awaiting his reinstatement to the bar. (Case material furnished by courtesy of Dr. Norman Reider.)

e. *Congenital brain syphilis*

When Eddie Ramsey was four years old he chopped a live cat in two with a hatchet. When his sister tearfully protested, he laughed and jeered at her. This is a typical instance of his childhood, which was replete with atrocities and offences against his family and society. He stole from his parents and from the neighbours, cruelly abused his dog, taught younger boys to use tobacco, which he charged to his parents' account, and was expelled from school because he swore continually. Then he began chasing children at night, frightening them with terrible cries and threats.

He led a gang of boys who obtained money by raising the way-bills on chickens. When detected he ran away to the harvest fields, where he made fifty dollars gambling with the harvesters. When he came back, he forged a cheque and ran away again. When he was arrested for this, he only laughed, and pointed out the advantages of being in jail and not having to work. He was sentenced to the boys' reformatory, where he was very difficult to control, stirred up trouble among the boys, and was indifferent to punishment and reward alike.

Eddie is another case of brain syphilis; this time the syphilis was inherited from the parents rather than personally acquired.[15]

Martin Mendenhall was assistant professor of English in a large Eastern university. His students liked him, his faculty associates admired him, and he was regarded as a brilliant man whose achievement of an assistant professorship at thirty was prophetic of a great future. He supported a widowed mother, who idolized him.

Without warning and without particular provocation Professor Mendenhall's health began to fail. He lost weight and strength, ate and slept poorly, and suffered from numerous anxieties and needless fears. He worried lest he were doing less than justice to his school-work, and dreaded to meet his students or his confreres.

His mother finally persuaded him to consult a physician, but an examination revealed no cause for his difficulties. A verdict of "just nerves" was given and he was advised to take a vacation. He got a leave of absence and started for the mountains, but was removed from

---

15 It should not be forgotten that most patients who have syphilis acquired it innocently, in a sense that they themselves did nothing to acquire it. I once knew a man who in the one extramarital affair of his life contracted syphilis and communicated it to his wife and by kissing to three of his four children. Fortunately, it was discovered and he and they were treated before he communicated it to unborn children, as many do. (See Harry and Maida Solomon: *Syphilis of the Innocent*, Washington: United States Interdepartmental Social Hygiene Board, 1922.)

the train because of a queer attack of sleepiness from which he could not be awakened.

A more technical and expert examination was made and a specimen of the spinal fluid removed and subjected to laboratory tests, which indicated the presence of syphilis. He was horrified at this discovery and went at once to his mother with the news and with protestations of its impossibility. She then brought out the family skeleton and told him in detail of his father's infection from syphilis, and his death through neglect of treatment, and her vain hope that her son might escape infection. (Cf. Ibsen's *Ghosts.*)

Professor Mendenhall was immediately placed under treatment and returned to his position the following year. He has remained in good health since that time.

Ludwig Beethoven probably had congenital syphilis. Unfortunately, however, Beethoven and Professor Mendenhall are the exceptions rather than the rule, for most congenitally syphilitic children die young or live profitless lives.[16]

f. *Hookworm and Malaria*

Impairment of energy, activity, and intelligence resulting from a generalized infection of the body with the hookworm parasite is estimated to have affected as much as fifty per cent of the population in certain Southern communities. Fortunately this condition is curable if recognized and much progress has been made in that direction.

The psychological manifestations of malaria have not been adequately studied, but in view of the fact that this disease has been one of the great medical problems of World War II we can expect to learn more about it soon. It is not encouraging to read this observation made years ago: " There is nothing more striking to a cursory traveller than the appearance of age which occurs at a very early period of life . . . and the expression keeps pace with all else; being that of unhappiness, stupidity and apathy; an habitual melancholy which nothing can rouse, and an insensibility to almost everything which operates on the feelings of mankind in general." [17]

---

[16] *Juvenile Paresis*, a comprehensive technical monograph on general paresis from inherited syphilis, has been written by my brother, William C. Menninger, to which those are referred who wish to investigate this topic further (Baltimore: Williams & Wilkins Co., 1936) .

[17] From an essay by Macculloch (1827) , who introduced the word " malaria " into the English language; quoted by William K. Anderson: *Malarial Psychoses and Neuroses* (London: Oxford University Press, 1927) .

2. THE HYPOPHRENIC TYPE

(STUPID PERSONALITIES)

A personality handicapped by deficiency in capacity for thinking, learning, reacting to perceptions, making decisions — such
a personality belongs in a group long designated by the term
feeble-minded, but better called *hypo-* (insufficient) *phrenic*
(mind). Mental deficiency varies in degree, as well as in kind,
from complete " lack of brains " (*idiocy*) up through gradations
called *imbecility* and *moronity* to *subnormality,* the latter being
just perceptibly less than " average intelligence." No one knows
precisely what " average " or " normal " intelligence is, so these
border-line cases are often very difficult to recognize and label.
Some of them even get to college. Several cases of " feeble-
mindedness " were discovered among commissioned officers in
World War I, according to the official reports.[18] Ex-soldiers
tell me they have no trouble in believing this.

Morons

The " moron " grade of feeble-mindedness can be recognized
fairly definitely by tests; morons possess the intellectual capacity
of children from eight to twelve years old.

Stationed regularly at a busy corner in a certain city is a dwarfish
man with cold, red, wet hands, narrowed eye-slits, and coarse features.
He is familiar to everyone who habitually passes that corner in the
evening. The newspapers regard him as one of their most faithful
newsies. Occasionally he disappears for a year, but sooner or later
he returns and is once more regularly on the job.

He is well known to the charity organizations. Many jobs have been
got for him, but he works only a few days. When sent to carry out
ashes, for example, he sets the bucket down and walks off, forgetting
his mission entirely. Dispatched to the store on an errand, he forgets
what he is sent for. What little money he gets from time to time he
spends all at once without any concern for the future.

When he is asked why he does not hold his jobs better, he says:
" Oh, I don't know; I just do that way. There is something wrong
in my head; I can't think of anything. I don't know what I want to

[18] *The Medical Department of the United States Army in the World War,*
Vol. XV, *Statistics,* Part 2, " Medical and Casualty Statistics Based on the Medical
Records of the United States Army, April 1, 1917, to December 31, 1919, inclu-
sive "; prepared under the direction of Major General M. W. Ireland, by Albert
G. Love (Washington: Government Printing Office, 1925) , pp. 90–1, item 68 B,
columns 3, 9, 14.

do. I pick on the smaller boys when I ought not to. They say I am feeble-minded. I don't think I am. I've made my own living for four years. Anyway I'm not crazy. But there is something wrong with my head."

"Chuck had met Flora on the street and said 'How about a show, Blondey?' to which she had replied, 'O Boy!' With this introduction matters had gone far before she even knew his last name — a name which she was now to assume under a wedding bell of Easter lilies. We social workers did not approve of the wedding any more than we had approved of others about which our opinion had been asked. But both high contracting parties were of legal age, however low their mental ages might be (Flora's was between ten and eleven as it happened, and Chuck, who was very dull but not quite so feeble, scored a scant year higher), and they wanted to marry, so there was nothing to do but ring the wedding bells, turn on the 'Lohengrin' record, throw rice and old shoes, and wait for the inevitable. Incidentally, let no one underestimate the value of an elaborate wedding for morons, if wedded they must be. The mere signing of a license is essentially too abstract and trivial a formality for those who cannot grasp the idea of law. It takes more than a scrap of paper to hold the family together after a quarrel. But if the veil is long enough, enough jokes are made by the best man, and enough shrieks uttered by the bridesmaids, the impression is made upon the dimly-endowed pair that something really important socially has taken place. They are helped thereby to remember that somehow the clergy and the police will see to it that the bride does not sell the household furniture behind her husband's back, and that he will not leave her with the rent to pay. So Flora married Chuck on $20 a week, and they went to housekeeping in two furnished rooms.

"Flora had been getting $12 and her lunches as a dishwasher in a restaurant, but that could not continue for long. This aspect of the case, however, was not discussed very much, for Chuck seemed genuinely fond of his Flora, and was marrying her under no outside pressure. Ultimately therefore, Flora must budget his $20 a week to cover rent, food, clothes, movies, gas, tobacco, lipstick, chewing-gum — and layette. . . .

"Flora's good nature had often led her into difficulties, not only with agents in the way of rash purchases, but with friends in the way of picking up joy-rides, calling out of the windows to people she did not know, wearing ultra-conspicuous dress when she and Lucille (whom she soon took as a boarder) went shopping, and over-indulgence in matinées which neither could afford, and in which her flirtations with the trombonist made Chuck very jealous. Lucille, as a temporary widow, felt that she had a right to flirt with whom she chose, and Flora, from long habit, followed her example. In what words shall one urge the laws of morals and good taste upon a moron of flaming cheeks and healthy appetites, whose inclinations are those of an adult body with a child's mind? Unfortunately there is no value in exhortations unless one's auditor understands the words in which they are phrased, and what do Flora or Lucille (or Chuck for that matter) understand? All of them stuck in the fifth or sixth grade in school until they were so large that they were ashamed to be seen with the smaller children, and were tired of being scolded for not getting their lessons." [19]

Morons are considerably limited in powers of adjustment; they can succeed only under favourable conditions, and hence social and economic failures are frequent.

The following table deserves careful study. It is slightly out of date so far as precise wage figures are concerned. The important thing to notice is the close approximation of the percentages in each column, reading across the page. This remarkable correlation may indicate that the amount of schooling and salary that one receives depends largely upon one's intelligence, or it might indicate that intelligence, as measured by the test used in the army, depends upon the amount of education obtained. I be-

WAGES	SCHOOL	INTELLIGENCE
Of 100 average wage-earners	Of 100 average children	Of 1,700,000 soldiers
9% earn $150–200	13% leave in 4th grade, age 10	10% in "D" group, mental age 10
12% earn $250–300	13% leave in 5th grade, age 11	15% in "D" group, mental age 11
16% earn $350–400	14% leave in 6th grade, age 12	20% in "C" group, mental age 12
31% earn $450–600 (per year)	27% leave in 7th & 8th, age 13, 14	25% in "C" group, mental age 13, 14
68% earn less than $15 per week	67% do not finish 8th grade	70% are below mental age of 15
27% earn $750–1000	10% attend high school	16.5% in "C" group, mental age 15
3% earn $1250	3% graduate from high school	9% in "B" group, mental age 16, 17
2% earn over $1250	1.5% attend college	4.5% in "A" group, mental age 18, 19

[19] Eleanor Rowland Wembridge: " The People of Moronia," *American Mercury,* Vol. VII, no. 25 (January 1926), pp. 2, 3–4.

lieve it is the former, although the correlation is probably not quite so close as this table would indicate. To accept it literally would lead us into the fallacy which for a time misled the psychometrists, as discussed in Chapter I, in connection with "the psychological fallacy."

Statistically, 40 per cent of the occupants of the alms-houses of Georgia were found to be feeble-minded (chiefly morons), and 34 per cent of the county jail prisoners; 17.5 per cent of the men and 43 per cent of the women in the state prison; 24 per cent of the boys and 27 per cent of the girls in the state reformatory. Similar statistics have been derived from mental-hygiene surveys of various other communities, east and west.

Morons frequently get caught for crimes that smarter persons "get away with." Their mental deficiency is related both to the offence and to the capture. Few judges, however, give it any consideration in the subsequent disposition of the case. Much crime would be prevented if they did.

The Fosters were one of the richest families in the county. The three brothers and their two sisters held between them many thousands of acres, and their influence in political, religious, and social matters corresponded to their affluence. If the Fosters had a certain opinion, most of the villagers had that opinion.

Edward Foster was the adolescent son of the oldest brother. He was an only child and the sole interest of his simple-hearted, simple-minded mother. She was proud of everything he did and everything he was. When he brought home more squirrels than anyone else in the party, when he was elected captain of the grade-school football team, when he whittled a little windmill out of a pine beam, she went into ecstasies of maternal pride and pleasure.

In school, however, Edward was not so successful. Before he finished the seventh grade his work was becoming increasingly unsatisfactory. Several times he was put back to complete some of it.

A marked change seemed to take place in his disposition. As he was increasingly baffled in his school-work, he became increasingly active in certain less commendable directions. A group of boys about his own age who were regarded as the "bad element" of the neighbouring towns were glad to include him in their gang. It was in connection with frequent association with them that a small quantity of liquor was found to have a disproportionately severe effect on him and it was one of the amusements of the crowd to see what a variety of manifestations could be stimulated by this means. Such experiments, however, only cemented him the more firmly to the group. The fact that he was the son of a wealthy man and even had his own automobile made him particularly desirable to them, and the exaltation which they made him feel because of this adulation compensated in some measure for the inferiority he felt in school.

He began disappearing from home for long periods without giving notice beforehand or explanation afterwards. The neighbours began to say he was a little wild. His father was distressed, but, being a quiet and very busy man, he did nothing about it. His mother didn't believe it.

Meanwhile his amiability had made him a convenient tool for a chain of bootleggers, who prevailed upon him to use his car to transport liquor across the state line. These trips were the occasion of his introduction to opportunities for sexual promiscuity. Having wandered thus far from the standards and ideals of his home, it was not a great step to the stealing of automobile tires, jewellery, and similar articles in company with the "gang." It was on account of such thefts that he was finally taken in hand by the state authorities.

The judge admitted himself much puzzled by the fact that a man of wealthy parents and good upbringing, with an opportunity for a useful and prosperous life, should be involved in such petty and persistent delinquencies. He made an excellent appearance and impression, his physique was above the average, and it was not surprising that the judge, with his lack of information regarding the boy and regarding the motivation of human conduct in general, should have been satisfied with the explanation of bad company and sentenced him to the industrial school.

Careful examination revealed the fact that Edward was definitely feeble-minded, with an intelligence equal to that of a ten-year-old child, which of course could not be raised by the best industrial school in the world. The recommendations of a psychiatrist that Edward be given supervised parole were approved by the Governor. Edward now manages his own farm, unassisted, and has never given his guardian the slightest anxiety.

(Can a feeble-minded man run a farm? No, not as a rule, any more. The financial stress of recent years has forced most of the feeble-minded into other vocations or into unemployment.)

But ninety per cent of the morons are peaceful, law-abiding citizens; most of them usefully employed. Much of the simple, tedious work of the world is done by cheerful morons, and with special supervision and training they can be used even more advantageously.

For example:

——, Ia., Nov. 24, 1930 — (A.P.) — Thirty-five years ago Samantha Woods came to Dallas county home and was given a job peeling potatoes.

She peeled a bushel and a half every day until her death, never missing a day. For the 12,784 days that would make 19,175½ bushels, or enough to fill 32 freight cars. Incapacitated and with death drawing nigh, the aged woman worried about her task, asking:

" Are the potatoes being peeled as well as I did them? "

— Topeka *Daily Capital,*
November 25, 1930

A certain restaurant in Boston was reputed at one time to be giving intelligence tests to every prospective applicant for the position of waiter. Applicants who made an intelligence rating above a certain point were rejected, because it was found that the morons made the best waiters. Once trained to the task, they were steady and dependable and were not likely to become dissatisfied and leave to take better-paying positions.

It is probable that vast numbers of factory employees and men and women doing common labour would be classified as morons technically. Textile industries are regarded by those in charge of the training of frankly feeble-minded girls as an excellent opportunity for remunerative employment for them. At Rome, New York, for example, Dr. Bernstein, superintendent of the State School for Mental Defectives, found it possible as early as 1917 to introduce girls whom he had trained in his school into knitting-mills at Oriskany Falls, Richfield Springs, Clayville, and other mill towns.[20] Their efficiency was found to be seventy-five to one hundred per cent of that of the so-called normal operators. Dr. Emily Burr, director of the Vocational Adjustment Bureau, New York City, which is an organization for finding employment for maladjusted girls, has found that subnormal girls find many openings in textile trades, as illustrated. Compare this with the waste at the average state school for the feeble-minded.[21]

[20] *Industrial Psychology,* June 1927.
[21] A very complete list of industries operated by adult morons, imbeciles, and idiots at the Walter E. Fernald State School in Waverley, Massachusetts, is given by Dr. C. Stanley Raymond, in *Industrial Psychology,* September 1927.

DIAGNOSIS

Mental deficiency can sometimes be recognized early in life by certain symptoms of retardation.

Mr. and Mrs. George Smith had looked forward eagerly to the arrival of their first-born. The little child came into a home where he was very much wanted and very much prepared for. Mrs. Smith had read everything she could get her hands on with regard to the bearing and rearing of children. She knew precisely when the first tooth should come, at just what age the child should be permitted to stand up, just what words were first to be expected, and when.

But none of these things happened according to Hoyle or Holt. The child's birth had been uneventful and the first few months were like those of any child, with perhaps a little more than the warranted amount of crying and restlessness at night. There was some difficulty in feeding and there were some attacks of croup and some bad colds, but these the parents took as part of the bargain and it was not until the child was nearly two years old that they realized that something was not quite as it should be. Little Tommy cried a great deal and made no effort to talk or walk. Friends told them that this was frequently the case, that some children did not talk until they were several years old. This helped them to keep up their courage for another year, but Tom was a dull and uninteresting child; he did not reach for things; he did not want to play with his daddy, or laugh when tickled, or smile. He was nearly three before he said any words and they were almost inarticulate. He did not take any interest in other children; he preferred to sit by himself on the floor, aimlessly clasping his hands together, or pounding the floor with a little stick.

Kind neighbours thought he must be deaf. Unkind relatives said he was badly brought up. By the time he was seven it was clear that he was a very backward child. He said only a few words. He was listless, apathetic; occasionally he screamed and fought vigorously against the most obvious necessities. He was in no way capable of caring for himself. He would not dress or undress himself and he fed himself only in the most crude and inefficient fashion.

There may or may not be physical stigmata; that is, sometimes anyone, and sometimes no one, suspects mental deficiency from facial appearance or physical development.

There is a widespread belief that it is possible to detect feeble-mindedness by facial appearance. " Why, you can tell it from his looks," people will say; or, more frequently, they will insist that a specified individual cannot be feeble-minded because of his fine appearance. How erroneous this is can best be illus-trated by citing the experiments of Lloyd N. Yepsen at the re-nowned training-school for the feeble-minded at Vineland, New Jersey. Yepsen selected twenty-five feeble-minded boys and twenty-five normal boys of the same general age group; he combed their hair and standardized the background and garbed them all the same, and then photographed them. Then he sub-mitted these photographs to groups of students, including some experienced with the feeble-minded. Their efforts to pick out the feeble-minded from the normal were no more successful than would be the selections of a blindfolded judge. In other words, the selections made from photographs, although made after care-ful scrutiny, were in the same ratio as would have occurred in random picking according to the laws of chance. These results might be slightly different if motion pictures were made so that the mobility of the features, the gait, posture, and carriage, were compared. But the feeble-minded are not conspicuous except in the extreme cases.

Idiocy and Imbecility

Idiots have practically " no brains " at all. This is sometimes literally true; an examination of the brain cortex shows obvious gross deficiencies in size, form, and configuration which one who had never seen a brain before could recognize. In other cases the brain *appears* normal; and although we can postulate that in such cases microscopic examination would reveal a conspicu-ous absence of nerve-cells despite the well-formed supporting structure, curiously enough such researches as have been con-ducted do not always confirm this postulate. It may be assumed that idiocy, the lowest grade of feeble-mindedness, is practically always dependent upon defective brain structure.[22] Imbecility is a degree of deficiency midway between moronity and idiocy.

The following are some of the well-recognized types:

Mongolian, characterized by Chinese appearance and other physical signs, plus a sweet, cheerful disposition (many " Mongo-lian idiots " are really imbeciles rather than idiots); *Amaurotic,* characterized by congenital blindness; *Familial,* characterized by

[22] See the incomparable studies of Fernald, Southard, Taft, Canavan, and Raeder, the "Waverley Researches in the Pathology of the Feeble-minded," *Memoirs of the American Academy of Arts and Sciences,* Vol. XIV, nos. 2 and 3 (May 1918 and December 1921).

sudden appearance and persistence in tainted families; *Hydro-cephalic,* characterized by huge heads, caused by "water on the brain"; [23] *Microcephalic,* characterized by small heads (under-developed skulls); *Little's Disease,* characterized by paralysis and convulsions; *Encephalitic,* characterized by the residual symptoms of an inflammation of the brain; *Syphilitic,* char-acterized in most instances by no special ear-marks, except those disclosed by chemical laboratory tests; occasionally certain physi-cal signs; *Cretinous,* characterized by other evidences of in-sufficient thyroid-gland secretion; *Fröhlich's,* characterized by excessive fat deposits in the body, and deficient genital develop-ment; *Cerebral Agenesis* and *Aplasia,* characterized by incom-plete brain development.

HEREDITY

Some kinds of feeble-mindedness may be hereditary — that is, transmissible by heredity from parents who may or may not show it themselves. Such families as the following show why segregation of the feeble-minded is strongly advocated by some.

"Bennie B. 18 years old. Mentality 9. Has been here 8 years. Ameri-can born; nationality of parents unknown.

"Bennie has gone through about the usual course for children of his mentality. In eight years he has learned to count a little, and manipulate figures, learned to read a little, and write a simple child-ish story; his penmanship is very bad, also his figures, and his papers slovenly looking. . . . On the industrial side he has steadily improved and can make nice baskets and do good work in the woodworking room. . . .

"With these children it is always a question of instinctive interest; we cannot rely upon their doing things to any great extent from any associated interest, consequently the efficiency with which they work in any given line depends on how much they enjoy it and how much they are interested in it. . . .

"Bennie's family chart shows an unusually bad condition of things, possibly because we have been more than usually fortunate in trac-ing his people. Bennie is one of seven children; the father and mother were both feeble-minded and . . . have defective brothers and sisters and the father is in turn the child of two feeble-minded parents, while the mother's mother is also feeble-minded. . . .

23 Hydrocephalus does not always result in idiocy; some normal and even supernormal individuals show evidences of congenital hydrocephalus.

" In this family we have twenty feeble-minded individuals. . . . In spite of all that, this boy had to be dismissed from the Training School, is now at large and will almost certainly continue the race of defectives to which he himself belongs." [24]

" Malcolm W. 22 years old. Mentality 10. Has been here 3 years. American born, of American parents. Had convulsions at four months, whooping-cough at four years, measles at seven, scarlet fever at nine. Has had pneumonia. Illness is given as the cause of the condition.

" Malcolm is a typical moron; learned to talk at the age of five; has slightly defective speech. He came here when he was nineteen years old; has learned to be generally useful about the barn and the cottage. . . . He can read and write a little, but his spelling is bad; he evidently has not been trained to do as much as he might have done, and yet he is quite as happy and quite as useful as he would have been had time put upon this phase of his education. The following short letter is representative of Malcolm.

Vineland, N. J.
Aple 29, 1910

Dear Mother
    I hope you got home save I wood like to
have gorne with you.
We have a new boy and look to be a nice won. I
wood like to com hom on my birthday it is not fare
of We had som moveing picture on Wesday and thay
were pretty.
With time did you get back home it mich of been late?
from your Loving son
Malcolm

" The family history is a most interesting one. Malcolm is the only living child of his parents, although there have been nine conceptions. The rest resulted in miscarriages or stillbirths. The mother is a normal woman and seemingly of a normal family; the father is also a normal man but evidently a carrier of defect, since his mother was feeble-minded. . . . To confirm our theory that the father must have been a carrier of feeble-mindedness we have only to look at an older brother who is feeble-minded and married a feeble-minded woman. They had twelve children of whom two died in infancy and all the rest were feeble-minded. There is no doubt that Malcolm has inherited this defect thru his paternal grandmother." [25]

[24] Goddard: *Feeble-mindedness, Its Causes and Consequences* (New York: The Macmillan Co., 1914) , case 16, pp. 96–7.
[25] Ibid., case 14, p. 94.

In contradistinction to this, however, the progeny of feeble-minded parents sometimes turn out surprisingly well. Some years ago Dr. Walter Fernald, then superintendent of a state school for the feeble-minded in Massachusetts, made a study of the offspring of some of the older children who had escaped from his institution and got married. To the considerable discomfiture of the eugenists, he found that a number of them had achieved considerable distinction, that several were holding public office, that at least two were teachers in high school, and that many of them were economically independent.

Clarence Darrow has vigorously exploded the myth of the Jukes versus the Edwards families, which is so often and so tiresomely repeated in this connection.[26]

BORDER–LINE CASES

George Smith had graduated from high school at seventeen and worked three years in order to save up money to go to college. He clerked in a store where he was regarded as efficient and dependable. He entered college with a full program. By scurrying around before school started, he lined up enough work to make himself self-supporting. He got up at half past three in the morning and distributed a morning paper. He attended classes from eight until twelve and spent the afternoon clerking in a store. From six to seven he served as a waiter. From seven to ten he tried to study.

He couldn't study very well. He thought it was because he was so sleepy from having got up early to carry papers. He didn't seem to be able to grasp the subject-matter. Possibly, he thought, it was because he had been out of high school three years and had forgotten how to study. At any rate he was soon reported as doing failing work in about two thirds of his classes.

At first sight, there would seem to be many reasons why George was unable to keep up with his work. But before jumping to conclusions and trying to arrange other ways for him to finance his schooling, it would be well to look into his psychological-test rating. The mean score for his (freshman) class on the intelligence test known as the Army Alpha was 137. His score was 82. Soldiers with such a score were placed in what is called the C-plus group. It is not impossible for them to graduate from college, but it is exceedingly difficult and it is probably inadvisable for them to make the effort.

[26] "The Edwardses and the Jukeses," *American Mercury*, Vol. VI, no. 22 (October 1925), pp. 147–57. See also the scientific studies of Abraham Myerson, op. cit.

Harry Emerson was the son of a farmer who, having been deprived of a college education himself, was determined that his son should have one at all costs. Accordingly he and his wife had denied themselves for years in an effort to save up enough money to send Harry to school. His father was very proud on the day that he brought him to college and enrolled him in his freshman subjects. Harry was likewise quite proud of himself. He seemed to have no doubt whatever that he would march right through, as he had done in high school.

Later we found that his high-school achievements had not been so rosy as they had appeared. His willingness and determination had impressed his teachers favourably to a point that influenced their judgment of the real merit of his work. And so it was only a few weeks before it was quite evident that he could not do any of the college work. He was totally lost in his foreign-language course, his English essays were impossible, his laboratory work in chemistry was altogether unacceptable. In all classes he was reported as failing.

He was tremendously upset by it, but declared that he would study harder and make his parents proud of him yet. He seemed to have no fear of the future, but on the contrary he seemed to think that all that was necessary was for him to try a little harder and study a little longer, in spite of the fact that he was already putting about twice as much time on his work as any of the other students.

An intelligence test showed that he had done well to finish high school and could never in the world be expected to do college work. It was impossible to tell his father this in view of the circumstances; so while it would have been simpler in some ways to have redirected his life, after six weeks' trial we felt it advisable to let the natural laws of college take their course. At the end of the semester he failed in everything, but, nothing daunted, he re-entered again the following fall, only to fail in most of his subjects. Several conferences with his father followed, in which it was tactfully suggested that something less academic and more practical would be better suited to Harry's personality requirements.

One should not jump to conclusions even on the basis of apparently definite presumptive evidence.

There are numerous recorded instances of children being regarded as feeble-minded who subsequently proved their intellectual superiority. James Watt was considered dull by his schoolmates; William Lloyd Garrison was surpassed in learning the alphabet by his much younger sister; William Warburton was considered by his first teacher to be " the dullest of all dull

scholars "; Thomas Aquinas as a child was called, for his slowness, a " dumb ox." [27] I know a very competent physician, who
graduated from his university with honours, who was considered
feeble-minded as a child and kept in the first grade several years.
Professor Thomas Edward Shields has written up his own case
in an autobiographical volume. [28] From nine until nineteen he
was considered hopelessly stupid; at the age of sixteen, he says,
he could not write his own name. And here is a case I remember
well:

Mary Mason was sent to me by the dean because she was failing in
most of her work. I found that in addition to great difficulties in
studying she was having trouble with her room-mate, was burdened
down by jealousy of her sister, was alternately tearful and cynical, and
was regarded by the students as moody and disagreeable. She was
totally discouraged with college and was homesick, and thought she
could never be popular or successful in her work.

Upon looking up her intelligence-test rating, I found that it was
about the same as those of the two cases described above, indicating
that her intellectual capacity would probably never exceed that of a
fifteen-year-old girl. Accordingly I wrote to the dean that it was probably not worth while struggling on with her, because she lacked the
intellectual capacity to do college work and was having adverse
emotional reactions to her difficulties.

What actually happened is that she developed influenza and pneumonia and had to leave school for a semester; when she came back,
she got down to work with such energy that a year later she was
doing average or better than average work in every subject.

Another case with deceiving appearances:

Dr. Seif of Munich, Germany,[29] reported the case of a boy who was
brought before the juvenile court because about one hundred and
forty cases of truancy were charged against him. The school for the
feeble-minded felt hopeless about his future because the boy had a
very peculiar lack: *he could not read at all*. When he tried to read,
what he brought out was pure nonsense and nobody could under-

[27] See Catharine M. Cox: *The Early Mental Traits of Three Hundred Geniuses*
(Stanford University Press, 1926) ; and J. J. Walsh and J. A. Foote: *Safeguarding
Children's Nerves* (Philadelphia: J. B. Lippincott Co., 1924) .

[28] *The Making and Unmaking of a Dullard* (Washington, D. C.: Catholic Educational Press, 1909) .

[29] In discussing a paper by Dr. Neil A. Dayton (see *American Journal of
Psychiatry*, Vol. VII, no. 5, March 1928) .

stand it. The teacher who attended the educational conference was absolutely sure that a boy so feeble-minded was hopeless.

Yet this boy who couldn't read after eight years of training, learned to read very well in nine weeks! His parents, who had lived in Switzerland, went to Germany when the boy was about six years old, and he had to go to school. He had spoken a certain Latin dialect and could not understand German and so he did not make good progress in the German school. He was laughed at and the teacher was not at all satisfied with him. The same thing was true in the second year; the third year he was sent to a school for the feeble-minded.

His situation at home was found to be very bad. His sister was only a year younger than he. She came to Germany when she was five years old, and so she had a full year in which to learn the language, with the result that when she entered school she was much better prepared than her brother had been. The mother always praised the girl, and the boy was entirely discouraged. Little by little the teacher came to despair of his ability to develop, thus closing the last opportunity. And of course the jealousy, the envy towards his sister, and the deprecation by his mother and teacher accomplished the result that seemed to be feeble-mindedness.

In at least one extraordinary case the intercurrence of influenza apparently brought about great improvement in a child previously regarded as unmistakably feeble-minded.

Helen, aged six, was the daughter of college-bred parents. Her maternal grandfather and his four brothers all had had " nervous break-downs." She was born with difficulty and had had a stormy infancy, with pneumonia at ten months, delayed dentition, etc. She had never learned to talk or to control her excreta. She had learned to walk after three years.

She was admitted to a school for feeble-minded children when four years old. Physically she was practically normal. " She sits and gazes at the end of a colored stick, waving it back and forth. She gazes fixedly at the ceiling. Screams violently if crossed in her play." The psychometric test rating was ten months.

In October 1918, at the age of five, she was taken ill with influenza, followed by broncho-pneumonia, and this by empyema (purulent pleurisy). During the long convalescence she began to talk and to be tidy, learned to feed herself, learned the letters of the alphabet, attended kindergarten, and co-operated with teacher and physicians. The Binet test rating in April, seven months after the influenza, etc., was two years and four months. In January 1920 it was three years and ten months, an improvement of four hundred and fifty per cent, thus measured! In 1922 it was approximately six years, and she continued to gain! [30]

TREATMENT

Imbeciles and idiots, unlike morons, are a total loss if left to their own devices, and must be specially provided for. Hence our state and private schools for feeble-minded children. It is amazing how much can be done for some of them by properly adapted educational methods and adequately trained workers.

The following case was observed in a private school for mentally retarded children.

When Bernard was admitted to the special school he was a noisy, restless, erratic, disobedient, clumsy little fellow who was the despair of his mother and teachers. From early delicacy and frequent illnesses he had grown to be physically sturdy, and because he was active and talkative he appeared to be superficially an average child. But a year in kindergarten and two years in the first grade had been a total failure. He could not count above ten and could write only a few digits. He could repeat parts of a few jingles with much prompting, could read reluctantly a few sentences, but absolutely refused to write.

His manners and social behaviour were correspondingly untutored. He galloped instead of walking. He carried on his incessant conversation in shouts. He displaced the other children in games and was openly defiant.

Examination showed him to have a mental age of four and a half years. His actual or chronological age was nine years. After several months of careful individual training the child was almost transformed, and, although he still made vigorous efforts to attract attention, his boisterousness and excitability had practically disappeared. He memorized twenty-six Mother Goose rhymes and the words to nine songs, which he sang more or less correctly. In school-work he learned fairly soon to write numbers through twelve and to count to fifty. He said he was interested in numbers so he could " figure up the cost of tractors." " They cost such a bloomin' lot of money," he remarked.

[30] For a technical report of this case see K. A. Menninger: " The Amelioration of Mental Disease by Influenza," *Journal of the American Medical Association,* Vol. XCIV, pp. 630–4 (March 1, 1930) .

He developed a good sense of order and was so much interested that often after school-hours or on Saturdays, when there was no attempt at routine work, he would say: " What shall we do now? " He was finally very proud of having learned to write and read with only slightly less ease than a normal child.

The vast majority of the stupid personalities in the world get along quite satisfactorily. Those whose handicap brings them into conflict with an environment too complicated for their powers of adaptation find refuge in flight or failure, like any other personality. Some of the pictures of failure resulting have been indicated in the foregoing.

Feeble-minded people may " go crazy " — that is, the distress of a too difficult situation may break down the unity of the personality so that the behaviour is grossly incompatible with social life. But this is not the rule.

The typical extreme failure in the stupid personality is inadequacy, inability to learn, and failure to develop mentally. This, in children, is a situation demanding our help. The help needed is proper environment and proper training.

Provisions for the feeble-minded who need institutional care are very inadequate. There are at least four low-grade feeble-minded persons to each thousand of the population in this country. No state in the Union has provided for more than ten per cent of its dependent mental defectives, and most of them for less than ten per cent. More and better schools, state and private, are needed. Special classes in the public schools for cases with favourable homes, for training in habit-formation and manual training are commendable if properly conducted and supervised. Just thrusting all of the eccentric, unstable, backward, and problem children into one so-called " opportunity room," or " ungraded class," as is done in so many cities, without psychiatric study or specialized attention to the individual, is an atrocity and a crime. It is comparable to the creation of a " fever room " in hospitals into which all patients whose temperatures were found to be above ninety-nine degrees were thrust, regardless of any other symptoms or complaints. In such a room all receive one sort of treatment, regardless of diagnoses.

A child whose mind is confused, clouded, or unhappy needs help more than a hungry boy. The hungry boy will seek for food; the misunderstood child does not know for what to search. Ordinary schooling, ordinary training methods, are of little value and sometimes even harmful. His problems and the problems of his parents in fitting him into a place in society require the knowledge and skill of those who are expert in such work. Such experts and such expert training are available only in special schools.

Such schools have the further advantage of grouping together children with similar difficulties.[31] This affords the mentally crippled child an environment which does not crush him with a painful sense of inferiority; he is surrounded by little friends who are just as baffled as he, whose wistful strivings toward goals that some find so easy are just as slow and just as difficult as his own. They laugh *with* him instead of *at* him; they are happy together because they understand one another and are understood.[32]

3. THE ISOLATION TYPE

(LONELY PERSONALITIES)

Among the personality types prone to failure in social adjustments, the seclusive, withdrawn, queer, eccentric, grotesque, odd, unsociable ones are both conspicuous and numerous. Analysis discovers that these are really of two sorts. Some are " temperamentally " unsocial and really prefer to be left out of it, although they may possess graceful social technique; the other group is made up of wistful " outsiders " who long to dive into the swim and either don't know how or are held back by restraining fears which have been inculcated.

The former are called schizoid, of which I shall say more later. The latter deserve a technical designation, and I have suggested the use of the name " isolated personalities." They are those who have been artificially withheld from human contacts to the point of developing curious deficiencies, mannerisms, attitudes, oddnesses, which serve to preclude their absorption or amalgamation into the group when, later, opportunities develop.

The " rube " is an example. However funny on the stage, in

---

31 Some of the better private schools for mentally retarded children are united in the Special School Association, 120 East 41st Street, New York City.

32 Nathan W. Ackerman and C. F. Menninger: " Treatment Techniques for Mental Retardation in a School for Personality Disorders in Children," *American Journal of Orthopsychiatry*, Vol. VI, pp. 294–312 (April 1936) .

Leona M. Chidester and Karl A. Menninger: " Application of Psychoanalytic Methods in the Study of Mental Retardation," *American Journal of Orthopsychiatry*, Vol. VI, pp. 616–25 (October 1936) .

real life the "rube" is a tragedy — a painful failure in social adaptation. He sometimes comes to college, as some of us know, and sometimes leaves college only a little less "rubish" than when he entered. It is a task indeed to alter a mould that has been setting for eighteen years.

The farms of the West and the great cities of the East develop two different types of provincialism, or "isolation," equally extreme. It is in the towns and small cities that socialization reaches its height. But geography and transportation facilities are by no means the sole determinants of breaking the shell. Isolation may result from many other things.

There are many examples in history of the "constructive compromises" of these lonely personalities struggling with a world for which they were ill prepared. Newton Arvin has pictured Hawthorne as the product of "abnormal seclusion," due partly to invalidism, partly to a morbid mother, eloquently proclaiming in all of his writings that "the essential sin . . . lies in whatever shuts up the spirit in a dungeon where it is alone, beyond the reach of common sympathies and general sunlight. All that isolates, damns; all that associates, saves." [33]

Similarly Sir Walter Scott was deflected by illness from the practical affairs and personal contacts of life and wrote himself into fame by setting down on paper his romantic fancies. Beethoven's deafness, Erasmus's illegitimacy, Byron's lameness and his incredible mother, Pope's stature, Swift's deformity, Samuel Johnson's psychopathic parents and defective sight — add these and many others to the list; the vast majority of isolated personalities lead lives no less lonely but far less productive.

Isolation by reason of a pathological parent

"A boy about ten years of age was at a summer camp, and the question came up whether or not he should come back home. He had been there eight weeks and was unhappy. He spent a good deal of the time by himself, and was looked upon by the other boys as queer, peculiar, eccentric. He had not participated in swimming, riding, and playing games; and, on the whole, he had been an undesirable comrade. When he first came, some of the other boys teased him, but, soon, he was passed by and ignored. The question was, why should a boy ten years of age be queer, peculiar, and eccentric, standing out alone among sixty other boys?

"In order to understand each type of individual . . . we must

[33] Newton Arvin: *Hawthorne* (Boston: Little, Brown & Co., 1929).

interpret his conduct in terms of past experiences. Now, going into the past experiences of this boy, we find the father is a professor who has a position of prominence. Five years ago the boy's mother died of an acute infection. The father was so emotionally upset that he began to build this boy's life around ill health. He got a nurse for the boy and she was told that this child must be protected against every possibility of sickness. The boy was not allowed to go to the public school or the private school, but had tutors at home. He was not allowed to ride on public conveyances, and only occasionally permitted to play with other boys. So his whole life was built around the problem of ill health.

" The emotional reaction in this father was, of course, in response to a serious situation; but most individuals are able to recover and adjust themselves, even in the case of the loss of a person much beloved and very near to them, and to make the experience a part of their lives. It is a part of our plasticity in life to be able to do this; but here was a man, a professor, an intellectual man, who stands out as a leader in his particular field, whose emotional reaction was so intense that he could not do so; and he planned the life of his boy around his emotional reaction," with the result described.[34]

Isolation by reason of poverty

All through the grades Lucile had two anxieties: the anxiety of keeping up in her studies, and the anxiety of poverty. These were the two topics which she heard discussed in her home. Her parents were poor and hard-pressed and her mother was a woman of high idealism who expected Lucile to make up in intellectual brilliancy what she lacked in glad raiment and finery.

Unfortunately Lucile was a normal child and hence couldn't make this extraordinary compensation. The constant reminders of her poverty which she received from her mother's tears, her father's complaints, and the obvious comparison of her clothing with that of her schoolmates combined to produce in her a marked sense of inferiority. In order to avoid the unpleasantness of comparisons, she quietly withdrew from situations in which opportunities for them were afforded. In high school, when the students' social life began to develop, she voluntarily excluded herself by declining invitations and avoiding opportunities. Because of her pretty face and sweet manner, she was in a way to be very popular, but she would decline dates and resort to various subterfuges and circumlocutions to avoid the humiliation of having her friends see the shabbiness of her home.

[34] Douglas A. Thom: " Moulding Personality in the Pre-School Years," *Mental Hygiene of Normal Childhood* (Buffalo Mental Hygiene Council, 1927), p. 40.

During her senior year in high school a relative died, leaving her mother considerable money. It was decided that Lucile should go to college. She outfitted herself prettily and her mother bought her a Ford for her own private use, so that she entered college with considerably more than the average personal comfort. The old habits, however, were hard to break. She was shy, diffident, retiring, and self-distrustful. These traits, together with her evidences of prosperity, stimulated the envy and dislike of her companions, who had formerly loved her for her very meekness. Her life was lonelier than before. She left college in her sophomore year.

Isolation by reason of wealth

" An example will show us the effect of the opposite type of home atmosphere on a girl who was fundamentally normal. In this case, as so often, the person developed an inability to make friends, and lacked self-confidence. She is always inconspicuous in a group, in spite of attractive dress, pleasant face, and kindly disposition. The girl is longing for friends and companionship, but as no one goes out of his or her way to talk to her she simply goes more into the background. At times she has developed a really dangerous despondency as a result.

" The fact is that the parents laid emphasis on the material side of life and built their home atmosphere on it. None of the three children were anxious to remain at home, though they loved their parents and the parents provided liberally for them. There was no friction between father and mother.

" What was the matter? The atmosphere was simply the atmosphere of a fine store or hotel. The furnishings were tasteful, rich, and beautiful. The children grew up in it and were taught to think that if they looked and behaved well they would grow up to marry and live happily ever after. From the start the girl was known at school as the most spick-and-span child in the class. Her dresses were always white and starched. She learned her lessons with the same mechanical precision and could rattle them off faster than anyone else.

" To her parents, dirty clothes meant inferior people not fit to play with. Consequently she, like her older sister, lost her childhood companionship. They could not play with or know the children at school or in a large part of their neighborhood. The parents were unaware of the spiritual malnutrition of their children, and did not even attempt to make up for the lack of playmates by themselves playing with the children. And if quarreling and harsh words were unknown in the household, so were noise and laughter.

" The girl fortunately possessed a good physical, emotional and intellectual makeup, which has helped pull her through a very difficult period. Now, at twenty-eight years of age, still unmarried, she has become aware of the deficiencies of her early life — and with unusual intelligence she has changed her business life to one of work with children, which is helping greatly to satisfy her lonely longings and giving her greater ease with people of her own age. She is practically free from her previous spells of depression." [35]

Isolation by reason of " religion "

The youngest son of a " Holiness " sect minister, Tom Schnell, was the only one of four sons not to follow in the footsteps of his father. He had always felt outdistanced by his brothers, and so dominated by his rigid and fiery father that he decided to go his own way and carry on his religious life privately. His mother, as much a crusader as her husband, was always too busy with her missionary activities to pay much attention to any of her children. She was proud of her older sons, but as for Tom, the youngest, it was enough that he was quiet and caused her no trouble.

Following his " conversion " at twelve, Tom spent more and more of his time alone, ruminating and pondering. He became convinced of the sinfulness of almost every usual interest for a boy of his age. He refused to go to school parties, was horrified at the thought of dancing or playing cards. He stayed away from groups of boys who tried out smoking and other forbidden activities. When he finished high school and went to work for a local contracting firm, he was out of step with the men around him. They, in turn, considered him queer and found it easier not to include him in their after-hour games and recreational evenings. Political issues and events of the day were also too worldly for Tom.

He married a matter-of-fact woman who said (later) that she married him because he always seemed so lonesome and she felt sorry for him. Though she went to church with him, she had little extra time to listen to his long discourses on religion or to engage with him in his private rituals. When he began to lose time from work because of stomach trouble and headaches, Mrs. Schnell had to take a job to help with their support. A simple-minded adolescent girl was obtained to help with the housework. Shortly after this Tom Schnell's attacks of indigestion became more frequent and he remained at home more and more, where the girl not only took care of him but, more important, listened with rapt attention to his long dissertations on religion. She was easily persuaded to take part in some of his rituals. At last he had found one person with whom he could share his inner life, which since early years had

[35] Hallowell and Davis, in the *Harvard Alumni Bulletin,* 1928.

become so much more important to him than the world around him. The girl became pregnant, the community became aroused, the girl was removed from the home, and Tom Schnell became so deeply depressed that he attempted suicide.

Isolation by reason of deafness

When Alice Burton was still in the grades she had repeated attacks of earache which resulted in a considerable reduction of hearing. It was necessary for her to obtain a front seat in each of her classes in order to be able to hear the teacher. Her school work had been of a high order and continued so in spite of her difficulty because she applied herself with special diligence to reading and home study at the expense of play hours and social recreation. Unfortunately her deafness progressed, and by the time she had reached her senior year in high school it was necessary for her to obtain an electrical hearing device. This helped her materially, but wearing it seemed to cause her embarrassment and she would avoid doing so whenever possible. This, however, meant that she missed or misunderstood conversations. She would do her best to conceal her confusion and bewilderment under such circumstances and was in a constant conflict as to whether to remain with the group or retreat from social situations altogether.

In the end it was the last alternative that won out. She obtained a position in the library, where she had a minimum of contact with the public and limited requirements of conversation with her associates. She did a vast amount of reading so that she became a very well-informed person in spite of her lack of college opportunity.

After some years she met and married a man as shy and retiring as herself and they moved to another community. With her husband, her subsequent children, her garden, and her reading she apparently lived a full and fairly satisfying existence for some years. Some of her neighbours were able to make allowance for her eccentricities and seclusiveness and became friends of a sort. Thinking to improve her community adjustment and lessen her loneliness, they importuned her to attend meetings of a local woman's club. This she did with a commendable bravery, but soon began to react unfavourably. She could not dismiss from her mind a suspicion that she was being talked about, that some of the conversations which she could not hear related to criticisms of herself. She began to have attacks of indigestion and physical discomfort and at one of the meetings fainted and was taken home. The confusion of so many people talking, the sustained effort of trying to understand some of the conversation, the embarrassment about her handicap combined to defeat the effort. She retreated again to her home and garden.

Isolation by reason of real or fancied defect or unfavourable comparison

The isolation of the deaf or crippled child is an obvious tragedy, to avert which systematic efforts are now made in most civilized communities.

Far more frequent, more devastating, and more inaccessible are the isolation and suffering caused by the *sense of inferiority* based (usually) upon *fancied* defects, or upon the emotional reactions to defects which of themselves are not isolating. This is the most important, the most frequent, the most serious of all factors conducive to the development of this personality type. Hence we shall now take it up in considerable detail.

THE SENSE OF INFERIORITY

From the time when one of the earliest Adams shivered in fear before the threatening forces of nature and compared his puniness with the incalculable power of the universe, man has been subject to disagreeable sensations dependent upon his awareness of the discrepancy between his fantasy of power and his relative helplessness in the hands of natural forces. Having reconciled himself to this with the aid of various devices — religions, philosophies, inventions, regional conquests over nature, and the like — he encounters the same discomforts in comparing himself with individual men, stronger, quicker, or more astute than himself. In childhood parents represent omnipotent gods, toward whom inferiority feelings first develop, only to be assuaged by compensations of dependency, and it is the brothers and sisters who then excite envy by comparison.

Ideally the results of such comparisons are an intellectual adjustment of one's given powers to one's given tasks in the most productive way possible with a minimum of dissatisfaction. But in actuality the occasional surrender to painful fantasies of relative incompetence and weakness probably replace productiveness to a lesser or greater extent in everyone. It is easy to see how these arise from envy and from the omnipotent ambitions of infancy, but even realizing these things does not make anyone totally immune from them. The expressions " inferiority complex," " the sense of inferiority," and " inferiority feelings " coined by psychiatrists and psychologists during the past few decades were seized upon as technical designations dignifying the unworthy and disquieting emotion they were supposed to describe and indicating it to be a unique phenomenon in the self-diagnosed individual (and perhaps a *few* others). The fact is, as I have tried to indicate, that compared to certain other powers and certain other persons in the world we *are* inferior, all of us, and the sensible person is aware of this, without pain.

It is, therefore, no distinction and no credit to one to recognize or proclaim one's inferiority feelings. To pity oneself because one lacks something that someone else has is a far less flattering way of viewing the situation, but one much more likely to lead to an investigation of its origins. The clinical fact is, as we all know, that whether they proclaim it proudly or deny it vigorously, many people do suffer constantly and sometimes acutely with feelings of inadequacy, diffidence, self-dissatisfaction, so-called hypersensitiveness, and a pervading discouragement because of such feelings. To call these merely " a sense of inferiority " is not enough. They should be called an illusion and alibi of inferiority, disguising envy, hate, guilt feelings, and other emotions which in turn arise from fundamental misconceptions and self-mismanagement.

Feelings of inferiority *consciously* center on comparisons of the subject with other individuals. Usually these comparisons are originally of tangible, visible things — that is, *physique* and physical accomplishments. The child early compares himself, his little body, his physical equipment, with that of his omnipresent and omnipotent parents; later, also, with siblings and playmates. Necessarily he is constantly aware of discrepancies in size, in height and weight, in strength. His obvious inferiorities are associated with his obvious dependency and subservience. Since what Father and Mother say " goes," he is early taught without words that " might makes right." This could as well be written " height makes right."

The child's first reactions to the constant reminder of his littleness take many forms. There comes to be a resentment of being called " little." There is much talk of " when I grow up " — Mamma and Papa games are indulged in; long dresses and trousers are donned, and various types of rebellion and insubordination are indulged in, in spite of foregone conclusions of ultimate defeat.

These compensations which the child makes become gradually less necessary as the child becomes aware of his growth.

" Soon I shall be as big as they," he thinks — and so he is often told.

There are certain other comparisons which the small child makes — comparisons which, from the covert or coy behaviour of his parents, he infers should not be made. They relate to the tabooed areas of the body. The axillary and pubic hair, for example, are never-failing sources of mystery and humiliation. It is so definitely *there* on his parents and so definitely *not there* upon his own little person. What is wrong that he is thus minus this attribute of the big and powerful folks? [36]

Other painful comparisons are also made by every child. The little boy compares himself with his father and wonders what is wrong with himself. Later he becomes conscious of pleasurable genital sensations and a sense of guilt develops with the theory that his under-development is a punishment. Similarly the little girl is puzzled by her discoveries. Psychoanalysis of many patients has revealed that the child spins fantastic explanations to account for these lacks, and develops innumerable compensatory defence mechanisms to save himself the pain of a realization of inferiority.

Now, such feelings of inferiority are common to nearly all children. They are based, to be sure, on misconceptions and ignorance, but the emotional response is there, and it has to be expressed. It may be handled very easily — a harmless discharge, as it were, especially where proper educational methods and manners are used by the parents. Or, on the other hand, the foundations of a neurosis may be laid.

These primary feelings of inferiority are ordinarily submerged in oblivion in the majority of persons. They usually become completely unconscious. But it is easy to revive these childish anxieties and add to their intensity a few years later by unfavourable comparisons made by someone in authority, such as: " Sam is not so bright as his sister," remarks his mother to a visitor. " George is unusually awkward and clumsy for his age." " Daughter, it's a good thing you're smart in your studies, because you certainly are the homeliest child on earth." " John's teeth are so ugly they make him look just terrible." " There's no use in paying out any more for your music lessons — you haven't any voice." (The girl to whom this last remark was

[36] Readers will be reminded that hair as the symbol of power runs through all history and legend — Samson, for a classical example; *The Hairy Ape,* for an O'Neill elaboration of the theme. It is well known how some wrestlers and other professional strong men grow and display heavy beards.

made became later a professional musician and concert singer.) [37]

Such comments are deadly. They often crush the child's hopes and efforts and self-respect completely. They rarely stimulate, because the authority of their source makes them incontrovertible.

Then there are other, less obvious ways in which parents build up inferiority feelings in their children. One is by constantly exhibiting their own inferiority feelings. Some parents are incessantly complaining of their misfortunes, comparing their acquisitions and opportunities with those of their neighbours, voicing their enviousness and unhappiness and disappointments. They may go further and berate themselves, or they may scowl and sneer at their envied friends. More frequently they complain that their neighbours dislike them, that their friends have lost interest in them, do not return their social overtures, do not appreciate their efforts. I remember one family that had moved seven times because of the wife's dissatisfaction with the neighbours. In any case, the effect on the child is the same — " My folks lost out; they're licked. They aren't as good as . . ."

The social organization of most American cities is built upon the existence of this sensitiveness. Many exclusive clubs keep their dues unjustifiably high and their membership dismally lonely in order that the members may gain consolation for their inferiority feelings by the realization that many who can't afford to join envy them in their exclusiveness.

Still other parents excite inferiority in their children by their delinquencies. The child feels much more keenly than his parents the social disapprobation which they incur. An alcoholic father or a divorced mother may serve as a burden of bitterness to the children throughout their lives. " I have always felt as if I must apologize for my father," one such remarked in discussing his self-consciousness. " I always have in the back of my mind: ' What if they knew! ' "

Finally there are certain physical conditions of which no one needs to speak — nor can the organic inferiority remain unknown to the subject. He knows because he can see himself in the eyes of strangers; he knows because the cruel taunts of the little animals about him — glad to find someone their inferior and someone to torture — won't let him forget. This group in-

[37] These are all actual quotations.

cludes speech defects, birth-marks on the face, dental deformities, crippled limbs, deformed bodies, cleft palate and hare-lip. So obvious are these things and so disfiguring that they permit of little real protection from exceedingly great mental pain.[38]

COMPENSATIONS AND CORRECTIONS

Many children early develop compensatory reactions to these inferiority feelings — patterns which continue to dominate their behaviour long after the original cause is extinct. Others develop them later. Enviousness, aggressiveness, penuriousness, acquisitiveness, flight reactions, anxiety states, bluffing, stealing, and all sorts of adventitious behaviour may result — do result. The roots of many neuroses of later life are to be found here. " Neurasthenia," in which a patient is sure that his or her eyes are weak, stomach ailing, legs impaired, etc., is a condition in which unconsciously these organs are used as substitutes for others concerning which, as a child, the sufferer had grave and painful misgivings.

The whole subject of compensation and over-compensation which so frequently results from feelings of inferiority will be discussed more fully in connection with the actual inferiority resulting from deficiencies in the perceptual apparatus — deafness, for example. (See pages 170–4.)

Unconscious refutation of inferiority feelings as represented by the " superiority complex " — that is, strenuous effort not so much to compensate for but to deny the very existence of any such feelings — is technically called reaction-formation. (See pages 295–6.)

When it is possible by means of medical, surgical, dental, or other devices to correct some of the actual inferiorities which go toward making isolation personalities, such treatment is, of course, indispensable. The plastic surgeons and orthopædists and orthodontists have done and are doing much in the direction of mental hygiene. Many such cases as the following are reported in dental literature:

A stenographer, aged twenty-four, had been under treatment for two years for a very bad disfigurement of the face caused by dental deformities. The mental effects were particularly marked. She had always taken a position in the back office where it would not be neces-

---

[38] Cf. Somerset Maugham's autobiographical masterpiece: *Of Human Bondage.*

sary for her to meet the public. Two years later, after the deformity had been corrected, she was working in the front office and wearing an engagement ring.[39]

Sometimes the " mental hazard," as the golfers would call it, remains the chief isolating factor. This can often be overcome by psychiatric technique, administered by a physician, a friend, a teacher; sometimes even by a football coach, to wit:

A student, Sny, " was frail and had a peculiar manner because his intimates were all adults. He was an object of ridicule and harsh treatment with his schoolmates. His first adjustment took the form of seclusiveness. He avoided all association with other boys and never played in the school yard. His recesses were spent in the assembly hall, where he might have, and actually did require, the protection of a master. Since he was physically incapable of protecting himself, it was not thought prudent to force him to go where the other boys were.

" The coach of the school football teams interested himself in the case. For many afternoons he devoted part of his time to Sny, training him in quarterback play. The boy developed with practice and was finally made a substitute on the third team. He showed special aptitude at forward-passing and was able to master a complicated play. In the last game of his team's schedule, he was rushed in to win the game in the last few minutes of play.

" The immediate effect of Sny's creditable performance was a complete change in the attitude of his companions. His frailness and queer manner remained for a time but were offset by demonstrated ability of a particularly desirable sort. For want of stimulus the inferiority reaction ceased to function. The same personality, after ten years, shows little trace of the original tendencies." [40]

4. THE SCHIZOID TYPE

(QUEER PERSONALITIES)

Consider the personality of a man believed by some to have been the greatest failure of history:

With intelligence superior to that of any other president of this country and with an opportunity for achievement greater than any human being has ever known, he went down in an ignominious and dismal defeat and died a lonely and broken-hearted man. Pitied by many.

[39] T. M. Robertson, in the *International Journal of Orthodontia, Oral Surgery, and Radiography,* Vol. XI, no. 9 (September 1925) , p. 848.

[40] English Bagby: " The Inferiority Reaction," *Journal of Abnormal and Social Psychology,* Vol. XVIII, no. 3 (October–December 1923) , p. 270.

scorned by more, he was worshipped to the end by faithful and puzzled millions, and understood by no one. He had been a solitary child, a child who " threw down the bat and wouldn't play " — a child who didn't know how to play with other children. That child became a university executive who couldn't get along with his faculty, a governor who antagonized his supporters, and a president who quarrelled with his counsellors. And while the masses bowed down to him as the Great Deliverer who would bring to Europe the democracy of America and to the world the peace of Utopia, his associates, the leaders of these people who worshipped him, suavely and expertly effected the utter defeat of his entire program and the extinction of his career.[40a]

Woodrow Wilson was a classical example of a well-established personality type. It is a type characterized by queerness, a queer sort of queerness, and there is nothing else like it in the world. Some people succeed because they are queer, and others fail for the same reason. Look, for a moment, at certain aspects of the lives of some successful persons of this type. Their unsociability, their self-sufficiency, their essential queerness, is always visible.

Napoleon Bonaparte was thus described by one of his biographers: " At nine years of age he was a shy, proud, wilful child, unkempt and untrained, little, pale, and nervous, almost without instruction, and yet already enamored of a soldier's life and conscious of a certain superiority over his comrades." [41] He loved most to play all alone, hidden in a cave.

At sixteen his instructors said of him that he was reserved, laborious, haughty, silent, egotistical, preferring study to pleasure, and loving solitude. He devoted his leisure time to the reading of history. Realier Dumas painted a picture of Napoleon at school, in which he walks silent and aloof from a group of schoolmates, doubtless finding consolation and a certain fierce sense of justification in the idea of his superiority to them which provoked them to laugh, sneer, point at him, and mock him.

He leaped to success, fought with the world, inspired millions, then passed rapidly through a series of anticlimaxes, and died a lonely, friendless man.

[40a] " His most disabling weakness [was] his pervasive suspiciousness. He believed in mankind but distrusted all men." David Lloyd George in *Memoirs of the Peace Conference* (New Haven: Yale University Press, 1939) .

[41] Ida M. Tarbell: *A Life of Napoleon Bonaparte* (New York: The Macmillan Co., 1923) .

Samuel Taylor Coleridge was a misfit among boys of his own age, taking little pleasure in their sports. He did not care for bodily activity, and said of himself that he was " a playless day-dreamer." His parents petted him, his brothers hated him, and his schoolfellows tormented him mercilessly. He became fretful, timorous, telltale, and vain, and despised boys of his own age. He is said not to have spoken a word until he was nearly two years old, when he surprised everyone by uttering a complete sentence.

Sir Isaac Newton was a sober, silent, thinking lad who never took part in the ordinary amusements of his schoolmates, but employed all his leisure hours in invention. As he grew older, his love of study increased, and he was constantly with his books, avoiding and ignoring those who might have been his friends.

Jeremy Bentham, the English jurist and philosopher, found his greatest joy in reading and disliked sports and games. From his earliest childhood he was sensitive and retiring, felt inferior, hated social pleasures, and was solitary in his play and work. He had few child associates and spent much time in reading and in gloomy meditation. At college he could discover little pleasure in the companionship of the other students. He was tormented by fear and suffered from almost morbid sensitiveness. His sense of inferiority was so strong that he shunned attention, and his father bitterly accused him of burying his talents.[42]

To get a more definite conception of the typical extreme picture of the schizoid personality, read the description of an unknown subject, by Kretschmer.

" Young Erich Hanner, the son of a well-educated family . . . was a pale, timid youth," of fifteen, " who had shot up to a great height, with long ungainly limbs, and a vague dreamy expression on his face. . . . He usually sat huddled up, bashful, and spiritless, so that one would think that he was dumb; if anyone spoke to him, he would look up surprised, embarrassed, and shy. Everyone was exasperated by his slowness and priggishness. . . . His conscientiousness and punctuality were almost pedantic.

" He was very quiet, and easily moved to tears, when anyone upbraided him. He never had any friends at school, and he became less and less able to get on with his brothers and sisters. . . . He never took

42 The data regarding these celebrities are taken from the excellent summaries of Catharine M. Cox in *The Early Mental Traits of Three Hundred Geniuses* (Stanford University Press, 1926) .

part in rough games. His school-fellows used to tease him a great deal; he made no protest, but suffered terribly under it. He quarrelled easily with his brothers and sisters on account of his oddity. He had a bitter feeling that he was different from the others. Speech was always a difficulty to him. He could not get hold of the words. ' If I speak a word as soon as it comes into my head,' he said, ' I have the feeling as if I were shouting insolently into the blue. . . .' He often drew back after shaking hands with the same feeling, as if it were an insult to grip a person's hand quickly. He laid great value on good clothes, and could never do enough with his own toilet.

"On the emotional side, he was tender, sensitive, and susceptible. When he was older he did not eat flesh any more, because it came from slaughtered beasts. . . . When he was away from home, he suffered dreadfully from homesickness. He clung very tenderly to his mother. Later on he developed a religious enthusiasm; he went every Sunday to church, and wanted to convert his family, and become a missionary.

" He had a favourite sister to whom he was very attached, especially in his younger years, and with whom he shared all his thoughts. His prematurely awakened intelligence produced excellent, original ideas, particularly of a technical variety. He liked to think out fleeting, fantastical inventions; for example, once he thought out a plan for a carriage which went with paddle-wheels upon the water. He tried a model of it in his bath, worked at it silently and passionately, and sent a copy to the Minister for War. The carriage did, as a matter of fact, go; it had been well thought out. He also drew and painted very beautifully.

" But he preferred to creep into a corner with his sister, apart from the other children, and build castles in the air with her. They would imagine princedoms in wonderful parts of the world, which they would rule, and there would be hunting, and enchanted creatures, a world of magic and an ether ship, that travelled forth to visit all the stars set in the spaces of the universe.

" He did not like people to touch him. He often felt as if he were made of glass." [43]

This queerness may go to great lengths.

On July 2, 1881 a man of no consequence, and never regarded or treated as of any, a wanderer without a home, penniless, and syphilitic, but who " appeared to . . . consider himself a great man . . . the maker of a President, the saver of his country, an evangelist who meant to save the world by a worthless book, a politician whose miserable little speech,

[43] Ernst Kretschmer: *Physique and Character,* translated by W. J. H. Sprott (New York: Harcourt, Brace and Co., 1925) , pp. 181–3.

delivered only once to a couple of dozen negroes, did much to elect Mr. Garfield, and insured him the right to one of the highest offices in the land " — this man, Charles Julius Guiteau, shot and killed President Garfield " as a political necessity under Divine pressure," as he said, " after two weeks of earnest prayer." [44]

What conceivable traits do these people have in common — a president, an emperor, a poet, a scientist, a jurist and philosopher, a queer stick, and the assassinator of a president?

They have this in common: they all possess traits of the schizoid type of personality. And they have plenty of company, good and bad; Calvin and Kant, Schiller and Rousseau, Erasmus and Spinoza, Whistler and Goldsmith, Wagner and Chopin, Robespierre and Adolf Hitler, Dickie Loeb and Jesse James, Van Gogh and Judas Iscariot, and a certain querulous congressman whom I am afraid to name, not to mention about two hundred and twenty thousand of the patients resident in state hospitals of the country with a diagnosis of " dementia præcox." They all " belong."

Reduced to its simplest terms, the common tendency of the members of this group is an inability to get along well with other people. This is almost too much simplified, because it might be applied to all of us at times, and to many criminals and " insane " all of the time. But this lack of social adaptability is of a very special kind. These people sometimes appear to want to mix with the herd. More often they obviously do not want to and they never do — successfully, at any rate. They may make gestures, go through the motions, even become extremists in social manœuvres, but " the pane of glass is always there." They never really make lasting contacts.

How does this make them appear? Well, variously, according to the combination of traits and reactions. Most of them are more or less seclusive, quiet, reserved, serious-minded, unsociable, and eccentric; many are timid, shy, very fine-grained, sensitive, " nervous," excitable, fond of nature and books and fine arts; others are dull, apparently (not really) stupid, indifferent, often quite pliable, but more often very stubborn; sometimes " stunty," again morose and grouchy, and all too frequently suspicious, envious, and jealous.

[44] Charles F. Folsom, M.D.: " The Case of Guiteau, Assassin of the President of the United States," Boston *Medical and Surgical Journal*, Vol. CVI (1882), pp. 145–53.

One word (other than " unsociable ") describes them — but it's a shifty word, variously understood by various people. That word is " queer." They are queer in that they are not all like the rest of us and don't seem to care to be. They may achieve great things and they may not — we may acclaim them and pay them due respect — but we never love them very much. We can't. They won't let us.

Such people are technically called *schizoid*. It is a word derived from the same Greek stem that gave us " scissors." It means split or broken. The implication is that the queerness of these folk represents a break or split in the internal harmony of the personality so that an external disharmony also results and the schizoid person is noticeably out of tune with the rest of the world. Their behaviour, their expressed ideas, and their emotional reactions do not harmonize.

This is because these personalities are afflicted with a curious split, a duality, a " surface and a depth," as Kretschmer says. They are " like Roman houses and villas, which have closed their shutters before the rays of the burning sun; perhaps in the subdued interior light, there are festivities." [45] They maintain one kind of front for the world to look at if it cares to (they don't care), but the real self, having looked at the world and renounced it, retreats into an inner unseen life. This life we never get to know, except when an explosion occurs.

" I have lived with that man for twenty years, and I don't know him at all," says a wife.

" A shy girl, pious, gentle, lamblike, serves with satisfaction in a country home for years. One morning the three children of the house lie murdered. The house is in flames. She has not lost her senses, she understands everything, she smiles uncertainly when she realizes her act.

" A young man dreams away the lovely days of his youth. He is so clumsy and loutish that one could shake him. If he is put upon a horse he falls off. He smiles in an embarrassed way, rather ironically; he says nothing. One day there appears a volume of poetry that he has written; exquisite feeling for nature, beautiful diction. Every blow that some fat lout has given him as he passed by is moulded into an inner tragedy; the polished rhythms flow on full of quiet." [46]

[45] Kretschmer, op. cit., p. 146.
[46] Ibid.

The seclusive variety

Consider more closely some of the characteristic manifestations of the schizoid make-up. None is more typical than *seclusiveness*. It isn't quite human constantly to prefer one's own company. But the schizoid does. " I prefer to be alone," they admit. " I never did care to mix with people." This is particularly noticeable in childhood.

Until he was seventeen the famous historian Gibbon had associated with no one but his parents, an aunt, and his tutors. When sent away to school he was " nearly overwhelmed by the strangeness and confusion," and stood aloof from the other students. Fichte, the celebrated German metaphysician, was, from an early age, fond of solitary walks and quiet contemplation. Sent away to school at the age of eighteen, he tried to run away because of the bullying he received there. Ralph Waldo Emerson's chief recreation, even in childhood, was omnivorous reading. He was not popular with other boys and rarely joined in their games. His best friends were grown people.[46a]

This seclusiveness as it appears in such notables as those cited will be immediately familiar in the behaviour of scores of the reader's acquaintances. It may even describe the reader himself. But its significance is usually not so familiar. Many unhealthily seclusive children are regarded as models of behaviour, studiousness, and ability. Their seclusiveness keeps them out of the scrapes and tangles and pranks in which normal children become involved.

The child often prefers adult company to companions of his own age. Carlyle, for example, who was a serious, silent lad with few boy friends, sought adult companionship, as did also René Descartes, Kepler, George Eliot, and many others. Such children (Descartes and Carlyle notoriously so) are stimulated to excel all other children, and often do so to their great satisfaction — and unpopularity. This, too, misleads adults into supposing them unusually healthy instead of the reverse.

For example, Kepler, the celebrated German astronomer, was, as a boy, mystically religious and superstitious and punished himself when he felt convicted of sin. At fourteen he was already deeply interested in

---

[46a] The seclusiveness of these great scholars and those listed below was not necessarily that of the schizoid personality which we are here trying to illustrate. See Isolation Personality, p. 64.

theological questions and won the enmity of his theology-teacher by openly trying to convert him. At one school the students envied and hated him because of his superior abilities; at another they made life miserable for him because he reported their misdemeanours. He loved gaming, but gambled only with himself.

Associated with seclusiveness, then really a part of it, are certain tendencies which of themselves or under certain circumstances are "normal," but which occur to excess in schizoid individuals. These are the over-studious, bookish, pedantic tendencies; the aloofness from sports and games and social activities, the compulsion toward excelling, taciturnity and conspicuous reserve, shyness and self-consciousness, and hypersensitiveness. The latter is frequently the most painful symptom and many college students who are aware of no other faults consult the mental-hygiene counsellor because of their distress on this score. Others make no complaint, but are forever getting their feelings hurt and pouting, or fighting unsuspecting foes, or running off.

The hard-boiled variety

It may be a little difficult to conceive it, but it is nevertheless true that in this same category belong some hard-boiled, unsensitive, heartless, ruthless, cruel individuals. The connection depends upon the fact that in both instances the personality is split or broken, so that the surface feelings and behaviour are grossly different from the real self within. Napoleon's self-seeking hardness, Lepke's and Loeb's callousness in their bloody crimes, the poise of the trained surgeon, and the penetration of the skilled psychologist are alike examples of a detachment which, whatever its fruits, is scarcely human. Utter objectivity is the aim of every scientist — it is a correct and fruitful but inhuman attitude and typically schizoid. Because many men are too human or too little schizoid in make-up, they fail of great achievement in science.

The artistic variety

The artist and the poet are similarly detached from "normal" life — to their own sorrow, often, and to our profit. They submit to us fragments of their inner world — bits of dreams and visions and songs that we — out here — do not hear except as they translate them. But this same esotericism, this same otherworldliness, may appear as religious fanaticism, artistic grotesqueries, pseudo-psychological bunk, spiritualism, mysticism, and all sorts of fad faiths and cures. Still more extreme are the totally incomprehensible productions of certain schizoid mental diseases. For example:

George Sand (Aurore Dupin), as a child, attempted to satisfy a desire for strange mental experiences by conjuring up hallucinations. Solitude delighted her, as did the reading of religious or fantastic books. She became known as an eccentric because she wandered about the countryside alone. At the time of receiving her first communion she learned the catechism like a parrot, resolving not to retain any of it. At seventeen she found Parisian life intolerable and married a man she did not love in order to escape it. At twenty-one she began a Platonic friendship which lasted four years.

The apparently stupid variety

As Kretschmer says, when faced by social necessities some schizoids " growl, or run away, or sit there and feel tortured, or else display a monumental peace of mind and are just dumb."

This " dumbness " is often a false front — a pseudo-stupidity. (There is also a type of schizoid personality combined with genuine stupidity.) There is an unresponsiveness, a lack of appreciation, which leads others to do the excluding. Its victims lack interest in their surroundings, take little part in social or civic affairs, manifest no initiative and no progress. They often brag about their conservatism, their fondness for the old-fashioned things, their dislike for modern innovations. They prefer to work alone with their own tools.

Many such are to be found amidst the welcome isolation of the prairie farms. It is their peculiar personality trends that makes it so difficult for the progressive, socially-minded farmer to effect rural co-operation even to the extent necessary to secure relief for the present agricultural distress. In a sense the social-minded persons make for the cities — that is, for groups of other people — and the schizoid personalities prefer the isolation of the farm. This is a tendency only; it should go without saying that many city dwellers are schizoid (particularly in larger cities, which afford the greatest of all opportunities for isolation), and many country dwellers, on the other hand, are notably gregarious.

The grouchy variety

The " growl " which Kretschmer speaks of is an armour of defence for the really sensitive skin of the schizoid. To ensure seclusion he erects a barrier of grouchiness, crabbedness, crochetiness, and makes himself as disagreeable as possible. Whether as bank presidents or as isolated grocerymen, whether as tramps or misers, these individuals are unpopular.

In any situation requiring contacts with others, they are apt to be painful misfits. They are a familiar problem in the daily life of every employment manager, often being retained only because of some propensity or knowledge or skill which makes them valuable in spite of the mental inflammation they cause in the surrounding personnel. If, as occasionally happens, the wheels of chance whirl them to the top or if they frighten and annoy away all except subordinates and become masters of the machine, they are often highly successful — as the world judges. Bankers and executives often belong to the category.

John Blakely was an example of this. When he was fifteen he ran away from home and went to the Middle West, where by one hard job after another he eked out an existence. Gradually he secured a little property, and by tremendous exertion, close dealings, and long hours of hard work he increased his holdings until he was accounted a man of means. With his wife and children he was irascible and mean. His wife did not know until after his death how wealthy they really were. At the time he died he had accumulated many sections of land and was known to many thousands of people, but aside from the few whom he patronized with his money he cannot be said to have had a single friend.

Old Mrs. Collins was another example. She was the neighbourhood crank. She kept a rabbit-hutch with several hundred rabbits in it. She collected old newspapers and magazines and piled them up in great stacks in her attic and barn. She was famous for flying into a rage at the grocery boys and postmen and accusing them of all sorts of villainy. At the time of her husband's death she accused the gravedigger of having cheated her with regard to the time spent in making the excavation for her husband's grave. The family lived with her only by dint of the most discreet silence and tact. They were accustomed to many outbreaks of accusation and vituperation.

In spite of all this, the old lady became well known as an authoress and accumulated considerable means through her shrewd business dealings.

The radical variety

Then there are the rebellious, those of the " queer " who forge through the mass of humanity about them with conspicuous aggressiveness, waving the battle-ax and shouting the war-cry, stirring up resentments and hostilities, making enemies if they find none, baiting and nagging and criticizing and challenging and attacking — these constitute another group of schizoids. Here again there are occasional successes, successes for which the world is grateful — Savonarolas and John Browns and William Lloyd Garrisons and John Knoxes and Patrick Henrys and John Husses and Martin Luthers and John the Baptists.

But these same traits may lead to failure, producing scandal-mongers, " hatelerites," backbiters, political rebels, and generally unconstructive trouble-makers. It is rare, however, that such obvious psychiatric cases get to psychiatrists.

In a large railroad strike in the Middle West a few years ago, one of the most prominent characters was a tall, angular, loquacious man who was always explaining. He explained elaborately to many of the workers wherein they were being defrauded, and explained to them in innumerable stump speeches and doorstep harangues the advantages and disadvantages of a strike; and then, when the men had about come to a decision that they would strike, he began a campaign to show them the foolishness of striking. By this time it was too late to head the strike off, and after the men had struck he went about organizing the strikers and suggesting proposals of reconciliation. Later he went to the railroad people and told them, correctly of course, that he had done his best to stop the strike and for that reason ought to be re-employed by them instead of being black-listed. When the railroad refused to employ him he carried the matter from union to union and from lawyer to lawyer. He agitated the matter for years. Finally he consulted a psychiatrist because he felt that his nervous system had been ruined by the stress and strain of the affair.

The suspicious variety

It will surprise many readers to learn that undue suspiciousness is one of the most serious symptoms known to the psychiatrist. They will have supposed that anger, rage, visions, delusions — some other less familiar and more vivid manifestations — were more important. Not so. The symptoms called " paranoid " constitute the cancer of the mental life.

Paranoid is a technical word, so apt, however, that it has been taken over into popular speech. It should be. No other word so well describes, with implications of their mental unsoundness, such folks as the man who eternally suspects and accuses an innocent wife, the student who is sure the teachers discriminate against him, the merchant who suspects a plot among his competitors, the athlete who believes the coach is playing favourites to spite him, the farmer who hides in the shed to prove by catching him red-handed that his neighbour is stealing his grain (or chickens or wife), the woman who just knows her neighbours are gossiping about her, or the one who is sure she was not invited to the party because the women in her suburb have it in for her, or the man who always demands a receipt and is sure all filling-station employees steal gasoline.

Do we not all entertain paranoid ideas? Yes, of course, but not for long, and not incessantly, except those of us who are schizoid. Persistent paranoid ideas are evidences of a breaking, if not a broken, mind. To be able to throw off promptly such an idea and see its absurdity is an evidence of a healthy mind.

But the schizoid " suspicioner," once he takes this route, is for ever tortured by suspicions, doubts, fears, constructions, and resolutions of self-defence. To illustrate: If I am " normal," I shall never suspect that my wife is putting poison in my coffee. I shall one day be inexplicably dead if it be true, or I shall go on trustfully living if it be not true. But the paranoid individual suspects it and expects it, in vain of course, for years — the poor fellow has his wife dumping arsenic in his coffee and cyanide in his potatoes every day for months or years. His delusions burn into his soul, and he becomes obsessed with his bitterness and plans for defence and revenge. He tries in innumerable ways to prove them or to disprove them and accumulates masses of useless data as evidence of her evil intentions.

Frequently the paranoid symptoms appear not in actual delusions but in what are called *ideas of reference;* everything that happens is interpreted by the victim as having special reference to him; an article in the newspaper, the chance words of a passer-by, the peculiar sound of an automobile horn, all of these have some meaning especially related to him.[47]

Paranoid tendencies may develop into full-fledged *paranoia,* an insidious and malignant " insanity " characterized by a slowly progressing tendency to regard the whole world in the light of a system of delusions, chiefly delusions of persecution which enhance the importance of the ego. First a feeling of being slighted and unappreciated and then of being avoided and disregarded,

[47] Cases illustrating paranoid delusions, paranoid ideas, paranoid tendencies are given at some length on pages 93 to 102 in connection with the discussion of the disintegration of the schizoid (sometimes called paranoid) personality.

then of being watched and pursued, then slandered, insidiously attacked, openly attacked, plotted against, etc. This often includes other types of delusions, such as that of being the defrauded descendant of royalty, the discoverer of great secrets or revolutionizing inventions, religious convictions of divine inspiration, or ideas of sexual control or implication. Such individuals often come into all sorts of conflicts with society and law, but they regard this as the natural outcome of their great but unrecognized importance and the jealousy of an ignorant world.

Because some of them manage to get along in the world in spite of their extraordinary distortions of reality, the pages of history are dotted with paranoiacs, many of them frankly recognized as such. Peter the Great of Russia certainly and several of the Roman emperors and the English kings were probably paranoiacs. Adolf Hitler is regarded by many as being one. The great hero of my own state, John Brown, was undoubtedly a paranoiac. Although it offends the feelings of their followers, it is none the less probable that the founders of numerous religions correspond in every way to the conception of paranoia which lands many a less gifted victim in the asylum.

For example, Mrs. Mary Morse Baker Glover Patterson Eddy, on June 5, 1882, gave out this interview:

" ' My husband's death was caused by malicious mesmerism. Dr. Rufus K. Noyes, late of the City Hospital, who held an autopsy over the body to-day, affirms that the corpse is free from all material poison although Dr. Eastman still holds to his original belief. I know that it was poison that killed him, not material poison, but mesmeric poison.'

" Mrs. Eddy was confident that she could have saved her husband by counter-thought, if only she had not been so occupied with her work, and had realized the power of the mesmerists. She says: —

" ' Oh, isn't it terrible, that this fiend of malpractice is in the land! . . . After a certain amount of mesmeric poison has been administered, it cannot be averted. No power of mind can resist it. It must be met with resistive action of the mind at the start, which will counteract it.'

" ' The atmosphere of Mrs. Eddy's house derived its peculiar character from her belief in malicious mesmerism, which exerted a sinister influence over every one under her roof. Her students could never get away from it. Morning, noon, and night the thing had to be reckoned with, and the very domestic arrangements were ordered to elude or counteract the demoniacal power. If Mrs. Eddy had kept in her house a dangerous maniac or some horrible physical monstrosity . . .'[48] the situation could not have been worse. If the water-pipe froze, or the wash-boiler leaked, or her servants were negligent, or her dressmaker was awkward in fitting, it was all the work of her enemies, accomplished by mental projections. Her mail, certain letter-boxes, certain streets, became infected with mesmerism. At one time she was convinced that the telegraph office at Boston was in the hands of her enemies, and sent a message to Chicago from West Newton via Worcester. She wanted her students to remain in Boston on the Fourth of July, a day when 'mortal mind was in ebullition,' to help her oppose the evil. She believed in a real 'printer's devil,' and attributed the delays in printing her 'Science and Health' to mesmerism. She set her students to treating mentally the pressmen against delays, and when the sheets were ready, asked them to turn their thoughts from the press-room to the bindery. Her letters are full of it; and nothing seems to irritate her more than a slighting of this essential dogma of her creed." [49]

Mass paranoia

In the first edition of this book I went on at this point to say that large groups of people, even whole nations, may develop paranoid delusions. I little suspected at that time that we should so soon have a vivid illustration of this in the amazing psychosis of the German nation, which pervades at least the lower middle class (as well as the psychopathic rulers). It seems incredible that anyone but savages and persons in a hospital for the insane would seriously accept such absurdities as truths (for example, that the Jews spread peculiar loathsome diseases, rape gentile girls, "taint the blood of Aryans," control the courts and government offices, etc., etc.), much less act upon them in a wild, barbaric fashion.

[48] Georgine Milmine: *The Life of Mary Baker G. Eddy* (New York: Doubleday, Page & Co., 1909), p. 301.

[49] Joseph Jastrow: *The Psychology of Conviction* (Boston: Houghton, Mifflin Co., 1918), pp. 201–2. For a vivid picture of this extraordinary personality see the remarkable biography by Edwin Dakin: *Mrs. Eddy — the Biography of a Virginal Mind* (New York: Charles Scribner's Sons, 1930), which her adherents vigorously but ineffectually attempted to suppress, and the more recent account of John V. Dittemore and Ernest S. Bates: *Mary Baker Eddy: The Truth and the Tradition* (New York: Alfred A. Knopf, 1932).

I cannot agree, however, that the capacity for group paranoia is peculiarly German, as is maintained by Dr. Richard Brickner in a recent popular book, *Is Germany Incurable?* (Philadelphia: J. B. Lippincott Co., 1943). The anti-Semitism, Jim Crowism, anti-Japanese-Americanism of the citizens of the United States is of precisely the same *genre*. The vivid German example, however, enables us to point out several facts about paranoid delusions. First, they are sometimes contagious. Secondly, it would seem clear that the paranoid delusions represent an expression of unendurable hate which must be justified by projecting accusations against others: " It is not I who am so wicked, it is they." The third obvious inference is that the persons suspected and accused are scapegoats; it is really not the Jews whom the Germans have reasons for hating, but the French and the Americans and the British and (more immediately) their own imperialistic rulers. Something like this the paranoid person always does; he defends himself against his own hostilities by projections which for all the malignancy of their nature and of their implications are nevertheless a device with which he contrives in desperation to protect himself against himself. This is the reason that paranoid delusions are both an evidence of disintegration and an evidence of a weak but struggling effort at self-salvation.

From this it can be seen why we regard paranoid delusions as dangerous. They are emergency defence measures against waves of terrific destructiveness. If they hold, well and good; we can put up with queer *ideas* in our friends, we have some ourselves. But if they break down, as also happens, the aggressions are apt to be released directly on innocent victims. (See p. 99.)

WHAT LEADS TO THE SCHIZOID MAKE-UP?

How much of the schizoid personality make-up is due to faulty home training and how much to inherited constitutional make-up and how much to accidents in childhood, psychiatrists are not all agreed. Some psychiatrists believe in the inheritance of an inborn schizoid constitution, characterized by a certain (" asthenic " and " athletic ") [50] physique, plus the mental symptoms we have been describing. It is probable, however, that to a con-

---

[50] It was the idea of Ernst Kretschmer (see footnote 43 on page 78) that a certain body structure and certain personality traits and with these the potentiality for certain types of mental illness were associated in a direct way, so much so that one could say, for example, that people of a certain build were likely to

siderable extent (if not entirely) it is determined by the attitude and technique of the parents during the formative years of life. Some parents frighten or bulldoze or shame their children into seclusiveness. Anything which stimulates a child's sense of inferiority beyond the reach of education ordinarily received at the hands of playmates is bound to have unfavourable consequences. The isolation type of personality discussed heretofore is one such reaction; the schizoid type is another. The latter is a reaction of flight, pulling into one's shell like the snail. Psychiatrists formerly saw these cases only in late stages; now, thanks to the child-guidance clinics and similar efforts, they see many of them in the process of development.

John, aged eight, was so much more interested in his own day-dreams than in what was going on around him that only rarely could his attention be attracted for school work. He spent hours alone drawing endless pictures of army tanks and planes, or carrying on imaginary conversations with his soldier toys. His toilet training had never been completed and this plus his absentmindedness made him so much of a burden to his school-teacher that his parents were asked to keep him at home and it was suggested they take him to a child guidance clinic, where his mother calmly explained that they really never had had time for John; since he was four months old his care had been almost entirely taken over by an elderly maid. During the day the two were alone in the apartment, or walked in a near-by park; by the time the parents arrived home in the evening John had usually been put to bed. When he was five his mother was home for a few months, but this was because of the birth of a baby sister, who received not only all of the mother's attention but the maid's as well. John's father, an energetic, ambitious man, had never been able to tolerate his lethargic son and early ceased paying any attention to him.

Mary walks to and from high school alone and spends her evenings alone, studying. Her schoolmates do not dislike her; they simply do not understand her. She plans to go to law school. "It's too bad you're a girl," her father has often told her. "Women cut no ice in this world and I wanted a son. A pretty girl has some chance if she's lucky, but you're not even pretty. Maybe you can make something of yourself as a lawyer."

have similar dispositions and in case of a "breakdown" similar mental disease pictures. Kretschmer and others who agree with him proceeded to confirm this hypothesis by examining the body structure of many psychotic patients, demonstrating that the large proportion of those of a certain diagnosis fell into a certain type of body structure. The methodology of this demonstration has many logical errors, and there were many errors, too, in the selection and collection of material data. On the whole, the theory has relatively few supporters in this country.

Lest what I have said add too heavy a burden of guilt to the already grief-bowed shoulders of parents of young people afflicted with a schizoid personality or its decompensated psychotic manifestations shortly to be described, I should like to make very clear that many times the unbearable disappointment which traumatizes the child's early life so that he is never able to face life with courage or meet his comrades on an equal basis is something over which neither child nor parents have any control.

I remember a man, for example, whose great seclusiveness later in life could be traced to the following circumstances:

When he was two years old his father went away to the World War and never came back. The relatives did not even have the satisfaction of ascertaining definitely that he had died on the battlefield. A pall of mystery always hung over the circumstances. In the meantime the mother died, shortly after giving birth to another child conceived before the father had gone to war. Thereupon the older child was taken to the home of an uncle and aunt who were very kind to him and provided a peaceful family circle for a few years until the aunt died suddenly, making it necessary once more to find a home for the little orphan. He was adopted by another family in which he was kindly treated, but where he was faced with the inevitable competition of a foster brother and sister. Such a series of losses, which must have seemed to the child to be desertions by those who had first given him some hope and expectation of continued love, brought about terrible injuries to the soul of the child, injuries from which he never recovered, although for some years he gave the semblance of an integrated personality.

I have referred in the previous case to the hazard of competition with another brother or sister, particularly one who is or seems to be more favoured. The magnitude and wide prevalence of this traumatic situation are not sufficiently indicated in this one brief illustration, nor should it be inferred that the outcome of sibling rivalry is always the schizoid personality or schizophrenia. One may say, however, that it is one of the most difficult adjustment problems the child meets; if he is able to solve it only fairly well, the results may show later in a neurosis; if he solves it very badly or feels utterly defeated, the result is more apt to be schizophrenia.

There were once twin girls, Mary and Maud (there has been a great deal of nonsense written by scientists on the evidences of heredity based upon the study of twins; none of these studies — at least none that I have ever seen — take any account of the *psychology* of twins), who had a very happy home so far as anyone knew until the death of their mother, when they were seven. They were cared for then by an aunt of whom they were very fond; then the father remarried and they came to live with a stepmother, who had a child of her own and, in addition, bore their father two more children. The twins, who had been very much the centre of attention, were exceedingly unhappy. Ultimately they were sent away to college in the East — an opportunity which they apparently welcomed because it took them away from a stepmother whom they regarded as cruel and selfish. They had been in college only a short time, however, before first one and then the other began to act in a very peculiar fashion, claiming to be the Virgin Mary, mother of Jesus, insisting that the people about them were not who they pretended to be, that every man in the college was in love with them, and, in short, manifesting definite evidence of the breakdown of schizoid personalities.

More careful analysis of the situation showed that their breakdowns, although occurring almost simultaneously, were by no means identical. Mary had always been her father's favourite. She had always felt guilty about her mother's death, as if she were in some way or other responsible for it, and had never forgiven her father for re-marrying. Maud, on the other hand, hated Mary for the preference which the father showed her, and attempted to compensate for it by winning the good graces of the stepmother, but in this, too, she failed. During their illnesses they were outspoken in their expressions of hatred for each other. It became clear that Mary found life intolerable because of the final conviction that the man whom she had loved most of all (her father) had not been faithful to her and had taken a stranger as his wife; this disappointment and this notion of the faithlessness of man spread to a feeling about all men which was temporarily contradicted in her illness by the delusion that all men were interested in her. Her sister Maud fell sick, as it were, through a conviction of the meretriciousness of all women. Had not her mother died and deserted her? Had not her stepmother rejected her? Had not her own sister stolen her father's love from her? During her illness she used to scream at and curse her sister, saying: " You are not my sister. No one ever had such a sister as you are. No sister would have done as you have done."

SCHIZOID BREAKS

Some schizoid personalities succeed and some fail; some bend and others break. There are certain fields of human labour for which seclusive and unsociable people are best fitted. Invention, exploration, music, and art are examples. There are others also in which the necessity of objectivity, of detachment, is best fulfilled by a schizoid make-up. The scientist himself may be an example. The surgeon, the banker, the judge — these are other easily recognized examples. All too familiar is the man who is a better judge or banker, for instance, than he is a human being. One of the best-informed psychiatrists I know has no practice. He is skilful, excellently endowed, excellently trained, but too schizoid to get on with people.

For most of the walks of life schizoid traits in abundance are a great disadvantage. Yet in spite of them some succeed. They succeed by reason of special talents which they call into service. But unfortunately not all schizoids have inventive genius or musical genius or some other talent to capitalize, to redeem the threatened failure.

Again, some schizoids who would otherwise fail avert disaster by the grace of fortuitous or deliberate advantages in the selection of environment. Granted an environment specially modified to fit his particular needs, modified *for* him, the schizoid may succeed. In fact, his success will be roughly proportionate to the felicity of the setting into which he is placed. And of those who fail, why do some fail financially, some in their marital life, some with mental illnesses? Here again the particular constellation of abilities and the peculiarities of the environment determine.

As we have seen, the schizoid personality has been so intimidated and so wounded in his earliest attempts to make a contact with the outside world that he has been reduced to a large dependence upon himself. The thin, frail bond which keeps him in contact with reality may easily be overtaxed or ruptured.

The first evidence of such a break is a period of anxiety and sleeplessness, with increasing denial of reality and the gradual substitution of fantasies, imaginings, hallucinations, and delusions. Such individuals often act and speak strangely; one gets the impression that they are living in another world from us. This is because they are at the point of abandoning the struggle to repress their unconscious wishes or to adjust them to the world as it is. This[51] is the stage of *acute schizophrenia,* formerly called *dementia præcox.*

As such, it usually has a brief duration. One of two things happen: the patient recovers (see page 103) or his condition becomes chronic. It may become chronic in two ways — either (1) he accepts his fantastic world peaceably and lapses into a queer, silly, or stupid reserve with a minimum of contact with other people (*hebephrenia* and *catatonia*) or (2) he fights against the acceptance of these strange impulses within him by projecting them upon other persons, a state of *paranoid maladjustment* characterized by delusions of persecution, ideas of being slighted, unappreciated, avoided, watched, pursued, slandered, insidiously attacked, plotted against. With these are frequently combined other types of delusions calculated to combat the fancied attacks, such as delusions of great power, authority, divine connection, or sexual omnipotence (see page 83). If a relative degree of equilibrium can be achieved by such delusional defences, the condition known as *paranoia*[52] develops; what appear to be the symptoms in this condition are really the patient's unconscious, automatic, and partly successful attempts at self-cure (see page 89).

The following examples will make this more vivid:

" The next patient whom I will bring before you is a merchant, aged twenty-six, who comes into the room under guidance, with closed eyes, hanging head, and shuffling gait, and at the earliest opportunity sinks limply into a chair. On his being spoken to, his pale, expressionless features do not show any animation; he does not reply to questions or obey orders. If I stick a needle into his forehead or his nose, or touch the corneæ, there follows at most a slight blinking or flushing, without any attempt at defense. But during this the patient quite unexpectedly breaks into a slight laugh. If you raise his arm in the air, it falls down as if palsied, and remains in the same position that it took accidentally. After much persuasion the patient at last opens his eyes; he now also gives his hand, advancing it by jerks with still angular movements, and remains like that. If you bend his head back, he stays in this uncomfortable position, and his leg, which I have lifted up, he also keeps stiffly stretched in the air. By degrees one succeeds in calling forth still further signs of automatic obedience. The patient

---

[51] Following the conception of H. S. Sullivan; see " Schizophrenia, Its Conservative and Malignant Features," *American Journal of Psychiatry,* July 1924, and " Peculiarity of Thought in Schizophrenia," same journal, July 1925.

[52] *Paranoia* is not ordinarily considered to be a form of schizophrenia.

raises his arms if anyone does it in front of him, and imitates pushing and turning movements, whirling his fists with great exactness and rapidity. On the other hand, he does not utter a word, presses his lips together when he is asked to show his tongue, cannot be induced to write, and apart from sudden repeated grins, remains quite mute, but repeats some words shouted out loud to him with his mouth closed. He obeys the order to go immediately.

" His father was temporarily 'insane,' and could not on that account finish his college course. The patient himself learnt with difficulty, after struggling through typhus fever in his youth; was easily excited, anxious, and inclined to hypochondriacal broodings. He fell ill mentally six months ago. *As the result of differences of opinion as to plans of marriage* [53] (the impending situation to which adjustment was impossible), he became anxious, believed himself to be mocked by everyone, was afraid of coming into contact with the prosecutor, and finally, because he looked upon his life as threatened, sprang out of the window one night, fracturing his heel. On admittance to the hospital the patient was decidedly dull; he declared himself quite ready to remain, although he was not insane but only suffered from delusions. He had thought he would be murdered; everything appeared to him so changed; voices spoke to him about all sorts of family affairs. There was no demonstration of physical disturbance except an old scar on the head and a newly-formed callus on the foot.

" In the further course of the illness the patient's want of judgment, as well as his emotional dullness, became more and more marked. He thought that the meat placed before him to eat was human flesh; everything in the newspapers was about himself; the assassination of the Empress of Austria, and the Peace Conference had to do with him, his mother wanted to murder him; he was the worst man alive. The doctor he designated as the German Emperor, who had dyed his beard; another gentleman as Christ — all in quite an indifferent tone of voice, without a trace of emotion. Sometimes he said senseless rhymes to himself — ' Nem, bem, kem, dem, schem, rem ' — over and over again, or he repeated this incomprehensible sentence: ' One for all, and all for one, and two for all, and three for all, here and there everywhere,' and ' Almightiness,' and ' Almightiness,' and ' Almightiness,' and so on. Gradually he became more and more quiet, and gave up speaking and eating, hid himself under the bedclothes, took up extremely uncomfortable attitudes, and allowed the saliva to run

---

[53] The italics are mine. The extension of oneself, the increased responsibilities and demands incident to marriage, are frequently the precipitating rock upon which the schizoid personality crashes.

out of his mouth. He has only latterly become rather more active again."

A different phase is presented by this girl, aged twenty-nine. " When brought into the room she lets herself slide on the ground, throws herself about, kicks with her legs, claps her hands, plucks at her hair and makes it untidy, pulls out a whole bunch of it, makes faces, hides her face, and spits round about her. She does not generally react at all when spoken to or pricked with a needle, but resists violently if you try to take her hand. She obeys no kind of orders. She will not show her tongue, and shuts her eyes as soon as you want to examine them. But, from isolated remarks, and answers quickly thrown out, it appears that she not only understands the questions, but is also pretty clear about her surroundings. But generally she calls out disconnected words, having absolutely no relation to her position, loudly and quite senselessly: ' Pup — pups — moll — you know — temperature — fire insurance — water — Weinheim — water — creolin — God damn you! — twenty marks — say, what is — away with it — thank you very much — twenty marks — say what you want — God damn you! — water — not I — twenty marks — so God damn you! — dear child — so fire-shy — stay at home with your wife — treasures — oh — sow— say what you want — thank you very much,' etc. Meanwhile she croaks and crows, then suddenly begins to sing a hymn with expression, changes to a street-song, laughs without restraint, and breaks off abruptly with loud sobs. She is slightly built and very badly nourished; her lips are cracked and covered with scabs; her head is flushed and her pulse hurried." [54]

What causes the break?

A variety of " causes " may precipitate these breakdowns in schizoid individuals. Schizophrenia, or dementia præcox, is a serious mental disease, because many patients never recover. It may come on insidiously, a gradual " slipping," or it may occur suddenly as the result of a situation requiring more adaptation than the personality is capable of, or as the result of an injury to the personality by grief or disappointment or physical disease. Influenza,[55] for example, may do such things as this:

[54] Dr. Emil Kraepelin: *Lectures on Clinical Psychiatry;* edited by Thomas Johnstone (New York: William Wood & Co., 1912), pp. 33–6. This is an oldish book, but Kraepelin's descriptions have never been surpassed for clarity. I commend this collection of psychiatric word pictures to any beginning student of the subject.

[55] I have been especially interested in the mental disturbances provoked by influenza for the past twenty years and use these examples because of this per-

Patient J. J. was born in Vermont in 1901. In temperament and disposition he is described by his brother as having been always of a quiet, seclusive disposition, never mixing with others, but preferring to remain alone. He was, however, considered mentally normal by his employers, friends, and family, and he was not regarded as particularly eccentric.

He developed influenza and pneumonia at Camp Devens, where he was a private in the infantry. He was delirious and did not regain his mental faculties. An interested friend wrote: " I am informed that when he took sick he was out doing trench work, was missed at roll-call, but was not found until the next morning, lying in the trench, where he had been working, after having lain out all night in a cold rain."

The military authorities sent only the information that subsequent to the influenza " he has been in a catatonic stupor; eats little; unclean in his habits; absolutely mute and unresponsive to external stimuli." He had been in the psychopathic ward of the base hospital for two months.

He was never accessible. He lay passively and apathetically in bed, responding to no questions by look or word. He obeyed simple orders, however, and co-operated in a fair way in the neurological examination. He made very mildly resistive manœuvres at times. After the first few days he was up and about the ward and was seen to look through magazines. He continued to show queer behaviour and lack of interest; when addressed, he presented his hand and shook hands listlessly. He could not be urged, persuaded, or forced to speak, smile, laugh, or cry. His facial expression remained fixed and impassive and his thought process showed complete blocking. He seemed at no time unaware of his environment; his reception of external stimuli was not interfered with. Thus, when told to indicate by signs his interpretation of some object, he did so slowly and uninterestedly, but quite correctly.

Physical examination and all laboratory (chemical) examinations were negative — that is, showed nothing wrong.

Another illustration of how the break may be precipitated by the sudden necessity of an adjustment beyond the individual's powers, already sorely taxed:

A girl reared in the lap of luxury had been transferred from a finishing school to a co-educational college. She was very active socially,

---

sonal interest. Influenza is not an important cause of schizophrenia; it merely illustrates one mechanism of breakdown. See also the last case of this section, pp. 105–6.

but owing to a technicality was not initiated into her sorority. Simultaneously she failed in one study, a unique experience for her. Finally there was " a poor young professor " with whom, out of sport at first, and then seriously, she began a flirtation. His financial incompetence and other such matters militated against a full development of the affair and she and her friend broke off over a misunderstanding, but with much distress and pain.

Suddenly, soon after, she leaped to her feet in the middle of the living-room and screamed at the top of her voice, assigning irrelevant explanations. She soon began to hear " voices " which told her that there had been a wedding at the college, that she and the professor had been married, that everyone was looking for Mrs. S., herself. She wrote this letter to her imaginary husband:

" My darling Kenneth:
" The days are so long without you. My babies are not well. I wish you would take a different attitude toward my position in life. You know May Ward has custody of my children and since she has hers, my babies are running at large in the city.
" Of course you know I left nothing in my will to you and I'm dying rapidly without the enjoyment of ever having taken care of my babies. My social obligations are no longer evident and I do expect you to act differently in regard to my position in the future."

Many other queernesses and delusions followed. She was pregnant; she had had a child. She was a queen or even an empress; her father was a Negro potentate who had inherited much wealth, now to be hers; she was hypnotized, infected with syphilis, poisoned; gas was being shot into the keyhole, arrows were fired at her, etc.

Usually she walked and talked in a stiff, stilted, over-polite, and gracious way, as if she were a princess. Occasionally she would do extraordinary things, sometimes silly, sometimes serious. For example, she suddenly rose up one afternoon and crashed two tumblers at another patient who sat drinking lemonade near by. Often she would order the nurse and doctors out of the room with curses and a stamp of her foot to emphasize them.

This is a sample of her talk:
" I am going immediately. Have you noticed the constellation of the stars this evening? It is very dangerous and should be watched closely. After the crucifixion of Christ and supposedly of some others, probably from a social point, there was a constellation of stars — that is, a gathering of stars and an extra star appears in the heavens. When there is

constellation of the stars it is a sign that some person or group of persons is in very great danger."

This is a sample of her writing:

" The test therefore is this: that if in the past we have met with the glorious success of example and time we steadily acquire so law along men. To proceed, I am illegitimate, being an orphan in society I was taken at five years of age by England to be the subject of a hypnotic test most guards of Chicago are being brutally poisoned she's place so are my darling brothers the blue-eyed Congressmen. . . .

" If my life was to have been sacrificed for the European why was the General Marchand to have received $300,000 of mine forwarded by the French government to stop the hypnotism and to be my asking shuns equal in society? Why did you take me so cruelly? My dearest hope is that the American Legion will love and understand my attitude toward those who have so cruelly murdered civilization, but in the first instance, why should New England or the dirt of London kill me in America? "

Dangerous aspects of schizoid breaks

Schizoid personalities once broken down demand help and protection. The stuporous types, the silly and stunty varieties, are helpless; the paranoid types are dangerous. The victims of paranoid breaks are burning with hate and fear and revenge. They are forever erecting defences and plotting retaliations. Sometimes, too many times, they carry out these plans. The murders of Garfield and McKinley were tragedies of this type. Twenty-three persons were shot in one day in a city of my own state by a man who believed himself to be the victim of persecution. A doctor friend of mine was shot by his own son, whom he refused to believe to be dangerous. The son had repeatedly hinted that he thought someone was after him, " doping " him, " trying to blackjack " him, etc., and the father foolishly pooh-poohed the idea and assured him that all he needed was a vacation. Vacations do not cure paranoid mental breaks.

A man whom I once examined in one of the state hospitals for the criminal insane was known by his relatives to have been " queer " for five years before he walked into a doctor's office one day and accused him of hypnotizing his wife. The doctor rather testily asked him to leave. He returned some days later, marched into the doctor's office, and emptied a gun into the doctor, saying: " You'll not hynotize any more women and ruin homes for real men! "

The late Dr. W. A. White, in his stimulating book *Insanity and the Criminal Law* (New York: The Macmillan Company, 1923), collected a number of these cases as they occurred in the army. For example:

A twenty-nine-year-old private had done so well that he had been promoted to be a corporal after three months. But then a change was noted in him. He began to fall short of his previous efficiency. For a minor offence he was tried by court martial and fined twenty dollars. He applied for a transfer to another post, but this was several times refused him by Captain R. He went one day to the basement, loaded his gun, put it in his pocket, and said he going to get the soldier who had taken two dollars from him. While he was looking for this soldier he was summoned to see Captain R. because of a report for misconduct. He told the captain that he would like to resign. The captain said: " Very well, that will do, corporal. That is all." Instantly the soldier shot the captain and then turned and shot two other men who were standing in the room, whom presumably he believed to be additional enemies.

An old farmer (a patient of mine), who was very well thought of in the community where he had spent all his life, and who was entirely deaf, began to " hear noises in his head." " Sometimes they sound like dogs barking or like the wind blowing." At other times they seemed like the noise of a train, or people talking, or like someone running after him.

One night they sounded like footsteps upstairs. " I heard you go into the hired man's room last night," he said to his wife the next morning. " You are unfaithful to me, I know you are." This the innocent woman earnestly denied, and he said no more about it at the time.

A few weeks later he told two neighbours that three of his nine children really belonged to old Dr. Peabody. The neighbours refused to believe this, for his wife was of irreproachable character. " Oh," he said, " I can see you're all against me." After that he told all his friends that each of his children had a different father. Besides the old doctor there was old man Schmitz, the blacksmith; one Sam Jonson, who had moved away; and a schoolmaster whose first name was Oscar. He couldn't be sure who the others were.

He kept trying to get his wife to confess her infidelity. " If you don't I'll blow your head off, and mine too. But first I'll kill some others. It'll be one of the biggest murders you ever heard about." One day he put a gun to her head and said he would kill her unless she admitted her guilt.

The poor woman said he'd have to kill her, then, for she wouldn't confess a lie. He put the gun away, but told her she would have to get down on her knees at the church bazaar, before everybody, and confess, or he'd yet carry out his threat. Fortunately he was sent to a hospital before disaster occurred.[56]

The public rarely recognizes the seriousness of paranoid symptoms. A man in Washington, D. C., applied at a hospital for treatment for an injured foot. Appropriate treatment was administered, but he developed the idea that one of the doctors " had it in for him." He sought out the doctor and shot him three times, but not fatally. He was arrested and put in jail, where he was so untidy, restless, and confused that he was transferred to the government hospital for the insane. He continued to give expression to ideas of being persecuted, said " wrong thinking " had been " put on him "; cried, listened to imaginary voices, which he said accused him of being a pervert, attacked other patients.

Yet some of his relatives insisted that he was not insane and succeeded in hailing him before a court on a writ of habeas corpus. The jury, after hearing the symptoms and the opinion of the doctors, unanimously found him *sane* and released him. Thus released into the world, the paranoid patient sooner or later gravitates into trouble, and this dangerous man, released, against the advice of all the doctors who had studied the case, by a jury of laymen who assumed to know more about it than the doctors, shot and killed, a short time afterwards, a total stranger of whom he suddenly became suspicious (White).

How difficult it is to convince relatives that this is not an occasional and exceptional occurrence is clearly illustrated by the following experiences of my own:

A young man, aged twenty-nine, had been under observation in the hospital for less than a month when his father insisted on taking him home in spite of my protestations. Although the patient had shown considerable improvement in his short stay in the hospital we warned the

---

[56] This case also illustrates the fact that schizoid personalities may reach advanced years before they undergo decompensation. Such schizoid breaks in connection with the disintegrative processes of old age are not called schizophrenia, partly because they seem so much more definitely related to the organic brain changes and partly because their clinical manifestations are somewhat different. Instead they are called by many different names — involution paranoia (Kleist), involution paraphrenia (Serko), pre-senile paraphrenia (Albrecht), senile paranoid psychosis (Seelert). (See Jelliffe and White: *Diseases of the Nervous System,* sixth edition [Philadelphia: Lea & Febiger, 1935], Chapter xxiii.)

father that he was still very ill and that we considered him dangerous. A few weeks later the young man rose from the table around which the family were seated and shot his father fatally.

A young farmer, Mr. Gray, kept his wife a virtual prisoner on their lonely farm during eight years of married life, never permitting her to go to town or to visit even her relatives. He discouraged neighbours from calling upon her, and upon those few occasions when his relatives visited the house, he flew into violent rages, accusing his wife of flirting with his brother and his father. These accusations were patently false, as his wife was unassuming and extremely anxious to please her husband.

One morning the rural mail-carrier put some of the neighbours' mail in the Grays' mail-box. He had not gone far along the road before he discovered the mistake and drove back to correct it. When Gray saw the car returning, his suspicions were aroused and he got his shotgun. As the mail-carrier straightened up from exchanging the mail in the box, Gray shot him, wounding him in the forehead and shoulder. Mrs. Gray, who was standing a few yards from her husband, holding her baby in her arms, screamed, whereupon Gray turned and shot her, killing her instantly. Afterwards he took his four children to a neighbour's home and then drove to town, where he gave himself up and asked to be locked in jail. Gray was sentenced to life imprisonment in the penitentiary.

This man was known by his relatives and friends to be mentally ill, jealous, and dangerous. Yet no one was sufficiently concerned to take the necessary steps to avert a terrible tragedy.

PROGNOSIS

Once the schizoid personality has completely renounced reality, abandoned his defences, and turned his back upon real life in favour of an unreal world of phantasy, delusion, and hallucination — once the schizoid has broken — the chances are against his ever returning to the real world — that is, recovering. It is not difficult to see why. For in spite of the apparent suffering which is sometimes manifested, such a state was sought as a refuge from a less obvious but certainly greater suffering incurred in the world of reality. In this respect schizophrenia differs from ordinary fever delirium, which is a temporary flight induced by the toxæmia and usually passes over. Schizophrenia is a long delirium.

But while it is true that most cases of schizophrenia do not recover, it is also true that many cases *do* recover. In the first edition of my book I felt that I had to apologize for declaring that a considerable number of them get well, because the general psychiatric opinion was such that many psychiatrists believed that a recovery in supposed schizophrenia disproved that diagnosis. Such pessimism, I believe, actually prevented some recoveries. I am glad to be able to say that it is now well recognized that this dread disease is by no means hopeless, granted the availability of prompt and skilful treatment.

Schizophrenic patients frequently appear to recover quite spontaneously. I reported several such in the first edition of this book. During the influenza epidemic in 1918 I was in the Boston Psychopathic Hospital and there made a study of a group of acute cases of schizophrenia that were observed by us during an early stage of the disease; subsequently most of them were transferred to state hospitals in Massachusetts. Five years later I made some follow-up inquiries and discovered to the amazement of all of us that three fourths of these patients were well. Sometimes the recovery occurred promptly; for example:

A twenty-year-old girl, with a negative family history, during a very severe attack of influenza developed a delirium which became rather more extreme than usual and shortly afterwards she became entirely mute and would have nothing to say or to do with anyone. She stood about in queer poses and attitudes, appeared to be listening to mysterious voices; she smiled and gesticulated to unseen visitors in a way very familiar to all psychiatrists. After about six months she began to show improvement, which continued until a year later, when she was well enough to return to her work as a stenographer.

Every psychiatrist could cite many such cases. Formerly we were wont to explain them either as spontaneous recoveries from schizophrenia or as recoveries from a chronic delirium, wrongly diagnosed as schizophrenia.

Some psychiatric opinion at the present time would say that there is no essential difference between a chronic delirium and schizophrenia, and probably also that there is no such thing as a spontaneous recovery. There are indeed recoveries for which we are unable to give our plans any credit and which we are unable to say just what specific means brought about. But it is a fair presumption that wittingly or unwittingly something was done for such a patient that encouraged the reacceptance of reality.

Fortunately the growing feeling of hopefulness in regard to this disease is spurring scientists all over the world to pursue research concerning it along biochemical, psychological, and psychoanalytic lines; for notable example, that at the Worcester, Massachusetts, State Hospital under the direction of Dr. R. G. Hoskins. An excellent résumé of this work is contained in N. D. C. Lewis's *Research in Dementia Præcox* (New York: The National Committee for Mental Hygiene, 1936). This book is the beginning of work made possible by a grant from the Supreme Council of the 33rd-Degree Masons of the Northern Jurisdiction of the United States, under the direction of the National Committee for Mental Hygiene.

TREATMENT OF SCHIZOID BREAKS

Ideally the schizoid personality should have the benefit of psychiatric help before any break occurs. Such treatment is based upon an effort to make up for the unutterable heartbreak and the feeling of unendurable disappointment of love that the patient has suffered as a young child. One must remember, however, that the person who has experienced these feelings has been crippled in his emotional development so that he cannot accept love in an adult way, but must be treated much as one would treat a child — with kindness, indulgence, and, above all, faithfulness. One author has said that such patients wait patiently day after day to see if the physician's kindness is what it seems to be and if he means what he says; one mistake, one reproach, one evidence of unfairness or unkindness, and the patient's confidence is lost forever and with it his hope of recovery. He cannot bear another disappointment.

Once the schizoid break has occurred, one must decide certain practical questions which arise from the patient's repudiation of reality. He must be protected from the environment, and from his own apathy, unreasonableness, aggressiveness, or self-destructiveness. This usually means hospitalization in an institution prepared to detain and care for him, and at the same time provide treatment. For while the patient is protected the schizophrenic process must be treated. There are several approaches to this, which have been used separately and in conjunction. The first is based on the principles of psychoanalysis — that is, of the scientific study of interpersonal relationships — and endeavours to help the patient to see how he has misjudged the world of reality on the basis of his own peculiar unfortunate experiences and interpretations. This is possible only in the hands of gifted and experienced workers. Of its success the late Dr. George H. Kirby, formerly professor of psychiatry at Columbia University, wrote in 1930 that "it has been demonstrated that patients, even those with pronounced symptoms may under (psychological) treatment show progressive improvement, may increase remarkably their ability to externalize their interests, establish better contacts with reality, and in general make the most of what appears to be an inferior affective (emotional) capacity." [57]

Another form of treatment depends upon an emotional reeducation accomplished by so arranging the patient's environment as to favour the elective repudiation of the psychotic world for the world of reality as the rest of us see it. This implies and requires the creation with intimate pains of a milieu in which an attitude of unfailing kindness prevails, and with it the opportunity for and the encouragement of the expression of the patient's hostilities and resentments without any fear of punishment or disapproval, and opportunities for transferences (that is, meaningful personal relationships) to trained and intelligent personnel. [58]

The case of a twenty-nine-year-old housewife studied by one of my colleagues, Dr. C. W. Tidd, shows pretty definitely how her recovery was related to this type of treatment.

" There was little in the history of the examination to indicate the underlying factors in this patient's illness. Treatment recommendations had been of a general nature designed to encourage the patient to express her true feelings in a friendly environment. During the first few

[57] From the foreword to Leland B. Hinsie: *Treatment of Schizophrenia* (Baltimore: The Williams & Wilkins Co., 1930). For technical reports of the psychoanalytic treatment of schizophrenia, see the book by Hinsie just mentioned and also H. S. Sullivan: " Modified Psychoanalytic Treatment of Schizophrenia," *American Journal of Psychiatry*, Vol. XI, pp. 519–40 (November 1931); G. Zilboorg: " Affective Reintegration of the Schizophrenias," *Archives of Neurology and Psychiatry*, Vol. XXIV, p. 335 (August 1930).

[58] The question of the proper personnel for such patients was first effectively stressed by H. S. Sullivan: " Socio-psychiatric Research; Its Implications for Schizophrenic Problem and for Mental Hygiene," *American Journal of Psychiatry*, Vol. X, pp. 977–91 (May 1931); " Environmental Factors in Etiology and Course Under Treatment of Schizophrenia," *Medical Journal and Medical Record*, Vol. CXXXIII, pp. 19–22 (January 7, 1931).

weeks there was a marked response to treatment; then without apparent provocation she relapsed and became exceedingly and aggressively disturbed. She attacked the nurses frequently, tore their uniforms, struck at them, threw feces, urinated on the floor, etc. This period of aggressivity was met on the part of the hospital personnel with unfailing kindness. The patient was seen daily by one of the physicians who, even though the patient did not show evidences of responding to him, continued to show a kindly interest in her. Very slowly the patient began to show improvement. She began to acknowledge the presence of the doctor; later she began to talk a little, and then to enter some of the activities that had been prescribed for her. She began to work in the occupational therapy shop, at first engaging herself in ripping and later in knitting. By the end of the fifth month her day was entirely taken up by various prescribed activities and her general condition, including the mental state, was quite good. She remained in the hospital for a few weeks longer and was then discharged. Several months later she was reported to be well.

"Perhaps the most important single factor in the recovery of this patient was that she became able to express her aggressive feelings without fear of punishment or retaliation. The kindness she received in spite of her disagreeable activity seems to have enabled her to bring such feelings to the surface and gradually learn to dissipate them in more socially acceptable forms. Just how much of this was effected through the person of the physicians and nurses (transference) cannot be definitely stated, but it is probable that a large part was due to the positive relationship that became more apparent as she progressed. Occasionally a schizophrenic patient will select a nurse or a therapist as a love object and in such instances the situation is carefully guarded and encouraged. Often irrational elements in the behavior of the patient toward his object of choice are impossible to understand and the relationship may be distressing to the object unless this person is properly trained. For that reason it is important that special instruction be given to all who come in contact with the patient.

"Her activity in the occupational therapy shop . . . served as a rough index to her general activity and feeling. In the beginning of her treatment her interest in destructive activity was predominant. Later the character of her work changed and became constructive. The possibility for the expression of *destructive* feeling in occupational therapy is unlimited and at the same time is subject to some regulation. Opportunities to encourage the development of *constructive* desires are then also available and the problems encountered in working out a combination of destructive and constructive activity consistent with the patient's condition and ability are worthy of a great deal of time and effort." [59]

A third method of treatment used recently, with and without the two just mentioned, is "shock treatment." It is described at some length in the new material of Chapter V (see pages 413 ff.).

5. THE CYCLOID TYPE

(MOODY PERSONALITIES)

Moodiness predisposes to failure only when it becomes extreme. There are moods and moods, as everyone knows, but the characteristic moods centre about the two poles of gaiety and sadness. Instead of the environment provoking the emotional reaction, moody people seem to arrive independently at a state of gloom or elation, and it determines their behaviour. Frequently it is an alternation between the two extremes. "I'm on top of the world one week and down in the depths the next," people often complain. "One week I can do anything and get lots accomplished, and then during the depression everything will slump."

This is typical. The pendulum action has been a familiar phenomenon to students of the mind for thousands of years. It was noticed as long ago as Hippocrates, several hundred years before Christ. Presumably Saul suffered so. Domination by emotional extremes and the cyclic alternation of moods characterizes one great group of personalities, the "moody" we will call them, and a corresponding group of mental illnesses, the *cyclothymias* or *manic-depressive* psychoses.

Harvey Behring is an extreme case in point. He was a stout, florid man who gave the impression of great ability and power. His conversation immediately stamped him as a superior individual. When he was only thirty-three he had acquired nearly forty thousand dollars by his enormous activity, working nightly until one o'clock in the morning, month after month. He became over-sanguine, invested the

[59] Charles W. Tidd: "Recovery Process in Schizophrenia," *Bulletin of the Menninger Clinic*, Vol. I, pp. 56–7 (November 1936). See also Charles W. Tidd: "Increasing Reality Acceptance by a Schizoid Personality during Analysis," *Bulletin of the Menninger Clinic*, Vol. I, pp. 176–83 (May 1937); and Robert P. Knight: "Psychotherapy in Acute Paranoid Schizophrenia with Successful Outcome: A Case Report," *Bulletin of the Menninger Clinic*, Vol. III, pp. 97–105 (July 1939).

money all in one project, lost heart in it, became depressed, and lost all of his money.

He recovered from this and started in business again on a small scale. A few years later the building which his business occupied was destroyed by fire and he was plunged into another depression, in which he remained a year. After that there occurred attack after attack, with and without provocation.

His characteristic cycle would begin with a phase of prodigious activity in which he would exert himself to the utmost. His efforts were usually crowned with a good deal of success, and this success would only stimulate him to greater exertion. At the same time, however, his judgment would become impaired by an overdose of optimism and he would make wild plunges and risk large sums of money. Sometimes these speculations turned out well, but more often they turned out badly. Then he would be plunged into a depression in which he would be quite incapable of doing any work at all. He would wake up in the morning groaning, crying out for God to spare his soul, heaving long sighs, and bursting into tears when spoken to. This depression would pass and he would again work himself up to great enthusiasm and industry.

In one of his depressed phases he shot himself.

This is an extreme example of the moody personality type. Its possessors may be predominantly gay, gloomy, irascible, or alternating. Those prevalently gay are apt to be highly distractible, but care-free and self-confident, given to jests, chatting, pranks, sports. They are very approachable and communicative, although often overbearing, arbitrary, impatient, and even belligerent. They are quick and animated, talk readily, easily, and abundantly, and often write in the same way. Their brilliancy and alertness, their versatility, their multiplicity of ideas, their kind-heartedness and sunny disposition, are likely to make them many friends in spite of their faults. They are always prone, however, to depressions, just as the depressed types occasionally experience periods of elation.

Typically, the chronically moody person of the depressed sort takes life seriously; he takes things hard and sees the dark side of things. Life seems to him to be more or less of a burden. Each task seems gigantic. He bears with conscientious self-denial obligations of life without any of the pleasure of living. He usually becomes anxious and despondent, feels useless and unfit He lacks self-confidence and decision and seeks the advice of others on the slightest occasion. He is prone to have physical complaints and anxieties.

The oscillating type of moody personality swings back and forth between the two extremes, today lively, sparkling, and radiant; tomorrow depressed, listless, and dejected.

The hotheads, who carry to extreme the emotion of anger, are still another variety. They are strongly affected by everything and often unpleasantly. Every little thing offends them, or at least they are apt to become offended at some little thing and pass over much bigger things. A slight provocation will be sufficient to provoke rage and storming, sometimes outbursts of cruelty and retaliation. There are likely to be violent scenes, with scolding, shouting, yelling, threatening, cursing, etc. Kraepelin describes a patient he knew who in such a fit of rage threw a whole pile of plates on the floor, hurled a burning lamp at her husband, and then attacked him with a pair of shears. These individuals are ordinarily serene, self-confident, self-assertive, but ill-controlled, and subject to attacks of sullenness, crossness, unhappiness, and excitement.

The " up " phase

A certain doctor friend of mine is celebrated for being able to say more words to the minute, drive more miles per hour, and treat more patients per day than it is given to most of us even to imagine. And I have a real-estate friend whose annual salary is in six figures, who earns it chiefly because of his prodigious supply of cheerful enthusiasm, energy, and industry — in short, " pep." It almost kicks him over sometimes (in fact, that's how I met him).

But failure does come to many of these accelerated and ex-hilarated types.

A brilliant, exuberant college student doing everything on the campus and making " A " work in all his studies was carried beyond the limits of good judgment and became uncontrollably over-active. This propensity is likely to be accompanied by bad judgment, and so my young friend soon announced his extremity by stealing successfully and successively ten or twelve automobiles. When the police finally apprehended him, the swiftness and skilfulness of his thefts and the noisy gaiety of his demeanour convinced them that he was a super-crook.

Fortunately the judge was easily convinced otherwise, and this man is now occupying an important public position. During his convalescence I secured a position for him in his old home town, and he wrote me many remarkable letters, some of which are excellent illustrations of the accelerated machinery of this type and condition of mind. I quote a representative passage, which excellently describes " how it feels ":

" My emotional experiences here have not been great or many. It is a new environment, and I am rather limited in my associations and amusements. I seem, however, to have become ' settled,' or at least to have lost much of that soul-built intensity that was so characteristic of me but a short time ago. I fear my tool of imagination with which I cut so many a delicious — although precarious — slice out of life, is becoming dulled. I no longer seem to possess that fervid compassion towards life. I would say that I was becoming ' middle aged.' Maturity, anyway, is a matter of experience rather than of time, and I have lived precociously.

" Perhaps this new turn that I describe is a symptom more hopeful than otherwise; but at times it really frightens me when I think of myself as no longer a Crusader or a Don Quixote. Sara Teasdale reminds us that life finally gives us Truth and takes in exchange our Youth! I believe I may now be making just that barter with life, and I cannot help but think that in many ways I am pressed to a hard bargain by the exchange. I have found a great enjoyment in my new and old friends here who have been so splendid to me, but I still like at times to get away from the whole press of social environment, and take a momentary refuge in lonely thought. Christ went to the mountain, and Mohammet to the desert for meditation — perhaps I am cursed with an introspective vice; but you know our vices are always such pleasant things.

" I believe, however, I am pruning the more psychotic elements, for I have not been subject to any sweeps of melancholia or tides of depression. My emotional schematic curve would now, probably, be tending towards a more even course, considerably above the gulfs of despair to which I have so often dropped, but still far below the Parnassian heights that I have known; and if I am to strike that level we call normal, if I am no longer to be thrown between Hell and Heaven, then I have achieved a certain inglorious peace which could never be happiness; but — ah! — I have also lost a certain torment of ecstasy, a deliciously mad confusion of soul — which, if at times it played me fiendish tricks, at others, brought to me angelic ages compressed into a single flash, that years of redeeming contentment can never know! "

The extreme of the " up phase " is called *mania;* this man was, technically, a maniac. They are not always so pleasant. The phase of excitement may be dominated by irritability and pugnacity; many inexplicable fights, both fistic and legal, have occurred because such a personality in such a phase encountered an unsuspecting and uncomprehending irritant.

The " down " phase — melancholy

Much more frequent, much more serious, much more understandable, are the swings to the opposite pole. This is how it *feels.* Later we shall see how it *looks.*

" Dedicated to Anyone who Feels the Same

" Given: a body with an aching, aching back and shot through with endless lassitude and a desire to end the back-ache and make itself a matter of no concern to

— a restless mind, which functions on a low plane, where it gives more dismay and dissatisfaction than healthy-minded joy. A mind which sees too well but yet not well enough to satisfy

— a weary ego whose respect for itself is lost in the knowledge that it merits no respect or praise from others and feels it must have unwittingly played the hypocrite to gain them

— a personality which like an aged horse is better put out of its gnawing misery.

" Come sit on top of the world with me, barefooted, with hair flowing free, and with the clear pure winds whirling round this strangling world. Let's dangle our toes in the clouds, and puncture the air castles which drift up from earth's children who are not yet cursed with wisdom. But oh! we needn't limit ourselves to such little mischiefs. When we look at this earth which we have just appropriated as a bench — don't you see, after all, it's only the same stupid, stifling world in which we used to live? Remember its pettiness, its paltry complacencies at its simple-minded achievements? Don't you remember how it was built without plan into a grotesque ruin where no one knew how to get what he wanted, no one wanted what he got, and those most nearly wise saw nothing worth their wanting? Oh, to be quite philosophically fair, as we used to be at rare moments, it is the dynamics of the thing we abhor. A few of my sentimentalities concerning bits of its structural sublimities still cling to me. But, shucks! we cannot forgive this earth the miseries it perpetrates. I know what we can do. You don't want to sit on such a wretched world either, do you? Let's bang it and sliver it and slash it to pieces with our heels. That would be lots of fun.

Oh, you say, where would we sit afterwards? Shame on you for such a sensible thought! We shall have so much fun battering this old earth to pieces and pulverizing it that we shall just effervesce into the clouds; and then, my dear, we shall have had our gay good time and there will be no more things to tangle people up, and no more people to tangle things up. Come on — let's start! " [60]

It is likely to be forgotten by the healthy-minded person that the moody man's ideas are dictated by his moods and feelings, because we ordinarily assume the reverse. In the following passage the reader may think: " Well, he's not so far wrong at that." Even the patient's disparaging description of himself is oftentimes largely correct; because as Freud [61] remarks of the melancholiac:

" When in his exacerbation of self-criticism he describes himself as petty, egoistic, dishonest, lacking in independence, one whose sole aim has been to hide the weaknesses of his own nature, for all we know it may be that he has come very near to self-knowledge. We only wonder why a man must become ill before he can discover truth of this kind."

Nevertheless, the same patient who wrote the following could at other times make an equally convincing argument for the beauty and happiness of life. In both cases, right or wrong, his ideas were determined by his mood rather than vice versa.

" Ultimately, I know, I must return to that paltry world where there is nothing either good or bad enough to inspire a soul which wanders helplessly between romance and reality and finds neither satisfactory.

" One doubts that it is more cowardly to die than live.

" The idea of doing again the petty things which somehow go to gain the high esteem of witless fellow mortals, the pin-pricks which mount to agony as one ignores them with a twisted, painted grin — how infinitely weary and disheartened it makes one feel!

" If I could but dip a quill in vitriol and curse a God who planned this cosmos and the feeble human beings who act in it! These deluded human beings who feel themselves masters of all they survey, little dreaming of reality or of the true nature of their surroundings! But no, I cannot feel that any god planned the world. I must be rather grate-

60 D. P. H. May 1929.

61 Sigmund Freud: *Collected Papers* (London: Hogarth Press, 1925) , Vol. IV, p. 156.

ful that men are given the limitations, the illusions, which keep them comfortably complacent, unable to see what might be, blind to half the unbearable stupidity of the whole mess, and worshipping power and prettiness when power makes slaves of half the souls, and beauty fades unheeded." [62]

Fortunately for the world, Abraham Lincoln, characteristically a " moody personality " type, was preserved from a wretched failure by the intelligence and decisiveness of his friends. This is an aspect of the life of Lincoln which many persons do not know, although it is recorded by most of his biographers. After the death of Ann Rutledge he was incapacitated for months with melancholia. Again in 1841 he was plunged into so deep a depression that he was taken by his friends into guarded seclusion at the advice of physicians, and all knives and dangerous instruments were removed from his reach. His wedding day had been set and had arrived; preparations were all made; the guests assembled, but Lincoln did not appear. He was found in his room in the deepest of dejection, entertaining delusions of unfulfilled obligation, of unworthiness, and of hopelessness. He is quoted as saying that he was the most miserable man living, and that " if what I feel were equally distributed to the whole human family, there would not be one cheerful face on earth. Whether I shall ever be better, I cannot tell; I awfully forbode I shall not."

Nor were his friends too sanguine. His law partner, Stuart, described him as a " hopeless victim of melancholy." His future wife's relatives frankly considered him " insane." A specialist in Cincinnati was consulted, although Lincoln found most relief from confiding in his friend Dr. Henry, who, he said, was necessary to his existence. [63]

He himself called his affliction hypochondriasis, but it was assuredly more than that. It was typical melancholia. The possible consequences to this nation and to the world of this episode in Lincoln's life, had it been otherwise than so judiciously handled, are terrible to consider.

Yet the affliction that engulfed Lincoln is no stranger to mankind. Creeping upon its victims insidiously, or seizing them like a storm, the grey clouds of depression settle down upon many thousands [64] every year. This refers not to the wave of sorrow that fate and fortune and the laws of nature bring to every

---

[62] D. P. H. May 1929.

[63] L. Pierce Clark: " A Psychologic Study of Abraham Lincoln," *Psychoanalytic Review*, Vol. VIII, no. 1 (January 1921) .

[64] About two thousand cases are committed in New York State each year; it is safe to say that this means that ten thousand or more cases actually occur in New York State annually.

human being, nor to the mild depressions of spirits that are said to be characteristic of Monday mornings. Melancholy moods are familiar to us all, such poets as Poe, Thomson (*The City of Dreadful Night*) , and Robinson have verbalized them, and Chopin, Tchaikowsky, Sibelius, and others have put them into music. But the mood may grow stronger than the man, and more frequently than not it is expressed in futile tears and groans instead of melodies and verses.

The depressions that overtook Lincoln and King Saul and others great and near great and not at all great are definitely recognized illnesses of a type with which psychiatry is intimately familiar. How does melancholia differ from " the blues " with which we are all familiar? Chiefly in degree and in direction. Usually, also, the " blues " depend to a greater extent than real melancholia on some external event — a loss, disappointment, frustration, physical illness, or the like.

But the melancholy man is usually unconscious of the real reason of his sadness and invents false reasons which he believes. His sadness gets worse rather than better with the passage of time. Environmental factors are of relatively little importance; they may contribute to it and may precipitate it, but they only mask the real, buried causes. The loss of a love object causes us all grief, and but few of us melancholia. For the *grieving* person the ego is unaffected; it is the outside world that is poor by reason of the loss. For the *melancholy* person the outside world is good enough; it is the ego that is destitute.

MOODY PERSONALITIES OFTEN FAIL — USUALLY ONLY TEMPORARILY

(1) *Melancholy failure: in school*

When she was sixteen years old, Esther Oliver entered college and in addition to a lively social life, including sorority, dancing, movies, and dates, she made an honour rank along with her brother. In the second year they played more and studied less. Toward the end of the year her brother died of appendicitis, and grief detracted from the patient's interest in college. So she stayed out of school for several years and was quite happy in so doing, having found a pleasant occupation in her home city. When she returned to college she found everything very difficult. She tried to study, but could not keep her mind on her books. Neither could she sleep at night. In the evening she would feel better and believe she could go on, but in the morning she would feel as if it were futile to carry on any longer. A physician was consulted, who advised that she quit college. She did so, but almost immediately became more depressed. She burst into the bitterest sobs and self-recriminations. " I have disgraced the family," she said, " I have proved myself yellow; I am a quitter, and everybody will know it. I can't bear the shame and disgrace of it. It will ruin us all."

Her depression went from bad to worse and she became exceedingly ill for a period of some months, but recovered completely and was able to resume her work the following year.

Grover Reeves graduated from the university with the highest honours. He was also winner of numerous prizes and fellowships. A great future seemed to be opening up.

Despite this he suddenly became tremendously blue, felt that it was all of no use, that he might as well quit. He rejected various scholarships and other opportunities that had been offered to him and went to work at a small job in a rural district. He began to feel better then and made a big success out of his seemingly unpromising position. In addition to his own business, he got control of the newspaper and the local theatre and ran all of them. He not only made money, but made himself a great name in the community. He was exceedingly happy. He took a pleasure trip to Europe and returned with the idea of resuming his post-graduate education. No sooner had he opened a book, however, than he began to doubt his powers and wonder if he had will-power enough, stamina enough, and character enough to keep up his study. The further he went in the semester, the more distressed he felt. He became so blue he thought he must quit. He took the bus to the next city to consult a physician, but became so distressed on the way that he had the bus-driver let him out before arriving at his destination and walked into the city with tears streaming down his face.

These are rather typical examples of varying degrees of depression as seen in college students. Students of the high-school age are much less frequently depressed, but this should not lead us to assume the non-existence of depressed personalities among younger people. I have seen sharp depressions in the early teens. Anxieties about maintaining one's status, which means, in essence, maintaining one's hold upon certain love objects, are very apt to develop in college years and then again in middle life (see page 118)

(2) *Melancholy failure: in love and home life*

Failures in the achievement of successful love-pursuits and the maintenance of happy home life are frequently associated with depressions.

Mrs. Wayne was a home-loving, shy little woman who made few close friends and went out very little. She was exceedingly domestic and quite devoted to her husband, of whom she had always been extremely jealous. He was absorbed in his career and gradually came to neglect her more and more, spending his evenings in social circles where he was very popular although she was scarcely known. She became increasingly sad and listless, crying a great deal and even losing interest in keeping her home neat, although it had always been her greatest concern.

She began to suspect that her husband did not love her and did not wish to live with her. One day Mr. Wayne was called home and told that his wife was dying. He hurried home to find that a suicidal attempt had not been successful and that she was moaning and begging to be allowed to die. Feeling that this was a histrionic effort on her part to keep him from leaving her by threatening him with suicide, he took her to a general hospital and left after assuring himself that she was receiving good care.

Those who attended her were aware, however, that the suicidal attempt, although calculated to appeal to her husband's sympathy, was not an idle threat and that she would eventually carry it through successfully if she were not sent to a mental hospital. She protested when she was taken to a sanatorium, saying that she was not crazy, that she had nothing to live for, and that no one cared whether she lived or died; therefore she should be allowed to do away with herself. As she said this she lay back in her chair as if exhausted, her head thrown back, her eyes closed. Her normally pretty face was drawn into an expression of extreme sadness and she turned her head from side to side while she talked, as if she were tortured. Tears came to her eyes frequently and rolled down her sunken cheeks, falling unheeded on her dress. There were no plans for the future, no hope of building a new life, and yet no reproaches for her husband. And so she remained for many months. (She ultimately recovered.)

Mrs. Louis Miller had been married for twenty years. One day her daughter came home and said that she had seen her father in an automobile with another woman. Thenceforth Mrs. Miller became increasingly sad. She cried much, moaned, wrung her hands, walked the floor, or sat gnawing her fingers and trembling. She was quite inconsolable.

Her husband was tremendously distressed by the whole affair and was utterly bewildered as to what to do. She said she had always been immensely fond of him — " she was just wild over men " — and afraid she would lose him or that he would cease to care for her.

Like so many of these cases, this patient subjected herself to an abdominal operation with the idea of being cured of her depression, without effect. She did not recover for several years.

(3) *Melancholy failure: in success*

We all know from personal experience that disappointments and failures make us sad. We are apt to assume that if one succeeds, one is happy, and if one fails, one is sad, that depression represents a reaction to extreme failure. I have been trying to show here that frequently failure is a result of a depression rather than the cause. This is most vivid in those frequent occurrences in which definite sadness, depression, and even failure are precipitated by the sudden arrival of success! There are several popular phrases to describe this inability to " endure prosperity."

The following cases will illustrate this as it is seen by the psychiatrist:

Walter Hale had just been promoted to the position of manager of a chain of grocery stores. For six months he had filled the new position with credit to himself and profit to the management. " Suddenly," as he put it, " something seemed to break; everything slowed up; I couldn't think; I couldn't work as fast as usual; I lost my pep. I didn't want to see anyone and I thought they didn't want to see me."

Thinking his work was responsible for his depression, he gave it up and tried one job after another, giving each up in the same way. He grew increasingly depressed. " The whole world seemed very dark, very dark. And all life seemed useless and purposeless." Vague fears of various sorts assailed him — that the theatre in which he sat would be burned down, that he was infecting people around him with disease, that he had lost his chance for ever in the business world, that he was to be poisoned, that he was losing his mind. He decided to kill himself by jumping in front of a train.

Severe as this case sounds, the treatment was not very difficult. Mr. Hale consulted a psychiatrist, who had many conferences with him, pointing out the psychological factors underlying his sudden panic and depression and tracing them back to childhood experiences which tended to undermine his self-confidence in certain situations. He was counselled to give up his work entirely for a year and put himself passively in the hands of certain intelligent friends, who were given specific instructions as to how they could best help him overcome his depression. Travel of all kinds was absolutely prohibited, and quiet seclusion with constant but unobtrusive companionship was provided for. A year later he was his old self again, had re-established himself in business, and was doing as well as, or better than, before.

Horace Larson, although a son of well-to-do parents, had largely supported himself since the age of nineteen. He was a handsome, amiable lad and very popular in his department of a large commercial house. When he was twenty-four years old he was promoted to a better job in a branch office, with a fifty per cent increase in salary.

The new tasks seemed to upset him completely. He felt increasingly incapable of holding the job, complained bitterly of various features connected with it, came home several times on visits, and was finally discharged by his employers, who regarded him as inexplicably lazy and incompetent.

The picture of melancholia became increasingly obvious to everyone after his discharge. He talked constantly about his failure, his disgrace, his loss of prestige, the hopelessness of his position, the emptiness of the future. He broke his engagement to be married and gave up all social life. To his parents' amazement, he frankly confessed when questioned that he would like to kill himself.[65]

He, too, recovered under treatment.

(4) *Melancholy failure: in middle life*

Depressions are so frequently associated with the period of middle life that the older psychiatrists believed and some still believe that the changes in endocrine-gland functions which occur in the middle forties and which in women bring about the menopause or " change of life " in some way or other affect the personality and produce the depression. Others believe the middle-life depression to be a psychological reaction to the senescent changes consciously or unconsciously perceived by the individual in himself, the realizations of diminishing powers

---

[65] As a sidelight on the family influences in this case and on the peculiar problems of the doctor, I should add that when Horace's parents were making arrangements to place him in a hospital, his father returned after everything was settled to ask: " Now, if Horace *should* happen to kill himself on the way to the hospital, would I get my money back? "

and of reduced opportunities for winning love. There comes then a dawning realization of the fact that we live but once, which until the forties or fifties few people really believe. Then they suddenly become aware of the fact that they no longer have the flexibility or the power that was once theirs to alter themselves and to adjust themselves to the environment, and these realizations plus any threat or example of decreasing effectiveness produce in some individuals panic and despair. In others, to be sure, it stimulates a revival of compensatory strivings.

These depressions are not to be explained by simple reference to a precipitating factor such as material losses,[66] although it is true that the loss or threatened loss of the objects in which the individual has invested the major portion of his love and hate (and these *may* be money) often precipitates a depression. Some examples:

Blanche Burns finished school at an unusually early age and then taught school for some years before marrying. Her life with Mr. Burns had not been especially happy, for, although he was a kind man and an excellent provider, he was not interested in social affairs, but attended strictly to business. Mrs. Burns, on the other hand, was much interested in social activities as well as in the raising of her three children, whose lives she dominated. As her children grew up and went away to school she became more and more active in social and political organizations. Several years before, her husband's business failed, and as though in reaction to some premonition of it, she had run for state senator and had been defeated. A little later she was nominated for president of a state organization, but was not elected. In order to console her some friends persuaded her to accept the position of historian of another state society. In this position she was expected to write a book, which she found herself unable to do. Gradually she lost interest in the things around her and even in her personal appearance. Within a few months she became exceedingly depressed, convinced that she had lost all of her personal beauty and intellectual prowess. " Oh, my beautiful mind! What has happened to it? " she moaned repeatedly. Never once did she seem concerned with or inspired by the tenderness expressed by her family.

---

[66] It is interesting that fewer cases of mental illness showing a direct relation to financial loss occurred during the great depression, 1929–31, than during a comparable period of national economic prosperity. See W. C. Menninger and Leona Chidester: " The Role of Financial Losses in the Precipitation of Mental Illness," *Journal of the American Medical Association*, Vol. C, pp. 1398–1400 (May 6, 1933) .

Mr. Patrick Bryan was an Irish peasant immigrant, a simple, honest, hard-working man whose only interests were his wife, his work, and his church. Though married, he had no children and he and his wife lived in a simple, frugal manner. For thirty years he had been a labourer in the stock yards, with few holidays and almost no recreation, so that by the time he was middle-aged he had been able to buy a home and have a small savings account. At this time American industry was partially paralysed by the depression, and Mr. Bryan was " laid off." Immediately he became anxious and disturbed. One day he went away from home and got drunk — for him a very unusual procedure. Following this he was more and more disturbed, obsessed with the fear that he had syphilis, that he might be the cause of suffering to others — many of whom he did not even know — or that some great catastrophe was just about to befall him. So strongly was his feeling of security rooted in his work that the loss of his job, the feeling of failure, rendered him no longer able to face life normally. He reacted to it as many people react to the loss of loved ones — by depression. His security was shattered.

Symptoms of melancholia

The first symptoms of depression are usually a slight reduction in energy, a mild tendency to inactivity, a suggestion of undue preoccupation, a little disturbance of sleep; later a loss of weight and appetite, a suggestion of restlessness or irritability, and loss of interest in things. Obsessive worry and especially a preoccupation with some real or imaginary physical symptom are common. Later come feelings of inadequacy, uselessness, futility, wrongness, sinfulness, poverty. I have purposely said " feelings," because the mood largely determines the ideas, rather than the ideas explaining the mood, as naïve observers, such as relatives and friends, are apt to think. The ideas entertained are not always entirely false, although they usually become so. These false ideas (delusions) of melancholy tend to be of three general sorts: those dealing with the past, in which the individual is self-accusatory and blames himself for sins of omission and commission, sometimes exaggerating insignificant offences and sometimes manufacturing terrible non-existent crimes; those dealing with the present, in which the patient is self-disparaging and believes he is diseased or ruined, that he is morally worthless, despicable, unclean, etc.; and, finally, those dealing with the future, in which the patient believes that there is an impending disaster, or feels convinced that ruin and desolation await him and his friends inescapably, or that he and his loved ones are doomed for destruction, crucifixion, or hell-fire.

In the extreme states some patients are too overwhelmed to speak or eat, and others are agitated by the terror of their thoughts. After some weeks or months the cloud passes. Little by little the false ideas disappear; the ordinary ways of life and the customary attitudes toward things and persons return. The old zest comes back and the patient becomes just as well as he ever was in his life. He realizes that he has passed through a morbid period, recalls much of his suffering, but is loath to discuss it and is glad to go on in the former happy channels of life as if nothing had happened.

Psychological mechanisms of melancholia

Until the studies of Freud and his students, particularly Karl Abraham, we knew nothing definitely as to the cause of mania and melancholia. They were attributed to all sorts of things, originally — as the name indicates — to an excess of black bile. Painstaking and extensive studies have shown definitely, however, that melancholia is an exaggerated response to a real or imaginary loss in the love life. It happens to people who, because of childhood experiences, are particularly incapable of bearing such a loss and react to it, therefore, terrifically. They react to it in a double way, first by feeling that their ego has been impoverished, that there is no use in living, or that they are not worthy to live, and at the same time reproaching or attacking themselves as if they were guilty of something connected with the loss of this loved object. It has been found that they feel this way because the unconscious hate concealed in the feelings of love for the lost object is now reflected upon themselves so that they attack the loved person, as it were, for having gone away and at the same time punish themselves for this attack and hatred. The girl who, when jilted by her lover, knocks her head against the wall or puts a bullet into her head is taking vengeance on her lover and punishing herself for doing so.

The melancholiac suffers greatly, because with his loss and with his resentment he has an over-developed conscience. Mania is a rebellion against the tyranny of this conscience and is essentially the same condition as melancholia with the conscience overthrown.

SUICIDE

All deeply depressed people are potential suicides! The responsibility is with relatives and friends! Many of the suicides ascribed in the newspaper to financial worry, disappointment, etc., are undoubted cases of melancholia; the victims would probably have recovered and gone on to spend useful lives had their conditions been recognized and the proper steps taken by their friends or relatives.

Suicide is a serious problem. In spite of all the clamour about crime waves, few realize that murder is of much less frequent occurrence than suicide. Moreover, the victims of suicide are, generally speaking, far more desirable members of society than the victims of murder. Many of the latter are underworldlings, killed in quarrels or arrests, whereas the victims of melancholia — many of whom attempt suicide, and not a few of whom succeed — are usually of a distinctly higher, however warped, mentality.

Every psychiatrist has scores of experiences like this:

Mr. X. brought in his son for examination because he was " nervous." He was told that his son's nervousness was really a manifestation of a melancholia and that he might kill himself if he were not watched, and ought to be confined in a sanatorium. Mr. X scoffed at the idea of so intelligent, sensible, and seemingly self-controlled a person as his son doing such a thing. Six days later the son was found hanging from a rafter. The papers said he was worried over finances. The father regards it as an inexplicable tragedy. The psychiatrist regards it as another instance of preventable suicide which ought to be called manslaughter.

Suicide is a form of death which should concern physicians no less than do tuberculosis and cancer, and the public no less than murder and rape. In 1923 sixty-two physicians died of this cause, forty-eight lawyers, fourteen ministers, twenty-five editors, fifty clubwomen, and over two hundred business men. Every day the newspapers herald the reports of suicidal deaths among respected and ill-spared citizens.

To the psychiatrist, familiar with mental sickness in all forms, suicide is an ever-present spectre. It is a frequent cause of death among his otherwise recoverable patients. Knowing them intimately, he knows how inadequate any simple explanation of the act must be. In general, it is the solution a certain type of personality makes for an unbearable situation. The psychiatrist today considers mental disease to be indicated by unhappy or inefficient adaptation to life, and in this hectic struggle the psychopathic patient is likely to choose suicide as one of the ways out. There are other ways — morphine, delirium, day-dreaming, an alcoholic spree, a good cussing, or perhaps just a fishing trip.

The psychiatrist sees many suicides and attempted suicides among his patients and ex-patients. They are, in a sense, his failures. But sometimes he fails because he lacks co-operation. He lacks an understanding on the part of relatives (and sometimes of doctors!) of what the pre-suicidal state looks like. If this situation could be remedied, much suicide could be prevented. The novels and newspapers have very definite ideas about suicide, most of which are wrong, for the motives impelling a man to this unhappy solution are never so simple as newspaper reports would indicate. Suicide is never caused by a single thing, such as ill health, unrequited love, grief over an erring daughter, etc. Nor is suicide ever the first symptom of the mental state which it terminates.

If asked about it, depressed people will often admit their plans or hopes for death; they occasionally mention suicide spontaneously, but more often deny it, thus throwing the relatives off their guard. They are suffering intensely, silently, and death looks sweet. Family and friends try in vain to cheer them up, and plan trips and parties and vacations and visits, all of which only increase the suffering. All the more they are impelled to find a way out when opportunity presents itself to escape the family. They will elect or devise all sorts of methods to do this. Innumerable examples of this could be cited: a patient who stuck his head in the bathtub after his nurse had bathed him and left him for a moment; a patient who hanged herself with her shoe-string; a patient who cut his wrists with a broken electric-light globe; a patient who battered his head against the wall; one patient who drank several ounces of hydrochloric acid, some in ginger-ale, some undiluted; and any number who shot, hanged, and poisoned themselves.

They rarely attempt suicide in the presence of another person. Hence it is usually not difficult to prevent it if the danger is recognized. Properly treated, these depressions gradually lift, and the patient recovers his normal emotional balance and has no more urge toward suicide. Great care should be exercised, however, not to assume too quickly that the temptation is gone just because the patient appears cheerful. Some of our greatest tragedies have occurred under these circumstances.

Not all suicides are melancholiacs, although most of them are. There are suicides with inferiority complexes, with sexual abnormalities and psychopathies, with various types of brain disease, such as paresis; and, most important of all, some are apparently " normal " persons. But such persons belie the adjective " normal " by the act of suicide, and those of us who are familiar with the hidden struggles of persons passing as " normal " know what great pain they may be silently enduring.

The public is apt to jump to superficial conclusions about the motivations of suicide based on explanations which appear logical but which do not explain it. The notion that the fear of poverty, a disappointment in love, a feeling of guilt about business dishonesty, and the like cause suicide is a naïve and totally inadequate assumption. People who commit suicide for these ostensible reasons have generally begun their self-destruction long before these things occur. If one takes the opportunity and the pains to investigate with great patience and persistency all the circumstances, internal and external, connected with a suicide, one finds a very different basis for its etiology.

Suicide is the grand and ultimate example of cutting off one's nose to spite one's face. It is a combination of hate, rage, revenge, a sense of guilt, and a feeling of unbearable frustration. Meeting with reverses, irritations, or disappointments too great for his personality to absorb or to deal with rationally, the suicide solves them by a flight from reality — that is, by an irrational, unrealistic act of spite in which he impulsively strikes a blow which cannot be rescinded, thereby expressing *toward himself* the resentment he feels toward something or someone in his environment and simultaneously exhibiting a dramatic submission to punishment.

One hears much of a longing for peace as a motive for suicide; Hamlet said long ago what is still inescapable truth: namely, that we do not know that there is any such peace in death. Those who fantasy peace, consciously or unconsciously imagine death to be a kind of Nirvana, a return of the comfort of the intrauterine state of existence to which they may by this self-elected route hasten.

It should not be overlooked that killing onself, cutting off one's nose to spite one's face, does actually accomplish indirectly one of its intended purposes. It does hurt the " other fellow," the relatives, the lover, the employer, the doctor. The revenge is a childishly dramatic but a fearful and effective one.

Is suicide or a tendency toward it hereditary? There is no scientific evidence in that direction and there is much to show that cases of numerous suicides in one family may be explained on a psychological basis. Superficially there is the element of suggestion, but deeper than this is the well-known fact that unconscious death-wishes reach their highest development toward members of the family and when these are unexpectedly gratified by a suicide of one of them, a sudden and overpoweringly strong wave of guilt feelings is set in motion in all of the others, replacing the death-wishes. This wave may be so great and so overwhelming as to make it necessary for the culprit to punish himself by death. Sometimes this is done, as every psychoanalyst knows, by dreams of being executed, hanged, killed in some other way, or sentenced to life imprisonment. In other instances the element of suggestion points the way for the actual self-infliction of the death sentence.

There are such things as unconscious suicides — " accidents " and diseases brought on by the patient with an unconscious motive. Some of these appear to be accidental (and inevitable) even to the perpetrator. Many fatal accidents must be regarded by an impartial student aware of all the facts as " accidentally on purpose." Some of the most eminent phthisiologists believe that tuberculosis is often quite clearly a form of unconscious suicide on the part of a patient who has conflicting wishes both to live and to die, but is unaware of his success in gratifying the latter — underhandedly as it were — in a capitulation to the bacilli of Koch.[67]

[67] For a full discussion of the psychology of suicide, the reader may consult an article by the author, " Psychoanalytic Aspects of Suicide," *International Journal of Psychoanalysis*, Vol. XIV, pp. 376–90 (July 1933) ; and articles by Gregory Zilboorg, for example his " Differential Diagnostic Types of Suicide," *Archives of Neurology and Psychiatry*, Vol. XXXV, pp. 270–91 (February 1936) ; also the practical work of Ruth Fairbank: " Suicide, Possibilities of Prevention by Early Recognition of Some Danger Signals," *Journal of the American Medical Association* Vol. XCVIII, pp. 1711–14 (May 14, 1932) ; and Raphael, Power, and Berridge: " The Question of Suicide as a Problem in College Mental Hygiene," *American Journal of Orthopsychiatry*, Vol. VII, pp. 1–14 (January 1937) ; and others of the numerous references collected in the excellent book by Louis I. Dublin and Bessie Bunzel: *To Be or Not to Be. A Study of Suicide* (New York: Harrison Smith & Robert Haas, 1933) .

Very shortly we may expect scientific information in regard to suicide as a result of the work of the Committee for the Study of Suicide, Inc., a foundation formed for the promotion of scientific research concerning this form of death.

TREATMENT OF MOODY PERSONALITIES

Knowing something of these deep unconscious psychological causes of melancholia, we can arrive at some general principles to be avoided in dealing with them. The following may be set down as axioms:

A. *Melancholy persons cannot be " cheered up," or jollied, or reasoned with.*

B. *Home treatment is usually inadvisable; these cases need hospital care, treatment, and protection.*

C. *Almost as bad as no treatment, or perhaps a little worse, is " trip treatment."* To illustrate this:

A woman of fifty complained of nervousness, despondency, lack of interest in life, flatulence, back-ache, headache. She was examined by several very capable physicians and was told to take a trip to Colorado, that it would do her good to get away from home. This is exceedingly dangerous advice for mentally sick patients. Try as they may, they cannot get away from themselves, and very few of these cases are actually made sick by their environment. This particular patient made the trip as advised, but dived out of the car window on the way.

Treatment of the proper sort is exceedingly important for the depressions and excitement of the moody personality, because the great majority of them subside. This recovery sometimes occurs under the worst of conditions; that is, the patient gets well in spite of misunderstanding, mishandling, and mistreatment. It is obviously better, however, to give him the best possible opportunity for the expediting of his recovery. This usually means isolation, protection against visitors (even relatives), physical support, the best of selected food, careful nursing, a variable amount of sedation by baths, electricity, and medicines, and, above all, psychotherapy of the right sort. Those cases in which an organic disease is a factor require still more specific treatment. All of this is more fully discussed in Chapter V.

Patients are frequently removed from the hospital too soon, before they have fully recovered. For example:

Mrs. K. had been in a hospital for three or four months and had made apparent recovery from a very severe depression. Her husband was importunate and we consented to his removing his wife on condition that he get someone to stay with her constantly for the next three months.

He said she seemed so cheerful and so like her old self that he scarcely thought it necessary, but would do so if we insisted. All went well for about a month, when one day the woman whom he had hired to stay with his wife in the day-time was ill and could not come. He thought he would take a chance because his wife seemed perfectly well. She got his early breakfast, and when the children got up she prepared their breakfast, washed them, dressed them, and sent them to school. Then she cleaned up her house neatly, put everything in order, went to the barn, and hanged herself.

Often no one but the afflicted ever knows he is depressed and he must help himself unaided. How?

Of course one can argue with oneself. Failure and frustration, defeat and disappointment — these are experiences common to the human race. It is an old saw that success depends upon reacting to them with equanimity.

One may sometimes regain composure and self-confidence by recourse to an old trick. Everyone is a master of something. He may comfort himself with that. For instance: A Harvard profes-sor, who is world-famous for his achievements and popularity, was obscure and self-disparaging until he discovered that he could play chess better than any other man of the school. This gave him a sense of assurance that helped him to give freely to the world great work in the scientific field. Not everyone can be a chess champion, but some can excel at golf and some at making a cake and some at music and some in entertaining children. It is a great gift to be able to recognize one's own excellencies. It is said that some men don't know when they are licked, but it is even more useful to know when one has really succeeded.

And as for the frustrations and losses sustained, it is helpful to apply a revised version of the fox and the grapes; not to call them sour, because this is an idle self-deception and cold comfort. The fox could not get the grapes, nor could he bear to face the fact that the failure lay in himself and not in his stars, as Cassius could have told him. He might have crawled away with his tail between his legs, thinking how impotent and worthless he was not to be able to get those grapes, shedding tears and meditating suicide. He might, on the other hand, have made various other more satisfactory solutions. He could have got a certain amount of satisfaction from smelling the grapes if grapes it must be, or he might have jumped just a little higher or hunted up a box to stand on. However, a little intelligent reflection would have reminded him that grapes are a poor diet for a carnivorous beast like a fox, and a beefsteak would be not only more palatable but more easily obtained. And finding himself baffled in what must have been a rather ludicrous spectacle — that of a fox jumping up at a cluster of grapes — he might have accepted the situation with a sense of humour and had a good laugh over the flips of fate in a puzzling but lovable old world as he trotted on down the road!

Such reflections will be of help to some, but for those more deeply depressed we must look further. What is the rational application of the theories about the origin of depression elaborated in the preceding pages?

It has been said that hate causes depressions, inexpressible, often unrecognized hate aimed at an outsider, but reflected upon the self. Logically, the thing to do would be to express this hate, if possible. It is of some benefit often merely to recognize that depression is hate and to ponder upon the curious paradox that hating someone else makes us feel so badly ourselves. There are usually very good reasons for not expressing hate toward the person who originally inspired it, but there are many innocuous ways in which hate can be expressed. Many athletic contests represent nothing else; this is recognized where the crowds cheer the players to "fight," "kill him," and similar savagery. We cannot all play football, but there is some benefit even in vicarious indulgence in sport, and most of us could take more exercise if we only would. Even exercise without an antagonist is of some definite relief to most depressed people.[68] Plain hard work will (and does) serve equally well for many and self-imposed penances of many kinds.

Even then all is not said, and some of us will still be blue. The ideal of serenity in the face of all events is an impossible one for some temperaments. Try as they may, they cannot "treat those two impostors just the same," but must over-react to both success and failure. There is some help in the thought that comforted Lincoln, that "this, too, will pass." Religion of some kind, the love of something ineffable — God, beauty, nature — the devotion to a task — these save some from depression. Some

---

[68] This principle has been used very successfully in treatment of hospitalized patients with severe depressions, as will be elaborated in the chapter on treatment. See W. C. Menninger: " Individualization in the Prescriptions for Nursing Care of the Psychiatric Patient," *Journal of the American Medical Association,* Vol. CVI, pp. 756–61 (March 7, 1936) ; and footnotes # 19 and 21 in Chapter V of this book,

think that it is the relinquishing of the intensity of religious faith, or its failure to engross its adherents as formerly, that has brought about the increased number of depressions in these latter days. There are fewer now who can say with Job: " Though He slay me, yet will I trust in Him." Job and Jesus knew grief, but not melancholy.

In general the thing for the melancholy man to do is to seek the most proficient counsel available and act upon the advice given. If suicidal thoughts occur to you, you owe it to yourself, your family, and the world to tell someone about it whose emotions are stable enough to guide you through the shoals of danger. That is what good friends are for. And a wise friend will not be presumptuous. He will take you to a psychiatrist. Modern psychiatry has developed to a point comparable with the better-known and more spectacular achievements of major surgery. Surgery of the mind is often as necessary and as feasible as surgery of the abdomen.[69]

6. THE NEUROTIC TYPE

(FRUSTRATED PERSONALITIES)

The word " neurotic " is fairly familiar to most intelligent people, but it is variously interpreted. For many it is a dignified synonym for " nervous." Some people consider it something of a distinction to describe themselves as neurotic. For others, particularly doctors, it is a word of opprobrium describing those individuals whose propensities for complaining outdistance all conceivable degrees of actual physical disease, and who cry their symptoms to high heaven in spite of the flimsiest evidence of organic trouble.

In truth, the neurotic is both of these, and neither of them, and much more in addition. Theoretically the neurotic patients are those whose childhood development was such that the conflicts between their instinctive tendencies and the environment were never resolved in a way wholly satisfactory to the ego and who are, therefore, constantly impelled to indulge in behaviour which gives them a needed satisfaction at an exorbitant cost. The neurotic is one who always contrives to defeat his own aims,

[69] Some of the cases and paragraphs in this section are taken from the author's chapter on " Depressions " in *Why Men Fail* (New York: The Century Co., 1928) , edited by Dr. Morris Fishbein, editor of the *Journal of the American Medical Association* and of *Hygeia,* who has gathered some excellent illustrations in Chapter VIII.

to spike his own guns, to lay his own pitfalls. He does this by treating persons and situations of 1944 as if they were the persons and situations of 1910, the period of his childhood. He suffers, as Freud says, from " reminiscences " — unrecognized ones. The gratifications he obtains are usually so disguised, so unsubstantial, so costly that healthy-minded people cannot understand or believe that the neurotic patient is actually the victim of an illness (more correctly, of a personality defect).

Hysteria, which is the typical neurosis, comes from a Greek word for " womb." It is very interesting to note that several thousand years ago, when the word was coined, it was recognized in some way or other that there was some connection between it (and all the neuroses) and the sexual instinct. The first theory of this was that the womb (*votépa, hyster*) got loose from its moorings in some way or other and wandered about over the body and thereby produced symptoms in this or that region, according to where it maliciously nestled. This very well symbolizes the modern view that the neuroses are essentially a displacement, not of the womb, but of the sexual instinct, or, rather, of the outlets for the sexual instinct. This will be made more clear in the chapter on motives; it must suffice here to say that *the neurotic personality is one whose primitive instincts (sexual and aggressive) have been modified to meet social requirements only with painful difficulty and with the development of numerous disadvantageous substitutions.*

Civilization has immensely elaborated the opportunities, the fruitfulness, and the significance of sex, and it has also greatly increased the difficulties of achieving its ends. In the days of our ancestors, in all likelihood, a man who felt so inclined simply sought a woman for mating-purposes, as any of the quadrupeds do today. He might have to do some fighting to get her, but no more than that. Today there are multitudes of obstacles to be overcome before a man may marry a maid, and great responsibilities devolve upon him once he has taken the step.

Now, this increase in the complexity of the expenditure of sexual instinct is only half of it; civilization has also greatly increased the opportunities for the development of the individual's self-expression aside from his physical propensities. For primitive man life was a matter of eating, sleeping, hunting, fighting, and procreating. Life today has infinitely more diversions.

And it will be seen upon a little reflection that this elaboration of interests and forms of self-expression which we call civilization could have been possible only at the expense of the sacrifice of the simple, easy, direct self-satisfaction methods of primitive life. It is only when resistance is placed in the course of an electric current that heat and light are developed. And it was only by the imposition of certain repressions that the interests of mankind became extended to their present and ever-increasing range. In other words, civilization and culture owe their existence to the thwarting of primitive tendencies, particularly the sexual and aggressive instincts, and in this sense *civilization itself is a neurotic product.*[70]

Now, it is not remarkable, considering how recently we have arrived from the stage of simplicity just described, that many of us should have difficulties in adapting our instincts to the elaborate code of twentieth-century civilization. This is characteristically true of the neurotic personality. He wants to have his cake and eat it. He wants to achieve the fruits of culture, but he also wants to retain more primitive forms of satisfaction.

As I have written this, it is altogether too simple. For it is too easy to say that the neurotic is vacillating between culture and animalism. Rather it should be said that the neurotic is confused and torn and distraught among a variety of opportunities. He is not defective or moody or withdrawn; he is thwarted. His unconscious mind is the scene of a terrific battle between unreconciled tendencies and opposing trends.

This battle goes on in the unconscious of every person, but in the neurotic personality it is closer to the surface of consciousness, the sides are more evenly matched, the fray is bloodier. For the " normal " person it is quickly, quietly, painlessly settled one way or the other. He eats his cake or he has it. He kisses the girl or he lets her go. He likes poetry or he doesn't like it. But the neurotic can't decide. He appears to want one thing and to do the other. He seems to create obstacles for himself and to stumble over his own feet. (See discussion of ambivalence, page 277.)

But the normal man or woman *does* find someone to love, and in the course of defending such a love probably finds someone to hate, and does both with a net result of success and happiness. The difficulties of the neurotic man or woman in accomplishing this may take the form of *flight* or of *attack;*

---

70 Cf. Freud's stimulating essay, *Civilization and Its Discontents* (New York: Jonathan Cape & Harrison Smith, 1930) .

some men fight the wives and sweethearts whom they think they love or should love and surrender themselves amiably to men or women who do them harm. Some take flight into physical illness, others into fears and absorption in their nervous indigestion and constipation, others into a preoccupation with physical culture and athletics or even art, music, and literature. These things are not forbidden to anyone, because no one living under civilized conditions can expend all of his instincts in a direct undisguised way.

Some individuals, however, unnecessarily and unintentionally surrender *all* direct sexuality and all conscious sexual feeling. Medically such conditions are known as *impotence* in men and *frigidity* in women. Women especially are subject to this affliction and frequently believe that it is physical in origin (which it never is) or that women " are not supposed " to have conscious sexual feelings (which is absurd). These people are not lacking in sexuality; they are merely under the spell of intense repression, which, as I have already said several times but cannot over-emphasize, does not mean *suppression*. They are inhibited by too much civilization, a special private civilization of their own which is not fruitful and which is a caricature or an exaggeration of real civilization. The fact that a mother prohibits all sexual activities in a boy when he is eight years old is no reason for his maintaining the same abstinence when he is thirty years old, but this logic often prevails in the unconscious, nevertheless, and prevents such a man from marrying or from being a good husband when he does marry. The same is true of women.

Inhibitions in sexual life are often explained away and ascribed to idealism, lack of opportunity, physical abnormality, glandular inadequacy, or incompatible companions. People are sometimes encouraged in this by conscientious but misinformed physicians. Such explanations are more comfortable, but leading urologists and psychiatrists now agree that usually they are false and the condition is a psychological one which requires psychological treatment.

I have gone into this at some length because such afflictions are so typical of the neurotic personality; that is, he thwarts his own instincts. Sometimes he thwarts his own instincts voluntarily and too much. To some extent he substitutes for these gratifications neurotic symptoms. The symptom acts as an excuse, and it also acts as a vehicle for expression of physical sensation and of bodily interest which should be expended in a more fertile direction, either in direct sexual expression or in a *sublimation* of direct sexual expression. If instead of dyspepsia this man would make poetry his outlet, his bride, so to speak, the world would be better off and he would be much more comfortable. He could still be described as having a neurotic personality, but not a neurosis. A man with nervous indigestion, however, has a neurosis.

Compromises of a sort valuable to society are called *sublimations* and it is upon sublimations that culture depends. To repeat the formula in a simple way, sexual instinct must in the nature of things be more or less thwarted. If this thwarting or frustration is followed by the turning of the energy into an unproductive channel, the individual is said to have a neurosis. If it is deflected into a productive channel, he is said to be sublimating. The school-teacher and the nurse represent simple forms of sublimation of their maternal instincts. The artist and the author are creators in no less definite a sense than the famous Austrian who was the father of forty-three children. The fact that the surgeon, the lawyer, the actress, and the minister are afforded opportunities for sublimation by their professions is a little less obvious until one remembers that sexual instinct involves many more tendencies than merely that of possessing a person of the opposite sex and procreating children therewith. The many forms which sexual emotions may take would carry us far afield into a matter which belongs to the chapter on motives.

I know of a club composed of distinguished and accomplished men. There are a bank president, the manager of a corporation, some lawyers and doctors, an editor or two, authors, journalists, business men. They are intelligent; they are educated. Their conversation is brilliant. They are the wise men of their community, the advisers and counsellors, the strong, sane men. Some of these gentlemen give evidences of possessing in addition to their high degree of culture neurotic personalities. None of them can be said to be out and out neurotic. Any of them might easily become so.

Look closely at one of our friends. He is so kind and so honest that he would certainly not deceive anyone in the world. He is amiable, soft-voiced, and gentle, and yet he is a lawyer famous for his fierce and courageous fighting in the court-room. But he allows himself to be tyrannized over by a hard, bitter, selfish, relentless wife who gives him no peace, yet from whom he is powerless to escape.

Here is another one: He is immensely fond of his wife and devoted to his children, but perfectly incapable of resisting any attractive woman. Time after time he is dragged out of messes by the heels, and only the extraordinary forbearance of a remarkable wife has saved him from the ruin that her desertion would certainly mean to him.

That newspaper man over there who knows so much about almost everything is interested in nothing so much as that about which he knows the least — namely, medical science. His own health is by far the most important topic in the world. He is alarmed at rainy weather on account of the possibility of colds; he believes that dry weather is likely to promote epidemics. He fears cold weather on account of pneumonia; hot weather on account of heat strokes. He has a propensity for wearing rubbers and heavy underwear. He is anxious about his food and suspicious of it. He eats far too much and immediately regrets it. He has never been sick in his life, but he is always expecting to be imminently.

Rather than spend more time in detailing examples of neurotic personalities who give clues to their maladjustment in these simple, single ways, I propose to proceed directly to describe the full-blown collections of compromise formations which we call the *neuroses.*

THE NEUROSES

THE BREAKDOWNS OF NEUROTIC PERSONALITIES

The older (pre-Freudian) classification of neuroses included hysteria, neurasthenia, and psychasthenia. This is still the accepted medical classification although it does not correspond precisely with psychoanalytic discoveries. *Psychasthenia* was (is) used to describe those illnesses in which the symptoms were entirely subjective — in which, that is, the patient suffered fears, doubts, and anxieties, which had no external manifestations except in certain acts which the patient frankly admitted to be defensive. According to the nature of their origin these are now called by the Freudians *anxiety hysteria, anxiety neurosis,* or *compulsion neurosis.*

In what was (is) called *neurasthenia* the patient also has nothing to show and a great deal to complain of, chiefly physical symptoms, pains, weaknesses, fatigue, etc. But whereas the psychasthenic knows that his troubles arise within himself, the neurasthenic is sure that his do not. Neither one has anything physical to demonstrate, but the psychasthenic doesn't try to have, whereas the neurasthenic is constantly seeking to prove that he does have. Doctors examine him over and over and tell him nothing is wrong — but he doesn't believe it and goes elsewhere.

But, in *conversion hysteria* the patient has nothing to say; he lets his symptoms speak for themselves. They are always gross, conspicuous physical and functional changes. No less than the neurasthenics, the hysterical patient is sure that there is nothing mental about his trouble — it is purely and surely physical. I shall illustrate each of these neuroses.

PSYCHASTHENIA

(DOUBTS, FEARS, ANXIETIES, OBSESSIONS, ETC.)

Obsessional neurosis

Mr. Robert Harrington was in charge of the credit department of a large and prosperous wholesale firm. He was regarded as one of the most intelligent and efficient business men in the city. His judgment was relied upon not only by his own firm but by many related business concerns. He was a director of one bank and one other corporation. None of the men with whom he had been associated for twenty years had the slightest idea that he was a patient of mine.

Yet, according to his own story, he had been a constant sufferer since childhood. "Never," he said, "have I been free from a pervading sense of unreality, a feeling that things were not right, that I am only partly here and partly in some other world. I can't seem to shake this funny feeling out of my head. My life is filled with presentiments and fears. I am distressed at a thousand possibilities which never happen. When I go to bed at night, I never go to sleep until I have worried and stewed over a score of things which have happened during the day, or which I fear may happen as the result of something I did during the day. I wake up in the night with feelings of anxiety and terror. Every night is full of the most hideous dreams, in which incredible terrors and adventures of indescribable horror involve me and seem to have been brought about by me.

"Occasionally I get the notion that I am going to die. I realize that it is absurd, as there is every indication that I am in the best of physical health and have no chance of dying, but I get so frightened at the thought that I see possibilities of death in every little thing. I think something in my food may give me acute indigestion. I wonder as I wash my face if I might get some water in my ears that would give me an infection; I think of the possibility of being wrecked on the way to work. The thought comes that the building may tumble in, or that an earthquake or lightning or some other act of God may occur that will end things. Sometimes I even look at the men in the office and think what if they might accidentally shoot me. I know such things are impossible, or at least improbable, but all sorts of such fears come to me. Then I wonder if I may have accidentally caused someone's death at some time in my life. I have actually driven back as far as ten miles to see if a car I passed at the side of the road might accidentally have been grazed by me as I drove by. I have spent hours trying to make sure that I have not made a mistake that might injure someone, realizing, even as I do it, that there is no probability of it and that I am punishing myself for something. I look back over pages and pages of correspondence to make sure that I am right about a certain client upon whom I am to pass judgment, and waste a great amount of time on something that should be done offhand. I make elaborate preparations each night in case of my unexpected death, which of course never occurs.

" No one in my firm has any idea why I have never married. They often joke me about it and most people think I am so engrossed in business that I lack any of the finer sentiments and affections. As a matter of fact, I have thought a thousand times I would get married and I have fallen in love with a score of girls. I never get further than an introduction, however. I have the feeling that if I should try to talk to a woman, or to interest one in myself, I should make a horrible and shocking failure. I should be covered with humiliation so intense that I should nearly die.

" As long as I keep my mind on the details of our business and devote myself assiduously to that and nothing else, I am relatively comfortable. It is not real peace of mind, but just relative comfort. I remind myself that I must always keep from the world the fact that I am suffering so intensely. I have broken scores of social engagements without an explanation; I have let the world think I was hard-boiled and socially indifferent; I have jeered at the antics of nervous people and at the theories of psychiatrists, and no one realizes that I am constantly struggling to maintain a camouflage, behind which cringes a tortured worm."

Compulsion neurosis

The general manager of a large corporation came to see me about eight years ago with this story:

" Doctor, we are very much disturbed about a problem that has arisen in our business. We have in our employ a young woman whom I regard as one of the most capable business women I have ever known. She is really a brilliant girl. She never has got along very well with the other employees, but she can grasp the principles of a problem extraordinarily well and she is conscientious to a painful degree. She just must have things perfect.

" A few weeks ago the head of her department said something to me about her queer behaviour, but I presumed it was some little attack of hysterics such as women have, although I thought it a bit unusual that she should have it. I really forgot all about it. But so much has happened since then that I have come to realize that it is a case for a psychiatrist.

" It seems that for some time she has been increasingly irritable and unsociable with the other employees. She went about her work as if much troubled by something. One of the men in charge asked her if anything was wrong and she rather irritably but emphatically denied it.

" A little later some of the employees saw her shaking her head and moving her lips, clenching her fists, clutching her hands over her breasts, and in fact acting just a little ' goofy.' We would notice her doing various stunts, each one repeated the same number of times, three I think it was. For instance, she'd tap her foot on the floor three times, or fold and unfold her hands, or get up and sit down again, or cross her knees and give three little kicks with her foot.

" You might think offhand that it is just a plain case of a girl losing her mind and developing some form of insanity. But, a funny thing about it, you can see it isn't that if you talk with the girl five minutes. She's just as sensible, intelligent, and self-possessed as ever. I don't know much about mental trouble, but I know that girl isn't crazy. Yet, when you ask her why she does those things, she just hangs her head and says nothing. I want you to see her."

I did see her. I saw her something over two hundred times within the next year or so and I could fill a book twice as large as this one with details of the symptoms and their unconscious significance and motivation.

In the first place the manager was quite right in saying that the girl was not " insane " in the popular sense; that is, she was not in any sense a menace either to herself or to society. She certainly was, however, tied up with a terrific " compulsion neurosis," which is one form of psychasthenia. In addition to the peculiarities of behaviour which my informer described, there were numerous other performances which she told me about herself. One of these was a very elaborate method of getting undressed to go to bed. By the time she had arranged her clothes precisely as she wanted them, read certain passages in her Bible a certain number of times, and assumed certain postures in the bed, it was nearly two hours from the time she started before she was able to fall asleep.

Anxiety hysteria

" My wife called me home from work one morning about ten o'clock. I thought something terrible must have happened. Her eyes were dilated, her mouth was white, she was gasping. She just looked like someone who was literally scared to death. Of course I asked her what was the matter, and all she would say was: ' I am dying, I am dying.' I called two or three doctors and they examined her over and over. In fact they put her in a hospital for a week, but they never could find anything wrong with her. She finally confessed that she had taken a tablespoonful of grated nutmeg to bring about an abortion, but in the first place she wasn't pregnant, and in the second place the doctors said nutmeg wouldn't hurt her anyway. But from that time on she has complained constantly about her heart palpitating, her pulse being weak, and she feels as though she were going crazy and thinks she is going to die any minute. She will break out in a sweat and tremble all over. She will get so dizzy she nearly falls down. She gets terribly passionate and then totally frigid. She has attacks of diarrhœa, and then for days she will worry over being constipated. Doctor, I didn't know a human being could have so many symptoms and be so nearly scared to death without knowing what she's afraid of! "

In the case just cited, the sexual energy was aroused, thwarted, and given no satisfactory outlet at all. In the following case it is directed back on to the patient's own body instead of in the normal direction of interest in her husband.

NEURASTHENIA
(MULTIPLE COMPLAINTS OF PHYSICAL AILMENTS, ON LITTLE OR NO ORGANIC BASIS)

With mild anxiety

" Ever since I have been married I've been nervous. If I didn't have the finest husband in the world and one who takes most wonderful care of me and puts up with all my complaining and all my sickness, I'd be a grass widow. The average man just couldn't stand it. I haven't been a wife to him at all. I've been too sick. First there was that awful headache. Oh, I can't tell you how terrible it was! It just knocked me down, and I thought the end of the world had come. It never really has gone away in all these eight years, but it's nothing like what it used to be. But there's been a lot of other things. There's a sort of an internal trembling, you know, a kind of inward nervousness, and I just feel as though all my organs were quivering. One doctor told me my nerves were tied in knots.

"I don't know why it is, but I can't stand anything. I haven't strength enough to walk from here to the street-car and back. I may get up in the morning feeling pretty good, but by the time I get breakfast for my husband and have started in on my morning's work I'm nearly exhausted, and by noon I'm just completely played out.

"And then I'm so terribly constipated. I really think I could go a week without a bowel movement if I didn't take something. And I've tried all the cathartics there are. My husband says that whenever there's a new cathartic invented, I hear about it and go and try it. Even then I have to take enemas every day or two. If I don't I just suffer terribly. Why, once I was down on my back for six weeks, simply because I neglected my bowels. Of course some doctors say there's nothing to this, but I know there is. I've been through it and I know.

"I guess I told you about my sweating and getting so hot and then so cold. Did I tell you about that funny twisting feeling? It runs right through my right side down into my leg. Once I noticed it come clear up to the top of my spine. I think it's a nerve loose or something like that. None of the doctors know what to make of my case. I've been to dozens of them. Yes, and I've tried osteopaths and chiropractors. I even went to the new psychology school and I don't know what all else. Some say I ought to try Christian Science, but you can't tell me these things are imaginary, and they are not in my mind either. I'll admit I'm nervous, but there's a cause for these things somewhere. I know I never had 'em before I was married."

Hypochondriasis
The following is a letter from a neurasthenic patient to her palpitating relatives:

"Dear Mother and Husband:
"I have suffered terrible today with drawing in throat. My nerves are terrible. My head feels queer. But my stomach hasn't cramped quite so hard. I've been on the verge of a nervous chill all day, but I have been fighting it hard. It's night and bedtime, but, Oh, how I hate to go to bed. Nobody knows or realizes how badly I feel because I fight to stay up and out doors if possible.

" I haven't had my cot up for two days, they don't want me to use it.

" These long afternoons and nights are awful. There are plenty of patients well enough to visit with but I'm in too much pain.

" The nurses ignore any complaining. They just laugh or scold.

" Eating has been awful hard. They expect me to eat like a harvest hand. Every bite of solid food is agony to get down, for my throat aches so and feels so closed up. They feed me at 7:15, 12 and 5.

" With supper so early, and evening so long, I am so nervous I can't sleep until so late. I haven't slept well since I've been here. My heart pains as much as when I was at home. More so at night. I put hot water bottle on it. I don't know if I should or not. I've been wanting to ask some Dr.

" I had headache so badly in the back of my head last night and put hot water bottle there. My nurse said not to.

" They don't give much medicine here. Mostly Christian Science it seems! Well I must close or I never will get to sleep. My nurse gets off at 8:15 so she makes me go to bed by then.

" My eyes are bothering me more.

" Come up as soon as you can. My nose runs terrible every time I eat.

" The trains and ducks and water pipes are noisy at night.

Annie

" P.S. I don't mean to be so partial by addressing this to Mother, they are for all."

Here is a fragment of another letter, a list of symptoms recorded by a patient anxious to enter a Wisconsin hospital. These are typical neurasthenic complaints.

" A severe Pain in the Crotch of the Brest.
A Pain at the top of the Stomic.
Falling Backwards.
Awful sick throughout the whole Body.
Bloating at Bottom of Bellie.
Languid — fretful — of long suffering.
Crazy Dreams see things that never was.
Worry nervous inside.
My breathing Springs right Back to me." [71]

A distinguished-looking merchant from another city who had a very characteristic variety of neurasthenia consulted me some years ago. His chief complaint was dual (most neurasthenics have a dozen or more

---

[71] " Tonics and Sedatives," *Journal of the American Medical Association.*

symptoms) : For eighteen years he had had a persistent pain in his eyes, which he described as coming from the back of his head, piercing the eyeball from behind. It had been so severe and so persistent that he had given up all reading, all theatres, and all sports requiring the use of his eyes. I have four pages of notes describing the various fluctuations in intensity which he had observed in the pain under various circumstances. His other symptom was that he could not get his wife to be interested in him. He deplored her stupidity, her failure to sympathize with his sufferings, her lack of interest in social and political affairs, and her general incompetence, but, above all, her refusal to give him as frequent sexual satisfaction as he desired. She cohabited with him out of a sense of duty, and the sexual act was followed every time by a renewed wave of mutual antagonism and discontent.

He had been to literally dozens of doctors, some of whom prescribed one thing and others another. Several had suggested that his illness was neurotic, and this particularly irritated him.

This case had a rather curious and illuminating outcome. I suggested that he try the effect of discontinuing sexual relations with his wife for a time, explaining that it was possible that these two symptoms which he believed to be entirely unrelated might, after all, have something to do with each other. I also prescribed some other treatment. Some months later I saw him again. He was delighted. He said that he felt better than he had for years. He was profuse in his expressions of appreciation. He paid a part of his bill.

I heard nothing from him for a time. The book-keeper sent him a statement for the balance of his account and an announcement of my change of address. Imagine our surprise at receiving in reply a letter of bitter denunciation. He wished me to know that he was not concerned with my change of address unless kind Providence would remove me from the community entirely. He was convinced that this would be a blessing to the State of Kansas. He had taken great pleasure in advertising over the state how deceptive and unscrupulous we had been, how members of my clinic had contradicted each other, and how much I had charged him for doing nothing at all; the sooner the institution went on the rocks, the better he would be pleased; and would I please refrain from speaking to him if I saw him on the street?

The moral of this case is " Hell hath no fury like a woman scorned " except a neurotic relieved of his one pet symptom. Samuel Johnson warned us to " *Depend upon it that if a man talks of his misfortunes there is something in them that is not disagreeable to him; for where there is nothing but pure misery there never is any recourse to the mention of it!* "

HYSTERIA

(PHYSICAL SYMPTOMS, USUALLY VISIBLE, AND USUALLY WITHOUT
COMPLAINT BY THE PATIENT)

Hysterical fits and varia

When Annabelle Atkinson was fifteen years old she was a senior in high school and everyone was very proud of her. One day she developed a pain in her side. The doctors thought it might be appendicitis, so they took her to a surgeon, who thought he would observe her for a while before operating. Then the pain disappeared.

A few weeks later it came back. This time a lot of other symptoms came with it. She had what her family called " the shakers "; she began to jump and jerk as she lay on the bed until it appeared that unless held she would throw herself clear off of it on to the floor. The doctors thought this must be St. Vitus's dance.

She had a dozen or more of these attacks of shaking and leaping; then they disappeared. Instead of them came waves of uncontrolled crying and laughing. She would laugh for thirty minutes at a time and cry for twice as long. Then she became so stiff all over that she couldn't move, and the doctors suspected rheumatic fever.

She was hauled about from one hospital to another in search of a diagnosis. Some of the doctors told her parents that the trouble was nervous (by which they meant hysterical), but the parents couldn't believe it.

More and more symptoms kept developing. She couldn't bear to have certain people look at her. Once she had a sudden fit of excitement and threw a chair at her mother because her mother happened to look in her direction. For several weeks she refused to speak to anyone. Then for a week she talked constantly without stopping. Suddenly all of these symptoms disappeared and her only complaint was a pain in her stomach.

Finally this symptom also disappeared and she was left perfectly (?) well.

Hysterical lameness

There was a dispute among the doctors over the case of a pretty little nine-year-old girl. The girl had developed a limp in one leg and it appeared to be hip-trouble. Along with it she had become pale and lost weight. She complained of pain in the hip, and X-rays suggested some changes in the bony structure. It looked very much as if she might have tuberculosis of the hip-joint. For this reason some of the doctors advocated a plaster cast.

Certain things about the case, however, gave some of the doctors another notion about it. For example, the child complained of a variety of pains, and sometimes when touched ever so gently by her mother she would scream out of all proportion to the justification. She would have limp spells in which she would drop into her mother's arms and lie motionless. At other times she would grow bitter toward her mother, make faces at her, and even throw things at her.

The mother was sure the child had tuberculosis of the hip, as some of the doctors had suggested. This we assured her was not true. A week after the child had been placed under treatment the leg was perfectly well!

Limitation of space prevents detailing the methods of treatment except that the child's confidence was secured and she was encouraged to ask questions. One of the first things she wanted to know was the meaning of the word " whore." This led to the uncovering of the fact that the father and mother had staged any number of dramatic fights in front of all the children, and that upon several occasions the father had referred to the mother as a whore in front of the children and then tried to explain to the children something of what that meant. He told them that their mother wore her dresses too short, that she wanted to show her legs off in public, that women who wanted to show their legs to other men were called whores. Hence the child's concern over legs.

Hysterical somnambulism

One of the most interesting examples of hysteria I ever saw occurred in a successful insurance man of thirty. He was the youngest of ten living children. The other nine had all gone off and left him to take care of his parents. His parents had done well by him and he took good care of them; everything was very satisfactory.

He decided to have a family reunion on his parents' golden wedding anniversary. He corresponded with all the brothers and sisters, and as a result of his energy and persistence a week's celebration was arranged and the children came from all over the United States, bringing with them their wives and families. Everyone enjoyed himself immensely, and particularly our entrepreneurial patient.

Shortly after the big party, however, he began to be a little upset. There were no particular complaints, but he just didn't feel like going to work. Then, to the consternation of his parents and his wife, he began to walk and talk in his sleep. Shortly after he went to bed he would get up, sometimes dressing himself, but usually not, and spend the rest of the night walking or sitting in his room talking and singing exactly as if he were wide awake and as if there were someone there to talk to. He kept this up for several weeks. When questioned about it the following morning, he always denied it vigorously, denied even its possibility, saying that he had slept well and felt fine.

The relatives observed him carefully during these nightly demonstrations. They discovered that his entire conversation dealt with persons and affairs of his childhood. Apparently he was reliving the days when his parents had to care for him instead of him caring for them. And apparently this regression to childhood had been provoked by the unconscious feelings of jealousy incident to the return of his older brothers and sisters, which had for the time being removed him from the centre of his parents' interest.

Hysterical paralysis (industrial shell-shock)

Hysteria is frequently the explanation of certain incapacitating injuries received by soldiers, workmen, and others in their line of duty, and in regard to which serious legal fights often occur. This can best be illustrated by the following case of a common labourer, forty years old, examined at the request of the attorneys on both sides of the case.

This man had attempted to throw an electric switch which was reputed to carry several thousand volts. In some way or other (elaborate details of all possibilties and particulars were secured, but will be omitted) he believed that he received a shock such that the electricity went through his left hand and left leg. He was thrown to the ground severely.

He got up, however, walked about half a mile, got into a friend's car, and was taken home. He felt weak and sick at his stomach and had a pain in his back. All at once he discovered he could not use his left leg. He had a rapid pulse, pains in various parts of his body, and loss of sensation on the left side.

For two months he was absolutely bedfast, unable to empty his bladder unassisted, and completely paralysed in his leg and thigh. During the next six or eight months he was able to get up and about with the aid of crutches and later wore an expensive and elaborate brace. He bought electrical treatment machinery and had all sorts of massage and chiropractic manipulations.

When examined, he had been paralysed, as he called it, for over a year. He was very anxious for an examination which would tell him how to get well. He had been out of work since the accident, and the allowance made by the company was not large enough to keep his family in comfort. He was a very discouraged and depressed man. His theory was that the electricity had gone through his leg and destroyed a nerve, causing it to be paralysed; and since it had occurred in the line of duty, he was entitled to compensation. He was asking fifty thousand dollars.

Now, this is a fairly typical case of industrial shell-shock or hysteria. It looked like an obvious, serious, pitiable injury to the leg. But let us see. In the first place, the electrical current in the switch which he was handling was not nearly so strong as he had supposed it to be. In the second place, even if it had been, it is almost impossible to conceive of any way in which he could have received a shock from it.

Waving these points entirely, in the third place electricity never paralyses nerves; it may burn the flesh but it never hurts the nerves! Electricity could not possibly have injured the nerves in his leg.

In the fourth place, had the nerves of this man's legs been injured in the way he believed them to have been injured, it would have produced what we call flaccid paralysis, in which the entire limb lies inert and flail-like, and all the tendon reflexes are absent. But this man's leg was not limp and the reflexes were not absent.

Fifth, sensation and motion are carried by two different sets of nerves and they could not be combined in the way in which his complaints combined them. Exactly why this is so is rather too technical to make clear here, but take my word for it.

In the sixth place, the paralysis of the kind this man believed himself to have — that is, one caused by nerve injury — is always accompanied by more or less shrinking of the muscles, but careful measurement showed him to have no such shrinking.

In other words, medical examination showed that this man could not possibly have any nerve injury, and that his leg was not paralysed as he supposed. On the other hand, however, it would be inaccurate to say that the man's symptoms were assumed. His pain and his paralysis and his disability were very real to him. Thirty years ago hysteria was regarded as a mixture of affectation, exaggeration, and deceit, but no intelligent physician believes this any more. We know now that the hysterical patient is fooling himself just as much as he is fooling anyone else; in fact, he fools himself first and last and fools the rest of us in between times. He isn't faking consciously; he is faking unconsciously.

In the example just cited we have a man never very successful, probably never very well satisfied with his occupation or his opportunities, who is suddenly very sharply frightened. In the twinkling of an eye he believes himself to have been shocked by an enormously powerful current. (Everyone knows the news story which is repeatedly turning up about the man or woman who is startled by the report of a revolver at close range and goes to the hospital for treatment, only to discover that he has no wound.) Believing this, conjuring up in his mind all the terrible possibilities he believes this may have, he promptly develops the anticipated symptoms, which have the very useful advantage of being at the same time a means of escape from arduous labour and an easier method of obtaining money.

I don't see how any industrial insurance company can handle its cases without psychiatric examination of nearly every applicant. Rarely are neurotic elements entirely absent. In this case instead of fifty thousand dollars the man was paid three thousand five hundred dollars. A few months afterwards he was reported to be perfectly well.

We may not conclude from this, however, that money is the chief object of hysterical illness. It never is. It is a secondary objective, as are also many of the apparent advantages of neurotic illness. Consider such a typical case as this, for example (*hysterical blindness*) :

" Helen D., a charming, curly headed girl of 14, was the only daughter in a rather large family of boys. On her shoulders fell the drudgery of housework. She resented doing the dishes and the cleaning, and came home every day from school unwillingly to perform her tasks. One day she was scolded by her mother; she replied sharply, and received a stinging smack across the face. Immediately she became blind." [72]

The wish to evade work did not cause the blindness, but it is a secondary gain of the illness for the child, and incidentally a method of retaliation against the harsh mother. But the real cause lies deeper, as we shall see later.

Epidemics of hysteria

The symptoms of hysteria are particularly susceptible of being evoked or dispelled by suggestion. For this reason epidemics of hysterical attacks occasionally spread through closely knit groups such as the army, where shell-shock cases sometimes occurred in showers. I once saw fourteen telephone girls who developed hysterical aphonia (speechlessness) in rapid succession. The witch scares were probably of the same nature. The following quite typical account of epidemic hysteria by a famous medical historian was written a hundred years ago:

[72] J. Fetterman in the *Journal of the American Medical Association*, Vol. XCI, no. 5 (August 4, 1928) , p. 317.

" At a cotton manufactory at Hodden Bridge, in Lancashire, a girl, on the fifteenth of February, 1787, put a mouse into the bosom of another girl, who had a great dread of mice. The girl was immediately thrown into a fit, and continued in it, with the most violent convulsions, for twenty-four hours. On the following day three more girls were seized in the same manner, and on the 17th six more. By this time the alarm was so great that the whole works, in which 200 or 300 were employed, was totally stopped, and an idea prevailed that a particular disease had been introduced by a bag of cotton opened in the house. On Sunday, the 18th, Dr. St. Clare was sent from Preston; before he arrived three more were seized, and during that night and the morning of the 19th, eleven more, making in all twenty-four. Of these, twenty-one were young women, two were girls of about ten years of age, and one man, who had been much fatigued with holding the girls [*sic!*]. Three of the number lived about two miles from the place where the disorder first broke out, and three at another factory at Clitheroe, about five miles distant, which last and two more were infected entirely from report, not having seen the other patients, but, like them and the rest of the country, strongly impressed with the idea of the plague being caught from the cotton. The symptoms were anxiety, strangulation, and very strong convulsions: and these were so violent as to last without any intermission from a quarter of an hour to twenty-four hours, and to require four to five persons to prevent the patients from tearing their hair and dashing their heads against the floor or walls. . . . As soon as the patients and the country were assured that the complaint was merely nervous, easily cured, and not introduced by the cotton, no fresh person was affected.

" To dissipate their apprehensions still further, the best effects were obtained by causing them to take a cheerful glass and join in a dance. On Tuesday, the 20th, they danced, and the next day were all at work, except two or three, who were much weakened by their fits." [73]

ALCOHOL AND DRUG ADDICTION

In the same way that certain unstable personalities whose sexual life is not well managed take refuge from the problems of life by a flight into illness, other individuals of similar make-up take refuge in a flight into alcohol or morphine. Alcohol and morphine are drugs which temporarily remove the individual

[73] J. F. C. Hecker: *The Black Death and the Dancing Mania* (written in 1832); translated by B. G. Babington. Cassell National Library edition (New York, 1888), p. 174.

from the immediate prospect of his problems. For a little while he has surcease from the struggle. Alcohol and morphine are self-administered anæsthetics. To these could be added many other things, such as nicotine, moving-picture shows, vacations, and wild parties.

The use of drugs, particularly morphine, is a peculiarly disadvantageous way of escaping reality. It involves the user in many costly complications, and leaves him less able to face his problems than before. This necessitates increasingly frequent recourse to their use. This is what constitutes addiction.

Psychiatrists do not all feel that alcohol is an unmitigated curse, but they are unanimous in believing that the use of morphine as a habit is the very ill wind that blows no one any good. The users of morphine, and many of those who think they know something about morphine addiction, are apt to think that its use is an end in itself. This is not so; it is always a means to an end; morphine is used to relieve pain. But if the pain comes from a broken leg, it will no longer be necessary when the leg is healed, whereas if it comes from a broken mind or, more accurately speaking, from a deformity or defect in the personality, morphine will always be necessary, because the pain will never cease. This is why most morphine addicts are incurable.

The public has many erroneous ideas about drug addiction. There are not nearly so many cases as is generally supposed, and the number is steadily decreasing. Very few criminals are drug addicts, and relatively few drug addicts are criminals. They are not dangerous or loathsome, but they are monstrous liars.[74]

Alcohol presents a somewhat different problem. It is a very serviceable psychic anæsthetic, and this utility easily leads to its excessive use by individuals whose unconscious struggles are particularly painful. This, in turn, is apt to lead to a psychopathic state of addiction, which is a deplorable kind of failure, complicated secondarily by the damage that alcohol does to the tissues of the brain.

The psychology of the addiction to alcohol is the psychology of insatiable needs and can only be understood by reference to the insatiable thirst of the little child who cannot live if he is deprived of the milk from his mother's breast and the love from her heart. The alcoholic addict is quite often a lovable, charming fellow who has never grown up, who is utterly dependent

---

[74] Cf., for example, A. Kossef (chief physician at Clinton Prison, New York), in *The Nation's Health*, January 1925 (Vol. VII, no. 1).

for his existence upon love administered to him in a maternal fashion (sometimes by men, however). Denied this or thwarted in it to some extent, he shows the same distress that one sees in the thwarted suckling and, just as a baby turns to its fists or toys or any other object that it can put in its mouth, so the alcoholic addict turns to liquor. In doing so, not only does he find a satisfactory substitute, but the anæsthetic effects of alcohol lull the craving for love or enable him to experience it in some other form (homosexual contact, prostitution, etc.). Moreover, it accomplishes a revenge upon the person who thwarted him — we all know how much the wives and parents of alcoholics suffer.

Theoretically, alcoholics, like other neurotics, are curable.[75] In practice a cure is exceedingly difficult. Alcoholics rarely take their addiction seriously, and their optimism is so contagious that, frantic as relatives may be during or immediately after a spree, they are easily won over by the patient's optimism into accepting the vain illusion of the promise that he will never go on one again. Alcohol addiction is an extremely serious affection, comparable with the psychoses ("insanities"). Recently alcohol addicts have been studied and treated with psychoanalysis, and considerable understanding of their special neurotic conflicts has been gained. Usually proper institutionalization must be associated with the psychoanalytic treatment. While some encouraging results have been seen, it is too early yet to evaluate the success of this form of treatment, which attempts to remould the personality make-up and resolve the neurotic conflicts that lead to addiction.[75a]

TREATMENT

Theoretically, all of the neuroses are completely curable. Practically, the cure is sometimes easy and sometimes impossible. Of this we shall have more to say in detail in the chapter on treatment.

Always it must be remembered that the neurotic patient is escaping conflict and expressing his wishes by his symptoms; that

[75] See the studies of Dr. Robert P. Knight, "Psychodynamics of Chronic Alcoholism," in the *Journal of Nervous and Mental Diseases,* and "Dynamics and Treatment of Chronic Alcohol Addiction," *Jour. Internat. Psychoanaly. Assn.* (1937).

[75a] The published work of the Research Council on Problems of Alcohol is of increasing scientific importance; on the practical side, the semi-secret, semi-religious activities of the organization of former alcohol addicts, "Alcoholics Anonymous," seem to be effective in some cases.

these symptoms represent the compromise necessarily arrived at as a result of terrific unconscious struggles helped along by certain external considerations, irritations, and precipitations. Fifty per cent or more of the people who go to doctors to be healed of their sicknesses are suffering from neuroses. Most of them can be helped, many of them cured. Many others would not under any circumstances dare to permit themselves to be cured. They live only by the grace of their symptoms.

7. THE ANTISOCIAL TYPE
(PERVERSE PERSONALITIES)

There is yet one more group. It has had many names — " psychopathic personality," " constitutional inferiority," " moral insanity," are some of them. None of these terms is adequate.

" Perverse " describes these folk better than any other single word. They are headed across-stream; they play at the game, but break all the rules. They are oftentimes possessed of good bodies, good looks, good manners; they lack neither intelligence nor perceptual powers. Their defectiveness is in their emotional and volitional functioning. They cannot keep out of trouble. They may achieve some good in the world, but the world pays dearly for it, and the net total of the individual's life is in the red.

Psychoanalytic studies have thrown considerable light on the nature of perverse personalities, especially the work of Franz Alexander, who has given them the designation *neurotic characters*. He means by this to distinguish them from neurotic *personalities,* a distinction which loses force in the English language because of the different connotation we give to the word " character," which has been literally translated from the German. The name is not important, however; what Alexander was able to demonstrate as to the psychology of these perverse personalities (neurotic characters) is that they substitute behaviour abnormalities for symptoms; that is, instead of the phobias, obsessions, back-aches, stomach distress, fears, and so on which characterize the neurotic types described above, these individuals present *behaviour* which is just as pathological and which is motivated in the same way — although apparently directed against the outside world, it always brings its perpetrator to grief. Troublesome and even dangerous as these individuals may be, they themselves always suffer worst of all, and a study of their behaviour shows that unconsciously they prearrange this. They are at cross-purposes with themselves and seem to carry out an aggressive program of defeatism.[76]

Some famous characters in history illustrate the perverse personality — Casanova and François Villon in particular — but there are better examples close at hand, more susceptible of detailed study.

One of the most notorious of these is a man picked up as a runaway boy in New York City at the age of eight and shifted about from one institution to another until he ran away and began a career of posing as a member of the European nobility without funds. He hoodwinked innumerable persons, some of them men of national importance, in spite of the fact that he was repeatedly arrested, exposed, threatened, and imprisoned. The details of his life fill many pages of extraordinary reading, throughout which one is struck by his rapid leaps from successful rascality to the ignominy of poverty and imprisonment. Over and over this cycle is repeated; the same fellow who was so clever in swindling was so unbelievably clumsy at other times as to make it certain that he unconsciously tried to get himself punished. For example, he is reported to have stolen and sold a valuable tapestry, for which he was sent to prison; immediately upon his dismissal from prison he went to the man from whom he had stolen the tapestry and sought employment in the tapestry department! When this was refused he calmly asked for the loan of some money. Once while eluding arrest he was captured in a particular place where he was recognized because of his predilection for a certain kind of imported tobacco. Some years later he went back to the same store to get the same tobacco and was on this very account again recognized and re-arrested.

Another case:

Harold was an intensely religious boy, carefully reared by a minister father and a pious mother. He was inspired to be a missionary and was already almost a pillar of the church. But in spite of his religious training Harold stole everything he could get his hands on. He was seldom suspected, for he seemed anything but a thief, and it was difficult to be-

[76] See Franz Alexander and Hugo Staub: *The Criminal, the Judge, and the Public* (New York: The Macmillan Co., 1931); and Franz Alexander: *The Psychoanalysis of the Total Personality* (Washington: Nervous & Mental Disease Publishing Co., 1930); and see Leo H. Bartemeier: " The Neurotic Character as a New Psychoanalytic Concept," *American Journal of Orthopsychiatry*, Vol. I, no. 5 (October 1931); also, Alexander: " The Neurotic Character," *International Journal of Psychoanalysis,* July 1930.

lieve that the president of the Christian Endeavour society would take money from the collection box and steal mufflers and gloves and purses from the pockets of the worshipping brethren.

As a leader of his Sunday-school class, he attended every meeting and every party. But always he came away with some piece of jewellery or with money taken from his classmates. At college he stole athletic equipment from the gymnasium. He picked up books other students left around. Even at college Y.M.C.A. meetings which he attended, things were missed.

The president of the college became interested in him and invited him to his home. During the evening Harold was caught stealing money from a drawer. He insisted he had never stolen before. His show of regret over the matter was obviously superficial, however, and he acted as if nothing serious had happened.

Under pressure, he admitted many other thefts, but did not seem sorry for them. He said he did not know why he stole; it just seemed easy and he did it. He had been stealing for a long time. His mother declared that Harold came from a family in which there had been many pilferers and thieves. His grandfather and great-grandfather, his uncles, and several cousins had all been habitual stealers.

Three years after he was dismissed from college he was occupying a church pulpit.

The female of the species

The daughter of a New York millionaire had been given everything that money could buy, without, however, effecting the happy adjustment to life which her family desired for her. From the cradle up she was a trial and a grief to her parents.

"She was not like other children, doctor," her quiet-mannered, seamy-faced old father told me. "She was born wrong. She has always wanted her own way in everything, and her way was the way of trouble and rebellion. Remonstrance, severity, threats, pleadings, punishments — they were all ineffectual. I've tried everything I know of or heard of or was advised, and all methods failed. I've taken her to schools and clinics and doctors all over the country. I've been through a thousand sessions of tears and remorse and forgiveness and promises. The outcome is always the same. She put her mother in the grave, and she has broken my heart. But one last time before I die, I'd like to make an effort to get her headed straight."

Now let us look at the girl of whom this father has such a despairing opinion. When I first saw her, she was twenty-four years old; she had a beautiful face, a shapely body; she was adorned with expensive but tastefully selected clothes. She moved with a cultivated grace and would have attracted attention anywhere because of her beauty and poise.

Only her voice would have attracted attention as out of harmony with an otherwise charming personality. It was a little hoarse, a little strident, a little tired. I might have overlooked this but for the words with which she greeted me. " So you're the doc that's going to look me over, are you? " she sneered. " Well, why doesn't the God-damned old coot have himself examined? He's the one that needs it." I could scarcely believe that she referred to the quiet, grey-haired gentleman to whom I had just been talking, but I came to realize that this was a very mild sample.

For swearing was certainly among the least of her vices. Every item on the catalogue of social sin could be charted upon her ledger. Experiences, any one of which might well form the central tragic catastrophe of a novel, had occurred in her life by the dozen. Adventurous marriages, rapid divorces, abortions, rapes, drunken debauches, scandals in high places, venereal infection, acid-throwing, detective-evading, escapades with members of the underworld — these and many other experiences made up her life story. For a long period of time she had consumed daily from one to two pints of gin and whisky, and at times this amount had been trebled.

I knew all of this to be undoubtedly true about her; what others did not tell me she told me herself. Yet knowing it, and knowing it without any question of a doubt, I could scarcely persuade myself, as I looked at this beautiful girl sitting quietly beside her austere old father, that it could possibly be true.

In the press
" If you care for romantics in bandits, Russell Scott is your man. An actor at twenty, he was a millionaire at thirty and head of a $20,000,000 corporation organized to construct a bridge from Windsor, Canada, to Detroit. A year later, Russell Scott was a cheap hold-up man robbing drug stores in Chicago's Loop. The bridge venture had bankrupted him and in the months after the crash Scott and his brother Robert coasted precipitately into crime. Russell had been successively a confidence man, a bootlegger and a drug peddler. Convicted of murdering a clerk during a small robbery and sentenced to death, Scott three times won a reprieve — twice on questions of his sanity. Funds were raised by clubwomen for his defense; all the syrupy tenderness that envelopes a good looking murderer was in evidence. And Scott was good looking. . . . Six months after his admission [to the state hospital for the insane], alienists at the institution announced that Scott had

duped the State and had never been other than sane. It was two years before Scott went to his death, and even then he cheated the law's vengeance. He hanged himself with a leather gift belt in his prison cell." [77]

Wanderlust type of perverse personality

Tramps, hoboes, vagabonds, gypsies, itinerants, ne'er-do-wells — these are usually members of this group, seeking to avoid the realities of life by perpetual flight and usually leaving society worse off for their occasional contacts with it.

> I shall smell lilac in Connecticut
> No doubt, before I die, and see the clean
> White, reticent, small churches of my youth,
> The gardens full of phlox and mignonette,
> The pasture-bars I broke to run away.
>
> It was my thought to lie in an uncropped
> And savage field no plough had ever scored,
> Between a bee-tree and a cast deer-horn.
> It was my thought to lie beside a stream
> Too secret for the very deer to find,
> Too solitary for remembrance
> It was a dream. It does not matter now.
>
> Bury me where the soldiers of retreat
> Are buried, underneath the faded star,
> Bury me where the courtiers of escape
> Fall down, confronted with their earth again.
> Bury me where the fences hold the land
> And the sun sinks beyond the pasture-bars
> Never to fall upon the wilderness-stone.
>
> And yet I have escaped, in spite of all.

— Stephen Vincent Benét: *John Brown's Body* (Garden City: Doubleday, Doran & Co., 1928), p. 341.

Successful exceptions

Some perverse personalities appear to have achieved a kind of success notwithstanding their antisocial peculiarities. Some of the following were probably perverse personalities:

Gebhard von Blücher, the famous Prussian field-marshal,

[77] Milton MacKaye in the *Outlook and Independent,* February 6, 1929, p. 205.

when a boy, was constantly engaged in adventures and duels, and failed of early promotion in the Prussian army because of his wild life.

Andrew Jackson, at the age of fifteen, dissipated in gambling, races, drinking, and cock-fighting.

Wallenstein, the famous Austrian general, was always a leader in pranks during his school and university days, was called unmanageable and rowdy, and was put in jail for damaging property.

Ben Jonson killed another actor in a duel and went to prison for it.

Richard Wagner, from his earliest years, was fond of pranks and adventures. At the age of sixteen he threw himself into all kinds of youthful excesses.

Voltaire began at the age of seventeen to drink deeply of the gay life. His father sent him away for a time, but when he returned to Paris he dissipated even more than before.

The perverse personality may have the redeeming grace of a talent or many talents. Such personalities are sometimes (wrongly) called geniuses. They occasionally accomplish great things, but always at great cost, and meantime vast armies of them fill jails, poorhouses, and freight cars.

THE TREATMENT OF PERVERSE PERSONALITIES

Until the advent of psychoanalysis we had no satisfactory treatment for these individuals. They were universally regarded by psychiatrists as hopeless. Now, however, since the clinical demonstrations of Alexander and others, we are more optimistic about their rehabilitation. Some extraordinary changes have been observed in such personalities as the result of psychoanalysis. Under such treatment they come to see that their aggressive misbehaviour is motivated by attempts to gain attention and love for which they feel so guilty that they must obtain punishment. The forces of attack, counter-attack, aggression, and submission to punishment surge back and forth through the personality like a race riot through the streets of a city, hindering the development of all legitimate business. When the origins of such resentments and aggressions are brought clearly to consciousness and compared with the altered reality situation of mature years, then and only then is it possible for the perverse personality to give up his infantile methods of obtaining love, expressing hate, and assuring for himself punishment. It takes many months for the reconstruction of such a personality but, granted some co-operation from the patient and some from his relatives, creditors, and friends, it can sometimes be accomplished.

SUMMARY OF THE CHAPTER

To summarize, seven types of personality that frequently fail have been described.

More frequently, of course, they don't fail. Failure may threaten, may impend; or it may never be more than a remote possibility. None of these personality types are *bound* to fail. Some of them, in fact, make glorious successes. I have suggested some of the famous successes under each type-heading.

And those that seem about to fail do not always do so. There are always the constructive compromises discussed at the opening of the chapter. This includes those who capitalize their weaknesses, who turn their flight into propitious directions, who divert their attack from society to the enemies of society.

Albuquerque, New Mexico, is full of doctors who have saved themselves from death by tuberculosis through healing others of it: *crippled* personalities magnificently redeemed.

I know a most typical *stupid* personality who has spent his life organizing schools for certain neglected classes of society; thousands love him, and the world honours him.

The chairman of the most successful social committee I ever knew of is an *isolated* personality — ashamed of his lowly origin and fearful lest a slip may betray the fact that he was not to the manner born.

There are *schizoid* personalities running banks and writing books and discovering bacteria and painting pictures, for whom these things are life. They know there are other people in the world, but they don't know them. They can't. But they can run banks and write books and discover bacteria and paint pictures. And they do.

And as for the *moody* people — they fascinate us just as a child does, because of his unrestrained abandon to his feelings. They lend colour and charm and variety to life with their merriment, their quick sympathy, their versatility and sparkle. Everyone knows them and everyone loves them. In fact, their lavish generosity and their great popularity often conceal from their world their childlike dependence upon others; for the moody person will do anything to gain love, but when it is denied him he reacts with bitterness and sorrow.

And the *neurotics* — that's nearly all of us — all the rest of us, anyway. How neurotics convert their miseries into other things than groans and worries has already been set down. But they, too, succeed — by compromise and struggle. Sometimes they write books about their symptoms, like William Ellery Leonard and Émile Zola. Sometimes they write books about other people's symptoms, like James Joyce and Sherwood Anderson. Sometimes they write about the world's symptoms, like Oswald Garrison Villard and Eugene O'Neill. But always — even if his work is labelled fiction — the neurotic writes about himself. He is ourself, too; so we like it. It projects our own struggle. That helps.

And *perverse* personalities that make a go of it, some way? I have just cited a list of some, and the reader knows many more. " There's Bill Chilson, the old rascal — the pest of the town, a bully, a ne'er-do-well, a social outcast in spite of his money. Look at him! A hero, now, dead in France, with monuments all over the country to his valour, and flowers about his memory. He found his niche."

But we come back to the cold fact that many *do* fail. They may fail, as we have said, by a flight which damages themselves — or by an attack which damages society. Some personalities can't " make " certain situations, and, failing even at a compromise, they become broken or breakers.

The broken personalities are the " neuroses " and the " psychoses " and the " nervous breakdowns " and the " physical breakdowns " — in short, the illnesses. They are illnesses, but they don't always turn up in the doctors' offices. It is the family physician who most frequently discovers the breakdowns from physical disease. The stupid people are first identified often by the psychologists. And the lonely personalities, whose oddities are made, not inborn, are usually discovered by the public itself. The queer (schizoid) and moody (cycloid) types are generally not discovered at all until the relatives or the police take them in hand. Sometimes they go to psychiatrists.

The neurotics may go almost anywhere — and everywhere! — to relieve their distresses. The osteopaths and chiropractors see millions of them; every living doctor is treating (often successfully) many of them; a small but fortunate minority are in the hands of the psychoanalysts.

And finally the great group of the perverse, those formerly labelled " psychopathic personalities," those that damage every-one and everything without much self-injury or suffering — these the policemen know the best, the police, judges, wardens, parole officers, county attorneys, and newspaper reporters. Not that they are all criminals, or that all criminals belong here, but a fourth to a half of all criminals are of this type.

What happens to these personalities broken in their efforts to adapt themselves to the environment? What do such wrecks look like? As I have already tried to illustrate, *they look like the personality in which they occur.*

Twenty-five years ago we thought we had discovered some-thing very important. We thought we recognized in " normal people " (whoever *they* may be) personality types which faintly resembled some of our classical psychoses (" insanities "). In-tensive study followed and some scientists even proved various physical measurements and proportions to be identical in the sane and in the sick paralleling certain psychic resemblances. The more we studied, the more we felt sure that there were per-sonalities to match each one of our more definitely delimited mental-disease pictures.

But now we believe that it's just the other way! There are psychoses — that is, mental upsets — which carry to extremes the tendencies and traits of the various personalities.

In the evolution of psychiatric thought, this is of immense im-portance. It signalizes the transfer of emphasis from the final stages of mental disaster to the study of the constituents of per-sonality. It means that we no longer think that diseases malevo-lently attack and invade certain chance individuals, any more than do witches or devils. What we call the " disease " is the logical outgrowth of the particular personality in its efforts to solve a particular problem (or perhaps several problems). The disease, the psychosis, is a part of him, not an intruder or an in-vasion from without.

Since people's minds undergo these catastrophes from which we have learned these general principles, some study of their appearance under such circumstances properly belongs here. What are the detailed manifestations of broken minds? What are the signs and symptoms? Turn to the next chapter.

CHAPTER III

SYMPTOMS

ANALYTIC SECTION, DEALING WITH THE PARTS OF THE
MACHINE DISMANTLED

"Many people are suffering from a mental disorder, who in the current estimate of their friends are considered only as eccentric, model, disagreeable, extreme, wicked, virtuous, emancipated, etc. . . .

"Is it possible that our intense devotion to a philanthropic cause may in some instances be a disorder, rather than an indication of a healthy moral superiority? Is it possible that suspicion of employers and accusations of social injustice may be a disorder, and not the expression of an enlightened and impersonal grasp of economic and social relations? Can raucous patriotism and so-called pacifism be scrutinized in the same way? Is anti-vivisectionism not altogether to be explained by a surplus of the milk of human kindness in those who level virulent and ill-founded accusations at men, working earnestly in the interests even of those who revile them? Is intense intellectual activity, in apparent devotion to the pursuit of abstract truth, sometimes

the expression of a disorder, rather than the wholesome activity of a well-balanced personality? Can the blameless and model individual, following smugly in the parental footsteps, be the victim of a disorder consisting essentially in the repression of the most productive elements in the individual's nature? Can the emancipated and unconventional individual, who is expressing his personality to the amazement of his social circle, be the victim of illusion and be really in the throes of a mild mental disorder? Is it possible that many of our beliefs, attitudes, emotions, habits, standards, are not as valid as we have assumed them to be, but are of the same stuff of which mental disorder is made?"

—C. MACFIE CAMPBELL, M. D.: *A Present-day Conception of Mental Disorders* (Cambridge: Harvard University Press, 1924), pp. 14–16

CHAPTER III

SYMPTOMS

The " parts " of the mind are not discrete like parts of an automobile. They are more like the parts of the human body. There are no sharp divisions between perception and intellection, for example, any more than between wrist and forearm. In fact, we commit a logical crime when we make such divisions — there really is no such thing as perception, for example, apart from intellection, emotion, and behaviour. But for practical purposes the delimitation is useful. It is particularly useful in studying the symptoms of disorder; we know well enough how very definitely a broken wrist differs from a broken forearm. And the same is true of the various parts of the mind and of the psychological processes.

For purposes of classification [1] all human activity can be reduced to what is called the S–R formula, where S (stimulus) stands for all the incoming forms of energy which are transformed by the body, and R (response) stands for the new forms of energy thus produced. This " response " is human behaviour, human life. How the human machine uses oxygen and sugar and fat and water in the direction of this response is the province of physiology. How it receives and acts upon light-waves, sound-waves, etc., to satisfy certain instinctive cravings is the province of psychology.

We are made aware of the world about us by sights and sounds and smells, *sensations* which our aerials catch like radio antennæ and transmit to the brain over nerve-fibres very comparable to telephone wires. Each " wire " is an elongated cell called a neurone, the minute description of which may be found in any text-book on neurology. There are three kinds: incoming or

[1] The researches of the Gestalt theorists — Köhler, Koffka, Wertheimer, *et alii* — have conclusively shown that psychological behaviour cannot be explained as the summation and correlation of discrete stimuli and discrete responses. But descriptive nomenclature never keeps pace with advance in theory and concept, so that for didactic exposition the " S–R " and " P–I–E–V " designations serve us conveniently.

sensory nerves leading from receiving apparatuses called receptors, connecting nerves or connectors, and outgoing or motor nerves leading to glands or muscles called effectors.

The brain is being bombarded constantly by millions of stimuli coming in over the receptors from inside the body and from the outside world. Most of these it disregards, so far as visible consequences indicate. But those stimuli that are important enough to be recognized are called *perceptions*. The processes of receiving stimuli and identifying or recognizing them constitute perception.

Some stimuli produce a response, muscular or glandular action directly, before they are perceived. These are called *reflexes*. The impulse enters the spinal cord in the sensory nerve and is immediately relayed to motor nerves, which carry it to its destination, thus:

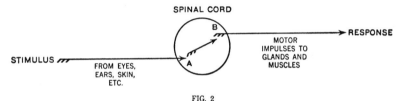

FIG. 2

In the spinal cord there are numerous junction points (*synapses*) where other nerve-fibres make connections. In order for a sensory stimulus to be *perceived,* a connection must exist from

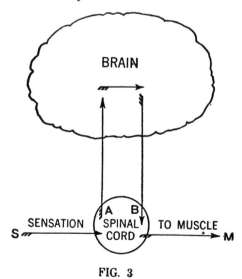

FIG. 3

the point of entrance in the spinal cord (at A) to the brain. Then in order for a motor response to result, outgoing nerve-connections must exist to carry impulses from the brain down the spinal cord and out (at B) to the muscles and glands, as in Figure 3 above.

Actually the interpolation of the brain between S (sensory stimulus) and M (motion) is much more complicated than here indicated. The psychic effect of the sensory stimulus is a *sensation,* which must be recognized by comparisons with stored memories to make *perception* possible. Such a comparison may go no further than is sufficient for recognition. It may, however, include the forming of some new groupings of ideas (memories), and incidentally the new sensation itself must be recorded. This comparing and regrouping and registering process is called " thinking," or cognition, or *intellection.* You see how difficult it is to separate it from perception; actually no sharp separation can be made. This diagram looks complicated, but it is very simple compared with what actually occurs.

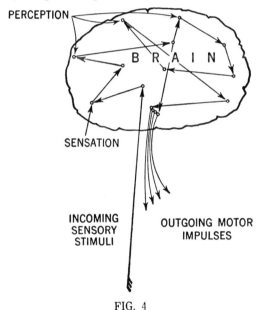

FIG. 4

Very little of what goes on is felt or known by the individual. That of which he is aware is called *consciousness;* it is a thin shell of fringe, perhaps as much in proportion as the skin of an apple is of the whole fruit. It is like the image which the eye sees of itself in the mirror, a small part of the whole optic apparatus.

But both conscious and unconscious intellection result in certain messages being sent to muscles, and also to glands, to increase or decrease their activity. The messages sent are decided upon much as the forces that move a push-ball which is being shoved about by a mass of players; some are pulling and some opposing, and the resultant or summation of them all determines or resolves the final decision. We know how this feels when we are faced with several opportunities at once, or with a pleasure-versus-duty problem. Actually all decisions are problems, but we are usually not aware of them if the forces vary greatly in strength.

The resolving of the impulses into some sort of outgoing stimulus or stimuli, which are sent to muscles to produce motions, these motions to form acts, and these acts to make up behaviour — this resolving and bringing to a focus is what *will* or *volition* or *conation* really is. It usually follows certain set patterns called habits, and hence some psychologists say that will = habit. Others make will = wish; that is, we do (hence will to do) what we wish to do, even though it may not appear to be so. But the wishing is a force far back of the resolving process —

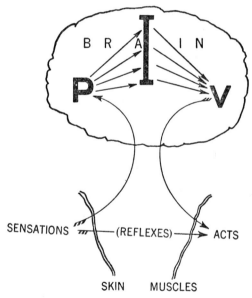

SENSATIONS —(REFLEXES)— ACTS

SKIN   MUSCLES

P = PERCEPTION   I = INTELLECTION   V = VOLITION

FIG. 5

back in the instinctive energy-transforming urge which runs the whole machinery. We do what all the forces active in the case, including our own memories, prejudices, beliefs, ideals, habits, and weaknesses, make us do. — Will ought to be used to describe this integration and resolution of forces resulting directly in motor responses. At the back of it, as we shall see, are energy drives or trends which determine the main direction and goal.

So far our diagram would appear as in Figure 5 above.

But there is another part of the cerebration. Linked to our memories, and hence to our perceivings and resolvings, there are certain secondary sensations and bodily changes called *emotions*. There is much disagreement among psychologists and

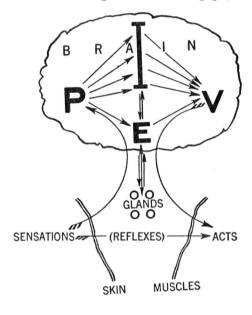

E = EMOTION

FIG. 6

physiologists as to just where emotional reactions belong in the scheme. We do know that they are dependent in some degree upon the endocrine glands of the body, so that for practical purposes they may be shown in our diagram as a connection of the brain and the body, thus emphasizing again that the mind involves the function of the entire body and not merely the contents of the skull.

So much for a review of the names of the main " parts." And what can happen to them? Wernicke, a brilliant psychologist-psychiatrist-philosopher, said that all misfunction could be classified as quantitative (that is, too much or too little) and qualitative (that is, of the wrong sort) . Irrespective of its logical faults, this classification is convenient. It covers most of the known facts. Memory, to take for example a part of one of the parts, may be deficient (one may forget) or excessive (one may remember too much, too many details) or distorted (one may remember falsely) .

So it is easy to make a little gridiron like this, containing, by implication, almost all we know of the symptoms of abnormal psychology. The words in quotation marks are the synonymous Greek stem words; those in parentheses are the technical scientific vocabulary derivatives.

	PERCEPTION "Æsthesia"	INTELLECTION "Gnosis"	EMOTION "Thymia"	VOLITION "Bulia"
DEFICIENT "Hypo"	Deficient perception (Hypoæsthesia)	Deficient intellection (Hypognosis)	Deficient emotion (Hypothymia)	Deficient volition (Hypobulia)
EXCESSIVE "Hyper"	Excessive perception (Hyperæsthesia)	Excessive intellection (Hypergnosis)	Excessive emotion (Hyperthymia)	Excessive volition (Hyperbulia)
DISTORTED "Para"	Distorted perception (Paraæsthesia)	Distorted intellection (Paragnosis)	Distorted emotion (Parathymia)	.Distorted volition (Parabulia)

FIG. 7

Instead of these general concepts like " deficient perception," " deficient intellection," etc., let us substitute in each square, just as an illustration, *one* of the familiar symptoms belonging in that category.

	PERCEPTION	INTELLECTION	EMOTION	VOLITION
DEFICIENT	Deafness	Stupidity	Apathy	Inertia
EXCESSIVE	Sensitiveness	Genius	Elation	Over-activity
DISTORTED	Hallucinations	Delusions	Phobias	Compulsions

FIG. 8

Now we shall proceed to study and illustrate these various symptoms. Sometimes they are best seen in clinical cases of maladjustment but many of them are to be observed in ourselves and others whom we consider to be essentially well adjusted. In most books on the subject the author takes up first perceptual disorders, then intellectual disorders, then emotional disorders, and finally volitional disorders. I have found from teaching-experience that it is easier for the student to grasp the idea if we take up first the *deficiencies,* then the *excesses,* and finally the *distortions.*

DEFICIENCIES

DEFICIENT PERCEPTION

Anything that impairs the antennæ with which we keep in contact with the world will, of course, impair our ability to adjust ourselves to it. Radios with bad aerials, submarines with broken periscopes, and human beings with deficient perceptual machinery are in comparable states of disadvantage.

Hence diminished acuteness of vision, hearing, and all the rest of the senses constitutes real and important difficulties in the effecting of smooth life adjustments. These defects may be merely transitory. Physical illness, drowsiness, alcoholic intoxication, and other conditions may temporarily induce these limitations. But many individuals are permanently handicapped by one or several types of perceptual deficiency, particularly deafness. A survey of school-children in 1928 disclosed that there are over three million deafened children in this country. This means three million children whose mental functioning, whose adjustment to the demands of life, is definitely impaired at the outset by a limitation or crippling of the receiving apparatus.

Deficiencies in perception — deafness, for example — cause trouble in three ways. First of all, they cause the individual to lose entirely certain stimuli, certain signals, certain information. Secondly, they make necessary a considerable waste of energy in the effort voluntarily to overcome the handicap. Eye-strain, headaches, and ear-strain are familiar examples of this. And, finally, all such deficiencies, like all other human deficiencies, bring about emotional reactions on the part of the individual which are usually unhappy. Some cases will illustrate this.

Visual defect, handicap, depression

Janet had always been popular. When she graduated from the art-school and went to work with an interior decorating firm, she became the most successful and most popular interior decorator in the city. She was invited out a great deal by her wealthy clients, and life seemed very rosy to her.

A sudden illness left her, at twenty-eight, with her eyesight seriously impaired. She was able to continue her work, but she was haunted by a terrible fear that her eyes would become worse and she would have to be financially dependent upon someone else. Her eyes became her chief thought. She would not go to movies or read even the headlines of the newspapers. Even being in the dark, she thought, strained her eyes.

She became very depressed and despondent. She could never again enjoy the things that her friends enjoyed. She could never marry, for who would want a half-blind wife? She refused all social invitations and avoided her friends; she felt remote from them; they lived in a world of happiness that she had once known and would never know again. There was really very little reason for her to live.

To make it clear that this patient was crippled chiefly by the secondary effects of the affliction, I may add that after four years of such suffering she was given an entirely new start in her life-work by some properly administered psychotherapy.

Deafness, handicap, delusions

Guy Reynolds was thirty years old when he first began to suspect that he was getting hard of hearing. He noticed that in conversation he often missed one or two important words and was forced to ask that they be repeated or else lose the conversation. As it became increasingly difficult for him to hear everything that was said, it occurred to him that perhaps his friends were purposely dropping their voices in order to humiliate him by forcing him to ask what had been said. He determined to watch closely and thought several times he detected them laughing at him behind his back when he did not understand what was said. Sometimes they said things and laughed uproariously; he was sure that they were laughing at him. Sure enough, it was just as he had thought. They were trying to make him the laughing-stock of the town. Probably they made jokes at his expense in his very presence and then told him that they had said something else. Probably everyone in town was talking about him and bringing about occasions to make him appear ridiculous. He began refusing all invitations; people only asked him so that they could laugh at him, taking advantage of his deafness.

Visual defect, handicap, inferiority feelings

When Charles was a baby, it was discovered that there was something seriously wrong with his eyes. By the time he was two years old he had had four operations, and the difficulty had been corrected to some extent, but it had been found necessary for him to wear very thick-lensed glasses for the rest of his life. Because he could not see as well as the other children he played with, who could therefore excel him in all games and sports, he avoided playing with them and withdrew into an imaginary world of his own where his imaginary playmates treated him as their superior. Throughout his boyhood he continued living this seclusive life, firmly convinced that his visual defect was an insurmountable barrier between him and those who would otherwise have been his companions. When he went to college he was self-conscious, diffident, and very sensitive to slights. He worried for fear he would fail to recognize people he knew and not speak to them. He felt left out because the other boys, realizing that he was not like them, did not include him in their activities, and he looked on at them from the side-lines, never joining them "because my eyesight is so poor I can't do the things that other people do."

On the other hand, many people with perceptual deficiencies do not recognize their own handicaps. They may recognize that they are failing, but they don't know why. They blame it on the weather, or their liver, or their ancestors. A young woman was once referred to me because, although alert and intelligent, she had never been able to interest herself in any literature aside from newspapers and short stories. No emotional causes for this disinclination could be found, but an eye-examination — she had never had one before — revealed a visual defect of about ninety per cent! Glasses reduced this to about twenty-five per cent and she developed an immediate and grateful fondness for books!

This girl did not know she was nearly blind, and many people do not know they are deafened. There is this much to justify the routine examination of school-children. But they should be examined from the point of view that their hearing is a part of their mental functioning, and not merely as a criterion for deciding to move their seats or to extract their tonsils.

There are numerous other clinical forms of perceptual deficiency based upon some structural injury to the receiving apparatus, the terminal sense organs, the nerves that connect these organs with the spinal cord, the spinal cord itself, the various association tracts in the brain, or the recognition centres of the brain. These things are properly the field of neurology. Neurology means two things in science: neuroanatomy and clinical neurology. The former is the anatomical study of the central nervous system and all its connections and extensions, microscopically and macroscopically examined. In this sense it is the most complex department of anatomy. *Clinical* neurology is the branch of medicine which deals with diseases of these same structures. It has been carried to a very high degree of precision by many generations of patient, conscientious clinicians working in conjunction with experimental physiologists, anatomists, and neuropathologists. In theory, neurologists are not particularly interested in total personality adjustments or maladjustments, the field of psychiatry, but in practice they *are* interested in it, and many of them have made important contributions to psychiatry. Freud, it will be remembered, began as a neurologist.

Neurology and psychiatry cannot be sharply separated. To understand psychiatry, it is important to have a basic, well-grounded knowledge of neurology. For this reason recommended texts have been included in the Bibliography.

Apparent deficiency in perceptual functions may result from what we will call emotional interference. A man may become blinded with rage, for example; a child may be too overwhelmed with anxiety to hear or see correctly. These phenomena are of enormous importance and will be thoroughly discussed from several viewpoints later in the book. For our present purposes, however, we shall assume that perceptual deficiencies either are of organic (structural) origin or appear to be and are reacted to in precisely the same way as if they were structural. In either case the personality has within itself certain resources which are consciously called upon to assist in the maladjustment which results from a failure to perceive correctly the external world in order to make the best immediate adjustment to changes in it.

COMPENSATION

Fortunately there is a mechanism deep in the interior of the human mind which automatically endeavours to make up for deficiencies of any sort — perceptual, physical, social, or whatever. This compensation is sometimes automatically and unconsciously accomplished, but sometimes it is a deliberate, conscious process. In either case it tends to make for more satisfactory adjustments than had been achieved in the few cases cited above.

For the purpose of illustrating these compensations as they apply to perceptual deficiencies, let us narrow our attention to deafness and blindness, since they are the most common and most important.

Perceptual accommodations to deafness may take the form of conscious, deliberate over-development of another faculty or function, such as lip-reading. Lip-reading should be taught to every deaf, or deafened, child as early as his condition is discovered. The sense of touch similarly may be developed far beyond ordinary necessities and to incredible degrees. Thus a blind girl has recently been studied [2] whose tactile acuity was so great that she could do feats no less remarkable than that of reading the newspaper headlines by feeling them with her fingertips.

Intellectual shifts are another means of compensation. These are the various philosophical attitudes and attacks, the point of view that hearing, for example, is not an end in itself, but only a means to an end, and, provided the end can be otherwise obtained, is not worth having. Earnest Elmo Calkins, a very successful business man of New York who is completely deaf, says in an eloquent dissertation that he finds the balance-sheet of available joys for the average deafened person leaves him still happily solvent.

The trouble with such philosophizings is that, in spite of the most ardent presentation, they leave the actual sufferer somewhat cold. They are analogous to the silly exhortations which every nervous patient is obliged to endure from all his relatives and friends who are sure that if he would only buck up and get control of himself and try not to be sick, and so forth, all his troubles would disappear. Anyone who understands the essential psychological nature of nervous diseases knows how much this is like telling a man in mid-ocean that if he will swim to shore he won't drown.

There is a second type of intellectual accommodation to handicap which is in the nature of a flight, but a worthy flight.

[2] T. J. Williams in the *Journal of the American Medical Association,* Vol. LXXIX, p. 1331 (October 14, 1922).

This is the development of a refuge in some avocation or hobby. The reading of books is one of the best. As a therapeutic measure as well as a hygienic preventive, this is exceedingly commendable. Gardening is even better.

Among emotional compensations the saving grace of a sense of humour ought to be mentioned first. If the temperament of the patient is such that he can laugh with the crowd, even at himself, he will be spared much suffering, and the very laughter will help him in a more general adjustment. Unfortunately, it is too often the case that this is impossible for him. Such persons then are the more deeply wounded, and the element of wishing not to hear complicates the organic deficiency. All deafened people know that it is easier to hear pleasant than unpleasant things.

Over-compensation

Some individuals achieve veritable success, not only in spite of their handicap, but because of it. This is called *over-compensation*. Sometimes it is quite unconscious, as, for example, in the case of Mozart, Beethoven, and Bruckner, all of whom were deaf, but became great musicians notwithstanding. The Adlerian theory holds that it was an unconscious but premonitory warning of their deafness which stimulated their interest in beautiful sounds; similarly, visual anomalies and defects are reported by Adler to be very prevalent among art-students and artists, pulmonary diseases among singers and actors, etc. Be that as it may, there are many who have achieved greatness in spite of perceptual deficiencies. The sculptor Gonnelli, who became blind at the age of twenty, was able to execute excellent portraits in terracotta, it being sufficient for him merely to pass his hand over a face to produce an exact likeness. " Dr. Nicholas Sanderson, who lost his sight before he was twelve months old, became professor of mathematics and optics at the University of Cambridge. It is recorded of him that his sense of touch was so exquisite that in a collection of Roman coins he could distinguish the genuine from the false by feeling them, though counterfeits had deceived the keen eyes of connoisseurs. Nor was his hearing less acute; he was able to determine the dimensions of a room into which he was introduced for the first time, and his distance from the wall at any point from where he might be placed." [3] Sir Joshua Rey-

---

[3] Robert Kingman: "A Study in Variation," *Long Island Medical Journal,* Vol. XXII, no. 10 (October 1928) . Cf. Alec Templeton, the great (blind) pianist.

nolds, the most popular painter of his time, who in one year had over six hundred sittings for portraits, became deaf at twenty-seven; the Earl of Chesterfield, Governor General of Ireland and one-time patron of Samuel Johnson, was deaf all his life, and in his old age became blind. Other great figures who were deaf, or deafened, include Harriet Martineau, philosopher, economist, and author; Pinturicchio, a great painter of the fifteenth century; Julius Cæsar; George Washington; Kitto, of *Pictorial Bible* fame; and, in modern times, Theodore Roosevelt, Ismet Pasha, Carolyn Wells, Grace Ellery Channing, Dorothy Canfield Fisher, and Thomas A. Edison.

Among sixty prominent New Yorkers who are known to be deaf, I found thirteen physicians — most of them otologists! Eleven are lawyers, so that these two professions, in both of which hearing is so important, comprise forty per cent of the list. Of the others, seven are bankers and seven are business men, six are journalists, four are novelists, three are manufacturers, two are in religious work, and there is one in each of the following vocations: architecture, cartooning, farming, politics, teaching, general science, and music.

There are many illustrations of various over-compensations for physical injury, defect, and disease. Ted Shawn seems to me to be one of the most remarkable. Shawn had infantile paralysis and became a great dancer! A lesser but more versatile genius recently died in Louisville, Kentucky.

Charles Lee Cook, who never walked a step, so turned his handicap into an asset that he could turn down a forty-thousand-dollar-a-year job. From a hopelessly crippled child, taken out of school at the age of seven because his parents thought he would never live to be benefited by an education, he became an invalid business man of international reputation. Cook numbered among his accomplishments the invention of an automatic lubricating device that has since come into use on almost all engines, and a machine which enables one unskilled workman to do as much work as had been accomplished by thirty skilled mechanics. He was an authority on the history of languages, had a vocabulary of over thirty-seven thousand words, and reproduced in miniature Rembrandt's *Night Watch* so accurately that enlargements thrown on the screen show not one of the figures a quarter of an inch out of place or proportion. Yet he was unable to hold in his hands anything weighing over a few ounces. He designed and constructed at Brunswick, Georgia, creosoting works which are remarkable for vision and technique in architecture. One of his last accomplishments was to design and build a miniature river-steamer of the old-style type, which has 3,500 horse-power, a maximum speed of twenty miles per hour, and a capacity of 3,000 tons net burden, and yet can navigate in seven feet of water when fully loaded. (Abstracted from an article in the *American Magazine* for April 1920.) [3a]

Decompensations

But while a few are succeeding like this, a great many more are failing. The fact of the deficiency remains larger than the fact of the compensation. The battle for supremacy is a continuous conflict. There are all degrees of victory, as we have seen; similarly, there are all degrees of failure. Space prevents illustrating this here, since these mechanisms are the subject of another chapter, but for the sake of completeness the chief stages or types of failing compensation should be listed and briefly described. In order [4] of increasing severity of degree, they are:

1. A simple *failure in suppression,* with a painful awareness of the conscious aspects of the complex — for example, hypersensitiveness as regards the fact of being partly blind or deaf;

2. Mild *failure in repression,* manifested in a painful awareness of what should be unconsciously solved conflicts — for example, the psychic pain of the sense of inferiority engendered by blindness or deafness;

3. Inadequate *compensatory efforts* made as a defence against the pains just described; for example, strivings to win social esteem stimulated by fear of failure, inferiority, ridicule; accompanied by varying degrees of tension, fear, shame, hate, fear of competition and of being exposed, suspiciousness, and various bodily symptoms;

4. *Regression* to a still lower adaptation — that is, a partial failure to compensate in spite of all these strivings is relieved by

---

[3a] Extraordinary over-compensatory reactions not only to perceptual deficiencies but to other handicaps are always highly inspirational and, hence, frequently cited in the lay press and in some books on popular psychology. The career of Glenn Cunningham, the Kansas boy whose legs were so burned in childhood that he was expected never to walk again but who became the fastest mile runner in the world, is well known to many. (See *Reader's Digest,* November 1934, and *Liberty* Magazine, August 4, 1934.) Wayland F. Vaughan in *The Lure of Superiority* (Holt) and V. E. Fisher in *Introduction to Abnormal Psychology* (Macmillan, 1937), cite numerous other excellent examples.

[4] This series was pointed out and elaborated by E. J. Kempf in *The Autonomic Functions and the Personality* (New York: Nervous & Mental Disease Publishing Co., 1921).

permitting the whole mental organization to slip back into earlier, easier, and more comfortable irresponsible ways. The individual becomes more childlike — a condition known as psychic infantilism. There is a tendency to the evasion of duty and of responsibility and toward inefficiency, apathy, and, above all, depression;

5. *Dissociation,* a further flight from adjustment, really an almost complete failure to compensate, so that the individual is dominated by the uncontrollable elements of the unconscious. Then there appear, as if they were a part of real life, such very unreal things as delusions, hallucinations, etc. These, in short, are symptoms popularly known as " insanity." This is a theoretically possible but very rare consequence of deafness, blindness, and other perceptual deprivations.

DEFICIENT INTELLECTION

We have seen that the perception of a need of a new adjustment to changing reality situations may be quantitatively deficient. Naturally this impairs the subsequent thinking, feeling, and behaviour reactions in such a person. The receiving apparatus may be intact, however, and a deficiency appear in the handling of the messages received — that is, in the process of intellection or in the product, intelligence.

Psychologists and philosophers have wasted much time and paper trying to decide just what constitutes intelligence, whereas almost any school-child can tell you in a minute that it is the ability to learn and to use appropriately what has been learned. Knowledge is the material stored; intelligence is the capacity for using it. Hence one can understand why knowledge may be added to as long as one lives, but the learning capacity — that is, the intelligence or intellectual ability, — reaches a maximum early in life, generally before twenty, and thereafter it remains essentially unchanged. Defect of knowledge constitutes ignorance; defect of intellect constitutes stupidity.

Intelligence measurement

A curious thing about intelligence is its direct relationship with the time element — that is, with the individual's age. Just as there is normally an increment in physical growth with time, so there is likewise normally an increment in intellectual growth with time. It should be remembered that growth does not necessarily take place at the same rate in all individuals nor is the rate of growth of either physique or intelligence absolutely constant. But since the conditions under which most people live are fairly constant, so the rate of growth is fairly constant for certain periods of their lives. It was assumed that these ratios (I.Q.'s) were unchangeable in the course of the life of one individual. Recent studies,[5] however, have conclusively demonstrated that if conditions change (neglected children placed in good foster homes, for example), the I.Q. changes.

In the beginning of the century Simon and Binet were engaged in the task of developing a method of ascertaining the number of mentally retarded children in the French schools and of measuring the degree of the stupidity more accurately than just calling them half-wits (and quarter-wits and three-quarter-wits). Binet and Simon worked out some tests that gave us a scale of measuring intelligence on an age basis. They tried out various groups of questions until they found some that most ten-year-old children could pass, then another set that most eleven-year-olds could pass, then another for twelve-year-olds, and so on.[6]

The score achieved by a child on such a test may be compared with his actual age and they should be approximately the same. A child of twelve should pass the tests for twelve-year-olds, etc. The chronological age divided into the test-score age or " mental age " gives what is called the intelligence quotient, or I.Q. It is usually expressed as if it represented so many hundredths, or, in other words, it is practically equivalent to percentage. For example, a ten-year-old boy who could only pass tests for six-year-olds would be said to have an intelligence quotient of 6 divided by 10, times 100, which equals 60. Sixty is the I.Q. of this boy; he might also be said to have sixty per cent of the normal intelligence for that age, but this expression is never used. Strictly speaking, it is incorrect.

Compare the distribution of intelligence among individuals (freshmen) in a college, and the individuals (soldiers) in the United States Army, as indicated in the following table:

---

[5] George D. Stoddard and Beth L. Wellman: *Child Psychology* (New York: The Macmillan Co., 1934).

[6] This was done early in the twentieth century, and, although much elaborated and varied since then by hundreds of psychologists, the original tests have not been greatly improved.

Alpha Score	U. S. Army Soldiers (1917)	Washburn College Freshmen (1927)	Approximate Mental Age [7]
135—212	4%	46%	18 and over
105—134	9%	35%	$16\frac{1}{2}$ to 18
75—104	17%	17%	15 to $16\frac{1}{2}$
45— 74	25%	2%	13 to 15
25— 44	20%	0	11 to 13
15— 24	15%	0	$9\frac{1}{2}$ to 11
0— 14	10%	0	Below $9\frac{1}{2}$

It can be seen from this that college attracts a population about half of which is in the highest ranges of intelligence while in the army, a cross-section of the general population, only about four per cent fall into this high stratum. Looking at the other end of it, these figures would indicate that seventy per cent of the population would find itself unequal to college requirements (with a two per cent exception). This gives an inkling of present information regarding the distribution of intelligence ranges.

There is nothing mysterious about intelligence tests, although they appear to have perplexed and irritated mightily some of the intelligensia whose prejudices exceed their information.[8] Intelligence isn't personality — it's just intelligence. And it can be measured just as one measures wheat or height or volts, except that our scales are not yet quite so definitely marked off. Wheat shrinks in the bin, and voltage may vary on the wires — and so with the evidences of intelligence. But in general it can be measured.

The use of intelligence tests has been much abused, however, because of a lack of understanding of their specific value and limitations. On the one hand, they have been supposed to test and diagnose the total personality of the subject completely. They were never designed to test personality, but only one aspect of it, intelligence. On the other hand, it has been supposed by some that the test scores, since they apply to intelli-

[7] As explained above, mental age is an arbitrary designation, varying somewhat with the tests used. The generally accepted maximum is somewhere from 16 to 20. It is impossible to correlate these arbitrary figures exactly with definite figures, such as the score made on an Alpha test.

[8] " I hate the impudence of a claim that in fifty minutes you can judge and classify a human being's predestined fitness in life. I hate the sense of superiority which it creates and the sense of inferiority which it imposes." Walter Lippmann, in the *New Republic*, December 27, 1922, pp. 116–22.

gence primarily, were wholly unaffected by other personality factors such as emotional conflicts, endocrine disturbances, fatigue, anxiety. Yet common sense tells us that one cannot think so well when worried, tired, or ill. This brings up the greatest folly that has pursued intelligence testing: namely, the erroneous belief in the infallibility and unchangeability of the I.Q. In no other fields, even that of physical measurement, where the measuring instruments are so much more accurate, is so much faith placed in the results. Educational programs, court decisions, medical diagnoses, and even institutionalization of children have been decided in some instances solely on the basis of test scores. Yet it is well known by psychiatrists that the test scores made on intelligence tests may vary greatly according to the physical, social, and emotional conditions under which the test was given. I saw the intelligence quotient of an eleven-year-old boy rise from 65 to 90 over a period of three years while under psychoanalytic treatment.[9]

The intelligence quotient is probably the least important information given by intelligence tests, since the score of a tested individual may be impaired by anxiety and maladjustment. Technical details within the test itself, inconsistencies, and discrepancies are used by the skilled psychologist as clues for the diagnostic appraisal of these impairments.[10]

Other kinds of psychological tests

In the last ten years psychology has turned its attention to the study of aspects of the personality other than merely intelligence. This has come to practical expression in a number of personality tests of great usefulness in clinical psychiatry.

The *personality questionnaires* (Bernreuter, Bell, Minnesota, *et al.*) constitute one group of these newer tests. These require the subject to answer a considerable number of direct questions about himself. They are, in short, self-administered, standardized interviews. On the basis of statistical experience they are

[9] See Leona Chidester: "Therapeutic Results with Mentally Retarded Children," *American Journal of Orthopsychiatry*, Vol. IV, pp. 464–76 (October 1934); and Nathan W. Ackerman and C. F. Menninger: "Treatment Techniques for Mental Retardation in a School for Personality Disorders in Children," *American Journal of Orthopsychiatry*, Vol. VI, pp. 294–312 (April 1936).

[10] Our information on this subject has recently been summarized in practical and extended form. See Rapaport, Gill, and Schafer: *Manual of Diagnostic Psychological Testing* and *Diagnostic Psychological Testing: The Theory, Statistical Evaluation and Diagnostic Application of a Battery of Tests*, both to be published in 1944.

scored and yield a certain measurement of neuroticism and of introversion-extroversion tendencies. While both of these concepts are rather vague, these tests can be quite useful in the hands of an experienced examiner; used mechanically or as a parlour game they can be very misleading and do more harm than good.

The tests known as *projective techniques* are of a much higher order, scientifically and practically. They are based on the postulate that when a person reacts to unfamiliar material or organizes it to a greater or lesser extent for interpretation, his mode of doing so is characteristic of him, characteristic of his reactions generally. Various materials (called " unstructured situations ") have been tried out for such tests in an attempt to develop objective scoring systems for them and to establish the principles by which the unique features of any particular individual's performance can be translated into a description of his personality. Among these tests the most important are the following:

In *play-techniques* a child's use of toys and the form of the game he develops are observed and used not only diagnostically (Bühler,[11] Ackerman) but therapeutically (Erikson, Levy).

In the *Rorschach Test* the subject's perceptual organization of inkblots is reflected in his answers to the question: " What could this be? " This test has become the one most generally known and used of all the projective tests. (See Bibliography.)

In the *Thematic Apperception Test* [12] the subject is shown photographs of situations regarding which he is asked to make up a story. The structure of the stories, the strivings expressed in them, and the figures described in them allow for interpretations of the subject's deepest yearnings and his picture of his world.

Tests utilizing free or restricted drawing, painting, finger painting, and allied techniques have been also extensively experimented with (W. Wolf, Schmiedl-Wahner), although they have not become as definitely crystallized or useful as the preceding. Even graphology, so often discredited, seems likely to prove of some value as a diagnostic test, although its scientific analysis still lags.

[11] Charlotte Bühler: *Kindheit und Jugend.* Leipzig: S. Hirzel, 1931. See also Wally Reichenberg: "The Bühler Test as an Index of Environmental Influence on Child Development," *Bulletin of the Menninger Clinic,* Vol. I, pp. 70–7 (January 1937).

[12] Henry A. Murray: *Explorations in Personality* (New York, Oxford University Press, 1938).

Still another line of psychological testing is for the purpose of vocational advice. Of course intelligence and personality tests are used here, but they usually do not suffice for specific counsel; vocational interests and aptitudes must be explored. Tests have been prepared (the best is Strong's) that require the subject to express a number of preferences as between different activities, hobbies, and occupations, and these replies are scored on the basis of material obtained from persons successful in different occupations. The results of this apparently mechanical procedure are often surprisingly valid and understandable in dynamic and psychological terms. The aptitude tests investigate such things as motor skill, speed, orderliness, and mechanical grasp in persons likely to enter occupations in which these play a role.

Achievement tests should be mentioned; these are standardized indicators of acquired knowledge and information and are useful in checking, for example, school grade accomplishment.

SPECIAL DISABILITIES

Quantitative estimates of intelligence must be supplemented by qualitative studies. It has been found that certain individuals have what are called specific disabilities of intelligence. The public knew this long before the psychologists would admit it. That arithmetic is particularly difficult for some otherwise intelligent persons should be no more surprising than that some good athletes cannot play football.

Failure to learn to spell, for example, is frequently symptomatic of general incompetence, though not so frequently as failure in reading. " Quite a number of children will be found whose achievement in spelling shows marked discrepancy with general capacity. Spelling is more mechanical than reading, so that the stupid may more easily master it by tireless drill, while the intelligent are not likely to derive so much pleasure from it or to practice it so much." [13] Hollingworth cites two cases illustrating discrepancy between general intelligence and ability to spell: (1) a boy, fourteen years and two months of age, who had been in school since his sixth year, was of average intelligence, but he scored below first grade in spelling; and (2) a girl, aged twelve and a half years, who had been in school six years, had a

13 Leta S. Hollingworth: *Special Talents and Defects* (New York: The Macmillan Co., 1923).

mental age of seven years and four months, but in spelling was of fifth grade ability.

Now compare their spelling performance, as indicated in the two columns below:

Boy (Mental age 14 years)	Girl (Mental age 7 years, 4 months)
canmat	cannot
Supteber	September
bande	burned
howsus	houses
centeer	center
——	thoundred
fefety	fifty
——	familys
tefomter	defends
peavely	bravly

Recently some interesting discoveries have been made in studying these children who cannot read or write well. Apparently some of them never overcome an innate tendency to do things, including reading, from right to left instead of from left to right, so that *cat* is seen by them as *tac; dog* as *god; come* as *emoc; here* as *ereh; now* as *won.* Sometimes they read alternately from left to right and then from right to left. This is the course followed by the ploughing oxen of old Greece, whence Orton [14] coined the term *strephosymbolia,* from the Greek *boustrophedon* (*bouz,* ox; *strepho,* I turn; *strophe,* a turning) .

Interesting and valuable as this work is, however, the inhibiting effect of emotional disorders on the development of the intelligence is vastly more important. It is more important because it is a more general principle, affects far more children, and has even better therapeutic possibilities. According to this theory (it has really gone far past the theoretical stage) , the children's capacity to learn depends in a large measure upon the emotional attitude, toward the teacher and toward reality, and

[14] Samuel T. Orton: "The Development of Speech Understanding in Relation to Intelligence," *Child Research Clinic Series in the Woods Schools,* Vol. I, no. 6 (1936) ; " 'Word-Blindness' in School Children," *Archives of Neurology and Psychiatry,* Vol. XIV, pp. 581–615 (November 1925) ; "Physiological Theory of Reading Disability and Stuttering in Children," *New England Journal of Medicine,* Vol. CXC, pp. 1046–52 (November 22, 1928) ; "Special Disability in Spelling," *Bulletin of the Neurological Institute,* New York, Vol. I, pp. 159–92 (June 1931) .

if these emotional attitudes are seriously disturbed, the learning process is disturbed. A college freshman who develops a violent love-affair cannot be expected to master calculus, a high-school girl whose father is accidentally killed cannot be accused of stupidity if she fails that year in Latin. Yet the emotional storms that brood over the seas of early childhood, without any such tragic external events as these are far more disturbing and find the child far less prepared to withstand them.

There are now plenty of reports of painstaking work uncovering in particular instances the precise nature of the emotional conflicts which brought about special learning disabilities.[15] We shall have more to say about this in Chapter VI.

DEFECTS OF MEMORY

All that goes to make up intelligence we do not know, but that memory is a very important constituent we do know.

All intelligent people have good memories, although they may not be able to use them well, and hence think they haven't. " I keep forgetting," or " I cannot memorize anything," they say. But these are rough and misleading tests.

Real deficiencies of memory are of three kinds, corresponding with the three phases of the memory process:

1. Defective recording;
2. Defective retention;
3. Defective reproduction.

1. *Defective recording* (granted a normal receiving apparatus) is chiefly a matter of lack of attention. Experiences, or stimuli, are not remembered because they were not adequately perceived in the first place. This is the common type of memory fault in students. Of course there are usually reasons to be sought as to *why* the attention is so errant; these are emotional, physical, environmental, etc. The deafened child who does not

15 See, for example, Ralph C. Hamill: " Emotional Factors in Mental Retardation," *Archives of Neurology and Psychiatry*, Vol. XXXVI, pp. 1049–67 (November 1936) ; Emanuel Miller: " Emotional Factors in Intellectual Retardation," *Journal of Mental Science*, Vol. LXXIX, pp. 614–25 (October 1933) ; Edward Liss: " Libidinal Fixations as Pedagogic Determinants " *American Journal of Orthopsychiatry*, Vol. V, pp. 126–32 (April 1935) ; Melanie Klein: *Psychoanalysis of Children* (New York: W. W. Norton & Co., 1932) ; Anna Freud: *Introduction to Psychoanalysis for Teachers* (London: George Allen & Unwin, 1931) ; and Mary Chadwick: *Difficulties in Child Development* (New York: John Day Co., 1928) .

hear without special effort becomes fatigued, his attention flags, his memory-recording suffers, his progress slackens.

Take the case of Helen Smith, who had done superior work in college during her first three years. In the latter part of her junior year she fell violently in love. The summer brought this to a climax and she returned to college engaged to be married and much puzzled as to whether or not she should leave college for this purpose. She sat through her classes and recited in a perfunctory manner when called upon. At the time of final examinations she found herself unable to remember anything about the details of her courses. She failed completely in ten hours of work. Her attention had been so distracted by her personal problems and day-dreaming that although she had been present and heard every recitation, she could recall nothing.

Sometimes what appears to be defective registration is not just that, but an interference with the process of recollection. There are many cases on record in which, under hypnotism or anæsthesia, an individual relates long-forgotten trifles or is able to describe minutiæ of a friend's clothing or other environmental details at which he had had but a fleeting glance. Theoretically, one glance at the newspaper photographs it on the mind so that under hypnosis various unread portions may be " seen " in imagery and read; but, fortunately for the efficiency of ordinary living, this hypermnesis (excessive memory power) rarely becomes consciously active, however valuable it might be in certain situations.

2. *Defective retention* is always due to an injury to the brain causing " organic " or structural changes. It occurs familiarly in concussion of the brain, skull fracture, etc., and in the less acute and more progressive injuries, such as the atrophic processes of old age. Even in some of these cases, however, spontaneous or hypnotic recovery of the loss indicates the participation of psychological mechanisms.

Bert Anderson was playing his third year on the varsity eleven. In one of the more strenuous games of the season he was thrown heavily to the ground by an opposing tackle, his head striking sharply. He got up promptly and after a few minutes' encouragement by the other players resumed play. It was necessary to remove him, however, after about fifteen minutes because of his increasing irritability and inclination to quarrel with the other players. He was taken to his fraternity house, where he remained somewhat delirious for several hours. He recognized me immediately and thought it was absurd that he should be confined in bed and wanted to know why he should be and why he was there. The next day he still had no recollection of why he had been put to bed. He did not remember any of the football game, either the part in which he played *before* he was injured, or the part in which he played *after* he had been injured. There had been a loss of memory retention for events both prior and subsequent to the injury, technically called *anterograde* and *retrograde amnesia*.

A successful merchant of about fifty-five, who apparently was in excellent health, began to be distressed by the fact that he could not remember the names of customers whom he had known for years.

When they came to his store he found himself quite unable to think who they were or what previous business they had had with him. In order to prevent his embarrassment, he developed a habit of jocular persiflage. He did much back-slapping, hand-shaking, and joking in an effort to cover up the fact that he did not know precisely to whom he was talking or what the business in hand might be. This tendency seemed to progress and became increasingly distressing to him. Persons with whom he had begun business transactions only a few weeks before would return to complete them, only to meet with puzzled forgetfulness on the part of the old merchant. His forgetfulness extended slowly so that he could not remember his own telephone number or his own street address, then the names of his neighbours and closest friends and the names of the streets of his city.

Within a few years his retention of the ordinary facts of his environment had been so completely lost that he had to be taken to work by his wife, being quite unable to find his way about the town in which he had lived all his life; and when he was once at work, his chief function was confined to signing his name and discussing trivial matters of immediate concern.

In spite of this extraordinary stripping of memory, really leaving the poor fellow quite helpless in the world, he was able, by means of jocular loquaciousness and affability, to maintain his social position fairly well; he was a member of a prominent luncheon club and attended regularly. His condition was entirely unknown to the majority of the members. He would carry on a patter of unimportant remarks about the weather and their state of health and the program of the day, which he could remember five or ten minutes after he had heard it, and his friends thought of him as a kindly, amiable, somewhat childish old gentleman.

This case was probably caused by hardening of the arteries of the brain so that the supply of blood nourishing the cells of the brain became diminished and the cells dried up and ceased functioning. Something similar to this in less extreme degree takes place naturally in many cases of senility, and older people expect to become slightly forgetful.

Occasionally it occurs in middle age. No one knows the cause.

For example, a woman we will call Mrs. Brown was admitted to the Topeka State Hospital in her forty-third year. She was a beautiful woman, in excellent physical health, and made a very fine first impression. She sat so quietly and with such poise and self-assurance that it seemed incredible that her alert face should hide such amazing vacuity. As a matter of fact, over a period of two years she had lost almost every memory that she had. She could not remember the names of her three children, nor even how many she had, or if she had any; she had no idea what her husband's name was, where they had lived, what he did, how she came to be in the hospital, or, in fact, anything about herself or the people about her. When asked her name, she laughed somewhat nervously and gave it hesitatingly, as if she were not quite sure even of that. This was a case of what is known technically as *Alzheimer's disease.*

Instead of an even, generalized loss, the memory may be defective in " patches," most commonly seen in diseases of the brain which attack it in spots (for example, syphilis).

Frank X. quit school to go to work as a telegrapher. He became very successful. He dispatched trains and had in his hand the lives of a great many unsuspecting passengers and train crews. As far as anyone knows, however, he had never made any serious mistakes.

During the summer of his thirty-second year he astonished his wife one day by driving home in a new Packard automobile. No one knew better than she that, although in comfortable circumstances, they were in no position to afford a Packard. She broached this to him and he calmly announced that he had given a cheque in full payment for the car. " You know we have about ten thousand dollars on deposit and I thought we might as well be using a little of it." Actually they had on deposit about fifteen hundred dollars, and even this was not in a checking account. " Don't you recall," she asked him, " that the ten thousand dollars that you are talking about is not to come to us until your mother dies? "

He was easily persuaded to call off the deal, and no more disturbances of memory were noticed for a month or so, during which time he continued to dispatch trains.

Then one evening he disappeared. He was found the next morning in a town ten miles from his home, apparently having walked the entire distance. He hadn't the slightest idea of what he had started out to do or why he had gone out bare-headed at night. He was put in the hospital and carefully observed. While there, he gave a very elaborate history of his life to the doctors. When this history was compared with his wife's account, it was found that while he gave many details which she had long since forgotten, he had completely omitted two or three of the most important incidents of his life, and concerning his running off he hadn't the slightest recollection.

He gave a very complete account of his duties with the railroad, but couldn't for the life of him remember the name of his boss or the time at which the limited train was due. He thought that if you subtracted 7 from 100 you had 86, and if you subtracted 7 from 86 you would have 66.

In many of these cases of defective retention due to organic brain-injury the structural injury produces a certain amount of perceptual defect which increases the memory weakness because of the resulting inattention. In other words, not only is the memory function injured but also the receiving function which must precede memorizing.

3. *Defective reproduction* (amnesia of recollection) is the ordinary " forgetting " of well-known things which we all experience every day. In contrast to the amnesia (defect in recording) just described, this type is very rarely due to brain-injury. The nerve-cells are intact; the memories are there, but something interferes with their recall at a needed moment. What is this interference? Freud first showed us what practically all psychiatrists and psychologists now believe: namely, that it is a wish *not* to remember that derails or blocks the wish to remember. Nietzsche summed it all up, both the process and its psychological basis, in his *Beyond Good and Evil,* thus: " ' I *did* that,' says my memory. ' I *could not have done that,*' says my pride, and remains inexorable. Eventually — the memory yields."

The girl knows this whose lover has unluckily forgotten an engagement and thus " broken a date." In vain he may plead excuses, or even frankly confess forgetting. She knows, perhaps even better than he, that unconsciously (if not consciously) he didn't really want to come. She may know nothing of abnormal psychology, but she " feels " it, and she is right.

Similarly, we forget debts — that ten dollars I owe my friend; that bet on last week's golf game; that account at Greene's. We forget the things we don't want to remember.

Even in science it happens, all the time. Darwin wrote in his autobiography that for many years he " followed a golden rule, namely, that whenever a published fact, a new observation or thought came across me, which was opposed to my general results, to make a memorandum of it without fail and at once; for I had found by experience that such facts and thoughts were far more apt to escape from the memory than favourable ones."

A medical friend related to Dr. Ernest Jones the following instance:

His wife was seriously ill with some obscure abdominal malady which might well have been tuberculous, and while anxiously pondering over the possible nature of it, he remarked to her: " It is comforting to think that there has been no tuberculosis in your family." She turned to him much astonished and said: " Have you forgotten that my mother died of tuberculosis, and that my sister recovered from it only after having been given up by the doctors? " His anxiety lest the obscure symptoms should prove to be tuberculosis had made him forget a piece of knowledge that was thoroughly familiar to him.[16]

Sometimes the process of association leading to the forgetting of one and the substitution of other memories can be clearly dissected. (This occurs daily in the course of the psychoanalysis of patients.) It is usually too complicated and detailed to present as illustrative material. The following case, however, given from his own personal experience by an analyst, Dr. Homer Frink, is a beautiful example, not only of the phenomenon of repression amnesia, but of the process of recall by free association and the identification of the motives for forgetting.

" A friend once asked me if I knew of a firm which could supply a certain commodity he desired, but upon replying that I did, I found myself unable to remember the name of the firm, although I did remember the location of their place of business — a large downtown office building.

[16] Ernest Jones: *Papers on Psycho-analysis* (New York: William Wood & Co., third edition, 1923) , p. 72.

" A few days later, as I happened to be passing this building, I stepped in, and upon consulting the directory of its tenants found that the name I had been unable to recall was Pond. I attempted afterward to analyze my forgetting with the results that are here recorded.

" My first association with the word Pond was that a certain Dr. Pond had been a pitcher on the old Baltimore baseball team. Next I thought of Indian Pond, where I used to go fishing as a small boy, and I had a memory picture of myself throwing into the water the large stone used as an anchor for the boat. Then I thought of a man named Fischer who is at present a pitcher for the New York Americans.

" Continuing, I thought of Pond's Extract and of the fact that it contains witch hazel. This reminded me that I used witch hazel to rub my arm when in my school days I was pitcher on a baseball team. I also thought of a certain fat boy who was a member of the same team and recalled with amusement that in sliding to a base this boy once went head first into a mud puddle, so that as he lifted his face plastered with dirt this, combined with his marked rotundity, had given him an extremely laughable and pig-like appearance. I further recalled that at that time I knew a boy nicknamed ' Piggy ' and that at a later time I had been nicknamed ' Pig.'

" At this point I was interrupted for a few moments, and when I returned to the analysis the word Pond brought the associations: Ponder — think — ' sicklied o'er with the pale cast of thought ' — Hamlet — the memory of my having referred to a certain village as a hamlet — the recollection that a farmer in this village once told me that a spiteful neighbor killed two pigs and threw them into his (the farmer's) well.

" Then there suddenly occurred to me the following incident from my seventh year, which appears to have been the cause of my forgetting the word Pond.

" At the time I refer to I had a dog to which I was greatly attached. My brother and I were playing one day on the edge of a small pond near our house, and this dog was in the water swimming. We began to throw small stones into the water in front of the dog, and as each stone struck the surface he would jump for the splash, try to bite it, and bark in joyous excitement. Finally, I was seized with the malicious desire to scare the dog and, picking up a stone weighing three or four pounds, I threw it, intending it to strike just in front of him and frighten him by its enormous splash. Unfortunately, my aim was bad. The big stone struck the dog squarely upon the nose and stunned him, so that he sank beneath the surface and was drowned.

" My grief over this incident was without question the greatest that

I experienced in my childhood. For days I was utterly inconsolable, and for a long time there were occasions when I would be so overcome with sorrow and remorse as to cry myself to sleep at night. I suppose, however, that my grief seemed greater than it actually was. That is to say, it was exaggerated to serve as a compensation and penance for the painful perception that a cruel impulse on my part was responsible for the dog's untimely end.

" At any rate, as is plain, the memory of the incident was a very painful one, and, in consequence, I had good reason to wish to forget not only the incident itself but also any word (such as Pond) which might serve to bring it before my consciousness.

" A matter that is not without interest in this analysis is the relevancy of my seemingly irrelevant associations. For instance, my first association — that of the pitcher, Dr. Pond — contains three ideas connected with the repressed memory; viz., *Doctor* (myself), *Pond* (the place of the incident), and *pitcher* (one who throws). My second association — concerning Indian Pond and my throwing into the water the big stone used as anchor — is equally relevant. Indian Pond is in the same town as the other pond in which the dog was drowned; my memory of throwing overboard the anchor is connected with the memory of throwing into the water the other big stone which caused the dog's death, etc.

" The association *pig* which came up several times in the latter part of the analysis seems at first glance to have no connection with the concealed memory. A connection does exist, however. The letters P-I-G reversed are G-I-P, which spells the name of the dog. Thus the association concerning the pig-like boy and the mud puddle — which contains the elements *P-I-G*, baseball *(i. e., throwing)*, and *water* — or that of the farmer and the pigs — *P-I-G, death, throwing*, and *water* — is seen to be perfectly relevant. ' Hamlet ' and the quotation from it gain a mediate relevancy through the drowning of Ophelia." [17]

FUGUES

There is a certain curious, exceptional kind of memory defect frequently appearing in the newspapers under the erroneous caption of " aphasia." [18] What is usually referred to is an episode in which a previously healthy and presumably happy individual

[17] H. W. Frink: " Some Analyses in the Psychopathology of Everyday Life." *Journal of Abnormal Psychology*, Vol. XII, April 1917.

[18] " Aphasia " really means loss of the power of speech. " Amnesia " is probably the intended word, but even it is scarcely specific enough.

suddenly disappears and when discovered is found to have lost his identity and all recollection of previous happenings, at least for the period of the *fugue* (the correct technical designation), which may last an hour or ten years. Many such cases have been reported; some typical illustrations from my own file may be briefly cited: [19]

A young man was working on his uncle's farm in Ohio. He started to the house on Saturday afternoon, to quit work until Monday morning. He recalls no more until he found himself in bed in a hotel in California. Upon investigating he found that three weeks had elapsed. The card of a travelling man in his pocket gave him a clue. He wrote to the man and received an incredulous reply, saying that when he had exchanged cards he had appeared to be a perfectly normal young man going about his business in a matter-of-fact and self-confident way, giving such and such a name, destination, and program.

The case just cited is probably classifiable as hysteria, but the same phenomena occur in certain other diseases, such as epilepsy, migraine, and — as in the case cited a few pages hereafter — mania.

A much more dramatic and tragic case is the following:

A vivacious girl of eighteen fell in love with a farmer twenty years older than she. They were married and had a son, and later two daughters. She was happy with her husband and devoted to her children.

They had been married perhaps fifteen years when she began to flirt with men who came to the farm on business. Her husband reproached her for this, and they quarrelled about it often.

One day they had quarrelled bitterly, but that night had made up and decided to try to live more harmoniously. The next morning, while the husband and son were milking, they heard shots. They rushed to the house. There they found the two little girls, shot through the heart, lying in great pools of blood. Their mother lay across a bed, a shotgun in one hand and a bleeding wound in her side. " What have I done? " she moaned, and lost consciousness.

She remained unconscious for several days. When she awoke she could remember nothing about the shooting. When I told her that her little girls were dead she burst into tears and demanded to know what had happened to them. I told her. " But," she cried, " how could

[19] A review of the literature and an investigation of certain selected cases of fugue states was recently made by three of my associates — Elisabeth Geleerd, F. J. Hacker, and David Rapaport. See *American Journal of Psychiatry,* 1944.

I do such a thing? Surely I couldn't! My God! How could I do that? " She still insisted that she could remember nothing about it.

Of course the prosecuting attorney expected the family quarrel to prove to be the origin of a guilty motive. But examination disclosed that for years she had been subject to severe sick headaches, of the type known as migraine, which were often accompanied by periods of amnesia. When suffering from one of these headaches she had several times done peculiar things which she later could remember nothing about. Once she had milked a cow in the afternoon and had thrown the milk in the horse trough. Another time she had gathered eggs and had then put them back in the nests. For several days before the murder of her children she had had one of these headaches and it had been unusually severe. To this day she has never been able to recall anything about the tragedy.

Judgment defect

So much for the various kinds of memory defectiveness. But not all who have good memories can be said to have good minds. There are the so-called *idiot savants* who can perform extraordinary feats of memory and yet have " no sense at all." Intelligence is more than memories properly received, recorded, and reproduced. It is the capacity to use them in facilitating the adjustment of the whole personality to the requirements of a situation. The piece of mental machinery which serves to select the appropriate memories for the particular moment is called by a very inadequate term *judgment*. *Judgment* means one thing to lawyers, and quite another to psychologists. The latter define it as " the ascription of meaning to the given," whatever that may mean. Psychiatrists use the word only in a very practical sense, best illustrated by the following cases:

Oliver Goldsmith, with only a few shillings to his name and any number of impending debts, was wont to give away to a passing beggar some or all of his precious pennies. When only a little more prosperous, he is said to have squandered his much needed pittance for unnecessarily extravagant and elegant clothes. Precisely the same type of defective judgment characterizes Madame Ranevsky in Tchekov's *The Cherry Orchard,* such that she flings gold to a tramp because she has no silver handy, and "just can't help it," gives a ball with not enough money even to pay the musicians, and by a career of such performances loses forever her beloved cherry orchard.

May Thompson was a senior, and should therefore have known better, the students all said. She came to class in party dresses; she wore ball-room slippers on the campus; she skipped her lunches to have money enough for two manicures a week; and she was for ever inciting gossip by " happening " into " compromising " situations *and* being discovered!

George Davis is worthy enough — everyone says he means well — but his gaucheries are notorious. He chooses precisely the right moment for the wrong remark. He bungles everything. He hurts his friends' feelings, he insults strangers, he shocks the unsuspecting, he bores the crowd. All of it is unintentional; no one regrets it so much as he. He is, as his friends say, the " prize bone-head artist." But he is not stupid. He simply has " rotten judgment."

A certain peculiar crudeness and bad taste are characteristic of patients with certain kinds of brain disease. I remember a puzzling case in which the correct diagnosis was first suspected because of such a breach of etiquette. The patient was a refined old lady, genteel and decorous in ordinary life, who had been stricken with a partial paralysis of a queer type. In making some neurological tests I asked to see her tongue. She protruded it promptly, and I examined it closely, when she suddenly drawled: " Look out! Don't bite it off! You know, you look awfully hungry! " She lay back and chortled gaily over this while her mortified daughters gasped and stammered in an effort to smooth over the situation. But we had a hint of the diagnosis (general paresis), which subsequent observation confirmed.

The first symptoms of the breakdown of Mrs. Frank Smith, which terminated in a hospital for mental disease, were a series of such episodes as these: She bought five gallons of white paint and painted the coal-bucket and the kitchen stove in order " to make the kitchen look less dirty." She seemed to have lost her skill at estimating the quantity of food to cook for her family and once prepared four great bowls of rice and baked them with three small Irish potatoes. She invited in some callers and entertained them gowned in her kitchen apron, with her dress unhooked. She ordered several hundred artificial flowers from the ten-cent store, saying that she was going into the millinery business.

DEFICIENT EMOTION

Perceptual and intellectual deficiencies may exist quite independently of any quantitative or qualitative variation in the *emotional* reactions of an individual, and vice versa. Since the human being is, in real life, a unit and *not* a collection of parts, there is always a connection, but it may not be apparent, and in this dissection we may neglect it for the present and consider deficiencies now of emotional capacity.

The adequacy of emotional response to a given stimulus can only be measured roughly as (1) average, (2) more than average, and (3) less than average. This average must necessarily be only a rough approximation, strongly influenced by our own subjective experiences. It is a matter of common knowledge that some "take things harder" than others and that we all react differently under different circumstances and at different times. Nevertheless the extremes are recognizable. (See Figures 10 and 11, page 194.)

If during war-time the national anthem is played at a public meeting, we feel thrilled and show our feelings by standing promptly and remaining standing during the rendition. Some, to be sure, will be even more prompt and ceremonious than ourselves; they will salute, or bow, or applaud enthusiastically. Still others will be less evidently moved than ourselves. They may rise reluctantly or not at all; they may appear bored or indifferent, or even show signs of resentment.

Now, resentment is an emotional expression, and the fact that it is not the same as ours, or as that of the majority of persons in the audience, does not make it any less so. But the presumption is that those who showed no interest whatever in expressing by the standard gestures their sympathy and enthusiasm lack in capacity for emotional response, at least in this particular test. Persons living with these individuals, or psychiatrists accustomed to watch for and estimate such reactions, would be able to say whether or not such indifference was a habitual reaction (or, rather, lack of reaction) to stimuli which arouse more feeling (or more evidences of feeling) in other people — that is, in *most* other people — and whether it was a general deficiency of emotional response or a specific emotional inhibition *in re* nationalism.

Such a habitual apathy constitutes emotional defect. It is exceedingly abundant. It appears in early school life in the child

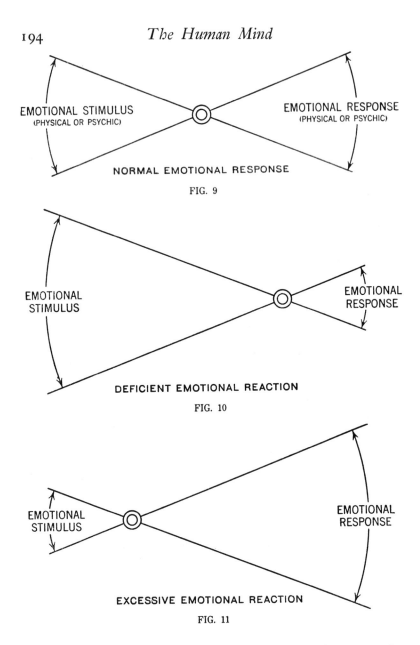

FIG. 9

FIG. 10

FIG. 11

who cannot be interested — in the older child who cannot become enthusiastic and aroused — in the aimless and desultory
high-school student and in the blasé college student. Silliness is
another form, especially common in women; callousness is a
more usual type in men. Psychiatrists describe this in their pa-

tients with such terms as " emotional flattening." It is a common symptom of the schizoid personality and of schizophrenia, discussed in the previous chapter, because such individuals are really not very much concerned with the events and opinions of the outside world. It must be distinguished, of course, from a culturally determined stoicism such as that of which some of the American Indians were so proud. It is not normal for a young man of contemporary American culture to react like this:

" The patient sat quietly on the edge of his bed staring out of the window. The expression on his face was one of complete abstraction. The approach of the physician was not acknowledged, apparently not even noticed. To a conventional greeting he responded with a nod. To interrogations regarding his illness, his presence in the hospital, his participation in the Tunisian campaign, his wish for food and the like, he responded with uninflected, ambiguous monosyllables. Suggestions by the physician that he might like to go home, that he would see his mother again, that he might be discharged from the Army, that he might not be discharged from the Army but sent back into active duty were all acknowledged perfunctorily without evidences of enthusiasm, pleasure, fear, anger, or regret. He seemed to be completely indifferent as to his past, present or future."

How much of this lack in a given case is due to a lesion in the physiological machinery of the organism — the basal ganglia of the brain, the endocrine glands, the autonomic nervous system — and how much of it is due to conflicts of emotional streams which neutralize each other, it is impossible to say from *a priori* evidence. Certainly there are both types. We see those whose shallowness or callousness or silliness seems to yield nothing upon analysis; there are a few superficial layers and nothing beneath.

Others, on the contrary, are trussed on the barbed wires of terrible battlefields. " I'm worried," said one college girl, " because I'm not more worried; I ought to be worried. I've plenty to be worried about. But nothing seems to matter much. I am enthusiastic about nothing, nothing interests me, nothing depresses me. Not even life itself appears very interesting, nor people, nor ideas, nor places, nor things. I don't believe I love anyone — my parents, my sisters, my sorority friends — or even myself." This child grew up in a home in which the father and mother were bitterly antagonistic, and each had tried for years to align the children on his or her side. "We'd hear it from Mother; then we'd get a tale from Father; then Mother would lay out Father and Father would tell us why he couldn't endure Mother. We were just torn this way and that until we were old enough to disregard all of it. Perhaps this has something to do with my indifferent feelings towards the world."

Some of those who did not rise when *The Star-Spangled Banner* was played may have been torn by conflicting emotions, or dulled by the conflict of more important emotional currents. Still others may be overwhelmed by an *excess* of feeling. But in all probability many, if not most, by reason of either native lack or educational lack, felt less keenly the emotional surge.

Do not some persons who feel deeply disguise the expression of their emotions? Yes, they substitute the effort of suppression or repression for the effort of expression. But essentially the James-Lange theory is true, and we feel what we express as well as expressing what we feel. That expression may be disguised, but it is never really absent. Even the best poker-player cannot inhibit the dilatation of his pupils upon completing a straight flush on a two-card draw. Freud put it this way: No one can keep a secret if we are able to read all the signs, and this applies not only to conscious but to unconscious secrets (and their concomitant emotions).

Deficiency of emotion as Masefield saw it:

" Tragedy at its best is a vision of the heart of life. The heart of life can only be laid bare in the agony and exultation of dreadful acts. The vision of agony, or spiritual contest, pushed beyond the limits of the dying personality, is exalting and cleansing. It is only by such vision that a multitude can be brought to the passionate knowledge of things exulting and eternal.

" Commonplace people dislike tragedy, because they dare not suffer and cannot exult. The truth and rapture of man are holy things, not lightly to be scorned. A carelessness of life and beauty marks the glutton, the idler and the fool in their deadly path across history. . . . Our playwrights have all the powers except that power of exultation which comes from a delighted brooding on excessive, terrible things. That power is seldom granted to man; twice or thrice to a race perhaps, not oftener." [20]

[20] John Masefield: Introduction to *The Tragedy of Nan* (New York: The Macmillan Co.. 1921).

DEFICIENT VOLITION

Theoretically, we no longer recognize such a thing as the will. Practically, it is helpful to consider that the mental process resolves itself into action at a point of convergence or resolution, and it is convenient to call this point the will. (See discussion on pages 163–4.)

Mary never rises until she is called. She gets no lessons unless driven. She goes to no parties unless urged. She accomplishes nothing of her own initiative.

Nellie is a patient at the state hospital. She has been there many years. She never moves except when she is pushed. Put her hand or arm or leg in a certain posture, and, no matter how uncomfortable it might be supposed to be, she will leave it there for hours rather than exert the will-power to replace it.[21]

There are those who seem to have no faultiness in their sensory and perceiving apparatus, who cerebrate accurately and rapidly, whose emotional reactions are quite comparable in kind and in degree to those of their fellowmen, who yet fail of life adjustment by reason of a defect. The defect is not perceptual, not intellectual, not emotional, but in the resolution of these functions into action. Descriptively it is easy to recognize pictures of a weak will. I am considering will, not as a discrete function of mind, but as the resolution of the perceptual-cognitive-emotional process preceding it. And in some persons the fuse burns and the powder is dry, but there is no explosion. This is what one sees:

a. An individual who apparently could and should accomplish something, or everything, but who actually accomplishes little or nothing. He initiates nothing, or he completes nothing that he initiates. He is inoffensive and often amiable and popular, but he is a negative factor except as filler or buffer material.

b. A similar personality, who may or may not contribute something from spontaneous initiative, but who is incapable or relatively incapable of resisting suggestion, particularly of certain types. This is the can't-say-no individual. He is at the mercy of his environment. If alcohol is the thing, it is alcohol to excess, and often to ruination. But

21 This is called *cerea flexibilitas,* and is a classical but uncommon symptom of advanced schizophrenia.

the toxic agent may be hard work or it may be subservience to a wife, or extravagance for a daughter.[22]

This is the picture. Let us grant immediately that since the will is only a convergence of forces, so to speak, the behaviour is to be explained by reference to intrapsychic mechanisms — emotional and intellectual — not visible to the ordinary observer. They may or may not be understood by the subject, though commonly they are recognized by him as existing. Usually he can't change them unaided, but such defects can often be remedied by re-education.[23]

EXCESSES

Most people assume that mental faculties are like money, in that it is easy to conceive of too little, but difficult to imagine too much. Excess implies imbalance, however, and it occurs in connection with mind as well as with money.

EXCESSIVE PERCEPTION

Excess in the acuteness of perception, for example, is all well enough if it takes the form of the fabulously keen vision of the plains Indians, the Lilliputians, or the giant who could see seven leagues. Unfortunately, however, that is not what happens. With the exception of certain compensatory over-developments of some of the senses, as described below, excess of perceptual function occurs chiefly as the clinical condition of hypersensitiveness.

Jacqueline had not slept well for several nights. Whether it was owing to an oncoming cold, or anxiety over her mother, or something else, she did not know, but she felt " bum." Everything seemed to irritate her. The slamming of doors in the dormitory made her jump with pain; the sunlight which she usually welcomed at her window seemed dazzling and disagreeable. Her room-mate seemed to talk unusually loudly and to stir about blusteringly. Her skin felt raw and rough; the very weight and friction of her clothes were almost unbearable. As she walked down the hall, her own footsteps jarred her

---

[22] For illustrations of both types, see Chapter II, under the perverse personality type (7).

[23] An early important book on psychotherapy was entitled *The Education of the Will,* by Jules Payot.

head. Everything was too keenly felt. She retreated to her room and to bed.

Georges Lamiers had been " shell-shocked." [23a] After a huge shell explosion he was found by his comrades dazed and speechless and was taken to a base hospital. I saw him many weeks afterwards. He gave the impression of a trapped rabbit. If one were very gentle with him he could be engaged in a quiet broken conversation, but let a door slam, a lock click, a heavy footfall sound, and he would jump as if shot. His leap would be followed by most pitiful tremblings and shakings; in a minute or two he would be quiet again. Even a loud cough or sneeze was sufficient to pull the trigger, and his amiable comrades had amused themselves in the hospital by clapping their hands to see him jump and scream and shiver. He told us that each ordinary sound of average intensity seemed to him as loud as a cannon. He could hear thirty feet away a watch-tick which most of us lost at twenty inches! (This condition is called *hyperacusis*.)

Such experiences are familiar to everyone who has been acutely ill physically, and, indeed, physical illness is the usual cause. They result from a decrease in the normal sensory inhibitions — that is, the ordinarily existing buffers which protect the receiving apparatus from over-stimulation. Physical illness, recognized or unrecognized, will produce this. So will fatigue. But so also will various types of mental disease, particularly hysteria and hysterical states. Emotional stresses of various sorts will do it, and these may be conscious or unconscious.

EXCESSIVE INTELLECTION

Fortunately for the world, and thanks to the statisticians (for this is, of course, a mathematically inevitable conclusion), there are as many persons whose intelligence is above the average as there are persons whose intelligence is below the average. Calamity howlers, ignorant of arithmetic, are heard from time to time proclaiming that two thirds of the people have less than average intelligence, failing to recognize the self-contradiction of the statement.

[23a] " Shell-shock " is an inaccurate term coined during World War I to describe acute mental disabilities precipitated by combat situations. The symptom here described was frequently but not regularly present. For a vivid description of such reactions in World War II, see the account of Lt. Commander E. Rogers Smith of the psychiatric patients returning from Guadalcanal (*American Journal of Psychiatry*, July 1943) .

Excess of intelligence is the spice of the pudding for the down-trodden, routine-burdened school-teacher. The bright girls and smart boys who require no attention, who learn faster than the rest of the class, and who grasp immediately what she is trying to make clear, brighten up the otherwise drab days to a degree of tolerability. The average teacher would rather have a few I.Q.'s (intelligence quotients) of 125 in her room than a new set of blackboards or a spring coat.

For all that, the teaching profession should hang its official head in shame at the way in which the superior child has been neglected. The thwartings and curbings of the members of this group by the teachers whose concern was necessarily concentrated on the problem of bringing up the stragglers has been even worse than the wretched mishandling of the intellectually defective.

Jane was the eight-year-old daughter of very matter-of-fact parents. It had never occurred to them that she was any different from the rest of the family or from the playmates with whom she associated. They knew that she was the youngest in her class and "a little old for her age," but they gave her no special credit for this and were much astonished when they learned from her teacher that her intelligence was forty per cent higher than that of the average child of her age.

She had learned to read when she was five and had always been particularly interested in the precise meanings of words and the relations of numbers. She collected calendars and almanacs and had many dates and weeks marked and labelled. She was given to thoughtful replies to abstract questions, showing a recognition of the complex relationship of things. For example, she would frequently say: "Well, now, that depends . . ." Sometimes when she would seem to be slow it turned out that she was merely attempting to be particularly accurate. Her younger brother would look at the clock and say promptly: "It's about half past seven." She, on the other hand, would look thoughtfully at the clock and then announce: "It was just thirty-six and one-quarter minutes past seven when I finished looking." [24]

We do not really know, as Mrs. Hollingworth points out,[25] what becomes of gifted children. We do know that they do not

[24] This precision and the meticulousness of her reply give us a hint of what may lie behind some, if not all, such precocity. It is a neurotic compulsion — that is, such a child is being driven to these great efforts by unconscious fears, often the fear of being considered stupid, inexact, unacceptable, unlovely.

[25] " Who are Gifted Children? " *Child Study*, November 1927.

become mediocre or worthless as they become older. But they probably make up the leading college students and then the leading physicians, lawyers, teachers, and business men and women of their generation.

Aside from the difficulties arising from the fact that the superior child has to drag along in his education with average and less than average children, a difficulty which he fortunately surmounts to some extent by very reason of his superiority, there are hazards in superior intelligence arising from imbalance. Where there is a corresponding superiority of emotion and perception and volition, we find genius; too often, however, superior intelligence and perception are joined with defective emotion and volition to produce a Nathan Leopold.[26] There can be no doubt about the enviable superiority of Leopold's intelligence; it is impossible for some people to conceive of brilliancy and versatility such as his being combined with the callousness and disorder of judgment which would make possible the murder of a child.

EXCESSIVE MEMORY (HYPERMNESIA)

Just as there are those whose memory is, or becomes, defective in patches or as a whole, so there are those who remember too much and too well. In view of the prevalent belief that all experience is recorded somewhere in the brain, granted a reasonably intact brain, there can be no such thing as an excess of recorded memories. Superiority of memory must relate only to a superiority of recollection (power of recall). This may occur:

1. *Episodically,* under certain conditions of great stimulation.

"When one is drowning, for example, the events of one's past life sometimes rush with incredible swiftness and accuracy through the mind. Many of these details have not been recalled for years, and some of them have been long forgotten, in the ordinary acceptance of the word. Such an experience of Rear-Admiral Sir Francis Beauford is related by Harriet Martineau. During the brief period in which he

26 The murder of Bobby Franks by two of his neighbours, Nathan Leopold and Richard Loeb, attracted great attention in 1924, the more so because psychiatrists were called into trial to testify as to the psychopathology of the murderers and first drew wide public attention to the fact that men could have irrational, criminal impulses without being, in the popular sense, insane. (See Maureen McKernan: *The Amazing Crime and Trial of Leopold and Loeb;* Chicago: Plymouth Court Press, 1924.)

was sinking for the third time it seemed as if every event of his past life was reviewed. 'The course of those thoughts I can even now in great measure retrace,' he told Miss Martineau. 'The event which had just taken place; the awkwardness which had produced it; the bustle it must have occasioned; the effect it would have on a most affectionate father; the manner in which he would disclose it to the rest of the family, and a thousand other circumstances minutely associated with home, were the first series of reflections that occurred. Then they took a wider range: our last cruise; a former voyage and shipwreck; my school, the progress I had made there, and the time I had misspent, and even all my boyish pursuits and adventures. Thus traveling backward, every past incident of my life seemed to glance across my recollection in retrograde succession; not, however, in mere outline, as here stated, but the picture filled up with every minute and collateral feature. In short, the whole period of my existence seemed to be placed before me in a kind of panoramic review, and each act of it seemed to be accompanied by a consciousness of right or wrong, or by some reflection on its cause or its consequences; indeed, many trifling events which had been long forgotten then crowded into my imagination, and with the character of recent familiarity.' " [27]

2. *Constitutionally* — that is, regularly and habitually by reason of superior cerebral endowment plus effort. The old rabbis used to memorize the Bible and other religious writings and pass these on orally to their students; similarly vast quantities of material were memorized by people for transmission to the next generation, which the advent of printing, libraries, the development and dissemination of periodicals, and last the radio have made less necessary and hence less frequent.

In that remarkable study of the mental traits of three hundred geniuses,[28] Catharine Morris Cox has recorded superior memories in only twenty of them, including Balzac, Abraham Lincoln, Jean Paul Marat, Edmund Burke, Thackeray, James Watt, Francis Bacon, Cuvier, and Coleridge, as well as the following worthy of special mention:

Fichte, the German philosopher, was able at the age of eight or nine to repeat from memory the whole of a sermon given by the village pastor, arranged by heads and including illustrative texts. Erasmus

---

[27] Edgar James Swift, in *Psychology and the Day's Work* (New York: Charles Scribner's Sons, 1926), pp. 205–6.

[28] *The Early Mental Traits of Three Hundred Geniuses* (Stanford University Press, 1926).

learned Horace and Terence by heart in his teens. Racine, the French poet, is said to have been able to quote entire plays from memory, and once after the sacristan had burned two copies of a long Greek romance found in his possession, he got hold of another copy and committed it to memory. Friedrich Wolf, the founder of scientific classical philology, when only five years old, could recall ten to fifteen lines of verse after a single reading. At twelve he committed whole cantos of Tasso. The same year, while studying the English language, he had an English dictionary for one month only; he committed two thirds of it and copied the other third. He was said to have learned the whole Greek dictionary by heart. " He could recite many rhapsodies from Homer and whole tragedies even before he got their complete meaning." Chateaubriand, the French author and statesman, could repeat almost word for word a sermon he had heard even when he had not paid close attention to it. He learned by heart the table of logarithms.[29]

3. *Eccentrically,* as to both registration and recall, as manifested in certain special directions by prodigies.

Mozart, after once hearing played the *Miserere* of Allegri, wrote it out from memory. Cæsar and Cyrus are said to have known all the soldiers in their armies by name, and Themistocles could address by name twenty-one thousand Athenian citizens.

I had a patient once who received an enormous salary, chiefly, I am sure, because he could recall the name of practically any and every person he ever met, no matter how long since. Of course this made him an invaluable salesman. There was a student in my class in medical school who failed in most of his work, but we all discovered, before he left us, that he could tell us the page or case number relative to any given topic, without a minute's hesitation. The entire class used the poor fellow for an index.

Just as we have seen that there are certain special disabilities, in arithmetic, spelling, music, etc., so there are corresponding superior abilities, or talents. Some of these appear to involve enormous powers of registration and recall. Arithmetic lends itself best to illustration.

Jedediah Buxton (born 1702) appears to be the first calculator on record in modern accounts. He lived at Elmton, England. " He labored hard with a spade to support a family. . . . In regard to matters out-

---

29 Marcel Proust has demonstrated his extraordinary hypermnesia in his autobiographical novel, *Remembrance of Things Past* (New York: Random House, 1934).

side of arithmetic he appeared stupid." In 1754, when he was taken
to London to be tested by the Royal Society, he went to see *Richard III*
performed. " During the dance he fixed his attention upon the number
of steps; he attended to Mr. Garrick only to count the words he uttered.
At the conclusion of the play, they asked him how he liked it. . . .
He replied that such and such an actor went in and out so many
times, and spoke so many words; another so many. . . . He returned
to his village, and died poor and ignored." It is said that he could
give an itemized account of all the free beer he had had from the age of
twelve years.[30]

Tom Fuller, "the Virginia Calculator " (born 1712), seems to be
another case of highly specialized ability. He came from Africa as a
slave when about fourteen years old. He is first heard of as a calculator at the age of seventy years, when it is stated that he reduced a
year and a half to seconds in about two minutes; and 70 years, 17 days,
12 hours, to seconds in about a minute and a half, correcting the result of his examiner, who had not taken leap years into the reckoning.
He also calculated mentally the sum of a simple geometric progression,
and multiplied mentally two numbers of nine figures each. He was
totally illiterate.[31]

Inaudi and Diamandi were two "lightning calculators " studied by
Binet and Meumann and reported in brief in Swift's interesting chapters on memory.[32]

The most famous calculating memory-wonder on record is a university student by the name of Rückle, who gave an exhibition before
the Congress for Experimental Psychology at Giessen.[33] He was able
to learn two hundred and four figures in thirteen minutes, so that he
could repeat them. Rückle differed from Inaudi and Diamandi in having an exceptional memory for other things than figures and numbers. He could learn a series of nonsense-syllables in less than half the
time usually required. With Rückle, however, as with some others,
recall was not based on mere memory. He made use of various devices
which gave the figures meaning. For example, he separated them into
two columns, and each column served as a unit; and in remembering
long numbers he divided them into their prime factors. Further than
this, his method was to change what he heard into visual images. Then,
as he put it, he saw the numbers as clearly as though they were written
on a blackboard.

---

[30] Hollingworth: *Special Talents and Defects,* pp. 123–4.
[31] Ibid.
[32] *Psychology and the Day's Work, vide supra,* pp. 249–59.
[33] G. E. Müller in *Zeitschrift für Psychologie,* Vol. V, pp. 177–253.

I personally talked with a lightning calculator once who was performing on the Orpheum vaudeville circuit. He could add prodigious sums of seven or nine digit numbers without looking at them, but laughing, talking, and answering questions as he did it. He had to do it a certain way, however — the numbers had to be written some forward, some backward, some in mirror-writing style, and so on. He hadn't the slightest idea as to how he arrived at the result; the answers simply popped into his head — or rather hand — *provided* he followed the certain curious routine of writing them down so and so.

4. *Psychopathologically,* in the forms of prolonged mental excitement, occurring in the disease pictures known as *mania.*

"From there we went over to Jane's apartment, 4137 Broadway, telephone Main 4521-W, second flight up — we went there and she wasn't home, but I said we'd wait, because it was only 3.30 — 3.27, to be exact — I'm sure it was because I looked at Jane's mantel clock — she has a clock that George got for her in Chicago — at a place on Michigan Avenue — let me see, I ought to remember the name of that store — oh, Abt's — that's it — on Michigan Avenue near — well, anyway, it keeps wonderful time but this day it was slow — half an hour slow — and I couldn't believe it was so early yet and so I called central and asked the time and she wouldn't tell me, but I remembered that Dixon's always . . . Are you listening to me? Well, we stayed there until Jane came — about four o'clock — no, it was after four, because I saw Mr. Smelzer go to work, and Jane says he has to be there at five and always leaves at four. He works at the post office, you know. . . ."

(The speaker is a girl of twenty-two, confined in a hospital for mental disease. She has talked on and on like this for months.)

EXCESSIVE EMOTION

Moods: Excesses of elation and depression, either as prevailing moods or as immediate feeling reactions, are essentially reciprocal — that is, one is the antithesis of the other, and often closely related to it, chronologically as well as etiologically.

Unlike fearfulness, which is a matter of education, or rage, which is usually a bad habit or else due to structural brain-injury, the tendency to elation and depression is *apparently* [34]

[34] The fact is that we don't know whether it is or not — it seems to be (see pages 23 et seq.). There is more belief than knowledge on this point among scientists.

inborn and "constitutional." Hence their association with the word "temperamental" as applied to musicians, poets, and artists.

A study of temperament or mood would indicate that there are two pillars between which the pendulum of human emotion swings back and forth. The figure is imperfect, however, because such regular oscillations are not the rule. There are many varieties of mood variation, best shown by diagrams. (See Figures 12 to 15 on facing page.)

Clinical experience has shown, however, that temperamental trends considerably modify this curve. There are those, for example, who in spite of innumerable set-backs, disappointments, and causes for anxiety describe an emotional curve which tends to be "above the line," as shown in Figure 13.

To match this type, however, there are those constitutionally or habitually depressed, as represented in Figure 14.

Another type consists in more or less regular alternations of mood, from which this personality type gets its name. This is diagrammatically represented in Figure 15.

In their augmented forms, excesses of emotional swings are clearly recognizable as psychiatric cases requiring hospital treatment (melancholia and mania).[35]

Less extreme cases are seen in everyday life.[36]

Bill Boardman was serious-minded. For this reason many of the students avoided him. "He's a nice fellow, and smart, but he'd crab the party," they said. "He'd rather read or talk religion or go hiking." But these same traits attracted certain other friends, and, on the whole, Bill could be called popular. He was the son of a successful doctor and had plenty of spending money. He bought all the new books and was generous about lending them. He got A's and B's in all his studies and was on the track squad and in the dramatic club.

But in spite of all this, Bill was subject to fits of unhappiness. He would leave the company of his friends and return to his room alone; he would try to read for a while, but soon there was nothing to do but stare out of the window and think. "I don't know what I sit there thinking about — just a few repetitious thoughts about what a failure I am and no good and a disappointment to Mother, and what's the use — and then the same things over again. Blue as midnight I get. No friends — don't want any. No interests, no hopes. After a while it goes

[35] See Chapter II, under Moody Personalities.
[36] See also Figure 11, p. 194.

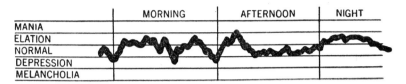

EMOTIONAL RANGE OF AN AVERAGE "NORMAL" INDIVIDUAL ON
AN AVERAGE DAY

FIG. 12

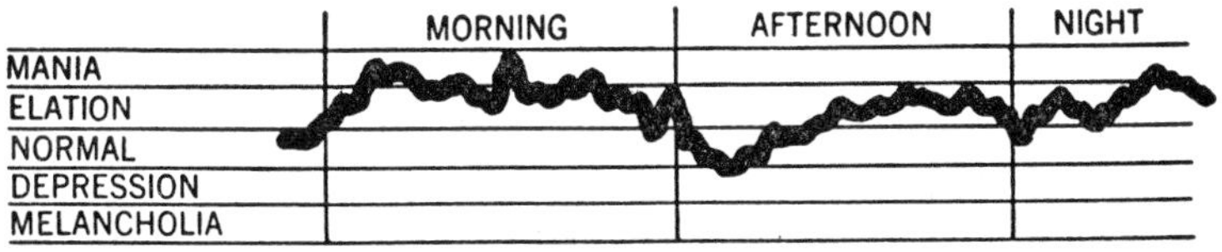

GRAPH SHOWING EMOTIONAL EXCESS (ELATION)

FIG. 13

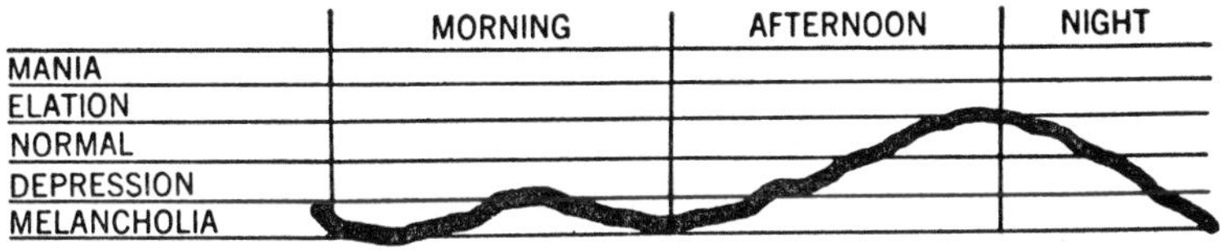

GRAPH SHOWING EMOTIONAL EXCESS (DEPRESSION)

FIG. 14

GRAPH SHOWING ALTERNATIONS OF PHASE
IN EMOTIONAL EXCESS

FIG. 15

away and I'm all right again." Sadness, which we all experience, may be experienced in excess as melancholy, depression — such as this.

George Hall went to the final examination in chemistry fully prepared for the worst. He had done superior work during the entire semester, and taking the examination should have been for him a mere matter of form.

But he was aware of a feeling of uneasiness. He drank three cups of coffee at breakfast to bolster him up. He was so restless that he could scarcely await the hour of the examination and went in fifteen minutes early and sat fidgeting in his chair.

When the time came for the distribution of the question sheets he became aware of the fact that he was scared. He felt chilly all over, his forehead was covered with a cool sweat, his mouth was dry, and his heart seemed to beat at the rate of a thousand beats a minute. He thought to himself that one look at the questions would reassure him. " After all," he thought, " I know this stuff. There's nothing to be afraid of." But his panic continued — it grew worse. He felt as if he would faint. The room was swirling and seemed insufferably hot. There was only one thing to do before he made a public scene. He rose from his seat, and without a word of explanation to his astonished instructor he left the room and did not return.

This illustrates excessive fear reaction; it is conceivable that an examination should inspire some amount of fear, but it should not provoke a panic.

Usually Annette was as amiable as a June morning. She was celebrated, however, for occasional outbursts of rage which were reminiscent of a stormy December night. One curious thing about them was the insignificance of their provocation.

One of her sorority sisters had agreed to accompany her, one evening, to a movie, with two men friends. As the hour approached, her sister found herself almost disabled with a severe headache and suggested that she and her caller might remain at home while Annette and her man went to the movie alone.

The suggestion was not out of the girl's mouth a second before anyone who knew Annette knew what was to follow. Her face turned white, then very red; she clenched her fists, she pounded her heels into the floor, she fairly foamed with fury. " That's the way you do, is it? " she hurled at the astonished sister; " you try to ditch me, do you? You frame up something and then crawl out of it, do you? I might have known it. Someone said you were yellow. You're pretending to have a headache and you're just a damned quitter, that's what you are. . . ."

And so on, for half an hour, at the end of which time her hair and clothes were in disarray, her face was stained with sweat and tears, her eyes bloodshot. The victim of the outburst had, in the meantime, quietly retreated to her room, and two impatient and puzzled gentlemen waited below.

Obviously the excess of anger was out of all proportion to the stimulus.

These are examples of emotional excesses. They are all related to subsurface mechanisms which are not visible to the naked eye of the passer-by, not visible or known even to the victim. This is the reason that the apparent cause or provocation of the attack is often so trivial, or even lacking altogether. It is there, but it is hidden.[37]

The man who became overwhelmed at the chemistry examination was reliving a childhood situation in which fear had been instilled into him by an over-anxious, fear-ridden mother, who robbed her son of his self-confidence. Or it may have been a hard-boiled, blustering father, well-meaning, perhaps, but intimidating. Some parents intimidate by silent disapproval, others by example, and still others by attack. Fears are educated into us, and can, if we wish, be educated out.

Similarly, temper tantrums are infantile reactions carried over into adolescence or adult life. Originally they served as a means of obtaining an objective; later they are retained, not so much because of the minor objectives, which they may or may not obtain, but because they have become emotional habits or patterns.

[37] For a tragic example of emotional excess (chagrin, anger, hate) from relatively trivial external stimuli, the extraordinary case of Mr. and Mrs. John G. Bennett of Kansas City is almost unparalleled if the newspaper reports of the incident are true. The story, according to the newspaper accounts, was as follows: the Bennetts had lunched and golfed with friends and in the evening had commenced a bridge game with them at a cent a point. The Bennetts were a little the losers; there had been some rather bad playing and hard words between husband and wife. Then came a deal of hands upon which Bennett opened with a one-spade bid, which Mrs. Bennett raised to four spades, laying down for dummy a very good hand, with which, however, Bennett failed to make the bid. " You're sure a bum bridge-player," snarled his wife. This provoked a retort, and there were more hard words, reaching a climax when Mr. Bennett rose and slapped his wife's face several times. Mrs. Bennett flushed crimson. " Only a dirty cur would strike a woman in the face in the presence of friends," she said. Then she rose, walked to the bedroom, obtained a revolver, returned to the living-room, and fired three shots, killing her husband on the spot.

(Information taken from the Kansas City *Journal-Post* and the Kansas City *Star* of September 30, 1929.)

Civilization and evolution have greatly diminished the opportunities for the exhibition of anger and the discharge of rage. Social weal requires that they be suppressed — released only in righteous causes as " indignation." This permits occasional terrible outbursts such as the Salem witchcraft persecution, the mobbing of Negroes, the hounding of the Nisei in this country, and the slaughter of Jews in Germany. It finds its grandest outlets in war, with its vilification and murder of the enemy, and in the abuse of social offenders (criminals). Those who believe that war can never be abolished justify this belief on the assumption that it is impossible wholly to suppress primitive emotional anger reactions.

The control of anger — that is, the preventing of wasteful emotional discharge in this form — is one of the aims and accomplishments of civilization. That this depends organically upon the development of the highest centres of the brain is prettily illustrated by the fact that these most highly developed are also the most vulnerable nerve-cells, and hence if they are injured, anger is a common symptom; irascibility and irritability are characteristic. Such symptoms appear in brain-injury due to syphilis, alcohol (everyone knows how some individuals become bellicose when drunk), brain tumour, apoplexy, and similar diseases. The most vivid examples occur in (1) hardening of the arteries of the brain, which starves to death the more vulnerable brain-cells, (2) brain syphilis, and (3) convulsive states.

In arteriosclerosis:

I had a patient once, a merchant who had always been an amiable Babbitt, who began to have such terrible outbursts of temper that he drove many of his customers away from his store. He would become angry over the merest trifles and get red in the face, stamp his feet, beat his fists on the table or against the wall, shout and curse, and actually tear his hair.

His friends avoided him as if he had the smallpox, for none of them cared to risk being the object of one of his attacks. He tried hard to control himself and be polite and pleasant, but it was evident that he was ready to explode at any minute. And explode he did, many times every day and night. His wife and children were puzzled and intimidated by his great irritability. He found fault with everything they did or said, ranted and raved, smashed dishes and furniture, and threatened to kill his family and himself. This is a typical example of the manifestations of arteriosclerosis, or hardening of the arteries, involving the brain.

In brain syphilis:

A certain conductor on a crack passenger train was retained for his experience and efficiency in spite of a reputation for ferocious temper tantrums. These tantrums seemed to have come on rather recently, and yet too early to be premonitions of old age, for he was only fifty. So fierce would he become over some trifle that even the engineers, the hereditary enemies of conductors, were a bit in awe of him.

On one occasion an old gentleman passenger became so engrossed in conversation that he rode past his stop. When our patient discovered this he went into a rage, stopped the train, and ordered the passenger off. It was dark and the old man had to walk the tracks back a couple of miles. On the way he fell into a ditch. The claim agent settled.

A year later, because the railroad company still stupidly disregarded the possible causes of this man's impossible disposition, his family, convinced that something was wrong, took him to a psychiatrist. He proved to have an advanced case of brain disease of the type known as general paresis. As previously discussed herein, this disease, unless vigorously treated — and often even then — ends in " insanity " and death. In the meantime it frequently leads to terrible examples of bad judgment and bad temper. Such men should never operate trains.

In convulsive states:

A soldier awoke one morning feeling " down and out "; he could not exactly describe his feeling, but he asked permission to go on sick-call. While he was standing in line waiting for his turn to see the doctor, he fell over and was unconscious for five hours. When he roused he was in bed in the hospital. Aside from feeling light-headed, he said he noticed nothing else. He was in the hospital for ten weeks. He had attacks like that nearly every day; on some days two or three attacks a day, lasting from a minute or two to half an hour. They usually came on at night, but occasionally during the day. He bit his tongue during such spells and frothed at the mouth.

One night he was lying apparently asleep, but suddenly got up and demanded to be let out. He pounded on the door with his fists, then piled up all the pictures, covers, chairs, and rugs in the middle of the floor and became very violent and threatening. He was finally persuaded to go to bed, and the next morning could remember nothing of the demonstration.

Thereafter the attacks, instead of being the ordinary convulsions or faints of epilepsy, consisted in sudden violent anger, usually without cause. He would become furious, throw the furniture, knives, clothes, or anything he could get his hands on, frightening his comrades and family nearly out of their wits. A few hours later he would be quite calm and deny any knowledge of the affair.

EXCESSIVE VOLITION

Excess in the function of resolving the mental process into action may appear in various forms.

Over-impulsiveness — sudden erratic bursts of activity

Most of the time Mayme Wilson preserved the even tenor of her way. No one knew, however, when a notion would strike her. When it struck, something happened. Everyone knew when Mayme had a new inspiration. The college had almost to stand still and let her and her cohorts sweep by. This thing or that, whatever it was, must be done, done at all costs, and done immediately. She would suddenly take to art and stay up all night studying it; next it would be a little-theatre play; now a special intimacy with the dean of women; now a wonderful new " date."

A sweet, demure patient of twenty-three was sitting on her bed in the hospital sipping iced lemonade with a friend — another patient. Suddenly, without the slightest warning, she hurled the glass, which was half full, straight at the visitor's head. The astonished guest dodged and dropped her own glass. Our lady quietly picked it up and hurled it, too, at her friend, and then she resumed her seat on the bed and went on quietly talking of the difficulties of cross-stitch.

Excessive determination

We are all familiar with the positively determined individuals who must have their way " in spite of hell and high water." A certain idea will occur to them, a certain method, a certain objective, and no obstacle seems great enough to daunt them, no argument powerful enough to dissuade them. Sometimes they pursue worthy and commendable ends by worthy and commendable methods, but they are just as frequently set and determined to accomplish something useless or to utilize other than the best possible method. Sorrell senior in Warwick Deeping's *Sorrell and Son* doggedly persisted in his purpose to advance his son, and in a very similar way Mamba in Du Bose Heyward's *Mamba's Daughters* was invincible. We all know students who plough their way through college in the face of almost superhuman difficulties.

Usually such individuals are of superior endowment, but not all of them. Sometimes they have nothing but determination.

Such an individual as this with a less worthy aim can cause lots of trouble. A few of them become John Browns, Jeanne d'Arcs, and Florence Nightingales.

Negative determination

Old Mrs. Gilbert sat quietly in a chair at the sanitarium, doing nothing, wanting only to be left alone. But let anyone try to get her to eat or to go for a walk or to go to bed and she would begin protesting loudly, absolutely refusing to do whatever was asked of her. For months at a time it would be necessary to feed her by means of a stomach tube, and she was forcibly undressed and put to bed at night. True, if the nurses could fool her into thinking that they didn't want her to do something, she was only too ready to do it. If they left food near her and warned her not to eat it, she ate it as soon as they were out of sight. If they told her that under no circumstances would she be allowed to go to bed, she stealthily undressed and crawled into bed. But unless tricked or forced into doing something, she would sit in her chair day after day, disturbing no one. (*Negativism*)

Passive aggression

How extreme passivity may represent in actuality intense aggressiveness, a negative expression of terrific volitional power, is spectacularly demonstrated in such a case as the following clipped from a newspaper.

SPITES HIS WIFE BY STAYING BLINDFOLD IN BED SEVEN YEARS

J., Ind., Nov. 16. — The strange story of Harry Havens of J., Ind., who went to bed — and stayed there — for seven years with a blindfold over his eyes because he was peeved at his wife, was revealed here today when he decided to get out of bed.

Havens was the kind of husband who liked to help around the house — hang pictures, wipe the dishes and such. His wife scolded him for the way he was performing one of these tasks and he resented it. He is reported to have said:

" All right. If that's the way you feel, I'm going to bed. I'm going to stay there the rest of my life. And I don't want to see you or anyone else again."

His last remark explains the blindfold.

He got up, he explained, when the bed started to feel uncomfortable after seven years.

— Chicago *Herald Examiner,* November 17, 1930

The first edition of this book described a celebrated case of this type; a thirty-three-year-old woman after many quarrels with her husband and after many frustrations one day became very angry at him and at his father and went to bed avowedly to spite them, remaining there until her death forty years later. Similar motives are frequently discoverable in the illnesses of both psychiatric and general medical cases but are rarely acknowledged with such candour or carried out with such extreme face-spiting vindictiveness.

General over-activity — pressure of activity

Elizabeth is constantly bustling and hustling about, enthusiastic and chattering, taking part in a score of college activities, and helping to plan a dozen more. She wastes vast energy and accomplishes much, but fails to finish much that she starts. She can't sit still. " I just must be doing something," she says. The girls envy her energy, deplore her inefficiency, laugh at her bluster, and love her for her good nature.

In mild degrees this is a familiar personality type — the town busybody, the " life of the party," cheer-leaders, etc. But the same symptoms may develop in a previously quiet nature and reach great extremes, as in the following case:

A pretty young school-teacher went home for the Christmas holidays. As she got off the train she was observed to be talking and laughing excessively. " Hello, everybody," she cried, " I can hardly wait to tell you everything that's happened to me. How's everyone? How are you, Mother — I've been worried about Father. I went to Columbus last Sunday and saw a man that reminded me of Father, riding on a bus, and I haven't been able to get it out of my mind. Oh, yes, have you ever been in a bird-store? I want to tell you . . ." and so she continued, far into the night.

The next morning she flitted in to breakfast with " Oh, good morning! What a lovely day! How I love snow! Mother, you don't look well, eat this extra egg! My, how good it is to be back again. I feel like a lost kitten just getting home. Oh! that reminds me I ought to feed Towser." At this she flew off to give the dog a piece of meat, forgot what she had gone for, and began making a snow man. Then she remembered that she had not finished her breakfast. Back at the table, still talking, she took a few bites between sentences and then ran off to see whether the paper had come. On the way she remembered that she had not made her bed, but, going upstairs, she noticed a broom and went downstairs to sweep. Her attention was soon distracted by something else, and she did not finish the work. Thus it went on all day and half the night.

The next day it was the same, and the next and the next. Finally her parents became so alarmed that they took her to a physician, who referred them to a psychiatrist. He told them that she would probably recover shortly from this very typical and familiar type of illness (mania; see pages 110, 205) and advised them to place her in a hospital. This they did not choose to do.

About a month later the newspapers carried a story of an osteopath's completely curing a girl of " talking sickness, a disease almost unknown in America," by a series of manipulations. Later her parents wrote that the osteopath had " plainly worked a miracle; she is her sweet, quiet self again." A few months later they wrote another letter which said that she had finally been cured by a chiropractor; some weeks after that she was again brought to the psychiatric clinic, as disturbed and disturbing as ever.

DISTORTIONS

Thus far we have been considering quantitative variations in the various mental processes. Now we pass from excesses and deficiencies to qualitative variations — that is, distortions.

If my friend calls my name and I, being deaf, don't hear it — that, as we have seen, is a perceptual defect, which is one kind of handicap.

If he calls my name and I am not feeling well, a little tired or a little " nervous," and his voice startles and disturbs me and seems too loud, that is (as we have also seen) a perceptual excess.

But if he calls me and I understand him wrongly, if I think he has called my brother, or if I think he has called me a liar, or if I think he is speaking French, or if I do not recognize the voice to have been his at all, but think it perhaps the crack of a revolver or the crowing of a rooster — these are not deficiencies and not excesses. They are shifts in the accepted value and meaning of the thing, not in its quantity. They are *distortions* of perception.

These we shall now consider, and then, *seriatim*, distortions of thinking, distortions of emotion, and distortions of what we have called volition. In the main, these make up the more common important and significant symptoms of broken minds.

DISTORTED PERCEPTION

There are three principal forms of perceptual distortion: (1) illusions, (2) hallucinations, (3) disorientation. The first two will be considered together; the third separately.

Illusions and hallucinations

Everyone knew old Mrs. Berry. She wasn't so old — she had lived sixty-seven years, but she was as agile as a cat and took the best of care of her husband Joe, with whom she lived quietly in a little village in the farm country which had been her homeland for forty years. She was present at all of the funerals and most of the births in the township, and occasionally she travelled many miles to sit with old friends who were ill or in trouble.

One evening, as she and her husband were sitting before the fire, her husband smoking and she knitting, she suddenly rose and went to the front door and opened it. She looked out, uttered an exclamation of surprise, closed the door, and resumed her seat. "I guess I was mistaken," she said.

A little later she repeated the performance, looking rather puzzled and remarking to her husband: "I was just sure I heard someone knocking at that door." "You imagined it," said he, and dozed off again.

But it was only a few minutes before Mother Berry straightened up quickly and exclaimed: "There, Joe, don't you hear it? I was sure I did, and now I know I did. Go and see who it is playing a trick on us." But old Joe was no more successful than his wife had been. "I tell you I don't hear nothin' and you don't either — it's the wind if it's anything, and probably you just imagine it. Let's go to bed."

To bed they went, but not to sleep. Time after time Mrs. Berry would insist that someone was to be heard knocking at the door, and time after time she would clamber out of bed and go and look.

Night after night this was repeated. It was not long before she glimpsed her tormentors. As she would fling open the door she was sure she caught sight of human figures hastily disappearing round the corner or down the street. She could never convince her husband of this, try as she might. "If you'd move right smart and look quick, Joe, you couldn't help but see 'em. And I think you ought to have a stop put to it. It's pretty poor of you to sit by and let folks torment us that way."

But Joe couldn't be moved, and the torments went on. Mrs. Berry became certain that she heard jeering laughter as she opened the door, and once she thought she heard someone speak her name, together with fragments of a sentence which she couldn't quite catch. Night after night she ran to the door over and over again.

Nor were her tormentors then content. One day at lunch the old lady suddenly dashed from the table and emptied her mouth of a spoonful of soup. Tears sprang to her eyes. " To think they have even attempted to poison me! There is surely strychnine in that soup. Joe, you must not eat another drop! Such a bitterness! It is the work of the Devil or his agents."

And so it went, with one thing after another. Vile odours and pungent gases were released in her room. Even the flowers in her garden were doctored so that the rose gave off an odour of garlic, and the tulips smelled of dead flesh. Her furniture was disarranged, her bed linen molested, her clean clothes soiled.

Thus it continued for months; at times her molesters would cease for a brief respite, but soon they would begin their tricks again. Her husband shook his head in perplexity and despair; for a time he had believed his wife's explanations, but with the accumulating evidences of their incredibility, he could only doubt the integrity of her mind. And his grief and anxiety rendered him helpless.

Finally old Mrs. Berry suffered the last straw. She began to feel distinctly the nudges and kicks and slaps of unseen limbs; she was even pinched and tickled and tweaked. She would find and demonstrate to her incredulous friends the black and blue marks that such treatment had left upon her. If her friends would seem to have difficulty in seeing the bruise, she would become indignant with them and turn away in tears.

This case is presented to illustrate the occurrence of perceptual distortions of several kinds. Perceptual distortions are known as *illusions* and *hallucinations*. Where there is an actual object of perception which is misconceived, such as old Mrs. Berry's thinking the wind to be a voice, the misinterpretation is called an illusion. Where there is no external object or stimulus at all, so far as the outside world is concerned, the false perception is called a hallucination.

Illusions are, of course, common. All of us experience many illusions every day. Of some of them we are aware; for example, we have come to know that the sun's rising and setting are an illusion. Others we correct from time to time; for example, we mistake Mr. Brown for Mr. Smith, or we interpret Mrs. Smith's attempt to smile sweetly as a sneer.

A great many illusions are never corrected by the average individual; one of the functions of education is to point out some of the common ones and to teach students the technique of correcting them themselves. Unfortunately the existing educational system perpetuates almost as many as it destroys.

Hallucinations, on the other hand, are rare in everyday life. Most individuals have never experienced them, although twenty out of one of my classes of two hundred students claimed to have done so. Usually, however, they indicate rather serious mental ill health.

George Henry was a well-known coloured barber in Boston. To the consternation of his friends and to the amusement of great numbers of passers-by, he was seen streaking down Tremont Street one winter day minus shoes and socks, hat and coat. Reaching a telephone pole near the Common, he clambered up it as if pursued by wild beasts. He climbed clear to the top and hung on to the cross-bars, where he could be seen trembling and shivering. The police, looking in vain for a pursuer, exhorted and then ordered him to come down, without any effect. Finally linemen were called and they laboriously climbed the pole which George had mounted so nimbly, and forcibly brought him to the ground. He seemed immensely relieved to be surrounded by policemen, and explained volubly that he was being pursued by ten million little black automobiles, fifty thousand cockroaches, and seventeen red elephants. He still shivered and shook despite copious sweating, and it was easy to see that he was in a serious physical condition.

This case represents typical hallucinations of the *visual* type, as seen in the formerly familiar alcoholic mental disease *delirium tremens*.

Another kind of alcoholic mental sickness is characterized by the existence of *auditory* hallucinations only, and these occur quietly and fearfully and persistently in a patient who is usually quite free from evidences of physical sickness. To wit:

A busy accountant was sitting at his desk when he distinctly heard (as he thought) the voices of two men in an adjoining room completing plans for murdering and robbing him. He nearly swooned with fright, but climbed out a window and went down the fire-escape, to seek safety. He was about to give himself over to a sense of security and relief as he neared his home, when from behind some bushes he caught the words: ". . . as he goes into the house, and drag the body into the alley and no one will — " Again he was petrified with fear, but, thinking to elude the plotters, jumped into a taxi and hurried to the police station to get assistance. While waiting for the officers, however, he was sure that he heard a muffled voice from somewhere near him say: ". . . get him yet! "

The following case illustrates the much less frequent *tactile* hallucinations.

An old lady of sweet demeanour began to spend many hours a day brushing her body with a stiff brush, and picking, scratching, rubbing, and polishing her skin. She insisted that she was distinctly conscious of being covered with vermin; at first she said it was lice, but later she would hold up long (imaginary) wire-worms, and then ropy, snake-like worms, many feet long. These she would calmly strip and pick from her skin into a bowl, insisting that those who denied seeing anything in the bowl were purposely blind. " And you need not call me crazy," she would say, " because you all know that I'm pretty spry for my age and can remember everything of importance that has ever happened to me. I've proved that to you by writing it all out. And none of you can equal it."

Both illusions and hallucinations may be classified in various ways, but to no great advantage. Obviously there are illusions and hallucinations involving each of the various senses — auditory, visual, tactile, gustatory, involving a sense of pain, olfactory, kinæsthetic, sexual, and so on. The most common are auditory and visual; voices are heard, familiar or unfamiliar, coming from within the body or without, saying sense or nonsense. Sometimes the voice may repeat to the patient his own thoughts. Visual hallucinations may be of persons or things or animals, or fabricated symbols, gods, devils, or spirits. Hallucinations of taste and smell are usually disagreeable — poison is tasted in the food, foul gas is smelled in the room, etc. Painful pricks and proddings, stabs and shocks may be felt. The patient may feel as if he were flying through the air, or being dragged, or pressed down upon, raped or mutilated, and so forth.

Because hallucinatory experiences may be suggested to susceptible individuals, and because illusions may be favoured by mechanical and sometimes automatic tricks, and because to supposed supernatural phenomena great import is attributed, the study of miracles, spiritualistic seances, " thought-transference," and the like reveals many examples of both illusions and hallucinations, but particularly illusions deliberately produced by someone with ulterior motives. Houdini exploded and exposed many of these with consummate genius.

Disorientation

Examine the following illustrations:

Mr. and Mrs. Lochinvar Brandenburg marched in stately fashion from their front door to the waiting car and were driven to the home of the Gregory Smiths. It was four o'clock in the afternoon, and they were in formal afternoon dress. Mr. Brandenburg was to officiate at the wedding.

To their astonishment there seemed to be no preparations. Their hostess was not even at home. They looked at each other and gasped. " Something terrible has happened," they said.

All that had happened was that they were twenty-four hours too early. Both had been under the impression that it was the appointed day.

George Brown was a sophomore. He took everything but his school-work seriously. He lounged into his history class one morning just as it was beginning. He dropped into a rear seat as usual and gave perfunctory attention.

After the class the instructor approached him and inquired as to the reason for his presence. It was only then that George realized that he had been in room 317 instead of room 417, as he had supposed.

In the city in which I live there are three men, supposed to look something alike — a musician, a banker, and myself. About three years ago an acquaintance of mine chanced to sit beside me at luncheon at a club to which we all belonged, and for nearly half an hour I listened to a criticism of my concert series. After luncheon I mentioned this to my musician double and he laughed, saying: " That's better than being bored by a financial discussion, as I was." During the week I was telling the story to our banker, and he met it by declaring that he had thrice that week been hailed as " Doctor."

These are examples of *disorientation,* which is a disturbance of perception resulting in misunderstanding of our relation to the environment. It is commonly classified as spatial, temporal, and personal disorientation, each type being illustrated above by an example from everyday life.

We are all more or less disoriented in all these three spheres all the time. No one knows exactly who he is or where he is in the universe, and all time notions are relative.

> Sometimes when slowly from the deep sleep of fatigue
> a man awakeneth, he lyeth for awhile amazed,
> aware of self and of his rested body, and yet
> knowing not where he is, bewilder'd, unable
> to interpret sight or sound, because the slumbering guards
> in Memory's Castle hav lagg'd at his summons
> for to let down the drawbridge and to uplift the gate:
> Anon with their deliverance he cometh again
> to usual cognisance of the things about him,
> life, and all his old familiar concepts of home.
> So 'tis with any Manchild born into the world,
> so wondereth he awhile at the stuff of his home,
> so, tho' slowly and unconsciently, he remembereth —
> With ease of long habit his lungs inhale the air,
> his muffling wraps, his frill'd and closely curtain'd cot
> and silken apparel of wealth are stranger things to him
> than the rough contacts wherefrom they are thought to shield him,
> the everlasting companionships of his lang syne.
>
> Robert Bridges from *Testament of Beauty* *

Clinically, disorientation results from many causes and is seen in many conditions. The common sorts are associated with distractions of attention, repressed memories, and defects of perception. In more seriously sick individuals disorientation is associated with three general conditions:

a. *Disorientation in delirium* (acute brain-injuries resulting in dissociations).

Mr. Marks was a sedate, middle-aged banker. He contracted influenza and was very severely ill for several weeks. During the height of his fever he was almost continuously delirious. He seemed to think he was on a railroad train, *en route* to New York. Occasionally he would make vigorous attempts to rise, declaring that the train had entered the Grand Central Terminal and the passengers should all disembark and not delay the trainmen. He referred to McKinley and the World's Fair, and other indications showed that he thought it was 1898 instead of 1918. He called the doctors " porter."

* From " Testament of Beauty " by Robert Bridges. By permission of the Oxford University Press, New York.

b. *Disorientation from amnesia* (acute or chronic brain-injury, with loss of standards of comparison).

A personal friend of mine so considerably lost his memory that he could not recall my name, my occupation, my many contacts with him and his family; he could not be sure of the name of the city we live in or the day of the month or year. " I think it's Chicago, isn't it? About 1922? " This was due to progressive destruction of the cells of the association areas of the brain from the local anæmia produced by general hardening of the small arteries.

c. *Disorientation in delusional states* of various types in which the disorientation is dependent on and used by the disordered thinking.

To Mrs. Browning all Catholics and Masons were agents of the Devil. She was sure that they were groups of evil and conspiring men whose chief aim was to wreck the nation and destroy all good Christian Methodists, including, of course, herself. She had alarmed the neighbourhood by loud and fiery declamations on this subject, provoked by the unsuspecting iceman, who happened to be wearing a Knights of Columbus pin. So violent were her imprecations and denunciations of the Pope and his children that her husband was called to attempt to subdue her. In the end she was lodged for observation in a hospital for mental disease. " This is a jail, that's what it is," she'd say, " and a jail run by Catholics to pull off more dirty work. It's just like 'em. Nuns dressed up like nurses, priests pretending to be doctors, supposed patients all around spying and reporting — they can't fool me."

Morton Prince describes an interesting case.[38]

" She was alert, absolutely alert; could talk and act and move, just like any one of us here. . . . She could laugh, joke, reason, answer questions, and converse like any one. . . .

" There was a complete loss of every form of sensation, with the exceptions I have mentioned [hearing, and possibly vision]. She could not taste, smell, or feel tactually. She had no kinesthetic sensations and no cœnesthesis. She had absolutely no perceptions of her body. . . .

" She described herself simply as ' *thought in space.*' She did not know whether she was standing or sitting, or what part of the room she was in. It seemed to her as if she was just in space somewhere; that is, thought in space without any consciousness of body. She did not seem to herself to have a body. . . .

[38] *Journal of Abnormal Psychology*, Vol. XVIII, no. 3, pp. 239–40.

" If you told her to stand up, she stood up. Then she would say, ' Am I standing up? ' When told to raise her hand, she did so. When asked ' Are you raising your hand? ' the answer was, ' I don't know, am I? ' ' Sit down.' ' Am I sitting down? I don't know.' In short, though in response to commands she moved and had complete control of her muscles and body, she did not know it, for she had no kinesthetic sensations, absolutely no sensation of her body, no organic sensations, nor anything else. As I have said, she was ' thought in space.' "

DISTORTED INTELLECTION

Thinking straight is a rarely attained and oft quoted ideal. But the severe distortions which serve us as illustrations of the symptoms of mental misfunctioning fall into a few categories:

1. Obsessions
2. Distortions of memory
3. Disturbances of association
4. Delusions

Each of these will be successively considered.

I. OBSESSIONS

Two hundred senior students at the University of Michigan were asked: " Do you have, or have you had, any fixed ideas coming involuntarily and unsolicited and remaining in spite of efforts to get rid of them? " Twenty-five per cent of them answered in the affirmative.[39]

Two hundred freshmen students at Washburn College were asked a similar question. Twenty-nine per cent answered in the affirmative.

What sort of ideas are these beggar-lice which attack nearly a fourth of us — of college students at any rate [40] — and can't be got rid of? Here are some examples — all in " normal " people, remember — from Professor Berry's classes and my own.

One student wrote: " Almost two years ago I persistently over-evaluated the importance of taking care that I did nothing which might in any way injure another. Every time I crossed a railroad track I had to go back several times to see if there were any spikes or stones on the

---

[39] C. S. Berry: " Obsessions of Normal Minds," *Journal of Abnormal Psychology*, Vol. XI, no. 1 (1916) , pp. 19–20.

[40] It is probable that a much larger percentage of persons experience obsessions at one time or another. I should say fifty per cent was more nearly correct.

track that might wreck the train. That crossing of tracks was real anguish. Sometimes I would close my eyes when crossing to avoid seeing anything I might imagine could do harm. For a time I could not pass even a stone in the street (I rode a bicycle) without stopping to kick it over to the curb, lest some other bicyclist fail to see it and come to grief."

Another student wrote: " When I was about eight years of age I had a fixed idea. I thought I was going to cut my throat from ear to ear with a certain large butcher-knife in my grandmother's kitchen. I couldn't throw off the idea. I was afraid to go near the knife. This persisted for about two weeks, then gradually wore off. When fatigued, certain combinations of words or letters recur again and again. Often I am wholly unaware of their origin. For instance, the words ' sy ' and ' cip ' have come to me over and over the last few days, and I am absolutely ignorant of where or when I heard or saw them. Often at night when very tired just before I fall asleep I read page after page of a large magazine in which there is absolutely no meaning — just a jumble of words. Yet I feel no irritation and my mind is absolutely satisfied with the jumble. I read down the columns, turn the pages and am aware of a half-tone illustration in the middle of the page but never see it distinctly."

Another one: " For the past ten years I have repeatedly found myself when thoughtlessly scribbling, writing the name ' Claudius.' I have no idea why this is but it certainly has stuck."

" I cannot," said a forty-nine-year-old patient of Pierre Janet's, " perform a single new activity without representing to myself that it is going to entail diabolical consequences. If I buy new shirts it seems as if I were preparing for the assassination of my two children. If I rent an apartment it is only in order that I may place under the big entrance door the coffin of my wife where it will rest very nicely; I have selected the apartment (it would seem) only because of the convenience which this entrance way presents for the coffin of my wife. If I open this book it is with the idea that I am preparing a cataclysm which will involve the whole city of Paris. All this frightens me so that I take back my recent purchase of shirts with the excuse that they do not fit; I give up the apartment, and I close the book." [41]

Another one confessed: " It seems that I am offending against ethics when I prepare the soup. . . . I am flaunting morality when I put on my dress. . . . I am always doing forbidden things. . . . This book must indeed be very immoral, since when I read it I always have the feeling that

[41] Pierre Janet: " The Fear of Action," *Journal of Abnormal Psychology and Social Psychology,* Vol. XVI, no. 2 and 3 (June–September 1921) , pp. 153–4.

I am reading surreptitiously one of those books which I was forbidden to open at boarding school. Is it that I have not paid for my breakfast? For in eating it I have the impression of stealing something from poor people. . . . It is as if I were putting poison in the soup, pins in the bread . . . putting loaded bombs in the chimney to blow up the house." [42]

The obsessions of patients are usually a little more elaborate and vivid than those of the ordinary healthy-minded person. Hence they make good illustrations.

" A man killed a fly which annoyed him by buzzing about the room. Hardly had he done so when there came to him the thought, accompanied by an intense feeling of horror and fear: ' My God, what if I should kill a *person* like that! ' He was not conscious of ever having had a desire to kill any one; he was not really in fear that he ever would kill any one, but nevertheless the thought ' But wouldn't it be awful if I did? ' stuck in his mind for months at a time and he was utterly unable to banish it." [43]

" A young married woman, who happened to be watching another woman who was seated at a window across the street, suddenly discovered that she could not get the thought of this other woman out of her mind. She *had* to think of her, she did not know why nor to what end, but she could not stop it. These thoughts, accompanied by a sense of apprehension and depression, persisted for the greater part of the time for four or more years." [44]

EXPLANATION AND INTERPRETATION OF OBSESSIONS

It was long surmised, even before the dawn of the modern era of psychopathology, that obsessions (as well as their sister manifestations, the phobias and compulsions) were substitutive phenomena; that is, that the persistent idea of " Did I turn off the gas, I wonder," replaces some other doubt or problem, such as " Should I confess this thing? " or " Shall I be blamed for that? " Sometimes these substitutions were discernible. It was easy to see, for example, that Lady Macbeth's hand-washing symbolized the cleansing of her hands from guilt rather than from mere blood. But most obsessions are more subtle and less easily interpreted. It was not until the development of Freudian psycho-

---

[42] Ibid., p. 154.

[43] H. W. Frink: *Morbid Fears and Compulsions* (New York: Moffat, Yard & Co., 1918) , p. 271.

[44] Ibid.

pathology that anyone understood clearly how or why the substitution was made.

It is impossible adequately to explain obsessions without the postulation of an unconscious part of mental activity. An obsession is a relatively innocuous idea substituted for a painful one which has been pushed back into limbo, out of sight and recognition. The laws governing the choice of a substitute, laws of symbolic formation, of condensation or reversal, and others, will be dealt with in the next section of this book.

Phobias, similarly, are substituted *emotions;* for example, the fear of thunder may disguise a deeper and older fear relating to some other terrifying sound — profanity, obscenity, scolding, or less articulate physiological sounds.

Compulsions, in the same way, are substituted *acts.* As compulsions are much more easily demonstrated and interpreted than obsessions, although similarly produced, further explanation will be deferred until those topics are reached (pp. 260–2).

II. DISTORTIONS OF MEMORY

Distortions of memory are called technically "*paramnesia.*" There are four main types to be illustrated:
>   (a) False memories;
>   (b) Confabulation;
>   (c) *Déjà vu* phenomenon;
>   (d) Mythomania.

a. False Memories

The following scene was enacted before a small class in psychology.[45]

" The regular work of the class was in progress, one of the young women being engaged in making a report on an investigation which she had made. . . . A few moments after the beginning of the report an altercation was heard in the corridor, then the door burst open and four students, two young men and two young women, dashed into the room. Miss R., immediately after entering, dropped a brown-paper package on the floor. This package contained a brick so that the occurrence might not be too inconspicuous. K. flourished a large yellow

[45] Edgar Swift: *Psychology and the Day's Work* (New York: Charles Scribner's Sons, 1918), pp. 201–301. This type of experiment excited a great deal of attention from lawyers and others about thirty years ago — unfortunately shortlived and now too little known.

banana as though it were a pistol, and all struggled across the room to the side opposite the door. . . . [The instructor arose and] threw a small torpedo on the floor. . . . H. fell back, crying, 'I'm shot!' and was caught by Miss R. All then hurried out the open door, Miss T. picking up the brown-paper package which had been dropped near the door by Miss R. The entire scene occupied less than thirty seconds and it was startling to the class, all of whom jumped up and crowded back against the wall, believing that it was a real riot.

" . . . Of the twenty-nine ' witnesses ' only three knew that four persons dashed into the room. These three also realized that two were young men and two were women. To the others it was an indefinite number, to a few less than four, but to the majority more; some characterized them as ' a crowd ' or ' a mob.' That only three actually observed the number was conclusively shown again when they tried to name and describe the participants. . . .

" Though the four participants were well known to the class and no disguises were used, no one recognized all of them. The results so far as concerns recognition by the twenty-nine ' witnesses ' is the following: 7 recognized 3; 11 recognized 2; 7 recognized 1; 4 recognized 0.

". . . Eight ' saw ' persons who not only took no part in the performance, but who were either not present or who sat at a distance from the place where the scene was staged. . . .

" The descriptions of clothing were so general as to be worthless for purposes of identification. Only thirteen of the twenty-nine attempted any sort of description even of those whom they recognized. . . . Only two noticed a conspicuous red tie [worn by one of the men], and one ' saw ' that his shoes were muddy and his face dirty, neither of which statements was true. . . .

" The indefiniteness and vagueness of these descriptions indicate a state of mind that makes a fertile soil for suggestions in the form of questions, newspaper reports, and innuendoes in court trials. . . . Examination and cross-examination . . . are in their very nature suggestive, and with soil so admirably prepared for the purpose, an abundant crop of imaginary pictures and scenes will be readily grown. . . .

" Several things done plainly in front of the witnesses were either not observed or were wrongly observed. Six saw one of the young women drop something and, of these, four noticed who did it. Only one of them, however, was able to describe the package as a brown-paper parcel . . . but five of these said it was Miss T., while one thought it was H. This illustrates the tendency to fill in the outline memories. . . .

" Five heard or saw a pistol-shot. Three of the five saw the flash. ' I saw the blaze,' wrote one of the young men. ' I know some one fired a pistol because I saw the flash,' was the statement of a young woman. This, of course, was the result of suggestion. The yellow banana was flourished and then pointed at H. . . .

" Five of the reports did not contain an item of truth or fiction. These witnesses saw nothing except a mob bursting into the room, and confusion. Six others were unable to testify to anything more than the identity of one of the participants. To these, all else was a blank. . . .

" Identification is, of course, fundamental in criminal cases, and positive recognition by well-intentioned, uninterested persons is commonly accepted, unless the alibi is convincing. In our drama-experiment the observers were well acquainted with the participants, yet they were surprisingly incompetent as witnesses. Their minds were therefore prepared, had the affair involved a real crime, to recognize one against whom there might appear to be corroborative evidence. The ' witnesses ' had little definite knowledge of what actually happened. Had a crime been committed their testimony would have been of slight value. Yet it would have been accepted because they were eye-witnesses."

It has been repeatedly shown that forced memory gives twenty-five per cent or more of errors — that is, false memories. This in *" normal "* persons! Few lawyers and judges have ever learned this.[46]

b. Confabulation: apparently purposeless memory falsification associated with certain severe mental illness — for example, *Korsakoff's syndrome*

J. K. had been acutely ill in bed for several weeks with a fever and a variable delirium.

" Good morning," I would say to him, " how are things going? "

" Just fine, thank you. I left the folks all well this morning and came over on the street-car because I had a blow-out last evening on the way home from the show."

" What did you do down town this morning? "

" Oh, I ran up to the office and saw Jim Hodgson and his foreman and went over to the bank a minute and did an errand for my wife at Macy's — you know, just an ordinary sort of morning. Oh, yes, a little unusual thing happened, too; I nearly forgot to mention it — I guess old

---

[46] Experiments of this type were probably first used by von Liszt, criminologist at the University of Berlin, about 1901. These have been repeated in many forms since, but this and other illustrations of the unreliability of memory were forcefully brought to popular attention in this country by Professor Hugo Münsterberg of Harvard with his famous book *On the Witness Stand: Essays on Psychology and Crime* (New York. The McClure Co., 1908) .

Baker is about done for; he tried to keel over on us; I guess someone just pumped a little dope into him, I don't know. I ran over and called Dr. Rainey, but he couldn't do anything for him."

" What happened to him? "

" Oh, he died, I guess. They took him to the hospital and I've just been over there and they say he's low."

" I thought you said he died."

" Yes, he died. I'd better go by there again later and see how he is."

All this time the speaker was lying prostrate in a bed from which he had not moved for nearly a month.

c. Déjà vu *phenomenon — the illusion of false recognition*

" Some one may be attending to what is going on or taking part in a conversation, when suddenly the conviction will come over him that he has already seen what he is now seeing, heard what he is now hearing, uttered the sentence he is uttering, — that he has already been here in this very place in which he now is, in the same circumstances, feeling, perceiving, thinking, and willing the same things, and, in fact, that he is living again, down to the minutest details, some moments of his past life. The illusion is sometimes so complete that at every moment whilst it lasts he thinks he is on the point of predicting what is going to happen; how should he not know it already, since he feels that he is about to have known it? It is by no means rare for the person under this illusion to perceive the external world under a peculiar aspect, as in a dream; he becomes a stranger to himself, ready to be his double, present as a simple spectator at what he is saying and doing. This ' depersonalization ' is not identical with or necessarily a symptom of false recognition; it has, however, a certain relationship to it. Moreover, all the symptoms differ in degree. The illusion, instead of being a complete picture, may often present itself as a mere sketch. But, sketch or finished picture, it always bears its original character.

" There are on record many descriptions of false recognition. They resemble one another in a striking manner, and are often set forth in identical terms. I have in my possession the self-observation of a literary man, which he specially undertook for me. He was skilled in introspection, had never heard of the illusion of false recognition, and believed himself to be the only person to experience it. His description consists of some dozen sentences, all of which are met with, in almost identical words, in the published records of other cases. I congratulated myself at first that I had at least obtained a new expression of it, for the author tells me that what dominates the phenomenon is a feeling of ' inevitability,' a feeling that no power on earth could stop the words and acts about to come, from coming. But re-reading the cases recorded by M. Bernard-Leroy, I find in one of them an identical expression: ' I was a spectator of my own actions; they were inevitable.' Indeed, it is doubtful if there exists another illusion stereotyped with such precision." [47]

This phenomenon may be the result of psychic conflicts, but it is also seen occasionally in patients with tumours arising and developing in a certain part of the brain (temporal lobe). One personally observed complained of the *déjà vu* phenomenon [48] for many months before any other evidences of brain tumour were apparent.[49]

d. Mythomania

" Remembering " things that never happened is a kind of memory distortion which goes by several names, such as *pathological lying* and *mythomania*. It differs from ordinary lying in its apparent uselessness, and also in that the speaker comes to believe his own lies and seems unable to tell the truth.

A girl of sixteen, decidedly attractive, and capable of earning a fair living, was examined by Dr. Healy in the juvenile court in Chicago. " She first came to notice after much newspaper notoriety. During the course of revival meetings, at one session of which the scarlet woman was the subject of discussion, she became much excited, and went to her Sunday School teacher, and with her to the pastor, and gave a most circumstantial account of her own life as a clandestine prostitute. She gave times and places with apparent accuracy. On the strength of all this detectives set about making a raid upon the secret centers of vice which she named. At the time of the raid she went with the detectives to show them the previously described entrance to a certain house. When

[47] Henri Bergson: " *Le Souvenir du présent et la fausse reconnaissance* (Memory of the Present and False Recognition) ," *Revue philosophique,* December 1908, pp. 561–2.

[48] The *déjà vu* phenomenon is the basis of a play, *Berkeley Square,* suggested to the author by Henry James's posthumous fragment *The Sense of the Past* and made successful (1930) by the discerning delicacy of the acting of Leslie Howard. It is the story of a man of 1928 who returned to 1784 to live the role of one of his ancestors with whom he identified himself. Since he knew the family history intimately he had an uncanny ability to foretell to the people among whom he lived for a week what had not yet happened. For a scientific review of the topic see S. A. K. Wilson: *Modern Problems in Neurology* (Baltimore: William Wood & Co., 1929) ; and Hughlings Jackson in the *Medical Times and Gazette* (1876) and *Brain* (1888–9) .

[49] See the report of Dr. Leo T. Stone: " Paradoxical Symptoms in Right Temporal Lobe Tumor," *Journal of Nervous and Mental Diseases,* Vol. LXXIX, pp. 1–13 (January 1934) .

they got to this alleged place, it seems to have suddenly vanished, and the girl could not substantiate her story in the slightest detail. . . .

" Up to this time, by the girl's wishes, the information had been given unknown to the step-mother. The girl was detained in the station as the result of her self-accusation, and when the family appeared it was stated that, notwithstanding her story, she had never been away from home a single evening or night. There was not the slightest reason to believe she had ever been unchaste. It was her first stories as told to the police which got into the newspapers. The family said she came home from the evangelistic meeting, where conditions in the New York slums had been described, in a very hysterical state, and it appeared she had very soon afterward gone to these other people and made astonishing confessions about her own life. Her family stated that her memory was very peculiar. At one time she might repeat much of a long sermon she had just heard, and at another time would seem to be very forgetful of recent events." [50]

Three times during 1927-8 Governor Young of California granted reprieves to an obscure, penniless Negro by the name of George Watters. Watters was accused of murdering his wife, and, chiefly on the testimony of his nine-year-old daughter, was tried, convicted, and sentenced to be hanged. The case was appealed to the supreme court, where the judgment was affirmed.

Careful study of the evidence by a psychiatrist, Dr. Anita M. Mühl, on behalf of the Governor, indicated that it was more than likely that not only did Watters not commit a murder, but that no murder was ever committed! No body was ever found and the alleged " deceased " was later seen on the streets of Los Angeles. The nine-year-old daughter, who was the chief witness, was found upon examination to be hysterical, hypersuggestible, very self-contradictory, and probably afflicted with mythomania.[50a]

III. DISTURBANCES OF ASSOCIATION

If the word " king " is submitted to a group of 1,000 people who have been instructed to respond with the first word that

[50] William Healy: *The Individual Delinquent*, Case 168 (Boston: Little, Brown & Co., 1915) . See also William Healy and Mary Tenney Healy: *Pathological Lying, Accusation and Swindling* (Boston: Little, Brown & Co., 1915) , pp. 93-7.

[50a] The false accusations of a sixteen-year-old servant girl resulted in the hanging of twenty-four persons and the burning at the stake of fourteen others, plus the deportation of seventy-one. This in New York City in 1741. (See " The Slave Plot of 1741," *New Yorker,* August 23, 1930.)

occurs to them after hearing it, about 354 will be found to have thought of " queen," 150 " ruler," 50 " monarch," 50 " crown," 20 " power," 20 " England," and some scores of various other words.

Similarly, if the word " dark " be submitted, the majority of persons (at least one-half) will respond with the word " light," and another large group will say " night."

These may be said to be normal associations to stimulus words. Some individuals, however, will respond at variance from any of the score or more of normal reactions. For example, to the word " dark," some may be found who will respond instead of with " night," with " murder "; others with a girl's name, a senseless word — such as " dork " or " sork," a rhyme — such as "Hark, hark, the lark," or nothing, for a time; then a strange association — for example, " letter." Any one, or perhaps all, of these associations might be given by an individual who had, for example, recently been implicated in a crime. Delay in response is due to a struggle with the " censor " of our thoughts as to the propriety of the delivery of one of several thought-associations. The common association is, let us say, " night "; but if " night " of itself connotes a situation of fear or shame or some other painful emotion, there will be an internal mental struggle to prevent the emergence of this painful word. A substitute word will be used, which will be likely to be a telltale word, unless the censor is quick enough to head it off, in which case a nonsense word is apt to come forth which in itself is a telltale index to the experienced listener. (Standardized word lists and responses are in regular use by psychologists as a test method.)

The thing illustrated is a disturbance in thought-association. It appears in ordinary life in many ways. At a dinner-party someone mentions a hare. A fastidious lady whose emotions are sensitized to bodily references hears it " hair," glances at her food in alarm, and becomes nauseated. Someone mentions poverty, and the fellow who has just overdrawn his checking account is suffused with discomfort and can think of nothing to say. The girl with a guilty conscience is forgetting last night and having a lovely time until someone mentions " petting parties." She feels chilly all over and tries to laugh with the rest, but laughs too loudly and then becomes too silent.

For these individuals the idea A is followed, not by B and C, as ordinarily, but by ideas M or S, etc. — special experience-associations which disturb the ordinary sequence of association.

In extreme cases of association, patients may be unable to reply to questions, or to talk at all. Or they talk freely for a while and then suddenly, in the middle of a sentence, stop short unable to proceed. Or they may deflect the line of thought, or interrupt it, repeatedly.

" And when I had told him good-bye, I stepped into the taxi and said to the driver: ' I want — ' " (Silence.)

" Go on." (Silence.) " Go on." (Silence.) " Please go on."

" That's all." (*Blocking.*)

" Whatever they may do, they show you a good time. Good time doesn't describe it; it's glorious — glorious — glorious — morning glory — ous — Do you like flowers? I do. I like flowers all around me — on the table — on the mantel — on the ceiling — ha ha — on the light-fixtures — mistletoe — you know! Oh, boy! That's me. Maybe! Don't take too much for granted. I came here on the California Limited, but I'm not so fast. Fast and get thin. That's more important. Coolidge economy — that'll do it. Cal Coolidge. Cal or Al — what do you think of Al? " (*Incoherence.*)

Still more severely dissociated:

" Have just been to supper. Did not knowing what the woodchuck sent me here. How when the blue blue blue on the said anyone can do it that tries. Such is the presidential candidate." (From the letter of a patient with a mental disease, schizophrenia.)

Yet more:

" My dear dear dear dear dear dear dear dear my dear my dear dear." (From the efforts of a man to write a letter who had had a stroke of apoplexy, involving the writing centre of the brain.) (*Verbigeration.*)

Another type (also due to a brain-injury, the rest of the mental faculties being unimpaired) :

> " The Lord is my hospital
> I shall not want
> He marries me green pastors parters
> He leadeth me leadeth me leadeth . . ."

Group of ideas, together with their emotional concomitants, may become split off from the main personality in one way or another and continue a separate existence. This existence is always more or less dependent on the main constellations, and hence is something like the moon and the earth. According to the size of the satellite, these splittings have different names.

FIVE TYPES OF DISSOCIATION

The following classification of dissociations is based on one suggested by F. L. Wells.[51]

Type I. Dissociation, from the main consciousness, of a process ordinarily consciously controlled (motion, speech, sensation, etc.).

A pretty and formerly popular high-school student was brought to the mental-hygiene clinic with a useless leg; the parents related that for two years she had been unable to stand upon it or use it in any way while erect; they had to carry her everywhere. Lying upon the bed or couch, however, she was able to move it quite normally. Neurological examinations showed the nerves to be uninjured. (*Astasia.*)

A soldier in the trenches in France was stunned by the explosion of a large shell. He " came to " almost immediately, but felt that something had happened to him. He was at first unable to move any part of his body, but soon he found that he was twitching and jerking all over. His tremors continued after he had been removed to the base hospital. He appeared to be in a terrible fright, but said that he felt no fear. Neurological tests showed that he had lost all feeling for even so sharp a stimulus as a needle thrust deeply into the skin.

A school-child of nine suddenly began to scream and hold her hand to her head. Relatives flocked about her; doctors were called; all sorts of relief measures were tried in vain. The screams finally changed into prolonged wailings and loud crying. Suddenly it all ceased, the child rose and went about her play as if nothing had happened.

A woman of forty lay on a specially made springless bed, maintaining at all times as nearly as possible a motionless position. She was carefully fed and nursed by her solicitous farmer husband, who came in from his farm-work many times a day to attend to her special needs. She talked glibly and volubly of her " terrible condition " and recited in detail how five years previously she had permitted herself to make a slight move in the bed, which resulted in a sudden and terrible shock of pain in the head, blackness, feeling of imminent destruction, etc. Since then she had not ventured to repeat this rash act. This patient was hypnotized, and in this state she rose from the bed, in which she had not moved for five years, went to the supper-table, and ate with her family. For a few weeks she repeated this even when not in the hypnotic state.

[51] *Mental Adjustments* (New York: D. Appleton & Co., 1922), pp. 156-7.

Then she relapsed into the old conviction of helpless immobility. Five years have now passed; she is still lying motionless, fed and tended by her faithful husband.

Neighbours and relatives clustered about the bed of a woman who appeared to them to be dying. She gasped and struggled for breath; she writhed and groaned; from time to time she threw herself into the air and screamed and jerked her body convulsively. The family physician had suggested a consultation. The consultant arrived, examined the patient, conferred with the family physician aloud in the patient's presence, assuring him that she would recover both mentally and physically. The next morning the patient was as well as ever.[52]

There are many examples in literature — none better than the old woman in Selma Lagerlöf's *Jerusalem* who had taken to her bed and there remained, paralysed, for years. She was "cured" by a combination of prophecy (suggestion) and emergency — her child tumbles into the fire and she leaps to its rescue.

Type II. Dissociation, from the control of the main personality, of a process ordinarily controlled unconsciously and automatically (digestion, heart-action, etc.).

This is the explanation of many "functional" diseases of the body, such as goitre, gastric ulcer, "nervous indigestion," etc. Alexander reminds us that the nervous system divides its task so that the regulation of the body to the external environment is ordinarily managed by the cerebrospinal nervous system, and the regulation of the inner processes is managed by the autonomic or vegetative nervous system. Emotional disturbances, however, may bring about a confusion in this division of labour so that an impulse which would ordinarily lead to an external action becomes repressed, takes a wrong pathway, and instead of some voluntary nervous system response such as striking, or running, a vegetative nervous system response results. Unexpressed hate or fear, for example, may be converted into "organic speech" and appear as functional disturbances of the stomach or heart. Alexander compares this to the internal revolutions which so often follow a defeat in war with another country and the political stratagem of checking revolutionary tendencies by starting military movements against foreign nations.

[52] These are cases of hysteria, taken from an article by the author in *Hygeia*, August 1927, pp. 394–6. For additional illustrations see Chapter II, pp. 141–7 and Chapter V, pp. 379–86.

" The emotions and wishes to which the individual cannot give expression and relief in actions concerning the environment find expression in the unintelligible tacit language of inner organic processes." [53]

A student who was trying to make his way through college by means of a job requiring long hours at small pay stumbled and fell, tearing his one and only suit beyond repair. This and a few other unexpected drains on his slender resources put him into dire straits. He actually lived for a few weeks on about twenty-five cents a day. Even then it looked as if he were not going to be able to make the grade.

Suddenly he began to have a terrific pain in his head. He never had had headaches, but this one made up for all his years of exemption. It bore down upon him and prevented his doing anything — working, studying, or even eating. There was obviously only one thing to do — he must quit school, honourably discharged as it were, on account of illness.

But he didn't. A small loan was negotiated and the headache disappeared at once.

A very dressy woman marched into my office one day, trailed by a handsome but worried-looking little husband, whom I knew to be a fairly successful merchant. " I'm early," she announced, " because I wouldn't take the bus. I made *that* bring me." (" That " seemed to refer to her husband.) " He doesn't have to be at that business of his all the time; he works too hard anyway; the rest will do him good. So I just told him he had to bring me."

" Are you bragging? " I asked.

" Why, certainly not, certainly not! Why, what do you mean? I didn't come here to be insulted. My husband loves to wait on me. I am a nervous and physical wreck. My arms, my back, my head, all pain me constantly — I have nervous diarrhœa — my heart palpitates — I have the most terrible nervous chills; I just know I'm going to die! "

" But she doesn't die," sighed the husband. " She lives on, enjoying ill health. So long as I entertain her and indulge her in her self-centred life, she feels fine. If my efforts to amuse her and wait on her flag, if I let up one little bit in order to keep my business appointments, if I go out one evening to the lodge, she's all in again. But I've never dared say so until today."

A friend of mine has been courting a girl for many years, yet he won't marry her, nor will he ever take her to a public gathering. Once I asked

[53] Franz Alexander: " Functional Disturbances of Psychogenic Nature, *Journal of the American Medical Association,* Vol. C, no. 7 (February 18, 1933) .

him why. " Well," he said, " I'm ashamed to tell you, but the truth is I no sooner get seated in the theatre or church or social gathering with her than an overpowering desire to go to the toilet descends upon me and there is simply nothing to do but leave the room, and such embarrassment I simply can't bear, so I dodge all such situations — including marriage." It would do no good to explain to him that his unconscious had played a simple trick on him, and that his natural sexual impulses aroused by the girl were being represented in this urinary disguise — a childhood stage of sexual expression. It would do no good because he could neither understand nor believe it.

Mrs. R. was a well-poised, gracious, and intelligent woman who consulted scores of physicians, chiefly heart specialists, because of one curious, persistent symptom. Her heart would suddenly begin to palpitate and pound along at a rapid rate in a distressingly appreciable fashion. Most of the heart specialists agreed that there was no disease of the heart. They said it was "nervous" in origin. A little psychological study of Mrs. R. revealed the fact that the portals of her consciousness were periodically bombarded with repressed recollections of intense emotionalism — fright, shame, and anxiety — over incidents supposedly forgotten. Her consciousness never recalled them, but her heart did.

Type III. Dissociation of a group of ideas from the main mass or stream of controlled associations.

Automatic writing is a pretty illustration of how two different streams of thinking may coexist, without mutual acquaintance or dependence. Simple as the experiment is, many have not seen it and many can scarcely bring themselves to believe that a subject can be induced to write lines, pages, even whole books, without conscious knowledge of their contents. In fact, the best way to demonstrate the faculty is to divert the attention of the writer by conversation or reading, letting the hand on the tablet write as it will. As is well known, some whole works — notably those of a St. Louis woman, under the pseudonym of Patience Worth — have been written thus automatically. Ouija boards and planchettes depend on the same principle.

All of us are familiar with the emergence into consciousness of unconscious material, such as dreams. The dissociated nature of these will be discussed later; it is evident, however, in some notable instances, such as Coleridge's *Kubla Khan*, a poem conceived in his sleep. Edward Lucas White's long and elaborate novel *Andivius Hedulio* is stated by the author to have been largely dreamed. Mr. White's numerous other books were composed, I believe, without the interposition of the dream state. The following case cited by McDougall [54] is another illustration:

"A man in his early prime, who followed the calling of a stock-broker, lived a normally active social and athletic existence. His tastes were those of an average member of his class; he had no special literary interests; poetry he had always regarded with indifference as a thing rather for women than for men. He had the habit of lying in a half-waking state for some little time before rising each morning. He noticed that, thus half-awake, lines of what seemed to be verse would come into his mind. He was sufficiently interested to jot them down on paper, and found that they made connected and coherent verses, which seemed to him as good as other verses he had seen in print. He therefore sent some of the verses, thus subconsciously produced, to the editor of a magazine. To his astonishment they were accepted. At the time when he told me of these facts, a number of his poems, produced in this way, had been published in leading magazines, and — paid for. Such of these poems as I read seemed to me of considerable merit, in a bold romantic style. An interesting feature of the production was that often the lines of a poem would come into his consciousness as complete but detached lines in irregular order; these lines could then be sorted out in the fully waking condition, and arranged, without other change, to make the complete poem. This fact shows very clearly that the verses were designed and constructed before the several lines came to consciousness."

Type IV. Dissociation of a system of ideas which displace the main consciousness or "personality" in its control of the organism.

Here belong *fugues* (already discussed under defects of memory; see page 189), *automatisms, somnambulisms,* and occurrences of *multiple personality.*

Automatism in absent-mindedness:

All the absent-minded-professor jokes illustrate this. One told me by a friend will do as well as any. "My wife had reminded me one evening of a dinner engagement which I dreaded. But I went obediently upstairs to dress. This necessitated removing my street clothes in order to replace them with a Tuxedo. I recall having been engrossed in some reflections about a difficult case, and my wife says I was talking to myself when she last listened. I didn't appear downstairs and she came

[54] William McDougall: *Outline of Abnormal Psychology* (New York: Charles Scribner's Sons, 1926), p. 257.

up to investigate. I had carried the undressing to completion, donned my pyjamas, and gone to bed! "

Automatism in hysteria:

A new nurse was on duty in the children's ward. Suddenly she disappeared. About the same time the nurses in the convalescent women's ward noticed a new addition to their ranks. This new girl pitched right into the work without saying a word and went about her tasks as if thoroughly acquainted with them. When spoken to she stared and made no reply. An hour later she approached the head nurse and asked where she was and where the children's ward could be found.

Automatism in epilepsy:

An electrical engineer of considerable ability was referred for examination by the corporation for which he worked because of a very embarrassing episode. He had been engaged in some delicate experimental work in the laboratories of the company, which adjoined a small clerical room. He had entered this room, apparently engrossed in deep thought, and a moment later one of the stenographers uttered scream after scream. Other employees rushed in to find him gazing at her and at them in amazement. She declared that he had approached her as if to grasp or attack her, which he vigorously and persistently denied, but was unable to assign a reason for being away from his laboratory.

It developed, however, that upon numerous other occasions he had suddenly dropped his work for a few seconds and indulged in queer purposeless stunts. He would balance a chair on one leg, or dally with a light-cord, or run hastily to the front door or up and down a flight of stairs.

Somnambulisms:

Somnambulisms are similar to automatisms except that they appear to develop while the patient is and has been sleeping, and differ from fugues and cases of multiple personality, in which a larger part of the personality is split off so that the patient is able to pass for a normal individual. This is rarely true in automatisms and somnambulisms.

A professional woman of great ability once consulted me for a symptom which had been present for the second twenty years of her life. She would rise from her bed in her sleep and search about her own room for a lost " package," a package which she had never seen, but which she could vaguely describe — from remembered dreams — and of which she had the feeling that to find it would confer upon her wonderful blessing and satisfaction.

In the course of psychoanalytic treatment she discovered what the " package " represented and thereafter never walked in her sleep again.

The motif of somnambulism occurs rarely in literature. *Aebelö* by Michaelis and *Jörn Uhl* by Gustav Frenssen are modern novels in which somnambulism plays the dominant part. The notable German motion picture *The Cabinet of Dr. Caligari* is based on one of the many mediæval legends dealing with somnambulism. Such legends were common in the Middle Ages, when the unusual was commonly unexplainable and attributed to a divine or a diabolical intervention. *The Cabinet of Dr. Caligari,* in which the somnambulist commits murder and kidnaps and attempts rape, was supposed to illustrate the fact that sleepwalking fulfils wishes which are inhibited in waking hours.

The first two editions of this book included the report of a man of forty-eight who, according to the newspaper accounts, had shot and killed his wife during a sleepwalking episode. Similar cases have been reported in the newspapers several times.

I have never seen such a case professionally or known personally of any such instance. Newspapers have more recently carried the full account of a sixteen-year-old girl who was acquitted of the murder of her father on the plea that she committed it during a somnambulistic dream. This patient was thoroughly examined psychiatrically following her acquittal and it was then definitely established that she was not subject to somnambulism and that the murder of her father had not occurred under those circumstances. According to the history given, this same girl had been found tied and gagged some years previously and had claimed then that this had been done to her by housebreakers; it became quite certain that she had done it to herself. Clinical examination indicated that she was afflicted with a serious mental disease and she was later committed to a state hospital. Although this patient's youth, looks, and ability to enlist the sympathy of many people may have contributed, the fact that a jury would accept the defence plea as a mitigating circumstance is indicative of the mystery and ignorance that surrounds sleepwalking.

In certain ways there are marked similarities between sleepwalking and the unrealistic behaviour of patients affected with schizophrenia (see Chapter II) , but we know of no direct relationship. Sleepwalkers do not, so far as I know, ever become schizophrenics and, unlike the latter, sleepwalkers can be easily awakened. There is a widespread belief that sleepwalkers never injure themselves, even though they may take dangerous risks in their perambulations. This I can say, from clinical experience, is very definitely not true. We have studied cases in which sleepwalkers have seriously injured themselves by severe falls, not once but repeatedly.[54a]

Multiple personality:

Dr. Jekyll and Mr. Hyde is the prototype of alternating dual personality in " normal " persons. This should not be confused with alternations of mood from gay to sad, characteristic of the cyclic temperament. These are merely emotional swings; personality splits are far more comprehensive. The classical case in medical literature is that of Miss Sally Beauchamp, elaborately written up many years ago by that pioneer American psychopathologist Morton Prince. This girl was a patient of Dr. Prince's over a period of years, during which time he described numerous entirely distinct personality pictures appearing at different times.

More recently quite a few cases have been reported.[54b] It is likely that most of them have been artificially (although unintentionally) produced by suggestion (that is, hypnosis). It is well known that under hypnosis a second personality may be induced temporarily — that is, a subject may believe himself to be a butcher or a sailor and be induced to act in accordance with that belief.

Spontaneous (?) doubling of the personality with alternations or coexistence is well illustrated by the following brief abstract of a long and carefully studied case: [55]

Norma was an attractive girl of nineteen, whose normal personality sometimes changed to that of four-year-old " Polly." As Norma she was highly intelligent, well-mannered, modest, and obedient. As Polly she talked baby talk, could neither read nor write, and was coarse,

[54a] For a scientific study, see Sadger's *Sleepwalking and Moonwalking* (New York: Nervous & Mental Disease Publishing Co., 1920).

[54b] For a very carefully studied example see " Vera," by Dr. A. G. Ikin in the *British Jour. Med. Psychol.*, Nov. 1924.

[55] H. H. Goddard: " A Case of Dual Personality," *Journal of Abnormal and Social Psychology*, Vol. XXI, no. 2 (July–September 1926), p. 170; abstract by Roberta Smith.

selfish, outspoken, and wilful. In this last state she tested a little under four years old on the Binet intelligence tests.

These transitions from one personality to the other were made by way of a period of sleep. When in one state she had no memory of her life in the other personality.

While in the Polly condition she wrote a letter by automatic writing which was neat and well written, and in which she answered correctly questions which Polly knew nothing about. She wrote that she was fifteen years old and showed an intelligence of fifteen by the Binet test. The next day, still Polly, she wrote that she thought she was nineteen. There was, however, no change in her personality. For a few weeks after that she was Polly most of the time. Then came a change, and she was Norma again.

As Polly she began to be totally anæsthetic and could not even feel a needle thrust under the thumb-nail to the root of the nail. At other times motor control was lost.

Twice she passed from Norma to Polly without sleep. One day she suddenly changed from Polly to Norma without the usual transition period. Goddard questioned her and found that the two personalities had blended; she could now remember what she had done and said as Polly. She showed sincere regret for things she had done in the four-year-old state.

She soon passed into the Polly state again and was more difficult to manage than before. Changing to Norma, she was not so careful of her speech as she had been before when in that personality. Goddard found the plan of trying to keep her in the Norma state by hypnosis unsuccessful. He then tried the plan of restoring the memory of one personality for another, with more success. As Polly she was put in a hypnotic state, and when she awoke had full memory of her life as Norma. As Norma the process was repeated and she again remembered Polly.

After that she was Norma most of the time. Gradually the Norma personality was established, and the Polly personality rarely appeared.

Type V. Dissociation of one of several ideas which the main consciousness is aware of, but fails to recognize, and hence misunderstands, mislabels, and projects (a term to be more fully discussed in the next chapter). Here belong hallucinations, previously discussed under perceptual distortions, and also delusions, the most characteristic and typical distortions of the thinking process, now to be illustrated.

Delusions:

Saint Peter and his contemporaries believed that the end of the world would shortly arrive. Many times since then certain individuals have become convinced that they knew the precise date when this was to happen. They have usually been disappointed. Sir A. Conan Doyle and Sir Oliver Lodge were sure that they had communicated with the dead. Bishop Berkeley was convinced that water mixed with tar would cure most of the ills of mankind. Woodrow Wilson believed that the French and English diplomats were sincere. Millions of people believed that the Great War was a " war to end war," and a few thought that America entered it for moral and idealistic reasons only. All of these were delusions.

We may define a delusion in the conventional terms of being a false belief, but as used in psychiatry it is a false belief not generally shared by those about one and resisting all ordinary measures to correct it. We can become lost in philosophical abstractions about this; for practical purposes delusions are utterly and obviously mistaken ideas for which the sole authority is some inner feeling on the part of the subject. This inner feeling arises, of course, from deep unconscious trends, which will be explained a little later (see page 247) .

The delusion arises to make possible an adjustment of the personality to otherwise unendurable tensions. The ego thus makes an effort to alter reality in order to make it acceptable to itself; for this reason it is convenient to classify delusions (as below) on the basis of the place which the ego gives itself in the new system. Quantitatively one might also classify delusions by the degree of unreality or dereism which they imply; there is often a grain of truth in even the most absurd delusions (although it may be very hard to find) ; others are obviously much less extreme distortions of reality.[56]

Before discussing the significance of delusions, it will be well to illustrate some of the more frequent types encountered. This will be done in the form of quotations representing the ideas if

---

[56] I remember a patient who believed himself to be watched by the police, secret-service agents, and others, and insisted upon one occasion that the police were taking special notice of his automobile. This type of delusion corresponds so typically with one familiar to all psychiatrists and was so directly in line with other delusions of this patient that I discounted it entirely. A few days later he brought me documentary proof; it was actually true that at least *some* policemen had taken note of his car because it bore the license plate of a state relatively infrequently seen in this city and the patient had considerably overstayed the tax exemption period. He was, therefore, partly correct in fact, although not in theory.

not the actual words of some severely ill and severely deluded persons.

Centrifugal types (the ego is made the subject)
   a. Delusions of grandeur:

" I'm the richest man in the world. I'm worth ten trillion dollars. I've already given this town seven libraries and I'm going to give you four million dollars just to show you I think you're the best doctor in the world."

" Don't call me Henry. My name used to be Henry, but I've been promoted. I was King Henry for a while, but now I'm God Almighty Lord Jehovah. You can call me God for short."

" I had expected to leave for Chicago this morning had you folks not detained me. I expect to meet some fellows there who will put this thing across. They are big men, with big brains and big money, and when I explain this they will jump clear over their chairs to get first whack at it. They'll probably form a corporation, make me chairman of the board, and we'll have to organize a foreign sales department at once, because this is a world-beater. You think I'm crazy, but just remember — that's what they said about Fulton and James Watt and all the rest of us! "

   b. Delusions of deprivation and disease (hypochondriacal) :

" I'm not the man I used to be. Something has hit me hard. I've lost ground. I can't stand up against things. I think it's my heart. I feel funny around my heart, and there are queer sensations all through my chest. It may be high blood-pressure — my uncle died with that. They say that results from constipation and I'm fearfully constipated. No movement for days and days; full of poisons, that's what I am, full of poisons, and ruined. Just a shell of a man, a walking corpse, slowly decaying."

" Below my armpits I'm made of rubber — dead, lifeless rubber. My liver is petrified, my lungs are solid, my bowels have rotted away. Can't you see how my legs have turned crooked? All my blood-vessels have dried up, I'm a shrunken, shrivelled shell. I can't swallow; my throat is blocked. I have syphilis and every other foul disease."

" We've nothing left. We'll all starve. I haven't a cent — just debts, debts everywhere. I'm ruined, that's what I am. I've no right to be here, eating three meals a day with nothing to pay for it — an object of charity, my children somewhere starving. Oh, God pity my poor children, crying for food, and me feasting here in the hospital! Our hogs have all run away. The stock is dead, the wheat burned up, our home is gone. I've squandered our last penny. We're ruined! "

c. Delusions of sin and self-accusation:

" I am the cause of it all. Let God punish me as He may. It was I who started the Great War, and it is I who brought these horrors upon the world. I am the greatest sinner of them all — I have committed the unpardonable sin. God have mercy on my soul! "

" Once — it was thirty years ago — I stole a quarter from my mother's purse. A thief all my life! That's the kind of a man I am. I've been disloyal — I've turned my back on Christ. There's no use talking. Such a man is hopeless."

Centripetal types (the ego is made the object)

These are also called *paranoid* delusions, an interesting word derived thus: *para,* "beside" (i.e., distorted), and *noos,* "mind" = *paranoia,* a name first used (1863) by Kahlbaum to describe a disease characterized among other things by many delusions, chiefly persecutory. Then *paranoia* plus *oid* ("similar to," or "of the nature of") is *paranoioid,* elided for euphony into *paranoid,* and referring to delusional states similar to, but not identical with, those of paranoia.

d. Delusions of persecution:

" It was more or less gradual and insidious. At first I didn't think much about it. I just supposed I was having a run of hard luck or an off season. All at once, however, it dawned on me that there were too many coincidences. The window in my office was always open just a few inches more than I had left it. I'd leave my chair facing east, and I'd go out to come back to find it facing south. My pen would have dried ink on it — there were fresh spots on the desk blotter. All these things taken together convinced me. My deals all miscarried — my secrets all leaked out — my experiments all went bad. Why? Because I'm the object of an organized plot to annihilate me. I'm too dangerous to the aspirations of someone. And I'm going to have to pay the penalty. They're after me."

" Poison in your coffee — stinking gas injected into your room -- radio signals flashing all around — dirty looks and sneers from the neighbourhood children — hidden dangers everywhere — how would *you* like it? "

" This is not the first time that the Reds, Socialists, Pacifists, and their college-professor allies have attempted to prevent, and have actually prevented, murderers and other violators of the law from getting their just deserts. The leader of the movement to set these two murderers free is Felix Frankfurter, Professor at Harvard College. . . .

". . . So far as Red criminals are concerned our judicial systems are being scrapped, and the decisions of juries and courts are being supplanted by the decisions of the mob . . . and this is being made possible because college professors and ministers of the gospel are lending respectability to the mob! . . .

". . . I find that this bold, resourceful and able gang of enemies with ample funds are . . . instilling subversive doctrines into the minds. . . .

". . . A widespread assault is now being made on the sanctity of marriage and sacred family relations . . . with great success in the leading colleges for women. . . . We find the presidents and professors of most of them members of the Babrin-Foster Committee, or its allied organizations." [57]

e. Delusions of reference (i.e., referring back to " me ") :

" Everyone knows it. I come in the door of my home; neighbours are visiting, but they promptly leave. I kiss my wife; she coughs three times, meaning disgust. I pick up the evening paper and the headlines say: ' Baker will run,' which really means I had better run. I go out for a walk, and people stare at me and nudge each other as I pass; they whisper to each other and cast glances over their shoulders. At the movies they seem to see me coming and throw in a few jabs at me in the sub-titles. ' It won't be long now,' one of them said, and ' He wondered if she knew! ' They've got something on me — there's no doubt of that, and they are closing in on me; only I don't know what it is! "

f. Delusions of jealousy:

" She doesn't love me any more. I can tell. She doesn't smile at me like she used to, nor kiss me passionately any more. She is cold and indifferent — she's never home when I get there, and she makes no explanations — no adequate explanations, that is. There must be some other man in the case. I have no proof, of course, and yet — well, judge for yourself. Over and over I try to reach her by phone, and the line is busy. I come home unexpectedly and she looks startled and her

---

[57] From a speech made before the L —— Kiwanis Club, June 30, 1927, and distributed by the Massachusetts Civic Welfare Alliance in printed form, as published in the Boston *Traveler*, June 30, 1927.

face flushes. I say I'm going on a trip for a few days and she smiles and seems pleased.

" Well, that isn't all. She's for ever riding the bus to and from town — she says it's cheaper than driving the car, but that's not it. It's one certain bus — and one certain bus-driver — I know it is. They even have some sort of a signal system — I've heard a queer lot of tootings — three short ones and two long ones — and then I've seen her run to the window and peer out, not knowing that I was watching her. Of course when I accuse her of it she laughs and says I'm crazy. But I know a thing or two, and there's going to be a sad interruption in a little love game one of these nights. Kill him? Sure I would. Aren't they plotting right now how to get rid of me? Didn't you read about the Hall-Mills case? Well, I'm wise, I am. And I'll shoot first."

THE MECHANISMS OF DELUSIONS

Although a systematic consideration of the mechanisms behind all these symptoms is the subject-matter of the next chapter, a brief explanation of the *why* of delusions here will make them much more easily understood.

All delusions are to be regarded as dissociated fragments or systems of which the main consciousness is fully aware, but which it fails to recognize as such, and hence misunderstands, misinterprets, mislabels.

1. Sometimes these fragments are split off because they represent unattainable wishes. In spite of a cold world of reality which the main consciousness must face, certain dear fancies may endure providing they can be sufficiently dissociated. This type is represented by the woman who believes her dead husband to be merely sleeping and by the man who thinks himself a billionaire. In other words, if Mohammed won't come to the mountain, the mountain is brought to Mohammed. This mechanism is called introjection. More about it will be given later.

2. In other instances the dissociation takes place because the fragment split off is a fault or wish which is repugnant to the main consciousness, and hence to retain it would result in self-reproach. To avoid this conflict the dissociation is effected, the offending fragment (or wish or complex) is projected upon some " goat " who can be given all the abuse that the possession of such an obnoxious quality deserves. This explains the mote-and-the-beam parable — the gallant buck-passing of Mr. Adam

to Mrs. Eve. It is an excellent cloak for the skeleton in the closet.

In delusions of persecution the dissociated fragment is usually a secret desire, unknown even to its possessor consciously, but unconsciously recognized by him as a wicked and unworthy possession. The old maid's delusion of being followed by a man is a clear illustration. This mechanism is called projection. It, too, will be discussed later in greater detail.

3. Delusions of sinfulness, sickness, poverty, and the like represent combinations of projection and introjection. A man who erroneously believes himself to be ruined, for example, may have several unconscious reasons for believing this; in the first place, he may have such a *wish,* not as applied to himself, but as applied to someone else whom he thinks he loves. The conscious love overlays the conscious hate, hate which cannot be expressed because it is incompatible with conscious affection. He seems thus to identify himself with the person against whom he has uttered (perhaps silently) these destructive wishes, so that the delusion carries out at the same time the phantasy of an aggression and the appropriate self-punishment for such a phantasy. These, then, are really delusions of *hate*.

4. Paranoid delusions, on the other hand, *seem* to be delusions of *love* — a distorted, misinterpreted, conflictual love. They really mean something like this: " I love that person, or I did, and I want him to love me. But he doesn't. I hate him for this and I am justified in hating him or at least fearing him because it is clear that he hates me."

This roundabout way of changing " I love him " into " He hates me " has been worked out in great detail both in scientific and in literary contributions. Of the former, most thoroughgoing is Freud's study of the celebrated Schreber case.[58]

5. Finally there are delusions (and illusions and failures of memory) which exist to make life tolerable. Schopenhauer and others describe us as dashing about doing things in order to for-

[58] *Psychoanalytic Notes upon an Autobiographical Account of a Case of Paranoia,* English translation in the *Collected Papers* by Sigmund Freud, Vol. III, pp. 387–466 (London: Hogarth Press, 1924) ; and in literature, *Flight into Darkness,* by Arthur Schnitzler (New York: Simon & Schuster, 1932) makes clear the same mechanisms. See especially the revisions of the original interpretation made by Dr. Robert Knight in " The Relationship of Latent Homosexuality to the Mechanism of Paranoid Delusions," *Bulletin of the Menninger Clinic,* September 1940, which bring the explanation more directly in line with Freud's revision of his own instinct theory.

get how miserable an existence we lead and how certain is the death we must die. Perhaps the melancholiacs with nihilistic delusions are right in thinking life isn't worth living. But most of us want to go on thinking it is.

" For human memory and human optimism are adepts at the prevarications which everybody grasps, retails and tirelessly reiterates: these two it is who coin the fictions which every person weaves into the interminable extravaganza that he recites to himself as an accurate summing-up of his own past and future: and everywhere about this earth's revolving surface moves a circulating library of unwritten novels bound in cloth and haberdashery.

" The wholesome effect of these novels is patent. It is thanks to this brace of indefatigable romancers, it is due to the lax grasp of memory and to the perennation of optimism, that nobody really needs to notice how the most of us, in unimportant fact, approach toward death through gray and monotonous corridors. Besides, one finds a number of colorful alcoves here and there, to be opened by intoxication or venery, by surrender to the invigorating lunacy of herd action, or even by mental concentration upon new dance-steps and the problems of chess and auction bridge. One blunders, indeed, into a rather handsome number of such alcoves which, when entered, temporarily shut out the rigidity and the only exit of the inescapable corridor. Life thus becomes for humankind a far different matter from what it would seem to any merely reasonable creature, since life's monotonous main tenor is thus diversified by an endless series of slight distracting interests and of small but very often positive pleasures in the way of time-wasting and misdemeanor. And in addition, as we go, all sorts of merry tales are being interchanged, about what lies beyond the nearing door and the undertaker's little black bag." [59]

DISTORTED EMOTION

Emotional distortions to be discussed are of four types:

1. Schizothmyic, or inappropriate, reactions;
2. Phobias (morbid fears) ;
3. Anxiety states;
4. Perversions of affection and interest.

[59] James Branch Cabell: *Straws and Prayer-Books* (New York: Robert McBride & Co., 1924) , p. 28.

1. *Schizothymic reactions*

To respond to the aroma of broiling beefsteak with disgust or with fear may seem incredibly abnormal. The emotions of disgust and fear seem totally inappropriate to the stimulus which should evoke pleasurable anticipation.

Yet a seasick ocean voyager experiences disgust at such a small matter; so does a very strict vegetarian of certain persuasions. Some neurotic patients may react to it with fear. These twisted or inappropriate emotional responses are one type of emotional distortion. (*Schizothymia.*)

They appear in less vivid forms in all our friends. A salmon-coloured rose which delights us irritates Miss Brown; Mrs. Clark is bored by music; Mr. Dooley is made angry by the familiarity of pet dogs or cats; Mr. Erwin is tremendously interested in certain genera of worms which most of us find repulsive. These may be exaggerated in degree, but the shifting of emotional response is always of this general type.

One never knew, for example, how a certain patient of mine was going to react. Sometimes she would scream if one said " Good morning " to her; an hour later she would respond to the same greeting with peals of laughter. A box of candy from her husband might be thrown out the window, or offered politely to all the nurses and patients, or locked in a bureau drawer untouched. A pleasant smile was sometimes returned similarly, at other times ignored; upon still other occasions it might provoke streams of bitter and profane denunciation. Her emotional reactions were nearly always utterly inappropriate.

This symptom, schizothymia, is a very important one in psychiatry, because it is one criterion of the severity of the internal disharmony of the schizoid personality. In other words, when a schizoid personality begins to disintegrate, to break down, to " go crazy," the degree of schizothymia present is a rough index of the degree of mental damage. The patient just described, for example, is extremely broken of mind.

The newspapers said that Edward Hickman, the California murderer, laughed and joked about his crime, his trial, his mother's distress, and his execution. If this be true, it is more significant of mental disease than is the murder, even in the shocking queerness of its method.

2. *Phobias*

Quite different is the emotional distortion known as a *phobia*. Phobias, or morbid fears, are somtimes vague and general

(*panophobia*). " I just feel anxious and worried all the time."
" I feel as if something terrible were going to happen." " I get
along fine until it suddenly occurs to me that sooner or later
retribution and Nemesis will overtake me." " I'm constantly a
little uneasy — I start at every sudden sound. I feel like a young
girl alone in a big house at night."

Specific fears or phobias begin as such *free-floating* anxiety
which then becomes attached to specific objects and situations
secondarily. The objects or situations selected usually represent repressed (forgotten, unrecognized, unknown) wishes.
This is plain enough in the familiar caricatured man-phobia
of the old maid. To assure her that no man really is following her does not comfort or reassure her; to suggest that
such fears represent hidden wishes is apt to be equally displeas-
ing. Yet nothing is more obvious to everyone else.

Symbolization prevents this substitution from being so obvious in most cases. Thus a fear of dogs — dog-phobia — becomes understandable only when one learns what dog represents
to that particular individual.

There are all sorts of such morbid fears — fears of high places,
low places, open places, closed or narrow places — fears of thunder, of lightning, of blood, of dirt, of darkness, of light, of
crowds, of death, of persons. The statistics of our college students indicate that about twenty per cent of them admit having
or having had phobias. In most cases they sooner or later disappear.

Not always, however.

George Harris remembers that when he was twelve or thirteen he
became morbidly terrified by crowds of people — so much so that
he could not bear to remain in large congregations at church, and
once interrupted the service in making a hasty exit. This fear disappeared, however, until he was nearly through college, when he was
suddenly overwhelmed with fear one day in the confusing crowd of a
big football game. Thereafter he found it difficult to visit any large
city where the business streets were crowded; he could not bear to
enter or remain in a building containing an assembled multitude. He
had to give up eating in restaurants and riding in day coaches because
of the feelings of panic and terror aroused by these situations.

Something of the intensity and extensiveness of phobias may be inferred from the case of Mrs. Sellards, who at thirty-seven developed a
misophobia, or fear of contamination. At first she was made restless

anxious, fearful, only by the presence of broken glass. Then she began to fear the existence of particles of dirt of any kind. She scrubbed
her entire house, on her hands and knees, over and over and over.
She refused to permit anyone to wipe the dishes for her, or to handle
the food, lest they inadvertently contaminate it. She feared lest the
handling of the door-knobs might lead to the carrying of infections, and
scoured them many times a day. Within a short time she was so engulfed in her phobias that her entire life was spent in frantic efforts
to prevent the development of situations which evoked them.

The dynamics of phobia formation will be more fully discussed in the next section. To grasp their nature somewhat better, however, the following instance of *tracing* the phobia to its
origin should be considered.

" A young woman of good heredity developed during her childhood
a severe phobia of running water. She was unable to give any explanation of her disorder, which persisted without noticeable improvement from approximately her seventh to her twentieth year. The
general nature of the disturbance is readily shown.

" Her fear reaction to splashing sounds was especially intense. For
instance, it was necessary for her to be in a distant part of the house
when the bathtub was being filled for her bath and, during the early
years, it often required three members of the family to give the bath.
She always struggled violently and screamed. During one school session a drinking fountain stood in the hall outside of her classroom. If
the sound of children drinking was audible, she became very frightened, actually fainting on one occasion. When she rode on railroad
trains, it was necessary to keep the window curtain down so that the
streams over which the train passed might not be seen.

" During her twentieth year an aunt, Mrs. G., came to visit at her
home. This lady had not seen her niece in thirteen years. She was met
at the station by the mother of the girl, who told her of the daughter's
condition. On arrival at the house, she met the girl and her first words
were ' I have never told.' This served to provoke a recall of the following episode.

" The mother, the aunt, and the little girl — she was then seven
years old — had gone on a picnic. Late in the afternoon the mother decided to return home but the child insisted that she be permitted to
stay longer with her aunt. . . . The two then went into the woods
for a walk and the girl, disobeying her aunt's instructions, ran off alone.
The aunt followed, and after a search, found the child lying wedged
among the rocks of a small stream with a water-fall pouring down over

her head. She was screaming with terror. They proceeded to a farm house where the wet clothes were dried. The child expressed great fear that her mother would learn of her disobedience, but the aunt reassured her with the promise, ' I will never tell.' They returned home and the aunt left the house next morning without seeing her niece. The child was thus left with no one in whom she could confide and had a period of anxiousness. The phobia developed shortly after this.

" After recalling this experience of her childhood, the young woman found it possible to approach running water without discomfort. And gradually the special adjustments, which her phobia had necessitated, disappeared." [60]

This case which has been widely quoted appears to explain a long-standing specific phobia by relating it to an incident associated with painful emotions and therefore repressed. It illustrates the mechanism known as the conditioned reflex [61] — that is, the individual having once reacted in a certain way to a certain stimulus continues to react in the same way to that stimulus even although the reaction is no longer appropriate.

Psychoanalytic studies have shown, however, that such explanations as the above, notwithstanding the therapeutic efficacy indicated in the report, are incomplete. Behind all such apparently causative traumatic episodes such as the one described here are earlier and more significant episodes for which the one reported is a screen. It screens an earlier and more painful episode which cannot be so easily recalled because of its remoteness and its painfulness. Every psychoanalyst has similar experiences daily; his patient will describe a contemporary dream and he will first be able to relate this to a parallel experience in his contemporary life and then to parallel incidents or satisfactions at various epochs in his life, five years ago, twelve years ago, thirty years ago. The nature of these may be such that the original episode, even if it cannot be recalled, may be clearly inferred and in other cases it can be definitely recalled.

The incident described in Bagby's case is strongly suggestive of a *screen memory* for difficulties connected with the patient's birth — the head is wedged, the waters flow over it, etc. Such an experience cannot be recalled by the child and from a therapeutic standpoint it is sufficient if the patient is able to recall so

[60] English Bagby: " The Etiology of Phobias," *Journal of Abnormal Psychology and Social Psychology*, Vol. XVII, no. 1 (April–June 1922), pp. 16–17.

[61] See Ivan P. Pavlov: *Lectures on Conditioned Reflexes* (New York: International Publishers, 1928).

closely related a screen memory as in this episode in which the girl practically relived the birth experience. Probably an important factor was the emotional conflict aroused by the feeling of conspiracy with the aunt against the mother — that is, concealed hostility.

We know from extensive psychoanalytic study that the purpose of the phobia is to prevent the individual from getting into situations or from doing particular acts which for him represent " sins " — that is, satisfactions with which are connected a strong sense of guilt. The phobia or artificial fear protects him from an anxiety connected with the real fear. A woman with strong sexual temptations will connect the latter with, for example, a certain street, perhaps for some such reason as that she once saw a prostitute on that street. Then walking on that street comes to mean for her something like streetwalking — that is, yielding to her torturing temptations. Such yielding causes her real anxiety and fear and she protects herself by avoiding that street. Soon, however, this phobia is extended to other streets and finally to all streets, and some women with such a phobia cannot even leave their houses except in company with a protector.[62]

Superstitions are closely related to phobias, but spread through community life so as to become more or less stereotyped and conventional. Even college students are not free from them.

Two hundred and sixty-seven males and 290 females between 16 and 25 years, all college students, were examined by E. S. Conklin as to superstitiousness. Superstitious belief or practice was indicated in 40 per cent of the male and 66 per cent of the female subjects. Sixty-one per cent of those denying superstition

---

[62] Our first clear understanding of the nature of phobias, obsessions, and the like resulted from a study made by Freud in 1909 of a five-year-old boy. Freud did not himself see this child, but directed the parents in their observations and treatment of him. The parents made many mistakes in their dealings with the child, but they were honest enough to admit them. By comparing these mistakes with the child's misapprehensions and misconceptions about the world, it was possible to understand a very curious phobia which he developed in regard to horses. He became so afraid of them, so afraid that a horse might bite him, that for a while he would not even go out on the street. In spite of this fear, the boy would play horse in the house, pretending to be one. A painstaking study of the case ultimately revealed how little Hans was acting out with horses as symbols the various fears and wishes connected with his parents, particularly their sexual life and the birth of his little sister. The child, his parents, and Professor Freud, who, as it were, surveyed the case from a distance, discovered that the phobia developed about this symbol (horse) as a protection against consciousness of the unendurable anxiety relating to the original ideas. The interested reader is commended to the source: Sigmund Freud: *Collected Papers* (London: Hogarth Press, 1925) , Vol. III, pp. 149–289.

at the time state its former belief or practice. Men appear to outgrow superstition more easily than women; one-half the group assign former superstitions to the years 12–16. Slightly more superstitions per individual are mentioned by the women than by the men. Superstitions of women concern chiefly domestic activities. It is indicated that the superstitiousness is not due wholly to contact with superstitious people. " The persistence of superstition in spite of education and the development of reason, the prevalence of superstition, the variability of superstition forms, the slight coincidences or trifling events which give rise to new superstitions, the readiness with which incidents are accepted as proof, and the evidence of strange feelings and emotions which impel in spite of the reason — all point to a predisposition to such emotional reactions to the events of life as are conducive to belief in mystic interpretations." [63]

3. *Anxiety*

It is not abnormal to worry about things which threaten our safety or our ideals or our plans. It is because of this capacity to see ahead, to anticipate certain dangers and to avoid them, that man has achieved what he has. In this sense, worry is one of the ear-marks of civilization.

An unjustified amount of anxiety or worry — that is, a reaction not commensurate with the stimulus — is a type of emotional excess which is closely related to worrying about nothing at all, or worrying about something which we cannot name. This is pathological anxiety. It may exist in a chronic state; everyone knows the chronic worriers. Many who know nothing about psychopathology know that some of these worriers never have the slightest idea of the real thing they are worrying about.

This is much more evident, however, in the acute states of anxiety such as we see, for example, in the type of nervousness known as *anxiety neuroses*.[64] These distressing feelings or anxious expectation, uneasiness, dread, pessimism, sudden fears and panics, accompanied by all sorts of physical manifestations of fright, are perfectly appropriate for the unseen stimulus

[63] Edmund S. Conklin: "Superstitious Belief and Practice Among College Students," *American Journal of Psychology* (1919), Vol. XXX, pp. 83–102. For a study of superstitions from the psychoanalytic standpoint, see Ernest Jones's painstaking book: *Nightmare, Witches and Devils* (New York: W. W. Norton & Co., 1931).

[64] "Anxiety hysteria," in the more modern psychoanalytic parlance. See Chapter II, page 138.

which gives rise to them, but appear on the surface to be entirely inappropriate and therefore a " distorted emotional reaction." The simplest example is ordinary stage-fright, in which the poor sufferer often looks and acts and feels as if he were in danger of his life. The following is a more complicated example:

I had a patient once who had been a Chicago police officer of the big, burly, dreadnought variety. He had looked into the business end of many a revolver and shotgun, had dragged bootleggers out of closets by the pants and testified against gangsters, and had been through all sorts of exciting adventures with impunity. In fact, he enjoyed the life of excitement and said that he never once experienced the slightest fear.

Nevertheless, upon such insignificant occasions as the eating of his lunch at a cafeteria, or attending an innocuous motion-picture show, or even walking down the street, he would suddenly be seized with a panic which would actually bring him on the run to my office. He would dash in, panting and sweating, his face pale, his breath coming in jerks, his knees trembling, his voice quavering. He would demand an immediate audience, sink down in a chair, and call upon God to witness that he had barely got there in time.

And yet, when questioned, he hadn't the slightest idea of what it was he was afraid of, or of what he thought was going to happen, or what had frightened him, or what had made it go away. Sometimes he couldn't get to my office and he would call me on the telephone. After we had talked a few minutes he would feel all right again. It used to puzzle him considerably that my voice or presence had such a magical effect on his fears, but it puzzled him no less that these panics would come upon him in this inexplicable fashion. The case always used to make me think of the picture one sometimes sees of an elephant quaking at the sight of a mouse, except that it was only after vigorous and prolonged delving that this man ever came to see the mouse.

Since the first edition of my book I have had many inquiries as to what the " mouse " was in this case. It was a combination of things. Such powerful, pugnacious individuals as this are nearly always subject to great cowardice in spite of their bulk; to cover this up, to deny it, to disguise it even from themselves, they charge at the enemy with an apparent fearlessness which is actually not always sensible. George Bernard Shaw has shown in his play *Arms and the Man* how prevalent this same mecha nism is in times of war when those who rush forward with great apparent bravery are really the most timorous ones. But not only was this man afraid of his own timorousness, he was afraid of his own belligerency. This may seem like a contradiction, but the fact is that we all know that being belligerent is likely to incur some trouble for us, both from the person attacked and from our own consciences. For this reason people who really have much inner fearlessness of spirit and would like to attack someone often fear their own aggressive tendencies. One frequently observes evidences in policemen, detectives, criminal lawyers, and others who go hot on the trail after criminals that unconsciously they are trying to trail and capture their own criminal tendencies personified.

Finally, at the deepest level of his psychology this man had another type of fear which he realized when he discovered how his pursuit of these criminals was connected with his sexual life. It was, in fact, a form of repressed homosexuality which occasionally threatened to break forth into consciousness, so great was its strength and so tenuous this form of sublimation.[65]

4. *Perversions of affection and interest*

Nothing pertaining to man and his environment is foreign to the interest and devotion of some versatile geniuses. But most people are interested in relatively few things. The specialist is always regarded as a little peculiar — one who knows more and more about less and less. All psychiatrists are so regarded by their healthy-minded surgical and obstetrical brethren. Some think we should suspect the good judgment of the tuba and double-bass players, and I have several college friends who insist that to be a cheer-leader requires a special kind of craziness.

All of these are tolerable. The psychiatrist becomes familiar with many indulgences of sorts which society as a whole is unacquainted with, and of which it would be extremely intolerant.

Some are trivial — I recall a friend, a miser, who saves all the strings, ropes, wires, etc., that he can in any way acquire, and stores them away on carefully wrapped spools, in numbered boxes in his attic. He is an accepted and successful business man. (Unconscious *anal eroticism*.)

[65] For the most definitive treatment of the *psychology* of anxiety, see Sigmund Freud's *The Problem of Anxiety*, tr. by H. A. Bunker (New York: W. W. Norton & Co., 1936). For a discussion of the *physiology* of anxiety, see William B. Cannon: *The Wisdom of the Body* (New York: W. W. Norton & Co., 1932).

Others are more serious: A man of seventy is romantically in love with a ten-year-old girl. He sends her gifts, calls her up, sits where he can see her come and go, and feasts upon her longingly with his eyes. (*Pœdophilia.*)

A college girl becomes enamoured of her room-mate. Between them there springs up a romantic attachment which entirely displaces their interest in other things and other people. They attend each other like lovers. They have violent quarrels, demonstrations of jealousy, and rapturous reunions. (*Overt homosexuality.*)

A man collects girls' handkerchiefs. He displays them proudly to a few of his friends. He gloats over them, fondles each one tenderly, drops sly hints inferring passionate conquests, and kisses his favourite handkerchiefs as if they were the maidens who once possessed them. (*Fetishism.*)

A series of fires broke out in a Western city with such frequency and persistency and in such a limited area that incendiarism was suspected. A youth was finally captured in the act of setting on fire a large office-building. He was the son of wealthy parents and had recently married an adorable wife. He confessed to an irresistible thrill as he watched the flames mount. (*Pyromania.*)

A young civil engineer, a man of athletic build and masculine appearance, astonishes and horrifies his wife by bringing home lacy lingerie, silk nightgowns, and satin negligees and wearing them about his home in the evening. He is distressed by his wife's attitude, but undeterred. He says he loves women's clothes and has always wanted to wear dainty undergarments. (*Transvestitism.*)

(For examples of *sadism* and *masochism* see pages 341 to 349.)

One of the most curious examples of perversion is found in the Black Mass, which, I am told, is celebrated in Paris and New York City and probably in all other large cities, though an attempt is made to keep the rite absolutely secret. Satanism, the worship of the Devil, or of devils, instead of God, goes back into very early times, and devil religions exist side by side with such religions as Buddhism and Lamaism. The Black Mass, which is the type of Satanism existing alongside Christianity, consists of a parody of the Christian mass. In the common version the altar is the naked body of a woman. The celebrant is a deposed priest. A goat instead of a cross appears on the chasuble. The service follows the Christian mass, either Roman or Anglican, making it blasphemous in every place possible. The members of the congregation are naked throughout the service and at the end engage in both normal and abnormal sex relations. Sometimes, it is alleged, the blood or the ashes of a murdered child are used in the ceremony. Huysman's novel *Là-bas* deals to a considerable extent with the Black Mass. There is reference to Satanism, though of a different type, in the sketch of Charleston in Joseph Hergesheimer's *Quiet Cities.* The so-called witches' sabbath referred to frequently in literature, most amusingly in Robert Burns's *Tam o'Shanter,* consisted of Satanist rites.

Strange perversions are often openly indulged in by groups of people especially in the form of mobs. Then what is ordinarily looked upon with horror as socially unacceptable is indulged in with a unanimity of spirit. The wholesale systematized murder of war is such a perversion; even more obvious are the sadistic orgies of mobs (see for example the vivid description of Vernon C. Sherwin's "Souvenir" in the *American Spectator,* Vol. I, no. 5, March 1933). The treatment of criminals in prisons is socially approved sadism, occasionally brought to the uncomfortable notice of the public in such books as *I Am a Fugitive from a Chain Gang, Ann Vickers,* and *Georgia Nigger,* but quietly practised in a number of prisons throughout the United States. The cruelty of child-labour exploitation and that of the governmental robbery and starvation of the American Indians are other examples.

Mass masochism is also prevalent. The Crusades and asceticism of the Middle Ages have been replaced by self-imposed restrictions which may not be so conspicuous as the mediæval orgies but have the same unconscious origin.

DISTORTED VOLITION

All behaviour that is unseemly, all that is inexpedient, all that is purposeless or unachieving or antisocial or proscribed — in short, all " bad " behaviour — theoretically belongs here. It is still only a small minority of people who say of a given act of offence: " Why does he have to do that? " in the same spirit in which they speak of a convulsion, believing that proper scientific investigation can discover the answer. Yet both are examples of misdirected energy.

Of volitional distortions, the complicated series of acts, such as crime and delinquencies, are best left for presentation in Chapter VI. But there are certain small groups of acts indicating a misdirection and wrong release of energy which will be briefly dealt with here. These are: 1. Tics and other bad habits; 2. Compulsions; 3. Convulsions.

1. *Tics*

Tics can't be illustrated. But everyone knows what they look like. Persistent " batting " of eyes, screwing up one side of the face, stretching the mouth, shrugging the shoulders, etc., are frequently seen in children and remain characteristic ear-marks of some individuals throughout life. Those mentioned are quite properly called *habit spasms,* and represent the expression in a form easily learned and easily repeated of certain psychic and physical tensions which are denied (for unconscious reasons, usually) a more comfortable release. This is easier to understand in the case of *bed-wetting* and *nail-biting* and similar petty " bad habits " of children (although these are met with in college students and others of equal age) . They are all best treated by a combination of methods which aim at a decrease in the tension which produces them and an interruption in the habit of repetition which has been established.

2. *Compulsions*

Compulsions are still more complicated phenomena, with more conscious content than tics. They are closely allied to obsessions; they are persistent repetitious acts instead of persistent repetitious ideas (obsessions) . They are very common; here are some of those listed by my college students one year as being their particular pets:

Touching posts.
Counting blocks or bricks in sidewalks.
Counting out words or letters of a word on the fingers until the count comes out even.
Lighting matches one after another.
Setting something afire.
Tracing a design on the roof of the mouth with the tongue, or writing a word there.
Stepping on or over cracks or on every other brick in the sidewalk.
Keeping out of shadows of trees.
Counting trees, poles, mail-boxes, water-pipes, signboards, etc.
Walking on the edge of the sidewalk.
Counting bulbs in electric signs.
Moving to the beat of clock-ticks.
Returning by the same path or street as on the first trip.
Tracing the design of a carpet with the toe when standing or sitting.

Jumping off when on a high place.

Doing something to shock people.

When turning through magazines, turning back to look at something that does not interest much, just to see if it was seen right the first time.

Marking and drawing aimlessly while listening to a talk or lecture.

Then, some are more serious:

" A boy in high school was supplied with some second-hand books. He began to doubt the accuracy of them, for, as they were not new, he thought they might be out of date, and what he read might not be the truth. Before long he would not read a book unless he could satisfy himself that it was new and the writer of it an authority. Even then he was assailed with doubts. For he felt uncertain as to whether he understood what he read. If, for example, he came across a word of which he was not sure of the exact meaning, he could not go on until he had looked up the word in the dictionary. But as likely as not in the definition of the word there would be some other word with which he was not entirely familiar and he would have to look *that* up, so that at times half an hour or more would be taken up in reading a single page, and even then he would feel doubtful as to whether he had got the exact truth." [66] (Compulsive doubt — *Folie du doute.*)

My brother studied an interesting little coloured child, nine years of age. Following a severe cold she had awakened every morning to tell her folks that she saw dead people, her grandmother and others. This always occurred early in the morning before daylight. During the day she never saw any such visions, but occasionally would make some statement about not caring whether she died or whether everybody died, but that she must move her foot in just a certain way to keep people from dying, or must wrap a watch-chain round her wrist ten times or somebody would die.

Her history disclosed the fact that between the ages of four and seven she had attended five funerals and in each instance had viewed the corpse. One of these was her grandmother's. She had been very fond of her grandmother, who died from pneumonia, with pulmonary œdema and the characteristic death-rattle. Along with the rest of the family the patient had been present during the last few minutes of the grandmother's life and remained in the same house with the corpse for three days, seeing it often. The relationship of these experiences, her own respiratory-tract infection, and the subsequent hallucinations and compulsions seems close.

[66] H. W. Frink: *Morbid Fears and Compulsions,* pp. 163–5.

Prior to psychoanalysis, compulsions were described and classified in great minutiæ, particularly by French psychiatrists, but
understood not one tittle. The compulsion is a typical neurotic
symptom — an act or thought that an individual feels compelled
to make for reasons that he recognizes to be insufficient or irrational. The real reasons are unknown to him, unconscious. Many
studies have shown that these compulsions, like the phobias, are
methods of forestalling or neutralizing anxiety, the anxiety being
connected with the compulsion or phobia in a definite though
roundabout way. (See the discussion of neuroses on pages 135–8.)

3. *Convulsions*

The phenomenon of convulsions has been recognized through
the ages and has been erroneously regarded as an incurable disease, often accompanied by deterioration. In the light of recent
knowledge we now know this to be untrue. Convulsions may
occur as a symptom of a great many different diseases, some of
which can be identified by various examinations. The term
" epilepsy " is still used quite widely for those cases in which the
basic causal factor has not been discovered, but it has so many
false and depressing connotations that most neurologists and
psychiatrists now avoid its use. It should be remembered that
these idiopathic convulsions do not differ in any way from convulsions due to a known cause.

The tendency to have at irregular intervals certain more or
less similar interruptions of consciousness, usually with convulsions, is now generally believed to indicate the combination of
a particularly sensitive or irritable brain and some factor particularly irritating to that brain.[67] This theory gives us a practical
basis for rational treatment.

It is scarcely necessary to describe a convulsion. Anyone who
has ever seen one never forgets it. What happens is that all the
impulses from the brain which are ordinarily distributed to the
muscles of the body in an orderly, regulated way are released
suddenly so that all the muscles are stimulated at once, with the
result that the body is first pulled into stiff contortions and then
jerked spasmodically.

[67] The chief known factors which contribute to produce convulsions in predisposed individuals are (1) deficient oxygen supply to the brain; (2) chemical
changes in the blood (hydration, dehydration, alkalosis) ; (3) mechanical factors
disturbing the brain such as œdema, tumours, hydrocephalus, congenital brain
defects; (4) some drugs and infections, and (5) emotional factors. See Stanley
Cobb: " Causes of Epilepsy," *Archives of Neurology and Psychiatry*, Vol. XXVII,
pp. 1245–56 (May 1932) .

There is another very common manifestation of this condition which people often do not recognize. This consists in sudden brief absences or periods when the patient stops short and seems to be lost in a trance (*petit mal*). Sometimes he keeps on going but does not remember afterwards what he has done. These periods usually last only a few seconds. They may occur many times a day or only once in several months. They are just as characteristic of epilepsy as the convulsions and, in fact, are generally considered a rather more serious form from the standpoint of successful treatment.

Still another but less common manifestation is the " equivalent " in which, with variable degrees of disturbed consciousness, the patient displays strange, usually purposeless, but sometimes violent behaviour — running about, upsetting things, striking at people, pushing over furniture, and the like. In rare instances crimes, particularly murders, have been committed.

In recent years the study of convulsive phenomena has been greatly assisted by the discovery of methods to measure the form and frequency of the electrical brain waves (electroencephalography). It was long known that the muscles of the body generated faint electrical currents in certain rhythms, and this was discovered in 1874 to be true of the brain. But it was not until the past few years that technical devices were perfected which made it possible to record these currents in a practical way. The presence of the convulsive tendency and also the presence of localized brain disease such as tumours, abscesses, and hemorrhages cause a distinct variation in the form and frequency of these waves.

The psychological factors that contribute to the development of convulsive phenomena have been sorely neglected in medical research. Only recently have we come to realize how strong they are and how frequent. Sometimes there are perfectly obvious external situations which tax the patience of a potentially epileptic person beyond his endurance. Instead of doing something violent he has a convulsion. This explains only a few cases, for many are quiet, calm persons. In many such individuals, however, the conflict is all the greater because it is hidden. For such people the convulsion which results when the conflict can no longer be repressed and yet dare not be expressed is a terrific relief, but unfortunately only a temporary one. As the psychic tension again accumulates, the explosion recurs and soon a habit pattern is established which even the most diligent and prolonged treatment finds it difficult and sometimes impossible to alter.

The treatment of convulsions has been a subject of mystery, superstition, and quackery for centuries. Except cancer no other condition is so exploited by quacks, patent-medicine fakes, and those who prey upon grief and hope. The psychological elements are such that almost any type of treatment may afford temporary improvement of convulsions; consequently patients who are experiencing the joy of temporary benefit from some quack treatment or patent medicine often write testimonials or tell inquiring friends of their enthusiasm. By the time the improvement has disappeared and the symptoms are worse than ever, it is too late to change the testimony and others have bitten on the same bait.

Since convulsions are a symptom and not a disease, there is no specific cure. In some cases the underlying cause can be found and removed. When the cause cannot be found, the symptom is treated directly, often successfully. Treatment is directed toward decreasing the irritability of the brain through the use of specific sedatives, diet, and dehydration. In all cases, even those of known organic causation, psychotherapy and regulation of living habits may affect the symptoms favourably.[68] Whatever treatment is found to be the most beneficial in a given case must be carried out continuously over a long period of time in order to re-establish normal responses to those stimuli which previously resulted in a convulsion. To be most effective it should be administered early, before the habit of reacting with convulsions has been established. For those cases in which treatment for one reason or another has proved ineffectual it may be necessary to provide institutional care. The regulated regimen of the hospitals especially adapted to the treatment of convulsive tendencies often acts in a favourable direction.

It should always be remembered that many afflicted with this condition have accomplished much and not a few have achieved greatness. Among these are Julius Cæsar, Dostoievsky, Molière, Flaubert, Handel, Petrarch, Charles V, and Peter the Great.[69]

[68] See Harry N. Roback: " Behavior Disorder Associated with Brain Tumor," *Bulletin of the Menninger Clinic*, Vol. I, no. 3 (January 1937) ; and Leo H. Bartemeier: " Some Observations of Convulsive Disorders in Children," *American Journal of Orthopsychiatry*, Vol. II, pp. 260–7 (July 1932) .

[69] At our Clinic we make it a practice to recommend the reading of Dr. Tracy Putnam's enlightening and reassuring manual *Convulsive Seizures: How to Deal with Them* (Philadelphia: J. B. Lippincott Co., 1943) . For more technical treatises see the Bibliography of the present book.

CHAPTER IV

MOTIVES

DYNAMIC SECTION, DEALING WITH THE SOURCES AND
DISTRIBUTION OF THE POWER THAT DRIVES THE
MACHINE

*"I cannot but think that the most important step forward that
has occurred in psychology since I have been a student of that
science is the discovery . . . that . . . there is . . . a set of
memories, thoughts, and feelings which are extra-marginal and
outside of the primary consciousness altogether, but yet must
be classed as conscious facts of some sort, able to reveal their
presence by unmistakable signs. I call this the most important
step forward because, unlike the other advances which psychology has made, this discovery has revealed to us an entirely unsuspected peculiarity in the constitution of human nature. No
other step forward which psychology has made can proffer any
such claim as this."*
—WILLIAM JAMES: *The Varieties of Religious Experience*
(London: Longmans, Green & Company, 1902), p. 233.

M O T I V E S

Why does the trout want to get away?

What keeps the engine going?

Why do we live and love and fight and envy and play music and tell stories and plant potatoes and have delusions and hallucinations and bad dreams and ambitions and quarrels with the neighbours?

Prior to the discoveries of Sigmund Freud we [1] could only answer: " Instinct." We had a vague notion that there were several instincts — perhaps hundreds. Anyway, they drove us on toward certain goals, we thought — self-preservation and race-preservation.

But how? How could the same instincts appear as philanthropy and politics and poetry and paranoid delusions, in different individuals? There must be some hidden influences, some unseen moulding and guiding and repressing forces. This we knew long before Freud. But we knew of no way to get at it — no good way, at least. There were hypnotism and automatic writing and a few such tricks. But all they had taught us definitely was that there *is* a psychic underworld, a nether region, and that *we* are not aware of all that *we* are thinking.

THE DISCOVERY AND DISCOVERIES OF PSYCHOANALYSIS

What Freud discovered was a method for learning systematically about these hidden things in people's minds. This technique is called the psychoanalytic method. Psychoanalysis is the application of this method to a patient or to any of the phenomena of human life, such as a certain custom, or a tradition, or

---

[1] We wouldn't listen to the novelists and poets and philosophers. Some of them had guessed it.

a dream, or a picture, or a poem, the better to understand the unconscious motives and mechanisms which produced the external appearances.

From such applications the laws governing subsurface workings of the human mind have been derived through the work of many scientists. Freud's discovery of this subsurface material is quite comparable to the discovery of the minerals beneath the *earth's* surface. Important as was the first discovery of coal, or iron, or oil, the discoveries of Freud are perhaps, in the long run, of greater importance to the race.

It came about in this way: [2] Freud had been combining research and the clinical practice of neurology in Vienna. Although his researches had chiefly related to organic brain disease, he became much interested in the psychological factors in illness, working with an older colleague, Breuer. Breuer had a certain famous patient who came in to be relieved of typical nervous symptoms. She sat down to tell the doctor her troubles, her symptoms. She had a fluent tongue and before she had completed her story her appointment time was up, so she returned the next day and continued and again the next and the next. With the aid of hypnosis she told still more, including important details and events that she had forgotten. By the time she had told her story in full she was well! [3]

About that time the great French neurologists Charcot, Bernheim, Liebeault, and others were demonstrating that certain symptoms were psychological in origin, a startling innovation in medical theory. Patients with nervous symptoms of certain types could be commanded under hypnosis to abandon those symptoms.

Freud decided to go and see this work in Paris, and while there (1885–6) tried to interest Charcot in the theories that he and Breuer had evolved. In this he was unsuccessful, and returned home to continue the work he and Breuer had begun. Soon afterwards Breuer became alarmed and sceptical, withdrew

[2] See S. E. Jelliffe: " Freud as a Neurologist," *Journal of Nervous and Mental Disease,* 1937; and A. A. Brill: *Freud's Contribution to Psychiatry* (New York: W. W. Norton & Co., 1944) .

[3] This is a sorry commentary on the reluctance with which most of us listen to the other fellow until we hear him out. La Rochefoucauld and many others have said in various ways that while our friends (patients) are talking to us, we, instead of listening, are thinking up what we shall say in reply. Whether or not this has led to the deterioration of the fine art of conversation, it is partly responsible for the tardiness of this simple discovery of Breuer and Freud.

from the work, and left the subsequent development of psychoanalysis to Freud, who worked for about ten years before publishing his results.

The essence of Freud's great discovery was not merely that a
nervous patient was cured by being permitted to talk out his
troubles. It was that a patient and a physician could develop
a certain relationship with each other, with objectivity and
detachment on the part of the physician and deference and
trust on the part of the patient, such that the ordinary forces
which hold back memories could be recognized and eluded.
The painful, forgotten episodes were recalled in the course
of a friendly, uninhibited conversation in which *free associations,* passing thoughts and fantasies, were verbalized to an
attentive, noncritical listener who could detect and point out
unrecognized connections. The making conscious of this previously buried, fermenting material proved empirically to be
therapeutic.

Freud thus not only discovered a technique for relieving
distress of psychic origin; he discovered, with the use of this
technique, the existence of laws and principles governing unconscious mental functioning, the motives and mechanisms
within the depths of the human mind. He demonstrated that
all surface material was related to subsurface material by complicated, concealed bonds of linkage operating according to principles that could be definitely stated and related. He affirmed
the law of psychic determinism, that nothing psychological
happens by chance but everything always and only as the
result of pre-existing factors and forces, operating in a causal
chain, the links of which may or may not be evident or discoverable.

A slip of the tongue, an " accidental forgetting," day-dream
fancies, even the apparent nonsense of dreams at night, all
have definite producing causes, definite utility, and definite
meaning.

DREAMS

Freud's research [4] early centred about the way in which dreams
serve as indices of the unconscious trends of the mind. He
found that dreams could be interpreted in the light of earlier

[4] Freud's great monograph *Interpretation of Dreams* (New York: The Macmillan Co., 1921) was first published in German in 1913.

(forgotten) experiences and yearnings, and present conflicts and frustrations, just as symptoms could be thus interpreted. The technique was just the same. The laws of interpretation were just the same. It has long been recognized by thoughtful people that dreams represent in some way our forbidden wishes. Plato [5] discussed this, and even Heraclitus alluded to it.[6] What Freud did was to work out a technique whereby anyone who would could penetrate the disguises and discover these underlying wishes.

It strikes many people as incredible that there should be any serious significance to dreams. Dreams seem to be totally meaningless, utter nonsense, the excreta of the mind. We need only recall, however, that it would once have been considered ridiculous for a doctor to examine a patient's urine. Because it is the excretion of the body, chemical examination of the urine enables us to tell something of the condition of the body from which it is excreted. In a similar way, dreams, under the proper sort of analysis, indicate something of the condition of the mind which casts them forth.

The Harlequin of Dreams

Swift, through some trap mine eyes have never found,
    Dim-panelled in the painted scene of Sleep —
    Thou, giant Harlequin of Dreams, dost leap
Upon my spirit's stage. Then Sight and Sound,
    Then Space and Time, then Language, Mete and Bound,

[5] "Certain of the unnecessary pleasures and appetites I conceive to be unlawful; every one appears to have them, but in some persons they are controlled by the laws and by reason, and the better desires prevail over them — either they are wholly banished or they become few and weak; while in the case of others they are stronger, and there are more of them.

"Which appetites do you mean?

"I mean those which are awake when the reasoning and human and ruling power is asleep; then the wild beast within us, gorged with meat or drink, starts up and having shaken off sleep, goes forth to satisfy his desires; and there is no conceivable folly or crime — not excepting incest or any other unnatural union, or parricide, or the eating of forbidden food — which at such a time, when he has parted company with all shame and sense, a man may not be ready to commit." Plato, in the *Republic*, Jowett's translation, Book IX.

[6] "*Protagoras*. Do you not remember the saying of Heraclitus, 'For the waking there is one common world, but of those asleep each one turns aside to his own privacy'? And do you suppose that if we acted on our dreams, we could with impunity do what we dream? Is it not merely because we lie still, and do not stir, that we can indulge our fancies?"

From Chapter xiv, "Protagoras the Humanist," in F. C. S. Schiller's *Studies in Humanism* (New York: The Macmillan Co., 1912).

And all familiar Forms that firmly keep
    Man's reason in the road, change faces, peep
Betwixt the legs and mock the daily round.
Yet thou canst more than mock; sometimes my tears
    At midnight break through bounden lids — a sign
    Thou hast a heart; and oft thy little leaven
Of dream-taught wisdom works me bettered years.
    In one night witch, saint, trickster, fool divine,
I think thou'rt Jester at the Court of Heaven!

Sidney Lanier: *Poems of Sidney Lanier* (New York: Charles Scribner's Sons, 1924).

Freud discovered, as suggested also in Lanier's poem, that dreams had a symbolic language of their own, the symbols used being in many instances universal or at least similar in the dreams of many people (and also similar to the symbols used in mythology and folklore), and in other instances being apparently evolved out of the personal experience of the individual. In ancient times it was assumed that dreams conveyed a supernatural message; it remained for Freud to recognize that the dream is a fantasy of the dreamer, natural — not supernatural, but expressed in symbolic form and often pertaining to the primitive processes of procreation, birth, and death. Even in sleep the repressions are still alert, clothing forbidden thoughts and emotions in beautiful, comical, or even frightening disguises which usually prevent them from awakening the sleeper.

Although Freud was very explicit in setting forth the technique of dream analysis, illustrations of dream interpretation are very difficult to present for several reasons. In the first place, dreams involve the use of numerous disguises, elsewhere illustrated, which require study for full understanding. In the second place, dreams are highly condensed, and tie up with so many details in the lives of the particular individual who experiences the dream, that it is difficult to set forth in a small space convincing proof that the interpretation presented is correct. It is not difficult for the patient to believe this; in fact in a properly conducted analysis he frequently arrives at the interpretation of the dream himself. In the third place, because the dream usually represents the expression of forbidden wishes, it is apt to contain material which offends not only the taboos of the patient but the taboos of the average reader.

Nevertheless, at the risk of scepticism and criticism, I shall present a brief example which recently came to my attention. A patient who was having a good many indications of neurotic maladjustment in his married life dreamed that *he, his wife, and his superior officer were " travelling from Texas in a northeasterly direction. I was drowsy, so much so that when the train stopped at some station I turned lazily to them and asked where we were. They said it was McAlester, Oklahoma. Then the train moved on; I was still sleepy, but a man I used to know in Germany called me on the phone and talked with me about a benefit affair that was to be given."*

Now, without reciting all of this man's free associations (we ask for these in connection with each section of a related dream) , I think I can make this dream intelligible to the reader. In the dream he was "travelling in a northeasterly direction." Since he was born and reared in Chicago and had gone into a line of business that had gradually taken him to live in the *southwest*, where he is now located, this might fairly be assumed to represent a regressive trend toward his childhood, which was actually taking place in more ways than one. (Many of his symptoms were distinctly childish.) The analysis we were making of his troubles had been recalling childhood episodes closely associated with his present difficulties. Again, I live directly northeast of the state and locality in which he lives (Texas) .

" I was drowsy." This drowsiness refers to two things. Just before he related this dream to me, he had mentioned the fact that he was in a maze. " I'm so confused that I don't know which way to turn," he said. " I'm all mixed up about these things." The drowsiness, then, not only describes the state which he was experiencing in the dream, but an unnatural state which he was experiencing in actual life. It also of course refers to the whole confusion and disarray of his faculties incident to the nervous disturbance for which he had consulted me.

" I asked where we were." This is obviously a request of the analyst for a diagnosis. " Just where am I? "

" McAlester, Oklahoma." This town (my patient reminded me) was recently the scene of a very terrible mine disaster in which many men were killed. " Mine disaster " is not hard to interpret as meaning " my disaster " and also " mind disaster." What his disaster was, or what he expected it to be, we need not elaborate beyond the obvious.

The German friend is very probably myself (German by name

and by descent, foreign in the sense of being a stranger to him, living in a different state, and interested in a very different type of work). This is a polite demurral to the whole psychoanalysis.

The reference to the telephone conversation probably related to the talking nature of psychoanalysis.

" Some benefit affair " is quite obviously a punning reference to the object of the treatment.

The meaning of the whole dream, then, on the superficial level, is that " although I pretend to be a normal man, annoyed by his wife, I realize I am sick — confused — and perhaps a little indifferent. I want to get out of such a state, however, and start on this trip, this treatment which is administered by a man whom I don't know very well or trust fully, who warns me of possible disaster in my life and says this treatment will benefit me."

What is repressed about this? Chiefly his real awareness of the severity of his illness, his desultory attitude toward it, his distrust of psychoanalysis. More deeply the dream has to do with terrific hate, generated in his childhood, which he hesitates to loose upon the analyst, who might be a friend. The wife and superior officer referred in a deeper connection to the patient's father and mother, with whom he travelled as a child.

As might be inferred, this dream occurred in a very early stage of the analysis, which partly explains its trend and also the reasons for a lack of deeper interpretation. We may now consider a dream which occurred near the *end* of an analysis.

A patient dreams that *a friend of his is dead; the patient and others are attending the funeral. They discover, however, that the coffin is empty because the man who is supposed to be buried has come to life and is struggling and twisting. He has been transferred from the coffin to a couch. He has taken his coat off and the doctor is standing by him talking with him, perhaps encouraging him.*

The patient's associations to the man in question were that in age he was half-way between the patient and his father, that he was a successful business man such as the patient would like to be, that he was actually a very lively (not a dead) man. " Perhaps," the patient remarked, " he represents my father, whom I have always thought of as dead, coming to life, or perhaps he might be myself coming to life."

The struggling and twisting on the couch reminded the patient that he himself was lying on a couch at the moment he was telling me this. He had removed his coat so that he was very much in the condition of the man in the dream.

The doctor working with the patient reminded him that I was a doctor, working and talking with him.

From these an interpretation was not difficult to make. The patient dreams not only of what he wishes but of what he is actually doing in the analysis, coming to life, relinquishing the neurosis, which is really a kind of death, and identifying himself now with a living, active, successful father.

Since the early research of Freud, psychoanalysts have expanded the principle that dreams represent unconscious wishes, with which the public is so familiar. It is still considered to be true, but the word " wish " is apt to be taken in too narrow a sense. Dreams serve the purpose of allaying or forestalling anxiety, and thus making sleep possible. If the anxiety is not great, the dreams are usually forgotten; if it is very great and the dream function fails, we awaken with recollections of a nightmare. The anxiety may arise from external or internal conditions, and may be allayed sometimes by a pleasing or comforting dream, and sometimes by a dream that inflicts (harmlessly) an anticipated punishment; [7] again, the dream may refute or depreciate an unattainable wish. Dreams also set forth, at times, the dawning of insight into the patient's own actual condition, or his psychoanalytic situation, like those above. Theoretically all dreams may be interpreted in terms of the analytic situation, the reality situation outside of the analysis, and the infantile situation that gave rise to the particular conflicts represented in the neurosis.

LAWS OF THE UNCONSCIOUS

All these discoveries of Freud resolved themselves into a theory about the way in which instinct acts to motivate human conduct. We start out with the proposition that at the back of all living things there is an energic drive to accomplish certain ends, which brings about a state of tension within the individual until its gratification is achieved. There is no good reason why we should not go on calling this drive instinct, except that " in-

[7] That even punishment dreams may be the gratification of a wish and therefore conform to the original principle of dream function discovered by Freud was the contribution of Franz Alexander of Chicago. See " About Dreams with Unpleasant Content," *Psychiatric Quarterly,* Vol. IV, pp. 447–52 (July 1930) ; also his review of Freud's *New Series of Introductory Lectures on Psychoanalysis,* in *Psychoanalytic Review,* Vol. XXI, pp. 336–46 (July 1934).

stinct " is used in various other ways. Freud suggested that it might be called love and hate; someone else suggested interest, or the Latin word *libido,* which means desire. Whatever it is called, it means the stream of primitive energy.

Originally this stream of energy is an undivided one, directed back upon the individual himself. In this sense Herbert Spencer was right when he said that self-preservation is the first law of life. It is chronologically first. A baby is interested in nothing but itself.

A little later the race-preservative or social or sexual instinctive trend begins to develop. Gradually, as more and more opportunities appear for investing love in other creatures than in oneself alone, this stream assumes larger and larger proportions until the instinct for race-preservation rivals, competes with, and finally, in most cases, completely vanquishes the instinct for self-preservation. This is most clearly seen in the insects that spend months and even years in reaching maturity, then spend a few glorious minutes or hours in fertilizing or laying their eggs, and die forthwith.

The main tenets of this theory were generally agreed upon long before Freud came upon the scene. But the discoveries of Freud introduced certain new elements. In the first place, it had always been assumed that the sexual instinct lay dormant in human beings until late adolescence; that is, until the physical manifestations of sexual activity appeared. Freud was able to show that there are undoubtedly psychological indications of sexual instinct many years before this. He referred to sexual interests; that is, pleasure-seeking interest in the body, first one's own and then that of another. If Freud had only used the word " social " instead of " sexual," he would have staved off an enormous amount of criticism, but he would have perpetuated the very illusion which so long blinded us to the real significance of social behaviour. What Freud did was to show that the growing interest a child takes in the outside world is not a part of the selfish tendencies, but a part of the unselfish tendencies and is physiological as well as psychological in origin. The interest we are able to give to persons and things outside of ourselves represents love withdrawn from the great reservoir of affection which the new-born child invests entirely in himself. *Growing up emotionally* really refers to the increasing capacity to take from this self-directed love and invest wisely in externally directed love. In its essence this investment of love in external objects is sexual; that is, it relates to the creation and maintenance of life, the attachment of one person to another, the pleasurable giving and receiving of attention and care.

There always remains, however, a certain amount of conflict between these two phases of sexual instinct, the selfish and the unselfish. They come into an increasing amount of conflict and collision. Everyone knows that you can't have your cake and eat it, but apparently no one had stopped to consider the fact that neither can you have your cake and give it away to your best girl. Whether to eat the cake or give it to his girl, whether to go to a prize-fight or take Mary to a movie, whether to finish his college course and go on with his plans for a career or quit in the middle of things and marry his sweetheart, whether to play golf or take the children to the circus, whether to invest in life insurance or in a new stock company, these are some of the corresponding conflicts at different periods of life. Of course there are other kinds of conflicts. There are conflicts within the stream; there are conflicts of choice — shall I be a doctor or a lawyer? Shall I marry Mary or Helen?

As the psychoanalytic discoveries increased and the theory expanded, another suggestion of Freud's became increasingly obvious: namely, that along with these conflicts in positive interests or love — that is, as to the choice of a love object — there exist negative or *destructive tendencies*. It gradually became more clear that the so-called self-preservative and race-preservative, or, as they were technically called, ego tendencies and sex tendencies, were only differently directed forms of love and that greater than their opposition for one another was the opposition offered both of them by these destructive tendencies and their emotional representative, hate. A study of the relationships between people discovers that accompanying love there is always some hate and vice versa. One or the other wins the victory and may be the only visible and conscious bond. Sometimes there is an alternation; we all know how lovers alternately quarrel and make up.[7a]

The destructive tendencies, properly directed, have a great utility in the world, but obviously they must be invested in objects suitable for the carrying out of the destructive aim. Civilization itself exists only because of the well-aimed hatreds

[7a] For a detailed account of this conflict see K. A. Menninger: *Love against Hate* (New York: Harcourt, Brace & Co., 1943) .

of man against ignorance, pain, disease, and the malignant forces of nature, but when these hates are directed too strongly toward one whom we love, disaster results. It is therefore necessary to repress this hate. If the repression is successful, we are conscious only of one prevalent emotional attitude toward another person. Even when he gives us provocation, we do not get angry, but forgive him promptly. But if, on the other hand, there are very strong unconscious hostile elements in our relationship with this person, the repressing forces may be unsuccessful in restraining them and they may emerge at very inappropriate times and dominate the scene. They may even be so conscious that we can honestly say: " Sometimes I love that person and sometimes I hate him."

This is, perhaps, an extreme example:

" In Springfield, Missouri, Tom Escue, ' Watermelon King of the Ozarks,' and Sarah Sullins were (finally) married, aged 60. They were engaged at 17, but quarreled a few days before their wedding day. Said Tom Escue: ' That went on for 43 years.' "   (*Time*)

More often this *ambivalence,* as it is called, shows itself by a partial repression of the genuine feelings so that although we think we love a particular person with " one hundred per cent " loyalty and devotion, our occasional, perhaps quite frequent, behaviour shows that we have some hostility toward that person which we are not completely successful in repressing.

It is important to distinguish between this technical use of the word *repress* and the technical use of the word *suppress.* We speak of suppression when we refer to the deliberate, conscious renunciation of certain wishes or temptations. Repression, on the other hand, is a very different matter. It is unconsciously accomplished; what one has repressed one remains unconscious of; one does not even know that one has repressed anything at all. Repression is not necessarily harmful; in fact, it is absolutely necessary for the adult to keep in repression certain tendencies which, when he was a child, were permissible. The trouble is that most of us, through childhood misunderstandings, repress some things which it is not necessary to repress and, on the other hand, sometimes have difficulty in repressing what should remain repressed. Hate, for example, and the belligerency it leads to are normally repressed and sublimated (see page 280), but sometimes it breaks through the repression, overcomes the love attachments, and the individual must then either suppress his violent inclinations by a strong act of conscious will or else suffer the consequences of his infantile misbehaviour.

To accuse psychoanalysts or psychoanalytic theory of advising or implying the desirability of uninhibited self-indulgence is either frank libel or crass ignorance. Freud and the Freudians recognize even better than the rest of the world how necessary it is to suppress primitive desires except in propitious directions. Freud no more advocated promiscuous indulgences in sex than he did promiscuous indulgences in eating, for it is a failure on the part of the neurotic patient to be able to maintain his inhibitions that drives him to the need for help. Anita Loos understood Freud very well in this respect. Her " preferred " blonde, whose predatory erotic life was so engagingly confessed in her diary, went to Freud hoping for psychoanalysis, but received the advice that she use some suppression instead:

" So yesterday he took me to Dr. Froyd. So Dr. Froyd and I had quite a long talk in the english landguage. So it seems that everybody seems to have a thing called inhibitions, which is when you want to do a thing and you do not do it. So then you dream about it instead. So Dr. Froyd asked me, what I seemed to dream about. So I told him that I never really dream about anything. I mean I use my brains so much in the day time that at night they do not seem to do anything else but rest. So Dr. Froyd was very very surprised at a girl who did not dream about anything. So then he asked me all about my life. I mean he is very very sympathetic, and he seems to know how to draw a girl out quite a lot. I mean I told him things that I really would not even put in my diary. So then he seemed very very intreeged at a girl who always seemed to do everything she wanted to do. So he asked me if I really never wanted to do a thing that I did not do. For instance did I ever want to do a thing that was really vialent, for instance, did I ever want to shoot some one for instance. So then I said I had. . . . So then Dr. Froyd looked at me and looked at me and he said he did not really think it was possible. . . . So then Dr. Froyd said that all I needed was to cultivate a few inhibitions and get some sleep." [8]

8 Anita Loos: *Gentlemen Prefer Blondes* (New York: Boni & Liveright, 1925) .

STRUCTURE AND FUNCTION OF THE
UNCONSCIOUS

There is a continual striving on the part of the repressed instinctual tendencies to escape, to express themselves in spite of the prohibitions of the ego. These prohibitions are dictated, on the one hand, by the requirements of reality (the ego knows what the instincts do not — for example, that it is inexpedient to kill one's rival) and on the other by the strictures of the super-ego, that part of the parental ideology which has been incorporated into the psychic system so that it becomes the " still, small voice." Unfortunately this voice is not in contact with reality, as is the ego; we all know that our consciences do not keep up with the times. This is particularly true of that unconscious portion of the super-ego, which is far more unreasonable and troublesome than those conscious ideals which we sometimes call our *conscience*. It is the unenviable task of the ego continually to adjust these instinctual strivings to these internal and external " rules," and it is no wonder that it sometimes fails and allows repressed tendencies to succeed in escaping by means of modifications and disguises. To bribe one's conscience is such a device familiar to everyone. These tricks of the unconscious constitute what we call *mental mechanisms*.

To illustrate them and the technical terms employed, I know of nothing so illuminating as the stage metaphor.

Think of the mind as a theatre. Let the field of consciousness be represented by the stage. On it, from time to time, there come and go certain actors (ideas and desires), directed from the wings by a stage-manager (the censor or ego ideal), who has derived his standards and experiences from training and example and precept and pictured ideal — from the lives and mouths of parents, teachers, early friends, and other early influences.

All of the actors — and we infer that there are very many of them — want to act. They will get on to the stage, if possible. The stage-manager holds some of them off stage merely until the proper time for their appearance. They are suppressed *pro tem.*, and come or go as called. Others never get on the stage at all. They are poor actors, or unclothed and motley, or belong in another show, and so have no business clamouring for admission here. Most of them are not even in the wings (the *fore-conscious*), but are outside the theatre, thrown out, perhaps, in the course of previous rehearsals and performances. They noisily demand to be let in, hoping to get on to the stage, but the confusion they create is not heard on the stage or in the audience. These actors, locked outside, are repressed ideas and desires.

These, the repressed, and even the suppressed, actors may trick the stage-manager by disguising themselves in various costumes and masquerading as proper actors in the show. They are never wholly proper, and the keen eye may detect their real identity and trace their origin. But the average playgoer (the ordinary person) will think only that the play is here and there a bit shabby or clumsy or strange.

Essentially psychoanalysis is concerned with a study of the distribution of a person's instinctually directed energy, and the various modifications and disguises which cloak the original intentions, cloaking them from the person himself even more successfully as a rule than from the outside world.

Hence a study of these disguises is highly essential to an understanding of the dynamics of the mind. If they serve some external utility they are called *sublimations;* if not, they are called *symptoms. Reaction formations* are ego-accepted "symptoms" which have ceased to be painful, and often become *character traits.* Dreams and purposive accidents constitute other types of disguises.

The propensity to cut and shed blood, for example, may appear beautifully disguised in the surgeon (sublimation), less prettily so in the butcher (still a sublimation), and unhappily so in the neurotic who feels impelled to cut someone (symptom); and dangerously so in the Jack the Rippers who carry out such impulsions. The anti-vivisectionist may be voicing a protest against his own cutting propensities. And which of us has not, in a puny moment, fancied himself a St. George or a d'Artagnan?

DISGUISES AND MASKS

There are a dozen different ways in which the original instinctive purpose or intention is modified or disguised. Each of these will now be presented, with a definition and then one or several illustrations of the way they look.

(a) PROJECTION

One solution of a conflict brought about by self-criticism is to lodge the fault at someone else's door, to project it outside of the personality — " It is not I who am disagreeable to people, it is they who are disagreeable to me." This is tacitly recognized in the admonition: " Judge not that ye be not (thereby) judged."

Projection in Shakspere:
The Player Queen in *Hamlet* expresses her attitude toward a second marriage (already secretly contemplated by her) in this vigorous projection:

> The instances that second marriage move
> Are base respects of thrift, but none of love. . . .
> Nor earth to me give food, nor heaven light!
> Sport and repose lock from me day and night!
> To desperation turn my trust and hope!
> An anchor's cheer in prison be my scope!
> Each opposite that blanks the face of joy
> Meet what I would have well and it destroy!
> Both here and hence pursue me lasting strife
> If, once a widow, ever I be wife!

The real queen dryly comments on this, recognizing the psychological mechanism, although not by name: " The lady doth protest too much, methinks."

Projection in everyday life:
Everyone is familiar with the penny-wise housewife who does her best to take advantage of her grocer, butcher, and milkman, but is always scrutinizing their bills, determined to prove that they are cheating her. Many physicians are familiar with patients who go contrary to every bit of advice and seem to be bent upon defeating the treatment and who usually don't pay their bills, who are loud in their denunciations of the dishonesty and incompetency of the doctors.

The feeling that someone has it in for us is frequently a projection: it is we who have some secret (perhaps entirely unconscious) hostility for that person, and this prejudices us and leads us to reverse the truth. When, for unconscious reasons, we develop fear and dislike of someone or something, it is a psychological necessity for us to justify such feelings in order to save our face. Faults found with the feared or disliked person, even when they contain a modicum of truth, can be recognized quite frequently as mirror images of our own faults and feelings.

Women frequently complain that their neighbours do not call upon them or come to see them, and interpret this to mean that the neighbours do not like them. It is usually easy for an outsider to detect that such a feeling is a projection and that the neighbours do not call upon such a woman because she does not call upon them. Prejudice against the Jews or the Negroes or any other members of a distinctive group is clearly recognizable, in most instances, as based largely on projection.

Projection is frequently the mechanism in delusions:

" A young woman student had at various times a number of attacks which invariably began with her becoming attracted by one of her professors. She would for a time talk a great deal about him, of how able and attractive he was, but without intimating that she was falling in love with him. Then she would begin to think that he was falling in love with her. This would seem to please and amuse her at first, but soon she would get the notion that he was hypnotizing her, and her pleasure would be succeeded by anger. She would complain that through hypnotic influence he was putting into her mind all sorts of erotic fantasies about him, that by telepathic suggestion he gave her impulses to come to his apartment, etc., all of which would get her into a state of great rage and excitement and she would have to abandon her studies. Thereupon the attack would gradually subside, only to be repeated in connexion with some other teacher when she resumed her work.

" It is apparent that this patient's delusional ideas were nothing but a projection of her own erotic interests in her teachers. What she felt as a hypnotic or telepathic influence brought to bear upon her from without was simply an externalization of her own desires. Her anger against the teachers represented her pathological resistances against these desires. Presumably had she been able to regard her sexuality in a normal way, as something perfectly legitimate and wholesome, what appeared as delusional attacks would otherwise have been ordinary love affairs." [9]

A dramatic historical example of projection:

" The signs of the possession appeared in the Ursuline cloister of London (1632-39). The nuns accused a good-looking priest of the

[9] H. W. Frink: *Morbid Fears and Compulsions* (New York: Moffat, Yard & Co., 2nd edition, 1921) , p. 99.

town, Urbain Grandier, of having bewitched them. The principal role in the epidemic is played by Madame de S., the superior. She was a proud woman of lively intellect and marked hysterical temperament. The hallucinations began with her. During the night a phantom appeared to her in whom she recognized her deceased father confessor. The phantom explained to her that he had simply come to console her, and to instruct her about various matters which he had not had time for during his life. On the following night the phantom again appeared. But this time a change took place in it. She perceived suddenly a strange alteration in the person, and he spoke to her. He was no longer the person of her father confessor, but the visage and body of Urbain Grandier; who, changing his intentions with his countenance, spoke to her amorously and assailed her with enforced and shameless tendernesses. The sexual hallucinations of the superior were repeated not only every night, but also infectiously.

" 'And the majority of the nuns, as well as other girls annoyed by evil spirits, hallucinated that they received nightly visits from Urbain Grandier, and had carnal commerce with him. Their senses were deceived in such measure that the accusations which they brought against the innocent priest had the appearance of absolute truth and were well calculated to convince unprejudiced judges.'

" After being put to the most extreme tortures, Urbain Grandier was burned to death." [10]

(b) INTROJECTION

Introjection is not quite the opposite of projection. Instead of palming off our faults on someone else, we may award ourselves another's virtues, or even his faults.

The best-known example of introjection is the identification we make of ourselves with actors on the stage or screen, particularly those actors whom we admire and think of as doing what we should like to do. The little boy who aspires to follow in his father's footsteps, who takes up his father's profession or succeeds him in the business, the little girl who aspires to be as

---

[10] Paul Recher *Études cliniques sur la grande hystérie,* p. 816.

We have here cited projection as recognized in the Bible, Shakspere, history, and everyday life. Further discussion of the psychological mechanisms is given by Dorian Feigenbaum, who cites (*Psychoanalytical Quarterly,* Vol. V, pp. 303–19, July 1936) , " a Greek dramatist, a medieval ecclesiastic, a nineteenth century essayist, and a twentieth century novelist, as well as a pre-Freudian psychiatrist all speaking clearly, though intuitively, of projection."

motherly and as charming as her own mother, even to the point of excelling her, have, in a sense, grown into these identifications. The psychology is precisely the same as that which moves the savage to eat tigers' teeth for the purpose of gaining strength. In the child's mind all introjection is accomplished orally and may, therefore, be said to represent a kind of psychic cannibalism of a benign sort.

Mrs. Ward had struggled through a pitiful childhood and a painful adolescence. She and her husband early resolved that their children should have the privileges and pleasures they had been denied, just as far as possible.

Of course they must go to college. Mr. and Mrs. Ward had both wanted to go to college. Their children must do so for them. And so throughout their college life the Ward children were followed by the fond and wistful eyes of their parents, who suffered with them their every minor defeat and outdid them in rejoicing at every success. Every scrap of detail they eagerly devoured. Kindly friends said the Wards were getting more out of their childrens' college life than the children themselves.

"A young woman who came to me complaining of insomnia and a depression of two years standing, mentioned during the course of the second visit that the night before she had dreamed of Evelyn Nesbit Thaw. I asked her, very casually, what she thought of Mrs. Thaw, whereupon she at once launched upon a most vehement and passionate defense of that celebrated young woman. Since her emotion concerning Mrs. Thaw, whom she had never seen, was obviously excessive, I concluded the patient must identify herself with her. Inasmuch as her defense had to do entirely with the question of sexual temptations to which the lady had been alleged to have succumbed, I also decided that she too must have yielded to some temptations of that character, and that such was the basis of the identification. And this proved actually to have been the case. . . . Her defense of Mrs. Thaw was then in essence a defense of herself." [11]

(c) CONDENSATION

Multum in parvo. Several ideas may be telescoped into a single word or symbol or phrase; the Postal Telegraph and the Western Union code books contain excellent although arbitrary illustrations of this.

[11] H. W. Frink: *Morbid Fears and Compulsions*, pp. 169–70.

Condensation in a name:

A certain patient wanted to name her new baby Constadine. She said she had never heard the name before, but it came to her with a strong feeling that she must call her child that. Later we found out why.

Constadine is an elision of *constant* (and *constancy*), *Nadine* (a girl's name), *cod(e)ine* (a drug), and probably some other words. But each of these had an important meaning to my patient. I can indicate only briefly what was entailed.

Constant is what our lady had *not* been; and it is what she hoped and prayed that her daughter, on the other hand, might always be. Hence she wanted her to be called Constant.

Nadine turned out to be the name of a woman with whom her husband had once flirted. To justify herself for her own inconstancy she had tried to convince herself that her husband really loved Nadine or some other woman and that it was he who had been inconstant and hence justified her own intrigue. In this sense she wanted her husband to love both Nadines — the old Nadine and the new Nadine, this daughter.

Codeine is a narcotic drug; she had been so disturbed over her problems that she had been sleepless and had taken a few codeine tablets, thinking to force sleep. Now, codeine is a poor sleep-producer, and it is not a drug predisposing to habit-formation. But my patient didn't know this and was doubly worried over this additional sin and danger. And this, too, she wove into the name of the child in an obsessive fashion, because she felt she must confess (to the world) that she was a drug addict (which of course she wasn't). She also wanted to blame her sleeplessness, and hence also the codeine, upon her pregnancy — that is, upon little " Constadine."

Condensation in a dream:

Anna, a senior in college, who was having a rather unhappy time of it, reported to me that she had dreamed that her sister got married. This apparently simple dream actually condenses a great many ideas and wishes, quashed and withheld from the " stage " of consciousness until by means of this *condensed* disguise they escape. Here are some of the facts:

This girl's sister, of whom she dreamed, was much prettier than my consultant. She had immediately become popular and sought after; joined a sorority, entered into numerous activities, and had many dates. In sharp contrast to this, Anna had been distinctly unpopular and unnoticed. This painful differentiation had in a measure been present since early childhood, and Anna's heart was fairly eaten out with envy and jealousy. Yet her little sister was as amiable toward her as she was toward everyone else; in fact, more so, so that Anna was the recipient of all her confidences and served as comforter and adviser and foster-mother. This gratified Anna to a large extent and made her deeply affectionate, in spite of her jealousy toward her little thorn-in-the-flesh sister.

Yet for this sister to have got married, as Anna dreamed, would have gratified Anna in several ways. In the first place, Anna had for years lived her life in part through an identification of herself with her sister. "To have sister married as I dreamed," she said, "would be almost as good as being married myself." Thus it really was a wish that she herself might be married, using her sister as a sort of representative symbol. In the second place, it would have removed the sister from the competition for a husband. In the community in which they lived it was unavoidable that the two sisters should have been compared as to eligibility, with all the preferences in favour of Anna's sister.

There was a more subtle and still more reprehensible notion concealed in this dream. Anna's sister had come to her the day before with some anxieties. "Is it true," she had asked, "that having a baby is such a terrible thing for women? Maude Martine said her sister-in-law nearly died last week in the hospital. It sort of scares me, because I do want to get married some day. When I was a girl I used to think it was almost certain death to have a baby, and now all this talk gets me awfully worried, some way. I wish I really knew something about it."

Well, of course Anna reassured her sister, told her what she knew, pointed out the common-sense view that if childbirth were so terrible there would long since have been no people, and so on. Thirty minutes later the matter was forgotten. But now the facts of the matter are that Anna herself had also once entertained such notions about the fatal nature of childbirth; she had laid such childish misconceptions aside long ago, she thought, but she had carried them round in her unconscious ever since.

So it appears that behind the simple dream, as well as the less reprehensible but selfish meanings, were such sinister thoughts as these: "Let her go and get married to one of these fellows if she's so crazy about 'em. . . . It's as good as suicide . . . but that's O K — it clears the decks for me, anyway."

(d) DISPLACEMENT

The disguising of a wish or fear or hate by substituting another person or thing as the object of the emotion is called displacement.

Displacement from father to son:

Having teased and irritated his wife to the point of explosion, Mr. Baker put on his hat and left for the office. Mrs. Baker was thoroughly wrought up. Her husband had dodged like a coward; he flung these taunts and accusations at her and then lit out; she was chained to the house and the confining routine of it with no chance to get back at him. He could leave, yes, and he could forget it all in a few minutes, but she must wash dishes and sweep and make beds and do all the things that give you too much time to think. The smallness of that last remark, the insinuating nastiness of it! After all she had tried to do to help him get somewhere in the world — no more appreciation than that! To trump up all those taunts and accusations!

Just then her five-year-old son came bursting into the house from his play outdoors. " Mother! Mother! Listen. Harold and I have got a swell stunt. We're going over to his house and get the wheelbarrow and make it into — "

That's as far as he got. He had tracked a little mud on to the porch. It was not much, but it was infuriating. Mrs. Baker fairly screamed. She jerked the child into the house, she shook him, she pointed at the mud and at his feet and harangued the child as if he had stepped in blood. He burst into tears, which only made her the angrier. She seized a hairbrush and thwacked him vigorously. Howls of protest mingled with scoldings and recriminations.

No one ever knew — not the husband, certainly, nor the little boy, and not even the mother herself — that she had released a forbidden actor in disguise — the disguise of displacement.

Displacement from one part of the body to another:

An adolescent girl was brought to a psychiatrist by her mother on account of great preoccupation she had developed concerning her mouth. She thought something was wrong with it and kept looking at herself in the mirror, feeling her jaw, wiggling each tooth, exploring her throat, and in various ways indicating her fixation of interest on this organ. Along with it, she had developed a great fear of dentists and, derived from that, of other physicians. She had seen a moving picture in which men turned into werewolves, and this frightened her so much that she would not go again to the movies. The wolves' teeth frightened her most.

After the patient's confidence was completely won, she confessed that some time previously she had become very much interested in her own genitals, had examined them with a mirror, and had masturbated. She became secretly alarmed about the dangerous possibilities of the latter and ceased the practice immediately, only to develop this concern about her mouth, *displacing* the feeling that something was wrong, had been injured, was dangerous, and so on from the genitals to the mouth, where it was much more possible to demonstrate her anxiety about it. It should be remembered that this displacement was not accomplished consciously, but unconsciously; this girl did not think: " Well, now I will not worry any more about masturbation, but I will worry about my mouth because it also is an orifice," and so on. But some similar shift in the object of anxiety was accomplished quite unknown to her. She was assured that masturbation is an entirely harmless procedure, normal to all human beings, and the anxiety about her mouth and the extension of this fear disappeared at once.[12]

Displacement from parents to teacher:
    " Up to the age of fourteen or fifteen years he was the ' best pupil ' in the school but at that period a complete change came about. Study as he would he always had the feeling that he could not learn. At every examination he felt that the teacher was asking something he knew nothing about, which was set down in no textbook. ' Now what is this,' he asked himself, ' which is to be found recorded nowhere, which no one has told me but which I must answer nevertheless? All my thoughts were so penetrated by the emotion of dread that I was incapable of entertaining any clear idea. My mind seemed void and empty. What was it, then, that I was afraid of being asked? Nothing that I knew, certainly. Then it was something that had no connection with real life. Perhaps it is a certain question which I carry in my head, of which my head is full and with which my thoughts are constantly occupied. Of one thing I am certain — when I was fourteen or fifteen years old I was constantly afraid that the teacher would ask if I had any bad habits. I thought it was something connected with sexuality. I was also afraid, perhaps, that the teacher would go further and ask what else I did. Too, I was very unwilling to permit my mother to go to the teacher, even when my standing in the school was good.

[12] This case was abstracted from Robert P. Knight: " Application of Psycho-analytic Concepts in Psychotherapy: Report of Clinical Trials in a Mental Hygiene Service," *Bulletin of the Menninger Clinic,* Vol. I, pp. 99–108 (March 1936) .

I was afraid that the teacher might ask my mother what I did at home. Still another fear distressed me: if I should ever give the teacher the right answer he might spring at me, attack me, and then something awful would happen.' " [13]

Evidently this lad feared detection and punishment, presumably by his parents, for secretive sexual indulgences concerning which he felt painfully guilty. The displacement involves not only the person feared, but the *casus belli*.[14] The neurotic often treats his wife as if she were his mother, taking revenge on the wife for things she did not do, but which his mother *did* do.

(e) ELABORATION AND DISTORTION

The disguise of ornamentation and arabesques, and the disguise of partial alteration.

Strictly speaking, elaboration is the disguise of hiding the actor under a mountain of costuming — a needle-idea in a haystack of words. Distortion is the curved-mirror sort of thing — a disguise of slight but cumulatively important trifles.

The following illustration entails both of these closely related mechanisms. The kernel of the nut is the (unconscious) malevolent wish of some of the ladies against Mrs. King.

Mrs. Adams to Mrs. Beck: " Where is Mrs. King today? Is she ill? "

Mrs. Beck to Mrs. Clark: " Mrs. Adams wonders if Mrs. King may not be ill."

Mrs. Clark (who doesn't like Mrs. King) to Mrs. Davis (who does): " I hear Mrs. King is ill. Not seriously, I hope? "

Mrs. Davis to Mrs. Ellis: " Mrs. Clark is saying that Mrs. King is seriously sick. I must go right over and see her."

Mrs. Ellis to Mrs. French: " I guess Mrs. King is pretty sick. Mrs. Davis has just been called over."

Mrs. French to Mrs. Gregg: " They say Mrs. King isn't expected to live. The relatives have been called to her bedside."

Mrs. Gregg to Mrs. Hudson: " What's the latest news about Mrs. King? Did she die? "

Mrs. Hudson to Mrs. Ingham: " What time did Mrs. King die? "

Mrs. Ingham to Mrs. Jones: " Are you going to Mrs. King's funeral? I hear she died yesterday."

[13] J. Sadger: " Concerning Fears of Examinations and Dreams of Examinations," *Internationale Zeitschrift für Ärztliche Psychoanalyse*, Vol. IV, no. 2.

[14] For other examples of displacement, see the first illustration under (g) Rationalization and the third illustration under (j) Reaction-Formation, pages 295 and 291.

Mrs. Jones to Mrs. King: " I just learned of your death and funeral. Now, who started that? "

Mrs. King: " There are several who would be glad if it were true."

(f) REVERSAL

Saying or doing precisely the opposite of the real unconscious wish. This differs from hypocrisy or insincerity in that these are conscious deceptions.

The sleep-walkers:

" In the town where I was born lived a woman and her daughter, who walked in their sleep.

" One night, while silence enfolded the world, the woman and her daughter, walking, yet asleep, met in their mist-veiled garden.

" And the mother spoke, and she said: ' At last, at last, my enemy! You by whom my youth was destroyed — who have built up your life upon the ruins of mine! Would I could kill you! '

" And the daughter spoke, and she said: ' O hateful woman, selfish and old! Who stand between my freer self and me! Who would have my life an echo of your own faded life! Would you were dead! '

" At that moment a cock crew, and both women awoke. The mother said gently, ' Is that you, darling? ' And the daughter answered gently, ' Yes, dear.' " [15]

(g) RATIONALIZATION

Explaining away plausibly, but without reference to the unconscious reasons, or without loyalty to all of the facts.

" I had a patient who attended every concert given at the Yankee Stadium by a well known musician. She had never been interested in music before, and knew little about it. Asked why she never missed going, she replied that she loved music. ' She loved music.' She had subscribed to various musical journals and had studied day and night to understand music, so that eventually she was able to detect even minor imperfections in the technique of the different scores, and frequently would become emotionally disturbed when any mistakes were made by this musician. A study of her condition revealed that her expressed interest in the music was a *displaced* interest in the

[15] Kahlil Gibran: *The Madman: His Parables and Poems* (New York: Alfred A. Knopf, 1918) .
See also the second example under the next heading (Rationalization) .

conductor which she explained of course in other words and *rationalized* by saying that she loved music. She really loved the conductor." [16]

"One of my patients confessed to me that it had always been his intention to marry a rich girl, though as a matter of fact the girl he had married had no money at all. Before he became engaged he had taken advantage of every opportunity to meet, and be in the society of, rich girls, hoping to find one that would be attractive and at the same time willing to marry him. I felt somewhat surprised that his devotion and industry in this direction had met with so meager a result, and so expressed myself, whereupon he explained that all the rich girls he had ever met were so spoiled by their money and so utterly selfish that no matter how rich they were he would not marry any one of them. All of them, he said, put clothes and dances and yachts and cars, and all the other things that money could buy, ahead of love and sympathy and companionship, which, he assured me, were to his mind the vital features of marriage. But though I did not feel in a position absolutely to deny that great wealth may have a prejudicial influence upon character, the fact remained that this man had known a great many girls with money, and it did seem rather unlikely that every single one of them had exactly the same group of faults which he seemed to discover in them. His failure to carry out his intention to marry a rich girl (a thing he had many opportunities of doing) was, it appeared to me, due in all probability not so much to the alleged defects in the character of the young ladies, as to certain peculiarities of his own, while the explanation he offered was not the true one but a rationalization. The real determining factor, as at length appeared, was his own money complex. He felt that rich girls would be more interested in money than in companionship because to a certain extent he was that way himself. Since he doubted if he could care for a girl who was not rich, he was compelled also to doubt whether, since he was not rich, any such girl could care for him. He could feel sure of the love only of a girl who had no money at all, for such a one would appreciate, he felt, the moderate amount of money he did have." [17]

"There is nothing like a good moral attitude in such matters. Just settle it with yourself that it was the cat that ate the jam or the lightning that lit the match, and think no more of it," says Isabel M. Paterson [18] in discussing the rationalizations of Thoreau.

[16] Gerald R. Jameison in *Occupational Therapy and Rehabilitation*, Vol. III, no. 6 (December 1928).

[17] H. W. Frink: *Morbid Fears and Compulsions*, pp. 176–8.

[18] *New York Herald Tribune Books*, December 13, 1936.

She goes on to say: "The incident in Thoreau that gave him his chance to moralize himself out of responsibility . . . was when he set the woods on fire, through carelessness in making a campfire. All the neighboring farmers had to turn out and spend a whole day fighting the flames, scorching their hands and singeing their eyebrows — and one farmer lost a lot of cordwood. Altogether Thoreau's fire 'burned over a hundred acres or more and destroyed much young wood.' And how did the great moralist and naturalist feel about his own responsibility? Well, 'it was only half a dozen owners, so-called . . . and I felt that I had a deeper interest in the woods, knew them better and should feel their loss more, than any or all of them. Some of the owners, however, bore their loss like men, but other some declared behind my back that I was a damned rascal; and a flibbertigibbet or two shouted some reminiscence of burnt woods from safe recesses for some years after. I have had nothing to say to any of them. . . . Hitherto I had felt like a guilty person . . . . But now I settled the matter with myself shortly. Who are these men who are said to be the owners of these woods, and how am I related to them? I have set fire to the forest, but I have done no wrong therein, and now it is as if the lightning had done it. I at once ceased to regard the owners and my own fault — if fault there was.'"

(h) PURPOSIVE ACCIDENTS

Many acts are called "accidental" which can be shown to have purposes which must be ascribed to unconsciously active wishes, which take advantage of appearances of accidental or chance occurrence.

Such accidents may be in the nature of slips of the tongue or pen. These are among the most easily grasped evidences of unconscious mental functioning.

I am indebted for the following amusing *lapsus linguæ* to a friend who owned a department store. A woman had been accused by one of his floor-walkers of having stolen some goods from the counter. The case was dropped, however, whereupon she sued the company for false accusation and false arrest. On the witness-stand when asked why she was in the store on that day, she replied: "Oh, I just dropped in to do some *shop-lifting* — I mean *shopping.*" The case was dismissed immediately, because of a general recognition on the part of everyone of the truth of the unintentional confession.

Such slips are ordinarily overlooked in everyday life except by those who have gained some concept of the power of the unconscious. A very pretty example of this is given by Karin Stephen.[19]

One of her sceptical friends with whom she was discussing this question of the meaning of accidental occurrence remarked to her, rather contemptuously: "One or two instances like that would never *convict* me." Of course, what he meant to say was "*convince* me," but he gave himself away utterly. He showed that his inability to accept the implications of such interpretations of the unconscious was related to some secret sense of guilt which was involuntarily betrayed and expressed in this inadvertent way. After his slip the friend naturally was a little more convinced.

But some accidents are a great deal more serious and involve actual injury to oneself or others. It is much more difficult for the uninitiated to accept the possibility that these "accidents" are purposive; many of them probably are not, but some of them most certainly are. This has been demonstrated by intensive psychological study of individuals to whom such accidents have occurred. Sometimes, however, a similar inference can be derived merely from the facts of the case.

I knew two brothers once, one of whom was a very fine student and the favourite of his parents, and the other a poor student and something of a black sheep. It was no secret (at least not from me) that the poor student envied and hated his favoured brother. Nevertheless they played together and seemed to have many things in common. One day in preparation for a hunting trip the two of them were cleaning their guns. The younger envious and unfavoured brother *accidentally* discharged his gun, and his brother was shot through the spine and paralysed for life. There was really no reason to doubt that this terrible accident was accidental; but there was also no reason (for me, at least) to doubt that it gratified a deep, banished wish of the jealous brother.

Everyone knows examples similar to the following:

A patient from a distance had had a violent quarrel with her husband which made her loath to return home, but she felt obliged to do so in order to discuss certain matters with him. She was exceedingly reluctant to start and toyed with various plans for evading the unpleasantness. Her intelligence prevailed, however, and she started out bravely in her car; she had gone but a few miles when, in attempting to handle a

[19] Karin Stephen: *Psychoanalysis and Medicine: A Study of the Wish to Fall Ill* (New York: The Macmillan Co., 1933).

slight traffic irregularity, she collided with another car, upsetting her own. The conclusion is obvious, perhaps more so if I add that she was an unusually skilful driver.

We may suspect that not only automobile-drivers but even pedestrians who are involved in accidents are *sometimes* vaguely directed by unconscious intentions which masquerade as carelessness. In 1935 nearly seven thousand persons in the United States "jaywalked their way to death," according to statistics compiled by the National Safety Council. The Council calls this carelessness, but as psychologists we must suspect that something sinister and purposive lies behind much so-called carelessness.

And perhaps the most convincing evidence of all that many accidents are purposive is the way in which some individuals seem to fall victim to them one after another. Newspaper men describe such unfortunate individuals as "hard-luck champions." In my hand is a clipping enumerating the accidents which befell one man.

When four years old he fell off a horse and broke his right leg; at six, while trying to drive a stake with a hatchet, he cut his left foot severely; a year later he was gored by a bull (his own responsibility for getting in the way of the bull is, of course, not discussed); at seventeen he broke his leg again; when a little older he was caught under a train and his left arm cut off, nine of his toes severed, and his skull fractured. He lived, however, and a few years later, "while riding in a passenger coach, he tripped in the aisle and broke a vertebra in his spine and sprained both ankles."

I have a file containing many clippings describing characters of this sort. Unless one is superstitious or believes in demons or evil spirits, one must assume that such an individual has unconscious intentions to hurt himself "accidentally"; the consistency of trend and frequency of repetition is too great to allow us to attribute these events to pure chance or even "carelessness." [20]

[20] Karl A. Menninger: "Purposive Accidents as an Expression of Self-Destructive Tendencies," *International Journal of Psychoanalysis*, Vol. XVII, pp. 6–16 (January 1935); and in *Almanach der Psychoanalyse*, pp. 118–27 (Vienna: Internationaler Psychoanalytischer Verlag, 1936). See also N. W. Ackerman and Leona Chidester: "'Accidental' Self-Injury in Children," *Archives of Pediatrics*, Vol. LIII, pp. 711–21 (November 1936).

(i) REACTION–FORMATION

The chief purpose of some disguises appears to be not so much to fool the audience as to protect the pride of the actor, or of the show itself (the ego). These are called defence mechanisms. Reaction-formation is a defense mechanism characterized by activity precisely opposite in trend to that of the underlying impulses.

Too honest:

George Barro was regarded by everyone as scrupulously honest. For ten years he had been the cashier of the largest bank in his county. He was so conscientious that he even listed on his income tax a five-dollar bet he won on the election. He had the confidence of his superiors, his associates, and the customers of the bank.

Suddenly, without warning, he absconded. Even after the shortages were discovered and clearly demonstrated, it was difficult for many people to believe that honest George Barro had actually taken the money.

It will be recalled that Victor Hugo exploited a similar theme in his novel *Les Travailleurs de la mer.*

A familiar pair of examples:

R. L., a friend of mine, is one of the officers at a state prison. He was formerly a prisoner there himself and is now an executive. T. M., another friend of mine, formerly a policeman in Kansas City, is now a prisoner at the same state prison. R. L.'s reaction-formations were slow in getting under way; T. M.'s didn't hold.

The wolf in sheep's clothing:

The most proficient and sophisticated Don Juan whom I ever knew, a man who had had literally hundreds of ignoble love-affairs, was so effeminate in his appearance and manner as to have been an object of ridicule on the part of persons not familiar with his life. In fact, I think strangers usually suspected him of being homosexual (that is, feminine). And of course they were right so far as his unconscious is concerned. It was to overcome this that he made such extravagant gestures to show what a real man he was, after all.

The anti-vivisection movement is a clear-cut example of reaction-formation; people who over-react to their own impulses of cruelty by attempting to forbid activities on the part of others which they *believe* to be cruel, thereby actually increase the amount of suffering in the world. This is typical of all reaction-formation, as Freud [21] has pointed out; the reaction-formation only prevents the direct operation of that which is warded off; the indirect operation accomplishes its original effect nevertheless.

Fads can often be traced directly to reaction-formations. The pruriency of vice crusaders is acknowledged. Fenichel [22] had a patient who was a convinced vegetarian and for many years at the forefront of the vegetarian movement who finally decided to change his occupation and became a butcher! Morgan [23] describes vividly a preacher who, ordinarily calm and prosaic, became very intense on the subject of dancing, short skirts, flapperisms, bobbed hair, rouge, and vice, all of which in his mind represented sexual misconduct. He became almost violent and frenzied in his denunciation of these things. He forbade young boys and girls of his church to walk home together, often himself escorting them in order to prevent it. At times he would throw his arms about and almost scream in his repudiation of the seduction which he believed some women to be attempting with respect to himself. This example reminds one of the earnest and intense missionary in *Rain,* the well-known drama based on a story of Somerset Maugham's, who first denounces, then converts, and finally embraces a prostitute.

(j) SYMBOLIZATION

One thing used to represent another is a symbol. Usually the symbol is a great abbreviation, a condensation.

It is easier to illustrate symbolization than to define it with precision. Money, words, pictures, maps, many symptoms — these are some familiar examples. A dollar, we know, is a recognized symbol of so much value; the word "horse" is a symbol for a certain domesticated mammalian quadruped; the map of Europe is a representation of the territories occupied by certain diverse peoples and nations. Each of these symbols, as can be seen, is enormously condensed, and each of them, therefore, is capable of varying interpretations. The word "red," for ex-

[21] Sigmund Freud: "Inhibitions, Symptoms, and Anxiety," translated by Henry Alden Bunker, in *Psychoanalytical Quarterly,* Vol. IV, pp. 616–25 (October 1935); Vol. V, pp. 1–28 (January), 261–79 (April), 415–43 (October 1936).

[22] Otto Fenichel: *Outline of Clinical Psychoanalysis* (New York: W. W. Norton & Co., 1934), p. 410.

[23] John J. B. Morgan: *Maladjusted School Child* (New York· The Macmillan Co., 1924), pp. 155–6.

ample, is the symbol for the effect that a certain wave-length of light makes upon our eyes, and also for courage, danger, fire, debts, radicalism, and other things.

There are many reasons for the use of symbols; one of the most obvious is that they make for an enormous psychic economy. It is easier to look at a map of Texas than to run all over that state each time one wants to determine the precise relationships of various cities or counties therein. It is easier to say "red" than to define that colour sensation each time by citing the wave-lengths of the light. It is easier to use a dollar bill than to carry about with one the amount of wheat or food or gold or cloth which it represents in value.

But this convenience is not merely one of mechanics, the saving of time and effort. We know that a symbol has certain dynamic purposes, among them the furtherance of repression. For this purpose, symbols with a fairly constant meaning are apt to be used, especially those which have had an evolutionary basis both in the life of the individual and in the history of the race. For the same reason there are apt to be linguistic connections between the symbol and the symbolized idea (for example, the mammæ or breasts are often used as a symbol of the mamma or mother; again, the sea is a common symbol for the mother and in French this linguistic connection is clear — *mer* and *mère*). Further evidence of the repression value of the symbol is to be found in the latent meaning discoverable in myths, cults, religions, fairy-tales, and folk-lore.[24]

It should be remembered that the symbol is never an identity; it represents a substitution, a substitution of an incomplete and often ambiguous representative. Korzybski[25] has made the point that in the development of human speech these inadequacies and deficiencies of the word as a symbol are overlooked so that our language is dissimilar in structure to the facts of reality. Certain devices, called by Korzybski "extensional devices," tend to make our language more specific and the meaning of the symbols more definite; among these are indices, dates, quotation-marks, hyphens, and indicators of series, such as the expression "etc." But in spite of these devices, much confusion

---

[24] This is elaborately worked out by Ernest Jones in *Nightmares, Witches, and Devils* (New York: W. W. Norton & Co., 1931).

[25] Count Alfred Korzybski: "Neuro-Semantic and Neuro-Linguistic Mechanisms of Extensionalization," *American Journal of Psychiatry,* Vol. XCIII, pp. 29–38 (July 1936); *Science and Sanity* (Lancaster, Pa.: Science Press Publishing Co., 1933).

of thought which is essentially logomachical — that is, dependent upon the inadequacy of the language — has arisen to complicate scientific concepts. One of the most familiar of these in
our own work is the body-mind controversy; no such dichotomy
actually exists. Another one which the reader can experiment
with is the word " criminal "; I think it is impossible to define,
even with an unlimited number of words, the exact meaning
of the word " criminal " in such a way as to fairly represent what
the word now symbolizes, let us say for the people of this country in the year of 1944. Is it, for example, a man who is convicted of something, a man who plots something, a man who is
accused of something, a man who has been in jail . . . ?

Some examples of symbolism follow: [26]

The symbolism of the foot:
The attributes above mentioned may be seen to apply to the
various symbolic values of the foot, for example.[27]

In various parts of the world, ancient and modern, the foot has
been used as a symbol for speed, vitality, power, health, success
(in journeys and other undertakings) ; and as such we find the
foot inscribed on coins, amulets, tablets, outstanding rocks, etc.
Christianity took over this symbolism from its heathen predeces-
sors and uses the foot as a symbol for the passage into the new
life, the happy termination of the life in this vale of tears.

The foot is also symbolic of anything used as a basis or foundation, for something on which one stands or relies. Thus, for example, " to be on a good footing " means " to be well established," and " setting one's foot down " expresses determination.

From the fact that a strong man controls what he puts his foot
on, the foot is a very common symbol for power, rule, right,
domination. In personal combats it was customary for the con-
queror to plant his foot on the neck of the conquered foe. Many
idiomatic expressions are founded on this practice. A man took
possession of purchased property by setting his foot on it. When
a man married a woman, he was said to set his foot on her neck —
for example, in *Twelfth Night.* From the fact that a person is
rendered fairly helpless if his foot is impeded (*pes* = foot) in its
motions, it was the custom in the Middle Ages for the lord to
symbolize possession by stepping on the right foot of his vassal.
In the same way a bridegroom went through the ceremony of

[26] For symbolism in dreams, see page 271.
[27] What follows on foot symbolism is abstracted from *Foot and Shoe Symbolism,* by Aigremont.

stepping on the foot of his bride. The foot thus being a symbol of power, to kiss the foot or toe became a symbol of humility. A great sense of gratitude and great love often express themselves by a foot-kiss. The ancient Greeks and Romans used to kiss the feet of their gods, and, no doubt, their goddesses too.

In many parts of the world the foot, especially the foot of a woman, has been and still is used as a symbol for fecundity. This symbolism is very ancient. By virtue of the fact that the foot established a connection between the fecund and life-giving earth and the gods or heroes (goddesses, heroines, and saints) these deities and persons were credited with possessing a fecun·dating and healing power which enabled them to render fecund and to heal or strengthen those who won their favour. Woman was supposed to have derived her procreative power from con·tact with the earth, the mother of all things, and thus her foot came to be the symbol for the fecundating principle. In all probability the feet of male deities, kings, heroes, saints, princes, were credited with the fecundating principle subsequently, so that the dominant male lords and lordlings might not feel in·ferior to the females. After a while the fructifying power was possessed not only by the foot but even by the footprints, the sandals, and the shoes of kings, queens, saints, etc. This explains the large number of stories about fruits, grain, and flowers grow·ing on the spots where gods and heroes (Buddha, Jehovah, Mars, Hercules) had rested their feet. Kings and princes were credited with the power of curing the sick and removing sterility by touching the afflicted one with the right foot and, subsequently, with the hand. The Holy Anna's footprint is still the means of making women healthy, happy, and fruitful.

The mythologies and folk-lore of all nations and races are rich in material whose significance hinges on an intimate bond which links the feet and sexual ideas together. In some places at some times the natives have been more ashamed to expose their feet than their genitals. In many parts of the world it is considered disgraceful for a woman to expose her feet, even though shod, to the public view. It was formerly quite general to regard the exposure of the leg as the extreme of impropriety; presumably this was because of some erotogenic potentialities. There are numerous reasons for this connection, some of which are:

1. The foot connects the individual with the earth; the earth is earthy, gross, reproductive, hence phallic. That is why deities and spirits of

fruitfulness, wantonness, lechery, and sensuality are portrayed as having the feet of animals (horses, donkeys, steers, geese, goats, etc.) — for example, Bacchus, Hecate, Freya, the Devil, the Queen of Sheba, Lilith, etc.

2. Crippled feet have long been associated with excessive sensuality — for example, in Chinese women. Byron's sensuality has been referred by some to his lameness.

3. Some women cultivate a gait which emphasizes their femininity.

4. Women dress their feet and legs in such a way as to attract attention to them — for example, by flesh-coloured stockings, etc. This emphasizes their sexual significance.

5. The foot is a frank phallic symbol for numerous reasons — it is an appendage, it is dependent, it slips into the shoe, etc.

Well-known symbols may carry unsuspected values:

Take such a simple symbol as a letter of the alphabet; B, for example. For most of us it means a labial puff, an initial, an insect, a verb; and those are about all the connections we can think of.

Compare this with the discoveries made by a very intelligent patient of mine in regard to his B's.

In the course of his free associations one day he was trying to recall a name and remarked: "It probably begins with a B. I've always had such difficulty in remembering names which begin with the letter B. Words beginning with a small B do not so easily escape me." At that time he was unable to give any explanation of this phenomenon, and the immediate free associations were not particularly helpful. The problem gradually unfolded itself, however.

Consciously introspecting, the patient was able to find some fifteen or twenty B associations which would in some measure explain the lapse of memory. Some of them I will cite. There was a family physician who was called Doctor Bee. "I can easily understand why I should want to forget his name, for my childhood impressions of his office are ghastly. Here it was that I went to have my foot lanced, my teeth pulled, and God knows what other torments."

B was also the first letter of the town in which lived a boyhood sweetheart, whom he lost, and B was the first letter of the name of another girl whom he lost, and the first letter of his wife's name. B is the first letter of "banker," which is his much-hated father's profession, and "ball" is associated with his brother for a similar reason (ball-playing). "Bigot," "blood," "burial," "body," "bastard," "brother," and numerous proper names beginning with B were others in this list.

The great ogre of his childhood was the bugger-man. (He some-times spells this "bogger-man," sometimes "bogey-man.") The ter-rible fears of this hypothetical creature were recalled vividly, together with many associations. One was being put in a room where an autopsy was said to have been performed. The bugger-man was the token used to frighten him into good behaviour. It was related in dreams to Ne-groes, to buggies, buckets, butchers, burglars, and so on. Finally, bug-ger-man had a sinister connotation to my patient because of uncon-scious homosexual fears and feelings, and the shape of the letter B lends itself to a confirmatory interpretation.

What do you suppose " pipe " symbolized to this poor old burglar?
" An invitation from a patrolman to join a Bible class succeeded yes-terday in bringing a confession of burglaries from Warren E. McGlas-son, 60-year-old wanderer, after customary police methods had failed.

" ' I've been thinking about what that officer said about church,' he said. ' It's made me realize I have been wandering through life in a useless manner. I have decided to confess, take my punishment, and when I get out, get a job and go to work.'

" The man then confessed to burglarizing more than 100 southside homes from which he took principally faucets and other plumbing fixtures.

" He will be taken to the prosecutor's office today."
— Kansas City *Star*, February 7, 1923

Physical symptoms are often symbols:
Miss Everett came in complaining of a back-ache. She had had it for three years. With it were the usual neurasthenic symptoms of fatigua-bility and " peplessness." Thorough examinations, including X-ray, were negative. She had had various attempts at " suggestion " and manipulation treatments (osteopathy and chiropractic) which had failed.

" The back-ache began," she said, " when I came home to take care of Mother, seventy years old, who is an invalid." The patient was thirty-three and had been engaged to be married for several years. She had not married because she felt she ought to take care of her mother. The man to whom she was engaged became restive and did not want to postpone the marriage any longer.

The symptom of back-ache, in other words, was a symbolic way of saying that her burden was greater than she could bear and that, like the old man of the sea, her mother was on her back. Her self-respect com-bined with other factors to censor this from her consciousness. Treat-ment consisted in pointing out the obvious logic, advising her to face it frankly and make her decision consciously rather than unconsciously and to make some study of the psychological phenomena involved. She has been well ever since.

Symbolism in fairy-tales:

". . . Close by the king's castle lay a large, dark forest and in its midst, under an old linden-tree, was a deep well. One day the beautiful little princess went out into the woods and sat by the well and began to play with a golden ball, her favourite plaything. As she was tossing it up into the air and catching it again, it happened that the ball missed her hands, fell upon the ground, and rolled into the well. At this the princess began to weep as if she could never be comforted."

Whereupon, as the story goes, a frog appears and agrees to retrieve the ball, providing the princess will let him be her playmate, table guest, and bedfellow. The princess promises, but upon recovering her ball endeavours to evade the fulfilment of her promises. At her father's insistence, however, she is compelled to admit the repulsive frog to her house, to her table, and finally to her bedroom. When the frog, reminding her of the agreement, demands to be taken into her bed with her, the princess rebels and in a burst of anger picks the frog up with two fingers and flings it with all her strength against the wall.

" The next instant there stood before the princess a handsome young prince with friendly eyes. He fell on his knee before her and thanked her for his wonderful deliverance from the spell of a wicked witch. . . . And so they were married and lived happily ever afterwards." (After Grimm.) [28]

(The golden ball and the frog both symbolize the same thing. To understand this fully, one must remember that the child frequently has unconscious anxieties about his genital organs. The theme of this story is that a girl who has lost her " golden ball " can only regain her completeness, so to speak, as a result of surrender to what at first seems a repulsive aggression or seduction. It is a mistake to assume, as many amateur psychoanalysts do, that the frog, snake, cane, and other phallic symbols represent the male sexual organ and nothing else. It is more correct to say that such symbols stand for all that the phallus stands for; that is, for masculinity, power, authority, and procreation as well as physical sexuality. See Fantasy IX, page 353.)

These, then, are some of the disguises. The acts and the actors come and go — and the audience (the world) is often fooled,

---

[28] See the similar but somewhat more explicit tale of Oda and the Serpent, cited, along with many others, in Franz Ricklin's *Wishfulfillment and Symbolism in Fairy Tales* (New York: Journal of Nervous and Mental Disease Publishing Company, 1915) .

more often not fooled, by disguises and tricks which quite elude the stage-manager. " Everyone is queer but me and thee "; " She deceives no one but herself "; " Actions speak louder than words " — these and a score of other proverbs attest this truth. In fact, it is sometimes hard to convince impatient and irritated friends that a certain offender is quite unconscious of the obvious motives indicated by a certain untoward act or symptom or mannerism or attitude. " He can't suppose that we don't see why he does it," they will say. " His headaches (or tantrums or threats) disappear when he gets his own way. It's too obvious."

But as a rule it is obvious only to the outsiders. The offender himself is quite blind to this " obviousness." For him, at least, the disguises work perfectly. He believes himself sick or abused or in danger. In everyday life the disguises are usually not even suspected, let alone detected. Few persons suppose there is any relationship between Rockefeller's constipation and his wealth, or between Theodore Roosevelt's big-game hunting and his large family; few recognize the unconscious cruelty of the surgeon or the over-compensated criminal propensities of the prosecuting attorney. The woman who slowly chokes her husband to death [29] is often regarded as " sweet and lovely," [30] and the par-

[29] She took my strength by minutes,
　　She took my life by hours,
　　She drained me like a fevered moon
　　That saps the spinning world.
　　The days went by like shadows,
　　The minutes wheeled like stars.
　　She took the pity from my heart,
　　And made it into smiles.
　　She was a hunk of sculptor's clay,
　　My secret thoughts were fingers:
　　They flew behind her pensive brow
　　And lined it deep with pain.
　　They set the lips, and sagged the cheeks
　　And drooped the eyes with sorrow.
　　My soul had entered in the clay,
　　Fighting like seven devils.
　　It was not mine, it was not hers;
　　She held it, but its struggles
　　Modeled a face she hated,
　　And a face I feared to see.
　　I beat the windows, shook the bolts,
　　I hid me in a corner —
　　And then she died and haunted me,
　　And hunted me for life.
— Edgar Lee Masters: " Fletcher McGee " in *Spoon River Anthology* (New York: The Macmillan Co., 1916).
[30] Cf. Fran (Mrs. Samuel) Dodsworth, in Sinclair Lewis's novel *Dodsworth*.

ents whose children all remain unmarried because of their mutual adoration are praised for their success in rearing a beautiful and devoted (but perverted) family. Pictures and songs of a most primitive portent are innocently accepted if a few symbols are used discriminately. " My Wild Irish Rose " passes muster in polite society in spite of most obvious and ordinarily tabooed implications contained in it. The fact that flowers are the sexual organs of the plant kingdom is a disturbing (and hence a forbidden) thought to those for whom sex is an ugly thing, but the handling and giving of flowers a keen pleasure.

So much, then, for the disguises. The play's the thing, and what of the play?

The theme of the play is essentially the biography of the universal hero, the *Heldenleben,* which Richard Strauss has so graphically portrayed in music. It is a record of the birth, development, activities, experiences, successes and failures of the little individual who comes into a strange world believing himself to be unique and seeking throughout his life to understand and to adjust himself to the universe of which he is a minute part. The play that we speak of is the emotional essence of any and every biography, the story of the expression and the repression of human love and hate. In actual life there are infinite variations, and there is always some interference with ideal development and ideal adjustment. The play may go ahead too fast, it may lag or stop, it may actually reverse itself.

I. THE PLAY MAY GET AHEAD OF ITSELF (PRECOCITY)

" Charles Charlesworth, born of normal parents in Staffordshire, England, March 14, 1829 . . . reached maturity and grew whiskers at the age of four and died suddenly in a faint (syncope) when but seven years old." [31] This was a freak, of course — probably to be accounted for by a perversion of function of some of the endocrine glands. But it caricatures a process of precocity which in less extreme forms is very common.[32]

[31] Robert L. Ripley: *Believe it or Not!* (New York: Simon & Schuster, 1929), p. 15.
[32] The following scholarly summary is pertinent:
" Sirs:
" A recent issue of your magazine contained an interesting account of the precocious physical and sexual development of an American boy. Rare as such

" We don't know what to do with Bernard, doctor. He is nine years old, but you'd think he was twenty. He has learned the most terrible things! When I make him come in and go to bed, he swears — calls me incredible names. And when his father punishes him, he fights back and swears some more and says he'll kill his father! Then, when his temper cools down, he gets so serious — he looks at us reproachfully. He says he's worried. He talks so solemn! He tells great tales — we scarcely know what to believe. And then he has such nightmares and panics. He says he dreams of Jane, a schoolmate; he says he dreams he has kidnapped Jane and taken her away, into a wood all alone, and that he has kissed her a thousand times and married her there. And whether he dreams this or not, he acts it out, and some of the neighbours have been coming with serious complaints. He

---

a condition is, it is not altogether unheard of. There is a Greek description (Plegon. de Mirab. Cap. XXXII) of one who in the space of seven years was an infant, a youth, a mature person, an old man, married a wife, died, and left issue. Pliny records (Nat. Hist. Lib. vii–xxvii) a similar instance. A more detailed account of such a phenomenon is given in a curious tract in the Bodleian (Bodl. Pamph. Godw. 87. (4)) which bears the following title: Prodigium Willinghamense: Or, authentic Memoirs in the Life of a Boy, Born at Willingham, near Cambridge, October 31, 1741; who, before he was Three Years old, was Three Feet, Eight inches high And had the Marks of Puberty. With some Reflections on his Understanding, Strength, Temper, Memory, Genius and Knowledge. By T. Dawkes, Surgeon, London; Printed for C. Davis, over-against Gray's-Inn, Holbourn. Price One Shilling (not dated but apparently printed in 1747).

" This remarkable boy was carefully examined and measured by various ingenious gentlemen who made annual reports of his development to the Royal Society, for which they received a vote of thanks from that Learned Body. He was exhibited, particularly the marks of puberty, at market towns and fairs. At the age of three, we are told, his diversion was to throw a blacksmith's hammer weighing 17 lbs., after which he refreshed himself from a runlet of ale holding two gallons. Like others before him, however, he became a prey to strong drink and died, like Gilbert's precocious baby, ' an enfeebled old dotard at five.'

" Intellectual precocity though less rare is more interesting. Child wonders have actually performed mental feats which most adults could never hope to achieve. Eminent among them are Baratier, whose life was written by Dr. Johnson, Heinnecken, Quirino, Scaliger and John Stuart Mill, though the chief place must be accorded to the great Lipsius, of whom we are told that he composed a work the day he was born, concerning which there is the immortal remark of my Uncle Toby in Tristram Shandy (Chap. ii, Vol. II of *Tristram*).

" There are many instances of pious precocity — such as that of the unhappy little puritan girl who (so Cotton Mather in his Magnalia tells us, and with evident approval) spent eight hours a day in a dark closet weeping and praying for the forgiveness of her sins. Most remarkable though less authentic, is the refusal of the infant St. Nicholas to take his milk on Fridays, though the palm must be awarded to St. John the Evangelist whose pre-natal obeisance to Christ is a commonplace of medieval legendry.

Bergen Evans

University College
Oxford, England "

— Reprinted, with permission, from *Time*, January 5, 1931

denies them, but — well, he says: ' You take me to those lovely movies and I feel just like they do in the pictures. I can love and I can fight and some day I can kill! Only, gosh, it scares me when I dream about it.' " Nine years old!

Edward Porterfield is a man of sixty; he is rich, respected, influential. When his father died he was fourteen, and it was up to him to support the family. To this day he supports them all. His brothers and sisters are failures. His mother is penniless. They all look to Uncle Ed.

Porterfield had no childhood. He grew up without learning how to play, or how to live with other children. He married a wife who wanted to play — and she did and he didn't. And so they live together in armed neutrality, totally indifferent to each other. In recent years he bethought himself of his lacks, and, like the Æsop's ass that emulated the lap-dog, he made grotesque and pathetic efforts to dance and frolic. He gamed and he golfed, he danced and he flirted, he whisked himself to Europe and to Cuba.

But he is back in his office now, and his friends have stopped laughing. They dare not offend him, for they need his counsel and his favour, which are worth having.

II. THE ACTION OF THE PLAY MAY GET HUNG UP (FIXATION)

Instead of normal or supernormal progress, or instead of regressing or returning to earlier parts of the play (see next topic), the action may be interrupted by the overlong persistence of certain situations or characters. The play never moves on. The same lines and the same acts are repeated over and over with slight changes in the personnel.

To understand this perseverance the details of the family romance in its inception must be briefly recited:

The hero is cast forth upon the sands to begin the trip of life as a naked, helpless, new-born creature. He wastes no love on his environment. Presumably he is vastly displeased with the necessity of exchanging his warm, comfortable home within the mother for the cold, glaring world into which he emerges. This he proclaims in his first loud cry of displeasure.

Such love as the little new-comer is capable of he keeps to himself. So far as he is concerned, there is no world but his own microcosm. His hands, his crib, the walls and ceilings, even the nurses and passers-by, must seem to the child to be more or less remote parts of himself.

Gradually, step by step, he acquires, by experience, useful information. If indeed these things about him are all parts of himself, some of them are far more refractory parts than others. Some are noisy, some silent; some move, some remain fixed. Of those that move, some come, some go. Some seem to be capable of influence; they yield to cries and screams and do pleasurable or discomfort-removing things; others seem wholly indifferent to any and all protest.

Little by little the hard fact becomes accepted that some of this environment is really environment and not a part of the little self. From those detached portions of existence all interest, all love, is likewise detached. It is still for the self, or ego, alone that the child exhibits love. But this self still definitely includes certain moving, speaking, pleasure-furnishing creatures, one of whom is particularly available, particularly comfortable and gratifying. The mother, gazing at the child on her breast and thinking how much a part of her it still is and always will be, little realizes or considers how nearly identical are the baby's "thoughts."

Gradually, however, the child progresses further in its disillusionments and begins to appreciate a distinction between self and ministers to the little self, the mother in particular. But this time the intellectual discrimination is not accompanied by emotional discrimination. Separate, in a sense, she may be, but as a former part of oneself she is still of interest, still beloved; and as a supply of pleasure and comfort (the fruit of her own love for the child) she is still loved by it.

This love for the mother, then, may be seen to be, first, an extension of self-love to a detached part, as it were, of the self; next, a love for the source of personal comfort; and, thirdly, a reflection of the love felt and manifested by the mother.

Much later there comes to be a fourth stage or aspect of the attachment. This is the love for the mother (and father), not for the sake of subjective advantage, but for the sake of the pleasure of the love itself. This object-love has two elements: the desire to *have* the beloved individual, and the desire to *be* or be like the beloved individual.

It is easier to see this in adult love situations. A lover will desire to *have* his sweetheart (to marry her, be with her, kiss her, and order her about), and he will also desire to share things with her, cultivate the same friends and interests, adopt the same church, and so on. Lovers even come to look alike in their unconscious efforts to be identified with each other. A son may be seen to exhibit this type of love toward his father or any other idol. But both the elements of possession and of imitation enter into all objective love.

Let us return now to the growing child. As we shall discuss presently in another connection (page 317), his instinctual life has been developing through various stages of interest and with the aid of various organs of pleasure. Such a cycle of development reaches a tentative goal about the age of six, when an objective love relationship to the parents is developed. (This cycle is in a sense repeated during the next twelve years and other love objects are selected, ending normally in mating, but the instinctual mechanisms are the same.) The parents, being human beings, make distinctions of sex in their attitude toward each other and toward the child, and so the child begins to do

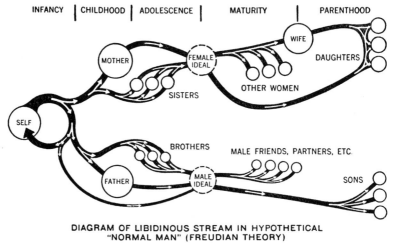

DIAGRAM OF LIBIDINOUS STREAM IN HYPOTHETICAL
"NORMAL MAN" (FREUDIAN THEORY)

FIG. 16

likewise. The father, for example, treats the mother as a woman; he loves her as a woman and she loves him as a man, and this is both implicit and apparent, in all their relationships. Of course they also love each other simply as human beings, but there is no such thing as a sexless human being, and hence no such thing as sexless, or purely Platonic, love.

Moreover, these parents, knowing that their child is a boy, or a girl, unconsciously — or perhaps even consciously — develop the attitudes toward him or her that they have had toward other boys or girls. If it be a boy, for example, the father will, to some extent, think of him and toward him as he did toward other boys and does toward other men, and the mother similarly.

Now the child, bathed in this cross-fire of paternal and maternal love, likewise develops attitudes and distinctions. He returns what he is given. Toward the father, who loves him in a masculine way, he returns masculine love; toward the mother, feminine love. Outwardly there may be little apparent distinction; unconsciously this is the beginning of the psychological differences of sex.

This is an important point, one which Freud himself overlooked for many years, or at least never emphasized until 1930. It would have saved some misunderstanding of his original thesis, which shocked many people because it attributed the erotic initiative and selection entirely to the child. The child does indeed turn toward the parent of the opposite sex, but this love is not something which springs spontaneously from an unstimulated mass of protoplasm; it is a response induced, encouraged, and directed by the attitude of the environment (the parent). This does not deny the existence of instincts. It only means that the direction of the child's affection is not exclusively dependent upon a specific and selective instinct, as was the inference many people drew from the delineation of the Œdipus complex.

Assume, for illustration, that the child is a boy. As he grows a little older, reaching the age of five or six or seven, a familiar triangle develops which has far-reaching consequences. There are himself and his mother and his father — two men and a woman. It is a commonplace that many men are jealous of their sons (of the attention and love their wives give their sons, subtracted, as it seems, from themselves). But it is none the less true that sons are jealous of fathers. This, however, is usually unconscious rather than conscious. It has been proved beyond question, by thousands of psychological investigators, but it still meets with scepticism and angry dispute from the uninformed.

What happens, of course, is that the jealousy of the child is largely repressed through fear of the consequences of its overt expression. He loves both father and mother, but his love for his mother is possessive, and for the father identifying, or imitative. It is as if he were striving to replace his father by himself. It is common to hear little boys announce this quite naïvely. They will say: " Daddy is gone, so I'll sit here and be Daddy," or " Mother, when I grow up I'll marry you and Father can stay at the office all the time," or similar things. But he does not dare to express all of his thoughts on the subject or to carry out his fantasies.

It is easier still to observe the secondary consequences of these attachments. Everyone is familiar with the preference mothers show for sons, and fathers show for daughters, but it is not so generally recognized that this is reciprocal, and that most daughters love their fathers more dearly than their mothers, and sons their mothers more than their fathers. Friction between daughters and mothers and clashes between sons and fathers are commonplace, everyday observations. That they go so far as to imply murder — in fantasy — is no longer a " shocking " or incredible observation, since it is indeed the theme of many plays and stories (for example, *Hamlet*). Essentially, these clashes are dictated by jealousy — the competitive striving of two persons for the love and attention of a third. Of this, however, the participants are practically never conscious. When the first baby arrives, some men will say to their wives: " Are you going to love him so much now that you won't have much time for me any more? " This fear is well justified by biological facts, but it is usually covered up. Many childless couples remain so because the husband and wife are too jealous of each other's love to risk the intrusion of a rival, even though that rival be their own child. Many divorces arise over this same conflict.

More important by far than the effects on the parents are the effects on the child, if these emotional conflicts are unsatisfactorily handled. The direct instinctive demands must, of course, be repressed. Affectionate or tender love must be substituted for acquisitive love (for the mother), and respect and emulation substituted for rivalry and jealousy (toward the father). To the extent that this repression and substitution fail, familial unhappiness, unsatisfactory substitutes, and " nervousness " result.

Then, subsequently, substitutions must be made for the original *dramatis personæ*. A son may not always confine his love to his mother; it is a law of social and biological and psychological nature that he begins in his teens to " like " girls and then to love them, and ultimately to love one woman more intensely and more fully than he did even his mother. This woman will probably be chosen by him because of the ways in which she fulfils his idealized memory-image of his mother, but he will not know this. He will scarcely see it or believe it if it be pointed out to him. Even when he has, in some measure, made a mother of his wife, he will probably only faintly recognize it. All this is worked out in the unconscious.

It appears most clearly when one of these hitches in the play occur — particularly a tie-up of the action, a *fixation*. Some children are unable to detach sufficient of their family love bonds ever to love anyone else. They are, as we say, *fixated* always on the mother or father, or it may be a brother or sister; or it may be someone who too closely represents one of these early pillars. This is the persistence of an infantile relationship, which in the unconscious workings of the mind becomes a romantic triangle, as outlined above. Because it is common to all mankind and because its repression and successful conversion into felicitous outlets is a keystone of mental health, it is very important in theoretical psychiatry. It is commonly called the Œdipus complex (the Elektra complex is the feminine equivalent) , after the Greek legend in which Œdipus unknowingly kills his father and marries his own mother, with dire consequences. In the old Greek plays this was represented as coming about through the blind determination of fate. Modern plays on the same theme — *The Silver Cord,* for example — take issue with such a deterministic explanation and lay an immediate responsibility upon the parents for the ruin of the child. In this they are confirmed by modern science; there seems little doubt but that parental attitudes largely determine the emotional patterns of the child.[33]

Fixation (on the mother — the Œdipus complex)

Sam Henderson was the town bachelor. Every girl in town knew him — they all liked him, but none of them took his attentions seriously. They knew from experience that it was idle to do so. Girl after girl he had pursued, but none of them seemed quite to satisfy his requirements. He seemed to be seeking a perfect woman for his wife. A psychiatrist could have told him that she was dead.

Fixation (on the father — the Elektra complex)

Marie was her father's daughter. From the cradle up she was his joy and pride, and he her slave and lover.

" When I was — oh, not twelve years old, I was constantly aware of my love for my daddy. If things went wrong in school, if I seemed to be left out of something, or ignored by someone, I clung to Father. His love made up for everything. His approval of what I did made me blissfully happy; his disapproval plunged me into despair and despondency. I doubt if he knew that. But Mother did! "

Mother was alert with the keen sensibilities of her sex. She saw her place in the emotional life of her husband usurped by her own

[33] The classic discussion of the psychosexual evolution of the child is Freud's *Three Contributions to the Sexual Theory,* published in English in the Nervous and Mental Disease Monograph Series. For an excellent summary with more recent discoveries incorporated, see Gerald H. J. Pearson " *The Psychosexual Development of the Child* " in *Mental Hygiene* for October 1931, Vol. XV, no. 4.

daughter. It was a situation in which she felt powerless. To be jealous of one's own daughter seemed despicable, incredible. She was cross with Marie — irritable, frankly uncongenial.

High-school days found Marie a developing girl of poise and beauty. She was apparently much more mature than her schoolmates. Her mother, glad to be able to oppress her daughter legitimately, piled household duties upon her which would have overwhelmed the average child of her years. But this delighted Marie; she acquired a skill and dispatch in sewing and dusting and cooking that astonished even her father. And of course he was delighted, and praised her for it. This was ample pay. "I felt as if my breast would burst with joy. I'm sure he never knew how much each word of his praise and approval meant to me. It made all of Mother's bitterness and hatefulness bearable; in fact, I sort of pitied Mother — poor, thwarted, vengeful Mother!"

For a time she was totally uninterested in boys and went through a series of crushes with various schoolmates. They were of short duration, however, and in the main Marie was not particularly popular with other girls, nor they with her. Her mother had soured her a bit on her own sex. But, rather earlier than most of the girls in her class, she began to be considerably interested in one boy after another. She seemed to get along excellently with them. They all liked her. Her natural exuberance of spirits made her various admirers believe her to be very much in love with them, and this response to her enthusiasm would speedily fan the embers into flame. Marie would become alarmed at this; her alarm would cool her ardour and soon there would be a new boy on the string and a perplexed, chagrined castaway trailing behind.

She continued this hectic social program into her college days. But, having acquired the reputation of being a flirt, she found herself attracting the attention of few of the more desirable men, although it was only the leaders who really interested her. This gave her some anxiety, because in theory she had strong matrimonial leanings and she was much distressed at her own inconstancy. She became somewhat more calculating in her manœuvres and developed an infatuation for a man much older than herself, but a particularly unworthy specimen, which lasted for a miserable year. Its termination left her thoroughly disgusted with the same male sex for which she had previously had so unbounded an enthusiasm.

She decided to renounce entirely the idea of matrimony. She gave up her course in domestic science and enrolled in a business course, from which she assured herself and everyone else she derived great satisfaction. Before she had completed a year of it, her father offered her an opportunity to go into business in his own store. She accepted at once. She opened up a millinery department and devoted herself to it assiduously. For several years she put her heart and soul into the business. The world thought her successful and happy.

But her father and mother, her family physician, and her pastor knew differently. They knew that she was increasingly miserable. "She isn't getting any joy out of living; she isn't really happy at all, but she won't say what it is."

"She thinks she wants to get out of the millinery business and teach or keep house. She really doesn't know what she wants to do. She wants to get married, but she won't look at a man," said her mother.

"She ought to go out with some of the boys," said her brother.

"Or girls," added her father.

"She needs her tonsils taken out," said the doctor.

"I think it would help her to do some work in the Sunday school," said the minister.

But in spite of suggestions and exhortations, in spite of a business success that would have overjoyed the average young merchant, the clouds of depression slowly lowered. Marie would rush home from the store at night and shut herself in her room. Her mother would timidly inquire about her supper and receive angry rebuffs. There were tears and long silences, sleepless nights of tossing; restless, fretful Sundays. With her mother, particularly, Marie was short and irritable. They came to avoid each other as much as possible by tacit consent. The old feud was still on, but Marie now felt vanquished. Her father was no longer her mentor. He seemed to have lost his power over her affections. Her brothers were as nothing. Life itself was as nothing. "There is only one thing to do with a fool like me," she wrote, "and I've got to do it myself. Some day I'll get up nerve enough to do it."

Thus it came about that Marie, whom everyone loved, came to be a recluse like her grouchy brother Charles, and in place of the poise and direction of her early life she was torn between conflicting desires and impulses, most of them only dimly conscious. Whether to go on in business or seek a home, whether to live with her irritating parents or take up with unfriendly strangers, whether to welcome a lover or to eschew all men, whether to yield as a woman or compete as a man, whether to live or die — all these wrestled in her heart till she could no longer endure the soul torment. Gradually she sank deeper and deeper into a depression of resignation.[34]

[34] This patient finally undertook psychoanalytic treatment; see pages 394–7.

Fixation (on the self — the Narcissus complex)

Most tragic of all, the love fixation may be upon the individual himself, so that he loves himself too much to spare any love to anyone else. This is called *narcissism* (really narcissus-ism) after the ill-starred youth who fell in love with his own reflection in the brook and vexed the pursuing goddess to the point of turning him into a flower. Hell hath no furies . . . even though the scorned woman realizes that those who so love themselves cannot love another or understand what such love is.

> When Arthur's slender lavender wife died in bearing a child,
> He wept decorously,
> Bore himself punctiliously in the ritual of the requiem,
> Gave the courteous young priest a gold coin,
> Then went home
> And composed, with the aid of a riming dictionary,
> A Ballade of Sorrow,
> And a rondel about death
> In the manner of Henley.
>
> —Nelson Antrim Crawford

This concentration of libido upon self is normal, it must be remembered, at certain stages in the psychosexual evolution. It is the *persistence* of the immature objective and immature expression into adult life that deserves to be called fixation and regarded as pathological. And this fixation may be conscious and overt or it may be altogether concealed by some of the disguises already described.

Masturbation, for example, is an obvious form of overt indulgence in self-love or narcissism. It is quite natural and normal in children, despite energetic condemnations by misguided parents and teachers. In the vast majority of individuals it ceases spontaneously, giving way to more extroverted, adult forms of sex expression.

But some persons continue all their lives to concentrate their love upon their own bodies rather than upon the body — and soul — of another person. In Benét's beautiful and faithful portrayal of Lucy, below, he clearly indicates not only her love of her own body, but her abhorrence of and incapacity for mature heterosexual love.

> *(The flirt, Lucy, was speaking to herself)*
> . . . You may dance.
> Play in the sun and wear bright gowns to levees,

But soon or late, the hands unlike to your hands
But rough and seeking, will catch your lightness at last
And with strange passion force you. What is this passion,
This injury that women must bear for gowns?
It does not move me or stir me. I will not bear it.
There are women enough to bear it. If I have sweetness,
It is for another service. It is my own.
I will not share it. I'll play in the heat of the sun.
And yet, young girls must marry — what am I thinking?

She stepped from her hoops to try on the rose brocade,
But let it lie for a moment, while she stood up
To look at the bright ghost-girl in the long dark mirror,
Adoringly.
　"Oh, you honey," she thought. "You honey!
You look so pretty — and nobody knows but me.
Nobody knows."
　She kissed her little white shoulders,
With fierce and pitying love for their shining whiteness,
So soft, so smooth, so untarnished, so honey-sweet.
Her eyes were veiled. She swayed in front of the mirror.
"Honey, I love you," she whispered, "I love you, honey.
Nobody loves you like I do, do they, sugar?
Nobody knows but Lucy how sweet you are.
You mustn't get married, honey. You mustn't leave me.
We'll be pretty and sweet to all of them, won't we, honey?
We'll always have beaus to dance with and tunes to dance to,
But you mustn't leave me, honey. I couldn't bear it.
You mustn't ever leave me for any man."
　　— Stephen Vincent Benét: *John Brown's Body* (Garden City:
　　　　　　Doubleday, Doran & Co., 1928), p. 275.

One form of narcissistic indulgence carried over into adult
life and exemplified upon all sides in the most varied disguises
is *exhibitionism*. Exhibitionism is the satisfaction taken by an
individual in the exposure of his personal charms to the eyes of
the admiring world. At the age of three this is regarded with all
the evidences of great delight by admiring relatives. But, unhappily, cuteness at three may become grotesquerie at twenty-
three, or sixty. Yet many adults get varying degrees of satisfaction out of various kinds of exhibitionism, and similarly many
other people obtain pleasure from beholding these exhibition-

istic performances. This offers some explanation of the bur-
lesque show, the musical comedy, and other systematic exhibits
of the human form. It may be a little less obvious that there are
ministers who love to preach because of the exhibitionistic opportunity it affords, and lawyers who love to argue and doctors
who love to operate in part for the same reason.

Exhibitionism may appear in an undisguised genital form in
adults, usually compulsive acts which, although causing the perpetrator himself embarrassment and humiliation, are nevertheless at the moment irresistible. This is technically called exhibitionism, but it represents more than the narcissism discussed
above; it is a compulsive denial of great unconscious fears, and
such individuals need treatment, not persecution.

Fixation (on body organs) [35]

Instead of investing narcissistic love upon the body as a whole
as in the case of Lucy quoted above or the first type of exhibitionism described above, or, on the other hand, upon the genitals
exclusively as in the case of masturbation, many individuals exhibit their narcissism only with respect to various organs of the
body which they select for a particular erotic attention. Everyone knows the man who has fallen in love with his lungs, so to
speak, and is incessantly protecting himself against tuberculosis
or pneumonia. Such men may pet their respiratory tracts into
giving good service in singing, public speaking, or some other
vocal ballyhoo. Similarly there are the cardiac people, the
hearty boys who whoop it up for athletics and exercises and
strength and courage (*cour* = heart), and who in their weaker
moments develop and succumb to heart afflictions,[36] angina
pectoris, and arteriosclerosis. The *oral erotics* are the mouthy
folk, the epicures and good livers, who like to talk and to chew
gum and suck their cigars and prolong their kisses, and who run
to tonsil operations and dental dallyings.

But most familiar of all are the belly types, the *anal* erotics,
who have reserved for their digestive tracts a large share of their
libido and exemplify this by an elaborate concern for all phases
of the process, from ingestion to excretion. Here belong the

[35] For a technical discussion of the way in which organs of the body are uti-
lized to express neurotic conflicts, physicians are referred to Chapter VI of Franz
Alexander's *The Medical Value of Psychoanalysis* (New York: W. W. Norton &
Co.; revised edition, 1936). (See also pages 235–7 of this book.)

[36] E.g., 32 per cent of 315 former college athletes died of heart diseases; less
than 20 per cent is the rule. See L. Dublin: "Longevity of College Athletes,"
Harper's Magazine, July 1928.

stomach-petters and belly-rubbers, the pill-takers and enema cranks, the dyspeptics and hyperacidics and the " bilious " and the martyrs to the piles. Their bowel movements are their most important daily activity and their most lustily enjoyed topic of conversation. Nothing could be more convincing of the thesis of organ-fixation, the genitalizing of a non-sexual part of the body and the concentration of libido thereupon, than the orgies of emotion poured out in direct and indirect fashion by this type of narcissist upon his lowly and long-suffering gut.

These organ-fixations represent vestiges of normal stages in the erotic or *psychosexual evolution* of the child. There is a time, as everyone knows, when his oral activities are his chief preoccupation. At first these are sucking in nature, later biting. With this latter mode the child's hostility can be expressed; his teeth are his chief weapon. But by this time his attention has been called to his excretory habits. The wishes of the parents are gradually imposed upon him. His adjustment of his excretory and retentive pleasures to these requirements replace the former dominance of the oral interests. Gradually other organs of the body, the skin, the hands, the eyes, the ears, occupy his interest and serve him as his major source of pleasure, until finally the beginning of genital sensations attracts him predominantly to that zone. The genitals are too interesting a piece of apparatus to escape notice and the necessary requirements of urination frequently call his attention to this region.

Now, any one of these phases or stages in psychosexual development may be complicated by peculiar attitudes on the part of the parents or unusual occurrences in the daily life of the child such that a normal or complete evolution does not take place. An over-anxious mother may place so much importance upon the time, place, method, and amount that the child eats as to develop a peculiar over-emphasis upon eating and oral activities in general; an overly fastidious mother may stimulate a child to excessive preoccupation with toilet habits. Even under ideal circumstances some of these activities are necessarily and normally carried over into adult life, but most of them are replaced either with other interests or with sublimations. For example, a fondness for exquisite wines may represent a continued seeking to gratify some of the excessive oral demands which were thwarted in childhood, but it is a socially acceptable form; biting one's finger-nails or chewing tobacco is less socially acceptable.

In regard to anal-erotic proclivities, the pleasure which one of my neighbours derived from collecting and hoarding short lengths of twigs from the elm trees on his estate and packing them in boxes always amused me. Reactions *against* these infantile erotic residiums are frequently conspicuous; over-cleanliness, for example, fastidiousness, punctiliousness, miserliness, and so on.

All these infantile tendencies or reactions from them may be represented only in attitudes — for example, by an attitude of dependence, stubbornness, curiosity, optimism, pessimism. This has led to the delineation by psychoanalytic writers of personality types based on the predominance of traits from one or another of these stages of development — for example, the *oral character* (that is, personality), the *urethral character,* etc. For our purposes it is sufficient to indicate that the traits represent fixations, often with reaction formations (see above), representing incomplete personality evolution.[37]

III. THE PLAY MAY BACK UP
(REGRESSION)

In yet a third way the play may go badly. Actors whose parts were played long since and who should have left the stage may force their way back, so that the play, instead of proceeding with the third act, let us say, reverts to a clumsy, anachronistic reproduction of Act I.

Technically the word *regression* is used rather loosely to describe two different things: the surrender of sublimation or a socially acceptable disguise of a primitive trait in favour of its more direct expression — for example, fist-fighting instead of debating; also reversion to one of the earlier infantile modes of obtaining satisfaction — for example, relinquishing personal friends in favour of greater attachment to money. In both senses a greater degree of infantilism is implied.

This is how it appears clinically:

Harry Emmet, a college freshman, came from a proud, seclusive family. He was timid, baby-faced, and very " green." His money made him popular, but a great deal more was expected of him than he could possibly deliver. He soon became frightfully homesick and wrote for his mother to come. She came, petted and comforted him, and took him home for a rest.

[37] The interested reader should consult especially the works of Ernest Jones and Karl Abraham; see bibliography at end of book.

George Babbitt was ordinarily a sedate, respectable business man. Upon certain occasions, however, under the influence of a few drinks of whisky and a convivial crowd, his sedateness disappeared and he became a boy again. He sang and yelled, shot craps and played tag, wrestled and tussled, laughed and played.

The late Frankwood Williams put eloquently what we shall some day feel like saying to some of the grown-up babies whose infantilisms distress us and handicap themselves:

" You have reached physical adulthood, and you have an unusually keen intellect. You could be a very useful individual. Your decisions in important matters, however, are made, not in accordance with the facts but in the light of the unsolved emotional problems of your own personal childhood. You act honestly enough, but you see the facts presented to you not as they are truly but as they are distorted through these personal lenses. You cause difficulty and confusion. Your keen intellect makes it possible for you to defend ably your improper decisions and your weak causes. Many problems which are brought to you could be fairly easily solved if they did not get mixed up with your own personal problems which have nothing to do with the issue at hand. Therefore you hinder rather than help. You need to grow up." [38]

In the same article the author gives an interesting list of those persons considered emotionally immature. A part of the list follows:

" Men who must love any woman briefly, and find it difficult or impossible to love one for any length of time.

" Men and women shy and self-conscious in the presence of each other.

" Women who do not believe that women are inferior to men, but who feel and act as if they were.

" Individuals who force sex in one form or another unnecessarily to the fore.

" Men and women greatly concerned over the salvation, one kind or another, of others.

" People living on Park Avenue on a Greenwich Village income.

" Social workers who wear out shoe leather rather than brain cells.

" Husbands who are not understood.

" Judges who wear horns and bellow.

" Ministers whose hearts bleed."

[38] Frankwood E. Williams: " Putting Away Childish Things," *Survey Graphic*, April 1928, pp. 14-15.

All of us recognize these childish traits cropping out in our-selves at times, and it is still easier to see them in our friends. One purpose of education is their recognition and renunciation. I asked my freshmen at Washburn College to tell me some of the infantilisms which they had detected in themselves. Here is a partial list:

"I'm always wishing I were like somebody else."

"I love to look at myself in the mirror."

"I always get what I want even if I have to shed barrels of tears."

"I enjoy saying things I think are humorous, especially if by so do-ing I can get the attention of the crowd."

"I get very annoyed when people interfere with my plans, intention-ally or otherwise."

"I laugh when the joke is on somebody else; when it is on me, I pout."

"I actually work to get out of work, especially if it's cooking."

"When I have a pet idea or plan, I expect everybody to agree with me, and I become very angry if they don't."

"I like to be begged and coaxed into things."

"If I don't get a lot of publicity for work in an organization, I quit working."

"I like flattery. Nothing makes me so happy as to have someone 'feed me a line' about almost anything."

"I hate awfully to admit my own faults, especially to admit I'm childish."

"Sometimes I do things just because somebody doesn't want me to."

"When I am angry, I over-condemn the thing or person that causes the anger, and then get sulky and feel miserable."

This clinging to infantilism or regressing to infantile methods of expression may proceed to alarming extremes. A few illustra-tions of this will indicate how much of a baby a grown-up woman (or man) may sometimes become.

Professor McDougall, of Duke University, has described some very vivid instances of this which took place in soldiers as a re-sult of their horror over war experiences. One of his cases has been very eloquently recast by H. A. Overstreet in his book *About Ourselves* (pp. 19–20), as follows:

"The first picture which we shall cast upon the psychoneurotic silver screen is that of a young Australian soldier. He had been sent to a hospital for complete loss of speech following shell-shock. He was recovering fairly well under treatment when there occurred a series of severe air raids, which threw the hospital into confusion and made necessary the hurried removal of the patients. As a result of this second fright, the young Australian underwent a startling transformation.

" He became as a child. Literally so. He lost completely the power to speak. Given a pencil, he was utterly at a loss to know what to do with it. He seemed even to have forgotten the use of the ordinary things about him, which he examined with a kind of mingled curiosity and timidity.

" He walked jerkily, with feet planted widely apart; and if he was not supported, he would quickly slip down and crawl about, as a child does, with the aid of hands.

" He could not even feed himself, and when fed by his nurse, insisted that she taste each spoonful first. ' He played in a childish manner with various objects, making toys of them, and he quickly adopted and became very devoted to a small doll kept as a mascot by a neighbor in the ward.'

" Here, then, is an instance of complete breakdown from adulthood. It is a case of so-called *regression to the infantile*. This young Australian was not feigning. He *was* a child. It was as if all that had been slowly built up in the course of his normal growth had been suddenly swept away and he had been pushed back to the physical and mental condition of a helpless infant.

" At first blush such a case seems to bear no likeness whatever to anything which happens in ordinary life. And yet a more careful scrutiny shows it to be only an aggravated form of what takes place with a fair degree of frequency in far more lives than we ordinarily imagine."

Another extreme case of regression:

Mrs. A. was thirty years old when she began to be depressed. Her melancholy gave way to an excited stage in which she acted out, in extreme forms, first the sort of behaviour characteristic of her at twenty and twenty-five, then things reminiscent of the period of her teens, and from this on back to her girlhood days.

" She repeated the slang and catch-words of that day, sang the now forgotten popular songs, and talked much of old friends — in brief she became again in many respects the young girl I had known before her marriage. Later she reached the period of nursery songs and rhymes, and the childish naughtiness in which she had all along indulged became more marked.

"Now more striking infantile characteristics were revealed. She talked very little, and then in a babyish fashion. She asked naive and child-like questions. She drooled at the mouth constantly, and would rub the saliva over her face. She displayed an incessant curiosity about everything in her environment, handling it awkwardly and attempting to place it in her mouth. She was constantly tearing things apart or taking them to pieces ' to see the insides.' She forgot the use of knife and fork, eating with her fingers and spilling her food. She seemed partially to have forgotten how to walk, falling and bumping against furniture or crawling on her hands and knees. She would sit on the floor and amuse herself for considerable periods of time by tearing books and magazines to pieces. Finally she began to soil the bed, and . . . smear the walls. . . . As she began to recover, these habits were replaced by a mania for taking enemas. The drooling habit also was replaced by a constant child-like spitting. We are all familiar with the interest little children often take in spitting as soon as they learn the trick, and how natural it seems to be for them to use it as a means of defense.

"Gradually she seemed to grow up. She no longer denied her marriage, but expressed no interest in husband and children. She seemed rather distraite, indifferent and dazed. After a time she expressed a desire to go to her sister's home. She was then allowed to go to live with her father and sister, just as she had before her marriage. Continued separation from her husband was advised. She now asked for her children, and they were brought to her. She began to correspond with her husband, and after her recovery seemed to be complete they began living together." [39]

PERSISTENT FANTASIES OR PLAY THEMES

Regression does not necessarily proceed to the infantile stages just described. There are certain other felicitous phases which the actors are prone to recall, and there is an ever-present propensity to lapse back into these older and easier situations instead of proceeding with newer and harder ones. The actors, finding the real words and acts of their parts difficult, substitute false lines. These substitutions are fantasies; fantasy acting replaces reality acting; and fantasy-formation replaces thinking.

For the child, thinking is synonymous with wishing; that is, all thought is an untrammelled expression of wishing. He recog-

[39] Ralph Reed: " A Manic-Depressive Attack Presenting a Reversion to Infantilism," *Journal of Abnormal Psychology*, Vol. XI, 361–7 (1917).

nizes no interferences, no need for consistency, no responsibilities to reality, no importance attached to distinguishing fact from fancy, and no necessity for making essential or significant discrimination between things which appear to be alike or which arouse similar emotional reactions (often for some superficial reason). This is typical of primitive thinking, wishful thinking, the thinking of children, savages, and psychotics. Ordinarily one learns from experience the necessity of modifying our wishful thinking to conform to the realities of existence; to change from thinking on the basis of the *pleasure principle* to thinking on the basis of the *reality principle,* as Freud put it.

But this is, at best, only imperfectly achieved even by the most mature adults. For all of us certain favourite fantasy themes persist to comfort and support us in a world the hard realities of which hurt us, especially in our peculiarly tender spots. There are some aspects of our past, especially our childhood past, which were so painful that we cannot repudiate or surrender the illusory plasters which we have applied to the wounds.

Some of these fantasy themes are indeed harmless, others more malignant. Some are acted out, some are proclaimed and even defended, others are only dreamed in the deepest sleep.

Each of these fantasies or themes or *complexes* (a complex is a group of associated ideas centring in an emotional nucleus) will be described and then illustrated in one or several ways. There are many other fantasies common to many people. Those dealt with here are some of the best-known.

I. THE JEHOVAH COMPLEX

" *I am God Himself, omnipotent, omniscient, inscrutable.*" [40]

In poetry:

> Out of the night that covers me,
>   Black as the Pit from pole to pole,
> I thank whatever gods may be
>   For my unconquerable soul.

> In the fell clutch of circumstance
>   I have not winced nor cried aloud;
> Under the bludgeonings of chance,
>   My head is bloody, but unbowed.

[40] See Ernest Jones: " The God Complex: The Belief that one is God and the Resulting Character Traits; " Chapter v of *Essays in Applied Psychoanalysis* (London and Vienna: International Psychoanalytical Press, 1923).

Beyond this place of wrath and tears
Looms but the horror of the shade,
And yet the menace of the years
Finds, and shall find me, unafraid.

It matters not how strait the gate,
How charged with punishments the scroll.
I am the master of my fate;
I am the captain of my soul!

— William Ernest Henley: *Invictus*

In prose:

The Egyptian astrologist in *Rasselas* had acquired from long study an ability to predict the overflowing of the Nile with such accuracy, time after time, that he came to believe that he himself controlled its movements. He fell sick, however, and the river continued to ebb and flow as it had always done, to his utter consternation.

In the hospital:

Dr. Alexander Van Petten Smith walked with immense dignity. He was the terror of the nurses and the joke of the other doctors. When he entered the hospital ward the nurses rose, stood at attention in utter silence, and trembled. He was famous for finding out some trifle and roaring about it. He gave the nurses long and tedious orders and insisted upon their minute and complete fulfilment. Once a nurse whispered to another as they stood awaiting his beck or nod. He looked up, flushed with anger; he rapped upon the desk with his knuckles a moment, then strode to the office and ordered the nurse's dismissal from the hospital.

Also in the hospital:

"If you want an answer, don't call me Dave Gerber," said a patient in the hospital. "Once I was Dave Gerber; now I am God Almighty. Address me as God. Treat me as God. That's who I am. I'm the most powerful person in the world; I can turn this building inside out. I'll write you a cheque for ten million dollars and you can build sixteen more sanitariums. I've got four hundred children by my first wife and they all work for me, and I rule them and rule the whole universe. I was running for governor, but I gave that up when I became God. I used to feel afraid of other people, but now I rule over all of them and it's a glorious feeling. Did you ever feel like that, doctor? You rule over your patients, don't you? But think of ruling the whole world. That's me. I'm God Almighty."

In the home:

Judge Jones sits proudly and stiffly at the head of his table, as if he were in his court-room. His wife and daughters scurry to bring on the food promptly. The small children sit meekly and quietly in their places. All look expectantly toward the lord and master, who in turn alternately considers critically the degree to which his comforts are being assured and the respectful dependency of his flock. At precisely ten minutes of nine he drives off to the court-house, where he poses and imposes and gives moral lectures on the majesty of the law and the vileness of its infractors.

In New York, U. S. A., 1936:
"FATHER DIVINE (GOD)"[41]

"'It is a privilege to live in the ACTUAL PRESENSE OF GOD, — to bring your bodies into subjection, that the Spirit of My Presence with all Divine Intelligence, might Teach you Wisdom, Knowledge and Understanding that cannot be criticized. . . . You will move spontaneously by the Spirit within you, and it will be according to My Mind, to My Will, and to My Pleasure.'"[42]

In Rome:

Commodus, Emperor of Rome from A.D. 161 to 191, was so proud of his achievements in the arena as a gladiator that he commanded the world to worship him as Hercules. He was eventually killed in a wrestling contest by a gladiator named Narcissus, but only after he had fought and won over a thousand battles.

In Austria:

Bernard Scheinberg, seventy-six, an Austrian, holds the world's record for paternity. He is the father of eighty-eight children, of whom eighty-four are living. Scheinberg was married twice and had seventy children by his first wife, who died at the age of fifty-six. He married the second time at the age of fifty-seven and by this union had eighteen children. The first Mme Scheinberg had quadruplets four times, triplets seven times, and twins sixteen times.[43]

II. THE JESUS COMPLEX (OR MESSIAH COMPLEX)

" I am not God, but His son, and the son of a virgin; destined to make all manner of sacrifices, to give my life, if necessary, to carry out my ideals and save the world from the other men in it,

41 Inscription on the buses between the Harlem and Newark " Heavens."
42 John Hoshor: *God in a Rolls Royce* (New York, Hillman-Curl, 1936), p. 56.
43 Topeka *Daily Capital,* January 8, 1927.

*who are mostly bad. I am like Jesus, that other Son of God, and
like Him I eschew women and bow my head to my Father's will."*

In poetry:

My good blade carves the casques of men,
    My tough lance thrusteth sure,
My strength is as the strength of ten,
    Because my heart is pure. . . .

How sweet are looks that ladies bend
    On whom their favours fall!
For them I battle till the end,
    To save from shame and thrall;
But all my heart is drawn above,
    My knees are bow'd in crypt and shrine;
I never felt the kiss of love,
    Nor maiden's hand in mine.
More bounteous aspects on me beam,
    Me mightier transports move and thrill;
So keep I fair thro' faith and prayer
    A virgin heart in work and will. . . .
    —Alfred Lord Tennyson (from *Sir Galahad*)

In college:

Frank O'Brien entered college with his head and heart lifted high.
He had always been a sensitive lad, given to dreaming and high
aspirations. It seemed to him as if there must be a special mission on
earth for him, that perhaps he would find it in college. He was not
a crusader, but was given more to grail-seeking than to dragon-slaying.
He had a pleasant smile, which won him friends, but he was not
enough interested in them to keep them, except a few who learned
to know him well and to esteem him highly.

These few joined him in the organizing of a new fraternity, in-
stigated partly by their resentment at having been excluded by the older
fraternities and partly by idealistic conceptions of a nobler order which
O'Brien painted. He was unanimously elected the first president, and
under his guidance it launched forth on a meteoric career of temporary
brilliancy. As its leader, O'Brien shone with redoubled lustre. He was
radiant with the satisfaction of achievement, strong and confident in
its leadership, tireless in his efforts at improving the order.

Suddenly in his senior year he resigned his membership and withdrew. "I do not think that it is in keeping with the highest purposes
and best good of mankind that a few of them should group themselves
together as we have done," he said. "I have come to realize my mistake.

For the rest of you it may be all right, but I don't feel that I can conscientiously continue in such a spirit of separatism. Democracy is the noblest conception of man. Fraternities are not democratic. I must hold to my ideals. This is a sacrifice that I must make."

Thence he and the fraternity passed rapidly into oblivion.

In the home:

" I have put up with it, doctor, for thirty years. After all, I thought, she's my wife — I chose her, I promised her, and I do love her. If I underestimated her capacity for meanness, for harshness toward me, for temper tantrums and hysterics, for flights of extravagance and spells of parsimony — if I little suspected this, it was my misjudgment, not hers. She came into my room last week, and, seeing the watch my firm gave me for twenty years of loyal service, she banged it down hard upon the floor. I suppose some men would have cursed or wept or fought. I didn't — I just went to bed in silence and to sleep. Oh, it's an old story — I don't mind so much any more. And you see, after all, it's not me, now, that's losing my mind — it's her. Curious, isn't it — after I've spent my life giving in to her whims and accepting her abuse in order to save her that much suffering."

In the hospital:

" And so, doctor, I just felt I ought to offer myself up as a sacrifice and I found that match and lit my dress and offered myself as a burnt offering unto the Lord. I must redeem some of the suffering in the world with my own. That's how it happened and that's why I'm here, I suppose in all these bandages."

III. THE THEORY OF SACRED AND PROFANE LOVE AND THE TWO KINDS OF WOMEN

" *I hold that there are two kinds of women: saints and sinners, mothers and prostitutes. The former are pure, sexless, dull, and good; the latter are wicked, passionate, interesting, and utterly taboo.*" [44]

In prose:

" This way of looking at the last embrace of love has always been repugnant to me. If the last embrace is not as sacred, as pure, as de-

[44] The reader is urged to read Freud's unusually clear essays on this theme: " Contributions to the Psychology of Love: (1) A Special Type of Choice of Object Made by Men; (2) The Most Prevalent Form of Degradation in Erotic Life; (3) The Taboo of Virginity "; in the *Collected Papers*, Vol. IV (London, 1925).

voted as the rest, there is no virtue in abstaining from it. . . . Can there be for lofty natures a purely physical love and for sincere natures a purely intellectual one? . . . To distrust the *flesh* cannot be good and useful except for those who are all *flesh*. . . . The magnet embraces the iron, the animals come together by the difference of sex. . . . Man alone regards this miracle which takes place simultaneously in his soul and his body as a miserable necessity, and he speaks of it with distrust, with irony, or with shame. This is passing strange. The result of this fashion of separating the spirit from the flesh is that it has necessitated convents and brothels." [45]

In poetry:

>	Think, when our one soul understands
>		The great Word which makes all things new,
>	When earth breaks up and heaven expands,
>		How will the change strike me and you
>	In the house not made with hands?
>
>	Oh I must feel your brain prompt mine,
>		Your heart anticipate my heart,
>	You must be just before, in fine,
>		See and make me see, for your part,
>	New depths of the divine!
>
>	But who could have expected this
>		When we two drew together first
>	Just for the obvious human bliss,
>		To satisfy life's daily thirst
>	With a thing men seldom miss? [46]

In legend:

"There was a difference between Lilith and her, however, a difference of character which showed in their appearance. Lilith was almost as young as Eve, yet she looked as though she knew more and had lived, not longer, but more thoroughly. The lines of her body were full and luscious, and the browns and pinks of her skin were lively colors, strongly marked. Eve was a slender, neutral sort of figure, by comparison; exquisite in surface, you might say, but also monotonous.

---

[45] George Sand. Quoted by Gamaliel Bradford in *Harper's Magazine,* January 1929, p. 205.

[46] Robert Browning: "By the Fire-side," xxvii, vii, ix; from *The Complete Poetical Works of Robert Browning,* edited by Augustine Birrell (New York: The Macmillan Co., 1907), p. 247.

Adam wondered if the strength or weakness of emotions, especially in women, affects the outer conformations. Perhaps Eve took her experience chiefly in the realm of nerves, or maybe she was the intellectual type. . . . That would be odd, since she got on so badly with life, and Lilith so well." [47]

IV. FANTASIES OF EXTRAORDINARY BIRTH AND ROYAL LINEAGE

" I am not the son of my alleged parents, but of nobler birth, to the promise of which I must aspire."

There is almost a standard formula for the birth of popular heroes. The hero is usually

1. The child of most distinguished parents, the son of a king or a god.

2. His origin is preceded by difficulties;

3. And by prophecies, cautioning against it or threatening danger to the father.

4. After birth he is surrendered to the water, in a box.

5. He is then saved by animals or lonely people and nursed, schooled, and cared for by them.

6. He grows up, finds his father, revenges himself unknowingly, and himself achieves rank and honour.

Recall, for example, the details of the stories of Moses, Karma, Ion, Œdipus, Paris, Telephos, Perseus, Gilgamos, Kyros, Tristan, Romulus, Hercules, Siegfried, Lohengrin, and Jesus. The oldest known hero-myth (about 2800 B.C.) concerns the birth history of Sargon I, founder of Babylon. A literal translation of an inscription presumably made by Sargon himself reads as follows: " Sargon, the mighty king, King of Agade, am I. *My mother was a vestal, my father I knew not,* while my father's brother dwelt in the mountains. In my city Azupirani, which is situated on the bank of the Euphrates, my mother, the vestal, bore me. *In a hidden place she brought me forth. She laid me in a vessel made of reeds,* closed my door with pitch, and *dropped me down into the river,* which did not drown me. The river carried me to Akki, the water carrier. Akki the water carrier lifted me up in the kindness of his heart, Akki the water carrier raised me as his own son, Akki the water carrier made of me his

[47] John Erskine: *Adam and Eve* (Indianapolis: The Bobbs-Merrill Co., 1927), p. 198.

gardener. In my work as a gardener I was beloved by Istar, I became the king, and for 45 years I held kingly sway." [48]

And since everyone fancies himself some kind of hero or heroine, these fantasies are subjectively applied and extended so that there prevails very widely in childhood a secret theory that one is not after all a member of one's family, but an illegitimate or adopted child, probably of noble parentage. (See, for example, Hardy's *Tess of the D'Urbervilles,* Maupassant's *Pierre et Jean,* Strindberg's *The Father,* Ibsen's *The Wild Duck,* Shaw's *Candida,* Mark Twain's *Puddn' head Wilson,* and *Il Trovatore.*)

In the doctor's office:
These fantasies sometimes crop out in nervous symptoms of adults. " She would look at her mother and wonder whether she were her real parent. Perhaps she was kidnapped in childhood."

"Wherever such a patient goes, he feels out of place," as if he just didn't belong. "' When I sit in the orchestra I feel that my place is in the balcony, and when in the balcony I feel that I belong in the orchestra. As a dinner guest, no matter where I am placed, I feel that I don't belong, and in my profession (of law), whatever case I am assigned to by my senior partner finds me in the same uncertainty. In fact I feel like an outsider, and even in my home I never felt that I was one of the family.' " [49]

A great many patients suffering from the severe mental illnesses reveal the same fantasies, stressing the insignificance of their origin, or its illegitimacy. Such patients often hear themselves called " bastards " and other derogatory names.

In the asylum:
" The woman that I knew as my mother made a death-bed confession saying that I was not her child, that the mother who brought me into the world was a Scotch girl, a Scotch princess. She was the grand-daughter of King George III of Scotland. She was also the daughter of the man known in the history of the Irish as the Lord Edward Fitzgerald. That was my real murdered mother, the mother that I have never seen, the mother that I have never laid eyes on. It is as true as the Almighty." (A patient in a New York state hospital.)

[48] Otto Rank: *The Myth of the Birth of the Hero* (New York: Nervous & Mental Disease Publishing Co., 1914), pp. 12–13.
[49] P. R. Lehrman: " The Fantasy of Not Belonging to One's Family," *Archives of Neurology and Psychiatry,* Vol. XVIII, p. 1015 (December 1927).

In the newspaper:

FIGHT IN LONDON CLUB OVER " WOLF GIRL " TALE

The story of two little girls found living in a wolf's den in Bengal British India, as told by the Westminster Gazette yesterday, brought the members of a well-known London club to fisticuffs today after heated arguments as to whether the story is to be believed or disbelieved. . . . The Westminster Gazette story repeated that of Bishop Walsh of Bishop's College, Calcutta, who told how the Rev. Jal Singh of Midnapur, Bengal, had discovered the two girls in a distant part of his district. They were described as about two and eight years of age, running on all fours, making guttural sounds, and in every respect living like wolves. The supposition was that they were abandoned as babies and adopted by the she wolf. . . . Lady Dorothy Mills, noted author and traveler, said that in West Africa she had often been told by natives of small children being taken and reared by a large species of monkey, but it did not seem possible to her that anything but a very small baby could be reared by a wolf.

— *New York Times,* October 23, 1926

And in fairy-tales:

" But Cinderella was only an adopted sister and so she stayed in the kitchen while her two foster-sisters enjoyed themselves in the parlour."

V. FANTASIES OF PATRICIDE, FRATRICIDE, AND MATRICIDE

" *I must (or do) , for self-protection or revenge, or from jealousy, kill my father (mother, sister, brother) , or his substitute.*" [50]

In poetry:

Yet each man kills the thing he loves,
By each let this be heard,
Some do it with a bitter look,
Some with a flattering word,
The coward does it with a kiss,
The brave man with a sword!

[50] The theme of father-murder is a part of the Œdipus complex, the nuclear complex of all neuroses. See pages 311 et seq.

> Some kill their love when they are young,
>   And some when they are old;
> Some strangle with the hand of Lust,
>   Some with the hands of Gold:
> The kindest use a knife, because
>   The dead so soon grow cold.
>   —Oscar Wilde (from *The Ballad of Reading Gaol*)

In fairy-stories:

". . . And then Cinderella's two wicked sisters were put to death (by her order, of course), and she and the Prince lived happily ever afterwards."

In the business office:

" I've noticed for several years that I get unreasonably irritated by my father, angry as can be without any cause. He's so good-natured, he thinks so much of me and does so much for me in his way, that I'm ashamed of myself. I get so mad over some trifling fault of his that I could almost tear him in pieces, and I'm afraid I do — with my voice and words.

" You see, he lives with us, since Mother died. He says it's so much less lonely, and of course we're glad to have him in a way — but he's a third party, and he's a grandfather, and — oh, I can't just say, but he disturbs us. At least he disturbs me — not my wife so much.

" He retains the title of president, but I do all the work at the office, without the title. That's all right — I don't mind. He lets me do about as I please now. But I can't shake off the memories of those days long ago when he was so hard-boiled and tyrannical. No wonder the townsmen all feared him — and we kids certainly did. He's harmless enough now, goodness knows, and I don't see why I let him get under my skin so."

In history:

Countess Elizabeth Bathory, the famous Hungarian " tigress " (1560–1614), killed 650 servant-girls in six years. Being a noblewoman she was immune from punishment (Ripley). Servant-girls probably represented daughters to this woman; many women kill their daughters in one way or another, and many would like to, but are prevented. Few, however, achieve the murderous debauch of Lady Bathory, who, of course, was definitely sadistic.

In the newspaper:

YOUTH WALKING IN SLEEP SHOOTS FATHER
TO DEATH

Lakeland, Florida, Nov. 15. — C. S. Whipple, a music store dealer, was shot and killed here early today as he lay sleeping in his home. The police investigating the case report Whipple was shot by his sixteen-year-old son, walking in his sleep. The father had planned to go hunting with a party of friends today.

— Topeka Daily Capital, November 15, 1922

Here, as so often in sleep, the unconscious repressed wishes became dominant. People very frequently dream of the death of their parents and other loved ones, and even that they themselves do the slaying. It is rare, however, for the dream to be carried out in action. See the discussion of dissociation somnambulism in Chapter III, pp. 238–41. Death-wishes, as carried out by this son, for example, are often implicit; fortunately, seldom explicit. See the poem by Oscar Wilde at the beginning of this section.

In contemporary folk-lore:

" Mr. Williams told me that, for the past quarter of a century, he had been especially maddened by the repeated recurrence in newspapers all over Europe of a story which never varied in essentials, and which might, for purposes of identification, be labelled The Adventure of the Returning Stranger. The date, the proper names, even the language might vary, but always the story concerned a native in some country in the eastern part of Europe returning from America after many years with his pockets full of gold, and seeking shelter for the night with greedy old peasants who promptly killed him for his money and then found among his papers evidence that they had murdered their own son. Doubtless it had been his pretty plan to greet them at breakfast with the Czechoslovakian equivalent of ' Surprise! Surprise! '

" At intervals of about six months, Mr. Williams said, he would come upon this story in some newspaper in England or France or Germany. Each time it would be published as having happened the night before, and each time apparently in good faith. Always he felt sure it had been despatched by some remote correspondent in equally good faith

— some too unskeptical correspondent who would also swallow whole the story of The Vanishing Lady or the story of The Triple Warning if someone in a tavern were to tell it to him as true. If you sit in any tavern in the world long enough, you will hear all these stories told to you as true.

"I assured Mr. Williams that The Adventure of the Returning Stranger was, to my notion, a perfect specimen of folk-lore, but that it seemed to have been confined to European circulation. Only two weeks later, published as hot news on the front page of the New York *Herald Tribune* — a despatch from Warsaw which had been cabled over at considerable expense by the Associated Press correspondent in the Polish capital — there appeared a breathless report with these headlines:

PARENTS KILL RICH SON POSING AS A STRANGER

Pole, Home after 18 Years in U. S., Goes Unrecognized

And the story which followed was none other than Mr. Williams's old favorite — as it was in the beginning, is now, and ever shall be, world without end." [51]

In the Bible:

"And it came to pass after these things that God did tempt Abraham . . . and he said: 'Behold, here I am.'

"And He said: 'Take now thy son, thine only son Isaac, whom thou lovest, and get thee into the land of Moriah; and offer him there for a burnt offering upon one of the mountains which I will tell thee of.'

"And Abraham rose up early in the morning, and saddled his ass, and took two of his young men with him, and Isaac his son, and clave the wood . . . and went unto the place of which God had told him.

"Then on the third day Abraham lifted up his eyes, and saw the place afar off.

"And Abraham said unto his young men: 'Abide ye here with the ass; and I and the lad will go yonder and worship, and come again to you.'

"And Abraham took the wood of the burnt offering, and laid it upon Isaac his son; and he took the fire in his hand, and a knife; and they went both of them together.

"And Isaac spake unto Abraham his father, and said: 'My father'; and he said: 'Here am I, my son.' And he said: 'Behold the fire and the wood; but where is the lamb for a burnt offering?'

[51] Alexander Woollcott in *The New Yorker*, December 12, 1931.

" And Abraham said: ' My son, God will provide Himself a lamb for a burnt offering.' So they went both of them together.

" And they came to the place which God had told him of; and Abraham built an altar there, and laid the wood in order, and bound Isaac his son, and laid him on the altar upon the wood.

" And Abraham stretched forth his hand, and took the knife to slay his son."

— Genesis xxii, 1–10

(This and the next illustration apparently reverse the Œdipus theme in that a father would kill a son, instead of the son his father, but it is understandable in the light of the fact that in the unconscious a father frequently regards his son in the same way as he once did his own father. See the discussion of transference, pages 391–4.)

VI. THE GUILT COMPLEX AND PROPITIATORY COMPULSIONS

" I have committed a sin which weighs heavily upon me — I must atone, I must pay the price. I must be punished, offer propitiation, or find a scapegoat."

In the psychiatric clinic:

" A mother observed her four and a half year old daughter eating chocolates which were forbidden to her. But every time she devoured a piece she struck herself a smart blow on her hand. When her mother asked her why she struck herself in this manner, she said: ' I spank myself because I am naughty.'

" This need for punishment often shows itself in a peculiar manner. Thus, a young girl of nine was seduced by her father's chauffeur and she visited him regularly in the garage. But following each visit she was seized with remorse to the extent that she often confessed to her mother such peccadilloes as spending too much money on sweets, neglecting her lessons, or breaking something valuable. The effect she displayed in these matters seemed so exaggerated that it led to the discovery of the true state of affairs." [52]

[52] A. A. Brill: " Psychopathology of Crime, Its Psychiatric and Social Implications," *Journal of the American Institute of Homeopathy*, March 1929. For a full development of the theme see Franz Alexander's *The Psychoanalysis of the Total Personality* (Washington: Nervous & Mental Disease Publishing Co., 1930) and *The Criminal, the Judge and the Public* (New York: The Macmillan Co., 1931).

Freud and since him several others, particularly Reik (*The Unknown Murderer*) and Alexander and Staub (*The Criminal, the Judge, and the Public*), have made an important contribution to the psychology of criminality by pointing out that many criminals confess or permit themselves to be convicted of minor crimes in order to relieve a sense of guilt related to a crime which *in their own minds* at least is greater. A criminal we recently examined was released on parole. He went home to find his mother disabled and dependent, making it necessary for him to remain in his home town and care for her instead of going to Mexico as he had planned. Shortly afterwards he broke his parole by committing several minor thefts and was returned to prison. It should be remembered that in the unconscious the intention, the fantasy, or even the mere wish to commit a crime entails a sense of guilt, not as great as if the crime were actually committed, of course, but frequently burdensome enough to drive the individual to acts of atonement or acts of aggression which result in punishment.

In the newspaper:

SORROW ENDS IN DEATH

Boy, 12, Hangs Self after Killing Red Bird

San Antonio, Texas, May 28. — Conscience stricken after he had shot and killed a red bird, Edward Perenot, 12 years old, hanged himself here last night. The body was found by his sister.

A signed note addressed to his parents told the motive for the act.

" I killed myself on account of me shooting a red bird. Goodby mother and daddy. I'll see you some day," the note read.

— Kansas City *Post,* May 28, 1928

Believe it or not:

SILENT FOR 30 YEARS

" Reb Frommer did not speak a word or utter a sound for thirty years. This remarkable penance was self-imposed. It seems that Frommer, in an outburst of temper, cursed his newly-wedded wife, who soon after met with a violent death which Frommer feared was brought about by his abuse. He was a celebrated local character of Czortkow, Poland, and when he died in 1928, the newspapers of Germany and Poland repeated again the story of his life and of the strange vow that he never broke." [53]

In the psychiatric clinic:

Mrs. Doolittle consulted me because she was " so nervous " she felt she " couldn't stand it another day." She thought the chief cause of her trouble was her overbearing employer, whose criticisms and tyranny hurt her so, and she wanted to be confirmed in her plan to seek a new position. " Then I think I'd be right. Because I really don't deserve the treatment I get. I don't know why I get it or why I take it so hard. My friend says she never knew anyone who could look so guilty and be so innocent! "

I told her that her own submissive attitude toward her employer and the impression she gave her friend led me to suspect that she had some feelings of guilt. This stimulated a confession of disastrous love-affairs which she thought filled the psychological requirements.

Then I pointed out to her that while she might justifiably feel some regret over them, the underlying principle of the various crashes was the same sort of theory which was troubling her now; she kept putting herself in a position of over-submissiveness, as if guilty before being accused, and brought her griefs upon herself as if she craved punishment. We see this very often in patients who complain bitterly of the suffering they endure at the hands of others, but do nothing to alter the circumstances.

She insisted that there was no adequate explanation. After a while, however, I learned this: She and her three children by one of several husbands were living with her mother, who had acquired property and money, which my patient had not. She depended upon this mother for financial help, because she was maintaining herself and her children on a far more comfortable and pretentious scale than her own wages would have permitted. And while this had its advantages, it had painful disadvantages. Her mother was glad enough of this dependence, because she was a tyrant who loved to tyrannize. And every act and movement of my patient and her children were scrutinized, criticized, and discussed. " We don't dare call our souls our own," she said. " And of course there's nothing to do but put up with it, because I've got to have the financial help — in fact, we couldn't live without it. Of course I'll inherit the money when she dies, but — well, frankly, I've often thought how nice things would be — I mean will be — Oh, I'm

[53] Robert L. Ripley: *Believe it or Not!* (New York: Simon & Schuster, 1929), p. 54.

ashamed to my toes to admit this — but, honestly, I've been low enough to wish sometimes that if she must die, she'd hurry up and do it."

In her death-wish and unconscious hatred for her own mother, was part of the guilt she kept propitiating.

In the university:

" A University sophomore sought assistance in connection with a strong impulse to bite his right hand. The tendency had been operating over a period of two months and already a large callous area had developed. [He] appeared to be quite ashamed of his inability to secure control over the tendency and said that he had been wearing a glove to conceal the scar although the weather had been quite warm.

" As a first step in treatment acid had been put on the callous surface. This technique was effective as far as the compulsion was concerned. However, the patient began immediately to complain of a new symptom. He found himself persistently beset by moral problems. The nature of these will be illustrated.

" He said that he had been walking on the street and saw in front of him an undergraduate acquaintance who was a social outcast. Behind him, he saw approaching a very prominent member of his class. He thought, ' Shall I walk with the attractive man in the hope of improving my personality and, consequently, my effectiveness in Christian work, or is it better to attempt to help the man who is without friends? ' He walked with the outcast but was later dissatisfied with his decision and was unable to get to sleep the following night because of nervousness.

" On another occasion he was troubled by the question of his obligation in the matter of neckties. Should he wear old ones in order that his financially poor roommate might not be embarrassed, or should he wear such ties as would attract prominent students to him so that he might develop a strong personality and thus gain in effectiveness in Christian work? The problem was not solved.

" The condition of moral uncertainty persisted for several days. Finally, the patient came to report that he was no longer troubled with moral questions but, during the conversation, it was observed that he had begun to bite his other hand. . . .

" The development of the new compulsion prompted a systematic study of the personality and the customary procedure was followed. An attempt was made to determine the occasion of the first occurrence of hand-biting. Through the use of many lines of questioning, recall was secured. During his fifteenth year the patient had had an attack of measles. This followed a period of private sex practice and, while the patient lay ill, he began to think with intense emotion of his recent misconduct. Under these conditions he had begun to bite his hand. As he said, ' I found that biting my hand kept me from thinking about my sin.' " [54]

In religion:

" He lived alone in a tiny adobe house. His bed was of boughs. One year he had been crucified, and of his many penances this had been the supreme ecstasy. Now the Lenten season drew toward Good Friday. In enacting the Passion and Death of the Saviour during Holy Week, he was the dominant figure; his back was covered with scars. The original three gashes down and three across had been all but obliterated by fresh disciplines. It was terrible and inspiring to see him scourging himself, the blood clotting and fresh blood running down; but when urged to abandon the annual scourging, he smiled; his passion for pain, as strong as when he had first come to the village. Yet all had experienced the benefit of his love for them. It was impossible to hurt his feelings. His prayers for the members were many. They in turn prayed for him. The brothers had waived precedent and he had been *hermano mayor* for the past fifteen years. His zeal in keeping order and settling disputes was unrivalled, his own penance the more severe."

(He is, in the course of the penance, fatally injured, and on his deathbed tells of the origin of his zeal.)

" ' That was a time, Padre, for your Church to save me. It was soon too late. I have lived along only because of this life here, not because I have wanted to. The power that my uncle's position gave him had its echo in my arrogance and extravagance. I rode Arabian horses; our estate was famous for its magnificence.

" ' I met Manuelita at a royal ball in Madrid. *Por Dios,* how beautiful! She wore the Spanish comb, her eyes flashed. I was inflamed not with love but with desire; I tried to seduce her but she drove me off. There was a woman good by a natural endowment. I knew later. At the time I was offended and left for easier prey.

" ' I went from bad to worse; I surfeited myself with sin, and went home to my uncle but it was not for long. From across the sea my parents voiced their anxiety and one day my uncle told me he had arranged a marriage for me. When he told me it was Manuelita I was to marry, I was pleased, nothing more. She was rich, beautiful, amiable, and would make the right kind of wife for a free-living man. I could show her off and thus gain prestige. She came to visit us and between my sins

[54] English Bagby: " A Compulsion and Its Motivation," *Journal of Abnormal and Social Psychology,* Vol. XXII, no. 1 (April–June 1927) , pp. 8–9.

I made love to her, thinking she cared no more for me than I for her.

" 'That was my first great mistake. My egotism was so monstrous a thing that I failed to see the sympathy in her eyes.

" 'We were married in my uncle's own chapel. The event was her-alded throughout Spain — echoes of it carried even across the sea. I re-member the cry that rose from my uncle's servants outside the chapel.' Alberto paused. 'Curious that I should remember that. The mind is treacherous with memories; faithful here and fickle there.

" 'It was a brilliant — a brilliant match. Everybody rejoiced but Manuelita and me. Yet I was pleased, for she was an ornament of which I might be proud, but in my mind I was planning escape and fell swiftly into my old way. Manuelita looked on with seeming indifference.

" 'She fulfilled her vows; I continued to be proud of her and to go elsewhere for my love. My sins were no secret. She knew but uttered never a word in reproach. I grew more abandoned; it did not occur to me that she cared. I urged her to take lovers as I was doing and failed to understand the look that she gave me; the wistfulness, the infinitude of sadness that was in it. My fortunes increased through the death of my family in the New World. I determined to remain in Spain and bought lands there.

" 'I had planned a festival for our tenth anniversary,' Alberto inter-rupted himself. 'Come closer, my voice goes. I am of you, *hermanos!*

" 'I had imported dancers, music from the city of the king and entertainers from Paris. A three-day *fiesta* was my plan, to end with a bull-fight, for which I built an arena big enough to hold all my guests and people without number from the countryside.

" 'God! that I should live to tell it, like this. In an enclosure half-way up the arena sat Manuelita. Arms waved and cries filled the air. In the midst of it all, the structure began to move, and crashed to the ground. She was pinned beneath an immovable beam of the platform I had made for her glory. It was then, for the first time, that I began to un-derstand. In her look was that sadness. She spoke my name, softly, and raised her eyes to heaven. " O God, forgive and save him! " she said. Her words plunged me in a transport of grief. I fell at her side asking what did it mean. " God forgive him," she said, and died.

" 'I sought escape from my conscience; I tried every form of forget-fulness. Then it came to me that these whom I had pitied as ignorant unenlightened self-torturers, had nearest communion with Him who died to save such as I. There is peace in acting the drama of Christ, Padre; it is ageless.

" 'Padre, leave us. Death comes; his mist is before me. Go now, that my brothers may prepare the way for . . .'

" On Sunday he was buried. Over the stony way they carried him to the Campo Santo, their voices rising in mournful *sudarios*. It was a great man going to his rest." [55]

VII. FANTASIES OF CRUELTY, OF BEING BEATEN OR GIVING BEATINGS, OSTENSIBLY FOR PUNISHMENT, BUT REALLY FOR PERVERSE PLEASURE

" I am being whipped — I am whipping someone."

That some people enjoy being cruel and that others enjoy being abused is well known.

To understand this we must consider how great and inexpressible may be the rage aroused in children by the treatment they receive from their parents. Parents who whip their children should not be surprised if those children, once they attain the power and authority for doing so, take their revenge upon the next generation. In some cases this revenge spreads to include others than the helpless children, animals for example, and weaker adults as well. Nor is such revenge limited to the repetition of childhood whippings; there are many other cruelties of which parents may be guilty which their children ultimately reinflict upon others with great zest.

Psychoanalytic study has shown that, for the child, acts of cruelty from the parents may be closely associated with sexual acts and sexual feelings. Children frequently interpret the sexual relation between the parents as being a sadistic one, a theory derived from numerous misinterpretations and observations (of domestic animals, for example). They think the female is being hurt. Thus they come to associate pain and sexual pleasure. One patient who was kindly but rather impersonally treated by her father always became very excited when her father whipped her brother, which he did quite energetically. She would become almost hysterical with anxiety and beg to be whipped in his place. Her puzzled father would occasionally accede to this. She got a supreme joy out of the experience and cried not one whit; in the first place, she had received from her father some of the violent and personal attention which for her had a definite sexual flavour, and, in the second place, she felt relieved in regard to malicious and envious feelings that she had had toward the brother, whose punishment she was now assuming.

[55] Raymond Otis: *" El Penitente,"* in the *Dial,* Vol. LXXXV, no. 5 (November 1928), pp. 406–7, 411–13.

Some vestiges of this association of infliction of pain with the sexual life are to be found in many people, possibly nearly all people; but in most civilized people they are completely repressed. Sometimes the repression is only possible by virtue of reaction-formations. This is the explanation of the almost fanatical anxiety that some people have in regard to the protection of animals from cruelty. Masochism is less well repressed than sadism because less blame attaches to it, and there are many who exploit the role of martyr, little realizing how much they enjoy the suffering they mournfully display to the world.

When I was a boy there was a man in our neighbourhood who was addicted to horsewhipping. He had invented an open box stall in which he could tie the horses up very short, then stand on the outside of the stall and beat them to death, or until the aroused neighbourhood and the police intervened. These episodes were very exciting to the whole community, and I thought at the time that they were unique. When I grew older I learned, as every child does, that no man has a monopoly on cruelty. I learned that millions of men take a frank and vivid pleasure in murdering helpless creatures, not for the food obtained thereby, but for the sheer pleasure in the scream and fall of the stricken animal. And in my adolescence I learned what this pleasure was and slaughtered beasts and birds with the callous abandon characteristic of most hunters.

I learned, too, that so prone were some parents to abuse their children that a society for the prevention of such cruelty had been organized in many cities by those more humane, more civilized. In the meantime I had read *Nicholas Nickleby* and later *Limehouse Nights* and then *Oliver Twist* (with the strange submission of Nancy to her sadistic husband, Bill) and by this time I had come to learn that in spite of the pleasure-pain principle — the instinctive striving to avoid pain and to find pleasure — some people find their pleasure in submitting to pain, and others in inflicting it.

It is customary to explain this paradox by rationalizations. Those who slaughter animals insist that there is a hunting instinct which human beings conceal from themselves by their civilized ways of living and that it is normal for men to indulge this instinct. They may say that they are out for food, or, occasionally, that they are ridding the country of predatory beasts which threaten the safety of man or domesticated animals.

SADISM

In industry:

" ' I feel like a good workout,' Lieutenant W. J. Lyster of the Pittsburgh Coal Company's private police is reported to have said on the night of February 9, 1929. The scene was the barracks of the coal and iron police at Imperial, Pennsylvania, and a miner named John Barkoski had just been brought in charged with stabbing a private policeman after the latter had invaded his house while drunk. The miner, badly beaten, was lying on the floor. Lieutenant Lyster, according to an eyewitness, stripped to the waist, walked to the coal box, and picked up a poker. He beat Barkoski over the head until the poker was bent almost double; then he paused, straightened the poker, and returned to his task. When the miner was beaten into unconsciousness, so it is charged, Lieutenant Lyster and Private H. P. Watts, the latter also of the coal and iron police, jumped upon the prostrate man's body. The miner died the next morning, and when his body was taken home to his wife and four children his hands were swollen to twice their size from warding off blows, his nose was fractured, his entire rib structure was broken, and his lungs were punctured in many places. . . . While sobbing over the body of her husband, Mrs. Barkoski said: ' Why they beat him I don't know. He never done nothing to nobody.' " [56]

In poetry:

First Death

He laid his head upon the breast,
He spoke in soothing tone,
He startled by his fierce caress,
And swiftly snapped a bone,

Methodically his hands moved on
While with his lips he kissed,
He bruised the unresisting arm
And snapped the brittle wrist,

With breast and hands quite powerless,
He sealed the mouth from cries,
Immersed his hands in frightened blood
And marked the shivering thighs.

He broke through flesh with skilful ease
As through the heads of flowers,

[56] The *Nation*, February 27, 1929.

Stripped off the blue wings of the heart,
And petals fell in showers.

Then with supreme ferocity
Satyric in his mirth,
Lifted the body by its stem,
And from its roots shook earth.
— Helen Pearce in the *Nation,* January 30, 1929

Still more explicit poetry:

Loving Kindness

Her flesh was lyrical and sweet to flog,
   For the whip blanched her blood, through every vein
   Flooded with hate shot a hot flow of pain,
And her screams were muffled by a brackish fog.
He loved her, yet his passion could but fret
   Unless he lashed her to an awkward rage —
   But when his hand wrote terror on her page
He knew exultant joy of feigned regret.

Theirs was a bond that poured the wine of fear,
   And he drained her stiffened limbs with cruel art.
He taught her that all tenderness had fled
Till she would beg the hurt to taste the tear,
   And when she bent to kiss her crumpled heart
It lit a Chinese candle in his head.
— Donald Evans: *Sonnets from the Patagonian*

In education:

" It is recorded of a Suabian schoolmaster that during his fifty-one years' superintendence of a large school he had given 911,500 canings, 121,000 floggings, 136,000 tips with the ruler, 10,200 boxes on the ear, and 22,700 tasks by heart. It was further calculated that he had made 700 boys stand on peas, 6,000 kneel on a sharp piece of wood, 5,000 wear the fool's-cap, and 1,700 hold the rod." [57]

In fiction:

" The door opened quietly and closed. A quick whisper ran through the class; the prefect of studies. There was an instant of dead silence and then the loud crack of a pandybat on the last desk. Stephen's heart leapt up in fear. — ' Any boys want flogging here, Father Arnall? ' cried

[57] Rev. William M. Cooper: *History of the Rod* (London, 1876).

the prefect of studies. ' Any lazy idle loafers that want flogging in this class? ' " [58]

In the pulpit:

" What was behind the terrific fantasies of Jonathan Edwards himself concerning the brutal torturings in hell of those pictured by him as sinners?

" The diagnosis, of course, is vicarious sadism. He who would otherwise have been a monster of sexual depravity gratified his ferocious lusts by sublimating his suppressed libido along lines that can be clearly indicated. His preaching orgies were substituted for sexual ones. His hellish imagery, preached with ecstatic fervor and frightful vehemence, released and put into action the tremendous sexual potentialities of the man which had been inherited in full store from the tribe of satyrs and Jukeses, or worse, who graced his family tree. But the harm done by the aristocracy of crime which produced Edwards pales into insignificance when compared with his ' spiritual ' depredations upon the race. The earlier band of degenerates were heavenly angels, in their obscure spheres, relatively speaking. The brilliant Edwards disdained to ravish the bodies of his kind. He tore their quivering souls to pieces with an obscene, frantic and gory ritual that today stands revealed in all its horrible putridity, with all the intolerable stench of its altar incense in the nostrils of civilized men.

" Sinners in the Hands of an Angry God got a terrifying warning: ' The wrath of God burns against them; their damnation does not slumber; the pit is prepared; the fire is made ready; the furnace is now hot, ready to receive them; the flames do now rage and glow. The devils watch them; they are ever by them, at their right hand; they stand waiting for them; like greedy, hungry lions that see their prey, and expect to have it, but are for the present kept back; if God should withdraw His hand, by which they are restrained, they would in one moment fly upon their poor souls. The old serpent is gaping for them; hell opens its mouth wide to receive them; and if God should permit it, they would be hastily swallowed up and lost.'

" ' The God that holds you over the pit of hell, much as one holds a spider or some loathsome insect over the fire, abhors you, and is dreadfully provoked; His wrath towards you burns like fire; He looks upon you as worthy of nothing else, but to be cast into the fire; He is of purer eyes than to bear to have you in His sight; you are ten times so abominable in His eyes, as the most hateful and venomous serpent is in ours.' " [59]

[58] James Joyce: *A Portrait of the Artist as a Young Man*, p. 51.
[59] Arthur C. Jacobson: *Genius* (New York: Greenberg, 1927), pp. 130–2.

THE OTHER SIDE OF THE SHIELD: MASOCHISM

In the doctor's office:

A big, strong farmer came to see me once and after some preliminary conversation prepared to tell me his troubles, but became so embarrassed that I thought he was never going to come to the point.

Finally he got round to it. " You see, I have a lot to be thankful for. I've got a fine farm and we're breaking even on it, which is more than most farmers are doing. I have the finest woman in the world and she's healthy and works hard every day to help us pay out on it. We have six children and they're all well, and everybody in the community treats us decent. We're really pretty comfortable. All but one thing.

" There is certainly something funny wrong with me. I don't understand it and I don't know if I can even explain it. I'd sooner be shot than tell you about it. But I promised my wife I would. So I'll try.

" You see I'm an average-looking fellow. You probably think I'm normal. I guess I act pretty sensible most of the time. But every once in a while I get a funny feeling. It's the funniest feeling you ever heard of in your life. I never heard of anyone else that ever had such a feeling. But it comes over me and I've just got to yield to it. First I go and get a board or a cane of some kind. Then I wait till all the children are out of sight, off at school or somewhere, or maybe asleep in bed. Then I take this stick to my wife."

At this point the poor fellow was so overcome with confusion that it required considerable reassurance to get him to continue. He finally did, however.

" Well, I make her sit down in a chair. Then I turn myself over her knees. Yes, sir, just like I used to when I was a little kid and my mother spanked me. And then I get her to give me a good hard licking. She hates to do it; she says I'm a fool and everything else, but she knows how strong the feeling is. And after she's done it I feel all right again. I'm grateful to her and I love her and I feel ashamed of having been so foolish. But when that feeling comes again, I'm a goner."

In poetry:

The Prayer of Women

O Spirit that broods upon the hills
And moves upon the face of the deep,
And is heard in the wind,
Save us from the desire of men's eyes,

And the cruel lust of them.
Save us from the springing of the cruel seed
In that narrow house which is as the grave
For darkness and loneliness . . .
That women carry with them with shame, and weariness, and long pain,
Only for the laughter of man's heart,
And for the joy that triumphs therein,
And the sport that is in his heart,
Wherewith he mocketh us,
Wherewith he playeth with us,
Wherewith he trampleth upon us . . .
Us, who conceive and bear him;
Us, who bring him forth;
Who feed him in the womb, and at the breast, and at the knee:
Whom he calleth mother and wife,
And mother again of his children and his children's children.
Ah, hours of the hours,
When he looks at our hair, and sees it is grey;
And at our eyes and sees they are dim;
And at our lips, straightened out with long pain;
And at our breasts, fallen and seared as a barren hill;
And at our hands, worn with toil!
Ah, hour of the hours,
When, seeing, he seeth all the bitter ruin and wreck of us —
All save the violated womb that curses him —
All save the heart that forbeareth . . . for pity —
All save the living brain that condemneth him —
All save the spirit that shall not mate with him —
All save the soul he shall never see
Till he be one with it, and equal;
He who hath the bridle, but guideth not;
He who hath the whip, yet is driven;
He who as a shepherd calleth upon us,
But is himself a lost sheep, crying among the hills!
O Spirit, and the Nine Angels who watch us,
And Thou, white Christ, and Mary Mother of Sorrow,
Heal us of the wrong of man:
We, whose breasts are weary with milk,
Cry, cry to Thee, O Compassionate!
— Fiona Macleod (William Sharp) in *From the Heart of a Woman*

In religion (masochism, plus exhibitionism):

HINDUISM

" A Hindoo ascetic, of Singapore, walked three miles in the blazing sun with fifty spears (each fitted with a very sharp point) embedded in his flesh. Imagine the excruciating agony that every footstep meant.

" Why did he do it?

" No difference. There is no sense in a Hindoo religious fanatic anyway. But the fact that he did it is interesting enough, and it all goes to prove how much torment the human body can stand under certain mental conditions." [60]

CHRISTIANITY

" O Lord, I am not worthy of Thy consolation, nor of any spiritual visitation; and therefore Thou dealest justly with me, when I am left poor and desolate.

" For if I could shed a sea of tears, still I should not be worthy of Thy consolation.

" I am not, then, worthy of anything but to be chastised and punished; because I have frequently and grievously offended Thee, and in many things have been very remiss." [61]

In the newspaper:

BURNED INITIALS IN LEG AS LOVE ACT FOR MATE

Then Husband Beat Her for Her Devotion Mrs. Hinton Sees Futility of Great Affection and Will Sue for Divorce

Wichita, Kan., Feb. 28. — How a bride of a few months, moved by an ecstatic love for her husband, sat in the light of a fire of a moonshine still and with a steel darning needle etched his initials on the white flesh of her left leg above the knee, then burned the scratch into an indelible scar by placing raw lye in the open wound, has been revealed by police here.

The initials " E. H." stand for Elmer Hinton, now in city jail here on a charge of wife beating, arrested when neighbors hearing screams called police.

Officers, examining big black bruises on the girl-wife's legs and body, discovered the initials. The scar-letters are two inches high and three

---

[60] Robert L. Ripley: *Believe it or Not!* (New York: Simon & Schuster) , p. 53.
[61] Thomas à Kempis: *Of the Imitation of Christ,* translated by W. H. Hutchings.

and a half inches long. First Mrs. Hinton, hysterical, accused her husband of branding her, but later denied this and told of her own love act.

She said, recalling the early days of their marriage, " He had a still near Owensburg, a short distance south of Wichita, and I begged him to stop making liquor. We quarreled.

" He kept saying he was doing it to make money for me and that I'd never done anything to show him how I loved him. He was jealous of me too.

" So I thought I'd show him how a woman can love. I thought if I did he would stop making and drinking liquor.

" One day I took a needle and scratched his initials on my leg. Then I put lye on it. No one will ever know the agony I suffered as that lye burned and burned as though it would never stop.

" I lay in bed for days, suffering. Finally it got well and left a pretty clean scar. For awhile after that I think Elmer loved me more than he ever did.

" He's just pure gold when he doesn't drink. I'd burn myself again if I knew it would help. Although my body is covered with bruises he put there I still love him."

— Topeka *Daily Capital*, February 28, 1928

VIII. FANTASIES OF IMMACULATE CONCEPTION

" I become contaminated — infected — vicariously impregnated."

The Immaculate Conception, according to Catholic doctrine, has to do with a special preservation of the Virgin Mary from the stain of original sin from the moment of *her mother's* conception. As commonly used, however, the phrase has a very dif-ferent meaning, often falsely ascribed to Catholic doctrine. It is used to mean pregnancy without intercourse; that is, sexless reproduction. This meaning, this fantasy, is of course based upon the prejudice that sex is something sinful, wicked, dirty, taboo — a necessary evil connected with reproduction, which is desirable. That such notions cannot be blamed on Catholicism, Puritanism, or any other religious philosophy is proved by the fact that the idea is implicit in folklore and mythology long antedating our present civilization. Venus, it will be remembered, sprang from the ocean without the indignities of either conception or birth; Sargon, the legendary founder of Babylon, Jesus, the founder of Christianity, and many others were believed to have been born of virgins (see page 329) .

The wish to have a baby is natural in both little girls and little boys. The latter yield to conventions and surrender or transform the yearnings while the former play with dolls and interest themselves in babies, secretly nourishing the fantasy of obtaining a real baby of their own in some magical, non-sinful way, since sex is something forbidden to them. This wish to be impregnated without sin combines with misinformation and misapprehensions in children concerning the mechanisms of birth, often fostered by the lies or evasions of parents. Such fantasies are common to normal children; they are persistent in neurotic children and neurotic adults. In the latter these may be perverted into the fear of contamination (see page 251) or combined with little-understood physiological mechanisms to result in the extraordinary condition of false pregnancy.[61a]

Society is partly responsible, of course, for the childlessness of many women, but in many instances the obstacle that blocks marriage or, even after marriage, blocks childbearing is an internal, psychological barrier. I should add, at the risk of sounding repetitious, that this psychological barrier is (usually) an unconscious one; such women *think* they want husbands and/or children, and grieve that they do not have, wondering what fate is against them. Not fate but unconscious fears and taboos of childhood origin are the real deterrents.

Oral impregnation:

A pretty and precocious high-school girl had developed a very puzzling stomach-trouble. She had kept insisting upon attempting a bowel movement at frequent intervals and had other distress which had kept her in bed over a month. Then a series of conversational interviews cleared up everything. It turned out that she had had the common childhood theory that conception took place in some mystical fashion, either by mouth or in some other vague way, the only definite thing about it being that it was associated with an erotic feeling. She and six

61a See George D. Bivin and M. Pauline Klinger: *Pseudocyesis.* Bloomington, Ind.: Principia Press, 1937.

of her schoolmates had had a " petting party " some time previously and she had been kissed for the first time in her life. She had been reared with great strictness, and conceived the idea that kissing was wicked because it was erotically pleasurable, and therefore entailed the danger of impregnation. Pregnancy, she thought, took place in the stomach somewhere and delivery took place by the rectum. This explains her anxiety about her bowel movements. She was perfectly well after discovering her unconscious misapprehensions and discharging the emotion stored up therewith. Consciously she was not misinformed about any of these details. Her conscious mind was sixteen years old, her unconscious ideas were those of a seven-year-old.

Aural impregnation:

" This warrior of gentle lineage, Pwyll, could not win the love of the maiden, Eigr, ' slender of eyebrow and pure of heart,' with cornsilk hair the color of pale sunlight. Success came to him too easily and she thought him vain and spoiled by adulation. ' The sight of him is hateful in my eyes. Better were he as a stable boy with broom-bush hair. I like not Pwyll's face, his deeds, his form — him.' Keening to have his Ladye, the Knight tried Joyous Magic. Through successive transformations, he became a war-horse, ' large of bone, high mettled, fiercely snorting ' — a sword of intricate design, venomous, sturdily-smiting, fiercely-wounding — next he was a lamb fed from her carven bowl — then her own dove held his spirit. ' Adamant is my heart, I like him not,' Eigr coldly declared. Finally Pwyll became a millet seed and hid in Eigr's ear — close, at last, to the warm beauty of her. It was many months before his whispered soft words of love and endearment, his gentle promises gave to him her heart. ' As I am loved, so shall I love,' Eigr said. Drawn from her ear as a small child, he grew by hours, not years. ' And that night,' the old tale ends, ' the gentian-eyed Eigr, daughter of Ffluvddur and Owyn, became Pwyll's bride and she continued to be his dear wife, as long as she did live.' " [62]

Gastric impregnation:

". . . ' Thou speakest truth,' said Caridwen, ' it was Gwion Bach who robbed me.'

" And she went forth after him, running. And he saw her, and changed himself into a hare and fled. But she changed herself into a greyhound and turned him. And he ran towards a river, and became a fish. And she in the form of an otter-bitch chased him under the water, until he was fain to turn himself into a bird of the air. Then she, as a hawk, followed him and gave him no rest in the sky. And

[62] Welsh folk-tale, recast by Mrs. Effie Logan.

just as she was about to swoop upon him, and he was in fear of death, he espied a heap of winnowed wheat on the floor of a barn, and he dropped amongst the wheat, and turned himself into one of the grains. Then she transformed herself into a high-crested black hen, and went to the wheat and scratched it with her feet, and found him out and swallowed him. And, as the story says, she bore him nine months, and when she was delivered of him, she could not find it in her heart to kill him, by reason of his beauty. So she wrapped him in a leathern bag, and cast him into the sea to the mercy of God, on the twenty-ninth day of April." [63]

Tactile impregnation:
"Well, doctor, the germ theory may have helped your patients a great deal, but it has certainly ruined my life. I suppose no one knows less about germs and thinks more about them than I do.

"For years I have been afraid I would become contaminated with germs. I don't even know what they look like, but I imagine them to be small, squirming animals like minute tadpoles. Of course I have seen pictures in books, and I have read how they stick to things. I am sure I carry this beyond all reason, but I can't help it. It is the obsession of my life.

"I never shake hands with people; I never give Christmas gifts; I rarely handle a letter for fear it will bring me some germs through the mails. If I touch a door-knob I must wash my hands immediately. I am constantly afraid that I will be infected, that these little germs will enter my body, my lungs, my whole system, and will grow inside of me, that I will have tuberculosis and die. I have died a thousand deaths already. If someone in the apartment coughs I want to move; if a man in a street-car looks pale or thin, I am sure I will have contracted the disease before nightfall; if someone comes to see me I cannot sleep for days, thinking of the possibility that they brought tuberculosis germs into the house and that we shall all die. You have no idea what agony one can suffer over such preposterous, unreasonable fears as this.

"I can't bear to have anybody touch me. I haven't let my bare feet touch the floor for years. My laundry bill is very great, because if I wear things for even an hour or two I must send them to the laundry. When I can bring myself to go to a theatre, I have to sit forward in the seat so that I don't touch the back. I can't eat any food that I have touched. When I take a slice of bread, I eat around the part where I

---

[63] From " Taliesin," one of the tales in *The Mabinogion,* a collection of Welsh folk-lore, translated by Lady Charlotte Guest (New York: E. P. Dutton & Co.; Everyman's Library series) .

have held it and then discard that part. Unless my dishes have been scalded I can't eat from them. I have to have a new cake of soap every time I take a bath, and I have to bathe several times every day. I know my fears are unreasonable and preposterous, but they completely dominate my life."

IX. THE THEME OF THE MAGIC WAND (GOLDEN BOUGH, ROYAL SCEPTRE)

" *There is a certain omnipotent sceptre, the badge of power and authority.*

(a) " *If I could but get possession of it, the world would be mine,*

(b) " *It is now in my possession, but might be taken from me,*

(c) " *It was in my possession, but was taken from me.*"

In mythology:

The legend of the Golden Bough concerned a method of succession to the priesthood of Nemi in the worship of Diana. On a certain oaktree in the midst of a forest there was a golden bough. It is believed that the bough was mistletoe because in some way or other it represented life. The tree was guarded by a priest, who never slept, called King of the Wood. But a runaway slave, no one else, might break off this bough, if he could catch the priest off guard, and having done so he was entitled to meet the priest in mortal combat. If he slew him, he succeeded to the priesthood, the title of King of the Wood, and the guardianship of the Golden Bough (Sir James G. Frazer).

In the Bible:

" Thy rod and Thy staff, they comfort me " (Psalm xxiii, 4).

". . . Aaron stretched out his hand with his rod and smote the dust of the earth, and it became lice. . . . All the dust of the land became lice throughout all the land of Egypt " (Exodus viii, 17).

" And Moses lifted up his hand, and with his rod he smote the rock twice; and the water came out abundantly, and the congregation drank, and their beasts also " (Numbers xx, 11).

In medical history:

It was long customary for physicians to carry canes. A certain goldheaded cane which was transmitted through many generations of a medical family was made the subject of a book by William Macmichael in 1827. Doctor Coriat, of Boston, has pointed out the symbolic origin of this custom. " Historically," he says, " the physician's cane is linked with the wig and ring as symbols of deep learning, wisdom, and power. It is doubtless related in symbolic meaning to the herald's staff, the caduceus of Hermes, the wand of Æsculapius, the sacred wands of primitive peoples, the mystic wands of fairy tales, the staves of constables and sheriffs, and the phlebotomist's staff. Possibly in ancient times the physician's cane and the surgeon's club were used actively. For centuries fustigation was believed in as a sovereign remedy for bodily ailments as well as moral failings, and a beating was prescribed for ague as frequently as for stealing. Such customs may have been merely incidents in the history of flagellation, into which there enters strong sadistic and masochistic components.

"The physician's cane was generally smooth, of moderate weight, and with a gold head in the form of a knob. Gold once was supposed to have medicinal properties, but the desire to make a good appearance on the part of the physician was probably the stronger motive. Often the head was hollow, and in the cavity it was the custom to carry some drug. A mystery about it was thus created in the mind of the people, some of whom believed that the head of the cane was the dwelling place of a familiar spirit which gave the owner extraordinary powers. The symbolism, therefore, is twofold: in the first place, the cane was a bit of magic, a charm, a sort of omnipotent instrument which had power over evil; second, it was the symbol of the office of the physician himself, like the caduceus, signifying that the owner has medical power and authority, is omnipotent in his calling. Gold was also the symbol of the sun, the all fertilizing divinity, Apollo, the father of Æsculapius. In alchemy, male activity is derived from gold, female from silver.

"Thus the goldheaded cane became a sort of symbolic carrier of the power of the physician or the immortal transmitter or bearer of power as it passed from one physician to another. Historically it was emblematic of the physician's profession but beneath this there was a hidden symbolism, whose meaning stretched back to the beginnings of medicine in magic and thus unconsciously betrayed the secret of therapeutic power. Such transitions from literal meaning to veiled symbolism are very frequently encountered in the development of civilization and culture. To cite only one example of these age old mysticisms, we have the throwing of rice at a newly married couple which symbolizes fertility." [64]

In fiction:

". . . 'And how does a king come thus to be traveling without any retinue or even a sword about him?'

[64] Isador H. Coriat: "The Symbolism of the Goldheaded Cane," *Annals of Medical History*, Vol. VI. no. 1.

" ' Why, I travel with a staff, . . . as you perceive: and it suffices me.'

" ' Certainly it is large enough, in all conscience. Alas, young out-lander, who call yourself a king! you carry the bludgeon of a high-wayman, and I am afraid of it.'

" ' My staff is a twig from Yggdrasill, the tree of universal life: Thersitês gave it me, and the sap that throbs therein arises from the Urdar fountain, where the grave Norns make laws for men and fix their destinies.'

" ' Thersitês is a scoffer, and his gifts are mockery. I would have none of them.'

" The two began to wrangle, not at all angrily, as to what Jurgen had best do with his prized staff. ' Do you take it away from me, at any rate! ' says Chloris. So Jurgen hid his staff. . . .

" ' Oh, oh! O wretched King,' said Chloris, ' I fear that you will be the death of me! And you have no right to oppress me in this way, for I am not your subject.'

" ' Rather shall you be my queen, dear Chloris, receiving all that I most prize.' " [65]

In society:

It made Mrs. Bruce Bricksten very uneasy to lose at bridge or, for that matter, at any other game. Each fall she went duck-hunting with her brother and brother-in-law and was a better shot than either one. She was proud too of being considered a good executive and could wield a gavel with the proficiency of an expert. She had two children, but could spare little time for them from her many civic activities. She disdained housekeeping and feminine pursuits generally. Her husband, like her women friends, meekly surrendered to her sovereignty; they admired her abilities and described her as a better business man than most men.

Mrs. Bricksten had one symptom that few of her friends knew about. She suffered from occasional attacks of vague uneasiness, which some-times became rather acute. She felt as if for some unknown reason she was in a precarious position, as if she might suddenly be exposed to hu-miliation or embarrassment. At such times she would be obsessed with the feeling that she had mislaid or lost something of importance and would search for it vaguely but incessantly throughout the house, angry at herself the while for yielding to so senseless an impulse. (See also p. 302.)

In fairy-stories:

" . . . And when she touched Cinderella with her wand the old tat-tered garments were instantly transformed into the most beautiful

[65] James Branch Cabell: *Jurgen* (New York: Robert M. McBride & Co., 1919), p. 193.

and wonderful apparel . . . and the pumpkin became a coach, and the mice eight magnificent horses . . .''

In all of the above illustrations the magic wand is a symbolic representation of the phallus, as an organ of pleasure and power. For some people power is equivalent to force and especially to destructive force, and the representation of the phallus as a sword is, therefore, for such individuals very appropriate. Phallic worship in which the sex organs are prized as a possession, as a source of magic power greater than man himself, is essentially a primitive, infantile conception, but many civilized adults persist in this infantile mode of thinking. The over-evaluation of the genitals, however, is accompanied by morbid fears of losing them, represented clinically by the anxiety that many women manifest in regard to menstruation and that many men manifest in regard to the sight of blood. These infantile and unwarranted fears are called technically the *castration complex*. The glorification of the magic wand, the golden bough, the beautiful sword, is reassuring and compensatory fantasy.

X. THE FANTASY OF REBIRTH

" *From the turmoil of the weary world I return at last to the mother that bore me and retreat into that haven of refuge, the quiet protective envelopment of her body, her womb; there I shall find perfect peace and happiness; Nirvana.*"

In the Bible:
" Jesus answered . . . ' Except a man be born again, he cannot see the kingdom of God.'

" Nicodemus saith unto Him: ' How can a man be born when he is old? Can he enter the second time into his mother's womb and be born?'

" Jesus answered . . . ' Marvel not that I said unto thee, " Ye must be born again." ' " (St. John iii, 3, 4, 7.)

In poetry:

Mighty Is Man

To the body of woman man turns and seeks deliverance
From his world grown strange since deliverance from her thighs;
To the womb he turns, to his infancy's paradise,
Blind with a dream, an outcast weary of severance.

From the body of woman man rises with exultation
Shaking his veins. Singing, he whets a sword.
He is freed of his weakness now, he has loosed the cord
That binds him to alien mysteries of creation.

Again he is mighty, he stamps for joy of his strength;
His words, his deeds will be clamorous round the earth.
Woman, who bore him, merely gives him rebirth
Who returns to spurn, and return again, at length,

To the grieved eternal breast that lulled him since life began,
To the eyes that smile in the dark on the baffled Antæus, Man.
    — William Rose Benét, in the *Nation,* August 15, 1928

On the street:
  "I'll tell you the kind of a vacation I'd like. I'd like to get clear off from everyone, in some quiet deserted place where I'd be all alone, and free from all interruptions and responsibilities and calls for this and that. I'd want to be comfortable — meals served and everything like that, and all I'd have to do would be to lie around and sleep and read and eat and eat and read and sleep. Just a nice, quiet, restful hibernation. That's my idea of a rest."

In the Church hymnal:
        O mother dear, Jerusalem,
          When shall I come to thee?
        When shall my sorrows have an end?
          Thy joys when shall I see?
        O happy harbour of the saints!
          O sweet and pleasant soil!
        In thee no sorrow may be found,
          No grief, no care, no toil.

        Thy gardens and thy goodly walks
          Continually are green,
        Where grow such sweet and pleasant flowers
          As nowhere else are seen.
        Right through the streets with silver sound
          The living waters flow.
        And on the banks, on either side,
          The trees of life do grow.[66]

[66] Translated from the Latin. "F.B.P.," 1583. *Hymns for the Living Age* (New York: The Century Co., 1925).

In adolescent fantasy:

Shortly after the publication of the first edition of this book I received a letter from the author of the following poem which read: " I thought you might be amused. . . . I wrote it many years ago in my young days long before I had any knowledge of psychoanalysis." She graciously permits me to quote it.

O My Mother!

I that cannot have full sunlight — all its seething tropic glory,
  Under golden-tinted palms and eucalyptus-trees,
Flushing with its blinding opal, moss-hung live oaks tossed and hoary,
  Touching to a moment's gilt the fluid turquoise of the seas —

Give me then no tepid half-light, oozing through a smoky curtain,
  But the cleansing, deep, deep darkness, from whose silent wings
Droops a warmth of peace and healing, that to starved eyes bring a certain
  Sleep and dreaming — deep-sunk dreaming, sweet with death's far murmurings.

O my mother! O sweet darkness! Through innumerable ages
  I have lain, a weary spirit, underneath thy breast:
Balsam for the thirsty fire that in my thwarted body rages: —
  Plunge me in thy cool embrace, the lightless depths where I may rest!

— Miriam de Ford

In the sanitarium:

" Yes, I've come back. I want to be readmitted to the sanitarium. I'm a little mixed up again. I feel it coming on, and I want to get in out of the storm. Some way I've felt better just to know I could come here if I got shaky, and be away from everyone and taken care of and no responsibilities, even for my behaviour. I just feel like telling the world to go to hell and let me alone and here I hide, and eat and sleep and take nice long warm baths. It makes me feel easier, sort of comfortable, as comfortable as I could with my craziness. I am glad I'm back again."

In the bedchamber:

" . . . We are not accustomed to give much thought to the fact that every night a human being removes the garments with which he has clothed himself, and also those complements of the organs of his body which as far as possible replace whatever is lacking in them; for instance, spectacles, false hair and teeth, etc. It can also be said that he

carries out a similar unclothing of his psyche on going to sleep—
he renounces most of his physical acquisitions. Thus in two directions
he brings about a remarkable resemblance to the situation in which
his life began. Sleep is somatically a re-activation of the sojourn in the
womb, fulfilling the same conditions of restful posture, warmth, and
absence of stimuli; indeed, many people assume in sleep the fœtal attitude. The psychic condition of a person asleep is characterized by an
almost complete withdrawal from his environment and all interest in
it. Does not this throw a new light on recuperation by sleep and on
the nature of fatigue? " [67]

> The babe is at peace within the womb,
> The corpse is at rest within the tomb,
> We begin in what we end.[68]

PSYCHOANALYSIS

A final word about psychoanalysis. It was by means of psychoanalysis that the laws, conceptions, mechanisms, etc., described
in this chapter were discovered. But while psychoanalysis is, to
be sure, a *technique* of subsurface exploration, it has come to
mean other things as well. It is primarily a method of *treatment*
for certain kinds of mental illness — this is how it was discovered. It is also a method of *research*, not only in psychology,
but in anthropology and comparative religion and other social
sciences. Moreover, it is a body of scientific data and hypotheses,
representing a certain dynamic point of view in medicine and in
psychology, and both are vastly richer and more fertile for its contributions of the past few decades.

Practically no intelligent and informed scientist today disputes the main thesis and findings of psychoanalysis. There is
still much controversial matter; and unhappily the problems
already unearthed are proving to be exceedingly complex, so
that few will be able to follow where even fewer may lead.

The original discovery of psychoanalysis and its subsequent
development by Freud have already been referred to (page 268).
It is incorrect by all standards to refer to various " schools of
psychoanalysis "; by definition there is only one psychoanalysis,
and that is Freudian. The various men who originally worked
with Freud and subsequently developed their own methods of

[67] Sigmund Freud: " *Metapsychologische Ergänzung zur Traumlehre,*" *Inter-*
nationale Zeitschrift für ärztliche Psychoanalyse, Vol. IV (1916–17) , p. 277.
[68] Shelley: *Fragment, Peace First and Last.*

psychological investigation or treatment do not themselves call their work psychoanalysis, nor regard it as related to psychoanalysis, and no one else should. Psychoanalysis, on the other hand, is a standardized scientific discipline, standardized to a much higher degree of precision so far as its clinical application is concerned than most people realize. This I make clear by sketching briefly the history of psychoanalysis in America.

It was introduced about 1908 by Dr. A. A. Brill of New York, Dr. Ernest Jones, then at the University of Toronto, and Dr. J. J. Putnam of the Harvard Medical School and its early development here is chiefly to be credited to their primary efforts, the masterly research and technical exposition of Dr. Smith Ely Jelliffe of New York, and the application of psychoanalytic discoveries to formal psychiatry and its interpretations to the medical public by Dr. W. A. White of Washington. Formal and systematic instruction of physicians in psychoanalytic theory and technique, aside from that given by the tutorial method by a few competent men, began with the introduction of psychoanalysis into the curriculum of the University of Chicago in 1930 by Dr. Franz Alexander, formerly of Berlin. In 1932 the Chicago Institute for Psychoanalysis was organized by Drs. Alexander, Bartemeier, Blitzsten, McLean, French, myself, and others, and subsequently similar institutes (patterned on those of Vienna, Berlin, London and Budapest) were organized in New York, Boston, Baltimore and Washington, Philadelphia, Detroit, and Topeka. Branch societies of the American Psychoanalytic Association were formed in these cities and in California and meetings of the Association with increasing attendance began taking place annually in connection with the American Psychiatric Association.

To become a psychoanalyst one must first of all be a physician. He must have had psychiatric training. He must have submitted himself to a psychoanalysis at the hands of an analyst recognized as competent to give such didactic training; he must have participated in a stipulated number of case seminars, attended representative courses of lectures, and acquainted himself with the psychoanalytic literature to the point of being able to sustain an oral examination on the theory. Furthermore, he must have carried through the psychoanalysis of at least four patients under the weekly supervision and control of a competent training analyst. Finally, in most societies, he is also required to have presented an acceptable thesis or presentation in psychoanalysis and to have practised under the surveillance of the group for a period of time. After this he is eligible to associate membership in a psychoanalytic society and entitled to call himself a psychoanalyst. Later, if approved, he is made a full member. Such high requirements for specialization exist in no other branch of medicine, to my knowledge.

SUMMARY OF THE CHAPTER

In this chapter I have attempted the presentation of some of the fundamental elementary rules and data of the workings of the power-distributing mechanisms of the personality. The method of presentation is partly new; the material is not.

I have said there were instincts behind it all; that these instincts, selfish and unselfish, egoistic and sexual, constructive and destructive, were striving at aims which entailed frequent collisions and compromises, and that this made necessary the suppression and repression of this and that instinctive drive.

To escape repression these instinctive trends, or wishes, undergo various kinds of modification, or disguise. Their disguises are effected in part to fool the super-ego or censor — who stands, as it were, on the border between the conscious and the unconscious parts of the mind — and in part to fool the public, which sees only the product, and never (?) guesses the motive. Even the individual himself doesn't recognize the motive any more (if he ever did) by the time it appears on the surface as some sort of act or feeling.

I have listed and illustrated the main varieties of these disguises. Some of them are harmless, as well as useless; dreams, for example. Others are useful; they are called sublimations. Still others are neither harmless nor useful; they are positively harmful, evil, dangerous. These constitute symptoms, to which I have already devoted one whole chapter of this book.

We have seen that there is a natural evolution or development of the manifestations of instinct in the " normal " human being, through various stages, with changing objectives. Some have difficulties in making the evolutionary changes; some even return to earlier loves. And many cling to souvenirs of the balmy care-free days when reality entailed no obligations. Thence spring certain persistent fantasies. Man wants but little here below, so they say, but included in that little is the desire to be God or His son, to possess the king's sceptre and his queen, to kill off all opponents, and to dwell in a comfortable heaven of perpetual peace.

Finally I have said that psychoanalysis as a research technique and as a scientific discipline is additional to psychoanalysis as a method of treatment. In the latter capacity it is applicable to those whose internal conflicts have brought about so much pressure that pain is produced, and harmfully disguised signals are released (symptoms) of a sort which give a key to the unlocking of the repression and a releasing of the pressure. Of this I shall have more to say in the next chapter.

CHAPTER V

TREATMENTS

PRAGMATIC SECTION, DEALING WITH THE TECHNIQUE OF
MAKING REPAIRS

"Quæ lædunt oculos festinas demere; si quid
Est animum, differs curandi tempus in annum."
(*"If anything affects your eye, you hasten to have it removed; if
anything affects your mind, you postpone the cure for a year."*)

—HORACE: *Epistles, I, ii, 38-40*

CHAPTER V

TREATMENTS

Can'st thou not minister to a mind diseased,
Pluck from the memory a rooted sorrow,
Raze out the hidden troubles of the brain
And with some sweet oblivious antidote
Cleanse the stuff'd bosom of that perilous stuff
Which weighs upon the heart?

— *Macbeth,* Act V, Scene i

I. PREVENTION

It is customary under the head of treatment to speak of the way in which the necessity for treatment may be anticipated. This is essentially the concept represented by the word *hygiene* and in our special field, therefore, by the phrase *mental hygiene* (see page 15). Before discussing the treatment of those individuals whose attempts at adjustment have already shown some evidences of pending failure we must discuss the possibility of some systematic self-regulation aimed at the forestalling of such a necessity.

Without meaning to detract in the least from the importance of popular education in regard to mental illness and its proper treatment, it must be said that this, rather than any actual preventive principles, has been the first accomplishment of the so-called *mental-hygiene movement.* This was clearly developed in a stimulating article by the late Frankwood E. Williams,[1] formerly director of the National Committee for Mental Hygiene, who pointed out (as I did myself in the first edition of this book, page 362) that such advice as " Avoid alcohol and you will avoid alcoholic psychoses," or " Don't worry," " Keep smiling," " Know thyself," and the like are both platitudinous and useless as methods of preventing mental ill health. To en-

[1] Frankwood E. Williams: " Is There a Mental Hygiene? " *Psychoanalytical Quarterly,* Vol. I, pp. 113–20 (1932).

courage the intelligent public to believe that mental hygiene means what its name implies when we have so little to support this is inevitably disappointing. There is no doubt that such an idea was oversold in the early days of the renaissance of psychology in medicine. Nevertheless, it would be inaccurate to imply that we have no faith in the prospect of maintaining good personal adjustments through self-help. The first edition of my book was not written with this idea in mind, but I received an astonishingly large number of letters assuring me that its perusal had definitely changed for the better the life or views or adjustments of readers. I am certain from observation that a similar effect has been produced by the books of other psychiatric writers. I have also seen positive benefit from lectures on mental hygiene to college students. I am obliged to believe, therefore, that to some extent education in regard to psychological principles, whether because it objectifies them or for some other reason, does accomplish good in a hygienic direction, does act as a preventive.

In spite of this some people question how much a conscious desire to eliminate unhealthy tendencies can actually effect. Some believe that all of our determinations to do better in this or that respect are merely salve to our wounded self-esteem, and that we can no more change our minds than we can change our statures. But there is just as much evidence to support the opposite opinion, that, unlike the leopard, we *can* change our spots, although not as easily as some enthusiasts believe.

Take the question of controlling one's temper. We have considered at length the personality disorder characterized by the indulgence in emotional excesses. We know that some people get unduly angry, to an extent which anybody recognizes as mentally unhealthy. We know that others get painfully depressed. Can one, indeed, by giving thought to the matter, by consciously wanting to change and trying to do so, learn to control one's temper or to alleviate a depression or to alter self-crippling behaviour?

Undoubtedly. If psychiatrists did not know this from experience, they would long since have abandoned their labours. And at that they see the worst cases. The conception of a driving unconscious over which the conscious ego has relatively little control is not so pessimistic as it appears. For were the unconscious *totally* unamenable to the ego, psychoanalysis itself would not have been discovered and would not be efficacious. " The voice of the intelligence," says Freud, eloquently, " is low, but it is persistent." In a sense one may describe the function of psychiatry as that of strengthening overburdened egos, egos too weak to deal with the problems that confront them in the environment or from their own instinctual conflicts.

The general tendency is the other way — to think of the conscious intelligence as omnipotent. "We can do whatever we want to do," etc. This is absurd. In a certain sense we do indeed do what we want to, but when the stronger part of the wanting is unconscious, contrary conscious wishes are thwarted and that is all the individual knows about. Many fortunate individuals who are free from neurotic tendencies give themselves unjustified airs and speak contemptuously of neurotic sufferers; "They ought to know better," they say, "and, knowing better, ought to do better." The real state of affairs might be likened to a boat in which the rudder is the conscious intelligence and the engines the unconscious part of the mind. No matter how good the rudder is, the ship cannot keep on its course if the engines fail, or great storms arise.

This false idea that one's intelligence is quite sufficient to guide one's conduct expediently is often exploited unknowingly; for example, by physicians who feel that it is only necessary for them to tell patients certain things in order for them to "snap out of it" immediately and who become provoked when the patients do not do so. More often it is exploited by quacks — medical, literary, and religious. In this form it has given rise to a flock of "cheer-up" books, most of which are not worth the paper they are written on, and to a number of religious groups in which God equals mind, equals love, equals beauty, equals happiness, equals "it ain't gonna rain no more."

I know some readers find this book a bit gloomy. They had hoped to read in it the key-notes and slogans of mental health and perfection. Instead they read that the human mind is a complex mass of motives and mechanisms apt to go awry, and if they do go awry they had best be taken to a psychiatrist.

Not quite so bad as that. The vast majority of ailing minds never see psychiatrists and never will, and many of them never should. But the principles of psychiatry should be applied all the same. Sometimes they can be self-administered; sometimes a friend will turn the trick. The family doctor or clergyman often does it. And sometimes a book will do it — a book like this, or a less technical one, like several which I could name (see bibliography), and which I daily recommend.

There are no rules of thumb, no standard prescriptions for preserving mental health. But here are a few general principles that some have found helpful:

Set up as an ideal the facing of reality as honestly and as cheerfully as possible.

Cultivate social contacts and cultural developments.

Recognize neurotic evasions as such and take advantage of opportunities for sublimation. (Substitute hobbies for habits.)

Learn to know the evidences of mental pathology and how best to deal with them.

Assume that the unhappy are always (at least partly) " wrong."

II. DIAGNOSIS: A PREREQUISITE TO TREATMENT

If the reader will refer back to Chapter II, he can refresh his mind as to the basic concept of modern psychiatry — namely, that we conceive of personalities attempting to adjust themselves, with all that their heredity, their instinctual urges, and their past experiences have made them, to a constantly changing environment which does a certain amount of adjusting on its own part. When this mutual adjustment fails, the environment or the individual suffers. Sometimes the sufferer is wise enough to seek help. Such help as is administered by physicians is called treatment. Sometimes others than physicians can and do offer help — social workers, for example, teachers, parents, lawyers, psychologists, legislatures — but to this help there is no legal or traditional justification for applying the word " treatment."

Whoever it is that provides help does so with scientific precision *only* after a competent diagnosis. To some people, to make a diagnosis means the application of a name to something. But because of the inadequate structure of our language, because of the shiftiness of the meaning of even well-established names, a diagnosis of name only is of very little value in psychiatry. Unfortunately, there are some who do not know this and who still believe psychiatry to be the science of calling people names: " insane," for example, " feeble-minded," " manic-depressive," " psychopathic."

In a proper sense, the word " diagnosis " implies a sufficient understanding of the nature and meaning of the suffering of a maladjusted individual to indicate the possibilities and the techniques most likely to relieve his suffering and to facilitate his readjustment. This implies that the diagnosis must be expressed in dynamic terms, terms which describe not only the personality but also the environment, past and present, and the nature of the interaction between the two. But here comes the rub. Words fail us and names do not exist which can properly describe all of these things. The least we can do, however, is to describe in a systematic way the personality and the environment involved in the failure, and — for statistical and classificatory purposes — indicate the general type of personality, environment, and failure, using empirical terms.

As a practical matter, our ability to speak of the environment in scientific terms, to describe social forces systematically, has been of such recent development [2] that psychiatrists have as yet no adequate technique or terminology with which to record it. We are a little more proficient in the *systematic description of the personality*. It begins with an elaborate investigation of the historical data relating to the development of that personality, with particular emphasis upon the more recent evidences of adjustment failures. This includes what is traditionally called in medicine a *family history*, establishing hereditary trends and stigmata and an approximate picture of the child's earliest social environment. Then follows a *developmental history*, an account of the pre-school and adolescent periods of life and the adjustment intended or accomplished in these epochs. A *vocational history*, with a definite record of the patient's experiences in various attempts to earn a living, and a *medical history*, representing the organic happenings in the adjustment process — infections, operations, special illnesses — are also a part of the history. Finally, an account of the individual's adjustment to other individuals in a social or erotic way (*social history*) is important, extending as it does from the family circle of childhood through the developing sexual life to the marriage, establishment of a new home, and adjustment to the marital partner and children.

And all of this is just *history*, leading up in longitudinal study to the *examinations*, which are like a cross-section, made at one given moment of a life and body and mind that have been developing for years.

[2] See J. F. Brown: *Psychology and the Social Order* (New York: McGraw-Hill Book Co., 1936).

The *examinations* are:

I. Physical examination, of the body itself — the head, the chest, the abdomen, genitalia, extremities, skin, pulse, temperature, blood-pressure, and so forth;

II. Neurological examination — a detailed observation of certain reflexes, movements, and sensations indicating the condition of the nervous system;

III. Chemical examinations — of the blood, urine, fæces, sputum, spinal fluid;

IV. X-ray, air encephalography, electroencephalography and other special examinations occasionally necessary;

V. Psychological examination — the most important of all in most cases and the most apt to be neglected. It consists in certain formal and certain informal procedures the object of which is to determine as accurately as possible what general patterns the patient's perceiving, thinking, feeling, and acting follow. They are both qualitative and quantitative and should include not only the determination of the extent of so-called " abnormal psychology," but psychometric and other evaluations which modern psychology has introduced (for example, Rorshach, Luria, Dembo, and other tests).

By summing up and digesting these data we know what the individual has in the way of a personality — we know what he has to react *with*.

The next examinational inquiry must be into what he must react *to*. The examination of the environment (social, physical, economic) is made by a combination of methods. To some extent we may learn of it through the sufferer himself — he may tell us about it, as he sees it. But the proper scientific method, the standard method, is through the eyes and brains of trained psychiatric social workers. These young professional women, in two short decades, have made themselves the indispensable adjuncts of every up-to-date community clinic.[3]

Finally we must study precisely what has happened when what our patient has to react *with* meets (or has met) what our patient has to react *to!* Doctors call it the *present illness*. It means an account of the particular kind of failure apparent at the moment. It is a study of the symptoms (Chapter III) and misdirected motives (Chapter IV) apparent in the personality under the adjustment stress.

[3] See page 420.

Now, the failures — complete, incomplete, and pending — which come to the psychiatrist are of certain sorts, and have been given names. These names are not very important; in fact, if they distract the doctor's attention from understanding the adjustment problems of the patient and concentrate it on the label given to the disease, they are more harmful than useful. But a *descriptive diagnosis* has certain utility providing it is complete enough for accurate classificatory purposes. It should include a conclusion with respect to:

1. The psychiatric syndrome or *disease-picture*. This will conform to a list of such names agreed upon by a committee from the American Psychiatric Association and accepted now as standard (American) nomenclature. I think of no object to be gained by the more precise delineation of the historical and contemporary concepts represented by these terms. Some of them have been discussed in Chapter II. For more technical students, more can be found in any psychiatric text-book; by others than technical students, they are best forgotten.

2. The general *personality structure,* often represented most clearly before the outbreak of the acute illness. This corresponds in general to the personality types described in Chapter II, although in practice we use a somewhat different terminology.

3. Coincident conditions of conventional *medical and surgical* interest.

But more significant than such descriptive diagnosis is, in my opinion, an *interpretative diagnosis* which is an attempt to interpret the meaning of the patient's maladjustment in terms of etiology, structure, and dynamic development.

To the extent that the *etiological factors* are considered to be *physical,* we must endeavour to specify their location, their character, and, if possible, their origin. To the extent the *psychological* factors appear to have been prominent in the development of the maladjustment, we must try to indicate the initial trauma or traumata which appear to have dwarfed or inhibited the normal personality development, as well as the major psychic traumata in the patient's subsequent life which acted as secondary or complicating factors. To the extent that unusual *social* or *economic* conditions acted in a powerful way to restrict or over-stimulate this development, they, too, are noted. Finally, the *precipitating* factor or factors related to the final stage in the maladjustment or the appearance of symptoms are carefully noted and compared with these previous experiences.

From the standpoint of *structure* similarly we must inquire what is the weakness or defect in this personality:

1. From the standpoint of physical structure (for example, tuberculosis) ;

2. From the standpoint of physiological or chemical functions (for example, rapid heart) ;

3. From the standpoint of psychological intention and inhibition (for example, retarded intelligence, paranoid ideas) .

Third, concerning the *dynamics* of the maladjustment, we endeavour to see how the original etiological factors and the damage done by them have in turn modified the environment so as to increase the difficulties of subsequent adjustment, and how this in turn has produced further attempts at adjustment, or, on the other hand, perhaps overwhelmed all subsequent efforts. To do this one looks to see how and against whom aggressions are directed, or perhaps we should say misdirected, because had they been properly handled these aggressions should have served to preserve the patient's equilibrium and defend him against the hostile elements in the adjustment. And since to the extent that such hate has been unwisely and inefficaciously invested, one expects evidence of a sense of guilt, as described in Chapter IV; one looks now for the expression of this need for punishment. Of lesser importance is the symbolic meaning of individual symptoms, delusions, and incidents of behaviour which have been so greatly stressed by some writers under the assumption that they were correctly applying psychoanalysis to psychiatry.

And, finally, a proper and complete interpretative diagnosis should be able to express the *primary purpose* of the illness. It should specify, also, the *secondary gains* which the illness accomplishes for the patient; in many cases these are so great as to dwarf or hide the primary motivations.

III. TREATMENT

So much for diagnosis; what are the treatments, once the diagnosis is made and the problem understood?

Psychiatric treatment must be thought of as adjustment facilitation.[4] What can be done, we must ask, to help the individual

---

[4] This really applies to all treatments for all diseases. Taking aspirin for a headache, for example, makes life bearable by a chemical suppression of some pain stimuli. And opening a boil is another kind of manipulation to facilitate a

to do what he has failed to do? Can we change him? How?
Must we — can we — change his environmental situation for
him? How?

1. *Medicine and Surgery*

Sometimes by drugs. Let's get this clearly and unmistakably
said. Psychiatry isn't faith healing, as some imagine; it doesn't
try to fool anybody, or to solve all human problems with a single formula, or dedicate prayer to the cure of constipation. It
does effect changes in people by means of drugs when drugs can
effect the changes needed.

A man with brain syphilis, for example, can (sometimes, not
always) be changed from a wild and worthless failure to a once
more efficient and successful human being by means of certain
drugs. A child, idiotic because of thyroid-gland deficiency, may
be unrecognizably altered — for the better — by being fed on
thyroid-extract tablets. People afflicted by certain kinds of obesi-
ties may be afforded enormous relief by proper pituitary-
gland-extract injections. Aspirin has added thousands of years to
human lives by alleviating pain temporarily; caffeine has undoubtedly stimulated much achievement that over-eating and
under-sleeping would have stifled; and the peace that sodium
bromide and luminal have brought into the lives of millions is
beyond calculation. Recently discovered sleep-producers such as
the barbituric acid series and old ones such as paraldehyde have
soothed many troubled pillows and spared much needless suffering.[5]

It is true, none the less, that psychiatrists use less medicinal
therapy than the general practitioner, whose chief concern is
with chemical and physical disablements. As a rule, one can't
medicate people into a better personality, a better frame of
mind, or a better adjustment. Sometimes one can! Don't forget that. But usually something else is necessary.

In the same category is surgery. Time was when ambitious
and obliging surgeons would attempt the solution of almost any
human problem by opening the abdomen and removing something. In the backwoods there are still a few such. But a host
of surgically mutilated men and women over the country are still

---

more comfortable adjustment. But this point of view can be neglected in general
medicine; in psychiatry it is indispensable.

[5] See R. M. Fellows: " The Use and Abuse of the Non-Narcotic Sedatives " (in
psychiatric patients), *Journal of the Kansas Medical Society*, Vol. XXXVII, pp.
408–11 (October 1936).

struggling with their fits and fights and flops, only with less vigour and less courage and less likelihood of ever achieving peace. These living rebukes have rather discouraged indiscriminate surgical psychotherapy.

Here again it is easy to become monistic and neglect the fact that surgery is sometimes the *sine qua non* of successful readjustment. Mentally sick people have bodies, and these bodies are subject to afflictions amenable only to surgery; and for them surgery is *the* treatment. Appendicitis, brain tumours, infections requiring drainage, deformities of face or limb amenable to correction — these and many other opportunities for surgical treatment exist.

Physiotherapy, hydrotherapy, occupational therapy, and other devices for calming the soul through soothing the body will be reserved for discussion under hospitalization.

2. *Psychotherapy*

Psychotherapy is the categorical name for various modes of attack utilizing the psychological machinery rather than the physical or chemical machinery of the personality.

The first principle of psychotherapy is that it is done by some *one* for someone *else*. It requires a saviour. This saviour may be almost anybody — many an intuitive woman has cured a neurotic husband or lover by psychotherapy. This is the theme of the short novel *Gradiva* by Wilhelm Jensen, which was specially interpreted in the light of psychoanalysis by Freud under the title of *Delusion and Dream* (New York: Moffat, Yard & Co., 1922). The ministers often accomplish magnificent mass-psychotherapy, and I knew a policeman once who knew more about soul conflicts than the district judge and had a way of resolving some of them. I know a college dean who disclaims all technical knowledge, but who is so adept at ministering to student maladjustments that he does much of the work of the mental-hygiene counsellor.

Of course the technically trained person has enormous advantages over the naïve psychotherapist. For one thing, he knows what *not* to do and what *not* to say. The human mind, especially one in distress, is a poor practice field for amateur explorations.

But even more important than technical training and knowledge is the cultivation of the proper attitude toward the patient. Without this, psychotherapy is impossible. One must really be interested in the sufferer — one must, in a way, really love one's patients. To be bored or annoyed or disgusted by the fancies and failures and queernesses of " nervous " people is to be foredoomed to failure. One has to be infinitely patient and genuinely interested, and yet detached enough — " cold-blooded " enough — to be objective in the handling of the sufferer. The same attitude must be preserved as that of the surgeon, intent upon an operation which interests him, fatigues him, concerns him, but moves him not a bit.

In the third place, one must have in mind clearly what one is trying to accomplish. Psychotherapy must aim at something more fundamental than the mere trying to make someone feel better. The conception of treatment as the facilitating of readjustment by an attack of some sort on the conscious and unconscious conflicts that produce the distress must never be lost sight of. The unconscious conflicts are the more numerous and the more powerful, but the solution of the surface difficulties often proves to be sufficient to restore peace. The symptoms for which psychotherapy is useful are those in which these struggles from the unconscious push their way into the conscious life, usually in painful disguise. Psychotherapy may strengthen a failing repression or it may remove certain unnecessary repressions and lighten the load, or, finally, it may change the form of the disguised escapes from the harmful to the useful variety.

To change a symptom into a useful activity is what one has in mind when one says of a neurotic patient: " If she had something to do to occupy her mind she would get over her symptoms." This theory is right as far as it goes; the difficulty is that it neglects the fact that the change from a symptom to a sublimation cannot be made simply as the result of an exhortation. There is a great deal of *resistance* (which is usually unconscious) on the patient's part to any such change, and it is as difficult or impossible for him to make the change without help as it is for a man in mid-ocean to swim to shore. He often knows well enough what would save him, but he usually feels it as the bitterest irony to be told so, just as a drowning man would feel about being told to swim to shore to save himself. It is true, but it is impossible.

An understanding of this difficulty is the fourth essential of intelligent psychotherapy. *Resistance,* as it is technically called, is one of the most important new conceptions contributed by psychoanalysis. Resistance is the existence in every individual of an opposition to relief of the very suffering of which he complains. The symptom is there for a reason; it has a purpose and satisfies a certain craving of the patient's unconscious. Consequently any effort to change it meets with opposition. A crippled beggar who has earned his living for twenty years by selling lead-pencils on the street would be in a terrible plight if suddenly cured by some miracle. He would have his legs back, but he would have lost his livelihood. He would be up against the necessity of a very difficult readjustment. He wouldn't want it. In a similar way every neurotic patient opposes a dissolution of his symptoms; in other words, in one sense he does not want to get well.

This may seem hard to believe. The neurotic patient, especially, finds it incredible. " Do you think I *want* to feel this way? " he will ask with dramatic emphasis and gestures.

" Not consciously," you reply, " but unconsciously your illness gratifies you — it is a solution, a compromise solution, of a problem. It is the lesser of two evils — so your unconscious thinks."

" Well, all I know is I feel wretched," the patient will reply, " and I know it's not imagination and I don't want it. I'll do anything in the world to get well, just anything! "

" All right. Be here at eight o'clock tomorrow morning to begin your treatment. I can assure you that you can get well."

" Well, now, doctor, I can't very well come in the morning because I promised my sister-in-law I'd go shopping with her. Couldn't I come the next day? "

Of course this is a little exaggerated, but not much. Many, many patients come to me (and to every other psychiatrist) for treatment who say they wish to get well and yet balk at the first recommendation. They really think they want to get well, they honestly believe it. They are as unaware of the reasons for their illness as everyone else is. And they shield themselves from finding out or from having their illnesses dispelled.

Even Jesus in attempting to treat the mentally sick two thousand years ago met with resistance:

" And . . . there was a man which had a spirit of an unclean devil, and cried out with a loud voice, saying: ' Let us alone; what have we to do with Thee, Thou Jesus of Nazareth? Art Thou come to destroy us? I know Thee who Thou art; the Holy One of God! ' And Jesus rebuked him, saying: ' Hold thy peace, and come out of him.' And when the devil had thrown him in the midst, he came out of him. . . ." (Luke iv, 33-5.)

". . . A man with an unclean spirit, who had his dwelling among the tombs; and no man could bind him, no, not with chains. . . . And always, night and day, he was in the mountains and in the tombs, crying, and cutting himself with stones. But when he saw Jesus afar off, he ran and worshipped Him, and cried with a loud voice, and said: 'What have I to do with Thee, Jesus . . . ? I adjure Thee by God, that Thou torment me not. . . .' And he besought Him much that He would not send them [the devils] away out of the country." (Mark v, 2-3, 5-7, 10.)

Resistance is shown in all sorts of ways other than in mere disinclination to take treatment. One of my patients recently began treatment with a great flourish, talked about it to everyone, and told what a wonderful thing he thought it was. But then he began to break appointments on one pretext or another and finally quit coming altogether. Another patient made several appointments and then found very good excuses for breaking them, but when she finally got to see me she told me she had been trying for weeks to get an appointment, and if I would give her another appointment she wouldn't break it for anything, no matter how inconvenient. She complained because I wouldn't begin the treatment that very day. She wanted an appointment the next day, which I gave her at considerable inconvenience. She never came back.

Many patients show their resistance by doing everything imaginable in the name of "treatment" except the thing most likely to cure them. A patient will very frequently enter the hospital in despair, hoping that three to six months of treatment will cure him, improve rapidly for a time, and then leave on account of "homesickness" just before a cure is accomplished.

Another form of resistance is to take a dislike to the doctor; still another is to have dreams in which the doctor is represented as a bad man. One of my patients said that the expression "That old devil!" kept coming to her mind constantly when she was in my office and she couldn't think whom on earth it could apply to! [6]

[6] For the best technical discussion of resistance, see Freud's *The Problem of Anxiety,* cited above.

TYPES OF PSYCHOTHERAPY

All methods of psychotherapy aim at accomplishing the overcoming of this resistance and the transforming of the patient's energy from harmful to useful forms. There are many methods and techniques.[7] Look at this list, for example:

I. Methods using the principle of *suppression*
    1. Terrorism
    2. Placebos
    3. Rest
    4. Hypnosis
    5. Suggestion
    6. Exhortation
    7. Persuasion
    8. Explanation
    9. Command
    10. Religious assurances
II. Methods using the principle of *expression*
    1. Mental catharsis
    2. Psychiatric counsel
    3. Psychoanalysis
    4. Hypnoanalysis
    5. Narcosynthesis

In the suppressive methods of psychotherapy the physician assumes an active attitude toward the patient's conflicts, and endeavours to push them back into oblivion. Expressive psychotherapy endeavours to pluck them forth, to remove them. It is something like the difference between palliative medical and remedial surgical treatment. In the suppressive types of psychotherapy — take Christian Science, for example, or suggestion, or " persuasion " — the patient is talked to, read to, exhorted, encouraged. He is given books to read, slogans to repeat, prayers to say, motions to go through. Everything possible is done to extinguish or suppress the conflict.

---

[7] For a patient's version of treatment by various of these methods, including, among others, " treatment by minimization," " treatment by sex appeal," " treatment by terminology," " treatment by encouragement and infinite patience," and " treatment by efficiency," see *The Layman Looks at Doctors*, by S. W. and J. T. Pierce (New York: Harcourt, Brace & Co., 1929). Every doctor should read this; it may seem exaggerated in places, but the search of the maladjusted patient for a genuine understanding of and help in his affliction is often truly pitiful.

The expressive types of psychotherapy — psychoanalysis is the best example — are quite the reverse. The patient does the talking, and he has very little said to him except that he should talk it out. He is usually advised not to read about mental illness; he is exhorted only to bring forth his own repressed material and have the courage to look at it for what it is.

In the expressive types of psychotherapy the patient is encouraged to remember and disgorge all he can; in the suppressive types he is told to " forget it," which really means that the conflicts are to be thrust deeper into the unconscious. The latter is a fine trick if one can turn it. It is quick; it is simple; it is inexpensive; and sometimes it is effective. In the vast majority of cases it doesn't " stick," for the obvious reason that conflicts, like mice, are apt to play as soon as the cat's away. Consequently unless some measure is adopted so that the patient is continuously held under the thumb of the suppressor, the symptoms often crop out again.

Sometimes, however, under suppressive treatment an internal change takes place so that the patient is thereafter able to take care of himself. This is a little like poulticing a boil. As every doctor knows, this sort of home treatment often does good. Every doctor also knows that most big boils, however, have to be lanced. In an analogous way the expressive method of psychotherapy aims to eradicate the conflicts — that is, to let out the pus. The disadvantage of this is that it takes time, skill, and money. The advantages are that it is permanent and that it makes the patient independent.

SUPPRESSIVE PSYCHOTHERAPY

Suppressive psychotherapy is of many types, of which the following examples taken from Southard's amazing collection of war cases [8] are typical.

Although these are all war cases, the same symptoms, the same pictures, and the same treatments are everyday routine in ordinary non-military psychiatric practice.

Cure by Terrorism

A French infantryman was wounded in the upper third of the right calf, and was subsequently operated upon twice in the next twelve

---

[8] E. E. Southard: *Shell-Shock and Neuropsychiatry* (Boston: W. M. Leonard, 1919).

months. He was then sent to a neurological centre walking on two canes, right leg in forced extension on thigh, in permanent and absolute contracture. All movements except leg flexion could be executed, though slowly and weakly; but positive movements were impossible, except flexion of the knees. There was no sensory disorder. Reflexes were normal save that the leg reflexes were a little stronger on the affected side, and the patellar reflex on that side was nullified by the contracture. Electrical reactions proved normal. There were marked trophic disturbances of the right foot and of the lower third of the lower leg. There was a certain amount of œdema, cyanosis, coldness, and thickening of skin; marked muscular over-excitability of the distal extremity of the leg. In short, Ferrand was here dealing with a case of Babinski's group of the so-called physiopathic cases. The man was somewhat feeble-minded and anxious and a trembling suppliant for cure.

He was put in a re-education room and by means of fatigue, induced by violent physical exercises, was (Ferrand states) " brutally conquered." The contracture after a half-hour of physical movement of flexion and extension of the leg ceased. The patient was shown how he could both flex and extend the limb himself; he was then caused to do this spontaneously. These active movements were aided and at times provoked by somewhat painful galvanic discharges. The patient then walked slowly and flexed both knees to the maximum. He was cured after a treatment of two and a half hours.   (Ferrand, March 1917)

Cure by Placebo

A soldier from Gallipoli was admitted to the Royal Victoria Hospital at Edinburgh, blind. He had been at Gallipoli from May 1, 1915 until August 12, when a shell explosion blew in his trench and buried him. He was dug out nervous and tremulous. Shortly afterwards there was the bright flash of a second shell, and amnesia set in, until he found himself in a hospital. He could not see at all with the left eye, and the sight of the other was poor. He arrived in Scotland, October 9. He was nervous, excitable, and now somewhat depressed, complaining of blindness and pain in the left eye, and headache. The left eyelid drooped. The fundus was normal. He had not been given an anæsthetic.

It was explained to him that the eye had not been injured; that it had become weak from the explosion; that he would be given a series of injections into the left temple of a strong drug which would restore the sight of the eye.

Gradually increasing quantities of normal saline (table salt) solution were given every morning. After four days he said that the treatment was doing him good. A week later he said that the eye was much stronger. After the fifteenth injection he could not sleep. The headache was worse, and there was "moving about inside his head." Early in the morning he went to sleep after a period of restlessness. He awoke at eight o'clock able to see perfectly, and was overjoyed at the result. There was some blurring and four days later he said he was becoming blind again. More normal saline was injected, causing pain. After that there was no relapse, and the man was sent back to his unit.

(Bruce, May 1916)

Cure by Rest

" A musketeer was deafened and stunned by a near-by shell explosion. On coming to, he found no wound, but was deaf and dumb.

" Speech returned after ten days, and hearing partially, but there was a [severe] stuttering. He had to hunt anxiously for words, talked like a child in infinitives and telegram style, although he could express himself in writing perfectly well.

" Hearing improved on the right side very quickly, but on the left side conditions varied from total deafness to subtotal deafness. There was a general hyperesthesia of the skin, pain on pressure on the temples, exaggeration of skin and tendon reflexes, marked tremor in both hands. The man was anxious, depressed, and irritable. During caloric tests of the vestibular apparatus in the course of the next few weeks, the man had an hysterical attack of crying twice, following which all the phenomena got worse.

" Rest and isolation from all such influences procured an almost complete recovery in several months." (Zanger, July 1915)

Cure by Hypnosis

An English private, twenty-two, was looking over a parapet, July 18, 1915. He afterwards remembered sand thrown in his eyes and a fall backward, hitting his head, after a shell had struck the sandbags in front of him. He was unconscious twenty-four hours. Upon recovery he found himself completely blind, save that he could just tell light from darkness with the left eye. His eyes were sore and his eyelids blackened; there were also severe headache and partial deafness.

Hearing returned and the headache improved shortly; but the condition of the eye seemed more permanent. On forcibly opening the eyes, September 14, they were turned far upwards so that the iris could scarcely be seen. Some sand grains were buried in the conjunctiva, not in the cornea. There was no inflammation about the sand grains.

In hypnosis he was told that he would see on waking. The moment he woke, this suggestion was repeated forcibly and his eyes were held open. He cried out that he could see; tears ran down his cheeks; he fell on his knees in gratitude. Three days later he said he was able to see as well as he had ever seen. There was, however, an opacity of the vitreous of the left eye, the result of a retinal hemorrhage. September 30, he had perfect vision in the right eye and 6/36 in his left.   (Hurst, November 1916)

Cure by Suggestion

A private, twenty years of age, lost speech and hearing after the battle of Neuve Chapelle. Eight days later he came under the care of the laryngologist in a very excited state, pointing to lips and ears and carrying a note with information concerning his deaf-mutism.

Dr. O'Malley wrote on a piece of paper that he would restore the patient's speech and hearing. He then used the mirror (that is, prodded the patient in the throat with an instrument) until the point of retching was reached, and wrote: " You can speak now; count up to ten loudly." The patient did.

Dr. O'Malley next used the cold-water douche to the right ear to the point of giddiness, then shouted through a speaking-tube into the patient's ear: " You hear now? " The patient then realized he could hear and tears streamed down his face; thereafter he was able to converse freely. (O'Malley, May 1916)

Cure by Exhortation

" A soldier, 25, a low menial when war broke out, developed ' dysentery and gastritis ' at the Dardenelles, although even before the dysentery his nerves had gone bad. He had diarrhea and vomiting, was sick every day, found himself unable to walk, and found himself always wet with urine dribbling day and night. Arriving in England and treated in a hospital, he still had vomiting. He had lived on milk and custard and had been kept in bed.

" The patient was convinced by earnest insistence that his legs were not as weak as he had supposed. He was encouraged to walk, put upon a light diet and then upon ordinary diet. He became an active worker in the ward, later going for five-mile route marches. Two months later he went back to duty in good health, weighing seven pounds more than before." (MacDowell, December 1916)

Cure by Persuasion

" A man on crutches, paralyzed completely in the right leg, partially in the left, developed paralysis in the right arm from the use of the crutch. There were marked vasomotor changes in the right leg and arm together with anesthesia to pinprick. Assured that he could move the legs perfectly he said he had tried and failed. After a persuasive talk in private he began to use the arm, and to walk perfectly. It seems that in the trenches he had a sharp pain in the right knee, after which he did not use the leg and it gradually became more and more useless. It had been paralyzed for three months. . . ." (Russell, August 1917)

Cure by Explanation

" An officer and his servant were blown up by a shell. The servant ran to fetch a stretcher for the officer, to whom he was much attached, but on his return the officer had made a few convulsive movements and died. Immediately after, the servant had a fit. During the next two months he had eleven more. The doctor made a diagnosis of hysterial fits result-ing from emotion, explained his idea of their origin and nature to the servant, and the convulsions then ceased completely."

(Hurst, March 1917)

Cure by Command

" A girl, whose hands were tightly clenched, and the nails of whose fingers were buried in the flesh of her palms, was also brought to him by her parents. For weeks she had been in that condition; and though the physicians who had been consulted endeavoured to open her hands, they tried in vain. ' Allow me, my dear,' said Father Mathew, in his winning voice; and taking her hand in his, and gently unlocking and extending her fingers, he brought it into its natural form. This was a case of pure hysteria affecting the limbs, such as is frequently seen in hospitals." [9]

Civil-life " shell-shock " cases, like the above, are cured by all sorts of things, some of them honest and sensible procedures carried out by intelligent men and others pure fraud and chi-canery. And it should also be added that the most intelligently selected and conscientiously applied treatment methods may in a given instance fail. Osler in his famous essay on equanimity counselled young physicians not to lose heart or faith in hu-manity when they accidentally observe on the bureaus of their most co-operative patients some patent-medicine pills or some literature of a faith-healing cult. For illness is a flight from reality, and the patient has conflicting feelings about the desira-bility of being brought back to it; for all its discomfort, his ill-ness may seem less formidable. One thing which will bring him back is a sufficient relaxation of terror such that his own intelli-gence can once more assume some authority for his life. Natu-rally this is the happier and better way. Another way in which it may be accomplished is through the confidence inspired by a Saviour, the belief in his predictions and his success, and an

[9] John Francis Maguire, M. P.: *Father Mathew* (1864), p. 532.

affection which encourages this. This is especially clear in the simple examples of religious healing which I cite only to show that this can be accomplished by religious authority no less than by scientific authority. For the most part, the following examples, unlike those reported in certain contemporary faith-healing cult journals and tracts, are credibly and honestly reported and their mechanisms clearly understandable in the light of the previous discussion.[10]

From these representative examples of more sudden and dramatic types of maladjustment precipitated by the extraordinary war situation, one perceives that there are numerous ways in which suppression of emergent instinctual tendencies and emotions may be encouraged and the acceptance of reality without regression favoured.

CURES BY RELIGIOUS ASSURANCES

Reassurance

"The life of the wise and genial Founder of the Oratorians [St. Philip Neri, 1551–95] contains many instances of spiritual healing. [Consider, for example, the case of] Caterina Ruissi, whose tumor seems clearly to have been of a hysterical nature. St. Philip's method of dealing with her could not be improved in the light of our modern knowledge: 'There, my child,' he said, 'don't be afraid. You won't be troubled with it any more. It will soon be well.' And so it was."[11]

Affirmation

"Lucrezia Grazzi had a cancer in one of her breasts and the physicians had determined to apply the hot iron to it, and ordered her to remain in bed for the operation. She, however, in the meanwhile, moved with faith in her holy father, betook herself to [Saint Philip Neri] and related her case to him. Philip answered, 'Oh, my poor child, where is this cancer?' She pointed to it, saying: 'Here, my Father.' Then the Saint, touching the diseased part, added, 'Go in peace and doubt not that you shall recover.' When she was come home, she said to those who were present, 'I feel neither pain nor oppression, and I firmly believe I am cured,' and so it proved to be. Soon after the physicians came to cauterize the cancer, and were lost in astonishment at finding not a trace of the disease."[12]

10 The following six cases are taken from Percy Dearmer's *Body and Soul* (New York, 1909), which contains many others.

11 P. J. Bacci: *Life of St. Philip Neri*, translated by F. Antrobus (1902), Vol. II, p. 168.

12 Ibid., Vol. II, p. 169.

Sign of the Cross

" Once when the man of God [St. Francis of Assisi] had come to Narni and was staying there several days, a man of that city named Peter was lying in bed paralyzed. For five months he had been so completely deprived of the use of all his limbs that he could in no wise lift himself up or move at all; and thus having lost all help from feet, hands and head, he could only move his tongue and open his eyes. But on hearing that S. Francis was come to Narni, he sent a messenger to the Bishop to ask that he would, for Divine Compassion's sake, be pleased to send the servant of God Most High to him, for he trusted that he would be delivered by the sight and presence of the Saint from the infirmity whereby he was holden, and so indeed it came to pass; for when the blessed Francis was come to him he made the sign of the cross over him from head to feet, and forthwith drove away all his sickness and restored him to his former health." [13]

Blessing

" There was a brother who often suffered from a grievous infirmity that was horrible to see. . . . For oftentimes he was dashed down, and with a terrible look in his eyes he wallowed foaming; sometimes his limbs were contracted, sometimes extended, sometimes they were folded and twisted together, and sometimes they became hard and rigid. Sometimes, tense and rigid all over, with his feet touching his head, he would be lifted up in the air to the height of a man's stature and would then suddenly spring back to earth. The holy father, Francis, pitying his grievous sickness, went to him, and after offering up prayer, signed him with the red cross and blessed him. And suddenly he was made whole, and never afterwards suffered from this distressing infirmity." [14]

Anointing

" A sister of Ethelwald, ' abbot of the monastery of Melrose,' had been ' during a whole year troubled with an intolerable pain in the head and side, which the physicians utterly despaired of curing.' Cuthbert [died A.D. 687], in pity, anointed the wretched woman with oil. From that time she began to get better, and was well in a few days." [15]

Consecrated Bread

" Hildemer, a prefect, lay ' apparently near death.' One of his friends mentioned that he had with him some consecrated bread which St.

[13] Thomas of Celano, in *Lives of St. Francis of Assisi,* translated by A. G. Ferrers Howell (1908) , Chapters xxiii–xxv.
[14] Ibid.
[15] J. A. Giles: *Patres Ecclesiæ,* " St. Cuthbert, Beda," Vol. IX, pp. 303–4.

Cuthbert had given him. Those present were very pious laymen: 'turning to one another, they professed their faith, without doubting, that by partaking of that same consecrated bread he might be well. They put a little of the bread in a cup of water, and gave it him to drink,' whereat immediately 'all his inward pain left him, and the wasting of his outward members ceased.' A perfect recovery speedily ensued." [16]

EXPRESSIVE PSYCHOTHERAPY

Most of the methods illustrated above are no longer used by modern psychiatrists. The types of maladjustment in which such methods are apt to be successful are relatively rare, but I have cited these cases at some length, even though I do not believe in the treatment methods used, because they serve to illustrate the importance of the emotional factors in physical disease, which are so much neglected in modern medicine aside from psychiatry. It is the doctor's task to heal sickness and relieve suffering, and to this end many treatment devices and techniques have been employed — medicinal, mechanical, surgical, thermal, representing technical progress in medical science. But the disturbing fact remains that a large proportion of the multitudes that fall into the doctors' offices daily are sick in ways which are not relieved by any of these. They present symptoms, they suffer, they complain, they seek relief, but frequently their illnesses are not represented by any structural pathology. To some physicians this represents a puzzling paradox, and such patients arouse in them various emotional reactions, from irritation and annoyance to exasperation, contempt, and even anger. Still other doctors react with over-solicitousness and extend themselves in all sorts of ineffectual directions to help patients whose maladjustments give sufficient physical evidences as to encourage treatment along medicinal and surgical lines.

Such emotional reactions result largely from the fact that we physicians were formerly (and in some backward medical schools still are) taught the fallacious doctrine that all pathology is structural and hence that such things as are complained of by these patients could exist; the patients become, therefore, *prima facie* liars. And just because they are so generally misunderstood and mistreated, such patients learn to exploit every slight advantage which their illness gives them, including the doctor's errors as well as the family's mystification. These secondary benefits are often so conspicuous that doctors, like the relatives,

[16] Giles, op. cit., Vol. IX, p. 307.

mistake them for primary causes and incorrectly label the patient a hoax and a fraud. Such a false accusation plays directly
into the hands of the patient's spirit of martyrdom. This exploitation of suffering for suffering's sake is such abnormal psychology, " such craziness," that it combines with the feeling that
he has been deceived to make the physician uncomfortable and
even resentful.

Naturally, we cannot understand such patients until we can
overcome such feelings, and yet we can overcome such feelings
only if we actually do understand the patient. To fully understand the patient means, of course, to understand the interferences with the adjustment process which we have discussed in
this book. This includes the unconscious motivations of which
before Freud we knew nothing, just as before abdominal surgery
we knew nothing of appendicitis and other types of remediable
abdominal pathology.

We have learned from cases studied by psychoanalysis that one
of the unconscious motives of those patients who come to physicians with symptoms of maladjustment is the wish to make others
suffer, and this impels a self-inflicted punishment so that the patient himself must suffer. To obtain this suffering he will often
unconsciously persuade doctors to inflict suffering upon him in
the name of treatment and hence many doctors fall victims to
such patients and undertake cystoscopies, allergy tests, painful
gynecological treatments, dietary restrictions, and even surgical
operations to gratify the patients' need for suffering. Unfortunately, however, there is no permanent therapeutic benefit from
these. The patient only adds the new treatment or mistreatment
to his list of grievances against doctors and goes on to another
doctor and becomes his victim while she makes him hers.

The more intelligent scientific way to handle such patients is
by means of psychotherapy based on the principles we have been
discussing in this book — that is, *expressive* rather than *suppressive*. There are three common types, really " stages," in this
form of treatment.

I. MENTAL CATHARSIS

Telling someone else about it is an ancient form of relief based
upon the principle that verbalizing our feelings enables us to
objectify them. There is added to this some relief of the sense
of guilt implicit in all maladjustment. The Catholic confes-

sional accomplishes commendable psychotherapy, and my friend Charles M. Sheldon once shrewdly suggested a Protestant confessional.

Confessing, talking it out, *mental catharsis,* as it is technically designated, is by no means a cure-all, or even a very effective treatment for most of the severe neuroses. This is because the neurotic illness arises, not from the superficial, conscious conflicts, but from the deeper, unsuspected, unknown conflicts. But it helps, and its simplicity commends it. Often it suffices for the psychotherapist to be a sympathetic, uncritical listener. I have a very intelligent patient, with a very bitter cross to bear, who comes to see me periodically, pours out a great burden of woe about which I can do absolutely nothing (as she well knows), and then pays her bill and takes her departure declaring that she feels much better.

Skeletons

Everyone's closet is full of skeletons —
Skeletons rattling their bones and laughing
Loud and cruelly,
Struggling to force the door and escape in an obscene riot,
And the struggle is pain.

Some of us hold the door with a long, brave effort,
Some have long ago locked it, and lost the key,
But skeletons still escape
In disguises —
Ugly disguises,
Or merely bizarre,
Or useful and beautiful often —
(Beautiful incognito!)

The skeletons lose their power when exposed,
Bared by the long, lean knife of a self-inquisition,
The pressure against the yielding door
Ceases, and with it the pain.
The door goes shut,
Closing the skeletons in,
Silent,
Once more entombed.

Outwardly all is well;
There is peace again,

And quiet, and freedom from pain
Even though skeletons may remain
Closeted.

K. A. M.

2. PSYCHIATRIC COUNSEL

Most maladjustments do not require psychoanalysis for their correction any more than most people need major surgical operations. The vast majority of maladjustments can be helped with far less radical procedures. The mental catharsis above mentioned will be helpful to some, but in many others one must go further. In what we call *psychiatric counsel* the physician endeavours to learn as much as he can about his patient in all the ways he can, as outlined in the previous section regarding diagnosis. On the basis of such understanding of the individual with whom he has to deal and the environment to which that individual has to adjust himself and with the aid of his knowledge of the principles of mental functioning and his experience with other cases, the physician (he does not necessarily have to be a psychiatrist) can give advice, adjuration, enlightenment, and encouragement. This differs from suppressive psychotherapy in that such advice is always preceded by an airing of the patient's problem in his own words to an unhurried, uncritical, sympathetic listener — the doctor. And this works. Often it works wonders in the way of " cures " that are no less dramatic and far more thoroughgoing and permanent than the clumsy, mystic, old-fashioned examples described in the shell-shock illustrations above.

This type of psychotherapy is available to every physician who will take the trouble to use it. It takes a good deal of time, but good results mean time well spent. One difficulty is that the doctor is too often willing to pass the matter off with a careless exhortation to " forget it." Or he says: " Oh, there is nothing the matter with you." This is never true; it is usually not helpful, it is rarely of permanent effect, and it often offends and wounds the patient. Or perhaps the doctor may say: " If you would stop thinking about yourself you would be all right." This is a very weak and futile psychotherapy. It is exactly this transfer of interest which the patient cannot make and which he must be taught how to make. This the doctor must aim to do. The fact that some ministers and teachers have done it more successfully than some physicians is not because they know more about it, but because they see the necessity and make the effort.

If I were to be asked (as I frequently am) for rules of procedure in psychiatric counselling, I should give the following:

First, show the patient that you are interested in him.

Second, don't lie to him, don't give him placebos or joke with him about his symptoms, and don't promise him anything.

Third, listen to what he has to say, listen a long time, and listen many times, alone and without interruption.

Fourth, listen without censoriousness in word or expression, without rebuke, ridicule, or amusement. Absurd as aspects of them may be, your patient's maladjustments are not funny to him.

Fifth, give no advice, no treatment, and no opinion until you know what the patient is really unhappy about; then tell him that such unhappiness *could be* (not *is*) the cause of such symptoms.

Sixth, gradually help the patient to see the connection between his unhappiness and his symptoms and to realize that he must assume the responsibility for such changes in his techniques or his environment as will be likely to give him greater peace. This, rather than allowing him to throw all responsibility on the doctor, is the rational and only permanently successful method of helping him.[17]

3. PSYCHOANALYSIS AS A TREATMENT METHOD

Carried to its logical extreme, the talking-it-out method leads to psychoanalysis. But psychoanalysis as a treatment technique involves much more than merely the confessing of memories. In fact, the "confessing" stage soon passes, and the patient begins to recall and relate a great mass of material that may seem unimportant and often seems highly fantastic. Parts of James Joyce's *Ulysses* sound precisely like the *free associations* of patients undergoing psychoanalysis. There may be much "filler" —many apparently meaningless trivia, much circumlocution, but eventually this and that memory begin to link up, and together with the recollections inspired by dreams, and the inter-

[17] The art of the psychiatric approach is nowhere more explicitly delineated than in Kenneth E. Appel and Edward A. Strecker's *Practical Examination of Personality and Behavior Disorders* (New York: The Macmillan Co., 1936). Chapter one should be read by every physician essaying this work. See also Footnote 7 on page 378.

pretation of those dreams, the patient gradually begins to complete the memory record of childhood in such a way as to understand the apparent meaninglessness of his present dilemma. He has discovered beyond any question of a doubt various unsuspected motives, wishes, fancies, fears, misapprehensions; and these, together with the emotional charges associated with them including the efforts necessary to repress them, are released, relinquished, and revised. The actual treatment comes to be a struggle between the patient's desire to get well and his desire to avoid that necessity — and in practice this means a struggle between his transference and his resistance.

Transference

During the course of the prolonged psychoanalytic treatment, not only does the patient review significant portions of his past life, but to a certain extent he tends to act them out. He does not actually reproduce the early situations and experiences, but he reads into contemporary happenings some of the meaning that earlier experiences held for him, and in doing so he takes the analyst as a prototype of persons who were the leading characters in his early life drama — usually his parents. This phenomenon of unconscious displacement of emotion from another time and situation and person to the psychotherapeutic treatment session and to the psychotherapist is known as *transference,* and it is one of the most powerful tools used in psychoanalytic treatment. In the hands of a clumsy and untrained amateur therapist it may well prove to be double-edged, for, unable to understand and interpret the illogical changes of mood, the apparently reasonless shifts of emotion from extreme graciousness and compliance to antagonism and stubborn resistance, he may react to this provocative behaviour subjectively, much as the patient's family and friends do, and thus lose control of the therapeutic situation. This control consists essentially in allowing the patient to express his emotional drives, under controlled conditions, to an objective non-censorious therapist who does not permit himself to react emotionally. Under these conditions the psychoanalyst is able to appraise the transference phenomena as indicative of the patient's dominant strivings and to interpret them to the patient who has never before been in a position to find out why he behaves as he does. It should be explained that the patient does not see the psychoanalyst as a dispassionate observer; his opinions of the analyst throughout a large part of the treatment are coloured by the strong emotion he attaches to him as first one and then another of the characters in his life drama. But this very emotion is one of the forces which the psychoanalyst uses in the reconstruction of the personality — first by diverting it from unworthy, unfruitful, or outdated outlets, and then by redirecting it into productive channels. When this result is accomplished, the patient no longer has need of the therapist and the transference situation automatically comes to an end.

This will be made more understandable by a superficial analysis of one of my own patients, whom I will call Mrs. Cooper.

Mrs. Cooper had been treated by a large number of methods, in the hands of a large number of doctors, for a large number of symptoms, without avail. One of her physicians sent her to me.

She insisted that I resembled her father, for whom she had as a child a boundless love and admiration. There were some physical resemblances; a moustache, a certain gait, a kind of fingers. Her father had been a school-teacher and she was always interested in the fact that I was teaching in college. Her father had studied medicine at one time, as of course I had. Her father had been interested in psychology, which is related to psychiatry. Her father had had two daughters and a son, which she ascertained to be true of me. Her father's views on certain subjects were, as she recalled them, about the same as my own.

But much more important than these factual details was the fact that she was acting toward me precisely as she had acted toward her father thirty years previously and toward numerous other men since then — including her husband — all of whom she *unconsciously* identified with her father.

Thus, for all the plausibility of this explanation, the astute reader will see that these discoveries are not the reasons for this patient's transference to me, but were discovered as the result of it. In other words, she found all these reasons to justify her for feeling as she did. She felt toward me as she once had toward her father. Patients expect physicians to have a maternal or paternal attitude toward them, to sympathize with them and want to help them out of their distress. This attitude more than the particular facts of similarity enable the patient to identify a doctor with his or her father or even mother and feel and act toward the doctor as they once did toward their mother or father.

A curious consequence of tranference, which will further illustrate the nature of the phenomenon, is what is called the *transference cure*. Every psychiatrist has had scores of patients who have been sick for a long time with a nervous illness and who are miraculously cured after a few interviews with him. He may or may not say anything worth saying. In these particular cases it doesn't matter. The patient is cured if he or she happens to develop a strong transference and feels that the physician's attitude is reciprocal. This does not mean that the physician must love him or her in the ordinary sense, but that he must be loving in the same way that the original person of the transference — that is, the mother or father — was loving.

The only trouble about these cures is that they last only so long as the transference lasts, and such a transference depends upon renewed contacts. This is why some people are well as long as they keep running to the doctor, even though he may appear to do nothing for them.

The fact that a patient under psychoanalytic treatment develops a transference to the analyst often becomes apparent first in the dreams related by the patient. Patients who would never admit any such conscious feelings will bring dreams which frankly involve them in affairs or situations with the doctor. Naturally these afford them some embarrassment, but this is because they only partly understand them.

Other patients are still more subtle in announcing their transference.

For example, a patient of mine dreamed that a certain Mr. Jones of her acquaintance had handed her a flower. Presently she recalled that Mr. Jones was an undertaker and mentioned with a smile that she thought I had undertaken a good deal when I had undertaken to analyse her neurosis. She went on to mention half a dozen characteristics of Mr. Jones more or less applicable to myself, and soon it became apparent that in the dream Mr. Jones represented me. The symbolism of handing a woman a flower probably needs no clarification. Its romantic meaning and its psychoanalytic meaning have precisely the same basis. The dream, like all dreams, represented a repressed wish delicately cast, and it indicated transference because, after all, it was not I she desired, but one for whom I stood.

A *negative transference* always underlies the *positive transference* and must be brought out if a psychoanalysis is successful. The Mrs. Cooper described above who thought so well of me at first began to find many a fault with me later on and denounced me bitterly for matters which careful examination proved to be unimportant or non-existent. Her real grudge against me was that I did not make her my favourite child or perhaps even my bride, and this was of course the same reproach which she had felt toward her father when she was a little girl. Much as she had loved him, she had been embittered because he did not make as much of her as she would have liked, but seemed to prefer her sister.

Thus it can be seen that the patient relives his childhood, fulfils ungratified desires and expresses the unmentionable hates of that period, using the analyst as a convenient peg to hang them on. Ultimately he becomes able to take an objective view not only of the analyst but of other people. Then he is well. This temporary emotional utilization of the therapist is what we mean by transference.

Let us return for another example to Marie Baker, the patient described at length in Chapter IV as illustrating the disastrous effects of over-fixation of the child's love and hate on the parents.

Marie was, in actual life, treated by psychoanalysis, and this is a telescoped account of what happened: After she had told the story of her life in detail, which took several weeks of daily talks, she ran out of subject-matter. But she was directed to go on talking, relating whatever occurred to her. At first this seemed absurd and meaningless to her. Gradually certain things were recalled in regard to her father's devotion to her, her antagonism to her mother, her aunt's evil-minded prudery, her misconceptions of sex, her first realizations of physical love, things which she had long since forgotten. She recalled definitely some of the actual incidents of her childhood which led to her over-attachment to her father and to her antagonism to her mother; she traced this dominant father-attraction through its various replicas in her superficial flirtations and Platonic love-affairs, and the obverse of it in her sudden passionate attraction to the one so unlike her father and so disliked by him. She came to see that when this last effort at satisfactory love-adjustment, this one real and yet unworthy outlet for her love demands was withdrawn, the currents of her love stream became totally disorganized. She was torn hither and thither by a storm of impulses, inhibited in their aim, and tending in all directions, so that the net result was impotent distress — her nervous illness.[18]

---

[18] Freud pointed out long ago that attacks of nervousness or " neurosis " are brought on by one of two situations (or combinations thereof) :

(1) The presentation of an opportunity for libidinous investment (that is, for

During the analysis Marie was frequently impelled to break it off, as she had broken off all other relationships in her life, prematurely. She was not always aware of this motive at first. She would suddenly feel as if it were useless to go on; she wasn't getting anywhere; it didn't do her any good; she was just as bad as when she started; it was silly, etc. None of these things were true, but she made them sound true, and believed them earnestly for a few days at a time. Then it would be finances — it was going to cost too much; she couldn't afford to go on; she wondered if the analyst wasn't charging her more than anyone else; she had heard rumours that sometimes he charged hundreds of dollars an hour; perhaps he would yet charge her on this basis. None of these notions were true, either, but at times they were serious obstacles.

Again she would wonder if there were anything to psychoanalysis, after all; perhaps the analyst was one of those quacks you read about; after all, who could tell? It would be easy to fool someone. Mrs. Smalley had a neighbour who said that the analyst was worse than a quack. Such lament as this served to voice her resentment by proxy; it also served to postpone looking at, verbalizing, accepting, or repudiating other material which was still too painful.

Again this resistance would appear in the form of long silences, refusals to speak, forgetting (?) to come or when to come, coming very late, etc. All of these efforts to dodge the hard work of analysis are typical of the experience. Sometimes they succeed in derailing the patient.

But usually the patient's persistence wins and a complete realignment and metamorphosis take place.

After a time Marie's sole interest was her analysis and her analyst. This continued until most of her conflicts had been ironed out. Then, in every analysis, comes the time when this temporary object must be properly displaced and ultimate objectives of a satisfactory sort substituted. The patient has to be permitted to walk on his or her own legs. The aim of psychoanalysis is to make the patient independent — independent of her neurosis and also independent of the various persons and things upon which she has always leaned. The last step is to make her independent of the analyst.

---

love, or for absorbing work, for achievement, etc.) which strains the powers of adaptation of the individual beyond his capacity; or (2) the withdrawal or loss of an outlet which has hitherto been satisfactory.

In Marie's case, of course, it was the second, as it is also in neuroses caused by the death of a loved one, jilting, etc. The first category includes such instances as those of the man who kills himself just after being promoted, and the woman who becomes ill immediately after getting married.

Marie had a hard time of it for a while. She dreaded to go — she fought against going — but she went. A year later she got the university degree which she had started out to get fifteen years before and which had been prevented by the neurotic crash. After graduation she first went home and spent a few days with the formerly intolerable mother and the over-fond but no longer enshrined father. Even her neurotic brother, Albert, with all his lamentations and complaints, did not in the least disturb her equanimity.

"You can get well, Albert, whenever you want to badly enough," she told him. "Just remember that. I moped around here for ten wasted years and look at me now. They all say I look that much younger. And I feel it. You can do it, but you've got to have the right help."

Marie then left the state and took a position in a store similar to that in which she had had so much experience. It was one of a chain of stores, and three years later Marie was cashier and auditor of the accounts of eight of these stores. This was nine years ago. Since then she has risen a little higher. She is well and happy.

So much for psychoanalysis from the doctor's, or analyst's, standpoint. How does it look to the patient? To answer this I know of nothing better than an article by Lucian Cary, a short-story writer and newspaper man, on "How it Feels to be Psychoanalyzed." [19] With Mr. Cary's permission, I am reprinting extracts from that article.

"I asked him [the psychoanalyst] if there was any cure, and he said he would see, and we started in.

"In the course of three or four sessions I told him the story of my life from my earliest memory on. I believed I was telling it honestly. The fact is, I made a pretty good story of it. The omissions were particularly well chosen.

"When I got through he told me to go on.

"I said: 'What?' Every child knows that trick. It gains time.

"He said: 'Go on with your story.'

"I said: 'I've finished.'

"He said: 'What's in your mind at this moment?'

"I said: 'It's a matter of no consequence.'

"He said: 'That's just what I want to know — the things you think are of no consequence, but that you don't want to tell.'

"'Well,' I said, 'it's about some rabbits.'

"He said: 'Go on.'

[19] *American Magazine,* May 1925.

" ' Once, when I was four or five years old, I was playing with a little girl of about the same age in our yard at home. A man plowing in a field nearby turned up a nest of new-born rabbits. He gave them to us and told us to drown them. We played with them until we were tired of them, and then she proposed that I drown them. She couldn't drown them but perhaps I could. Of course I would — wasn't I a boy? So I got a bucket of water on the back porch and drowned the rabbits.'

" I hesitated, feeling as if I were about to cry.

" ' Go on,' said the analyst.

" ' My mother came out of the house just then,' I said, with an effort not to cry, ' and saw the little dead rabbits in the bucket, and she said, " Lucian, how could you! " '

" ' How did you feel at the time? '

" ' I felt as if I had done something unforgivably wicked. I realize now,' I went on, ' that I've never mentioned that episode to another human being since. I've been ashamed to.'

" Telling the analyst the story as I have told it here gave me relief. I learned from him that all human beings carry around with them memories of their childhood too painful to tell — things they feel to have been sins no one else would commit. Getting these things out of your system, as the slang phrase goes, is good for you. And realizing that you aren't unique — realizing that you are human rather than wicked — is good for you.

" But confessing your painful memories is not psychoanalysis. The true psychoanalyst is interested in what you remember only because it stands in the way of what you cannot remember. The process of psy· choanalysis might be described as a process of helping you remember the situations of your childhood which were too painful to contemplate. The feelings that you have forgotten are said to be in the uncon‑ scious. The object of the psychoanalytic method is to make them conscious.

" Indeed, if I could have remembered the whole episode of the rabbits and all that it suggested, I should have remembered all the important feelings of my childhood. What is more, I might have been able to understand why I was suddenly unable to write any more stories.

" The chief method of helping you to remember what you have for‑ gotten is the analysis of dreams. I brought my analyst the following dream, written out:

" I was driving a car. I came to a cross street. The road I was travel‑ ing did not go any farther. I must turn either to the right or to the left.

A policeman stood at the crossing, in oilskins and a sou'wester hat. He pointed to the left. He said, 'You go that way.' I noticed that the road running to the right was crowded with traffic. The road to the left was free.

" The analyst asked me what came into my mind. After some difficulty, for I wasn't quite willing to tell him promptly the first thing that came into my mind, but preferred to tell him the second, or third or fourth thing, I began to do what he asked. I cannot set down all the things I said. It would take pages. But I can give you examples.

" ' Left,' said the analyst. ' What does that make you think of? '

" ' Right,' I said.

" ' Go on — fast,' he urged.

" ' Wrong — left-handed compliment — left-handed pitchers are better than right-handed — my father could write with either hand equally well — he shot from his left shoulder — he was a good shot — he made doubles on quail — I shoot from my right shoulder — my son, Peter, is left-handed — he is a fine boy.'

" That is what is called giving free associations. The method of translating a dream is a good deal like translating a foreign language. In translating a language you look up the words in a dictionary, and gradually dig out a meaning. In translating a dream you look up the words in your free associations — and gradually dig out a meaning.

" Your greatest difficulty in translating your dreams with the aid of an analyst arises from your unwillingness to find out the meaning. If you were perfectly free to announce to the analyst every idea that came into your head; if you weren't in the least afraid of what the dream might convict you of — you wouldn't need to be analyzed. You will not get very far in translating your dreams without discovering impulses in yourself that you would hesitate to hang on a hyena, no matter how noble your life has been.

" I continued for three or four months to take dreams to my analyst without learning anything very important about myself. My resistance was childishly stubborn and ingenious. I constantly inveigled my analyst into discussions of psychoanalytic theory. Such discussions between analyst and patient do not help any more than stopping to argue about the theory and practice of excavation in hard pan helps two men to dig a ditch.

" Instead of recognizing that I was more interested in arguing than in digging, I decided that I was practically cured. I thought that if I had a secretary I could work. I left off my attempt to find out why I couldn't work."

After a " lay-off," Mr. Cary tackled it again and this time went much further in discovering the contradiction between his conscious and his unconscious motives, traits, aims, etc. He discovered the reason for his persistent failure, and recognized other failures which he had previously failed to see. He goes on to list the changes he discovered in himself after his analysis — his greater honesty with himself, his greater willingness to face reality and renounce infantilisms, his greater efficiency, his better physical health, his lessened anxieties.

" But the result of analysis that interests me most is my increased enjoyment of life. The things I don't like, but have to do, such as going to the dentist, are less painful than they used to be. The things I like, I like better than I used to. I like my family better. I like playing tennis better. I like writing better.

" Nevertheless, I do not advise everybody to go and do likewise.

" An average analysis takes an hour a day, six days a week, for eight or nine months.[20] As long as you are being analyzed, and for six months or so afterwards, you are advised not to make any important decision; not to marry if you aren't married; not to start proceedings for a divorce if you are married; not to choose a new life work. This is because the important effects of analysis do not appear for some time after the analysis is completed. It takes time to make a new adjustment to life. At best, analysis will take a year out of your life. . . .

" Competent analysts are very scarce. I have just counted off a list of fifteen American analysts of whose equipment I have some knowledge. Of these fifteen, only five have met the essential requirement of submitting themselves to a thorough analysis, and of these five only three are using the improved Freudian methods. [There are many more, now. K.A.M.]

" Finally, psychoanalysis is an extremely painful ordeal. It forces you day after day to make admissions about yourself that you don't want to make; to give up, one after another, your dearest illusions about yourself; to see that your predicament in life is nobody's fault but your own; to face the facts about yourself. Your family and friends will not, as a rule, be sympathetic to your enterprise. They will tell you of people who have gone crazy or committed suicide as a result of psychoanalysis.

" In closing, I might mention the fact that psychoanalysis frequently fails. Many people who undertake to be analyzed fail to go through

---

[20] This is a minimum time; many analyses take a year or two for their completion, some even longer.

with it. Analysts are often compelled to dismiss patients simply because they are unable or unwilling to stand the pain of being disillusioned about themselves.

"Psychoanalysis, however successful, does not insure a happy or an easy life. All life is struggle. And all human lives involve painful choices. The attempt of psychoanalysis is to resolve the unconscious struggle in your own soul, and thus release the energy that is being wasted there, for your conscious purposes." [21]

4. HYPNOANALYSIS AND NARCOSYNTHESIS

These are discussed on pages 414–15.

TREATMENT BY CHANGE OF ENVIRONMENT

Sometimes we must change the environment before we can change the patient. But there are wise and unwise ways to do this — scientific ways and unscientific ways, safe ways and dangerous ones.

Too often doctors and laymen alike resort to "flight" methods of treatment without considering the real nature of the illness. No one is ever made sick merely by his environment — that is one of our fundamental principles. It is the combination of personality trends *and* environment, and the effects they have produced in each other in the past. Just taking a trip, as is so often foolishly advised, in no way solves the problems of the maladjusted. Travel as far as they like, they cannot escape the internal problems, they cannot get away from themselves. And frequently the trip treatment actually aggravates the trouble.

"Traveling is a fool's paradise," said Emerson, in his essay on *Self-Reliance*. ". . . At home I dream that at Naples, at Rome, I can be intoxicated with beauty, and lose my sadness. I pack my trunk, embrace my friends, embark on the sea, and at last wake up in Naples, and there beside me is the stern Fact, the sad self, unrelenting, identical, that I fled from. I seek the Vatican, and the palaces. I affect to be intoxicated with sights and suggestions, but I am not intoxicated. My giant goes with me wherever I go."

[21] For the inquirer who is unacquainted with psychoanalysis, *Psychoanalysis Explained* by Dorothy R. Blitzsten (New York: Coward McCann, 1936) is a clear, simple, non-technical explanation of the fundamental ideas which can be read easily in one hour. Another excellent book, especially for physicians, regarding the practical details of psychoanalysis is Kubie's *Practical Aspects of Psychoanalysis* (New York: W. W. Norton, 1936).

A change in the patient's residence, vocation, companions is frequently indicated. Temporary boarding home care for problem children is often of great benefit.[21a] More frequently it is necessary only to change certain conditions or attitudes that prevail in the environment, and in this direction the assistance of *psychiatric social workers* is now considered indispensable. The modern psychiatric social worker studies the patient with the psychiatrist and assists in his treatment by interpreting him to the environment and in some instances the environment to him. The functions of the psychiatric social worker now include counselling the members of the family or the employer, seeking the appropriate home or job, presenting opportunities for work and play to patients inhibited in spontaneously discovering these, and in some instances continuing therapeutic contacts with patients under the direction of a psychiatrist. (For a further discussion of the function of the social worker, see Chapter VI.)

By far the majority of the psychiatrists' patients are seen outside the walls of the sanitarium or hospital. But there are some who need hospitalization and do not get it. That a melancholy man or a suspicious, deluded woman needs to enter a hospital as urgently as does a person with acute appendicitis is not yet common knowledge.

Such patients need to be hospitalized:

1. To expedite recovery, since home treatment for such cases is worse than useless; it is apt to aggravate the illness;

2. To protect the patient from himself, from the uncomprehending relatives, from the meddlesome neighbours and friends;

3. To protect the public, because the mentally sick are prone to strange and antisocial acts in accordance with their delusions and feelings, and not in accordance with public welfare or expectations.

Once in a hospital for the treatment of mental sickness, what happens to the patient? How is he treated?

TREATMENT METHODS OF ONE HUNDRED YEARS AGO

Let us first recall how the psychiatric patient was *formerly* treated in a hospital, only a few generations ago.

" It is difficult for anyone familiar with existing conditions to realize the state of English asylums when George III. was king. We cannot

---

[21a] See " Boarding Home Plan of the Southard School," *Bulletin of Menninger Clinic,* March 1943.

understand how such appalling neglect and thoughtless cruelty could be tolerated. But in those times people were not easily moved by the sufferings of others, nor was the public conscience sensitive in respect to oppression, whether in asylums, prisons, or factories.

" Until 1777 it was one of the regular sights of London to visit the ' lunaticks in Bedlam,' and at one time a regular income of 400 pounds per annum was obtained from fees paid by sightseers. In the early part of the seventeenth century appeared a song, ' The Tower of Bedlam,' in which the ' licentiated beggar ' alludes to his asylum life:

> ' In the lovely lofts of Bedlam,
>   In stubble soft and dainty;
>   Brave bracelets strong,
>   Sweet whips, ding dong;
>   And a wholesome hunger, plenty.'

" The conditions under which the insane lived were indescribably bad. It was the universal practice to chain troublesome patients in dark cells; they were bedded with straw like cattle; their keepers were frequently persons of the lower class, and there was neither appeal nor hope of inquiry into their complaints. Unhappily, the medical men of the day defended the existing régime, and declared that no other course was possible. The routine treatment included blood-letting, starvation, purging, blistering, surprise baths, and whippings, and any method of inducing fear or terror was approved. Dr. Cox, in his book, ' Practical Observations on Insanity,' published in 1804, spoke highly of a machine into which four patients were strapped, which, when worked by a windlass, formed a sort of horizontal swing, revolving a hundred times a minute. . . .

" Even the King of England, when he became insane, did not escape ill-treatment. For the greater part of three months, he wore a straightjacket, he was flogged, his feet were blistered, and tradition says that he was knocked down by his attendant ' as flat as a flounder.' " (From Bedford Pierce, op. cit., *infra,* page 409.)

THE MODERN PSYCHIATRIC HOSPITAL

The atmosphere, equipment, and methods of the modern psychiatric hospital are very different [21b] from those of a hundred years ago and also from those of the modern general medical

21b Thanks in particular to Dorothea Dix. See Helen Marshall's *Dorothea Dix: Forgotten Samaritan* (Chapel Hill: University of North Carolina Press, 1937).

hospital. The patient enters an environment in which his peculiar sufferings are recognized as personal problems which deserve serious consideration, sympathy, and help. This is a great relief to the person who comes from the average community where his ideas and actions are considered queer, ludicrous, or disgraceful, as the case may be. In the hospital there is provided for him an environment suited to his wishes and needs, far away from the surroundings where his affliction developed. He is protected from the difficult and confusing everyday world and oftentimes from his own self-destructive tendencies; he is tended with unfailing kindliness and consideration no matter how combative or unresponsive he may be; he is made as comfortable as possible, both physically and mentally, so that he may find rest from the torment he is in; and he is surrounded by others whose sufferings are akin to his own, which helps him to objectify himself. The question is often asked by unthinking persons: " Does it make the patient worse to associate with other ill persons? " Actually the reverse is true; the tolerance and forbearance and helpful sympathy of the patients for one another is one of the rewarding and hopeful aspects of hospital life.

Of the relationships formed in the psychiatric hospital my brother, Dr. William C. Menninger, has said:

" It is not wisdom to maintain the mentally sick patient in this individualized environment indefinitely. He must gradually win his way back until he is able to leave the artificially created atmosphere and re-enter the world of reality.

" The emotional response which he develops toward the persons who provide this haven for him and who minister with such understanding to his wishes, conscious and unconscious, is the chief factor in the process of recovery. The hospital building and all the material armamentarium are of little importance compared with the personality relationships that exist between the patients and the members of the staff. Every doctor is familiar with the part that confidence plays in the treatment of his patients and he is aware also of the influence, adverse or favorable, of relatives and friends on his patients. This familiar principle must be capitalized and greatly reinforced by making it a matter of study and practice of every employee of the institution. Every member of the personnel must be interested not only in carrying out his particular routine function, but also in contributing something personal to this ruling principle.

SCIENTIFICALLY CONTROLLED FRIENDSHIP: THE DAILY SCHEDULE

"This principle must be carried out in a systematic way, with specific application to the needs of each patient. One way to insure this is to give each patient a schedule of assigned activities selected particularly for him at the beginning of each week. This not only informs him that he is being given individual consideration, but also maintains a continued plan of prescribed therapeutic attack with opportunity for successive personal contacts in occupational therapy, recreational therapy, physical therapy, reading, music, and other creative efforts, rest, psychotherapy, and study groups. The friendly relationships which the patient forms in the course of his schedule transform this daily plan from a progression from one unrelated unit of treatment to another into a continuous process of treatment facilitated by varied occupations." [22]

Certain technical things help to create the desired atmosphere of confidence and reassurance in the hospital and assist in rebuilding mentally sick patients. There is always a degree of exhaustion, both physical and mental, which must be counteracted by external measures such as ultra-comfortable beds, pleasant, attractively furnished, and well-ventilated rooms, easy access to toilet facilities, and day and night nursing care (there are no call bells in mental hospitals — the nurses are never far away from any patient). Clean, cheerful living-rooms, and appetizing, nourishing food are essential.

Special treatment:
Massage is valuable because of the stimulation it affords to the circulation as well as because of the soothing and agreeable nature of its effects. *Hydrotherapy* (bath treatment) is of even greater benefit in many cases, because of its sedative effect. It also has a definite psychotherapeutic effect which is as yet not fully understood, but empirically acknowledged.[23]

Occupational therapy: This is the training and guiding of patients in various handicraft work — weaving, basketry, carpentry, pottery-making, sewing, etc. This is not done merely to occupy the patient's hands or mind; in a larger sense, it brings to the patient the stimulus of accomplishment of a creative piece of work. The awakening effects of such treatment for souls dis-

[22] William C. Menninger: "Therapeutic Methods in a Psychiatric Hospital," *Journal of the American Medical Association,* Vol. XCIX, pp. 538–42 (August 13, 1932).
[23] See W. C. Menninger and M. Cutrer: "Psychological Factors in Physiotherapy," *American Journal of Psychiatry,* May 1937.

couraged and disheartened by long inactivity and incapacity in some instances are marvellous. Furthermore, it brings the patient into a social group and enables him to develop friendships.

" For example, Mary B's schedule on Wednesday at 10 o'clock reads, ' Occupational Therapy: sewing on a quilt; ' but Mary reads into this something far more personal and satisfying, because her doctor, who is interested in ships, drew for her pictures and diagrams of the many kinds of sailing ships. These Mary painstakingly traced on cloth of her own choosing and cut out white sails and appliquéd them on a blue sea with infinite care and devotion. This project was artistically conceived and executed by the patient as a gift for her doctor. The work began while she was lying listlessly in her bed, depressed and weeping, but as the quilt progressed, it necessitated contacts with other people; she must choose materials and use the sewing machine; finally she began to enter into the other activities of the hospital. Thereafter her progress was rapid." [24]

" A middle-aged man, a banker, with a similar mental picture, was persuaded to supervise the building of a croquet court. Even in the hottest summer weather he took pleasure in putting in long hours and much hard work directing the laying out and construction of the court. Before it was completed, he was ready for discharge but decided to stay an additional month until the job was finished. In another example, two men, one with a typical depression and the other with alcoholic addiction, worked over a period of weeks constructing an outdoor barbecue oven, which when completed was the scene of a christening party and many felicitations. Their initials were duly inscribed on the cement work of the oven. On each subsequent friendly visit of these two men they inspect and comment on this highly therapeutic experience." [25]

Recreational therapy: This method of treatment is carried out in recreational activities with particular success. The director of recreation skilfully leads the patient to express an interest in some sport or hobby and then uses this to establish a common bond and to draw him into a social situation where he co-operates with other players. In free play, preferably outdoors, the patient is often enabled to externalize his conflicts and to express

[24] Ibid.
[25] William C. Menninger: " Psychiatric Hospital Therapy Designed to Meet Unconscious Needs," *American Journal of Psychiatry,* Vol. XCIII, p. 539 (September 1936) . See also, by the same author, " Psychoanalytic Principles Applied to the Treatment of Hospitalized Patients," *Bulletin of the Menninger Clinic,* Vol. 1, pp. 35–43 (November 1926) .

his aggressions in friendly fashion. Parties, clubs, picnics, out-
ings, concerts, and plays are prescribed according to the individual patient's needs and preferences and furnish a powerful
socializing influence.

" In recreational therapy, there are also many opportunities for socially approved expression of hostilities or destructive tendencies. An
agitated depressed man, who complained bitterly of the unfairness of his
family and the neglect on the part of his physicians, was always greatly
relieved when he returned from a half hour session with the punching
bag. To facilitate the transfer of the aggression to the bag a face was
drawn on the bag with chalk. A schizophrenic girl had vented her
wrath and criticism on various members of her family, all of whom she
felt had meddled to the extent of ruining her life. Her most satisfying
relief was obtained when she would name her practice golf balls after
her relatives and swing at them with all the pent-up hostility she felt
towards these persons. Another schizophrenic girl had slammed the
doors at home for five years until every door in the house was off its
hinges. At other times she had kicked the radio off the table, broken
the furniture, smashed windows and had committed other destructive
aggressive acts directed toward her parents. In the hospital, she took
up bowling, and after she began naming the number one ten pin after
her parents became one of the best women bowlers we have had. I
should mention that she never bowled prior to coming to the hospital.
Her improvement was striking and we believe that no small part was
due to the recreational therapy. . . . Likewise, recreational therapy affords numerous outlets for fantasy expression, especially as applied to
dramatics and music. An acutely ill schizophrenic woman refused all
invitations to therapeutic activity except to sit at the piano and compose
music. Even while entertaining the delusion that she was the Virgin
Mary, she took up interpretative dancing which, without coaching or
training, she did with extraordinary grace and ability. Through these
two opportunities for expression she began an improvement that resulted in a social recovery." [26]

The way in which reading is employed as a means of securing
the patient's confidence is shown in this incident:

For many weeks after her admission to the hospital a hypomanic patient repulsed the psychotherapist, regarding his attempts to gain her
confidence as a repetition of what she called the insincere attitude of her
double-crossing relatives. Finally, he brought her a copy of *Moby Dick*
and discussed with her at some length his interest in the story and its

[26] Ibid.

significance as an allegory. A few days later with self-deprecating bravado she gave him a longhand copy of the chapter called " The Lee Shore," with the explanation that she had awakened early one morning and copied it because she liked it so much. In that eloquent chapter she found a sympathetic description of her own flight, which caused her to relax her resistance and thus allow a positive transference to begin.

Other interests which are often used to enlist the patient's interest include music, painting, writing, language study, nature study, etc. Of course all regular medical and surgical treatments and methods are also applied in mental hospitals as in any others.

The function of the psychiatric hospital is certainly not that of caring for the helpless, aged parents whose children are annoyed by the slight inconvenience caused them by those who once took such infinite pains to relieve their discomforts and fears.

The average person has no idea how frequently children attempt to " unload " their helpless parents on state hospitals in the pretended belief that they are mentally ill to a degree necessitating such treatment. Sometimes, of course, it is the wisest thing to do, but more often it is a method for gaining premature control of an inheritance or taking advantage of the generosity of the state. Fortunately, there is an increasing tendency among state hospital executives to decline to admit such cases.

THE PSYCHIATRIC NURSE

The development of the modern psychiatric hospital, with its emphasis upon individual diagnosis and individual treatment, is an enormous advance over the methods of caring for the mentally sick only a few decades ago.[27] But more striking, even, than the advances in equipment and clinical methods are the changes in the character of the nursing personnel and their attitude toward their patients. The personality of the nurse has much to do with the recovery of the patients in her care, for, as my brother has reminded us, she has twenty-four hours a day in which to in-

[27] Yet 1,500 years ago Cœlius Aurelianus placed his patients " under the best conditions of light, temperature, and quiet; and recommended that everything of an exciting character should be excluded. Of particular interest are his references to tactfulness in attendants for the avoidance of antagonism, and to the limited and cautious use of physical restraint. . . . Theatricals, entertainment, riding, walking, and work were all recommended, particularly during convalescence. . . . He denounced semi-starvation, bleeding, chains, and excessive drug therapy." D. K. Henderson and R. D. Gillespie: *A Textbook of Psychiatry* (London: Oxford University Press, 1927) , p. 2.

fluence the patients, while few doctors spend more than a fraction of this time with them. Not only her personality, however, but her training must be adapted to this type of work. A nurse skilful in the care of surgical patients, for example, cannot on the basis of this experience and her general hospital training be a competent nurse for psychiatric patients. Psychiatric nursing is a specialty within nursing just as psychiatry is a specialty within medicine.[28]

The following excerpts from a series of lectures to psychiatric nurses [29] give some idea of their attitudes and ideals.

" Now, it is quite true that some patients show a great deal of badness, or of what would be pure badness in you or me, but we must always remember that this is the result of their illness. . . .

" You must remember that it was this very illness which made it necessary to send them from their homes and place them here. You must therefore put up with them, and do your best for them. You cannot punish them as bad children, you cannot order them about as inferiors and command obedience. What are you to do? Well, you must earnestly set yourself to gain some influence over them and get them to help you in something useful or pleasant, so as to lead them unconsciously to forget their disagreeable habits and tendencies, to behave more reasonably, and gradually to regain the sense of what is right, and the wish to do it, which illness destroyed.

" I hear a whisper, ' I should like to see you influencing so-and-so! ' There never was a human being that could not be influenced. Never, never! But how is it done? Well, first of all, and chiefly, by what you are yourself. You will never influence anyone until they discover that you are worthy of their respect. Personal character is, after all, the basis of the whole thing — and patients are very keen judges, although you may not think so. Patients sum up a nurse very soon. If they see that he is a man trying to do the right, a man who always speaks the truth, who is never unkind, or rough or harsh, who is just the very same whether the doctor is about or not — they very soon learn that such a man is worthy of respect and of trust and they do respect and trust him, and yield to his influence and guidance. . . .

" I do not know what quality comes first — so many high qualities

[28] See Isabel Erickson: " The Psychiatric Nurse," *American Journal of Nursing,* Vol. XXXV, pp. 351–2 (April 1935) ; and William C. Menninger: " The Needs and Opportunities in Psychiatric Nursing," *Hospitals,* Vol. XI, pp. 43–7 (January 1937) , and " Postgraduate Work in Psychiatric Nursing," *American Journal of Nursing,* Vol. XXXVII, pp. 186–7 (February 1937) .

[29] Dr. David Yellowlees in *Addresses to Mental Nurses,* collected by Bedford Pierce (London, 1924) .

are wanted for this work. Very likely I should use a word which may be less familiar to you because it is a Scotch rather than an English word. I should not even say kindness so much as *kindliness*. Kindliness means kindness and something more. It means a pleasant way of doing a kind thing. There are some people who do kindnesses in such a grumpy manner, in such an unpleasant sort of way, that there is no comfort in getting kindnesses from them. The giving of kindnesses seems to give them no happiness, and therefore it gives little to the person who benefits by it. If you want to give pleasure you must do kind things in a kindly fashion. It doubles a kindness if it is kindly done. Let us therefore practice kindly patience — patience above all! I know your patience is often terribly taxed. I know well how difficult it is to be always calm and self-restrained. No one can sit long in a ward and see what the nurses have to do, without feeling how trying and difficult their work is, and that it requires very high personal character to live up to it, and do it well. . . .

" Depressed patients, as you know, always give great anxiety by their suicidal tendency, and need constant care and watching, but they are not the most trying. The most trying to the staff are the irritable, insolent, abusive patients. I have often and often felt sorry for the nurses on account of the language they had to listen to, and the nasty insinuations they had to bear from patients who to all appearance knew better, and could have behaved better if they had liked. There is only one answer to abuse, and that is silence, still silence; and if you cannot be silent without rudeness, ignore the abuse as if it had never been spoken, and be sure that you reply calmly and politely.

" The object of all the insolence and nastiness is to wound and hurt you and to make you writhe under it. But if you show that you are not hurt or angry the abuse has failed, and it is not worth while to continue it; so the patient stops, seeing that she might as well have scolded the chimney-piece. There should be no sign of resentment, and no angry retort; behave just as usual, and as if you had not heard the abuse. If you have to speak, let it be with perfect politeness."

It can be seen from this how different the work of the psychiatric nurse is from that of the general duty nurse and how important attitudes and psychological understanding are. Experience has shown that it is not possible to inculcate these attitudes in all nurses, no matter how competent the training, and the newer emphasis in nursing education is on the more careful selection of those nurses who are allowed to enter this specialty. Psychological tests are now used for this purpose, as described on pages

178–80. In general, higher requirements in the way of intelligence, education, and, above all, emotional maturity are essential in psychiatric nurses. Meanwhile the demand for them far exceeds the supply.

NEW DEVELOPMENTS IN THERAPY

In the years that have elapsed since the publication of the first edition of this book and especially since the second edition, the rapid extension of the interest in psychiatry has stimulated an increasing amount of research into methods of treatment. Many new treatment devices have been discovered or proposed, tried out, found useless and abandoned or found promising and extended. Meanwhile older methods of treatment have been improved. The experience of the psychiatrists in the military forces of the Second World War will undoubtedly lead to the introduction of many additional techniques, so that a record such as this is necessarily transitory in nature.

Recent developments in treatment can be divided into three groups — the " shock " therapies, the medical and surgical therapies, and the psychological therapies.

I. SHOCK THERAPIES

Back in 1928 an Austrian internist (Sakel) was experimenting with large doses of insulin, an extract of certain glands in the pancreas, deficient function of which results in the disease known as diabetes. Quite unintentionally and accidentally he produced a state of unconsciousness with convulsions in some of his patients. Even more unexpected was the observation that following these " shocks " an improvement in the mental status occurred.

This led to the development of a type of treatment in which six to twenty such shocks are deliberately induced with one· to three-day intervals. This was first done in Vienna in 1933 and in America in 1936. It rapidly spread and has been widely used in psychiatric hospitals all over the world. The induction of insulin shock is not a simple matter, however, and for this reason another method of inducing convulsions introduced by a psychiatrist, Meduna of Budapest, about the same time became even more popular. As a matter of historical fact, this treatment, called metrazol shock, was first tried out in 1781 (by William Oliver of London), but it became generally accepted only in the past ten years. In general, it is regarded as less efficacious than insulin shock in schizophrenia and more efficacious in states of severe depression, especially those occurring in late middle life, sometimes called "involutional melancholia." Its use in this connection was introduced by Bennett.[30] Cases of this type that we formerly thought of as averaging several years in duration are now frequently restored to complete health within a few months.

A still more convenient and somewhat safer method of in- ducing shock is by the use of electrical stimulation of the brain. This was first done by Cerletti and Bini in Italy in 1937; it is now the most widely used method of shock treatment in this country and elsewhere. It is free from the disturbing sensations of apprehensiveness and even terror which accompany metrazol shock, and has an equal, if not superior, therapeutic effect.

Because the severe convulsions induced by all of these meth- ods sometimes cause minor muscle and bone injuries, a method of reducing the intensity of the convulsion was introduced by Bennett,[31] who used the South American arrow poison, curare, which has the effect of diminishing the intensity of the muscular contractions and hence the severity of the convulsions. In our own institution, for example, no shock treatment is ever given without this adjuvant, although many competent psychiatrists feel it to be unnecessary.

It is difficult to evaluate the shock treatments at the present time, because our experience is still relatively small and still growing, and widely different opinions are held by equally com- petent psychiatrists. I think we can say this safely: Some shock treatment certainly benefits some cases of some types of severe mental illness and sometimes results in a complete cure. This does not occur in a majority of instances, however. It is a treat- ment not without danger and, in the opinion of many psychia- trists, it is not the treatment of choice. We have no definite knowledge as to why it has a therapeutic effect.[32]

[30] A. E. Bennett: "Convulsive Pentamethylenetetrazol Shock Therapy in De- pressive Psychoses," *Bulletin of the Menninger Clinic,* July 1938. For an excellent summary see: "An Evaluation of Metrazol Treatment," by William C. Mennin- ger, *Bulletin of the Menninger Clinic,* July 1940.

[31] A. E. Bennett: "Preventing Traumatic Complications in Convulsive Shock Therapy by Curare," *Journal of the American Medical Association,* January 27, 1940.

[32] See Byron Stewart: "Present Status of Shock Therapy in Neuropsychiatry with Special Reference to Prevention of Complications," *Bulletin of the Mennin- ger Clinic,* January 1942, for an excellent summary.

II. MEDICAL AND SURGICAL THERAPIES

The treatment of syphilis of the brain (see pages 42–5) has continued to make progress. Improvements have been made in the compounding of arsenic, mercury, and bismuth preparations which are poisonous to the organism and relatively non-poisonous for human beings. These are injected into the blood-stream and carried to the tissues where the spirochetes are multiplying. Another method of treatment, based on an observation made as long ago as 1819, but developed in 1919 by von Jauregg, consists in the induction of fever in the patient by inoculating him with malaria, or placing him under an electric blanket, or, still more recently, exposing him to high-frequency short waves which increase body temperature. All of these methods produce results; the spirochetes are killed or inhibited and the disease process tends to recede. The once hopeless condition of general paresis can now be said to have a fairly good prognosis if early recognized and properly treated.

Surgical therapy in psychiatry is a recent introduction, and while by no means as established as heat treatment or shock therapy, it should be mentioned because it has had wide publicity in the lay press. Freeman and Watts [33] tried the experiment of cutting certain fibre tracts in the brain of severely disturbed mental patients on the theory that disturbing impulses would thus be prevented from reaching consciousness. They faced the fact that these tracts would never be regenerated and that the treatment might, therefore, result in permanent damage to the brain. This is approximately what clinical observation demonstrated. According to the reports in the medical literature, a few patients have improved clinically, some of them considerably, but evidence of brain damage is apt to be more or less manifest. The idea of operations upon the brain appeals to the imagination of the public and to those psychiatrists who are still influenced by the antiquated views of Benjamin Rush, whose insistence upon the brain (rather than the mind) as the centre of interest in psychiatry retarded the development of American psychiatry for so many years.[34] Most psychiatrists are definitely opposed to this type of treatment, certainly in its present state.

[33] *Psychosurgery* (Springfield: Charles C. Thomas, 1942).

[34] See " The Beginnings: From Colonial Days to the Foundation of the American Psychiatric Association," by Richard H. Shryock, in *One Hundred Years of American Psychiatry* (New York: Columbia University Press, 1944).

Drug therapies, on the other hand, are probably rarely harmful; but neither are they usually very effective. Two in particular have been used rather extensively: benzedrine sulphate, a cerebral stimulant that has somewhat the effect of coffee only "more so," and dilantin, which is an extraordinarily effective sedative for the convulsive disorders. In addition to these, certain other drugs are used in conjunction with psychotherapy, to be discussed below.

III. PSYCHOTHERAPY

The advances in psychotherapy are, in my opinion, far more important than those listed above, but they are technically more difficult and hence appeal to fewer physicians. It is much simpler to say to distressed relatives that a patient will be hospitalized and given some shock treatments or a brain operation than to explain to them that the patient is distressed by the things he does not fully understand and can be relieved by being given an opportunity to talk these things out under guidance with a properly trained auditor.

Nevertheless, talking things out and obtaining an understanding of oneself is a method of treatment, the philosophical basis of which dates back to Socrates and the scientific advocacy of which antedates Freud. The techniques of psychoanalysis and other forms of psychotherapy have been acquired by an increasing number of psychiatrists and have gained enormous ground in the treatment of neuroses and physical illnesses based on emotional disturbances. They have also been applied to more serious forms of mental illness.[35]

Various methods have been used recently to hasten the process of psychotherapy, which is often so slow. In psychoanalysis a patient coming day after day to his analyst and speaking freely whatever comes into his mind begins to recall memories and material that have been buried in the unconscious for years and he is thus able to see things in a different light. It is possible to

[35] Gregory Zilboorg: "The Deeper Layers of Schizophrenic Psychoses," *American Journal of Psychiatry*, 1931; Harry Stack Sullivan: "The Modified Psychoanalytic Treatment of Schizophrenia," *American Journal of Psychiatry*, 1931; Robert P. Knight: "Psychotherapy in Acute Paranoid Schizophrenia with Successful Outcome," *Bulletin of the Menninger Clinic*, 1939, and "Psychoanalysis of Hospitalized Patients," *Bulletin of the Menninger Clinic*, 1937; Dexter M. Bullard: "Experiences in the Psychoanalytic Treatment of Psychotics," *Psychoanalytic Quarterly*, 1940; and Frieda Fromm-Reichmann: "Psychoanalytic Psychotherapy with Psychotics," *Psychiatry*, 1943.

facilitate this recall by producing a modification of the field of consciousness by some drugs that induce a partial anæsthesia. Everyone knows how light doses of ether or laughing gas cause people to express thoughts ordinarily suppressed or repressed. But there are better drugs for this purpose than ether or nitrous oxide: amytal sodium, pentothal, and others. An aviator shocked by the destruction of his entire crew, brought into the hospital in terror and confusion with a complete amnesia for all that has happened, can be given an injection of such a drug and be enabled then to recall and verbalize the experiences he has been through, receive reassurance from the listening physician, and awaken in a state of relaxation and serenity. It does not always work this way, but it does sometimes — often enough to make this treatment (narcosynthesis) [36] an extremely promising one.

Another method of altering consciousness is the time-honoured one of *hypnosis*. The existence of the hypnotic trance has been known vaguely for centuries, but its deliberate induction by a physician intending to use this peculiar state for the therapeutic benefit of the patient is generally credited to Mesmer, a brilliant, erratic, Viennese physician, who, like many other geniuses, failed to win appropriate credit during his lifetime. It was hypnosis in the hands of Braid and Janet that really laid the foundation for modern psychiatric psychotherapy. But the method pursued a devious course. Breuer and Freud became interested in it, and through it discovered the method of free association, which for Freud, and psychoanalysts generally, superseded hypnosis. This is partly because hypnosis, as understood in the nineteenth century and indeed until very recently, depended upon the use of suggestion or commands given the patient during the trance state. The idea that the same altered state of consciousness induced by hypnotic techniques could be used to uncover forgotten and repressed emotional disturbances was only occasionally and unsystematically utilized.

A few years ago a patient who had suffered from seven years of acute neurotic illness was studied by the staff of our clinic who felt that she could be cured by psychoanalysis. For practical reasons, however, psychoanalysis was for her an impossibility. She volunteered as an experimental subject for the use of hypnosis as a method of speeding up the recall of the disturbing

[36] Roy R. Grinker and John P. Spiegel: *War Neuroses in North Africa* (New York: Josiah Macy, Jr., Foundation, 1943).

events and conflicts that were believed to be the cause of her illness. No commands were made to her and no suggestions beyond that of trying to recall how her illness began and what really disturbed her, and the suggestion that she herself could understand and interpret such dreams as occurred to her. She was encouraged to express her feelings toward the physicians and to compare them with the recollected feelings toward her parents. The result was that in the course of a few months this patient brought forth the material and gained the insight that a psychoanalytic patient would be expected to produce over a period five times as long. Furthermore, she was completely cured.[37]

This and similar experiences by these workers and others [38] has led to a renewed interest in the use of hypnosis as an adjuvant to psychoanalysis, and psychoanalytic principles as an adjuvant to hypnosis. It is still in an experimental stage, but may prove to be particularly useful in the " psychosomatic " conditions requiring short but penetrating psychotherapeutic treatment.

Finally, a word must be said for that more subtle method of altering consciousness in the direction of greater receptivity which is effected by the mutual stimulation of people under the influence of a leader. Group psychotherapy, meaning the administration of therapeutic benefit to more than one individual at a time, is of course implicit in the professional work of the minister. To use this method with sick people is, in one sense, directly antithetical to the emphasis upon individualization that has characterized modern psychiatry. Nevertheless, it would be unscientific to ignore the fact that people do influence one another in groups and do respond to a group situation. Group psychotherapy [39] is still in its early stages. It has already taken on various forms or techniques. Lectures and discussion groups dealing with mental hygiene principles, specially adapted educational films, spontaneous dramatic presentations, and various

[37] Merton M. Gill and Margaret Brenman: " Treatment of a Case of Anxiety Hysteria by an Hypnotic Technique Employing Psychoanalytic Principles," *Bulletin of the Menninger Clinic*, 7:163–71, 1943.

[38] M. H. Erickson and L. S. Kubie: " Successful Treatment of a Case of Acute Hysterical Depression by Return under Hypnosis to a Critical Phase of Childhood," *Psychoanalytic Quarterly* 10:583–609, 1941; M. H. Erickson: " Hypnotic Investigation of Psychosomatic Phenomena," *Psychosomatic Medicine*, 5:51–8, January 1943, and other publications.

[39] S. R. Slavson: *An Introduction to Group Therapy* (New York: The Commonwealth Fund, 1943) .

forms of recreation and group project work have been and are being tried.

MILITARY PSYCHIATRY

The whole field of military psychiatry, including the development of new ideas and screening, abbreviated interviews, problems of evacuated children, air-raid reactions, fatigue and exhaustion states, war neuroses, aviation psychiatry, and many other topics is too much in a state of flux for any summary at the time of this revision.[40]

PROGNOSIS

In all medical treatises it is customary to say something about the outlook for recovery of the conditions treated. While I have tried to imply something about this *parri passu* with the discussions on treatment, I am constrained to add a final definite word about it because of the astonishing frequency with which I am asked such questions as these: " Are mental cases ever cured? Do any of them get entirely well? Can you do anything for any of them? "

Such questions come not only from the laity but from medical students and physicians who thereby betray their own inner pessimism and lack of information concerning the field. As a matter of fact, *no branch of medical science with the exception of obstetrics is blessed by so many recoveries as is psychiatry.* Most psychiatric illnesses recover; even the most severe illnesses have a much better prognosis, statistically speaking, than is generally known. More than half of the patients who enter state hospitals are returned to civilian life, most of them able to do as much as or more than they did before they entered, and it should always be remembered that only the most advanced cases go to state hospitals. The earlier the treatment, the better the prognosis. All of us have our nervous illnesses, our attacks of mental sickness, and most of us recover from them without going to a psychiatrist. That the psychiatrist can facilitate the recovery is implicit in the material of this chapter.

[40] For a review of the field of army psychiatry in general, see the articles by Colonel W. C. Menninger and associates in the *Bulletin of the Menninger Clinic* for November 1944.

CHAPTER VI

APPLICATIONS

PHILOSOPHIC SECTION, DEALING WITH THE EXTENSIONS
OF PSYCHIATRIC THEORY

"It would seem that there are dragon-slayers and Grail-hunters. There are those who would prefer to be St. George and others who would rather be Sir Galahad. . . . Nor should we wish to swerve these zealots of the Grail from their goal. . . . [But for the rest of us] evil is easier to perceive than good is even to conceive. . . . We should, therefore, take advantage of this ingrained destructive trend and endeavor in the first instance to destroy definite, concrete and observable evils rather than to construct indefinite, abstract, hardly conceivable good. Let the proximate task of evil destruction be accomplished and the ultimate task of constructive goodness will shortly follow. The formula might run 'Get the Grail, but first slay the dragon.'"

—ELMER ERNEST SOUTHARD in *The Kingdom of Evils*

CHAPTER VI

APPLICATIONS

We began with the proposition that human life could be conceived of as the mutual adaptation of human beings and their environment, shutting our eyes for the time being to the philosophical truth that only for purposes of discussion can we make this arbitrary distinction between man and his environment since, after all, man is a part of his environment and helps to make it. Mankind has grown up in this illusion and hence for practical purposes we continue to speak of the personality versus the environment. In this chapter we shall consider aspects of the environment likely to yield useful indications with reference to a happier and, shall we say, healthier-minded race. The principles of psychiatry can be and have been extended beyond the individual, to organized social structures.

Theoretically, it might be possible to derive and express in genotypical terms laws of general application regarding the various human situations to which personalities attempting to adjust themselves often fail. But since I am a physician and think by force of habit in what the field theorists [1] call phenotypical terms — that is, in terms of clinical experience and such convenient, although artificial, conventions as individual and environment — I shall discuss them from that standpoint. The psychiatrist has learned from experience of certain particularly dangerous reefs, or, shall we say, he has learned that within certain great categories of human activity and interest there are always dangerous reefs. Marriage is one of these, one which has appeared in many of the examples already cited in this book. Education is another — I mean formal education, the educational system as it exists, learning according to rules and at the direction of teachers employed to instruct according to rules. Industry or, for the individual, the general problem of getting and holding a job — this is another reef-strewn sea. Then there are the circumstances created by the existence of organized legal

[1] See J. F. Brown, op. cit.

enactments and adjudication, the situation in which failure means crime. Finally, there is the matter of health; adjustment to the requirements of hygiene breaks some personalities.

Ernest Southard, author of the quotation at the beginning of this chapter, used to speak of the members of the Kingdom of Evils as ignorance, vice, crime, poverty, and disease. It is natural to suppose that psychiatry, familiar with the patterns of failure, should be able to contribute something to the understanding of failures related to this kingdom — educational failures, industrial failures, criminal failures, health failures. To what extent, and with what success, may be gleaned from the following pages.

The social application of psychiatry has been facilitated in a practical way by the development of a specialized profession, that of *psychiatric social work*. The function of the psychiatric social worker in psychiatric treatment has already been referred to (page 401). However, most educational failures, economic failures, and social failures do not come to psychiatrists, and to the extent that the principles of psychiatry can be useful in the alleviation of such social problems the skilled techniques of the psychiatric social worker are more widely available and more extensively utilized.

Medical social work as a profession has been in existence for nearly fifty years but psychiatric social work as a specialty within the profession was the creation of Dr. Ernest Southard and Miss Mary C. Jarrett at the Boston Psychopathic Hospital in 1913. This was furthered by the inauguration of a special training course in psychiatric social work at Smith College in 1918. Since then about twenty approved schools for training in psychiatric social work have been developed. In addition to this, most other schools of social work offer courses in psychiatry and the principles of human behaviour as a part of the basic training for all social workers.

The original impetus for the expansion of psychiatric social work was the need for technical assistants for psychiatrists working with the large number of neuropsychiatric casualties of World War I. Shortly after this, through the financial support of the Commonwealth Fund and the professional leadership of Dr. Lawson G. Lowrey, the *Child Guidance Clinic* idea was developed and demonstrated. This was the association of a psychiatrist, a psychologist, a social worker, a pediatrician, and a secretary or record clerk who worked together as a group in the study of problem children. The practical usefulness of such clinics to schools, children's agencies, welfare agencies, juvenile courts, and many other institutions, to say nothing of parents and the children themselves, made the idea very popular and these clinics were established in many cities throughout the country. The function of the psychiatric social worker in these clinics was so important that it was often necessary to have as many as four or six of them attached to one clinic.

In my opinion, the chief advantage of the Child Guidance Clinics was to demonstrate to the psychiatrists the important functions of social work and to social workers the usefulness of psychiatry. More and more psychiatric principles were inculcated into the attitudes and techniques of social workers and an increasing minority of them joined the ranks of the specialized psychiatric social work group. Meanwhile psychiatrists engaged in special health activities of all kinds, including clinics, state hospitals, and mental hygiene departments, have made increasing use of psychiatric social workers. In all of the social applications of psychiatry about to be presented, the psychiatric social worker serves a very important function.[1a]

I. EDUCATIONAL APPLICATIONS

There has been much misunderstanding about what the application of psychiatry and modern psychology to the education of children means, and this has been the occasion of merriment among those who hold that common sense is a better guide in child-rearing than scientific theory.

Modern education, from the viewpoint of the psychiatrist, does not aim to free the child from all inhibitions or to lift all repressions, but to allow him a natural development which will bring him to emotional as well as intellectual maturity. A natural development does not mean a régime in which the child does exactly as he pleases, for that would probably preclude

---

[1a] One of the important functions of the social workers in the psychiatric hospital is to explain to relatives things which they do not understand about the emergency that has suddenly confronted them, the nature of the hospital routine and regulations, the proper attitude to take toward the patient, the meaning of words used by the psychiatrist, etc. An excellent manual for relatives embodying this information has been prepared by Miss Edith M. Stern and Dr. Samuel Hamilton entitled *Mental Illness: A Guide to the Family.*

much of the social adjustment which we regard as an important part of development. There is no incentive to develop when one has everything one wants without effort. It means a plan of education which takes into account the child's *needs* as well as adults' *wishes*.

It has been assumed in the past that these two were synonymous. The investigations of Freud and his theory of the instinctive development of the child and the work of his daughter, Anna Freud, in making educational applications of the theory, have brought to our attention the fact that the *wishes* of the child are actually directly opposed to those of adult society during the early years of his life, and it is only with great resistance and reluctance that he surrenders his own pleasure for the more considerate and constrained behaviour demanded by adults. He does so, however, with remarkable facility, provided his actual *needs* are satisfied. Foremost among these are the obvious needs for food, for shelter, and for care and the need for love. It is this last, the emotional relation between child and adults, that can hasten or retard the learning process immeasurably. The child accepts learning provided it is accompanied by certain tangible satisfactions. When he is thwarted or restricted too severely in these he may abandon the effort to please his educators.

The psychiatrist does not deny the value of knowledge and skills learned in school, but he believes that these can be useful to the individual only if proper adjustment is made to life. He considers that the first purpose of education in its broader sense is the facilitation of adjustment to reality. This may be said to be the fundamental tenet in the application of psychiatry to education.

For this reason the psychiatrist thinks that the child's education begins with the first day of life and that the most important period from the educator's standpoint is the early years before the child enters school. The parents are the child's earliest educators, and the teacher is not dealing with untouched material, but with an individual whose personality is already well determined.

For example, it has been rather definitely established that a baby seems to require sucking as an emotional satisfaction quite apart from the food obtained by that method. The child who has weaning difficulties and who is deprived of his thumb by some of the elaborate and ingenious devices which are used for the purpose of breaking children of thumb-sucking may feel cheated out of a fundamental satisfaction, and the experience of this period may have an important bearing upon his development, manifesting itself in some instances in an aggrieved, demanding, or dependent attitude. Again, the child who is trained too soon and too rigorously to cleanliness and sphincter-control may satisfy the adult's æsthetic sense, but may pay in the emotional investment he must make in order to deny his natural bent to be dirty, an investment disproportionately large for the result accomplished if one realizes that it is subtracted from the sum total of energy with which the child must encounter life.

By the time the child reaches school, however, he is usually at the stage where his interests have expanded to include a large part of the environment, and the teacher has a powerful ally in the child's curiosity about facts. Unfortunately in many instances the child has not been able to pass through the previous stages of his development successfully and the teacher finds that he has remained a " mamma's baby " who sucks his thumb and clings to her skirts and cries easily, or he may be aggressive, unwilling to conform to the group. These are evidences that the child's previous training has been such as to divert or thwart the course of normal development. But in most instances the teacher doesn't know this and if she did she wouldn't know what to do about it.

Ask a teacher why Mary cries in school or why John fails to pass in spite of his " smartness " or why Helen does good classwork and always fails on examinations, and the fatuity, the shallowness, the unhelpfulness of the replies will break your heart if you have been thinking with intelligence (or even if you haven't been, if it is your child). " She's just a peculiar child," " she doesn't apply herself," " he's spoiled," " he's lazy." All of which means simply that the teacher doesn't know, and doesn't know that she doesn't know.

And psychiatry, which could help her, is comparatively unknown in educational circles. True, of late there has been considerable demand in parent-teacher groups and in teachers' associations for information on mental hygiene, but usually it has been included as a kind of side line, not a part of class-room teaching but rather a valuable adjunct to be used in extreme cases. The visiting-teacher experiment, while unfortunately not widespread, has been very helpful in educating educators as to the functions of mental hygiene in the schools. The stimulating reports of these workers [2] should be a part of the reading of every teacher and in time we may hope that the visiting teacher will be a part of the educational system of every city.

" Mental testing " (meaning the measurement of intelligence capacity and of certain special abilities of performance and information) is used by teachers much as a clinical thermometer is used by some housewives; the only sickness she becomes alarmed about is something that registers a fever. Children whom these tests indicate to be having trouble are thrust into the " ungraded " rooms or " retarded " rooms, much as if all patients found to have a fever were herded by the doctors into a huge " fever " room and treated for " the fever." The amusing irony of it is that in many places these collections of the educators' failures are called " opportunity rooms "!

E. K. Wickman's study of *Children's Behavior and Teachers' Attitudes,* though made several years ago, describes a situation that unfortunately still exists in many schools. Wickman discovered that such things as this occur:

Of several different third-grade teachers, each having the same number of pupils, all in the same school, one reported 3 dishonest pupils, another reported 18 dishonest pupils, one reported 2 day-dreaming pupils, another reported 34 day-dreaming pupils, one reported 26 cheating pupils, another reported 43 cheating pupils. Now, something is rotten in Denmark, and presumably the trouble is not in the subjects, but in the queen.

Here is something Wickman discovered which is even more striking. He collected from over five hundred teachers their opinion of the relative seriousness of about fifty different behaviour problems such as stealing, truancy, laziness, quarrelsomeness, shyness, etc. Then he asked a group of psychiatrists and psychologists familiar with the beginnings and endings of behaviour-problem cases to rate the same symptoms as to relative seriousness. Of the first twenty-five *most serious* symptoms listed by the teachers, the psychiatrists listed as among the most serious only two! And the symptoms regarded by the psychiatrists as most serious nearly all appear at the bottom of the teachers' lists!

In other words, teachers are colossally ignorant of what mental health and mental ill health look like. For them transgression of rules, offences against authority and against orderliness, are more

[2] Jane F. Culbert: *The Visiting Teacher at Work,* 1929; Mary B. Sayles: *The Problem Child in School,* 1927, and *The Problem Child at Home,* 1928; all published by the Commonwealth Fund, Division of Publications.

serious than withdrawing, recessive personality and behaviour traits.[3] For them the ideal child is the one who gives them and their complexes the least irritation; that is, they prefer the less active, docile, compliant child and object to aggressive, experimental, independent behaviour.

Of course this is true only of the mass of teachers. It is quite natural, partly because they are human beings themselves, with their own complexes; and partly because they are ruled over by a hierarchy of " educators " who, as I have said, are totally blind and deaf to any mental-hygiene principles. But there are notable exceptions.

The progressive education movement has made a brave effort to change things, and a new type of school has sprung up here and there over the country in certain progressive communities. To be sure, progressive education has had to suffer perversions and distortions of its tenets, and the misapplication of its name to procedures that are not progressive education, if education at all.

I have been at some pains to expound my own ideas about education at greater length in my book *Love against Hate* in a chapter entitled " Hope." In it I have tried to answer such questions as these: " What do you expect the teacher to do? Can she change ' human nature '? How can she inspire love and ideals in children when her own life is barren and frustrated? " The summation of the whole point of view of psychiatry regarding education is that: what the teacher is is more important than what she teaches or how she teaches it. Attitudes are more important than the method, and the whole of educational philosophy, from that of local school boards, who are usually responsible for not allowing teachers to be other than barren and frustrated, to that of education departments in universities where archaic ideas about teaching and children are perpetuated, should be imbued with a sounder attitude about child guidance and development than is now prevalent.[3a]

Colleges and High Schools

To one interested in the motives and derailments of human beings, the college is a magnificent laboratory in which vast numbers of subjects run a gauntlet, with many glorious successes

[3] See Chapter II of this book on schizoid and isolation personality types.

[3a] Porter Sargent of Boston has long inveighed against sterile educational attitudes of many schools in his annual *Handbook of Private Schools for American Girls and Boys*.

and many dismal failures. It seems wholly logical that modern psychiatry, concerning itself as it does with the difficulties people have in living, should be applicable to the difficulties that the students have in living their peculiar four-year lives.

Each year thousands of college students fall by the wayside. Each year thousands more fail to derive from their college work anything like the satisfaction which they have a right to expect, or the development of their personalities which the world has a right to expect. The outright failures may be in curricular work, social adjustment, physical health, or the ability to preserve that degree of happiness and efficiency which we have called mental health, or the index of a good general adjustment.

For such failures many explanations have been given, some of which are undoubtedly accurate as far as they go. Many of us believe that too many students are going to college; certainly too many students are going to college who are not properly prepared for it. On the other hand, those who do the preparing are for the most part the products of previous college generations and so it doesn't help for us to pass the blame from one spot to another in the educational system. Certainly many students go to college who do not appreciate what they are getting. How to make them appreciate this is a worthy psychological problem, for which Antioch College has one practical answer and Bennington College another answer, and probably other answers will be forthcoming before we have the final one. Those of us who are in close contact with colleges know well enough that there is much frivolity and much wasted time and money, and some, like the author, feel that fraternities and sororities, as conducted in many colleges (and promoted and supported by many uninformed parents), do an inestimable amount of harm, not only in the formation of artificial social distinctions, but in the development of a local group-membership character which tends to subtract from the primary purposes of education. Whatever the causes, the fact is that college education is not entirely successful, and that many collegians fail.

A disturbing scientific confirmation of this was reported by a former director of the department of psychiatry and psychology of the Macy department store in New York City, whose experience was that the vast majority of college students were undesirable as executive material. For example, out of 442 college men and women applying to Macy's during the spring of 1931, approximately 15 per cent were accepted for employment and only

4 per cent were accepted for the training squad. From this and similar experiences and estimates Anderson says that 85 to 90 per cent of applicants from the colleges are rejected (by his organization) for *any* job and that from 95 to 99 per cent fail to be selected as potential executive material. Why? Because of the lack of one or more of the following characteristics: alertness, intelligence, good physical health, reserve energy, purposiveness, shrewdness, adaptability, good insight, good sense of reality, well-defined interests, and some evidences of achievement.[4]

It is, therefore, no wonder that many people are beginning to doubt if college education is worth all it costs.[5] Yet despite all its faults and lacks, the earnestness, sincerity, patience, and integrity of a majority of faculty members (not necessarily the executives), plus the fact that, because they are envied, college students are apt to be maligned, incline me to stand to their defence and look for ways in which psychiatry, applied to the individual, can prevent some of these failures. The loss of John Smith may mean little to the college; the loss of Mary Baker may not very greatly distress the world; but some John Smiths and some Mary Bakers are worth saving.

Mental hygiene aims at saving them. It aims at the prevention of failure. Efforts at such prevention must begin long before the student flunks or has a nervous breakdown or shoots his roommate or enters an asylum. Such prevention must anticipate by many months, if not by years, such shocking and often irrevocable extremities.

On the other hand, the college is not a sanitarium, and it is just as desirable, as Raphael remarks (*vide infra*), "to discourage inadequate, incompatible and defective material as to encourage that which is positive," for, after all, the major purpose of mental hygiene is not merely to discover impending failure but rather to increase efficiency and happiness. Many factors little suspected by the outside world complicate the difficulties of adjustment for the college student.

Consider for a moment what the college freshman faces. He leaves the high school to enter a college. From being a senior,

[4] V. V. Anderson and Willie-Maude Kennedy: "Psychiatry in College. A Discussion of a Model Personnel Program," *Mental Hygiene,* Vol. XVI, pp. 353–83 (July 1932).

[5] John R. Tunis: *Was College Worth While?* (New York: Harcourt, Brace & Co., 1936).

with all that it means, he becomes a freshman, with all that it in turn implies. From town or country he may transport himself to a city, and to a very sophisticated and complex group within the city. From living at home, with all its protection and consideration, he enters a rooming-house or a fraternity house. Meanwhile he (or she) is changing physically. (The average college freshman is almost but not quite an adult physically. This stage of *almost* is a very difficult one, as everyone knows except those who have never reached it.) There are many acquaintances to make of the same and of the opposite sex and there are certain attitudes to be taken, certain gratifications to be sought, certain new lines of inhibitions to be set up, and certain old ones to be broken down. There is practically a new spoken language to learn and a new set of taboos and a more or less thoroughgoing revision of perspective and objective.

In addition to these general problems, the collegians have special problems which the outside world knows nothing about, or else judges unsympathetically. There are problems of athletic ambition and disappointment (the world hears only of the successes). There are problems of Greek-letter fraternity complications, both inside and out, which only one in close contact with students can fully understand. There are problems of love-affairs dealt with in the immature fashion to be expected at this age, but also with an intensity which the unsympathetic may easily underestimate. There are problems of jealousies and envies inside and outside of the family, conflicts with parents, special antipathies to subjects and instructors, religious problems, curricular problems, physical problems real and imaginary, life-work problems, racial problems, sexual problems, economic problems — in fact, all the problems that older people have, plus a great many more. Think of all this faced by a freshman student of only average intelligence, of average emotional control and average ability, at the average American college or university, at the average age of eighteen.

" Flunking "

Why, for example, does a student fail in a subject? " Lack of brains " or " lack of interest " is the common formula; but they're too simple. It is easy to detect actual deficiency of intelligence, and most of the " dumb-bells " are weeded out early in the race. And as for " lack of interest," where has the interest gone, and why?

Anne Bacon had been a brilliant student in high school and came to college with a scholarship because of her fine record. She made an excellent first impression and started off well, with a moderately heavy schedule. At the end of the first six weeks she was reported doing poor work in three of her subjects and at the end of twelve weeks was reported as failing in two of them. Her teachers, her faculty adviser, the dean of the college, looked in vain for an explanation. She said that she studied, but could not retain the material. Her intelligence test showed her to be far above the average in intellectual powers. The girls at her sorority said she was a quiet, studious girl who was rather uninterested in social activities and could not be said to have wasted her time in them.

I talked to Anne without getting much below the surface. It was quite evident that her heart was not in her work. She denied any interest in other activities or persons. She was mildly depressed over her failure, but seemed not to realize the seriousness of it herself or not to care. After listening awhile I quietly asked her: " Anne, where is he now? " She looked at me for a moment and then burst into tears. This led to the unfolding of a romance that had ended in pregnancy, abortion, disillusionment, and separation, which she was doing her best to forget. She was labouring under the mistaken notion that by never mentioning a thing, by denying to oneself and to everyone else that it had ever existed, one could eliminate an emotional experience from one's life. That explosion in my office, the outpouring of pent-up emotion, and a few hints as to some correction in her attitude were sufficient to help her make the honour roll at the end of her sophomore year.[6]

Unpopularity, inferiority feelings, and " datelessness "
The struggle for recognition and approbation never ceases. Most of us are more or less consciously concerned with and at times worried over our standing in the esteem of our companions, neighbours, friends, and relatives. In college, where there is constant close association and a variety of opportunities for competitive self-expression, these questions are painfully prominent.

In general, students are distressed by (1) feelings of physical or intellectual inferiority, and (2) feelings of social inferiority, unpopularity, friendlessness, and the like. The latter group includes those pathetic cases of the girls who want " dates " and

---

[6] This is the treatment method known as " catharsis." See the previous chapter, p. 388.

lovers and get none, and of boys who are too self-satisfied or too diffident to take any interest in the girls.

The causes for "datelessness," a common and often serious college disease, are multiple and varied. All too often it depends upon an unwholesome home training with reference to social contacts. A father or mother fixation, a feeling of impropriety, a false conception of the opposite sex (see the section on "the fantasy of the two kinds of women"), an over-development of self-love — these and others appear in such cases as the following: [7]

"Esther is from a ranch and is highly sensitive about the fact. She is very bashful and self-conscious. She is especially conscious about her clothes, which are hand-me-downs from an older sister. Physically she is short and awkward; for a while she bore the nickname of 'the runt.' She never attends any social functions except church. In her small-town high school, she was very sociable and active in school affairs, not paying a great deal of attention to her studies. In the university, however, she has practically drawn into her shell and has become a veritable bookworm. In high school she was known as a 'good scout'; in the university she is considered queer."

"'A. Arthur' he writes his name, and this indicates his mental make-up to a remarkable degree. His high school career was quite ordinary.

"In the fall of his freshman college year, he tried out for football, with no success. Then he tried in turn to make a debating team and a literary society, with similar results. It was at this time that his name began to appear as 'A. Arthur.' He became boisterous, especially so in the presence of students prominent in college activities. He let his hair grow long.

"He pays homage to no one. When his fraternity president returned to college from a trip abroad, he refused to walk four blocks to the train to welcome him. His professors are 'dubs.'

"He tried for success in a dramatic production, which was a marked failure. He was ill the next day and had to go home to let his mother take care of him. He and his father dislike each other.

"He is, by vote of the students, the most unpopular man on the campus, largely because of his arrogant, haughty ways, which are definitely forms of compensation."

[7] The next three cases are quoted from a study by Donald A. Laird: "Case Studies in the Mental Problems of Later Adolescence with Special Reference to the Mental Hygiene of the College Student," *Mental Hygiene*, Vol. VII, no. 4 (October 1923), pp. 715-33.

" Thora was attending an exclusive girls' school in the East. She was very queer, upon her own admission and the description of those who knew her. She could not talk openly and seemed to be hiding something. She did not go with the boys, and did not dance with girls. She was very cynical and was affected with spells that much resembled hysteria.

" One evening, while some of the girls were holding a session in one of the ' dorm ' rooms, she registered her distinct disapproval of conversations pertaining to the opposite sex. She spoke with tears in her eyes: ' My mother has told me never to talk about such things or even to think about them. She has told me all the horrible disasters that result from companionship with boys. She has frightened me from ever doing it, and when I think of marriage, I grow faint.' "

In the first edition of this book it was pointed out that mental-hygiene counsellors and some type of mental-hygiene instruction had already been adopted by twenty or thirty colleges and universities, although at that time it was a matter of only some five years' development. Although Princeton led the way with the appointment of Dr. Stewart Paton, Yale with its budget of fifty thousand dollars a year for a mental-hygiene department carried the idea out most completely and gave great encouragement and stimulus to many other less fortunate but no less ambitious institutions. The economic depression of 1929 to 1932 crippled this work in many places, but in the last few years it is being resumed and in some places it continued throughout this period.[8]

What is actually being done in these schools falls into two general categories: first, didactic instruction in the form of lectures — for example, in conjunction with assigned readings and perhaps some such introspective exercises as " What have been my greatest difficulties in the adjustment to college life? " — secondly, personal contacts between the student and a mental-hygiene counsellor. The latter may be in the form of intro-

[8] In addition to the institutions mentioned, mental-hygiene instruction or counsel or both have been provided at Washburn College for the past twenty years; and for periods of time of which I am not precisely certain it has also been available at the University of California, the University of Chicago, Harvard University, Radcliffe College, Smith College, Wellesley College, the Universities of Michigan and Minnesota, Dartmouth College, the New Jersey State Normal School, Columbia University, Vassar College, Elmira College, Sarah Lawrence College, Syracuse University, the University of Pennsylvania, Bryn Mawr College, Brown University, Pembroke College, and the University of Vermont. These are listed alphabetically according to states and not in the order of their development. After the war there will undoubtedly be many others.

ductory interviews with each student at the time of entry into college, a routine procedure, or it may extend to one or more therapeutic conferences with students who become aware of special adjustment difficulties.

As a typical example, at the University of Michigan [9] the mental-hygiene department is a part of the student health service, employs a full-time psychiatrist, a part-time psychiatrist, two psychiatric social workers, two half-time social workers, and a secretary. A brief interview with a psychiatrist is a part of the routine entrance examination given to all students; subsequent conferences are held with those students who request or seem to need it.

Numerous other colleges follow this plan. In a large university it is impossible to give didactic instruction in mental hygiene to a large group, an advantage which smaller schools can exploit. For many years I have been among those who advocated such didactic instruction because, while I have many doubts about the efficacy of lecturing in general and popular lectures on scientific subjects in particular, I am convinced from experience (at Washburn College) that each year a considerable number of students are definitely enlightened, relieved, or encouraged by information received therefrom to a degree materially improving their college adjustment.

With regard to the benefit derived from personal conferences with the mental-hygiene counsellor, I think there is no doubt in anyone's mind. Many technical reports concerning this have appeared in the psychiatric literature, including some from the author's own experience. And as to the point of view of the college authorities, no one has put it more kindly than Dean Mildred Thompson of Vassar, who at the very outset of this movement ten years ago declared:

"I must here bear witness to the great debt of gratitude I owe our consultant psychiatrist at Vassar, for the constant help he has given me at difficult moments. I am sure his tutelage has sharpened insight and brought into focus situations that were blurred and obscure. I have sometimes heard him jokingly describe his position on the staff of Vassar as ' assistant to the dean.' And that he has truly been. I would recommend, therefore, that every college and university have a psychiatrist as assistant to the dean, whatever else he be.

9 T. Raphael: " Four Years of Student Mental Hygiene Work in the University of Michigan," *Mental Hygiene,* Vol. XX, pp. 218–31 (April 1936) .

" The advance of mental hygiene in colleges and universities has come with such rapidity in the last five or ten years that it is no longer progressive to have an expert in mental hygiene on the staff and to give as respectable a place in the curriculum to mental as to physical hygiene. It is reactionary *not* to do these things." [10]

Without any reflection, then, upon the laudable efforts of patient, wise, and friendly faculty members who sporadically assist by means of wise counsel those few students who consult them, the fact remains that the mental health of the college student is too important to be left to these intuitive and conscientious few. It has been a matter for research, endowments, official reports, and practical applications of fruitfully combined personal interest and scientific technique. The advance of the mental-hygiene movement may thus be said to have reached the citadels of the colleges.[11] We may have some hopes that it will some day reach the public schools (see page 424).

II. INDUSTRIAL APPLICATIONS

The application of psychiatry to industry dates back only a few years. Among the pioneers in this field was that genius

[10] C. Mildred Thompson: " The Value of Mental Hygiene in College," *Mental Hygiene,* Vol. XI, pp. 225–40 (April 1927).

[11] It remains for some a moot question as to whether or not mental hygiene is actually the responsibility of the colleges or of the state. Some colleges justifiably take the position that psychiatric advice and treatment for college students is expensive and that the promise to provide students with an education does not include free treatment or character-reconstruction. One may reply to this that a good many of the things for which mental-hygiene counsel is needed are not questions of character alteration, but of superficial problems of adjustment. But even for these superficial problems there is good reason to believe that a psychiatrist rather than a person without clinical training, no matter how wise or intelligent, is desirable, and psychiatrists are hard to find. Psychiatrists employed by the state, as a usual thing, have had the wrong type of training and experience for success in this type of work; furthermore, I, along with many other physicians, have some conscientious objections to the promotion of state medicine independent of more fundamental changes in the economic system. This leaves us, I acknowledge but regret to say, in the position of advocating that mental-hygiene counsel in colleges would be a helpful thing for the students and a step forward for the colleges and an interesting task for the psychiatrists, but exceedingly difficult of practical application.

For a comprehensive survey of the subject see:

A. H. Ruggles: " Mental Hygiene of College Students," *Proc. First International Congress of Mental Hygiene,* Vol. II, pp. 70–94 (1932) ; V. V. Anderson and W. M. Kennedy: " Psychiatry in Colleges," *Mental Hygiene,* Vol. XVI, pp. 353–83 (July 1932) ; F. E. Williams: " Mental Hygiene and College: Levels of Mental Hygiene Work," *Mental Hygiene,* Vol. XV, pp. 532–41 (July 1931). These articles contain references to many other reports on the subject.

Ernest Elmer Southard, the late professor of psychiatry at Harvard. " Why are employees discharged? " he asked himself, and set out to ascertain. From the records of a large department store he found certain causes assigned: [12]

The *employee* was dissatisfied because he did not like supervision, lived too great a distance from the store, was given temporary work, was to be transferred, resented criticism, did not consider his salary adequate, did not like working-conditions, found the work too hard; the *employer* was dissatisfied because of the following offences or circumstances: agitating, carelessness, dishonesty, drinking, fighting, financial difficulties interfering with work, indifference, insubordination, irregular attendance at work, poor or insufficient references, " reasons not divulged, kept in superintendent's private file," pilfering (suspected) , slowness, and necessity to reduce size of working force.[13]

Most of these " dissatisfied " reasons suggest psychiatric needs, said Southard. These needs, he believed, should be met by a unified program participated in by psychiatrists, psychologists, and social case workers.

To the reader of the foregoing pages of this book, the implications of these symptoms as to personality defects will be obvious. It has been difficult, however, to convince business executives unacquainted with the psychiatric attitude that they have anything to gain from its application to their activities.

Most large organizations now have personnel departments. Few of them have psychiatric consultants. Basic personnel practices of good standard should precede the introduction of psychiatric counsel. But the salvaging of employees who show symptoms of failure or maladjustment and, more particularly, the straightening out of maladjusted executives are problems beyond the best personnel departments.

Some concerns utilize psychological science chiefly in regard to efficiency only, seeking short cuts and methods of increasing output without regard to deeper psychological needs and problems. For the most part, this has been a disappointment. An

---

[12] An even more illuminating list, much more recently compiled (by John M. Brewer, of Harvard, in the *Personnel Journal*, Vol. VI, p. 172) shows that sixty-two per cent of over four thousand cases studied were to be ascribed to traits of social incompetence rather than technical incompetence. His list follows: insubordination, general unreliability, absenteeism, laziness, trouble-making, drinking, violation of rules, carelessness, fighting, misconduct, dishonesty, loafing or sleeping, dissatisfaction, habitual lateness.

[13] E. E. Southard in *Mental Hygiene*, Vol. IV, no. 1 (January 1920) .

extensive experiment by the Western Electric Company in Chicago [13a] over a period of five years shows that no external changes were as effective in increasing efficiency as the expression of a personal interest in the employee.

It is estimated that approximately twenty per cent of the employees of mercantile establishments are problems or failures, liabilities or potential liabilities to the employer.[14] Anderson [15] has shown that the application of psychiatry is advantageous, not only as a humane measure but from the financial standpoint. Of 500 " problem " cases studied in one store, he reports that 67 per cent remained in the store, 23 per cent were laid off, 8 per cent resigned, and two per cent were pensioned. Of the cases retained in the store 40 per cent were adjusted and were no longer problems and 44.7 per cent were still under treatment. He points to the saving in time, money, and energy in having these employees adequately studied before experimenting with transfers and training in a wasteful, hit-or-miss way.

That the employer is shortsighted who tries to promote efficiency by mechanical aids alone, without taking the state of mind of his employees into account is evidenced by a research done on groups of workers in America and Germany [16] on the effects of happiness and unhappiness on production. The American workers produced approximately two per cent more than normal when they were happy and seven per cent less than normal when unhappy, and the German workers showed much the same difference. The observations indicate that although anger or fear may stimulate production for a short time, they do not bring results over a long period. A study of the emotional factors producing crises in these groups was made, indicating that among the American workers conditions relating to the job, such as its nature, amount accomplished, relations with the foreman and fellow employees, were the dominant influence (34 per cent) ; that feelings connected with physical conditions such as sickness, fatigue, etc., were the second most powerful influence

[13a] See F. J. Roethlisberger and William J. Dickson: *Management and the Worker,* and T. N. Whitehead: *The Industrial Worker* (Cambridge: Harvard University Press, 1940 and 1938 respectively) .

[14] V. V. Anderson: " The Contribution of Mental Hygiene to Industry," reprinted in *Readings in Mental Hygiene,* edited by Ernest R. Groves and Phyllis Blanchard (New York: Henry Holt & Co., 1936) .

[15] V. V. Anderson: *Psychiatry in Industry* (New York: Harper & Brothers, 1929) .

[16] Rex B. Hersey: " The Mental Health of Workers," *Mental Hygiene,* Vol. XVIII, pp. 462–6 (July 1934) .

on the emotions (twenty-eight per cent) ; and that outside factors, including relations with wife, children, parents, sweethearts, etc., was third in its influence. Contrary to popular opinion, weather and financial problems exerted a comparatively small influence on the emotional state of the worker. The investigator explains, however, that the study was made during a time of prosperity, although the comparable study made in Germany during the time of depression showed the percentage of influence of financial problems to be only ten per cent, less than half that exerted by any one of the first three named — the job, the physical state, and the home. Such studies help us to evolve practical applications of psychiatry to industry.

SOME PRINCIPLES OF INDUSTRIAL PSYCHIATRY

I. *Sudden or progressive failure in efficiency may arise from a variety of causes, revealed only by psychiatric investigation.*

Loss of efficiency from acute transitory mental illness

" Miss A., age 26, resents authority, is uncooperative and has a feeling of being very important, according to the executive who referred her to the clinic. Miss A. proved to be a large, over-developed, fairly good-looking young woman, well dressed according to a rather florid taste. She came to the Conference Office with a broad grin on her face and an air of elation, refusing to submit to psychological tests or to talk with anyone except the director. ' I can't have my time taken up with trifling things,' she announced. Miss A. talked incessantly, changing from one subject to another so rapidly that she often left one sentence half finished to begin another. Her work showed that her job behavior corresponded with her mental caprice. She worked with a great pressure of activity, flying from task to task, but accomplished almost nothing. The clinical examination revealed that she was suffering from a well-known form of mental disease and was in need of sustained hospital treatment" after which she would probably be as efficient and agreeable as ever. " She was not a case for adjustment on the job." [17]

Loss of efficiency from chronic mental illness

" Mr. B., a man of sixty, though he gave his age as fifty-five, made a splendid first impression. He was tall, carefully groomed, with a low, well-modulated voice, a soft Southern accent, unusually good use of

[17] From " Psychiatry in Business," in the *Survey*, December 15, 1927 — report by V. V. Anderson, M.D., psychiatrist to Macy's department store, New York City.

language, and formal, courteous manners. Inquiry revealed that he had limited schooling but had read widely to gain a good vocabulary and a speaking acquaintance with a variety of subjects. He was unmarried and had spent his life as a clerk or floorwalker in New York department stores, staying only a short time with each, and punctuating his employment with Wall Street sprees, during which he speculated as wildly as his meager savings allowed. After each venture in the Street he returned to store employment, but was never able to remain longer than a year in one position because of the 'dishonesty, underhand plotting, secret manoeuvering and chicanery of personal enemies, people who imputed to me motives and conduct that were but the reflection of their own unethical lives.' In Macy's he had encountered the same difficulties. 'There are things going on in this store about which the management knows nothing. They are very subtle. They are secret, but a shrewd man can see through such people. Of course the management does not know a good man, because of the hordes of malignant people surrounding it.' Because of his unusually pleasant manners and his success in meeting the public, it seemed worth making an effort to help this obvious paranoiac. But every attempt to help him sublimate his obsession failed. The friction that resulted from his attitude toward his associates and his superiors finally compelled a 'lay off.'" [18]

Loss of efficiency from minor maladjustment problems

"Miss C., age 20, was referred to the clinic because of her unsatisfactory work, her poor health, and her 'stiff, formal, impenetrable attitude' which handicapped her in contacts with her customers. Miss C. was a nice-mannered French girl, but excessively shy and retiring, too preoccupied with her own concerns to be a success as a salesgirl. Her father is dead, her mother and brothers and sisters in France, and she herself leads a lonely life in a girls' club where she does not feel at home. She suffered from indigestion, headaches, and insomnia. The clinical director talked over her health and job difficulties with her. He taught her some of the principles of physical and mental health and arranged a careful treatment program. She was intelligently cooperative and began to improve after her first contact with the psychiatrist. Six weeks later the buyer reported to Dr. Anderson: 'Miss C. has astonished everyone by turning in the best books of the department. Her sales record has been excellent and the girl herself is much brighter and better. I am delighted with the results in her case.'" [19]

[18] Ibid.   [19] Ibid.

II. *Some employees fail because they are in the wrong job for their personality make-up.*

" Miss D. was taken on as a cashier. She was sent to the psychiatric clinic because of her inaccurate work. Intelligence tests gave her an I. Q. [Intelligence Quotient] 88. She proved to be slow in speed tests, fair in learning ability, and poor in accuracy tests. 'She does not concentrate well on the things at hand,' the assistant who examined her reported, 'showing a definite tendency to mental revery. She has a good general appearance. There is considerable emotional upset.' Miss D.'s mother is dead, her father remarried, and the home situation is such that she lives in a boarding house having, as she feels, been 'put out of my father's house.' On Dr. Anderson's recommendation Miss D. has transferred from the cashiers to the sales department. She liked selling and was said by her supervisor to be 'a good worker.' She remained under the care of the psychiatric department, her weight was brought up to normal and her attitude toward her situation has slowly but consistently improved. 'Her health is now excellent and her sales are good. She has received close psychiatric guidance and has done so well that recently she has been promoted to a junior executive job as head of stock.' " [20]

III. *Some employees have a pattern of repeated failures (comparable to the life pattern of the " habitual criminal").*

" A man of thirty-one came to the clinic at the request of the Red Cross, who reported that he did not work and did not support his wife. The patient himself complained that he was delicate and suffering from a general nervous breakdown. . . .

" He went only to the fourth grade in school, but claims to have obtained after that a 'good home education in engineering and chemistry.' His [mental] age was eleven years and six months, with an I.Q. of 72.

" He married at twenty-two and has three children. His first job was 'jumping' on a bread wagon. He was then messenger boy for the Pennsylvania and later in various telegraph offices, then clerk in the freight division, then call boy for the Pennsylvania Railroad. Then helper in R——'s bakery, then in C——'s bakery, then in W——'s bakery, then in H——'s, then C——'s again, then G——'s. Then went to North Carolina as a mail clerk. Then took a fish wagon. Then in various bakeries and breweries. He gave up his jobs often because he wanted to move around, often because he would get in a quarrel and

[20] Ibid.

' smash ' some fellow; but claims that he never acted so they would not take him back. At the time of his examination he was looking forward to being a brakeman on the Pennsylvania Railroad.

" In the meantime his wife complains that he beats her, sits around the house, refuses to go out and work and eats up what she gets by work and charity for herself and the children." [21]

IV. *Some employees suffer from unsuspected mental conditions dangerous to the public.*[22]

An engineer on one of the transcontinental trains suddenly pulled his engine to a stop in the middle of the plains one day and announced that he wouldn't proceed a foot until they got all those other trains off the track. There were no other trains in sight. His fireman managed to control him with the assistance of the conductor, until they could get to the next station, where he was removed. He had probably had brain syphilis for several years, a fact which could easily have been detected by examination some time before this episode, which might have turned out more tragically.[23]

The following item is clipped from a newspaper:

" Apparently suddenly becoming mentally deranged, Eugene F. Evans, railroad fireman, jumped from a window of a passenger train last night and soon afterward died in a hospital."

The following two cases were reported to the Tennessee State Health Department:

" A conductor who was admitted to a hospital with paresis had been allowed to run his train until he was so demented that he had stopped it between stations and refused to go on. In another case the patient, also a paretic, had been discharged from the railroad at the recommendation of the company surgeon, but had secured employment on another road. Not long afterward he wrecked a passenger train."

The tendency to convulsions is equally serious:

" A railway fireman, aged 28, came to the hospital September 28, 1912, because of having ' bad spells.' There was no history of nervous or mental diseases in the family. The patient was single, denied vene-

---

[21] T. V. Moore: " The Pathology of Will," *International Clinics,* Vol. II, 33rd Series (1923) , pp. 121–2.

[22] See also the case cited on page 211.

[23] This case was reported to me by Dr. M. L. Perry of the Topeka State Hospital.

real disease, and showed no history of trauma. He did not use alcoholics, but smoked a considerable amount of tobacco.

" May 27, 1912, he had the first attack of which he had any knowledge. He lost the power of speech, had a ' faint ' feeling through his stomach, his arms trembled, and finally he lost consciousness. He did not have incontinence, but bit his tongue in the attack and felt weak after it. About three weeks later he had another attack, similar except that he did not bite his tongue. About two weeks later he had still another attack. The attacks were all ushered in by the same aura and none of them occurred on the engine while at work. . . .

" During his stay in the hospital he had an attack in which he first became apparently speechless, pointed to one of his companions . . . mumbled and then fell out of his chair. He bit his tongue and made a few convulsive movements. He was unconscious altogether about five minutes. Following the attacks he could answer questions, but was dazed. He returned to his position because *he said he was about to be promoted to be an engineer* and did not wish to lose his place." [24]

A driver of a cross-country bus came home one day, after completing his regular run, complaining of a severe pain in his head. This was the harbinger of a terrific attack of excitement. Five men were required to hold him; he bent the iron posts of his bed, as he pleaded for someone to do something for the pain in his head. After several attacks of this sort he fell asleep and woke up later with no memory of what had happened. Other drivers who had seen him on duty just before the attack remembered that he had apparently not recognized them, although he was usually friendly. Such a history would lead a physician to consider the possibility of brain tumour. *Yet this man continued to drive a passenger bus!*

V. *In many instances the most serious maladjustment problems are found not in the employees but in the employers and executives.*

I was once employed by a corporation to investigate its force of employees and make recommendations for the improvement of efficiency. It ended when I recommended that the general manager and the vice-president, whose hatred for each other had created difficulties all through the plant, be reconciled or removed. They removed me (over the president's protest).

[24] Carl D. Camp: " Epilepsy and Paresis in Railway Engineers and Firemen," *Journal of the American Medical Association,* August 30, 1913 (Vol. LXI), pp. 655–7.

(For other illustrative cases, see the section on schizoid personalities, pages 75 to 107.)

The public often confuses industrial psychiatry with " industrial psychology " (which is largely the study and measurement
of certain aptitudes with reference to their utility in certain positions) , and with the reports of self-styled " character-analysts "
(which is plain bunk) . Industrial psychology is a considerable
body of doctrine and practice relative to the selecting of the
right man for the right job. It is closely related to vocational
guidance work, and both of these fields are distinctly the work
of psychologists rather than psychiatrists. The psychiatrists
really know very little about them. The psychologists, on the
other hand, have devised, applied, and standardized all manner
of performance tests to decide how best to use certain men, how
to shorten certain operations, how to choose certain candidates,
and so forth. For example, Mrs. Lillian Gilbreth of Montclair,
New Jersey, lectures at Purdue University on the elimination of
lost motion, and the discovering of " the one best way " to perform certain given tasks. There is much work being done, also,
with reference to training salesmen, and the Phœnix Mutual
Life Insurance Company has arrived at some astonishing figures
with reference to the most desirable traits in employees for selling insurance.[25]
But all this, while beyond the ken of psychiatrists, is commendable scientific work. Quite the contrary is such hokum as
the following case illustrates:

" Age fifty. Education, public school till age of fourteen . . . intelligence high B. Occupation, salesman, sales manager, adjuster of
commercial claims in credit field, and collector. Excellent health, superior physique. Financially successful, liked the field of salesmanship
[but] had always felt that if could but find the exact and proper vocational niche, he would be satisfied for the rest of his life, that he
would then no longer feel a striving for accomplishment, but would
sail on smooth waters. Family relations always satisfactory, but constantly troubled by this vocational problem.

" Subject had been to a character analyst in 1912, in 1915, and to two
in 1922. The last analyst told him that ' your vital temperament gives

---

[25] For example they found that older men are much more likely to succeed
than younger men. And by proper selection on the basis of the optimum age,
education, social adaptability, etc., " 500 salesmen now sell over three times as
much life insurance for us as 1700 sold previously."

you your arterial circulation,' and that he should be a public speaker if not a politician; that he should be in construction work; that his executive talent was strongly represented through his large destructiveness; that he could handle men and read people like a book; that he could become an efficiency engineer, an inventor, a consulting lawyer advising young men how to run their business; that he had all the requirements for a decorator, an art critic, or a connoisseur of antiques; that he made an excellent host; that he should cultivate his secretiveness, control his sublimity, and he would be a benefactor to all "! [26]

Many valuable employees who would otherwise be lost by discharge or resignation may be salvaged by proper psychiatric investigation and technique. The following cases were studied by Mary C. Jarrett, the dean of psychiatric social workers and one of the first to report industrial cases (this study having been made as long ago as 1917). [27]

Case 1. MACHINIST, age 29. Diagnosis: DEMENTIA PRÆCOX [schizoid personality, see Chapter II]

Status at the Time of First Observation:	Period of Psychiatric Study and Treatment, resulting in:
January 1916:	January 1917:
Industrial disability	Good health
Unemployment	Regular work
Debts	Out of debt
Suicidal attempts	Cheerful

Case 2. TAILOR, age 37. Diagnosis: ALCOHOLISM; DEPRESSION

Status at the Time of First Observation:	Period of Psychiatric Study and Treatment, resulting in:
November 1914:	November 1916:
Unemployment	Employment
Gambling	Wife now manages
Inebriety	Out of debt
Contentiousness	No love lost; tolerance
Debts	Cheerful
Family discord	
Suicidal attempt	

[26] Lorine Pruette and Douglas Fryer: "Affective Factors in Vocational Maladjustment," *Mental Hygiene*, Vol. VIII, no. 1 (January 1923), pp. 102–18.
[27] From *Medicine and Surgery*, Vol. VI, pp. 727–41 (September 1917).

Case 3. CLOTHES-PRESSER, age 41. Diagnosis: NEURASTHENIA

Status at the Time of First Observation:	*Period of Psychiatric Study and Treatment, resulting in:*
1914:	1916:
Unable to work	At work
Supported by charity	Set up in business
Philanthropy	Social service
Family without support	Family supported
Suicidal ideas	Cheerful

Case 4. TEAMSTER, age 32. Diagnosis: ALCOHOLIC JEALOUSY

Status at the Time of First Observation:	*Period of Psychiatric Study and Treatment, resulting in:*
January 1916:	January 1917:
Inebriety	Sobriety
Inadequate income	Increased wages
Suspicions of wife	Suspicions gone
Abuse of wife	Abuse over

Case 5. MACHINIST, age 47. Diagnosis: GENERAL PARESIS (Brain Syphilis)

Status at the Time of First Observation:	*Period of Psychiatric Study and Treatment, resulting in:*
October 1916:	January 1918:
Disabled for work	Employed
Inebriety	Sobriety
Marital discords	Happiness
No income	Adequate wages
Debts	Debts reduced
No money for therapy	Treatment

III. LEGAL APPLICATIONS

" *Despite all that the criminologists have done in the last generation the criminal law is still framed chiefly in terms of punishing the vicious will. Despite all that criminologists and physicians have shown as to the necessity of special institutions with expert management for many classes of delinquents, the legal theory of ideal equality before the law leads the criminal law, whenever it is in the hands of lawyers, to consign all to a common prison.*

" *Despite all that psychiatry and psychology have achieved, the law-*

yer can draw only a plain straight line between an artificial legal conception of insanity and a no less artificial legal conception of normal responsibility.

" *Where anything has been accomplished in the way of individualization of penal treatment in almost every case it has had to be done through administrative boards and commissions, acting on principles radically different from those of the criminal courts and with courts and bar largely out of sympathy with them.*" — Roscoe Pound, then Dean of the Harvard Law School.

As the science dealing with the queer and untoward behaviour of human beings, psychiatry is naturally much concerned with crime. But tradition and custom and legal precedent have greatly handicapped the approach of the psychiatrist to the criminal. He appears popularly as the partisan interceder for the occasional accused criminal; he turns up to " save " some wretch from his " just dues " by pronouncing him " insane." And this is so absurd, unjust, and irritating that Mr. Dooley's caricature of the psychiatrist in court is probably not far from the prevalent popular opinion.

" ' D'ye know this prisoner? ' says th' coort. ' I do,' says the alienist. ' How long have ye known him? ' ' I see him first an hour ago, but I have sized him up. This young sign iv a wealthy fam'ly is suff'rin' from parynoya, dementia precox, dementia Americana, submerged ego, repressed desires, inferyarity complexes, deeliryum threemens, an' congenital peevishness. In a wurrud, which ye'er honor will undherstand, he is completely bug. I think he ought to be locked up.' ' In an asylum? ' says th' coort. ' No, indeed,' says the Dock. ' That wud be crool to his worthy parents an' to a young man who has been brought up in luxury an' who, outside iv th' few thriflin' ills I have mentioned, is entirely normal. I suggest that he be sintinced to some quiet rethreat in th' country, where he will have ivry attintion that a young man iv his means requires f'r his comfort — dilicate food, a well stocked cellar, an' th' companionship iv his akels. I can direct th' coort to such an institution. It is pleasantly situated in a rollin' counthry, with tennis, goluf, swimming, et cethry an' so on. There this eccentric but on th' whole lovable young man can spind his days in manly exercise or in long walks an' talks with th' other afflooent cuckoos who rave undher its hospitable roof. I know just such a reposeful nook. In fact, I own it mesilf.' "

Now the psychiatric profession is far too dignified and idealistic for this to be true. But it certainly does appear to happen.
How can this be, and what *is* the proper relation of psychiatry to
the courts?

The old problem of good and evil

Let us approach the problem historically. Once all human
behaviour was accounted good or bad. The " good " included
the pious, the proper, the conventional, the routine, the harmless, and the inconsequential. The " bad " included the heretic,
the improper, the unconventional, the unusual, the delirious,
the antisocial, and the not-understood.

Ultimately the " bad " became subdivided into two groups,
the inexplicable and the explicable. In the one group were
placed those who did strange things. The evil they wrought
brought no evident profit to themselves. In damaging society
they gratified no familiar desires. Their conduct became uncontrollable, they expressed baseless fears, they mutilated themselves, they looked upon their best friends as enemies, they
attempted or committed unprovoked murders, they set fires gra-
tuitously, they stole profitlessly.

Because their conduct was mysterious, such people came to be
regarded with a certain awe, and the prophets proclaimed it
inhuman to punish them. Eventually, too, it was discovered that
drugs would abate some of these aberrancies. They were therefore relegated to the doctors, who were told to do with them
what they would and could. To justify this relegation legally,
the term " insanity " was coined and impressed into legal use.
Those who were relegated, certified, disposed of to doctors, were
to be known as " insane."

The other group of the " bad " did things apparently easier
to understand. They did what nearly everybody else at some
time had done, or had desired to do, but which conflicted with
social convenience and comfort. They stole useful and valuable
things such as most men might covet. They took revenge upon
those who injured them, and if they murdered, the victims were
their enemies. Though these things were forbidden by tradition, religion, and the law, they were instinctive with nearly all
members of the race. Even the " good " must struggle against
the same temptations, and every normal adult remembers more
or less painfully his juvenile offences in the same directions,

though his childish thefts were trivial and his murderous impulses did not result in killing.

Recent scientific discoveries indicate the improbability that these "obvious" offences are committed for the obvious, the apparently obvious, motives. Motivation of conduct is found to be much more largely unconscious than conscious, and the conscious explanations are apt to be superficial rationalizations. Nevertheless, the offences committed are of a sort which the public *thinks* it fully understands, and this in the long run decides its attitude toward the offenders.

Society, as we have seen, came to consider it inhuman to punish the wrongdoing it did not understand. But a host of avengers arose to clamour for the blood of the wrongdoers whose conduct seemed comprehensible. It was as if each one desired to crush someone else for yielding to what the avenger was so fiercely struggling against in his own soul.

To resume: the sinners whose sins are inexplicable to laymen are officially labelled "the insane"; those whom we think we understand, judging intuitively by our own struggles, are officially labelled "criminals." The former have been accorded increasingly efficient scientific study and treatment; the latter have been traditionally treated by punishment.

Both the "insane" and the "criminals," so labelled, have been increasing in numbers more rapidly than the general population. It is significant to observe the difference in the handling of the two resulting social problems. The increase in mental disease has been met with a scientifically planned program for the promulgation of mental hygiene; the increase in the allied type of misconduct has been met with hysterical squawking and fatuous preaching about the "crime wave." Amateur criminologists have advocated ten thousand remedies for the cure of crime, from compulsory Sunday-school attendance to the abolition of automobiles, cigarettes, and short bathing-suits. Out of thousands of articles on the subject in current American literature, few have in any degree evinced a comprehension of the scientific bases of human conduct.

The theory of punishment

Punishment of criminals is theoretically advocated for one or all of three reasons. It is supposed (1) to reform the criminal, (2) to protect society, (3) to deter others of similar inclination.

It is hard to believe that anyone at all familiar with jails and prisons supposes that confinement in them reforms the criminal. He knows that at the end of their terms prisoners are likely to be more dangerous men than they were at the beginning. Nearly every warden says so, and all but the most somnolent judges know it and regret it.

That society is entitled to protect itself from the depredations of evil-doers by confining them somewhere, no one disputes. But a prison term comes to an end at the expiration of a fixed sentence, or earlier at the whim of parole officers actuated by sentimental or political considerations or by the administrative necessity of emptying overcrowded cells to make room for new-comers. Neither the arbitrary length of the sentence fixed by statute, nor the date of parole capriciously bestowed, corresponds with any change in the prisoners by which, if a dangerous man, he becomes a safe one. Hence we have the tragicomedy of the offender, sentenced for a fixed period, serving a small part of it, and repeating time after time the offence from which society is supposedly being protected by the jail.

That the spectacle of punishment may deter some persons from committing crime is conceivable, although it has not been scientifically demonstrated. But obviously it does not deter all persons, or crime would have ceased long since. The criminals now occupying our prisons were not deterred. Only a casual in-spection of any prison population should convince the thought-ful that the persons whom punishment is intended to deter are incapable of the proper appreciation of deterrence. In other words, mentally intact persons may indeed be deterred by cer-tain legal threats (it is a question how much) ; but it may not be at present the mentally intact persons who commit crimes, and the mentally impaired are notoriously incapable of ordinary reactions of social adjustment.

In serious offences there is another element, itself ordinarily powerful enough, perhaps, to control those capable of being influenced by deterrents of any sort. That is the profound feel-ing of social disapproval, involving moral disgrace, manifested toward crimes really considered grave. Most of us are aware that our conduct is restrained in many particulars by a sense of social approval even in fields not covered by statute law at all, though some people are indifferent or rebellious to this kind of control as well as to law. There are some legal offences, on the other hand, which carry no moral stigma with them, such as minor violations of the traffic laws. It is only in these cases, relatively unimportant and outside the field of the usual discussion of the crime problem, that the specific penalty has an independent restraining influence, be it great or small.

It would seem, then, that present modes of punishment actually accomplish none of the things they are supposed to do, or, at any rate, do not accomplish them so well as some other system might. The reasons usually given to justify punishment do not explain why it exists. They serve only to conceal the truth, that the scheme of punishment is a barbarous system of revenge, by which society tries to " get even " with the criminal.

Science is not interested in revenge, and science is notoriously opposed to accepting traditional classifications. And psychiatry, the branch of science concerned with aberrant behaviour, has no respect for such stratifications of human behaviour as " good " and " bad," " criminal " and " insane."

Once it was sufficient to diagnose an illness as " the fever "; now medical science knows scores of fevers, each of different causes, course, and complications. Similarly the psychiatrist cannot regard theft or murder as a diagnosis; these are single symptoms appearing with other symptoms in a variety of groupings.

Originally, it is true, the psychiatrists were chiefly concerned with those types of wrongdoers who had been labelled " insane " by the law-makers and gathered into special institutions. But when they had studied this material according to scientific method, they discovered no such partitions between the " insane " and the " criminal " as had been erected. They found that the types and trends of abnormal psychology extended far out from the " asylum " into the court-room, the school, and even the home. They found their task as definitely defined in the terror-ridden child as in the maniacal youth, as much in the melancholy and unstable mother as in the suicidal or homicidal father. They found their experience and technique equally applicable to the irascible employee, to the retarded school-child, to the unhappy suspicious husband, to the deluded and hallucinated wife. The psychiatrists, face to face with the legal partitions of the misbehaved, found they had no technical interest in these partitions or general agreement with them. As scientists they are concerned with *all* the unpropitious trends of human character, with all acts, thoughts, emotions, instincts, and adaptations, socially and individually adverse. To the psychiatrists there are no " criminals " and no " insane."

The scientific attitude as shown in psychiatry must sooner or later totally displace existing legal methods. Formerly doctors treated patients, not by applied intelligence, but by precedents established by Hippocrates, Paracelsus, and Galen. The doctors have now left this method one hundred years behind them; must the lawyers still continue solemnly to apply mediæval stupidities in the name of " established precedent," " public policy," and other mouthy archaisms? Many of the ablest lawyers are earnestly striving to better this situation. But a large share of them, unfortunately, are indifferent to the problems of criminal procedure, because they never practise in the criminal field and have no interest in criminals as individuals.

" Justice " and " responsibility "

Meanwhile the declamation continues about the travesties upon *justice* that result from the introduction of the psychiatric method into court. But what science or scientist is interested in *justice*? Is pneumonia just? Or cancer? Or gravity? Or the expansion of steam? What criteria of " justice " can be applied to a broken arm or a weak mind? And to what good end? The scientist is seeking amelioration of an unhappy situation. This can be secured only if the scientific laws controlling the situation can be discovered and complied with, and not by talking of " justice," not by debating philosophical concepts of equity based on primitive theology.

This brings up the conception of " responsibility " with which the psychiatrist is often faced, but with which also he is unconcerned. He has no idea what it means, although he is constantly asked to testify concerning it. The psychiatrist asks not " Is that man responsible? " but " Of what is he capable or incapable? "

Responsibility in the legal sense means punishability. The sense in which responsibility is used is an echo of the antiquated legalization of primitive and infantile reactions known as the talion law. In other words, " He hits me, so I hit him " (in spite of the scriptural adjuration that vengeance is the Lord's). No scientist has a moment's consideration for such emotionally determined policies. To say that they effect nothing is redundant.

The idea of responsibility runs back to the practices of primitive religious systems and is founded on the mystical concept of atonement. Every transgression had to be compensated for by some tangible sacrifice — if not by the transgressor, at least by some kind of scapegoat. For every offence somebody had to pay.

There was a time when even inanimate objects were held to this kind of accountability. If a man tripped over a chair and injured himself, the chair was " responsible " and must be punished — by being burned or broken. Until comparatively recent times animals were held responsible for injuries they committed; they were tried and convicted and formally sentenced. But ultimately inanimate things and animals came to be excepted from the ritual of responsibility; and slowly but progressively children, idiots, and finally all the " insane." Various curious tests then had to be decided upon to determine the " responsibility " of persons suspected of " insanity." Once they were compared in appearance and conduct with wild beasts. A later test was comparison with the mentality of a fourteen-year-old child. This was actually the criterion of " responsibility "! Current today in some states is the " right or wrong " test, which undertakes to determine whether the individual knows the difference between right and wrong or knows that his act is one regarded as wrong. It persists, notwithstanding general knowledge that people are actuated by various compulsions to do things they themselves regard as wrong in the most shameful sense. The capacity to feel remorse does not imply power to control conduct.

The legal problem of responsibility evidently involves the philosophical problem of " free will." Philosophy still debates the difficult issues of the question, and science can hardly give a final answer to them now. But the law stubbornly maintains that the question is closed. According to the law, all persons of certain categories possess absolute freedom of will, and all persons of other categories possess none. Neither science nor philosophy can accept such a conclusion.

A scientist does not wish to participate in the ritual of punishment, though he has a professional interest in observing how it gratifies the craving of the crowd for atonement through vicarious suffering. For his patients the psychiatrist seeks, not punishment, but treatment. This, in a sense, is an inhuman attitude, in that it is a departure from the instinctive mechanism that rules most of humanity; the clamour for vengeance is more human. But treatment may sometimes be as painful as the sacrifice prescribed by the legal ritual. Opening a boil or setting a fracture may be painful, and the psychiatrist, too, may prescribe painful treatment; but it is never punishment.

Practical results

The advantages of a changed attitude toward criminals seem too obvious to elaborate. With every prison in the land half filled with repeating offenders, there seems to be justification for current newspaper alarms over the " crime wave." So long as offenders are sentenced according to the book instead of studied according to principles, the results will continue to be as inadequate as if doctors prescribed twenty days of aspirin for every case of pneumonia, six months of castor oil for every cancer, or five years of calisthenics for every case of imbecility.

Much experimental work remains to be done, both legal and mental. It seems certain, however, that an entire shift of attitude will be necessary rather than the various manœuvrings of criminal procedure that are sometimes advocated. One immediate practical step in the right direction could be taken with a minimum of legislative and administrative readjustment; before paroles are issued, prisoners should be examined by psychiatrists, and if evidence of mental disorder or defect likely to cause a recurrence of misconduct is found, paroles should be denied. Those who confuse the scientific point of view with a maudlin sentimentality may see from this that the period of treatment for many offenders would doubtless much exceed the terms of " punishment " fixed by the law.

Ultimately there will be no important administrative distinction between " asylums " and " jails." Both will have lost those atrocious names. Both will be institutions under state jurisdiction and under expert medical direction for the care of individuals committed to them by the state because of behaviour ineptitudes, failures, and incapacities.

A " sentence " will be as unthinkable for a murderer as it now is for a melancholiac. Unkindness will be as taboo for a felon as it now is for a woman in delirium. Release before complete recovery will be as irregular and improper for a thief or rapist as it now is for a paretic or leper.

The modern surgical operating amphitheatre developed out of dirty public barber-shops. The physicians took surgery away from the barbers a century ago; now they are taking criminology away from jailers and politicians.[28]

Back in 1917 the New York State Prison Survey Committee, headed by George W. Wickersham, recommended that:

[28] This much of this section is reprinted from an article by the author: " Vengeance or Vision? " in the *Survey*, April 1927.

"County jails should be abandoned as places of punishment. All prisoners should be sent to clearing-houses for a diagnosis of their conduct disorders and for classification. Thereafter they should be confined in specialized units of a diversified institutional system, including industrial farms and vocational training schools. Sentences should be made truly indeterminate. No paroles should be issued until the prisoner's problem has been sufficiently well met to warrant the belief that he will adapt himself in the community. Even after parole the prisoner's activities should be supervised by a psychiatric social worker."

Then a few years ago Massachusetts enacted a law making psychiatric examination a compulsory routine procedure for a capital offender or a second (proved) offender.

Since then other states have been trying out various changes in criminal procedure, on the whole rather unhappily. By far the most progressive proposal is the one made by Governor Alfred Smith, of New York, on December 7, 1927, at a meeting of the New York State Crime Commission, proposing to take the sentencing power from judges in felony cases and invest it in a special state commission composed of experts in law, psychiatry, and penology who will be charged with the responsibility of dealing with offenders after conviction.

The main points in the proposal, which has been characterized as probably the most far-reaching and fundamental change ever suggested in American criminal law, were summed up in the New York *Times* as follows:

"That the jury should determine only the guilt or innocence of the person on trial.

"That after a jury has returned a verdict of guilty the power of imposing sentence should be taken from the Judge who presided at the trial and given to a special State Board to be created by a constitutional amendment.

"That the members of the board should include legal experts, psychiatrists and penologists devoting their entire time to the work and paid as high salaries as any others in state employ — $25,000 a year.

"That this board should determine whether a convicted felon should go to a state prison or to an insane asylum; and that it should determine the length of punishment and the extent he may be subject to parole."

Psychiatrists have long been dissatisfied with the existing state of affairs with special reference to their own participation, and in 1924 a special committee was appointed by the American Psychiatric Association, whose report as finally adopted (unanimously) by the American Psychiatric Association in 1927 was the result of a very careful study and many conferences. Its general purport has been covered above.[29]

Then in 1926 and 1927 the Criminal Law Section of the American Bar Association entertained speakers from this committee of the American Psychiatric Association, and as a result of the discussion a committee was appointed to formulate a corresponding statement of position on the part of the American Bar Association. This committee made the following revised report at Memphis in August 1929:

" The committee from the Section on Criminal Law of the American Bar Association, after a conference with the committee from the American Psychiatric Association, recommends to its own association that it advocate:
" 1. That there be available to every criminal and juvenile court a psychiatric service to assist the court in the disposition of offenders.
" 2. That no criminal be sentenced for any felony in any case in which the judge has any discretion as to the sentence until there be filed as a part of the record a psychiatric report.
" 3. That there be a psychiatric service available to each penal and correctional institution.
" 4. That there be a psychiatric report on every prisoner convicted of a felony before he is released.
" 5. That there be established in each state a complete system of administrative transfer and parole and that there be no decision for or against any parole or any transfer from one institution to another without a psychiatric report."

The National Crime Commission, on June 9, 1928, published a report of its subcommittee on the medical aspects of crime, in which, after a discussion of the Massachusetts law and the objectives of psychiatry, it goes on to say:

[29] This committee was composed of the following psychiatrists: Dr. Herman M. Adler (now deceased), Dr. L. Vernon Briggs of Boston, Dr. Bernard Glueck of New York, Dr. William Healy of Boston, Dr. Smith Ely Jelliffe of New York, Dr. Raymond F. C. Kieb, Dr. Lawson G. Lowrey, New York City, Dr. Thomas W. Salmon (deceased, and replaced on the committee by) Dr. Winfred Overholser, Boston, Dr. Frankwood E. Williams (now deceased), Dr. William A. White, Washington, D. C., recently deceased, and Dr. Karl A. Menninger, Topeka (chairman of the committee from 1924 to 1929).

"We are reasonably certain that, were we to follow the logic of the psychiatrist in his diagnosis of the American crime situation and reform our criminal codes and our court technique accordingly, far from helping the criminal, as has been mistakenly supposed, it would result in considerably greater social protection than we have enjoyed for a generation. . . ."

Subsequent to all this, the American Medical Association joined with the American Psychiatric Association and the American Bar Association and unanimously endorsed the principles outlined on page 453, which as can be seen are only a beginning in the direction recommended by the original committee of the American Psychiatric Association or espoused in the reports of the New York State Prison Survey Committee, cited on page 452. With these elementary principles, then, the organized psychiatrists, the organized legal profession, and the organized medical profession of the United States of America unanimously concurred. *Yet what has come of it?*

Practically nothing. I have reprinted this material at some length and indicated how unanimously the principles were accepted in order to make the observation more emphatic that they have apparently had no practical consequences. In the first edition of my book I cited the survey made by Dr. Winfred Overholser for the National Committee for Mental Hygiene and the National Crime Commission revealing that something less than ten per cent of the courts in the United States described themselves as being served regularly by a psychiatrist. Small as this percentage is, it would be still more disillusioning to examine more carefully the nature of some of the psychiatric service claimed by these courts; in one instance with which I am familiar in which the court claimed to have psychiatric service, such psychiatric service has not been called upon for ten years. Some revisions of laws have been made in a few states, but in not a single instance, outside of Massachusetts, has this been done on any broad basis of scientific reform. I have before me a detailed account of the development throughout the United States since the first issue of my book, kindly compiled for me by Dr. Winfred Overholser, whose work in Massachusetts has been outstanding; these notes show that speeches have been made, committee meetings have continued, resolutions have been passed, appeals for research funds have been issued, but as for significant changes in the criminal procedure of the states, *not one!* The Honourable Sanford Bates, commissioner of prisons in the United States, is an intelligent and high-minded man, and has repeatedly gone on record as to his conceptions of penology, including the assistance of psychiatry, and in the federal prisons this has been to some slight extent attempted, but, in the main, progress in penology in the United States has been without benefit of psychiatry.

One cannot but be rather pessimistic about such a stout resistance to progress, and such pessimism the late Dr. William A. White, whose contributions to the subject are so important and significant, told me he shared. Why is it so? For one thing, my experience convinces me that the lawyers and the doctors, in spite of the official actions of their organizations, do not really understand or endorse the idea of treating criminals instead of crimes, or of dealing with the situation on a scientific instead of a traditional basis. The same is true of the official attitude of the newspapers; individual reporters are frequently among the most clever and intelligent members of the community, but the current newspaper ideal of making things comical, "snappy," and, above all, hypocritically moral, thus serving the purpose of amusement rather than that of information or intelligent guidance, makes it very difficult for the general reading public to substitute new ideas for old prejudices. The impulse to take out on the criminal what we unconsciously fear and expect for our own guilty wishes and intentions — the old "whipping-boy" principle in short — is too powerful to be changed by the reports of a few scientific committees and the publication of a few reflective articles in the "quality" magazines.

The public is reluctant to entrust the criminals to the psychiatrists because it does not want to be robbed of its satisfaction in wreaking vengeance upon the criminals; it does not want to have scientific methods applied, even though to do so might be to the ultimate good of all. Emotions are more powerful than intelligence. Furthermore, the community in general is still suspicious of psychiatrists; there is something of a taboo associated with them, and this is reflected in all sorts of jeers, gossip, slanderous accusations, absurd speculations, and the like which are current among the semi-intelligent. People are reluctant to turn even criminals over to these curious fellows, the psychiatrists, because of a tremendous fear of some supernatural and malignant abilities associated in their minds with men who know about psychology and psychiatry.

A final reason for the failure of the psychiatric recommendations to make progress lies, I think, in the incompatibility of the present social and economic system with the application of scientific ideas of this type. To apply psychiatry to problems of the community or the state implies an increasing development of state medicine, yet however dissatisfied we may feel with the workings of the present system, most of us (physicians) do not favour state medicine, under the existing economic order. We can see the logic, the theoretical advantages, and the idealism of wholesale employment of medical services by the state for just such things as we have recommended, but we also see the disadvantages. It would be more accurate to say that we *feel* them, because it is not easy to put into simple words the reasons for our opposition. Those who have attempted to be articulate about it have sometimes put us in a rather unfavourable light; what some of them say *sounds* like crass selfishness. It is therefore understandable that we doctors should be accused by many people of fearing state medicine and socialistic principles in general because they would interfere with the personal advantages of a few of us; it is understandable, I say, but it is largely inaccurate. Many of us are opposed, I believe, for the reason that we are convinced that unless other elements in our socio-economic set-up are also changed, it makes impossible a genuine and fruitful patient-physician relationship.

The real reason underlying the incompatibility of our present social and economic system with progressive ideas in criminology may lie entirely in the fact that that system shapes the manner of thinking of the people and makes it difficult for them to accept new concepts. The premium that our present system places upon ruthless individual aggressivity, subtle though its manifestations may be, prevents the mass of people from seeing that the psychiatrist is someone who can be of assistance to them, and that the criminal is anything but someone to be punished. Isolated and constricted educational measures attempting to place before the public a new concept are feeble dikes against the flood of turbulent, ever-increasing destructiveness and hate which is sweeping over the world at the present writing. Hence it seems all the more likely that fundamental changes will have to take place which will get rid of the barbarism in our present ideology which prevents the application of the knowledge we are acquiring.

In contrast with this pessimism concerning the practical applications of psychiatry to the prevention of crime, the efforts of the theoretical investigations as to the psychological factors have been highly fruitful. Incidentally, those few individual offenders who happened to be the subjects of this research as well as the communities in which they lived were fortunate, but it is such a pitifully small number as to have little practical conse, quence for all its immense theoretical importance.

Long ago William Healy wrote his famous book *The Indi-vidual Delinquent*,[30] which signalized the concentration of scien-tific study upon the internal forces impelling the personality to break away from the socially acceptable standards of adaptation. Since that book was published, our understanding of the mecha-nisms of personality development and social adjustment has been vastly expanded along lines I have tried to indicate in the preceding chapters. At the same time the whole concept of the environment as a social field has been developed, as represented in the brilliant exposition of J. F. Brown's *Psychology and the Social Order*.[31] Another type of sociological approach is repre-sented by the statistical investigations of Sheldon and Eleanor Glueck, which endeavoured to ascertain what actually happened to a representative sample of criminals following so-called treatment — first, treatment by the conventional reformatory method [32] and then treatment in or at least contact with a psy-chiatric clinic. The conclusions of the first investigations were that, contrary to the optimistic political ballyhoo of the average reformatory warden whose " boys " are always making good in a high percentage, approximately four-fifths of the men dis-charged from reformatories continued their criminal careers, a finding which, as the authors state, " reverses almost in perfect proportion the figures of ' success ' and ' failure ' customarily attributed to reformatories and parole officers in researches, annual reports and texts on criminology." However, it must be added that similar studies carried out in connection with the survey of crime and criminal justice in Boston by the Harvard Law School showed that " the treatment carried out by (psy-chiatric) clinics, (juvenile) courts, and associated community

[30] William Healy: *The Individual Delinquent* (Boston: Little, Brown & Co., 1915).

[31] J. F. Brown: *Psychology and the Social Order* (New York: McGraw-Hill Book Co., 1936).

[32] Sheldon and Eleanor T. Glueck: *Five Hundred Criminal Careers* (New York: Alfred A. Knopf, 1930); Sheldon and Eleanor T. Glueck: *Five Hundred Delinquent Women* (New York: Alfred A. Knopf, 1934).

facilities added very little effect in preventing recidivism." Of course, all this means is that at the present time no appropriate devices are being utilized in sufficient quantities for statistical survey which give evidence of combating crime.

On the other hand, the psychiatric approach combining the attitude of Healy [33] and others and the technique of Freud as applied by Alexander [34] and others has gone forward.[35] The actual experimental application of psychoanalysis to criminals has gone far enough to allow us to say rather definitely that criminality can be classified psychologically as the result of: (1) reaction of theoretically normal personalities to the moral standards of a criminal group in which they have membership character; (2) the reaction of theoretically normal personalities alone in special situations of sudden, unendurable stress; and (3) aggressive failure of adjustment on the part of personalities handicapped in any of the seven typical ways described in Chapter II. A man with brain syphilis may, with his impaired judgment and his diminished emotional restraint, commit a murder which the same man prior to the development of his paresis would not have committed. Similarly, a stupid or schizoid or moody personality may commit a crime in a way directly related to his incapacity to adjust himself to a situation which a less handicapped personality would have less disastrously solved. Of these the neurotic criminals are the most interesting and perhaps the most numerous among those incarcerated in prisons since the neurotic tendencies are influential in determining the fact that the offender gets caught. In other words, since we know from numerous crime surveys that by far the majority of offenders are never apprehended or convicted, we must assume that those who are caught and convicted and punished are more vulnerable for some reason, and our psychological experience enables us to see that in some instances at least this vulnerability arises from a sense of guilt which the "normal " criminal does not have. If one

[33] William Healy and Augusta F. Bronner: *New Light on Delinquency and Its Treatment* (New Haven: Yale University Press, 1936) .

[34] Franz Alexander and Hugo Staub: *The Criminal, The Judge, and The Public* (New York: The Macmillan Co., 1930) ; Franz Alexander and William Healy: *Roots of Crime* (New York: Alfred A. Knopf, 1935) .

[35] Psychiatrists, psychologists, and social workers whose particular interest lies in the correction of behaviour disorders are united in an active organization known as the American Orthopsychiatric Association. At its annual conventions, which are attended by large numbers, topics pertaining to the scientific study of antisocial behaviour are presented and discussed from medical, psychological, and sociological points of view.

is in the business of crime, whether it be by promoting weak public-utility stocks or stealing automobiles, and does so without any conscience reaction, he will do his work for what he can get out of it and it is his business to do it cleverly enough to avoid being detected or convicted. The neurotic criminal, on the other hand — that is, one who has conflict in his mind about his antisocial activities — unconsciously assists society in arresting and punishing him. This has been made very vivid in the studies by Alexander cited above. These studies also showed that beneath the hard shell of criminal activities there may exist a great yearning to be loved. This factor has been therapeutically exploited in a somewhat individual but successful manner by Hartwell [36] in this country and Aichhorn [37] in Vienna.

It will be helpful in conclusion to cite from a recent study by Healy and Bronner in regard to the categories of emotional disturbances, discoverable from a psychological investigation of offenders, conclusions which agree so precisely with my own more limited experience and are so much more authoritative and so well couched that I quote them verbatim:

" (a) Attempt to avoid, even as a temporary measure, the unpleasant situation by *escape* or *flight* from it.

" (b) Attempt to achieve substitutive *compensatory satisfactions* through delinquent activities. These satisfactions include the thrill of delinquent adventure and the gratification at obtaining special recognition or attention, perhaps even notoriety, as a delinquent. In some instances material gains figure as compensation for deprivation.

" (c) Attempt to strengthen or *bolster up the ego* wounded by feelings of inadequacy or inferiority. The aim then is to obtain *recognition and status* with the delinquent crowd; or, if the offender is more solitary in tendencies, by the individual proving to himself that he really is courageous and can in some way play a spirited role. . . .

" (d) Attempt to get certain ego-satisfactions through direct and conscious or even unconscious expression of *revenge attitudes* — perhaps through hidden desire to punish parents or others by conduct that will make life difficult for them.

" (e) Attempt to gain a *maximum of self-satisfaction,* to inflate the ego, by generally aggressive, antisocial attitudes, that is, by the exhibition of definite hostilities and antagonisms to authority.

" (f) *Response to instinctual urges* felt to be thwarted. While this

[36] S. W. Hartwell: *Fifty-Five Bad Boys* (New York: Alfred A. Knopf, 1931).
[37] August Aichhorn: *Wayward Youth* (New York: The Viking Press, 1936).

response may be exhibited in sexual misbehavior, more notably in our delinquents we have discovered the attempt to satisfy the urge for independence and emancipation which normally flares up as an adolescent phenomenon.

"(g) The *wish for punishment* . . . a response to a conscious or unconscious sense of guilt." [38]

IV. RELIGIOUS APPLICATIONS

In the first edition of *The Human Mind* I had planned to incorporate a section on the religious applications of psychiatry. But when I reflected how difficult it was to define religion or to describe its function or its values in a way likely to be acceptable to the majority of my readers, I gave it up as a difficult if not impossible task. As a result, some readers interpreted the attitude of psychiatry, as represented by this presentation, to be antireligious. Said they: " As a realist, you must admit that religion means much to vast numbers of people; it makes their lives more endurable, it gives them comfort, hope, and happiness. For them it is a reality. It has much to do with their successful adaptation. If your conception of the human mind is an accurate and realistic one, how can you ignore the religious factor? "

Such an objection is entirely valid. Psychiatrists would be egotistical indeed to believe that they have any " corner " on the art or science of counselling the unhappy or correcting the misguided. Unless they set themselves up to be the very high priests of civilization, which of course they do not, they cannot assume to be the final authority in telling people how to live.

If, on the other hand, they have, from empirical experience or from scientific research, arrived at a knowledge which can be used by anyone who will acquaint himself with it to improve the skill with which he helps a stumbling or fallen fellow human being, certainly they should, by the code of scientific ethics, impart that knowledge to all who would make use of it.

This, indeed, the psychiatrists have been entirely willing to do. To be quite truthful, it has been rather that those whose professional lives require them to serve in the capacity of guides, counsellors, correctors, admonishers, advisers, and the like have cast a suspicious eye at psychiatry. Perhaps they felt that we were too presumptuous; perhaps our enthusiasm aroused their distrust;

[38] William Healy and Augusta F. Bronner: *New Light on Delinquency and Its Treatment* (New Haven: Yale University Press, 1936).

or perhaps it was merely that old suspicion which art always has of knowledge, and religion of science.

Whatever the reasons, certainly in times past, religionists, like the lawyers, had little use for any suggestions psychiatrists had to offer, and were willing to relegate to their care only such human wrecks as were no longer susceptible to their influence or persuasion.

It should be added in all fairness that science is apt to put its nose in the air, especially in these days of its practical exploitation and its material success; there is no doubt that many scientists have forgotten that, for all their self-satisfactions, religion is older, more prevalent, and stronger in the lives of the vast majority of human beings than are the principles of science.

Times have changed, however; neither the scientists nor the religionists are quite so proud. At any rate there are evidences of reconciliation. Psychiatrists have started writing books for the ministers to read. The ministers have been reading the books and quoting psychiatrists to their parishioners.

And so it is quite natural, I think, that the ministers have turned to the psychiatrists for advice. " What do you know that can help us? " they say. " We must counsel our people; we shall not relinquish our belief that their faith in God is of help to them, but can you give us perhaps some more human, some more worldly, some more practical aids? "

Some have pursued the matter quite systematically according to their training; there is an increasing number of books and articles in print discussing phases of the interrelationship of traditional religion and the various scientific attitudes represented by the term " mental hygiene." Some of these books have been written by psychiatrists, some by ministers, and some by psychiatrists and ministers in co-operation. A list of them is included in our Bibliography, and Oliver [39] lists a more extended bibliography of this subject, which he has well called " pastoral psychiatry." (See also Holman [40] and the publications of the Federal Council of Churches.) A good many of these books err a little on the side of encouraging the minister to undertake more therapy than I believe to be wise. Several studies have been made of religious manifestations in the mentally

[39] John Rathbone Oliver: *Psychiatry and Mental Health: the Hale Lectures at Western Theological Seminary*, 1932 (New York: Charles Scribner's Sons, 1932).
[40] Charles T. Holman: *The Cure of Souls: a Socio-Psychological Approach* (Chicago: University of Chicago Press, 1932).

ill.[41] I feel a certain obligation, however, to do more than merely refer to some of the excellent things that have been written. I have tried to think what I would say were one of my clergyman friends to ask me the question cited above.

I think I should say to him: " Were I a minister, first of all I should acquaint myself with what is known scientifically about the human personality. You may read this with a complete conviction that there is much more to it than we know; you may retain steadfastly your faith that there is something divine about the human being and that his faith in God is an essential part of him. Many scientists would not agree with you, but that does not matter. You could still legitimately learn what the scientists do believe about human beings and very likely you would be able to accept all of it. You could, for example, read the foregoing pages in regard to the structure of the personality, the conception of adjustment, the symptoms of maladjustment, and some of the devices used by psychiatrists for the correction of such maladjustments. And, while you are not a psychiatrist, there is nothing to prevent your using some of the same methods, providing you do not confuse the role of minister with the role of doctor. Presumably you are dealing with healthy — that is to say, relatively well-adjusted — people. If their maladjustment is considerable, it is not your duty to treat them; it does not correspond with either legal or religious concepts for you to do so; and it is dangerous to do so before an adequate diagnosis of the exact nature of their difficulties has been made."

An important practical question is to what extent the minister should endeavour consciously to be a therapist for either physical or mental symptoms of maladjustment. Theoretically it certainly is his privilege if not his duty. Practically it has several serious objections, but these have not deterred some from attempting it. A few years ago churches of various denominations became inspired with the idea of taking psychiatric experience to heart and making it a part of the function of the church. Church

[41] A. T. Boisen: " The Problem of Values in the Light of Psychopathology," *American Journal of Sociology*, Vol. XXXVIII, no. 1 (July 1932). Idem: " The Psychiatric Approach to the Study of Religion," *Religious Education*, March 1928. See also J. R. Oliver: *Foursquare: The Story of a Fourfold Life* (New York: The Macmillan Co., 1929). G. W. Jacoby: *Physician, Pastor and Patient; Problems in Pastoral Medicine* (New York: Hoeber-Harper, 1936). E. Van Norman Emery: " Cooperation between Clergyman, Psychiatrist, and Social Worker, 24:624–630. *Religious Education*, Vol. XXIV, pp. 624–30 (September 1929). Karl M. Bowman: " Religious Problems in Clinical Cases," *Religious Education*, Vol. XXIV, pp. 631–35 (September 1929).

mental-hygiene clinics were started, sometimes presided over by a psychiatrist in the name of the church, but occasionally managed entirely by the minister. If, as scientists have declared, ridding oneself of certain hates and other undesirable mental attitudes may relieve one of depressions and even of physical illnesses, why should not the minister or priest whose idea it is to dispel hatred apply this gospel in a therapeutic way? In other words, why should he not boldly undertake to cure those whose sufferings correspond to what religionists, at least formerly, called " sinful " attitudes?

The objection that every physician will think of first is that scientific treatment assumes diagnosis as a prerequisite. The minister can, to be sure, acquire some diagnostic clues, but without special training he cannot make an adequate differential diagnosis, and to fail to do so may lead him into serious errors. This has happened many times in the sphere of faith healing. Relinquishing one's envy of a sister under the inspiration of a minister (or, for that matter, of a healer or a psychiatrist) may cure a neurotic headache, but it will not cure a headache arising from an incipient uremia or a brain tumour and may postpone the recommendation of the proper treatment until too late. Here again, if one is a religious extremist and literally believes that the future life is far more delectable than the present, this mistreatment probably makes no difference, but then it would be still more logical by these standards for all of us to commit suicide immediately.

Another practical objection is the fact that legally and traditionally treatment is in the hands of physicians who give evidence [42] of their competence by examinations, licensure, and reg-

[42] The public has a peculiar idea that the medical profession favours the registration of those giving treatment on the basis of examination because they fear " competition " of less well-prepared doctors or others. It should be remembered that it was the lawmakers and the general public who instituted this plan, and not the doctors. It was a very wise one and only ignorant people speak seriously of the doctors' fear of competition. The doctors are continually working against their own " business," if business it is to be regarded, by developing and promoting public health and in various other ways trying to decrease sickness and suffering. The doctors do resent, however, the intrusion of ignorant, unscrupulous, or mentally unsound individuals whose promises to do the impossible, or shall we say the improbable, arouse hope in many which cannot be fulfilled and which lead to a general distrust of all treatment.

I should have thought this footnote to be unnecessary in the twentieth century had it not been for a recent conversation with some state senators who refused to pass a bill requiring all those administering treatment to have certain basic education. They refused, they said, because they thought doctors ought to be willing to " face competition like the rest of us have to do."

istration so that proper accountability can be rendered. Physicians, including the author, believe steadfastly in the justifiability of this arrangement for reasons of public policy.

The final objection, however, and the one that will appeal most to the ministers themselves, is that the ministers have many other things to do — so many, in fact, that to devote the time required for therapeutic offices to the individual members of their congregations would be humanly impossible.

This brings us back again to the conclusion that the function of religion and the religionist is better represented by prophylaxis than by treatment. It were better for the minister to assume that the ideals of living he preaches, the beauty of the services over which he presides with their music, their dignity, and their reflective hush, are a positive aid in the better adjustment of those who look to him, than to assume that he is more necessary to those troubled few who cannot even with these helps find happiness and health. This does not preclude his function as a personal friend and counsellor, but it does imply that he might well draw a practical line of demarcation, as does the rest of the world, between those who are well enough to profit by his ministrations and those who are sick enough to require a doctor.

In addition to these general principles, were I a minister, I should familiarize myself with the particular ways in which religion or something which passes for religion is grasped at in an irrational, compulsive way by certain individuals whose maladjustment is not apparent. The need for which religion is sought may be an insatiable need, arising from a very turbulent unconscious psychic structure. This leads to what one might regard as an abuse of religion or at least to a strange and excessive use of it. In this sense the religiosity must really be regarded as a symptom rather than a solution. It may become a very serious matter.

Let us take, for example, the religious history of Mrs. Henderson. She was an aristocratic girl, whose father was a government official of some prominence whose duties prevented his giving any attention whatever to his daughter. This is a point of great psychological significance in what is to follow. Accordingly she was educated in private boarding-schools, since he felt that her mother, a nervous irritable woman, was a deleterious influence upon the child.

The patient was married when she was only eighteen years old to a young man who had not quite finished his training in law school. She

had a fashionable wedding and she and her husband and the two children that were soon born to them lived in a city in Ohio where her
husband developed a good practice.

She had been reared in the Methodist church and for some time continued to work in it. For reasons not very clear to anyone she suddenly
decided that the Protestant Episcopal church was more nearly in accord
with her religious concepts and she transferred her membership. She
became very active in the work of that church, attended all the services
and all of the regular and irregular meetings, never omitting Holy
Communion when it was offered. She spent long hours reading and
discussing religious matters.

After seven or eight years, during which time she had established
herself as one of the pillars of that church, she decided that she should
again change faiths and insisted upon joining the Catholic church.

What does such a shift in religious faith mean? There is no
doubt that to her friends it represented intense, perhaps somewhat erratic, but certainly very conscientious devotion to religious principles. To the ministers whose churches she left, it
must have appeared to be quite inexplicable. To the ministers
of the churches which she successively joined it must have
seemed an evidence of increasing appreciation of the true faith.

To the psychiatrist it would indicate a progressive disintegration and an increasing inner necessity for an absolutism in religion which even the Catholic church could not offer her. Let us
look at the patient two years later.

At this time she had declared herself to be a member of the " invisible
church " and announced it as her mission to destroy all Catholics. She
felt herself to be the head of the " eternal triangle," which she described
as God the Father, the Son, and the Holy Ghost. She also thought herself to be a supernatural teacher or a nun in disguise. Such convictions
were announced by her going to the church, kneeling in front of the
altar, letting her hair down about her shoulders, and remaining there
for several hours weeping and praying; she then returned home, knelt
before her husband, and announced: " Unto us a child is born; unto
us a son is given," explaining this statement by saying that she was the
Virgin Mary and was soon to have a child by immaculate conception.

It is not sufficient to dismiss this as being the irrational wan-
derings of a very sick woman. Indeed it was, but one should not
lose sight of the consistent trend, even progression, toward this
extreme religiosity and mysticism. No one would deny that

the Protestant Episcopal church makes more use of symbolism and mystical references than the Methodist church, that the Catholic church does so more than the Episcopal church, and that this woman's delirium contains more such symbolism than the Catholic church. We can see that her progressive steps in church membership were progressive steps in her surrender of reality in favour of symbolic, mystical values.

It should not be forgotten that the Catholic theologians frankly describe certain aspects of their faith as mysteries; and that such mystical concepts have for certain people an immense psychological value cannot be doubted. The point is that for certain other people no such mysteries are acceptable, but all seem to be irrational, unrealistic, and " untrue "; while on the other hand, for still other people, such as this patient, they are not sufficiently mystical to gratify their flight from reality.

If I were a minister I would study with the psychiatrist some of those instances in which religion has seemed to do harm rather than good for the individual; I should study them without prejudice and without fear. It is a matter of common knowledge that many mentally ill patients have built up elaborate religious systems. Indeed, in his *Varieties of Religious Experience* William James pointed out that the fact that the founder of a religious faith may be, according to the standards of the rest of us, a little mentally affected, does not necessarily discredit the usefulness of his religious constructions. But these manufactured religions are not always useful; they sometimes seem to the psychiatrist positively harmful. Mentally sick persons sometimes express in symbolic language certain deep hopes and wishes of us all, wishes arising in childhood which experience and reality have led most of us to abandon. For some people the authorization of these wishes by religion is comforting, even inspiring; for others it only excites fantastic hopes, selfish preoccupations and irrational thinking.

From the standpoint of the psychiatrist a religion which merely ministers to the unconscious cravings for self-punishment, the relief of a sense of guilt, the repudiation of unpleasant reality, or the feeling of a necessity for atonement to some unseen power, by the repeating of phrases and ceremonials, cannot be regarded as anything other than a neurotic or psychotic system. One would be perfectly justified, on the basis of some religious philosophy — the total denial of reality — in killing anyone he did not like and then pronouncing solemnly some incantation to the effect that "he whom I killed was not reality but only a spirit; one cannot kill the spirit, therefore I have done no sin," or some other incantation to the effect that "Jesus, who forgives all sinners, must forgive my sins; to show my penitence I will walk out of my house barefooted in the snow and then all will be made right."

This is not said in any effort to disparage or ridicule anyone's religion, but rather to point out that religion may mean different things to different people and that psychological mechanisms determine what type of religion will satisfy a particular individual. The manner in which a man utilizes his religion — whether it be to enrich and ennoble his life or to excuse his selfishness and cruelty, or to rationalize his delusions and hallucinations, or to clothe himself in a comforting illusion of omnipotence — is a commentary on the state of his mental health. The fact is that we do not live in a world by ourselves. No religion which does not take cognizance of people about us and our responsibilities to them (aside from trying to convert them to the same self-absorption which *we* believe) is really a religion; it is a neurosis.

This is precisely what one sees in the religious formulations which many patients in mental hospitals produce in quantities. For example, I quote from an elaborate manuscript written by a charming but totally ineffectual and entirely self-centred patient who wrote many pages of which the following is representative:

"The distinction before the fall and after the fall of man in the garden I found to be this: God, himself, although the truth is somewhat disguised, conceived in man and made woman. Even as Satan's ways cannot be in the way of God, after the fall of Adam and Eve into sin because they did not withstand the temptation by the Devil, the sin of disobedience caused them to know the difference between right and wrong, and down through the ages the conception through woman is the way of Satan. But if this is the truth, what about the promise God made to Abraham that he would give him a son, I thought. In rereading the story concerning this promise and how God carried out his promise to Abraham, I noted that God, himself, conceived in Abraham's wife, and a son was born unto them. So far as is recorded, the last time God conceived in woman was that conception in Mary, the mother of Jesus."

But the following I quote, not from a patient, but from a tract published by a religious sect and distributed by the thousands.

This particular one was tenderly vouchsafed to a patient of mine by one of her earnest friends to whom it evidently had deep meaning which she wished to share.

" The Universal Subjective mind is a certain phase of the infinite mind of God. A portion of the Universal Subjectivity is allotted to mankind to use."

" Suppose a man owes money. His home is mortgaged. He has no manner of raising the money to meet the mortgage. The main thing to do is to stop worrying." (And the creditors? K. A. M.)

" An individual's vibrations once established in a sufficiently positive manner should maintain a continuous flow from his subconscious to the universal and they are to be effective and attract to the individual the thing he desires. . . . As a matter of fact, man is not subject to anything except as he himself permits himself to become a subject." (This person has never heard of measles, earthquakes, or poverty. K. A. M.)

My objection to these is not merely their silliness and their total disloyalty to reality, but their complete and essential selfishness. Further I object to what seems to me to be their utter dishonesty. I know there are some, even physicians, who feel it justifiable in dealing with persons whose difficulties they do not understand to " kid them along." If it makes them feel better (they say) why not? The same physicians often regard all religion as a similar illusion. Many and probably most religionists, however, distinguish sharply between vain and deceptive promises on the one hand and unselfish idealism on the other, as the basis of religion. They object, and perhaps properly so, to the selfishness inherent in all sickness and all individual treatment.

There can be no doubt that the emphasis in religion is frequently displaced from the idealism to the vain promises (both of heaven and of hell) and the various conditions supposedly determining the fulfilment of these. This emphasis, in my opinion, is more likely to be a cause of maladjustment than a solution for it. For example:

Bert Bonnigan was a fairly successful small-town garageman. He was an earnest, honest parent who carried on his business with no great financial success, but with the respect and confidence of his neighbours. There was nothing remarkable about his existence until the summer of his forty-third year, when his wife and two children attended a revival meeting of an eclectic sect in which a fire and brimstone future life was predicted for the wicked. His wife, followed by the children, " went forward " and was thereafter described as having been " converted." The father, a severely conscientious man, felt it incumbent upon him to do likewise, but felt he ought not to commit himself to something about which he was not wholly convinced. His family talked much of their new religious joy and instituted family worship, regular pronouncement of grace at meals, and the surrender of all types of recreation, including attendance at motion pictures, of which the patient was very fond. There was continual discussion among the members of the family of the eternal punishment awaiting the unbeliever and the non-conformist. The church services which his wife and children attended lasted from three to five hours each Sunday.

He worried a great deal about this, trying to bring himself to reconcile his wishes and pleasures with his family's religious views. All sorts of physical ailments developed — pains in his stomach, pains in his limbs, feelings of exhaustion, headaches, sleeplessness. These took him from one physician to another, without, however, any permanent relief. Things went on this way for a period of nearly four years. There was some fluctuation in the religious intensity of the other members of the family, but his concern as to the proper course for him to pursue did not diminish. Gradually, however, his pain subsided. His worries seemed to mount and he gradually succumbed to increasing feelings of melancholy, forgetfulness, preoccupation, and sleeplessness. In this condition he was admitted to a sanitarium for psychiatric treatment.

One should not gather that this family was an ignorant or erratic one; on the contrary, both the wife and the patient were intelligent, although of course quite limited in their horizons. A full discussion of the way in which his conflict had been represented at first by physical symptoms and then by depression, together with caution to his wife about the necessity for each man's finding his own religious expressions, accomplished tremendous relief for the patient, who was dismissed very much improved, if not well, after a few months.

Finally, or perhaps first of all, I should inquire of myself, were I a minister, just what my motives, my deepest purposes, were in the pursuit of my calling. I should not assume that they were self-evident and I should try to avoid the self-deception of rationalization.

One might assume that from a study of the minister himself we could learn everything about the function of religion in facilitating the adjustment of human beings in life. But, upon reflection, one can easily see that this is not necessarily true. The minister, priest, or rabbi is not to be regarded necessarily as one to whom religion has meant much; he is one for whom the expounding or administering of religion has meant much. It is theoretically possible, and I dare say it exists more often than we know, that one might be an excellent minister and at the same time have no personal religious satisfactions. We are apt to condemn this as hypocrisy. To do so is quite unjustified. There are certainly many physicians who refuse to take any medicine themselves, and lawyers who in their private lives are disinclined to abide by some of their professional convictions. This is no reflection upon any of them; it is merely an indication that the impulse to help others is not necessarily related to any convictions arising from help of the same sort for oneself.

Nevertheless, it cannot but be helpful to examine the function of religion in the lives of certain clergymen who, in spite of their success and in spite of their religious faith, have undergone at least temporary periods of acute maladjustment. Every psychiatrist has encountered such cases in clergymen of all denominations and sects, not excluding faith healers. Except for the latter, of course, it is no contradiction of faith for these sufferers to seek help from psychiatrists.

A very intelligent Catholic priest had gone as a missionary to a foreign country where he had undergone tremendous privations, some of them quite unnecessary and self-elected, and had been disappointed at the relatively sparse results of his religious labour. He returned to this country and was assigned to a parish in which he had constantly the feeling that life was too easy for him, that he was not sufficiently devout or sufficiently industrious. He laboured very diligently, kept in constant contact with the members of his congregation, carried through the services of his church successfully, but could not overcome his feelings of failure and unworthiness. He was told by some of his superior officers that such a spirit was compatible with that of a good Christian, that all of us were indeed unworthy of the sacrifices Jesus had made. One wise superior told him he was taking an exaggerated and not entirely sensible attitude toward the facts of life and his religion. Neither of these counsels affected him very much, however, and his growing depression finally made it necessary for him to be temporarily removed from his post of duty.

It was clear that this fellow was suffering from a deep sense of guilt arising from unconscious origins, a sense of guilt which he was unable to relieve through any amount of penance or self-imposed hard work. It is quite certain that neither he nor his associates fully recognized how definitely this sense of guilt was related to unconscious hatreds engendered in childhood and kept secretly burning by circumstances in no way connected with his religion. On the other hand, one trembles to think how a man with such an overwhelming sense of guilt might feel impelled to arouse and exploit the unconscious guilt of others, by projection. There is no doubt but that this mechanism has frequently been used by evangelical leaders of all faiths at all times. When John the Baptist went crying in the wilderness that all people should repent, however justified such an admonition may have been to the Jews of that period, it is certainly to be inferred from our present concepts of psychology that it applied first of all to John the Baptist himself.

Another minister, this time an Episcopalian, made an enormous success of a large parish on the west coast. Suddenly he "broke down." He became sleepless, anxious, unable to make decisions, distrustful of his mission and his stability, and was finally given a leave of absence by his congregation for the purpose of receiving psychiatric treatment. In his case he was motivated in his religious zeal not so much by a sense of guilt as by an overwhelming ambition to be the best preacher in the world, with the largest congregation and the most effective parish work. He was an exceedingly popular man and at the same time one who did not sacrifice principle in order to achieve popularity; on the other hand, he was very opinionated and aggressive. It was difficult for him to see that building the largest church in his city was not necessarily any evidence of emulating in the most effective way the principles and example of Jesus Christ.

Psychoanalysis revealed a very good reason for such great ambitiousness and for his compulsive feeling that unless he were the best in the world he was not good at all. He had been brought up by a strong harsh father of great physical stature. The patient's original childhood sense of inferiority was correspondingly great. The meekness conventionally associated with the profession of his choice was then only a disguise beneath which he could express his terrific but previously stifled wish to achieve the omnipotence he had felt his father had. That in his conviction he gave credit to the *heavenly* Father was, of course, only another disguise; his own father had been pretty big and pretty powerful, but of course he wasn't quite God (except to him as a child)!

A Jewish rabbi of great ability had been invited to one of the leading synagogues of an Eastern city. He served it for a time with a success that attracted wide attention. Subsequent difficulties in his adjustment for which he was referred to a psychiatrist proved to be related to the fact that as a child he had been expected by his parents to bring honour upon the family by becoming a rabbi, and not only "a rabbi," but the very best of all rabbis. To his childhood notion of things, this was in part a device of his parents for promoting themselves and their own sense of importance and obtaining by proxy a degree of power and influence over the other Jews of the community. However, it was not these parental motives that later disturbed him so much as the feeling that he had in some way or another been unfairly treated by being forced into something for their satisfaction which was not particularly to his liking and entailed enormous personal sacrifices and arduous study. He solved his ambivalence in regard to this problem by doing the job excellently for a time and arousing even greater expectations in them and then disappointing everyone, just as he as a child felt disappointed by the attitudes of his parents, not only in the respect mentioned, but in other respects which it will not be necessary to detail.

A middle-aged " practitioner " of a faith-healing sect who had a wide circle of friends in a small community suddenly became sleepless following a lecture given one evening on a subject pertaining to the theories of this sect. His sleeplessness was so intense that literally days would go by in which he was unable to close his eyes restfully for more than a few minutes in the twenty-four hours. He became highly apprehensive and agitated, and lost weight rapidly.

At last, against his convictions, he took some harmless sleeping tablets which relieved him immensely for a time, but finally, in spite of rather large doses of these, the sleeplessness recurred. This began to alarm him, lest he was becoming what he called a " drug addict."

He was finally taken to a sanitarium, where the physicians gradually reduced his sedatives to the point where he was not getting any, and discussed with him some of the emotional factors which had given rise to the increasing anxiety. These proved to be related largely to disturbances in his sexual life which were relatively easily corrected, and his insomnia permanently disappeared.

I have given these illustrations of religious leaders who have themselves suffered maladjustment in spite of their faith, not because they are of frequent occurrence, but because the fact that their interests were primarily religious helps us to see more clearly how religious expression is determined by individual needs and purposes. The fact is that relatively few clergymen break down, or at least relatively few come to the psychiatrist. I don't know why this is.[43] Some would interpret it as evidence of the saving power of religion; but I suspect the feeling that it *should* be so interpreted deters some ministers from getting help which they ought to have. Instead they suffer in silence and re-proach themselves for lack of faith. At any rate, it is my observa-tion that those who do come to the psychiatrist are often dis-tinguished by their superior intelligence and courage.

It is too early to say what the further developments of the practical application of psychiatry to the work of the clergy-man will be, nor can I attempt in these pages to review the more theoretical side of the connections between religion and psy-chiatry. There are many people to be helped in the world, and even the most agnostic scientist should concede that what is genuinely helpful to people cannot be denied them. What they regard as religion has, no doubt, injured some people, but what others regard as religion has, no doubt, helped many more than has psychiatry. This is not quite a fair comparison, of course, because, like common sense, religion formerly had to function exclusively for many people; there was nothing else. That it did function and did so in a socially useful as well as personally helpful way is attested to by many features of our civilization, particularly our schools and hospitals, which are in a very real sense the gift of religion, a fact which scientists have sometimes been entirely too cavalier in dismissing. We need not close our eyes to the ways in which religion has occasionally obstructed both education and science, but its errors should not blind us to its virtues. Indeed it is the essential spirit of the prevalent

43 John Rathbone Oliver, the clergyman-psychiatrist referred to above, says of this phenomenon: " I'll tell you the kind of people that I don't see in my office, as a general rule. So far as my experience goes, the people who do not seem to be assailed and poisoned by fears are those who believe and practice the Chris-tian religion. And by the Christian religion, I don't mean a religion man-made or man-given, but the Christian religion as it was established and delivered to twelve eyewitnesses by a Person who was both God and Man. . . . I tell you that people who believe and practice the religion that centers around this Personality seem to have an antidote against fear. At any rate I never see them. Don't mis-understand me. I'm not asserting that this form of religious faith is objectively true. I'm not saying that I accept it myself. I am simply putting before you . . . a fact as clearly proven to me as any other fact of my long professional experi-ence." (*Fear.* New York: The Macmillan Co., 1931.)

religions of the earth — Buddhism, Confucianism, Judaism, and Christianity — that one cannot live to oneself, but must love one's neighbour. And this is the same conclusion that we have arrived at in psychiatry. How this love of one's neighbour is to be fostered and expressed is a matter of varied opinion.

Psychiatry and religion may be thought of as co-operative rather than antagonistic. It is true that some psychiatrists feel that all religion is an illusion which the healthy-minded person can to a large extent dispense with. But this is an arbitrary definition of mental health and of reality, since we know that some so-called illusions are necessary to life. Psychoanalysis has been accused of being a foe of religion because it has decreased the dependence of some individuals upon compulsive rites. But it also has the effect of confirming some individuals, sometimes the very same ones, in the validity of certain aspects of their religious faith which previously they had ignored or minimized.[44]

[44] One of the leading British psychoanalysts recently wrote:

" It is indeed remarkable how frequently the researches of the psychoanalysts into the deepest recesses of the mind confirm the conjectures of some of the world's deepest religious thinkers. Psychoanalysts have pursued the problem of conscience beyond the frontier of consciousness, and the further they go the nearer they come to the concept not only of original sin but of godlike perfection. In his introduction Dr. Inge expressed some regret that Freud had openly referred to religion as an illusion. . . . But Dr. Inge should not have confused the attitude of natural science with the attitude of psychoanalytic science. So far from being antagonistic to religion, psychoanalysis has done more to add vitality to religious principles than any official body in the world with the possible exception of the Salvation Army. Indeed, psychoanalysts are more logical in their application of principles than any cleric or reformer. The average religious-minded individual is inclined to be satisfied when he carries out his precepts in his relation to equals, that is to say, to other adults. Psychoanalysts having made contact with the powerful, reassuring and recuperating functions of Love in man's unconscious, have returned to everyday life with a renewed sense of conviction. They find that religious institutions have not had the courage of their own convictions. They have neglected one of the most obvious outlets for their love-energies, the reduction of fear in the younger generation. In short, to the injunction ' Love thy neighbor as thyself,' the psychoanalyst has ventured to add ' Love thy children better than thyself.' " (Edward Glover: *The Dangers of Being Human.* London: George Allen & Unwin, 1936) .

It is only fair to say that a competent reviewer of this book, himself a psychiatrist (and psychoanalyst) had the following to say in contradiction:

" To couple psychoanalysis with the Salvation Army as two forces which have added vitality to religious principles would convey to a listener or reader knowing nothing of psychoanalytic technique the impression that we practice some energetic and ' vitalizing ' method comparable with that of the Salvationists for reducing the tension of guilt, and those readers with a capacity for constructive skepticism may wonder whether psychoanalysis will prove any more effective as a method for dealing adequately with the needs of ordinary people than has the Salvation Army.

" What our science is concerned to show is that man's need is not so much a

As one patient said, " Before my psychoanalytic treatment I went through the motions of religious observance in the way I had been taught I had to, faithfully and wearily, sometimes even resentfully. But after my analysis I was able to take genuine pleasure in the beauty and social purpose of my religion. Instead of a compulsive and conventional duty it became a comforting satisfaction and inspiration." [44a]

V. MEDICAL APPLICATIONS

The Historical Development of Psychiatry

Are psychiatrists doctors? Yes, they are, first and last. But while it has always " belonged," psychiatry has been the Cinderella of medical specialties. For years she sat alone by the fire in the kitchen, while her proud sisters Ophthalmology and Pediatrics strutted in the parlour. Sister Surgery was there, too, quite the queen of them all, forgetful of her humble origin in the barber-shop, and Mother Obstetrics was never reminded of her poor relations the Midwives.

When, by the Fairy Godmother's aid, the transformed Cinderella appeared at the Great Ball (the war), she outshone all her sisters. It was there she won the Prince's favour (popular esteem), and thereafter she came out of the kitchen and consorted with her fashionable and now deferential sisters, and at last married the Prince.

This allegory [45] is peculiarly apt. It sketches the development of psychiatry from the sterile, stagnant " asylum " period to the present unparalleled popularity of a specialty, which, because of its inclusiveness and its intimate relationship with all other branches of medicine, might even be considered the keystone of medical science.

The fairy godmother responsible for these great changes is a

---

removal of aggression, nor a once-and-for-all escape from guilt by personal or vicarious sacrifice, as an increased capacity to tolerate and thus be in a better position to deal with the feeling of guilt which it is our inevitable lot to experience, especially in our early object-relationships." (John Rickman: in the *International Journal of Psychoanalysis,* Vol. XVII, p. 528; October 1936) .

[44a] I have discussed the function of religion from the standpoint of the psychiatrist at greater length in the chapter entitled " Faith " in my book *Love against Hate.*

[45] Suggested by Dr. Thomas Salmon.

melioristic philosophy which kept alive embers of hope in the hearts of the early psychiatrists, whose task was generally regarded as hideous and hopeless. The patients relegated to them were the mad, the moonstruck, the lunatic, the alien, the devil-possessed, the idiotic, the demented, the insane. The very words are hideous, and their origins and meanings indicate the prevailing sentiments of aversion with which those afflictions were held.

Such feelings of aversion emanated from

1. The hopelessness ignorantly ascribed to such cases;
2. The helplessness of early medical science to understand or relieve them;
3. The persistence of superstitions and religious hypotheses dealing with their origin, their relation to sin, devils, evil spirits, and the like.

Of these, certainly the third has been the most powerful. Madness has for centuries been taboo — that is, both sacred and accursed. The taboo still attaching to it on the part of the rabble is betrayed by the archaic language of the law, but the progress of medical science and the extension of knowledge have lifted the taboo for the intelligent. The victims were found to be less hopeless than at first they seemed, and the increasing demands of civilization upon poor mortal frames increased their numbers. Familiarity replaced taboo with toleration and with the crusading spirit of modern preventive medicine.

It was the far-visioned hopefulness and the indefatigable spirit of the early *innominata* who observed and examined and nursed and protected the "insane" that formed the basis of modern psychiatric prestige. In the years when leeches and blood-letting and purges were the stock in trade of the practising profession, Pinel in France and Tuke in England and Dorothea Dix in this country were insisting that, all signs and customs to the contrary, the mentally sick were really human beings and deserved consideration as such and treatment for their sicknesses (about 1800). It was one step to substitute beds for heaps of hay, and another to replace whips and nakedness with even primitive decency and comfort. The progressive addition of sedatives, dietary care, nursing efforts, antisyphilitic therapy, hydrotherapy, and so forth, followed slowly (1850–1900).

Meanwhile there were accumulating data of these allegedly sick persons — psychological data, historical data, chemical data. An American association was formed (1844) of those physicians interested in these phenomena. Notes were compared, cases reported, brains examined. Gradually an increasing nosology (delimitation and classification of disease forms) grew up. From the old unitarian conception of one kind of "madness" there was first a revival of the preceding Greek (Hippocratic) partitioning into mania, melancholia, and dementia. Then all manner of varieties of each were described, and, what with kleptomania, pyromania, hypomania, monomania, acute mania, puerperal mania, delirious mania, etc., together with similar multiplications of the melancholias and the dementias, the nomenclature of psychiatry became elaborate, formidable, and useless. Accordingly, the balance of the medical profession, previously disdainful, was left astonished, bewildered, but none the less thoroughly convinced that psychiatry was an illegitimate child, still deserving of kitchen service in spite of these evidences of erudition.

It was Dr. Emil Kraepelin of Munich whose synthesizing genius brought order out of chaos. In a series of editions of a comprehensive treatise he coalesced certain similar clinical pictures into what he regarded as disease entities, showing certain general similarities in origin, symptomatology, course, termination, and pathology. From a mass of thousands of syndromes and names, he finally achieved a classification of approximately a hundred psychiatric entities, his most familiar creations being "dementia præcox" (schizophrenia) and "manic-depressive psychosis" (mania-melancholia). Kraepelin also deserves the credit for those atrocious names (about 1900).

During the first twenty years of this century these new formulations of Kraepelin's were engaging the attention of psychiatrists the world over, and soon became the dominant conceptions. The doctors in state hospitals were chiefly engaged in observations and descriptions of cases to be placed in one or another of Kraepelin's groups. This indeed was the maturity of the era of descriptive psychiatry, the Golden Age of fundamentalism. Characteristic of it was the descriptive and diagnostic attitude of the observers. The perceptual, intellectual, emotional, and volitional faculties were scrutinized in all their pathological variations; groups of symptoms and groups of cases were analysed; brains sectioned and stained and correlations of various sorts attempted between symptom and structure. The heyday of the branch of science called *neuropathology* was coincident and was the bridge of contact with the *neurologists,* private practitioners whose established respectability lent some prestige to the rising sister specialty. The elaborate brain-tissue-staining methods of Alzheimer, Nissl, Pahl, van Giesen, Weigert, and Cajal, previously applied to structural lesions of the cord and brain in traumatic, infectious, and degenerative conditions, were applied in these increasingly interesting mental aberrancies. The poverty of results discouraged no one.

Meanwhile the administrative attitude toward the mentally sick had steadily improved. Asylum provision was made increasingly comfortable, and the hospital rather than the asylum became the ideal. Pathologists and clinical directors were added to the staffs. Numerous therapeutic agents were added — pharmaceutical, hydrotherapeutic, electric, etc. The small diagnostic unit or *psychopathic hospital* became the vogue in various states. Specialized institutions for certain forms of mental disease were established, such as hospitals for the epileptic and schools and colonies for the feeble-minded. This was the great era of the state hospitals. Diagnosis was the key-note.

The first World War turned the tables. Entering at the back door, psychiatry emerged with enormous experience, enormous accomplishments, enormous prestige. The psychiatrists learned for the first time that they could be useful outside of asylum walls. They demonstrated that they had a province in war almost as extensive as, and little less spectacular than, the great realm of surgery itself. Unnumbered legions of patients with mental incapacities were referred to hastily organized psychiatric centres, not for mere labelling or diagnosis, but for rapid rehabilitation. Thousands were sent promptly back to active service. The psychiatrists overcame their ancient sense of inferiority and demonstrated to themselves and to the world that they could do something, something more than labelling various types of institutionalized wrecks.

This practical demonstration of efficacy moved psychiatry into the major leagues of medical specialties. It established definitely the therapeutic rather than the merely diagnostic objective. This ushered in the beginning of modernism in psychiatry, and ushered out old conceptions and terms such as insanity and lunacy. Psychiatrists became physicians, healers of the mentally sick, and ceased to be " alienists," or mere legal quibblers and nominators. From keepers of the insane they became counsellors of the unhappy.

Once the mentally sick who needed to enter a hospital were

necessarily made wards of the state, like criminals, and the formalities of commitment are still conducted in court-rooms in many places. But this is rapidly changing. Once all psychiatry was practised inside state hospitals. Now most of it is practised outside state hospitals.

One or two names stand out prominently among those whose spirit, energy, and wisdom were responsible for guiding American psychiatry through this period of metamorphosis to its present pre-eminence. (European psychiatry lags far behind.) Among these Thomas W. Salmon was the great ambassador who carried the cause of psychiatry to the courts of scientific and popular opinion with dignity and charm. Adolf Meyer has patiently expounded the didactic principles of psychiatric science to thousands of students. Smith Ely Jelliffe and William A. White courageously carried the new ideas of psychiatry into the old forms and into neurology and other branches of medicine as well. But the greatest genius of all, the man who in my opinion is more than any other one responsible for the extension of psychiatry from the laboratory and the asylum to the fireside and the market-place was Elmer Ernest Southard. His untimely death at forty-three has made his name less familiar to many than the principles he introduced, but the inspiration imparted to those fortunate enough to have been exposed to his amazing intellect and his kindling enthusiasm still carries on.[46]

Thus, from exclusive application to those patients with obvious and extreme psychopathology, psychiatry was gradually extended to other fields — criminology, sociology, pedagogy, and now, recently, with increasing intensity, to the parent field, general medicine. To it psychiatry has brought techniques of approach to the patient, of personality evaluation, and of therapeutic management with which general medicine, for all its perfection of laboratory procedure and clinical measurement, had been only vaguely familiar. Here and there an intuitive old general practitioner had discovered for himself in the " art ", of medicine the importance of dealing with the *feelings* of the patient and of influencing his recovery by a proper consideration of these intangibles. But psychiatry, with the aid of psychoanalysis, has made progress in the reduction of this intuitive technique to systematic, scientific principles, the application of which need no longer be limited to a gifted few.

[46] See *The Open Mind*, a biography of Southard by Professor F. P. Gay (New York: Normandie House, 1938) .

Psychiatry in the general practice of medicine

As a result, the emphasis on *psychological* factors in disease (as in health) is slowly permeating the entire practice of medicine. No longer the exclusively *chemical* concepts of the Middle Ages and earlier, nor the chemico-*physical* concepts of the nineteenth century, but a concept of interacting physical *and* chemical *and* psychological factors begins, now, to characterize the theory and practice of medicine. Once it was considered ridiculous to record a temperature; later it was considered ridiculous to examine a specimen of urine; and when these procedures became generally accepted it was still considered ridiculous to inquire into the details of a patient's dream. Now we know that dreams and urine and fever may and *must* all be examined if we are truly and fully to understand a patient. No intelligent or informed physician thinks any of these procedures absurd today — even though in practice he may sometimes omit one or several of them. For every thoughtful physician knows that psychological factors are as real and as effective as physical or chemical factors. His training, however, makes him feel more proficient and sure of himself in the old traditional modalities of physics and chemistry and he is often afraid to venture into the psychological investigations that he fully realizes his patients merit and need.

The result is that certain rather sharp differences persist in the points of view and techniques of most medical men, on the one hand, and psychiatrists on the other. The psychiatrists sometimes feel that they alone actually look at the human being as a whole, instead of as a creature with certain extraneous pathological attachments or invasions. The general medical man, on the other hand, suspects the psychiatrist of ignoring or underestimating physical and chemical data and of exaggerating psychic factors beyond their proper degree of importance. They think, too, that psychiatrists are apt to see the whole world a little askew, as if all people were "more or less crazy" and this strikes them as ill-founded and distorted.

Then, too, the time concepts of the psychiatrists and most other medical specialties (phthisiology and orthopedics excepted) differ considerably. Psychiatry, along with the two specialties mentioned, thinks in long-time terms; treatment extends over a long period, prognosis considers a long interval; the patient's whole life is under consideration rather than an acute episode or relatively brief illness.

Again, the patients with whom psychiatrists deal are still unfortunately, under some degree of social taboo which does not apply to the patients of most other specialties, that of the urologists perhaps excepted.

Finally, the psychiatric modalities depend more upon aural than upon oral ministrations. Words — that is, ideas — are " poured into " the patient rather than drugs, with, however, no less palpable — often identical — effects. This is a difference which the general medical man accepts with grave misgivings, because he feels suspicious of anything which resembles, even remotely, the unsavoury procedures of quackery and faith healing. Unfamiliar with the deeper mechanisms of psychological reactions, he cannot understand the therapeutic results which shrewd cult-leaders often secure, but has a strong feeling of condemnation for them because of their unscientific and often obviously dishonest methods. Because psychiatrists work with the same raw material and must use scientifically some of the tools which have fallen into the hands of unscrupulous and unreliable persons in some instances, the reproach attached to the faith healers has often been turned against the psychiatrists unjustly.

But the essential differences that yet separate psychiatry from general medicine go deeper than this. *To the psychiatrist, how the patient acts and reacts (behaves and feels) are important data. To the average physician, they are not (or have not been).*

For example, a cardiac patient may describe in detail his subjective reactions during a moving-picture show or while visiting his uncle; in either case the average physician listens only from courtesy, if at all. The psychiatrist, on the other hand, puts great stock in such data. Similarly, the psychiatrist is just as interested in how a patient reacts to the making of a physical examination as he is in the other data obtained from such a physical examination. He is just as interested in observing what the patient's emotional reactions are toward his office nurse or the hospital manager or himself as he is in discovering what the patient's blood-pressure or leucocyte count or vital capacity may be.

The psychiatrist considers it the first task of a physician to observe these ordinarily neglected data, to recognize them, to appreciate that they have meaning, to seek this meaning, to try to evaluate them. He feels that only having done this can he decide what should be done next with any degree of scientific precision. This " next " may be a chemical manipulation, a mechanical adjustment, or psychological therapy.

The question naturally arises as to whether there is any justification for attempting to bring closer together the viewpoints of the physicians and the psychiatrists. Is it or is it not helpful to consider the instinctual, purposive, emotional factors in general medicine? To the physician they seem unnecessarily elaborate and cumbersome. To the psychiatrist it seems impossible to ignore them with scientific justifiability. Both physicians and psychiatrists are apt to fall back upon the explanation that after all they are dealing with different sorts of patients entirely. But is this really true?

I should not go so far as to say that there is not some pragmatic value in the distinction that is made between patients who consult psychiatrists and patients who consult general practitioners, but I am certain that these groups are not separated so widely as is ordinarily assumed. The fact of the matter is that the psychiatric approach has never been applied in any systematic or extensive way to the general medical cases confronting the general practitioner. Rapid progress in this direction, however, is now being made, as was discussed in the first chapter of this revised edition, and many internists have become interested in psychiatry by way of the catch phrase " psychosomatic medicine." To speak of the emotional factors precipitating arthritis, the psychology of colitis, or the psychotherapeutic cure of gastric ulcer would have been regarded as *prima facie* evidence of lunacy or chicanery a few decades ago. Yet all these have been matters of serious scientific consideration by eminent physicians within the past few years.

Only a few years ago no medical schools taught psychiatry.[47]

[47] Surveys of psychiatric education as offered in representative medical schools were made in 1931-2 and since by a committee representing the American Psychiatric Association and the Commonwealth Fund. Most of the work was done by my neighbour and colleague Dr. Franklin G. Ebaugh of Denver, to whom medical education owes, in my opinion, a great debt. Dr. Ebaugh was kind enough to summarize the present status of psychiatric education in the medical schools for me as follows — but interested readers will consult his various published reports, noted below.

" In our 1931–1932 appraisal of the teaching of psychiatry it was found that only 14 of the 68 medical schools visited were giving reasonably adequate instruction in psychiatry. From many points of view such an appraisal is discouraging and especially so when we realize that the main objective of a general medical education is to produce a practitioner who has acquired a sound attitude toward his medical duties and responsibilities along with an ability to deal reasonably well in the early days of his practice with the rank and file of his patients, those presenting mental as well as physical phenomena. At the time we made the rounds of the medical schools there was an unanimity of opinion among the deans, professors of medicine, professors of pediatrics, and the psychiatric

Now all medical schools give required courses in psychiatry, and some of them do more than teach students the names of the major psychoses. Some of them present personality defects, the nature of adjustment failures, problems in " child guidance," and the mechanisms of personality breakdowns. This is very

---

teaching personnel concerning the practical importance of psychiatry in medical education; this paved the way for progressive change in the teaching of psychiatry as a fundamental phase in the basic general training. During the current teaching year there is evidence that all but 20 of the 68 schools visited have made noteworthy advances in the teaching of psychiatry. Such improvement is reflected in the teaching personnel, the content and viewpoints of teaching, and the clinical facilities available. Several schools have developed so-called ' liaison departments,' where the mental phenomena encountered in out-patient medical clinics and medical wards are freely utilized for psychiatric teaching. Many other schools continue to use state hospitals in their teaching and a few of these unfortunately continue with clinical teaching in the junior year class without establishing the essential preclinical foundations.

" Psychiatry should be looked upon as one of the fundamentals of the basic training of every physician and should not be taught as a specialty, but should be a major division of the general medical curriculum, along with medicine, surgery, obstetrics and pediatrics. . . . In such teaching, in terms of psychobiological principles involved in personality study, the various reaction-sets based on the interplay of physical, psychological, toxic and organic forces, and economic and social features can be evaluated. . . .

" Knowledge of the different types of paranoia, of the various types of the schizophrenic reactions is of little importance to the general physician. It makes little difference whether he can differentiate dementia præcox and manic-depressive insanity. It makes considerable difference, however, whether he has some knowledge of temper tantrums, anxiety, fears and the common emotional reactions to be found in every patient who comes to him. It is this material made up of early manifestations of mental disorders which we consider basic in the general teaching schedule. When emphasis in early teaching has been placed on the so-called normal reactions types and the relation of these to social situations the student with further elaboration can readily enter the study of the psychoneuroses and functional psychoses. . . . Although at present the objectives of undergraduate teaching should be that of a brief, clear-cut orientation in relation to the major psychoses, there should be greater emphasis on the clinical problems that physicians must deal with daily. Beyond this point undergraduate teaching is specialized and becomes postgraduate in terms of training. . . . The teaching of clinical years (assuming that the preclinical foundations have been well laid) should center mainly around the following headings arranged in order of their importance:

(1) The psychoneuroses (anxiety states, hysteria, obsessional states) ;
(2) Toxic and organic reaction types frequently encountered in general practice;
(3) The psychopathological implications in chronic organic disease;
(4) Psychiatric aspects of convalescence;
(5) The psychopathological problems of childhood; and
(6) Instruction of a pertinent, orientation type concerning the major psychoses."

See F. G. Ebaugh: " Ideal Standards for the Teaching of Psychiatry in Class ' A ' Medical Schools," *Journal of the Association of American Medical Colleges,* Vol. X, pp. 46–8 (January 1935) ; " Some Present Day Trends in the Teaching of

wise. For the vast bulk of psychiatric treatment is done, not in state hospitals and not by privately practising psychiatrists and not by the various free and pay clinics, *but by the general practitioners and family physicians.* It is they who have the constant contacts with patients whose minor nervous ailments, whose infelicities and inefficiencies, whose psychological and psychologically produced aches and pains, bring them to the doctor for help. The majority of these he can and does benefit. Here and there will be an exceptional case which is too severe, too complex, too resistant for routine treatment, which must be referred to a specialist, just as major surgical cases are referred to a surgeon. Minor psychiatry, like minor surgery, the general practitioner can and must do. But some day it will be considered just as heinous for a family doctor to neglect a case of melancholia as it is now for him to neglect a case of appendicitis.[48]

THE WAR AGAINST SELF–DESTRUCTION

I should like to suggest a theoretical point of view which might go far toward reconciling these differences of viewpoint between psychiatrists and general practitioners. This requires a rather radical revision in the ordinarily accepted notions of what disease is and what we, as physicians, are trying to do. It is a hypothesis which has gradually developed of late on the basis, originally, of empirical observations. I can only sketch it briefly here; it is elaborated in *Man against Himself.*

It is generally assumed, I believe, that the sick man comes to a doctor because he has been overtaken by fate, ill fortune, bacteria, or some other invader — and the disease is looked upon as something the patient hates, fights, and wants to be rid of. He applies to the doctor, who accepts the responsibility and focuses his energies upon combating this foe. But there are many bits of evidence that such a view makes incorrect assumptions and ignores an important principle. It does not require

Psychiatry," *Journal of Nervous and Mental Disease,* Vol. LXXIII, pp. 384–94 (April 1931) ; " What Constitutes Fellowship Training in Psychiatry: Some Fundamentals," *Mental Hygiene,* Vol. XV, pp. 791–812 (October 1931) ; and " The Importance of Introducing Psychiatry in Medical Licensure," *Federation Bulletin,* Vol. XXII, pp. 104–9 (April 1936) .

48 Quoted in part from an article by the author, entitled " Psychiatry and Medicine," *The Bulletin of the Menninger Clinic,* Vol. I, pp. 1–19 (September 1936) .

great intuition to detect the fact that the foe with whom many patients fight is not something outside of them but something inside — a part of themselves. They are often ready enough to let the doctors do the fighting for them; some even do their best to oppose his effort and even though bacteria, bad food, and sharp corners do exist and do inflict wounds, it is often observable that such wounds are invited.

If, in addition to this, we think of the persistence with which some patients cling to their illnesses, the compulsive way in which patients frequently force surgeons to operate and re-operate upon them, the extraordinary repetitiousness of afflictions to which some patients fall victims — these together with such clinical syndromes as alcohol and morphine addiction, neurotic invalidism, voluntary asceticism from other than religious reasons, malingering, and finally that most dramatic of all human acts, suicide — if we consider these things, we must begin to suspect as Freud did that self-preservation is not the only instinct which dominates mankind. On the contrary it would seem as if a self-destructive impulse waged constant battle with the will to live and took advantage of every opportunity to wreak its purpose upon its possessor.

Ordinarily the self-destructive impulses are presumably held in abeyance. Sick people, on the other hand, may be conceived of as persons in whom the battle has erupted so that they are trying to destroy themselves and at the same time fighting against it, imploring aid in this from the doctor. Such a hypothesis might be applied to such immediate and sudden self-destruction as is represented by suicide, or to more gradual and diffuse self-destruction such as neurotic invalidism. Perhaps such a thing as tuberculosis in which the individual seems to yield, sometimes all too willingly, to the invasion of an available assailant, and even the more localized or focalized diseases of the body may be thought of as further illustrations. Such an extension of the theory to organic disease was not made definitely by Freud and we are not yet in any position to support it with convincing evidence; it is, however, a logical conclusion from the theory that if there is a self-destructive impulse with the strength which Freud has postulated and which much clinical evidence supports, then we should not be surprised to find that it had an active part in the production of physical as well as psychological disease. Concerning its activity in the latter (that is, " mental " disease) , we psychiatrists now have no longer any doubt. Concerning its function in the former, we must wait expectantly the result of research.

In terms of this hypothesis, the therapeutic indication is regularly the same, whether in psychiatry, orthopedics, criminology, or cardiology. The physician must throw the weight of his knowledge, his skill, his experience, his chemical, mechanical, and psychological adjuvants on the side of the embattled life-instinct and in opposition to the destructive tendencies. This is actually what is done at the present time and, in both medical and psychiatric fields, we know that it sometimes saves the day for the patient. This success, in turn, saves the life of the physician, in a very literal sense. It diverts his own destructive tendencies to the attack on the destructive tendencies of others. This probably accounts for the prevalent optimism characterizing physicians in spite of their often dreary experiences, and for their convictions they have this responsibility and this power. Whatever the reasons may be, we physicians well know that our deep feelings and our professional ideals do not permit us to stand by inactively in the face of a life-and-death struggle. Our daily lives consist in a participation in innumerable miniature wars between life and death, and our constant striving is to increase our perspicacity, our skill, and our discernment and, from all of this, our efficacy in the opposing of self-destruction.

This is my conception of psychiatry and of general medicine as well; a more comprehensive treatment of it I must defer for the present. I feel sure that no one of my colleagues, medical or psychiatric, will deny that from this standpoint we have more in common than in controversy. What techniques we shall evolve to discover and rout or counteract this self-destruction will differ widely, varying with our talents and our training. But with this concept of disease and medical science we are less likely to be misled by the naïve assumptions, false optimism, and easy discouragement which the older views of man versus environment inevitably induced.

And surely there is balm in Gilead. No greater illusion prevails than that mental sickness is usually hopeless or has at best a bad outlook. Precisely the reverse is true. Most of its victims recover. Most maladjustments can be corrected. Some of the afflicted will right themselves, some will turn to amulets and chiropractic, some will insist upon operations, and some will put their trust in prophets. But there are rational, logical, scientific methods, and gradually — beginning with the intelligent and the intelligently guided members of society — these methods will prevail. And " by their fruits ye shall know them."

Not all psychiatrists agree on details of diagnosis or treatment, or ever will, in the nature of things, because psychiatrists are scientists, not creedists. But we are of one mind in our endeavour to apply ourselves to the scientific understanding and correcting of human unhappiness and misbehaviour rather than merely to its description or to its denial or to its punishment. This is the spirit of modern psychiatry.

SELECTED BIBLIOGRAPHY

IMMEDIATELY after the appearance of the first edition of this book I received numerous letters asking for further recommendations in regard to pertinent reading-matter. Since I could find no fault with my publisher's arrangement or presentation of the bibliography I had carefully selected and included, I decided that this must represent a certain popular distrust of appended bibliographies.

Because of the increasing use of this book by physicians, medical students, psychologists, and others for whom a more complete and more technical bibliography seemed desirable, I have constructed the following book list upon a very different basis from that of the first edition. I have selected topics which represent the general categories of interest corresponding to the subject-matter of the text. Under each I have listed books I and a dozen colleagues whom I consulted regard as most valuable. These lists have had practical use from myself, my colleagues and students, and our resident psychiatric physicians. Some are much more technical than others, but I have found it impractical to attempt to subdivide them on this basis. Those starred are the ones to read first.

It is more than likely that I have unintentionally omitted a few titles which certainly should be included, perhaps even some books by my friends. Such errors I shall hope to correct shortly after the first printing as the result of suggestions received from kindly critical readers.

I. NEUROLOGY

*BAILEY, PERCIVAL. *Intracranial Tumors.* Springfield, Charles C. Thomas, 1933.

*BING, ROBERT, and HAYMAKER, WEBB. *Textbook of Nervous Diseases.* St. Louis, C. V. Mosby Co., 1939.

BROCK, SAMUEL. *The Basis of Clinical Neurology.* Baltimore, William Wood & Co., 1937.

BROCK, SAMUEL. *Injuries of the Skull, Brain and Spinal Cord.* Baltimore, Williams & Wilkins, 1940.

COBB, STANLEY. *A Preface to Nervous Disease.* Baltimore, Williams & Wilkins, 1936.

*FORD, FRANK R. *Diseases of the Nervous System in Infancy, Childhood and Adolescence.* Springfield, Charles C. Thomas, 1937.

FULTON, JOHN F. *Physiology of the Nervous System.* New York, Oxford University Press, second edition, 1943.

GIBBS, F. A., and GIBBS, E. L. *Atlas of Electroencephalography.* Boston, privately printed, 1941.

GLOBUS, J. H. *Practical Neuroanatomy.* Baltimore, William Wood & Co., 1937.

*GRINKER, ROY R. *Neurology.* Springfield, Charles C. Thomas, third edition, 1943.

HEAD, HENRY. *Aphasia and Kindred Disorders of Speech.* 2 vols. London, Cambridge University Press, 1926.

HERRICK, C. J. *Introduction to Neurology.* Philadelphia, W. B. Saunders, fifth edition, 1931.

*MERRITT, H. H., and FREMONT-SMITH, FRANK. *The Cerebrospinal Fluid.* Philadelphia, W. B Saunders, 1937.

MONRAD-KROHN, G. H. *Clinical Examination of the Nervous System.* New York, Paul B. Hoeber, fifth edition, 1930.

NIELSEN, J. M. *Agnosia, Apraxia, Aphasia.* Los Angeles, Los Angeles Neurological Society, 1936.

*OPPENHEIM, H. *Textbook of Nervous Diseases for Physicians and Students.* 2 vols. Edinburgh, T. N. Foulis, 1911.

PURVES-STEWART, JAMES. *The Diagnosis of Nervous Diseases.* Baltimore, William Wood & Co., eighth edition, 1937.

REA, R. L. *Neuro-ophthalmology.* St. Louis, C. V. Mosby Co., 1938.

SPURLING, R. G. *Practical Neurological Diagnosis.* Springfield, Charles C. Thomas, 1935.

TILNEY, F., and RILEY, H. A. *Form and Functions of the Central Nervous System.* New York, Paul B. Hoeber, second edition, 1923.

WECHSLER, I. S. *A Textbook of Clinical Neurology.* Philadelphia, W. B. Saunders, fifth edition, 1943.

*WILSON, S. A. K. *Neurology.* 2 vols. Baltimore, Williams & Wilkins, 1940.

II. PSYCHOLOGY

a. Fields and schools

BORING, E. G. *A History of Experimental Psychology.* New York, D. Appleton-Century Co., 1929.

*——, LANGFELD, H. S., and WELD, H. P. *Introduction to Psychology.* New York, John Wiley & Sons, 1939.

FROLOV, Y. P. *Pavlov and His School.* London, Kegan Paul, Trench, Trubner & Co., 1938.

GOLDSTEIN, KURT. *The Organism.* New York, American Book Co., 1939.

HEIDBREDER, EDNA. *Seven Psychologies.* New York, The Century Co., 1933.

KOEHLER, W. *Gestalt Psychology.* New York, Horace Liveright, 1929.

KOFFKA, KURT. *Principles of Gestalt Psychology.* New York, Harcourt, Brace & Co., 1935.

LEWIN, KURT. *Principles of Topological Psychology.* New York, McGraw-Hill Book Co., 1936.

MARQUIS, D. G., and HILGARD, E. *Conditioning and Learning.* New York, D. Appleton-Century Co., 1940.

PAVLOV, I. *Conditioned Reflexes and Psychiatry.* New York, International Publishers, 1941.

*WERNER, HEINZ. *Comparative Developmental Psychology.* New York, Harper & Bros., 1940.

*WOODWORTH, R. S. *Contemporary Schools of Psychology.* New York, The Ronald Press Co., 1931.

b. Personology

*ALEXANDER, FRANZ. *Psychoanalysis of the Total Personality.* New York, Nervous & Mental Disease Publ. Co., 1930.

*ALLPORT, G. W. *Personality: a Psychological Interpretation.* New York, Henry Holt & Co., 1937.

ANGYAL, ANDRAS. *Foundations for a Science of Personality.* New York, Oxford University Press, 1941.

BOWLBY, JOHN. *Personality and Mental Illness.* New York, Emerson Books, 1942.

*BROWN, J. F. *Psychodynamics of Abnormal Behavior.* New York, McGraw-Hill Book Co., 1940.

CAMPBELL, C. MACFIE. *Human Personality and the Environment.* New York, The Macmillan Co., 1934.

DOLLARD, JOHN. *Criteria for the Life History*. New Haven, Yale University Press, 1935.

HEALY, WILLIAM. *Personality in Formation and Action*. New York, W. W. Norton & Co., 1938.

*HUNT, J. McV. (editor). *Personality and the Behavior Disorders*. 2 vols. New York, The Ronald Press Co., 1944.

JUNG, CARL G. *Psychological Types*. New York, Harcourt, Brace & Co., 1923.

KRETSCHMER, E. *Physique and Character*. New York, Harcourt, Brace & Co., 1925.

LEWIN, KURT. *A Dynamic Theory of Personality*. New York, McGraw-Hill Book Co., 1935.

MALAMUD, WILLIAM. *Outlines of General Psychopathology*. New York, W. W. Norton & Co., 1935.

*MASLOW, A. H., and MITTELMAN, BELA. *Principles of Abnormal Psychology*. New York, Harper & Bros., 1941.

McDOUGALL, WILLIAM. *Outline of Abnormal Psychology*. New York, Charles Scribner's Sons, 1926.

*MURRAY, HENRY A., et al. *Explorations in Personality*. New York, Oxford University Press, 1938.

SHELDON, W. H. *The Varieties of Temperament*. New York, Harper & Bros., 1942.

STAGNER, ROSS. *Psychology of Personality*. New York, McGraw-Hill Book Co., 1937.

*WHITE, WILLIAM A. *Mechanisms of Character Formation*. New York, The Macmillan Co., 1920.

WOLFF, WERNER. *The Expression of Personality*. New York, Harper & Bros., 1943.

c. Psychopathology, experimental

ANDERSON, O. D., and PARMENTER, RICHARD. *A Long-Term Study of the Experimental Neurosis in the Sheep and Dog*. Psychosomatic Medicine Monographs. Washington, D. C., National Research Council, 1941.

DOLLARD, JOHN, et al. *Frustration and Aggression*. New Haven, Yale University Press, 1939.

KOEHLER, W. *The Mentality of Apes*. London, Kegan Paul, Trench, Trubner & Co., 1927.

LEWIN, KURT. *A Dynamic Theory of Personality*. New York, McGraw-Hill Book Co., 1935.

——, et al. *Frustration and Regression*. Iowa City, University of Iowa Press, 1941.

LURIA, A. R. *The Nature of Human Conflicts.* New York, Horace Liveright, 1932.

MASSERMANN, JULES. *Behavior and Neurosis.* Chicago, University of Chicago Press, 1943.

*MILLER, J. G. *Unconsciousness.* New York, John Wiley & Sons, 1942.

*RAPAPORT, DAVID. *Emotions and Memory.* Baltimore, Williams & Wilkins, 1942.

SEARS, RICHARD R. *Survey of Objective Studies of Psychoanalytic Concepts.* New York, Social Science Research Council, 1943.

SEMON, R. *The Mneme.* London, George Allen & Unwin, 1921.

*TOMKINS, SILVAN (editor). *Contemporary Psychopathology.* Cambridge, Harvard University Press, 1943.

d. Psychopathology, clinical

BABCOCK, HELEN. *A Short Form of the Babcock Examination for the Measurement of Mental Deterioration.* Chicago, Stoelting, 1933.

BENDER, LAURETTA. *The Visual Motor Gestalt Test and Its Clinical Use.* New York, American Orthopsychiatric Association, 1938.

BRONNER, A. F., et al. *A Manual of Individual Mental Tests and Testing.* Boston, Little, Brown & Co., 1929.

*BROWN, J. F. *Psychodynamics of Abnormal Behavior.* New York, McGraw-Hill Book Co., 1940.

GOLDSTEIN, KURT, and SCHEERER, MARTIN. *Concept Formation.* Evanston, Ill., American Psychological Association, 1941.

HANFMANN, EUGENIA, and KASANIN, J. S. *Conceptual Thinking in Schizophrenia.* New York, Nervous & Mental Disease Publ. Co., 1942.

*HART, BERNARD. *The Psychology of Insanity.* London, Cambridge University Press, 1922.

——. *Psychopathology; Its Development and Its Place in Medicine.* New York, The Macmillan Co., 1927.

*KEMPF, EDWARD J. *Psychopathology.* St. Louis, C. V. Mosby Co., 1921.

MERRILL, MAUD A., and TERMAN, LEWIS. *Measuring Intelligence.* Boston, Houghton Mifflin Co., 1937.

*RAPAPORT, DAVID, et al. *Diagnostic Psychological Testing; the Theory, Statistical Evaluation, and Diagnostic Application of a Battery of Tests.* In press.

*Rorschach, H. H. *Psychodiagnostics.* New York, Grune & Stratton, 1943.

*Wechsler, David. *Measurement of Adult Intelligence.* Baltimore, Williams & Wilkins, 1941.

Wells, F. L. *Tests in Clinical Practice.* Yonkers-on-Hudson, World Book Co., 1927.

———, and Ruesch, Jurgen. *Mental Examiners' Handbook.* New York, Psychological Corporation, 1942.

III. PSYCHIATRY

a. The field

Bentley, M., and Cowdrey, E. V. *The Problem of Mental Disorder.* New York, McGraw-Hill Book Co., 1934.

*Campbell, C. Macfie. *Destiny and Disease in Mental Disorders.* New York, W. W. Norton & Co., 1935.

*———. *A Present Day Conception of Mental Disorders.* Cambridge, Harvard University Press, 1929.

*Cobb, Stanley. *Borderlines of Psychiatry.* Cambridge, Harvard University Press, 1943.

Ebaugh, Franklin, and Rymer, C. A. *Psychiatry in Medical Education.* New York, The Commonwealth Fund, 1942.

Hinsie, Leland, and Shatzky, Jacob. *Psychiatric Dictionary.* New York, Oxford University Press, 1940.

Hutchings, Richard H. *A Psychiatric Wordbook.* Utica, State Hospitals Press, fourth edition, 1935.

White, William A. *Twentieth Century Psychiatry.* New York, W. W. Norton & Co., 1936.

*Zilboorg, Gregory. *Mind, Medicine and Man.* New York, Harcourt, Brace & Co., 1943.

b. Textbooks and manuals

Appel, K. E., and Strecker, E. A. *Practical Examination of Personality and Behavior Disorders in Adults and Children.* New York, The Macmillan Co., 1936.

*Bleuler, Eugen. *Textbook of Psychiatry.* New York, The Macmillan Co., 1924.

*Cheney, C. O. *Outlines for Psychiatric Examinations.* Utica, State Hospitals Press, 1934.

Gordon, R. G., Harris, N. G., and Rees, J. R. *An Introduction to Psychological Medicine.* New York, Oxford University Press, 1936.

*HENDERSON, D. K., and GILLESPIE, R. D. *A Textbook of Psychiatry*. London, Oxford University Press, 1927.

HENRY, GEORGE W. *Essentials of Psychiatry*. Baltimore, Williams & Wilkins, 1925.

HINSIE, LELAND E. *Visual Outline of Psychiatry*. New York, Oxford University Press, 1941.

JELLIFFE, S. E., and WHITE, W. A. *Diseases of the Nervous System*. Philadelphia, Lea & Febiger, sixth edition, 1935.

*KRAEPELIN, EMIL. *Lectures on Clinical Psychiatry*. New York, William Wood & Co., 1917.

——. *Lehrbuch der Psychiatrie*. Leipzig, J. A. Barth, eighth edition, 1915.

KRETSCHMER, E. *A Textbook of Medical Psychology*. London, Oxford University Press, 1934.

*MacCURDY, J. T. *Psychology of Emotion, Morbid and Normal*. New York, Harcourt, Brace & Co., 1925.

*NOYES, A. P. *Modern Clinical Psychiatry*. Philadelphia, W. B. Saunders, second edition, 1939.

ROSANOFF, A. J. *Manual of Psychiatry and Mental Hygiene*. New York, John Wiley & Sons, 1938.

STRECKER, E. A. *Fundamentals of Psychiatry*. Philadelphia, J. B. Lippincott Co., 1942.

*——, and EBAUGH, F. G. *Practical Clinical Psychiatry*. Philadelphia, Blakiston Co., fifth edition, 1940.

*WHITE, W. A. *Outlines of Psychiatry*. New York, Nervous & Mental Disease Publ. Co., fourteenth edition, 1935.

c. Special topics

Administration:

*BRYAN, W. A. *Administrative Psychiatry*. New York, W. W. Norton & Co., 1936.

Heredity:

*ASSOCIATION FOR RESEARCH IN NERVOUS AND MENTAL DISEASE. *Heredity in Nervous and Mental Disease*. New York, Paul B. Hoeber, 1923.

MYERSON, ABRAHAM. *The Inheritance of Mental Diseases*. Baltimore, Williams & Wilkins, 1925.

Sexual Pathology:

*ALLEN, CLIFFORD. *The Sexual Perversions and Abnormalities*. London, Oxford University Press, 1940.

Ellis, Havelock. *Studies in the Psychology of Sex.* 4 vols. New York, Random House, 1936.

*Henry, George W. *Sex Variants.* 2 vols. New York, Paul B. Hoeber, 1943.

Hirschfeld, Magnus. *Sexual Pathology.* New York, Emerson Books, 1940.

Krafft-Ebing, R. *Psychopathia Sexualis.* New York, Rebman Co., n.d.

Alcohol addiction:

Durfee, C. H. *To Drink or Not to Drink.* New York, Longmans, Green & Co., 1937.

Emerson, Haven (editor). *Alcohol and Man.* New York, The Macmillan Co., 1933.

Haggard, H. W., and Jellinek, E. M. *Alcohol Explored.* Garden City, Doubleday, Doran & Co., 1942.

*Jellinek, E. M. *Alcohol Addiction and Chronic Alcoholism.* New Haven, Yale University Press, 1942.

Peabody, Richard R. *The Common Sense of Drinking.* Boston, Little, Brown & Co., 1931.

Smith, W. H., and Helwig, F. C. *Liquor, the Servant of Man.* Boston, Little, Brown & Co., 1939.

Strecker, E. A., and Chambers, F. T. *Alcohol, One Man's Meat.* New York, The Macmillan Co., 1938.

Other syndromes:

Association for Research in Nervous and Mental Disease. *Manic-Depressive Psychosis.* Baltimore, Williams & Wilkins, 1931.

*——. *Schizophrenia.* New York, Paul B. Hoeber, 1928.

Bivin, George, and Klinger, Pauline. *Pseudocyesis.* Bloomington, Ind., Principia Press, 1937.

Blanton, S., and Blanton, M. *For Stutterers.* New York, D. Appleton-Century Co., 1936.

*Cleckley, Hervey. *The Mask of Sanity.* (Psychopathy.) St. Louis, C. V. Mosby Co., 1941.

Coon, G. P., and Raymond, A. F. *A Review of the Psychoneuroses at Stockbridge.* Stockbridge, Mass., Austen Riggs Foundation, 1940.

Coriat, Isidor. *Stammering.* New York, Nervous & Mental Disease Publ. Co., 1928.

Dublin, Louis, and Bunzel, Bessie. *To Be or Not to Be.* (Suicide.) New York, Harrison Smith & Robert Haas, 1933.

HENDERSON, D. K. *Psychopathic States.* New York, W. W. Norton & Co., 1939.

*JANET, PIERRE. *The Major Symptoms of Hysteria.* New York, The Macmillan Co., 1907.

*JUNG, CARL G. *The Psychology of Dementia Præcox.* New York, Nervous & Mental Disease Publ. Co., 1936.

KAHN, EUGEN. *Psychopathic Personalities.* New Haven, Yale University Press, 1931.

KARDINER, ABRAM. *The Bio-Analysis of the Epileptic Reaction.* New York, The Psychoanalytic Quarterly, 1932.

KRAEPELIN, EMIL. *General Paresis.* New York, Nervous & Mental Disease Publ. Co., 1913.

——. *Manic-Depressive Insanity and Paranoia.* Edinburgh, E. & S. Livingstone, 1921.

——. *Dementia Præcox.* Edinburgh, E. & S. Livingstone, 1919.

LEWIS, NOLAN D. C. *Research in Dementia Præcox.* New York, National Committee for Mental Hygiene, 1936.

MENNINGER, WILLIAM C. *Juvenile Paresis.* Baltimore, William Wood & Co., 1936.

MILLET, JOHN. *Insomnia.* New York, Greenberg, 1938.

PENFIELD, WILDER, and ERICKSON, T. C. *Epilepsy and Cerebral Localization.* Springfield, Charles C. Thomas, 1941.

*PUTNAM, TRACY J. *Convulsive Seizures.* Philadelphia, J. B. Lippincott Co., 1943.

*SOUTHARD, E. E., and SOLOMON, H. C. *Neurosyphilis.* Boston, W. M. Leonard, 1917.

STORCH, ALFRED. *Primitive Archaic Forms of Inner Experience and Thought in Schizophrenia.* New York, Nervous & Mental Disease Publ. Co., 1924.

TALBOT, FRITZ B. *Treatment of Epilepsy.* New York, The Macmillan Co., 1930.

*TREDGOLD, A. F. *A Textbook of Mental Deficiency.* Baltimore, William Wood & Co., 1937.

WECHSLER, I. S. *The Neuroses.* Philadelphia, W. B. Saunders, 1929.

d. Treatment (except psychoanalysis and nursing)

BARKER, L. F. *Psychotherapy.* New York, D. Appleton-Century Co., 1940.

*BRAMWELL, J. MILNE. *Hypnotism, Its History, Practice and Theory.* Philadelphia, J. B. Lippincott Co., 1930.

*Brenman, Margaret, and Gill, Merton M. *Hypnotherapy.* In press.

Brown, William. *Psychology and Psychotherapy.* London, Edward Arnold & Co., third edition, 1934.

Diethelm, Oscar. *Treatment in Psychiatry.* New York, The Macmillan Co., 1936.

Harris, Noel. *Modern Psychotherapy.* London, John Bale, 1939.

Hinsie, Leland, E. *Concepts and Problems of Psychotherapy.* New York, Columbia University Press, 1937.

Hull, Clark. *Hypnosis and Suggestibility.* New York, D. Appleton-Century Co., 1933.

Jessner, Lucie, and Ryan, V. G. *Shock Treatment in Psychiatry.* New York, Grune & Stratton, 1941.

Kraines, Samuel. *The Therapy of the Neuroses and Psychoses.* Philadelphia, Lea & Febiger, second edition, 1943.

*Levine, Maurice. *Psychotherapy in Medical Practice.* New York, The Macmillan Co., 1942.

Moll, Albert. *Hypnotism.* New York, Charles Scribner's Sons, 1890.

Rogers, Carl R. *Counseling and Psychotherapy.* Boston, Houghton Mifflin Co., 1942.

Schilder, Paul. *Psychotherapy.* New York, W. W. Norton & Co., 1938.

*—— and Kauders, Otto. *Hypnosis.* New York, Nervous & Mental Disease Publ. Co., 1927.

*Slavson, S. R. *An Introduction to Group Therapy.* New York, The Commonwealth Fund, 1943.

Wingfield, H. E. *An Introduction to the Study of Hypnotism; Experimental and Therapeutic.* London, Bailliere, Tindall & Cox, 1920.

Yellowlees, H. *A Manual of Psychotherapy for Practitioners and Students.* London, Black, 1923.

Occupational therapy:

Dunton, William R. *Occupational Therapy.* Philadelphia, W. B. Saunders, 1915.

*——. *Prescribing Occupational Therapy.* Springfield, Charles C. Thomas, 1928.

Ketcham, Dorothy. *One Hundred Thousand Days of Illness.* Ann Arbor, Edwards Bros., 1939.

RUSSELL, JOHN I. *The Occupational Treatment of Mental Illness*. Baltimore, William Wood & Co., 1938.

Physiotherapy:

JENSEN, KATHRYN L. *Fundamentals in Massage*. New York, The Macmillan Co., 1938.

*KOVACS, RICHARD. *Manual of Physical Therapy*. Philadelphia, Lea & Febiger, 1944.

*WRIGHT, REBECCA. *Hydrotherapy in Psychiatric Hospitals*. Boston, Tudor Press, 1940.

Recreational therapy:

DAVIS, JOHN E. *Play and Mental Health*. New York, A. S. Barnes & Co., 1938.

——. *Principles and Practice of Rehabilitation*. New York, A. S. Barnes & Co., 1943.

*—— and MASON, B. S. *Principles and Practice of Recreational Therapy for the Mentally Ill*. New York, A. S. Barnes & Co., 1936.

*MITCHELL, E. D., and MASON, B. S. *The Theory of Play*. New York, A. S. Barnes & Co., 1935.

e. Nursing

ANDERSON, CAMILLA M. *Emotional Hygiene*. Philadelphia, J. B. Lippincott Co., third edition, 1943.

BAILEY, HARRIET. *Nursing Mental Diseases*. New York, The Macmillan Co., fourth edition, 1939.

BENNETT, A. E., and PURDY, AVIS B. *Psychiatric Nursing Technic*. Philadelphia, F. A. Davis Co., 1940.

BIDDLE, W. E., and VAN SICKEL, M. *Introduction to Psychiatry*. Philadelphia, W. B. Saunders, 1943.

CHADWICK, MARY. *Nursing Psychological Patients*. London, George Allen & Unwin, 1931.

——. *Psychology for Nurses*. London, William Heinemann, 1925.

HARRIMAN, P. L., GREENWOOD, L. L., and SKINNER, E. E. *Psychology in Nursing Practice*. New York, The Macmillan Co., 1942.

*INGRAM, MADELENE E. *Principles of Psychiatric Nursing*. Philadelphia, W. B. Saunders, 1939.

*KARNOSH, L. J., and GAGE, EDITH B. *Psychiatry for Nurses*. St. Louis, C. V. Mosby Co., 1940.

*MOERSCH, F. P. *Neurology and Psychiatry for Nurses.* Minneapolis, Burgess Publ. Co., 1935.

*NOYES, A. P., and HAYDON, EDITH M. *A Textbook of Psychiatry.* New York, The Macmillan Co., third edition, 1940.

PIERCE, BEDFORD. *Addresses to Mental Nurses.* London, Bailliere, Tindall & Cox, 1924.

SANDS, IRVING J. *Nervous and Mental Diseases for Nurses.* Philadelphia, W. B. Saunders, 1937.

*STEELE, KATHARINE McL. *Psychiatric Nursing.* Philadelphia, F. A. Davis Co., 1937.

f. History

ALLEN, CLIFFORD. *Modern Discoveries in Medical Psychology.* New York, The Macmillan Co., 1937.

*AMERICAN PSYCHIATRIC ASSOCIATION. *One Hundred Years of Psychiatry.* New York, Columbia University Press, 1944.

*DEUTSCH, ALBERT. *The Mentally Ill in America.* New York, Doubleday, Doran & Co., 1937.

DEVINE, H. *Recent Advances in Psychiatry.* Philadelphia, Blakiston Co., 1933.

GAY, FREDERICK P. *The Open Mind; Elmer Ernest Southard, 1876–1920.* New York, Normandie House, 1938.

GRIESINGER, WILLIAM. *Mental Pathology and Therapeutics.* London, New Sydenham Society, 1867.

*LEWIS, NOLAN D. C. *A Short History of Psychiatric Achievement.* New York, W. W. Norton & Co., 1941.

*MARSHALL, HELEN E. *Dorothea Dix — the Forgotten Samaritan.* Chapel Hill, N. C., University of North Carolina Press, 1937.

SELLING, LOWELL S. *Men against Madness.* New York, Greenberg, 1940.

WINKLER, J. K., and BROMBERG, W. *Mind Explorers.* New York, Reynal & Hitchcock, 1939.

*ZILBOORG, GREGORY. *A History of Medical Psychology.* New York, W. W. Norton & Co., 1941.

g. Social case work

DAY, FLORENCE. *Social Case Work.* Social Work Year Book, 1941.

DE SCHWEINITZ, KARL. *The Art of Helping People Out of Trouble.* Boston, Houghton Mifflin Co., 1934.

*French, Lois M. *Psychiatric Social Work.* New York, The Commonwealth Fund, 1940.

*Garrett, Annette. *Interviewing; Its Principles and Methods.* New York, Family Welfare Association of America, 1942.

Hamilton, Gordon. *Theory and Practice of Social Case Work.* New York, Columbia University Press, 1940.

Heath, Esther. *The Approach to the Parent.* New York, The Commonwealth Fund, 1933.

*Hollis, Florence. *Social Case Work and Practice; Six Case Studies.* New York, Family Welfare Association of America, 1939.

Hutchinson, Dorothy. *In Quest of Foster Parents.* New York, Columbia University Press, 1943.

Lee, P., and Kenworthy, M. *Mental Hygiene and Social Work.* New York, The Commonwealth Fund, 1929.

Reynolds, Bertha. *Between Client and Community.* Smith College Studies in Social Work, Vol. V., No. 1, September 1934.

*———. *Learning and Teaching in the Practice of Social Work.* New York, Farrar & Rinehart, 1942.

———. *Short Contact Interviews.* Smith College Studies in Social Work, Vol. III, No. 1, September 1932.

Richmond, Mary. *Social Diagnosis.* New York, The Russell Sage Foundation, 1917.

———. *What Is Social Casework?* New York, The Russell Sage Foundation, 1922.

*Robinson, Virginia. *A Changing Psychology in Social Casework.* Chapel Hill, N. C., University of North Carolina Press, 1930.

*Towle, Charlotte. *Social Case Records from Psychiatric Clinics.* Chicago, University of Chicago Press, 1941.

Young, Pauline. *Interviewing in Social Work.* New York, McGraw-Hill Book Co., 1935.

IV. APPLICATIONS OF PSYCHIATRY TO OTHER FIELDS

a. Sociological applications

Alexander, Franz. *Our Age of Unreason.* Philadelphia, J. B. Lippincott Co., 1942.

*Bassett, Clara. *Mental Hygiene in the Community.* New York, The Macmillan Co., 1934.

*Brown, J. F. *Psychology and the Social Order*. New York, McGraw-Hill Book Co., 1936.

Dickinson, R. L., and Beam, Lura. *A Thousand Marriages*. New York, The Century Co., 1932.

Faris, R. E. L., and Dunham, H. W. *Mental Disorders in Urban Areas*. Chicago, University of Chicago Press, 1939.

Fry, C. C., and Rostow, E. G. *Mental Health in College*. New York, The Commonwealth Fund, 1942.

Groves, E. R. *The American Family*. Philadelphia, J. B. Lippincott Co., 1934.

——, and Blanchard, P. *Introduction to Mental Hygiene*. New York, Henry Holt & Co., 1930.

——, and Brooks, L. M. *Readings in the Family*. Philadelphia, J. B. Lippincott Co., 1934.

Lasswell, H. D. *Psychopathology and Politics*. Chicago, University of Chicago Press, 1930.

*Levy, John, and Munroe, Ruth. *The Happy Family*. New York, Alfred A. Knopf, 1938.

Queen, S. A., and Mann, D. M. *Social Pathology*. New York, Thomas Y. Crowell, 1925.

*Southard, E. E., and Jarrett, M. *The Kingdom of Evils*. New York, The Macmillan Co., 1922.

*Stern, Edith M. *Mental Illness; a Guide to the Family*. New York, The Commonwealth Fund, 1942.

Williams, Frankwood E. *Some Social Aspects of Mental Hygiene*. New York, National Committee for Mental Hygiene, 1930.

b. Educational applications

Adler, Alfred. *The Education of Children*. New York, Greenberg, 1930.

Fenton, Norman. *Mental Hygiene in School Practice*. Stanford University Press, 1943.

*Freud, Anna. *Psychoanalysis for Teachers and Parents*. New York, Emerson Books, 1935.

*Low, Barbara. *Psychoanalysis and Education*. New York, Harcourt, Brace & Co., 1928.

Menninger, K. A. *Love against Hate*. New York, Harcourt, Brace & Co., 1942.

*Prescott, Daniel A. *Emotion and the Educative Process*. Washington, D. C., American Council on Education, 1938.

*SAYLES, M. B. and NUDD, H. *The Problem Child in School.* New York, The Commonwealth Fund, 1927.

c. Legal applications

*ALEXANDER, FRANZ, and HEALY, WILLIAM. *Roots of Crime.* New York, Alfred A. Knopf, 1935.

*——, and STAUB, HUGO. *The Criminal, the Judge, and the Public.* New York, The Macmillan Co., 1931.

BARNES, H. E. *The Repression of Crime.* New York, George H. Doran Co., 1926.

BRIGGS, L. VERNON. *The Manner of Man That Kills.* Boston, Richard G. Badger, 1921.

DARROW, CLARENCE. *Crime, Its Cause and Treatment.* New York, Thomas Y. Crowell, 1922.

DOSHAY, LEWIS. *The Boy Sex Offender and His Later Career.* New York, Grune & Stratton, 1943.

EAST, W. N. *Forensic Psychiatry.* London, Churchill, 1927.

*GILLIN, J. L. *Criminology and Penology.* New York, The Century Co., 1926.

GLUECK, BERNARD. *Studies in Forensic Psychiatry.* Boston, Little, Brown & Co., 1916.

GLUECK, S., and GLUECK, E. T. *Five Hundred Criminal Careers.* New York, Alfred A. Knopf, 1930.

——. *Five Hundred Delinquent Women.* New York, Alfred A. Knopf, 1934.

——. *Juvenile Delinquents Grown Up.* New York, The Commonwealth Fund, 1940.

——. *Later Criminal Careers.* New York, The Commonwealth Fund, 1937.

——. *One Thousand Juvenile Delinquents.* Cambridge, Harvard University Press, 1934.

——. *Preventing Crime.* New York, McGraw-Hill Book Co., 1936.

HAYNES, FRED. *Criminology.* New York, McGraw-Hill Book Co., 1932.

*HEALY, WILLIAM. *The Individual Delinquent.* Boston, Little, Brown & Co., 1927.

——, and ALPER, BENEDICT. *Criminal Youth and the Borstal System.* New York, The Commonwealth Fund, 1941.

——, and BRONNER, A. F. *Delinquents and Criminals.* New York, The Macmillan Co., 1926.

*HEALY, WILLIAM, and BRONNER, A. F. *A New Light on Delinquency and Its Treatment.* New Haven, Yale University Press, 1936.

——, and HEALY, M. *Pathological Lying, Accusation and Swindling.* Boston, Little, Brown & Co., 1926.

LEVY, RUTH J. *Reductions in Recidivism through Therapy.* New York, Thomas Seltzer, 1941.

MORRIS, ALBERT. *Criminology.* New York, Longmans, Green & Co., 1935.

MURCHISON, CARL. *Criminal Intelligence.* Worcester, Mass., Clark University Press, 1926.

PARSONS, P. A. *Crime and the Criminal.* New York, Alfred A. Knopf, 1926.

SHAW, BERNARD. *Imprisonment.* New York, Brentano's, 1924.

SHOENFELD, DUDLEY. *The Crime and the Criminal.* (The Lindbergh case.) New York, Covici Friede, 1936.

SINGER, H. D., and KROHN, W. O. *Insanity and the Law.* Philadelphia, Blakiston Co., 1924.

SULLIVAN, W. C. *Crime and Insanity.* New York, Longmans, Green & Co., 1924.

*SUTHERLAND, E. H. *Principles of Criminology.* Philadelphia, J. B. Lippincott Co., 1934.

TANNENBAUM, FRANK. *Crime and the Community.* New York, Ginn & Co., 1938.

VAN WATERS, MIRIAM. *Youth in Conflict.* New York, Republic Publ. Co., 1925.

WHITE, W. A. *Crime and Criminals.* New York, Farrar & Rinehart, 1933.

*——. *Insanity and the Criminal Law.* New York, The Macmillan Co., 1923.

d. Industrial applications

*ANDERSON, V. V. *Psychiatry in Industry.* New York, Harper & Bros., 1929.

ELKIND, HENRY B. (editor). *Preventive Management; Mental Hygiene in Industry.* New York, B. C. Forbes Publ. Co., 1931.

*GINZBERG, ELI. *The Unemployed.* New York, Harper & Bros., 1943.

MAYO, ELTON. *The Human Problems of an Industrial Civilization.* New York, The Macmillan Co., 1933.

NATIONAL RESEARCH COUNCIL. *Fatigue of Workers; Its Rela-*

tion to Industrial Production. New York, Reinhold Publ. Corporation, 1941.

ROETHLISBERGER, F. J. *Management and Morale.* Cambridge, Harvard University Press, 1941.

*———, and DICKSON, W. J. *Management and the Worker.* Cambridge, Harvard University Press, 1940.

*WHITEHEAD, T. N. *The Industrial Worker.* 2 vols. Cambridge, Harvard University Press, 1938.

e. Religious applications

*BATES, E. S., and DITTEMORE, J. V. *Mary Baker Eddy.* New York, Alfred A. Knopf, 1932.

*BLANTON, S., and PEALE, N. V. *Faith Is the Answer.* New York, Abingdon-Cokesbury Press, 1940.

BOISEN, ANTON T. *The Exploration of the Inner World.* New York, Willett, 1936.

BONNELL, JOHN S. *Pastoral Psychiatry.* New York, Harper & Bros., 1939.

CABOT, RICHARD C., and DICKS, RUSSELL L. *The Art of Ministering to the Sick.* New York, The Macmillan Co., 1936.

FOSDICK, HARRY EMERSON. *On Being a Real Person.* New York, Harper & Bros., 1943.

FREUD, SIGMUND. *The Future of an Illusion.* London, Horace Liveright, 1928.

*———. *Moses and Monotheism.* London, Hogarth Press, 1939.

*HILTNER, SEWARD. *Religion and Health.* New York, The Macmillan Co., 1943.

HOLMAN, CHARLES T. *The Cure of Souls; a Socio-Psychological Approach.* Chicago, University of Chicago Press, 1932.

———. *The Religion of a Healthy Mind.* New York, Round Table, 1939.

*JAMES, WILLIAM. *Varieties of Religious Experience.* New York, Longmans, Green & Co., 1938.

MAJOR, RALPH H. *Faiths That Healed.* New York, D. Appleton-Century Co., 1940.

MAY, ROLLO. *Springs of Creative Living.* New York, Abingdon-Cokesbury Press, 1940.

MCKENZIE, J. G. *Psychology, Psychotherapy and Evangelicalism.* New York, The Macmillan Co., 1940.

OLIVER, JOHN RATHBONE. *Psychiatry and Mental Health; the Hale Lectures at Western Theological Seminary, 1932.* New York, Charles Scribner's Sons, 1932.

STUART, GRACE. *The Achievement of Personality.* New York, The Macmillan Co., 1938.

*WISE, CARROLL A. *Religion in Illness and Health.* New York, Harper & Bros., 1942.

f. Anthropological and ethnological applications

BATESON, GREGORY, and MEAD, MARGARET. *Balinese Character.* New York, New York Academy of Science, 1942.

DENNIS, WAYNE. *The Hopi Child.* New York, D. Appleton-Century Co., 1940.

*DOLLARD, JOHN. *Caste and Class in a Southern Town.* New Haven, Yale University Press, 1937.

*FREUD, SIGMUND. *Totem and Taboo.* New York, Dodd, Mead & Co., 1918.

GORER, GEOFFREY. *Japanese Character Structure and Propaganda.* Prepared for the Committee on National Morale and the Council on Human Relations. Mimeographed manuscript. 1942.

HENRY, JULES, and HENRY, ZUNIA. *Doll Play of Pilaga Indian Children.* New York, American Orthopsychiatric Association, 1944.

KARDINER, ABRAM. *The Individual and His Society.* New York, Columbia University Press, 1939.

LEIGHTON, A. H., and LEIGHTON, D. C. *The Navaho Door.* Cambridge, Harvard University Press, 1944.

LINCOLN, J. S. *The Dream in Primitive Cultures.* Baltimore, Williams & Wilkins, 1935.

*MALINOWSKI, BRONISLAW. *The Sexual Life of the Savages in Northwestern Melanesia.* 2 vols. New York, Horace Liveright, 1929.

*MEAD, MARGARET. *Coming of Age in Samoa.* New York, Blue Ribbon Books, 1934.

——. *Growing Up in New Guinea.* New York, Blue Ribbon Books, 1930.

PORTEUS, S. D. *Psychology of a Primitive People.* New York, Longmans, Green & Co., 1931.

REIK, THEODOR. *Ritual.* New York, W. W. Norton & Co., n.d.

ROHEIM, GEZA. *The Origin and Function of Culture.* New York, Nervous & Mental Disease Publ. Co., 1943.

——. *The Riddle of the Sphinx.* London, International Psychoanalytical Library, 1934.

g. Military applications

*Brown, Mabel W. *Neuropsychiatry and the War; a Bibliography with Abstracts.* New York, National Committee for Mental Hygiene, 1918.

Copeland, Norman. *Psychology and the Soldier.* Harrisburg, Pa., Military Service Publ. Co., 1942.

*Durbin, E. F. M., and Bowlby, John. *Personal Aggressiveness and War.* New York, Columbia University Press, 1939.

Farago, Ladislas (editor). *German Psychological Warfare.* New York, Committee for National Morale, 1941.

Fenton, Norman. *Shell Shock and Its Aftermath.* St. Louis, C. V. Mosby Co., 1926.

Ferenczi, S., et al. *Psychoanalysis and the War Neuroses.* London, Hogarth Press, 1921.

*Gillespie, R. D. *Psychological Effects of War on Citizen and Soldier.* New York, W. W. Norton & Co., 1942.

*Glover, Edward. *The Dangers of Being Human.* London, George Allen & Unwin, 1936.

Goldstein, Kurt. *Aftereffects of Brain Injuries in War.* New York, Grune & Stratton, 1942.

*Kardiner, Abram. *The Traumatic Neuroses of War.* New York, Paul B. Hoeber, 1941.

MacCurdy, J. T. *The Structure of Morale.* New York, The Macmillan Co., 1943.

———. *War Neuroses.* Utica, State Hospitals Press, 1918.

*Miller, Emanuel (editor). *The Neuroses in War.* New York, The Macmillan Co., 1940.

*Mira, Emilio. *Psychiatry in War.* New York, W. W. Norton & Co., 1943.

*National Research Council. *Psychology for the Fighting Man.* Washington, D. C., The Infantry Journal, 1943.

*Solomon, Harry C., and Yakovlev, Paul. *Manual of Military Neuropsychiatry.* Philadelphia, W. B. Saunders, 1944.

*Southard, E. E. *Shell Shock and Other Neuropsychiatric Problems.* Boston, W. M. Leonard, 1919.

Watson, Goodwin (editor). *Civilian Morale.* Boston, Houghton Mifflin Co., 1942.

V. PSYCHOANALYSIS

A. HISTORY

*BRILL, A. A. *Freud's Contribution to Psychiatry.* New York, W. W. Norton & Co., 1944.

*FERENCZI, S., and RANK, O. *The Development of Psychoanalysis.* New York, Nervous & Mental Disease Publ. Co., 1925.

*FREUD, SIGMUND. *Autobiography.* New York, W. W. Norton & Co., 1935.

*———. *History of the Psychoanalytic Movement.* New York, Nervous & Mental Disease Publ. Co., 1917.

———. *The Problem of Lay Analyses.* New York, Brentano's, 1927.

HEALY, W., BRONNER, A. F., and BOWERS, A. M. *The Structure and Meaning of Psychoanalysis.* New York, Alfred A. Knopf, 1930.

LORAND, SANDOR (editor). *Psychoanalysis Today.* New York, International University Press, 1944.

RANK, OTTO, and SACHS, HANS. *The Significance of Psychoanalysis for the Mental Sciences.* New York, Nervous & Mental Disease Publ. Co., 1915.

REIK, THEODOR. *From Thirty Years with Freud.* New York, Farrar & Rinehart, 1940.

WITTELS, FRITZ. *Freud and His Time.* New York. Horace Liveright, 1931.

B. PSYCHOANALYSIS AS A BODY OF KNOWLEDGE

1. GENERAL TREATISES

*ABRAHAM, KARL. *Selected Papers on Psychoanalysis.* London, Hogarth Press, 1927.

BREUER, JOSEPH, and FREUD, SIGMUND. *Studies in Hysteria.* New York, Nervous & Mental Disease Publ. Co., 1936.

BRILL, A. A. *Psychoanalysis.* Philadelphia, W. B. Saunders, 1922.

CORIAT, ISADOR. *What Is Psychoanalysis?* New York, Moffat, Yard & Co., 1919.

*DEUTSCH, HELENE. *Psychoanalysis of the Neuroses.* London, Hogarth Press, 1932.

*———. *The Psychology of Women.* New York, Grune & Stratton, 1944.

*FENICHEL, OTTO. *Outline of Clinical Psychoanalysis.* New York, W. W. Norton & Co., 1934.

*Freud, Sigmund. *Collected Papers.* 4 vols. New York, International Psychoanalytic Press, 1924.

*——. *A General Introduction to Psychoanalysis.* New York, Horace Liveright, 1920.

*——. *New Introductory Lectures on Psychoanalysis.* New York, W. W. Norton & Co., 1933.

FRINK, HORACE. *Morbid Fears and Compulsions.* New York, Moffat, Yard & Co., 1921.

GLOVER, EDWARD. *Psychoanalysis.* London, John Bale, 1939.

*HENDRICK, IVES. *Facts and Theories of Psychoanalysis.* New York, Alfred A. Knopf, second edition, 1941.

JONES, ERNEST. *Psychoanalysis.* New York, Jonathan Cape & Harrison Smith, 1929.

LAFORGUE, RENÉ. *Clinical Aspects of Psychoanalysis.* London, Hogarth Press, 1938.

2. SPECIAL TOPICS

*ALEXANDER, FRANZ. *Psychoanalysis of the Total Personality.* New York, Nervous & Mental Disease Publ. Co., 1930.

FERENCZI, SANDOR. *Contributions to Psychoanalysis.* Boston, Richard G. Badger, 1916.

——. *Thalassa; a Theory of Genitality.* (The Instinct Theory.) New York, The Psychoanalytic Quarterly, 1938.

*FREUD, ANNA. *The Ego and Mechanisms of Defense.* London, Hogarth Press, 1937.

*FREUD, SIGMUND. *Beyond the Pleasure Principle.* (The Instinct Theory.) London, International Psychoanalytic Press, 1922.

——. *The Ego and the Id.* London, Hogarth Press, 1927.

*——. *The Interpretation of Dreams.* New York, The Macmillan Co., revised edition, 1933.

*——. *The Problem of Anxiety.* New York, W. W. Norton & Co., 1936.

——. *The Psychopathology of Everyday Life.* London, Ernest Benn, 1935.

*——. *Three Contributions to the Theory of Sex.* New York, Nervous & Mental Disease Publ. Co., 1930.

*GRODDECK, GEORG. *The Book of the It.* (Psychosomatic.) New York, Nervous & Mental Disease Publ. Co., 1928.

GRODDECK, GEORG. *Exploring the Unconscious.* London, C. W. Daniels Co., 1933.

JONES, ERNEST. *Nightmare, Witches and Devils.* New York, W. W. Norton & Co., 1931.

——. *Papers on Psychoanalysis.* New York, William Wood & Co., 1923.

*KLEIN, MELANIE, and RIVIERE, JOAN. *Love, Hate and Reparation.* London, Hogarth Press, 1937.

*MENNINGER, K. A. *Love against Hate.* (The Instinct Theory.) New York, Harcourt, Brace & Co., 1942.

*——. *Man against Himself.* (The Instinct Theory.) New York, Harcourt, Brace & Co., 1938.

REIK, THEODOR. *Masochism in Modern Man.* New York, Farrar & Rinehart, 1941.

STERBA, RICHARD. *Introduction to the Psychoanalytic Theory of the Libido.* (The Instinct Theory.) New York, Nervous & Mental Disease Publ. Co., 1942.

C. PSYCHOANALYSIS AS A TREATMENT TECHNIQUE

*BLITZSTEN, DOROTHY. *Psychoanalysis Explained.* (For lay readers.) New York, Coward-McCann, 1936.

*FENICHEL, OTTO. *Problems of Psychoanalytic Technique.* New York, The Psychoanalytic Quarterly, 1941.

*FERENCZI, SANDOR. *Further Contributions to the Theory and Technique of Psychoanalysis.* London, Hogarth Press, 1926.

GLOVER, EDWARD, and BRIERLEY, MARJORIE. *An Investigation of the Technique of Psychoanalysis.* London, Bailliere, Tindall & Cox, 1940.

JELLIFFE, SMITH ELY. *The Technique of Psychoanalysis.* New York, Nervous & Mental Disease Publ. Co., 1920.

JONES, ERNEST. *Treatment of the Neuroses.* New York, William Wood & Co., 1920.

*KUBIE, LAWRENCE S. *Practical Aspects of Psychoanalysis.* New York, W. W. Norton & Co., 1936.

PECK, MARTIN. *The Meaning of Psychoanalysis.* New York, Alfred A. Knopf, 1931.

REIK, THEODOR. *Surprise and the Psychoanalyst.* London, Kegan Paul, Trench, Trubner & Co., 1936.

SHARPE, ELLA F. *Dream Analysis.* New York, W. W. Norton & Co., 1938.

D. PSYCHOANALYSIS AS A RESEARCH TECHNIQUE

ABRAHAM, KARL. *Dreams and Myths; a Study in Race Psychology.* New York, Nervous & Mental Disease Publ. Co., 1913.

*ALEXANDER, FRANZ. *The Medical Value of Psychoanalysis.* New York, W. W. Norton Co., 1932.

FLÜGEL, J. C. *The Psychoanalytic Study of the Family.* New York, International Psychoanalytic Press, 1921.

*FREUD, SIGMUND. *Civilization and Its Discontents.* New York, Jonathan Cape & Harrison Smith, 1930.

——. *Delusion and Dream.* New York, Moffat, Yard & Co., 1922.

——. *Group Psychology and the Analysis of the Ego.* London, International Psychoanalytical Press, 1922.

——. *Leonardo da Vinci.* New York, Moffat, Yard & Co., 1916.

——. *Wit and Its Relation to the Unconscious.* New York, Moffat, Yard & Co., 1917.

JONES, ERNEST. *Essays in Applied Psychoanalysis.* London, International Psychoanalytical Press, 1923.

MENNINGER, K. A. *Man against Himself.* New York, Harcourt, Brace & Co., 1938.

MONEY-KYRLE, R. *The Meaning of Sacrifice.* London, Hogarth Press, 1930.

RANK, OTTO. *The Myth of the Birth of the Hero.* New York, Nervous & Mental Disease Publ. Co., 1914.

*RICKMAN, JOHN. *The Development of the Psychoanalytical Theory of the Psychoses.* London, Bailliere, Tindall & Cox, 1928.

SACHS, HANS. *The Creative Unconscious.* Cambridge, Sci-Art, 1942.

SCHILDER, PAUL. *Brain and Personality.* New York, Nervous & Mental Disease Publ. Co., 1931.

——. *The Image and Appearance of the Human Body.* London, Kegan Paul, Trench, Trubner & Co., 1935.

——. *Introduction to Psychoanalytic Psychiatry.* New York, Nervous & Mental Disease Publ. Co., 1928.

VI. CHILD PSYCHIATRY

*AICHHORN, AUGUST. *Wayward Youth.* New York, Viking Press, 1935.

*ALDRICH, C. A., and ALDRICH, M. M. *Babies Are Human Beings.* New York, The Macmillan Co., 1938.

ALLEN, F. H. *Psychotherapy with Children.* New York, W. W. Norton & Co., 1942.

BAKER, H. J., and TRAPHAGEN, V. *Diagnosis and Treatment of Behavior Problem Children.* New York, The Macmillan Co., 1935.

BAKWIN, H., and BAKWIN, R. M. *Psychologic Care during Infancy and Childhood.* New York, D. Appleton-Century Co., 1942.

BAUDOUIN, CHARLES. *The Mind of the Child.* New York, Dodd, Mead & Co., 1933.

BERNFELD, SIEGFRIED. *The Psychology of the Infant.* New York, Brentano's, 1929.

BEVERLY, BERT I. *In Defense of Children.* New York, John Day Co., 1941.

BLANTON, S., and BLANTON, M. *Child Guidance.* New York, The Century Co., 1927.

BRADLEY, CHARLES. *Schizophrenia in Childhood.* New York, The Macmillan Co., 1941.

CRAWFORD, N. A., and MENNINGER, K. A. *The Healthy Minded Child.* New York, Coward-McCann, 1930.

ELLIOTT, GRACE L. *Understanding the Adolescent Girl.* New York, Henry Holt & Co., 1930.

*ENGLISH, O. S., and PEARSON, G. H. J. *Common Neuroses of Children and Adults.* New York, W. W. Norton & Co., 1937.

*FREUD, ANNA. *Introduction to the Technic of Child Analysis.* London, George Allen & Unwin, 1931.

*——, and BURLINGHAM, DOROTHY. *War and Children.* New York, Medical War Books, 1943.

GESELL, ARNOLD. *Infancy and Human Growth.* New York, The Macmillan Co., 1929.

GODDARD, H. H. *Feeblemindedness.* New York, The Macmillan Co., 1923.

*GORDON, R. G. (editor). *A Survey of Child Psychiatry.* London, Oxford University Press, 1939.

*HARTWELL, S. W. *Fifty-Five Bad Boys.* New York, Alfred A. Knopf, 1931.

ISAACS, SUSAN. *Intellectual Growth in Young Children.* London, George Routledge & Sons, 1938.

——. *The Nursery Years.* New York, Vanguard Press, 1937.

——. *Social Development in Young Children.* London, George Routledge & Sons, 1937.

*KANNER, LEO. *Child Psychiatry*. Springfield, Charles C. Thomas, 1935.

KLEIN, MELANIE. *The Psychoanalysis of Children*. New York, W. W. Norton & Co., 1932.

LEVY, DAVID M. *Maternal Overprotection*. New York, Columbia University Press, 1943.

*———. *Studies in Sibling Rivalry*. New York, American Orthopsychiatric Association, 1937.

LORD, ELIZABETH E. *Children Handicapped by Cerebral Palsy*. New York, The Commonwealth Fund, 1937.

MOODIE, WILLIAM. *The Doctor and the Difficult Child*. New York, The Commonwealth Fund, 1940.

*PIAGET, JEAN. *The Child's Conception of the World*. New York, Harcourt, Brace & Co., 1929.

———. *Judgment and Reasoning in the Child*. New York, Harcourt, Brace & Co., 1928.

POWDERMAKER, F., and GRIMES, L. *Children in the Family*. New York, Farrar & Rinehart, 1940.

*RIBBLE, MARGARETHA A. *The Rights of Infants*. New York, Columbia University Press, 1943.

RICKMAN, JOHN (editor). *On the Bringing Up of Children*. London, Kegan Paul, Trench, Trubner & Co., 1936.

ROGERS, CARL R. *Clinical Treatment of the Problem Child*. Boston, Houghton Mifflin Co., 1939.

SAYLES, MARY B. *The Problem Child at Home*. New York, The Commonwealth Fund, 1928.

*SPOCK, BENJAMIN, and HUSCHKA, MABEL. *Psychological Aspects of Pediatric Practice*. New York, New York State Committee on Mental Hygiene, 1938.

STRAIN, FRANCES B. *New Patterns in Sex Teaching*. New York, D. Appleton-Century Co., 1936.

SYMONDS, P. M. *The Psychology of Parent-Child Relationships*. New York, D. Appleton-Century Co., 1939.

WEILL, BLANCHE C. *Through Children's Eyes*. New York, Island Workshop Press, 1940.

WILE, IRA S. *The Challenge of Adolescence*. New York, Greenberg, 1939.

———. *The Challenge of Childhood*. New York, Thomas Seltzer, 1925.

WINN, RALPH B. (editor). *Encyclopedia of Child Guidance*. New York, Philosophical Library, 1943.

WITMER, HELEN L. *Psychiatric Clinics for Children.* New York, The Commonwealth Fund, 1940.

*WITTELS, FRITZ. *Set the Children Free.* New York, W. W. Norton & Co., 1932.

WOLF, ANNA W. M. *Our Children Face War.* Boston, Houghton Mifflin Co., 1942.

*——. *The Parents' Manual.* New York, Simon & Schuster, 1941.

*ZACHRY, CAROLINE B. *Emotion and Conduct in Adolescence.* New York, D. Appleton-Century Co., 1940.

VII. PSYCHOSOMATIC MEDICINE

*ALVAREZ, WALTER C. *Nervousness, Indigestion and Pain.* New York, Paul B. Hoeber, 1943.

ASSOCIATION FOR RESEARCH IN NERVOUS AND MENTAL DISEASE. *The Biology of the Individual.* Baltimore, Williams & Wilkins, 1934.

——. *The Interrelationship of Mind and Body.* Baltimore, Williams & Wilkins, 1939.

——. *The Role of Nutritional Deficiency in Nervous and Mental Disease.* Baltimore, Williams & Wilkins, 1943.

BENEDEK, THERESE, and RUBINSTEIN, BORIS B. *The Sexual Cycle in Women.* Psychosomatic Medicine Monographs. Washington, D. C., National Research Council, 1942.

BRAHDY, LEOPOLD, and KAHN, SAMUEL (editors). *Trauma and Disease.* Philadelphia, Lea & Febiger, second edition, 1941.

CANNON, W. B. *The Wisdom of the Body.* New York, W. W. Norton & Co., 1932.

CHADWICK, MARY. *The Psychological Effects of Menstruation.* New York, Nervous & Mental Disease Publ. Co., 1932.

*DRAPER, GEORGE, DUPERTUIS, C. W., and CAUGHEY, J. L. *Human Constitution in Clinical Medicine.* New York, Paul B. Hoeber, 1944.

*DUNBAR, FLANDERS. *Emotions and Bodily Changes.* New York, Columbia University Press, second edition, 1938.

*——. *Psychosomatic Diagnosis.* New York, Paul B. Hoeber, 1943.

*FRENCH, THOMAS, and ALEXANDER, FRANZ. *Psychogenic Factors in Bronchial Asthma.* Psychosomatic Medicine Monographs. Washington, D. C., National Research Council, 1941.

GRODDECK, GEORG. *The Book of the It.* New York, Nervous & Mental Disease Publ. Co., 1928.

JELLIFFE, SMITH ELY. *Sketches in Psychosomatic Medicine.* New York, Nervous & Mental Disease Publ. Co., 1939.

McGREGOR, H. G. *The Emotional Factor in Visceral Disease.* London, Oxford University Press, 1938.

ROBINSON, G. CANBY. *The Patient as a Person.* New York, The Commonwealth Fund, 1939.

*STEPHEN, KARIN. *Psychoanalysis and Medicine; a Study of the Wish to Fall Ill.* New York, The Macmillan Co., 1933.

*WEISS, E., and ENGLISH, O. S. *Psychosomatic Medicine.* Philadelphia, W. B. Saunders, 1943.

WOLF, STEWART, and WOLFF, HAROLD. *Human Gastric Function.* New York, Oxford University Press, 1943.

VIII. MENTAL HYGIENE (PERSONAL)

(For other concepts of mental hygiene, see sociological applications of psychiatry, biographies, child psychiatry.)

ADAMSON, ELIZABETH. *So You're Going to a Psychiatrist.* New York, Thomas Y. Crowell, 1937.

*AMERICAN ASSOCIATION FOR THE ADVANCEMENT OF SCIENCE. *Mental Health.* Lancaster, Pa., Science Press, 1939.

*CAMPBELL, C. MACFIE. *Towards Mental Health.* Cambridge, Harvard University Press, 1933.

*EDITORS OF FORTUNE. *The Nervous Breakdown.* New York, Doubleday, Doran & Co., 1935.

ELKIND, HENRY B. *The Healthy Mind.* New York, Greenberg, 1929.

FISHBEIN, M., and WHITE, W. A. (editors). *Why Men Fail.* New York, The Century Co., 1928.

GROVES, E. R. *Personality and Social Adjustment.* New York, Longmans, Green & Co., 1930.

———. *Understanding Yourself.* New York, Greenberg, 1935.

*———, and BLANCHARD, P. *Readings in Mental Hygiene.* New York, Henry Holt & Co., 1936.

HOWARD, F. E., and PATRY, F. L. *Mental Health.* New York, Harper & Bros., 1935.

*JACKSON, J., and SALISBURY, H. *Outwitting Our Nerves.* New York, The Century Co., 1921.

*LAIRD, D. A. *Increasing Personal Efficiency.* New York, Harper & Bros., 1925.

Laird, D. A. *Why We Don't Like People.* New York, Mohawk Press, 1931.

Langer, W. C. *Psychology and Human Living.* New York, D. Appleton-Century Co., 1943.

McKinney, Fred. *Psychology of Personal Adjustment.* New York, John Wiley & Sons, 1941.

Morgan, J. J. B. *Keeping a Sound Mind.* New York, The Macmillan Co., 1935.

Oliver, J. R. *Fear.* New York, The Macmillan Co., 1927.

Overstreet, H. A. *About Ourselves.* New York, W. W. Norton & Co., 1927.

*Preston, George. *Psychiatry for the Curious.* New York, Farrar & Rinehart, 1940.

———. *The Substance of Mental Health.* New York, Farrar & Rinehart, 1943.

Rees, J. R. *The Health of the Mind.* Cambridge, Washburn & Thomas, 1929.

Schmalhausen, S. D. *Why We Misbehave.* New York, Garden City Publ. Co., 1928.

Travis, Lee, and Baruch, Dorothy. *Personal Problems of Everyday Life.* New York, D. Appleton-Century Co., 1941.

Wallin, J. E. W. *Personality Maladjustments and Mental Hygiene.* New York, McGraw-Hill Book Co., 1935.

White, William A. *The Principles of Mental Hygiene.* New York, The Macmillan Co., 1917.

IX. BIOGRAPHIES AND AUTOBIOGRAPHIES

*Beers, Clifford. *A Mind That Found Itself.* New York, Doubleday, Doran & Co., 1936.

Bonaparte, Marie. *Edgar Poe.* 2 vols. Paris, Editions Denoël et Steele, 1933.

Brand, Millen. *The Outward Room.* New York, Simon & Schuster, 1937.

Brown, Henry Collins. *A Mind Mislaid.* New York, E. P. Dutton & Co., 1937.

Coignard, John. *The Spectacle of a Man.* New York, Jefferson House, 1939.

Coleman, Emily. *The Shutter of Snow.* New York, Viking Press, 1930.

Dakin, E. F. *Mrs. Eddy; the Biography of a Virginal Mind.* New York, Charles Scribner's Sons, 1930.

GUTTMACHER, M. S. *America's Last King.* (George III.) New York, Charles Scribner's Sons, 1941.

*HILLYER, JANE. *Reluctantly Told.* New York, The Macmillan Co., 1927.

HOSHOR, JOHN. *God in a Rolls Royce.* (Father Divine.) New York, Hillman Curl, 1936.

INMATE WARD 8. *Behind the Door of Delusion.* New York, The Macmillan Co., 1932.

KING, MARION. *The Recovery of Myself.* New Haven, Yale University Press, 1931.

KRAUCH, ELSA. *A Mind Restored.* New York, G. P. Putnam's Sons, 1937.

KRUTCH, JOSEPH WOOD. *Edgar Allan Poe.* New York, Alfred A. Knopf, 1926.

LAFORGUE, RENÉ. *The Defeat of Baudelaire.* London, Hogarth Press, 1932.

LEONARD, WILLIAM E. *The Locomotive God.* New York, The Century Co., 1927.

NORTH 3–1. *Pick Up the Pieces.* Garden City, Doubleday, Doran & Co., 1929.

*PIERCE, S. W., and PIERCE, J. T. *The Layman Looks at Doctors.* New York, Harcourt, Brace & Co., 1929.

*SEABROOK, WILLIAM. *Asylum.* New York, Harcourt, Brace & Co., 1935.

WALTERS, W. J. *Forbidden Path.* New York, Dodd, Mead & Co., 1938.

*ZWEIG, STEFAN. *Mental Healers: Mesmer, Eddy, Freud.* New York, Viking Press, 1934.

INDEX

Aaron, 353
Abraham, 334–5
Abraham, Karl, 121
Absent-mindedness, automatism in, 238–9
Accommodation, process of, 21–3, 29–32
Achievement tests, 180
Ackerman, Nathan W., 64n, 178n, 179, 294n
Adjustment to environment, *see* Accommodation, Struggle
Adler, Alfred, 172
Adler, Herman, xvi, 453n
Aggression, passive, 213–14
Agrippina, 24
Aichhorn, August, 459
Aigremont, 298n
Albrecht, 101n
Alcohol addiction: as form of flight, 31; and melancholia, 123; as a neurosis, 147–9; psychoanalytic treatment of, 148–9; cases of, 442, 443
Alcoholics Anonymous, 149n
Alexander, Franz, 150, 151n, 155, 235, 274n, 316n, 335n, 336, 360, 458, 459; quoted, 236
Alexander the Great, 32
Alvarez, Walter, 36
Alzheimer, 478
Alzheimer's disease, 185
Ambivalence, 277
American Bar Association, 453, 454
American Medical Association, 454
American Orthopsychiatric Association, 458n
American Psychiatric Association, 360, 482n; committee on medico-legal problems, 453, 454
American Psychoanalytic Association, 360
Amnesia, 182; anterograde and retrograde, 184; of defective recording, 182; of defective retention, 183; of defective recollection, 186; with disso-

ciation (fugues), 189–91; cured by hypnosis, 381–2
Anal character, 316–18
Anal eroticism, 316–18
Anderson, Sherwood, 157
Anderson, V. V., 427n, 433n, 435, 437; quoted, 436–8
Anderson, W. K., 47n
Anger, *see* Excesses, emotional
Anterograde, 184
Antisocial personality type, 150–5, 156–7, 197; examples of, 150–3
Anxiety hysteria, *see* Neuroses
Anxiety neurosis, 134, 138, 255–7; and sense of inferiority, 70, 74
Aphasia, 189–90
Appel, Kenneth E., 41n, 390n
Applications, 419–87; educational, 421–33; industrial, 433–43; legal, 443–60; medical, 475–84; religious, 460–75; social work, 420–1
Arc, Jeanne d', 213
Arteriosclorsis, 210
Artist, the, as variety of schizoid personality, 82–3
Arvin, Newton, 65
Association, disturbances of, 231–4
Athletes, heart disease in, 316
Attack, as solution of failure in adjustment, 30, 31, 32–3, 131
Augustine, St., 24
Aurelianus, Coelius, 407n
Automatism, 238–9

B, symbolism of the letter, 300–1
Babington, B. G., 147n
Bacci, P. J., quoted, 384
Bacon, Francis, 24, 202
Bagby, English, quoted, 75, 253n, 338–9
Balzac, 202
Baratier, 305n
Barkoski, John, 343
Barnard, Ruth, I., x
Bartemeier, Leo H., 151n, 264n, 360

Bates, Ernest S., 88n
Bates, Sanford, 455
Bathory, Countess Elizabeth, 332
Beauchamp, Sally, 241
Beauford, Sir Francis, 201–2
Beers, Clifford, 15n
Beethoven, 47, 65, 172
Behaviour: laws governing, 14–15; patterns, 28; relative seriousness of problems of, 424–5
Benét, Stephen Vincent, 314; quoted, 154, 314–15
Benét, William Rose, quoted, 356–7
Bennett, A. E., 411, 411n
Bennett, John G., 209n
Bentham, Jeremy, 77
Bergson, quoted, 229–30
Berkeley, Bishop, 243
Berkeley Square, 230n
Bernard-Leroy, 230
Bernheim, 268
Bernstein, Charles, 53
Berry, C. S., 223
Bibliotherapy, 406–7
Binet, 176
Biodynamic medicine, 39
Bivin, George D., 350
Blanchard, Phyllis, 435n
Blindness: hysterical, 146; and depression, 168; and compensation, 170–1, 172; cure by placebo, 380–1
Blitzsten, Dorothy, 400n
Blitzsten, Lionel, 360
Blocking, 233
Blücher, Gebhard von, 154
"Blues," the: difference of, from melancholia, 114; prevention of, 365–7
Boarding home care, 401
Boisen, A. T., 462n
Bond, Earl D., 41n
Border-line intelligence, cases of, 48, 58–62
Bowman, Karl M., 462n
Bradford, Gamaliel, 328n
Braid, James, 414
Brain syphilis, *see* Syphilis, brain
Brain tumour, *see* Tumour of the brain
Brenman, Margaret, 415n
Breuer, 268, 414
Brewer, John M., 434n
Brickner, Richard, 89
Bridges, Robert, quoted, 221
Brigham, Amariah, 15n
Brill, A. A., 360; quoted, 335
Bronner, Augusta F., 458n; quoted, 459–60

Brown, John, 85, 87, 213
Brown, J. F., 9n, 26n, 27n, 39n, 369n, 419n, 457; quoted, 26
Browning, Robert, quoted, 328
Bruckner, 172
Buddhism, 474
Bühler, Charlotte, 179n
Bühler test, 179
Bullard, Dexter, 413n
Bunzel, Bessie, 125n
Burke, Edmund, 202
Burns, Robert, 259
Burr, Emily, 53
Butler, Samuel, 21; quoted, 19
Buxton, Jedediah, 203–4
Byron, 65, 300

Cabell, James Branch, quoted, 249, 354–5
Cæsar, Julius, 173, 203, 264
Cairns, Lucille, x
Cajal, 478
Calculators, 203–5
Caligula, 24
Calkins, Ernest Elmo, 171
Calvin, 79
Camp, Carl D., quoted, 439–40
Campbell, C. Macfie, quoted, 159–60
Canavan, Myrtelle M., 55n
Cannon, Walter B., 36
Carlyle, 81
Cary, Lucian, quoted, 396–400
Casanova, 151
Cassius, 127
Castration complex, 302, 356
Catatonia, 94
Catharsis, mental, 387–9, 429
Cerea, flexibilitas, 197n
Cerebration, *see* Intellection
Chadwick, Mary, 182n
Channing, Grace Ellery, 173
Character traits, 280
Charcot, 268
Charles V, 264
Charlesworth, Charles, 304
Chateaubriand, 203
Chesterfield, Earl of, 173
Chidester, Leona, 64n, 119n, 178n, 294n
Child Guidance clinics, 420–1
Children: parental influence on, *see* Parental influence; superior, 199–201; *and see* Excesses, intellectual; *and see* Heredity
Chiropractic, 487
Chopin, 79, 114

Christianity, 474; *see also* Religious applications of psychiatry

Cicero, quoted, 3

Cinderella, 331, 355–6

Civilization, a neurotic product, 130, 131

Clark, Leon Pierce, 113n

Claw-hand, cured by command, 383

Clendening, Logan, xvi

Cobb, Stanley, 262n

Coghill, 36

Cognition, *see* Intellection

Colburn, Harry J., xvi

Coleridge, 77, 202, 237

College, mental hygiene in, 425–33; *and see* Education

Commodus, 24, 325

Common sense, as treatment for mental illness, 9–14

Commonwealth Fund, 420, 482n

Compensation: and deficiencies, 170–2

Compensation, and inferiority, 74; *see also* Over-compensation

Complex, 323–59, *and see* Fantasies; Castration, 302, 356; Elektra, 311–13, 394–6, 430; Guilt, 335–41; Jehovah, 323–5; Jesus, 325–7; Narcissus, 314; Œdipus, 311

Compromise: constructive, 31, 32, 33–4; of isolation personality types, 64–5; *and see* Sublimations

Compulsions, 260–2; propitiatory, 335–41

Compulsion neurosis, 136–7, 225, 226, 260–2; examples of, 260–1; *and see* Distortion, volitional

Compulsive doubt, 261

Conation, 163–4

Condensation, 284–6; examples of, 285–6

Conditioned reflex, theory of, 253

Confessional, Catholic, and psychotherapy, 387–8

Confucianism, 474

Conklin, Edmund S., 254–5

Connell, William M., 15n

Conscience, 279

Consciousness, 163

Contamination, fantasies of, 350–3

Convulsions and convulsive states, 210, 211, 260, 262–4; treatment of, 264, 413; cases of, 383, 385, 439–40; *and see* Distortion, volitional

Cook, Charles Lee, 173–4

Cook, George, 15n

Cooper, William M., quoted, 344

Coriat, Isador H., 353; quoted, 353–4

Cox, Dr., 403

Cox, Catharine M., 60n, 77n, 202

Crawford, Nelson Antrim, xvi; quoted, 314

Criminality, as result of failure in adjustment, 5, 31, 32–3; and moronity, 51–2; and drug addiction, 148; and volitional distortion, 259; and psychiatry, 336, 443–60

Crookshank, 36

Cruelty, fantasies of, 341–9

Culbert, Jane F., 424n

Cunningham, Glenn, 174n

Curare, in shock therapy, 411

Cure, by command, 378, 383; by exhortation, 378, 382; by explanation, 378, 383; by hypnosis, 378, 381–2; by persuasion, 378, 382–3; by placebo, 378, 380; by religious assurances, 378, 384–6; by rest, 378, 381; by suggestion, 378, 382; by terrorism, 378, 379–80; *see also* Treatment

Cuthbert, St., 385–6

Cuvier, 202

Cycloid personality type, 107–29, 156, 157; varieties of, 108–9; " up " phase of, 109–11; " down " phase of, 111–14; failures of, 114–26; examples of, 107–21

Cyclothymias, 107; *see also* Cycloid personality type

Cynicism, illustrated, 4

Cyrus, 203

Dakin, Edwin, 88n

Dangerfield, Alice, x, xiv

Darrow, Clarence, 58

Darwin, quoted, 187

Davis, quoted, 67–8

Dawkes, T., 305n

Day, John Warren, xiv

Dayton, Neil, A., 60n

Deafness, 167–9, 171, 172; and compensation, 171, 172, 173; cure of, by psychotherapy, 381, 382; isolation by reason of, 69; *and see* Deficiencies, perceptual

Dearmer, Percy, quoted, 384–6

Decompensation, 174–5

Deeping, Warwick, 212

Defence mechanisms, 295–6

Deficiencies, emotional, 193–6; intellectual, 175–8; perceptual, 167–70, 193,

Deficiencies, emotional, *continued*
  215, *and see* Compensation, Over-
  compensation; volitional, 197–8
De Ford, Miriam, quoted, 358
Déjà vu phenomena, 226, 229–30; *and
  see* Distortion, of memory
Delirium tremens, 218
Delusions, 243–9; of persecution, 85–9,
  223, 242–9; and paranoia, 86–7, 245–7,
  248; and melancholia, 120; and disorientation, 222–3; types of, with examples, 243–7; of grandeur, 244; hypochondriacal, 244–5; of sin, 245, 248;
  of reference, 246; of jealousy, 246–7;
  mechanisms of, 247–9; and projection,
  282; *and see* Distortions, intellectual,
  and Schizophrenia
Dementia præcox, *see* Schizophrenia
Dementia simplex, *see* Schizophrenia
Dentistry, and mental hygiene, 75
Depression, 211, 367, 442; in students,
  114–15; relief of, 128–9; result of hate,
  128; treatment of, 128–9; and percep-
  tual deficiency, 168; *and see* Melan-
  choly
Descartes, René, 81
Determination: excessive, 212–13; nega-
  tive, 213
Deutsch, Albert, 15n
Devils: as explanation of mental illness,
  7; worship of, 258–9
Dewey, John, quoted, 8–9
Diagnosis of mental illness, 368–72, 478;
  classification of, 371–2; descriptive,
  371; interpretative, 371
Diamandi, 204
Dickson, William J., 435n
Dimont, Joseph, x
Disabilities, special, 180–2
Disguises, 277, 280–304
Disorders, mental, 167, *and see* Defi-
  ciencies, Distortion, Excesses
Disorientation, 220–3, *and see* Distor-
  tion, perceptual
Displacement, 280, 287–9; examples of,
  287–9, 290–1
Dissociation, 175, 223, 231–47; exam-
  ples of, 221, 233–47; types of, 234–47;
  and see Distortion, intellectual
Distortion, 215, 289–90; emotional, 249–
  59; intellectual, 223–49; of memory,
  223, 226–31; perceptual, 216–23, 242;
  volitional, 259–64
Dittemore, John V., 88n
Divine, Father, 325
Dix, Dorothea, 402n, 476

Domitian, 24
Don Quixote, 110
Dooley, Mr., 444
Dostoievsky, Feodor, 264
Doyle, Sir A. Conan, 243
Draper, George, 36
Dreams, 269–74, 280; condensation in,
  285–6; and psychoanalysis, 393
Drug addiction, and melancholia, 123;
  as a neurosis, 147–9; treatment of, 149
Drugs, in treatment of mental illness,
  373, 413, 414; *and see* Narcosynthesis
Dublin, L. I., 125n
Dumas, Realier, 76
Dunbar, Flanders, 37n
Dupin, Aurore, *see* Sand, George
Dwiggins, W. A., xiv

Eastman, Dr., 87
Ebaugh, Franklin G., 482n, 483n, 484n
Eddy, Mary Baker, 87–8
Edison, Thomas A., 173
Education, application of psychiatry to,
  421–33; in grade schools, 421–5; in
  colleges and high schools, 425–33
Edwards family, 58
Edwards, Jonathan, 345; quoted, 345
Efficiency, loss of, from mental causes,
  436–7
Elaboration, 280, 289–90
Electroencephalography, 263, 370
Elektra complex, 311–13, 430; treatment
  of, 394–6
Eliot, George, 81
Emerson, Harrington, 13
Emerson, Ralph Waldo, 81; quoted, 400
Emery, E. Van Norman, 462n
Emotional: reactions, 164–7, 168, 194;
  compensations, 172; disorders, effect
  on learning, 181–2; deficiencies, 193–
  6; excesses, 205–12; distortions, 249–
  59
Encephalitis, as handicap to personal-
  ity, 41–2; behaviour disorders follow-
  ing, 41n
Endocrine gland disorder, case of, 39
Environment, vii, 419; change of, in
  treatment of mental illness, 400–10
Epilepsy, *see* Convulsions and convul-
  sive states
Erasmus, 65, 79, 203
Erickson, Isabel, 408n
Erickson, M. H., 415n
Erikson, E. Homburger, 179
Eroticism, anal, 257, 316–18
Erskine, John, quoted, 328–9

Eugenics, fallacy of, regarding mental illness, 8

Evans, Bergen, quoted, 304–5n

Evans, Donald, quoted, 344

Excesses, emotional, 205–12, 366; intellectual, 199–205; perceptual, 198–9, 215; volitional, 212–15

Exhibitionism, 315–16; plus masochism, 347–9

Expressive psychotherapy, *see* Psychotherapy, expressive

Failure, in adjustment, 30–4; personality types predisposed to, 34–158; in love and home life, 115–17; in middle life, 118–20; in school, 114–15; in industry, 433–43; in success, 117–18

Fairbank, Ruth, 125n

Fantasies of the unconscious, 322–62; *and see* Complex; of sacred and profane love, 327–9; of extraordinary birth, 329–31; of royal lineage, 329–31; of patricide, etc., 331–5; of guilt, 335–41; of cruelty, 341–9; of contamination and impregnation, 349–53; of the magic wand, 353–6; of rebirth, 356–9

Fear: as form of flight, 33; and sense of inferiority, 70–1; *and see* Phobias

Feeble-mindedness, 48–64; in the Army, 48, 50; and industry, 52–3; *and see* Hypophrenic personality type

Feigenbaum, Dorian, 283n

Fellows, Ralph M., 373n

Fenichel, Otto, 296n

Fernald, Walter E., 53n, 55n, 58

Fetishism, 258

Fetterman, J., quoted, 146

Fever therapy, *see* Paresis

Fichte, 81, 202

Financial loss, effect on mental illness, 119, 120

Fishbein, Morris, 129n

Fisher, Dorothy Canfield, 173

Fisher, V. E., 174n

Fixation, 306, 310–18; on the mother, *see* Œdipus complex; on the father, *see* Elektra complex; on oneself, *see* Narcissism

Flaubert, 264

Flight: as solution of failure in adjustment, 30, 33, 90; illness as, 383; treatment as, 401; *and see* Fugues

Folie du doute, 261

Folsom, Charles F., quoted, 78–9

Foot, symbolism of, 298–300

Foote, J. A., 60n

Francis of Assisi, St., 385

Franks, Bobby, 201n

Fratricide, 331–5

Frazer, Sir James G., 353

Free will, 449–50

Freeman, Walter, 412

French, Thomas M., 360

Frenssen, Gustav, 240

Freud, Anna, 182n, 422

Freud, Sigmund, vii, 121, 131n, 170, 186, 248, 254n, 267, 268–70, 271, 274–6, 278, 296n, 309, 311n, 323, 327n, 336, 359–60, 377n, 387, 394n, 413, 414, 422, 458, 485; quoted, 112, 358–9, 366–7

Freudian psychoanalysts, qualifications and training, 359–61

Frigidity, sexual, 132

Frink, Homer W., quoted, 187–9, 225, 261, 282, 284, 291

Frommer, Reb, 336–7

Fromm-Reichmann, Frieda, 413n

Frustrated personality, *see* Neurotic personality type

Fryer, Douglas, quoted, 441–2

Fugue, 189–91, 238

Fuller, Tom, 204

Galahad, Sir, 326, 417

Galdston, Iago, 39n

Galen, 449

Garfield, James A., 79, 99

Garrick, 204

Garrison, William Lloyd, 59, 85

Gay, F. P., 479n

Geleerd, Elisabeth, 190n

Genius, and perverse personality, 154–5

Geography, and isolation personality type, 65

George, David Lloyd, 76n

George, Saint, 418

Germanicus, 24

Germ phobia, 352–3

Germany, mass paranoia in, 88–9

Gestalt psychology, 28, 161n

Gibbon, 81

Gibran, Kahlil, quoted, 290

Giesen, van, 478

Gilbreth, Frank, 13

Gilbreth, Lillian, 13

Giles, J. A., quoted, 385–6

Gilgamos, 329

Gill, Merton M., 178n, 415n

Gillespie, R. D., 407n

Glover, Edward, quoted, 474n

Glueck, Bernard, 453n
Glueck, Sheldon and Eleanor T., 457
Goddard, H. H., 241n, 242; quoted, 56–7
Golden Bough, theme of, 353–6; legend of, 353
Goldsmith, Oliver, 79, 191
Gonnelli, 172
Grandier, Urbain, 282–3
Graphology, 179
Grazzi, Lucrezia, 384
Grimm, 302
Grinker, Roy R., 414n
Groddeck, Georg, 36
Grouchy variety of schizoid personality type, 83–4
Group psychotherapy, 415
Groves, Ernest, 435n
Guest, Lady Charlotte, 352n
Guilt complex, 335–41
Guiteau, Charles Julius, 79

Habits: and will, 163–4; and tics, 260; *and see* Distortion, volitional
Hacker, F. J., 190n
Hale, David, xvi
Hallowell, quoted, 67–8
Hallucinations, 216–20, 242; *and see* Distortion, perceptual
Hamill, Ralph, 182n
Hamilton, Samuel, 421n
Hamlet, 125, 310
Handel, 264
Hard-boiled variety of schizoid personality type, 82
" Hard-luck champions," 294
Hardy, Thomas, 330
Hartwell, Samuel J., 459
Hawthorne, 65
Health, mental, defined, 2
Healy, Mary Tenney, 231n
Healy, William, xvi, 457, 458, 459; quoted, 230–1, 459–60
Hebephrenia, *see* Schizophrenia
Hecker, J. F. C., quoted, 147
Heinnecken, 305n
Henderson, D. K., 407n
Henley, William Ernest, quoted, 323–4
Henry, A. G., 113
Henry, Patrick, 85
Hercules, 329
Heredity, vii; and feeble-mindedness, 8; and personality, 23–7; and schizoid personality, 89–90
Hergesheimer, Joseph, 259
Hersey, Rex B., 435n
Heyer, 36

Heyward, Du Bose, 212
Hickman, Edward, 10, 250
High Schools, mental hygiene in, 425–33
Hildemer, 385–6
Hinsie, Leland B., 105n
Hinton, Elmer, 348–9
Hippocrates, 107, 477
History-taking in mental examination, 369
Hitler, Adolf, 32, 79, 87
Hoboes, as types of perverse personality, 154
Holistic theory, 35
Hollingworth, Leta S., 180, 200; quoted, 203–4
Holman, Charles T., 461n
Home training, and schizoid personality type, 89–91
Homosexuality, 258, 295
Horace, 203; quoted, 363
Horn, Samson, x
Hoshor, John, quoted, 325
Hoskins, R. G., 104
Hospitalization, 401–10
Houdini, 220
Howard, Leslie, 230n
Howell, A. G. Ferrers, 385n
Hugo, Victor, 295
Human nature, no such thing as, 9
Huss, John, 85
Hutchings, W. H., 348n
Huysman, 259
Hydrotherapy, 405
Hyperacusis, example of, 199
Hypermnesia, 201–5
Hypnoanalysis, 378, 414–15; *and see* Hypnosis
Hypnosis, early use of, 268–9; cure by, 381; as treatment method, 414–15
Hypochondriasis, 139–40
Hypophrenia, *see* Hypophrenic personality type
Hypophrenic personality type, 48–64; breakdown of, 63–4; institutional care of, 63; examples of, 48–50, 51–3, 54, 56–7, 58–9, 60–3, 156
Hysteria, 130, 134, 135, 142; examples of, 142–7, 190, 234–5; epidemics of, 146–7; automatism in, 239

Ibsen, 47, 330
Identification, 280
Idiocy, 48, 55–6; early recognition of, 54; types of, 55–6
Ikin, A. G., 241n

Illness, physical, as form of flight, 33; *and see* Somatic personality type

Illusions, 216-20; *and see* Distortion, perceptual

Imbecility, 48, 55, 62-4

Immaculate conception, fantasies of, 349-53, 465

Impotence, sexual, 132

Impregnation, fantasies of, 349-3

Inaudi, 204

Incendiarism, 4-5

Incoherence, 233

Industrial applications of psychiatry, 433-43

Infantilisms, 318-22

Inferiority: constitutional, *see* Organic disease personality type; sense of, 70-5, 90, 169, 429-30; compensations for, 71-2, 74-5

Inflammation of the brain, *see* Encephalitis

Influenza: related to encephalitis, 42; effect on the feeble-minded, 61-2; and schizophrenia, 96-7, 103

Inge, Dean, 474n

Inhibitions, 277-8

Insanity: as explanation of mental illness, 9; and the courts, 445-50, 453, *and see* Legal applications of psychiatry

Instinct, 274-8, 280, 361

Institutes for psychoanalysis, 360

Institutional treatment of the feeble-minded, 63-4

Intellection, 21, 161-6; deficient, 175-92; distorted, 223-49

Intelligence, 191; measurement of, 175-8; quotient, 176, 178; tests of, *see* Tests, intelligence

Introjection, 247, 283-4; examples of, 283-4

Iola, Hyman, xiv

Ion, 329

Ireland, M. W., 48n

Ismet, Pasha, 173

Isolation personality type, 64-5, 70-5, 90; examples of, 65-9, 72, 74-5

Jackson, Andrew, 155

Jackson, Hughlings, 230n

Jacobs, xiv

Jacobson, Arthur C., 24n; quoted, 345

Jacoby, G. W., 462n

James, Henry, 230n

James, Jesse, 79

James, William, quoted, 265, 466

Jamieson, Gerald R., quoted, 290-1

Janet, Pierre, quoted, 224-5, 414

Jarrett, Mary C., 420, 442; quoted, 442-3

Jastrow, Joseph, quoted, 87-8

Jeanne d'Arc, 213

Jehovah complex, 323-5

Jelliffe, Smith Ely, x, xvi, 36, 41n, 101n, 269n, 360, 453n, 479

Jensen, Wilhelm, 374

Jesus, 7, 24-5, 110, 129, 329, 349, 357, 376-7

Jesus complex, 325-7

Job, 128-9

John the Baptist, 85, 471

Johnson, Samuel, 65, 173; quoted, 141

Johnstone, Thomas, 96n

Jones, Ernest, 187, 297n, 318n, 323n, 360

Jonson, Ben, 155

Jowett, 270n

Joyce, James, 157; quoted, 344-5

Judaism, 474

Judas Iscariot, 79

Judgment, defects of, 191-2

Jukes family, 58, 345

Justice, 449-50

Juvenile paresis, 47n

Kahlbaum, 245

Kant, 79

Karma, 329

Katatonia, *see* Schizophrenia

Kempf, E. J., 174n

Kempis, Thomas à, quoted, 348

Kennedy, W. M., 427n, 433n

Kenyon, Theda, 7n

Kepler, John, 24, 81-2

Kingman, Robert, quoted, 172

Kirby, George H., quoted, 105

Kitto, 173

Klein, Melanie, 182n

Kleist, 101n

Kleptomania, 5-6

Klinger, M. Pauline, 350

Knight, Robert P., x, 107n, 149n, 248n, 288n, 413n

Knox, John, 85

Korsakoff's syndrome, 228

Korzybski, Count Alfred, 297

Kossef, A., 148n

Kraepelin, Emil, 96n, 109, 477-8; quoted, 96-7

Kretschmer, Ernst, 83, 89n; quoted, 77-8, 80

Kubie, Lawrence, 400n, 415n

Kyros, 329

Lagerlöf, Selma, 235
Laird, Donald A., 430n
Lameness, hysterical, 142–3; cure of, by persuasion, 382–3
Lanier, Sidney, quoted, 270–1
Learning disability, emotional disorders and, 182–3
Legal applications of psychiatry, 443–60
Lehrman, P. R., quoted, 330
Leonard, William Ellery, 157
Leopold, Nathan, 201
Lepke, 82
Levy, David, 179
Lewis, N. D. C., 104
Lewis, Sinclair, 303n
Libidinous stream, 306–11
Liebeault, 268
Lincoln, Abraham, 113, 114, 128, 202
Linn, Peggy, xiv
Lippmann, Walter, quoted, 177n
Lipsius, 305n
Liss, Edward, 182n
Lodge, Sir Oliver, 243
Loeb, Richard, 79, 82, 201n
Logan, Effie, quoted, 351
Lohengrin, 329
Lonely personality, *see* Isolation personality type
Loos, Anita, 278; quoted, 278
Love, Albert G., 48n
Love: sacred and profane, theory of, 327–9; Freud on psychology of, 327n
Lowrey, Lawson G., xvi, 420, 453n
Luther, Martin, 85
Lyle, Jeanetta, xiii; *and see* Menninger, Jean Lyle
Lyster, W. J., 343

Macbeth, 365
Macbeth, Lady, 225
Macculloch, quoted, 47
MacKaye, Milton, quoted, 153–4
Macleod, Fiona, quoted, 346–7
Magic wand, theme of, 353–6
Maguire, John Francis, quoted, 383
Malaria, 47, 412
Malcolm, Ida, x
Man-haters, 5
Mania, 109–11, 205, 211, 477; its cause, 121
Manic-depressive psychosis, 107–8, 477; *see also* Mania *and* Melancholia
Marat, Jean Paul, 202
Marcus Aurelius Antoninus, 24

Marriage, as precipitation of mental illness, 95
Marshall, Helen, 402n
Martineau, Harriet, 173; quoted, 201–2
Masefield, quoted, 196
Masochism, 342; examples of, 346–9
Masons, 33rd-Degree, grant for research in dementia praecox, 105
Massage, in treatment of mental cases, 404
Masters, Edgar Lee, quoted, 24–5, 303n
Masturbation, 288, 314
Mather, Cotton, 305n
Mathew, Father, 383
Matricide, fantasies of, 331–3
Matthew, St., 24
Maugham, Somerset, 74n, 296
Maupassant, 330
McDougall, William, 320; quoted, 238
McGlasson, Warren E., 301
McKernan, Maureen, 201n
McKinley, William, 99
McLean, Helen, 360
Meckel, Clara Louise, x
Medical applications of psychiatry, 475–87
Medicine, and psychiatry, a conception of, 486–7
Meduna, 410
Melancholia, 211; and Lincoln, 113; difference from the "blues," 114; symptoms of, 120–1; psychological mechanisms of, 121; and suicide, 122–6; its treatment, 126–9
Melancholy, 111–14; and perceptual deficiency, 167–8; its treatment, 366–8
Memory: in man and lower organisms compared, 21–2; and perception, 162, 164, 166; defects of, 166, 182–91, 201–5, 238–9, 248–9; distortions of, 166, 223, 226–31; extraordinary, 191, 201–5; false, 226–8
Mencken, Henry L., 221
Menninger, C. F., xvi, 64n, 178n
Menninger Foundation, The, viii
Menninger, Jean Lyle, x
Menninger, Karl, 37n, 39n, 64n, 276n, 294n, 360
Menninger, William C., xiii, 39n, 119n, 128n, 405n, 408n, 411n, 416n; quoted, 403–7
Mental catharsis, *see* Psychotherapy
Mental health, rules for, 368
Mental hygiene, origin of, as a movement, 15n; and prevention of mental

illness, 365–8; and education, 421–33; and industry, 433–43
Mental hygiene counsellors, 425–9
Mental mechanisms, 279–304
Mental process, in human beings and lower organisms, compared, 21–2
Mesmer, 414
Meumann, 204
Meyer, Adolf, xvi, 36, 479
Michaelis, 240
Military psychiatry, 416
Miller, Emanuel, 182n
Mills, Lady Dorothy, 331
Milmine, Georgine, quoted, 87–8
Misophobia, 251
Moersch, Frederick, 40
Mohammet, 110
Molière, 264
Mongolian idiots, 55
Moody personality, *see* Cycloid personality type
Moore, T. V., quoted, 438–9
Moralists, view of, regarding mental illness, 7–8
Morgan, J. J. B., 296
Moronity, 48–53
Moses, 329, 353
Motives, 265–362
Mozart, 172, 203
Mühl, Anita M., 231
Müller, G. E., 204n
Münsterberg, Hugo, 228n
Murder, 100, 101–2, 209n, 231, 232, 325, 331–5
Murray, Henry A., 179n
Myerson, Abraham, 25n, 26n
Mythomania, 226, 230–1; *and see* Distortion, of memory

Nagging, 4
Napoleon, 32, 76, 82
Narcissism, 314–18
Narcissus (Roman gladiator), 325
Narcosynthesis, 378, 414
National Association for the Protection of the Insane, 15n
National Committee for Mental Hygiene, vii, 15n, 104
National Crime Commission, 453–4
Negativism, 213
Nero, 24
Nervousness, as form of flight, 33; *and see* Anxiety neurosis
Neurasthenia, 134–5, 138–41, 443; examples of, 138–41

Neuroses, 129–30, 134–50, 157; obsessional, 135–6; compulsion, 136; anxiety hysteria, 138; treatment and cure of, 149, 388; *and see* Alcohol addiction, Anxiety neurosis, Compulsion neurosis, Drug addiction, Hysteria, Neurasthenia, Psychasthenia
Neurosurgery, 40n, 412
Neurotic character, 150–5; treatment of, 155; *see also* Neurotic personality
Neurotic personality type, 129–50, 157; defined, 129–33; examples of, 133–4, 135–47; and resistance, 376
Newton, Sir Isaac, 24, 77
New York State Prison Survey Committee, 451–2, 454
Nicodemus, 356
Nietzsche, 186
Nightingale, Florence, 213
Nirvana, 125
Nissl, 478
Normal personalities, xiv, 131, 158
Noyes, Rufus K., 87
Nursing, psychiatric, viii, 407–10

Obsessions, 223–6; explanation of, 225–6; and compulsions, 260; *and see* Distortion, intellectual
Occupational therapy, viii, 107, 404–5
Œdipus, 311, 329
Œdipus complex, 309, 311, 331n
Oliver, John Rathbone, 461n, 462n, 473n
O'Neill, Eugene, 72n, 157
Oral character, 316, 318
Organic disease, self-destructive factor in, 485–6
Orton, Samuel T., 181
Osler, Sir William, 383
Otis, Raymond, quoted, 339–41
Over-activity, 214–15
Over-compensation, 172–4, 174n; examples, 173–4
Overholser, Winfred, 454
Oversensitiveness, 70–1, 174; and schizoid personality type, 82
Overstreet, H. A., quoted, 320–1

Pædophilia, 258
Pahl, 478
Pain, pleasure in, 341–2
Panophobia, 250–1
Paracelsus, 449
Paralysis, case of, cured by sight of the

Paralysis, *continued*
cross, 385; hysterical, *see* Shell-shock, industrial
Paramnesia, *see* Distortion, of memory
Paranoia, 85–8, 94, 245; mass, 88–9; involution, 101n
Paranoid: symptoms, 85–6; public indifference to, 101–2; delusions, 86–9, 94, 245–7, 267
Paranoid psychosis, senile, 101n
Paraphrenia, involution, 101n
Paraphrenia, pre-senile, 101n
Parental influence: in isolation personality type, 65–6; on sense of inferiority, 72–3; in schizoid personality type, 89–92
Paresis, general, 42–5, 439, 443; fever therapy of, 412; *and see* Syphilis, brain
Paris, 329
Passivity, as expression of aggression, 213–14
Paton, Stewart, 431
Patricide, fantasies of, 331–2, 333, 335
Patterson, Isabel M., quoted, 291–2
Pavlov, I. P., 253n
Payot, Jules, 198n
Pearce, Helen, quoted, 343–4
Pearson, Gerald H. J., 311n
Perception, 161–7; deficient, 167–75, 193, 215; distorted, 215–23, 242; excessive, 198–9, 215
Perenot, Edward, 336
Perry, M. L., 439n
Persecution, delusions of, 245–6; and paranoia, 86–7
Perseus, 329
Personality: constituents of, 23–4; method of studying, 27–8; adjustment of, to situation, 29–34; broken, 34–5; types of, predisposed to failure, 34–158; questionnaires, 178; multiple, 238, 241–2; *and see* Antisocial, Cycloid, Hypophrenic, Isolation, Neurotic, Somatic, Schizoid
Perverse personality, *see* Antisocial personality type
Perversions: of affection and interest, 257–9; mass, 258–9; *and see* Distortion, emotional
Peter, St., 243
Peter the Great, 87, 264
Petit mal, 263
Petrarch, 264
Phallic worship, 356
Phallus, wand as symbol of, 356
Philip Neri, St., 384

Phobias, 225, 226, 250–5, *and see* Distortion, emotional
Physical illness personality, *see* Somatic personality type
Pierce, Bedford, 408n; quoted, 401–2
Pierce, S. W., 378n
Pinel, 476
Pinturicchio, 173
Pituitary-gland disorder, 39
Placebo, cure by, 380–1
Plastic surgery, effect on personality, 74–5
Plato, quoted, 270n
Play techniques, 179
Pleasure-pain principle, 323, 341–2
Pliny, 305n
Poe, Edgar Allan, 114
Pope, Alexander, 65
Poverty, as cause of isolation personality type, 66–7
Precocity, 304–6
Pregnancy, false, 350; *and see* Impregnation
Preston, Raymond A., xiv
Prevention of mental illness, 365–8
Prince, Morton, 241; quoted, 222–3
Prognosis of mental illness, 416
Progressive Education movement, 425
Projection, 242, 247–8, 281–3; in everyday life, 281–2; in Shakspere, 281; examples of, 281–3
Projective techniques in psychological testing, 179
Propitiatory compulsions, 335–41
Proust, Marcel, 203n
Pruette, Lorine, quoted, 441–2
Psychasthenia, 134, 135; examples of, 135–8
Psychiatric counsel, *see* Psychotherapy
Psychiatric education, vii, 482–4
Psychiatric hospital, 402–7
Psychiatric nurses and nursing, *see* Nursing, psychiatric
Psychiatric social work, 420
Psychiatry: fallacy of, regarding mental illness, 9; and prevention of mental illness, 14–16, 158, 373; and general medicine, a conception of, 486, 487; history of, 475–9; *and see* Applications, Mental hygiene, Treatments
Psychoanalysis, 267–80, 359–62, 376, 379, 389, 390–400, 413; discovery of, 267–9; history of, in America, 360–1
Psychology, viii; fallacy of, regarding mental illness, 8; contributions of, 12–14; educational, origin of, 13; indus-

trial, 13, 441; *and see* Tests, psychological

Psychoses, 157, 158

Psychosexual development, 317

Psychosomatic medicine, 35–39, 37n, 39n, 415, 482; *and see* Somatic personality type

Psychosurgery, *see* Surgery

Psychotherapy, 374–400, 413–16; types of, 378–9; suppressive, 379–86; expressive, 378–9, 386–400; group, 415

Public indifference to paranoid symptoms, 101–2

Punishment, theory of, 446–9; *and see* Legal applications of psychiatry

Purposive accidents, 125, 280, 292–4; examples of, 272–4

Putnam, J. J., 360

Putnam, Tracy, 26n, 264n

Pyromania, 258

Queer personality, *see* Schizoid personality type

Quirino, 305n

Racine, 203

Radical, the, as variety of schizoid personality, 84–5

Raeder, O. J., 55n

Rank, Otto, quoted, 329–30

Rapaport, David, x, 178n, 190n

Raphael, T., 125n, 427, 432n

Rationalization, 290–2; and religion, 469–70

Ray, Isaac, 15n

Raymond, C. Stanley, 53n

Reaction-formation, 74, 295–9

Reality principle, 323

Rebirth, fantasy of, 356–9

Recher, Paul, quoted, 282–3

Recreational therapy, viii, 405–7

Reed, Ralph, quoted, 321–2

Reference, ideas of, 86

Reflexes, 162–6; conditioned, 253

Regression, 174–5, 318–22; *and see* Complex, Fantasies

Reichenberg, Wally, 179n

Reider, Norman, xiii, 45

Reik, Theodor, 336

" Religion," and isolation personality type, 68–9

Religion, and psychiatry, 460–75; and psychoanalysis, 474–5; and sense of guilt, 471, 475n; and sense of inferiority, 470–1

Religious applications of psychiatry, 460–75

Repression, 276–8, 280, 361

Research Council on Problems of Alcohol, 149n

Resistance, 375–8, 395; defined, 375–6

Response, 162–6; *and see* Distortion, emotional, Schizothymic reactions

Responsibility, as test of mental health, 7–8; refusal to accept, 33; in legal sense, 449–50

Reversal, 290

Reynolds, Sir Joshua, 172–3

Ricklin, Franz, 302n

Rickman, John, quoted, 474–5n

Ripley, Robert L., 332; quoted, 304, 336–7, 348

Ritter, 36

Roback, Harry N., 40n, 264n

Robertson, T. M., 74–5

Robespierre, 79

Robinson, E. A., 114

Rockefeller, John D., 303

Roethlisberger, F. J., 435n

Rogers, Charles E., x

Rome (N. Y.), State School for Mental Defectives at, 53

Romulus, 329

Roosevelt, Theodore, 173, 303

Rorschach test, 179

Rousseau, Jean Jacques, 79

" Rube," the, as isolation personality type, 64–5

Ruggles, Arthur H., 433n

Ruissi, Caterina, 384

Rush, Benjamin, 412

Rutledge, Ann, 113

Sadger, J., 241n; quoted, 288–9

Sadism, 259, 341–5; examples of, 332, 343–5

St. George, 417

Sakel, Manfred, 410

Salmon, Thomas W., 453n, 475n, 479

Salvation Army, 474n

Samson, 72n

Sand, George, 83; quoted, 328

Sanderson, Nicholas, 172

Sargent, Porter, 425n

Sargon I, 329, 349

Satanism, 259

Savonarola, 85

Sayles, Mary B., 424n

Saul, King, 107, 114

Scaliger, 305n

Schafer, Roy, 178n

Scheinberg, Bernard, 325
Schiller, 79
Schizoid personality type, 75–107, 156, 157, 425, 442; examples of, 75–88, 90–2, 95–106; symptoms of, 79–82, 85–7, 250; causes of, 89–92; successes and failures of, 93; breaks of, 93–107, 250; treatment of, 106–7; *and see* Schizophrenia
Schizophrenia, 93–107, 197*n*, 442; recovery from, 102–7; and dissociation, 233
Schizothymia, 250
Schizothymic reactions, 250
Schmiedl-Wahner, 179
Schneck, Jerome M., 25*n*
Schnitzler, Arthur, 248*n*
Schools for the feeble-minded, 63–4, *and see* Rome, Vineland, Waverley
Schopenhauer, 248
Schreber case, 248
Scott, Russell, 153
Scott, Sir Walter, 65
Screen memory, 253–4
Seclusiveness, as form of flight, 33, 75; and schizoid personality type, 81–2, 90
Seelert, 101*n*
Seif, Dr., 60
Self-consciousness, and schizoid personality type, 82
Self-destruction, 484; through addiction, 485; through asceticism, 485; through malingering, 485; through neurotic invalidism, 485; through operations, 485; through organic disease, 485; through suicide, 122–6, 485; war against, 484–6
Self-destructive impulse, 125–6, 484–6
Sensations, 161
Serko, 101*n*
Sexual instinct: and neuroses, 130, 132, 138; and sublimations, 132; and psychoanalysis, 275, 276
Sexual symbols, 299–300, 301, 302, 304
Shakspere, projection in, 281; quoted, 365
Sharp, William, quoted, 346–7
Shaw, G. B., 256, 330
Shawn, Ted, 173
Sheldon, Charles M., 388
Shelley, 361; quoted, 359
" Shell-shock," 199*n*; cure of, 379–83; industrial, 144–6
Sherwin, Vernon C., 259
Shields, Thomas Edward, 60

Shock therapy, 410–11
Shryock, Richard H., 412*n*
Sibelius, 114
Sibling rivalry, 91–2
Siegfried, 329
Simon-Binet test, 176
Singh, Jal, 331
Slavson, S. R., 415*n*
Slips of the tongue, 292–3
Smith, Alfred, 452
Smith, E. Rogers, 199*n*
Smith, Roberta, 241*n*
Social workers, psychiatric, viii, 370, 401, 420–1
Socrates, 413
Solomon, H. C., 43*n*, 46*n*
Solomon, Maida, 46*n*
Somatic personality type, 35–47
Somnambulism, 238, 239–41; hysterical, 143–4
Southard, Ernest E., xvi, 43*n*, 55*n*, 420, 434, 479; quoted, 379–84, 418
Special School Association, 64*n*
Spencer, Herbert, 275
Spiegel, John P., 414*n*
Spinoza, 79
Sprott, W. J. H., 78*n*
Staub, Hugo, 151*n*, 336
Stephen, Karin, 37*n*, 293
Sterilization, 25–6
Stern, Edith M., 421*n*
Stevenson, George S., 15*n*
Stewart, Byron, xiii, 411*n*
Stimulus, 161–5
Stoddard, George D., 176*n*
Stone, Leo T., 230*n*
Strecker, Edward A., 390*n*
Strephosymbolia, 181
Strindberg, 330
Struggle with environment, 3, 29
Stuart, John T., 113
Stupid personality, *see* Hypophrenic personality type
Stupid variety of schizoid personality type, 83
Sublimations, 132–3, 280, 361
Subnormality, 48
Substitution: and obsessions, 225–6; and phobias, 251
Success in adjustment, 30
Suggestion, 382
Suicide, 122–6, 484; as form of flight, 33; and melancholia, 122; cases, 122, 126–7, 336; motives of, 124–6
Sullivan, Harry S., 94*n*, 103, 105*n*, 413*n*

Superiority complex, 74

Superstition, 254–5

Suppression, 277–8; *see also* Psychotherapy, suppressive

Surgery, in treatment of mental illness, 373–4, 412

Suspiciousness: as form of flight, 33; as characteristic of variety of schizoid personality type, 85–8; as serious paranoid symptom, 85–8

Sweetser, William, 15n

Swift, Edgar James, quoted, 201–2, 226–8

Swift, Jonathan, 65

Symbolization, 251, 296–304; in dreams, 271–4; examples of, 298–302

Symptoms: of schizoid personality, 79–80, 81, 84–7; of disorder, 161–264; and disguises, 280, 361, *and see* Chapter V; physical, as symbols, 301–2; of personality defects, 434; *and see* Chapter III

Syphilis, 42–6, 210, 211; brain, 42–5, 210, 211, 412, 439, 443; congenital, 46–7; and defective memory, 185–6

Tarbell, Ida M., quoted, 76

Tchaikowsky, 114

Tchekov, 191

Teacher, visiting, 423–4, 424n

Teachers, 421–5

Teasdale, Sara, 110

Telephos, 329

Temper outbursts, excessive, case of, 211

Temper tantrums, 209

Templeton, Alec, 172n

Tennyson, quoted, 326, 355

Tests, intelligence, 8, 175–8, 424; psychological, 178–80

Thackeray, 202

Thaw, Evelyn Nesbit, 284

Thematic apperception test, 179

Themistocles, 203

Therapy, new developments in, 410–16

Thinking, *see* Intellection

Thom, Douglas A., quoted, 65–6

Thomas à Kempis, quoted, 348

Thomas Aquinas, 60

Thomas of Celano, quoted, 385

Thompson, Isaac, 42–3

Thompson, Mildred, quoted, 432–3

Thomson, James, 114

Thoreau, Henry David, 291–2

Tics, 260; *and see* Distortion, volitional

Tidd, Charles W., 107n; quoted, 105–7

Timidity, as form of flight, 33

Transference, 104, 391–4, 396; negative, 393–4

Transvestitism, 258

Treatment, 365–416; by change of environment, 400–1; by hypnosis, 414–15; by medicine and surgery, 373–4, 412–13; by narcosynthesis, 378, 414; by psychotherapy, 374–400, 413–16; by shock therapy, 410–11; in psychiatric hospitals, 401–10; of threatened mental illness, 367–8; of full-blown mental illness, 368–416; *and see* Therapy

Treaty of Versailles, 89

Tristan, 329

Tristram Shandy, 305n

Tuberculosis, as form of unconscious suicide, 125, 485

Tuke, 476

Tumour of the brain, 39–41, 203; cure of, by reassurance, 384

Tunis, John R., 427n

Twain, Mark, 330

Twins, mental illness in, 91–2

Unsociability, 64; and schizoid personality type, 79–80; *and see* Antisocial personality type, Seclusiveness

Urethral character, 318

Van Doren, Carl, x

van Gogh, Vincent, 79

Vaughan, Wayland F., 174n

Venus, 349

Verbigeration, 233

Vespasian, 24

Villard, Oswald Garrison, 157

Villon, François, 151

Vineland (N. J.), training-school for feeble-minded at, 55

Vocational Adjustment Bureau (New York City), 53

Vocational testing, 180

Volition, 164–5; deficient, 197–8; excessive, 212–15; distorted, 210, 253–7

Voltaire, 155

von Bergmann, 36

Von Jauregg, Wagner, 412

Von Liszt, 228n

Wagner, 79, 155

Wallenstein, 155

Walsh, Bishop, 331

Walsh, J. J., 60n

Wanderlust, as symptom of perverse personality, 154
Warburton, William, 59
War psychoses, 379–83
Washington, George, 173
Watt, James, 59, 202
Watters, George, 231
Watts, H. P., 343
Watts, James, 412
Waverley (Mass.) , State School at, 53n, 58
Wealth, as cause of isolation personality type, 67–8
Weigert, 478
Wellman, Beth L., 176n
Wells, Carolyn, 173
Wells, F. L., 234
Wembridge, Eleanor Rowland, quoted, 48–50
Wernicke, 166
Western Electric Company, 435
Whipple, C. S., 333
Whistler, 79
White, Edward Lucas, 237–8
White, William Alanson, xvi, 36, 100–2, 101n, 360, 453n, 455, 479

Whitehead, T. N., 435n
Wickersham, George W., 451–2
Wickman, E. K., 424
Wilde, Oscar, 137; quoted, 331–2
Will, 164–5
Williams, Frankwood E., xvi, 365, 433n, 453n; quoted, 319
Williams, T. J., 171n
Wilson, S. A. K., 230n
Wilson, Woodrow, 75–6, 243
Witches, as explanation of mental illness, 7
Wolf, Friedrich, 203
Wolf, Werner, 179
Woollcott, Alexander, quoted, 333–4
World War I, 15, 199n, 420, 478
World War II, vii, ix, 46, 199n, 410
Worry, *see* Anxiety
Worth, Patience, 237

Yellowlees, David, quoted, 408–9
Yepsen, Lloyd N., 55
Young, C. C., 231

Zilboorg, Gregory, 105n, 125n, 413n
Zola, Émile, 157

The main text of this book is set in Linotype Baskerville; the illustrative " cases " are composed in Linotype Granjon. The smaller heading material is in Linotype Janson; the larger capital lines are Baskerville. This use of different types was contrived to place the " cases " a little apart from the main argument without too great interruption of the theme. Inclusion of Janson provided a touch of lively " action " in the running-titles at the tops of the pages, also a slight change of texture, away from the body-matter, in the various headings. These manipulations of type " color " and texture were inspired by the aim to make the structure of the theme's organization easily *seizable,* and at the same time to make the pages lively and interesting *as* pages.

The typographic scheme was arranged by W. A. Dwiggins. The book was composed by The Plimpton Press, Norwood, Massachusetts. Printed and bound by The Haddon Craftsmen, Inc., Scranton, Pennsylvania.